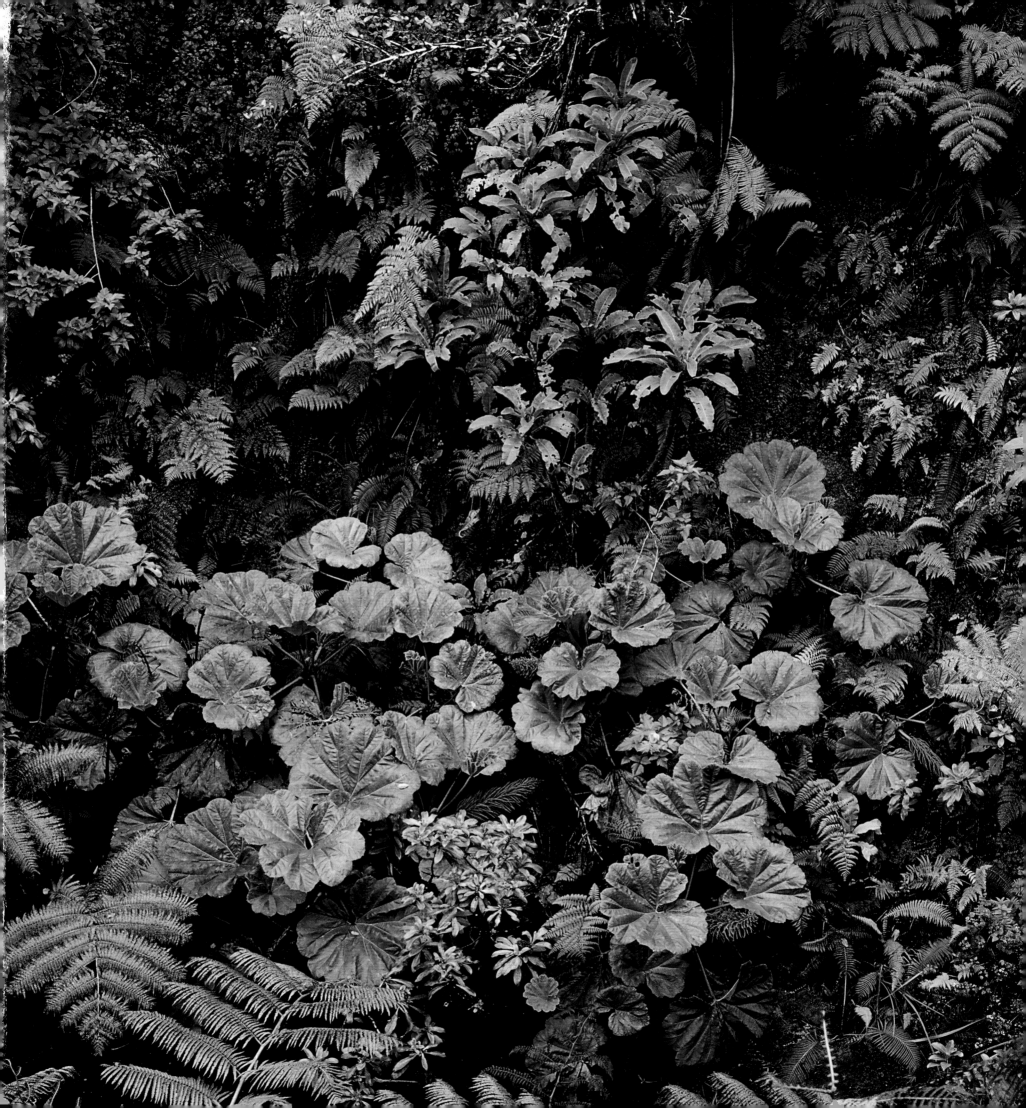

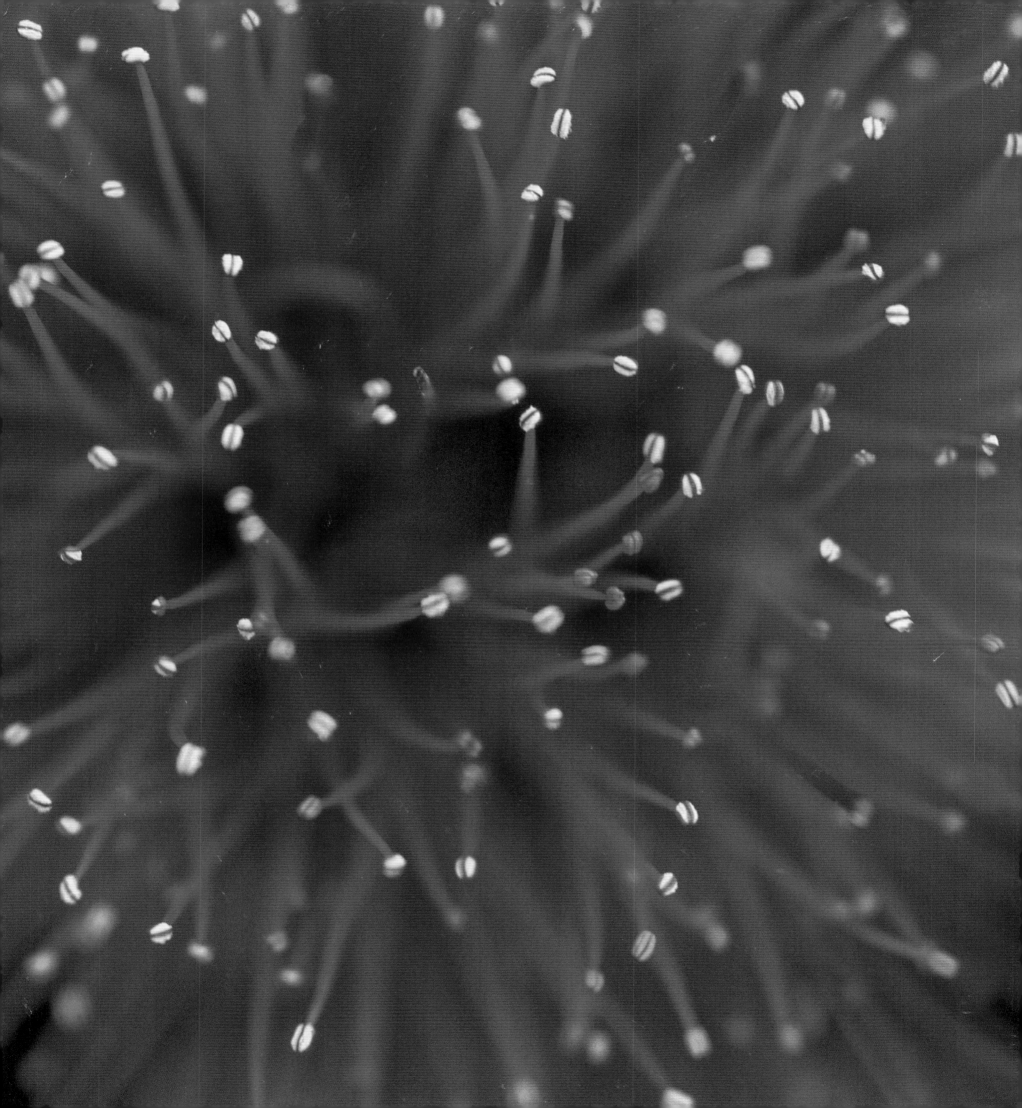

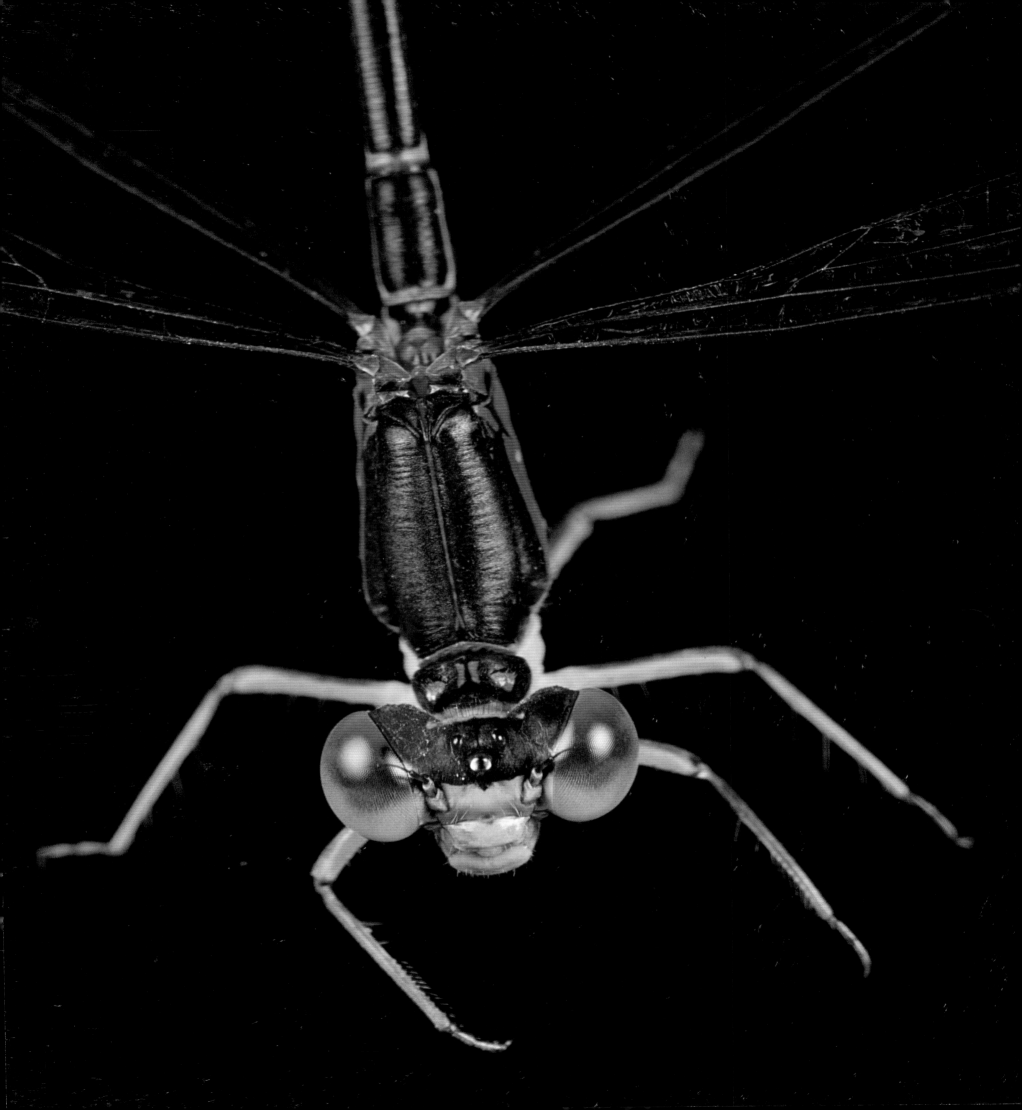

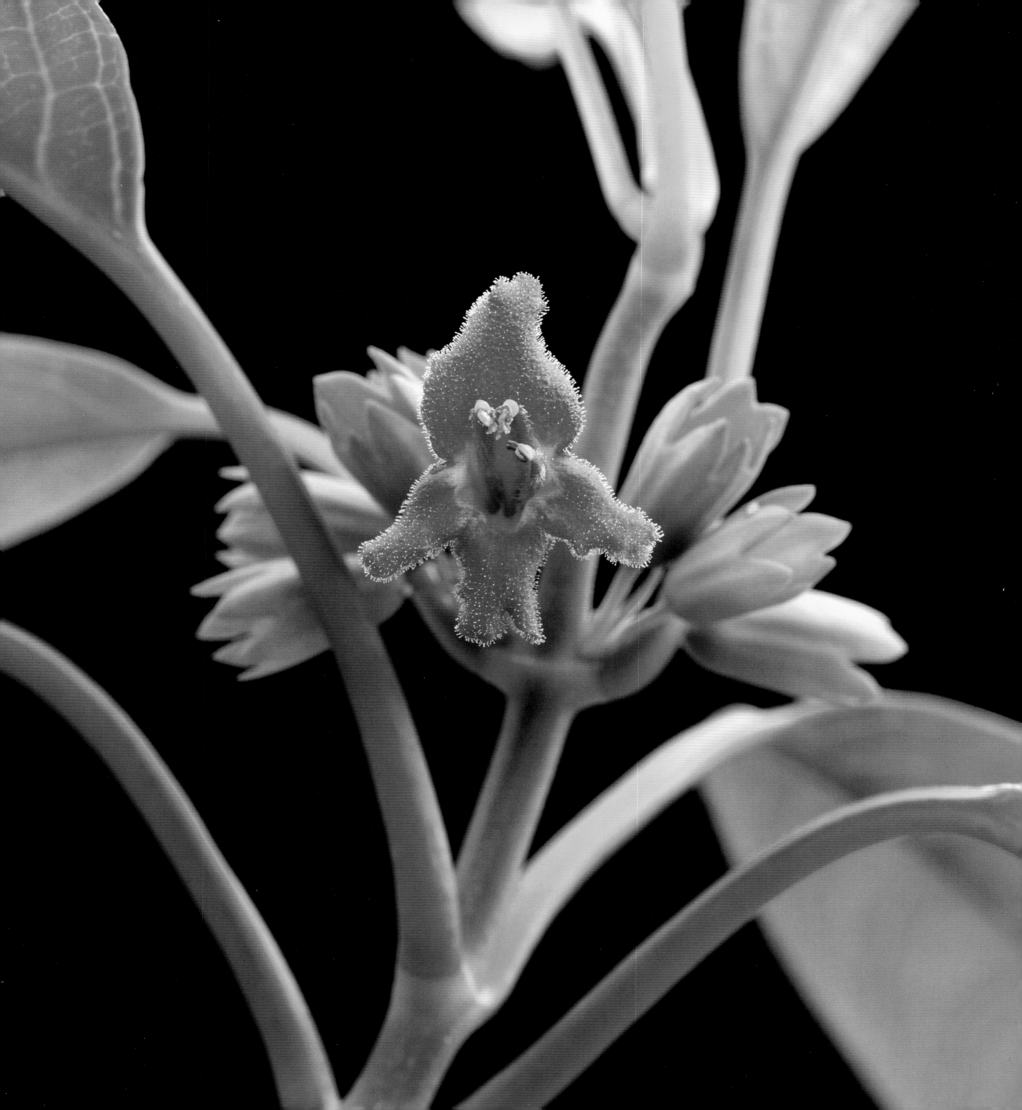

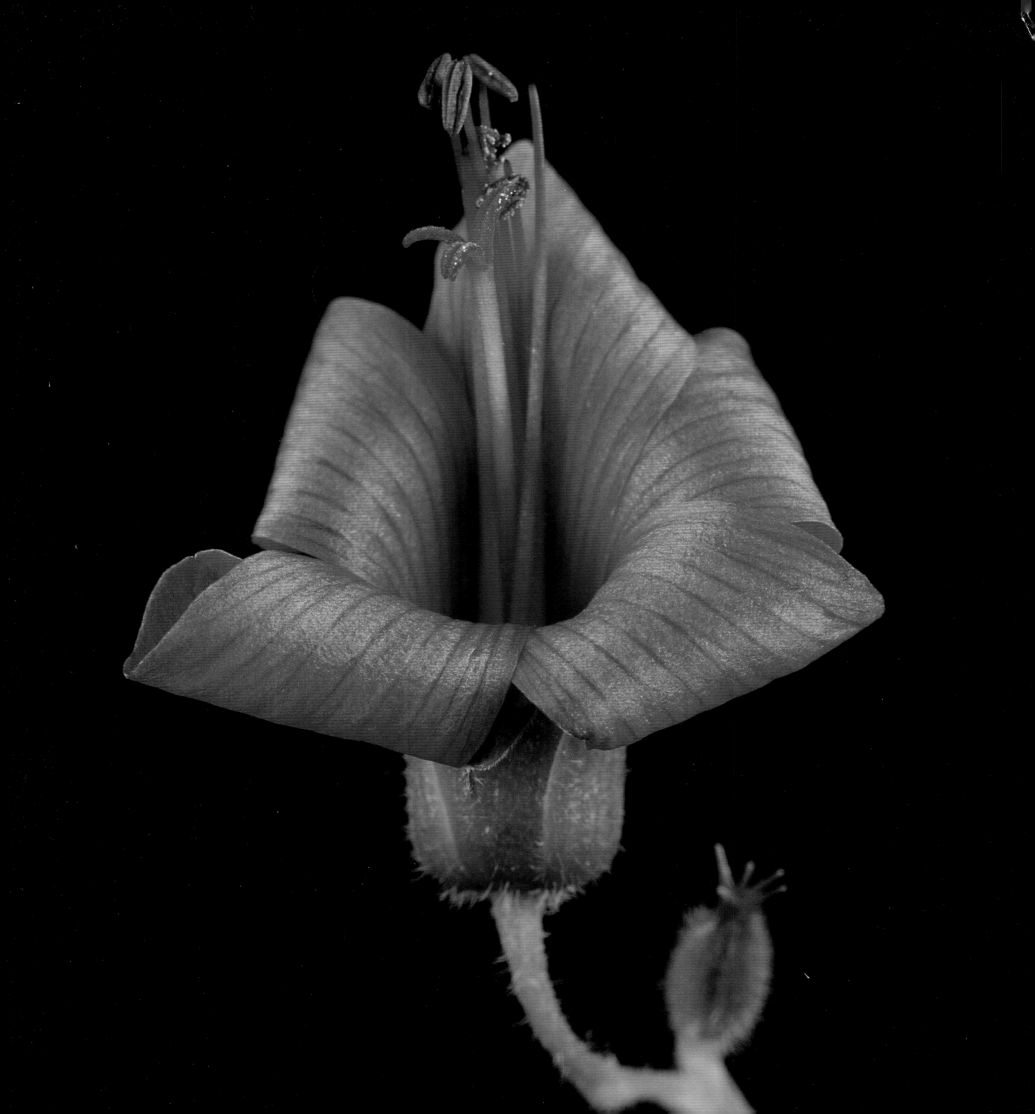

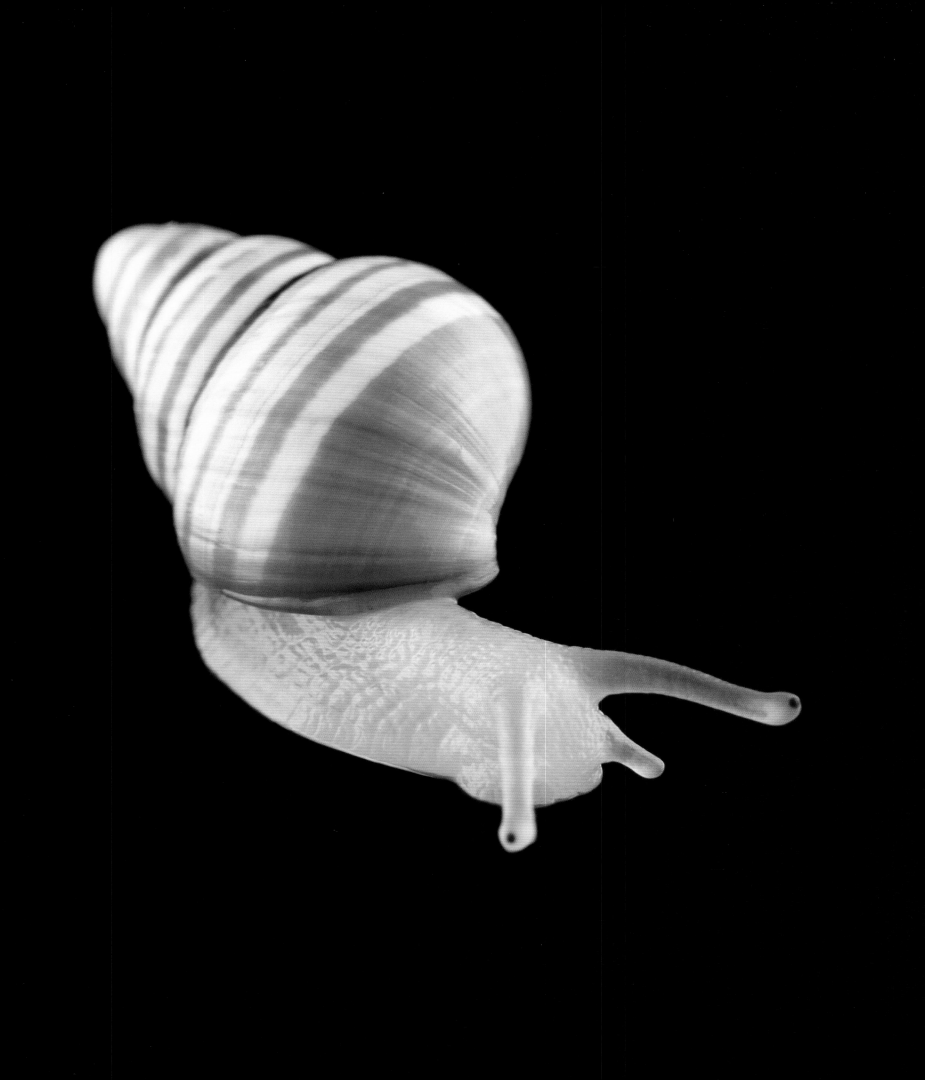

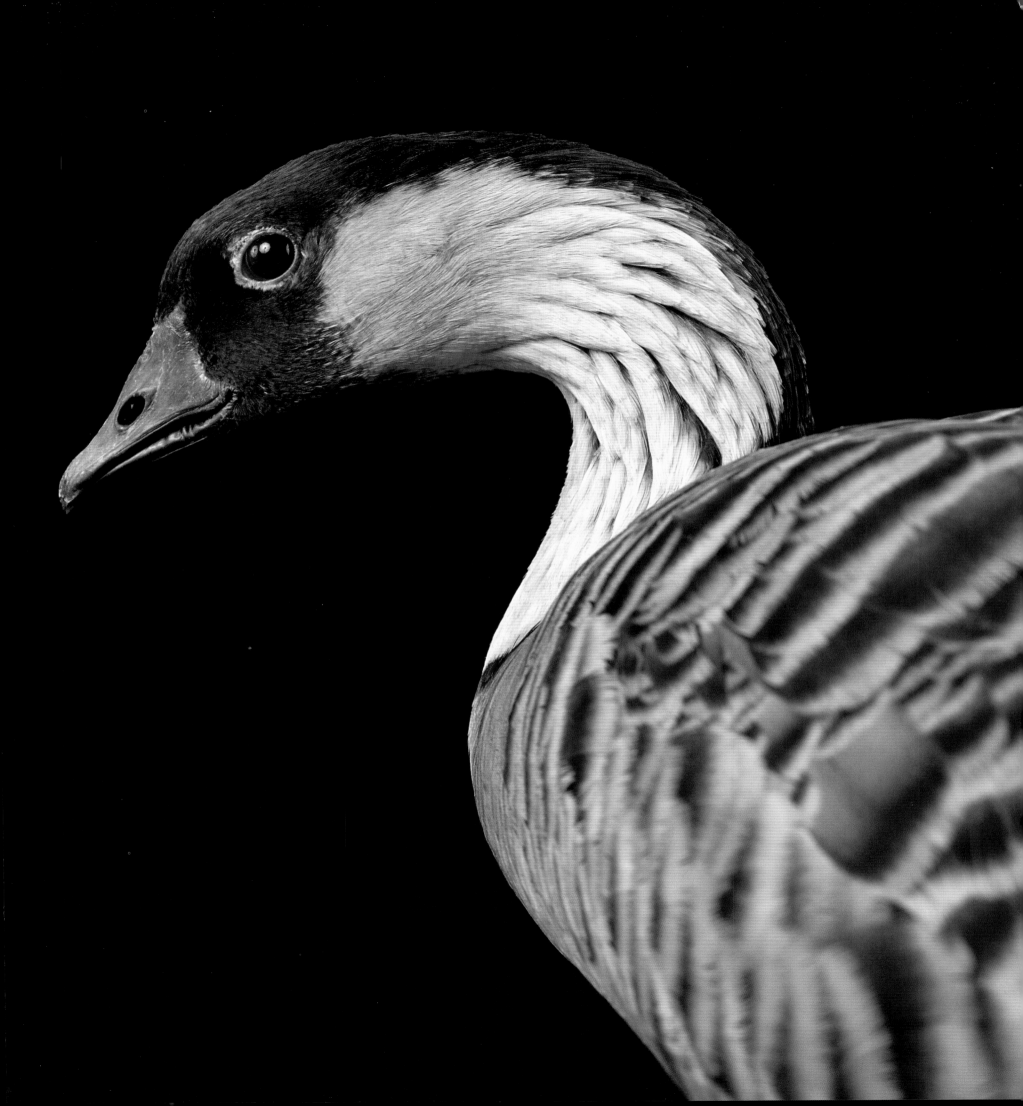

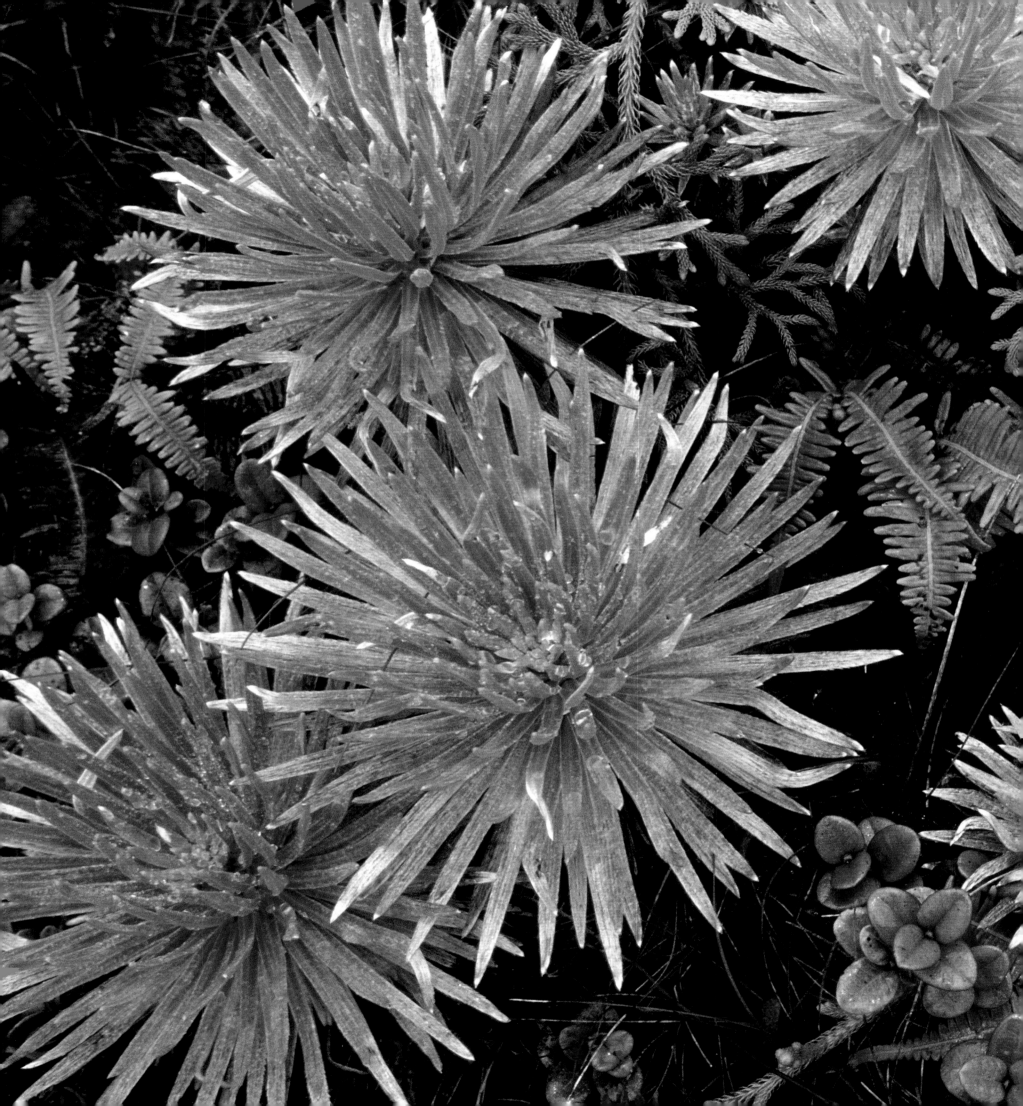

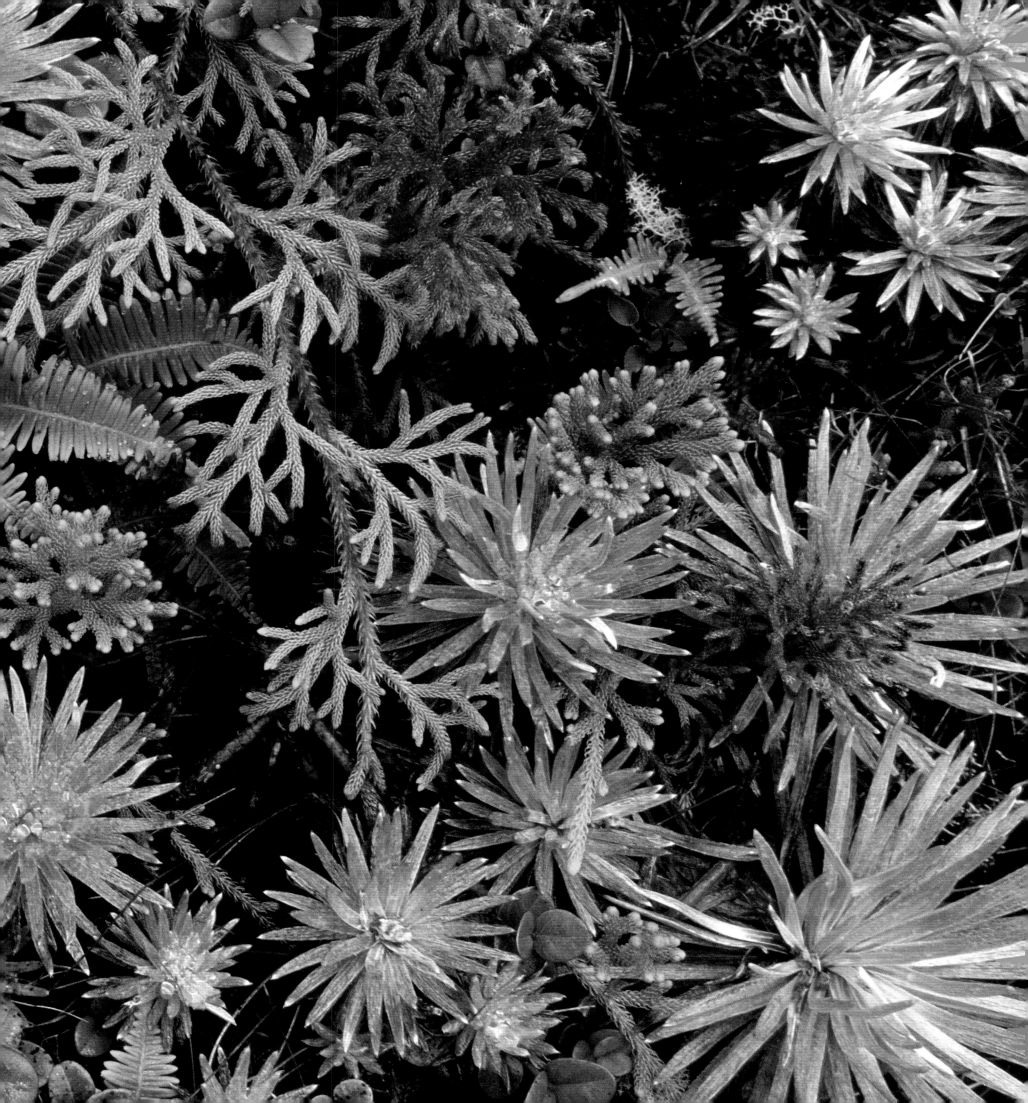

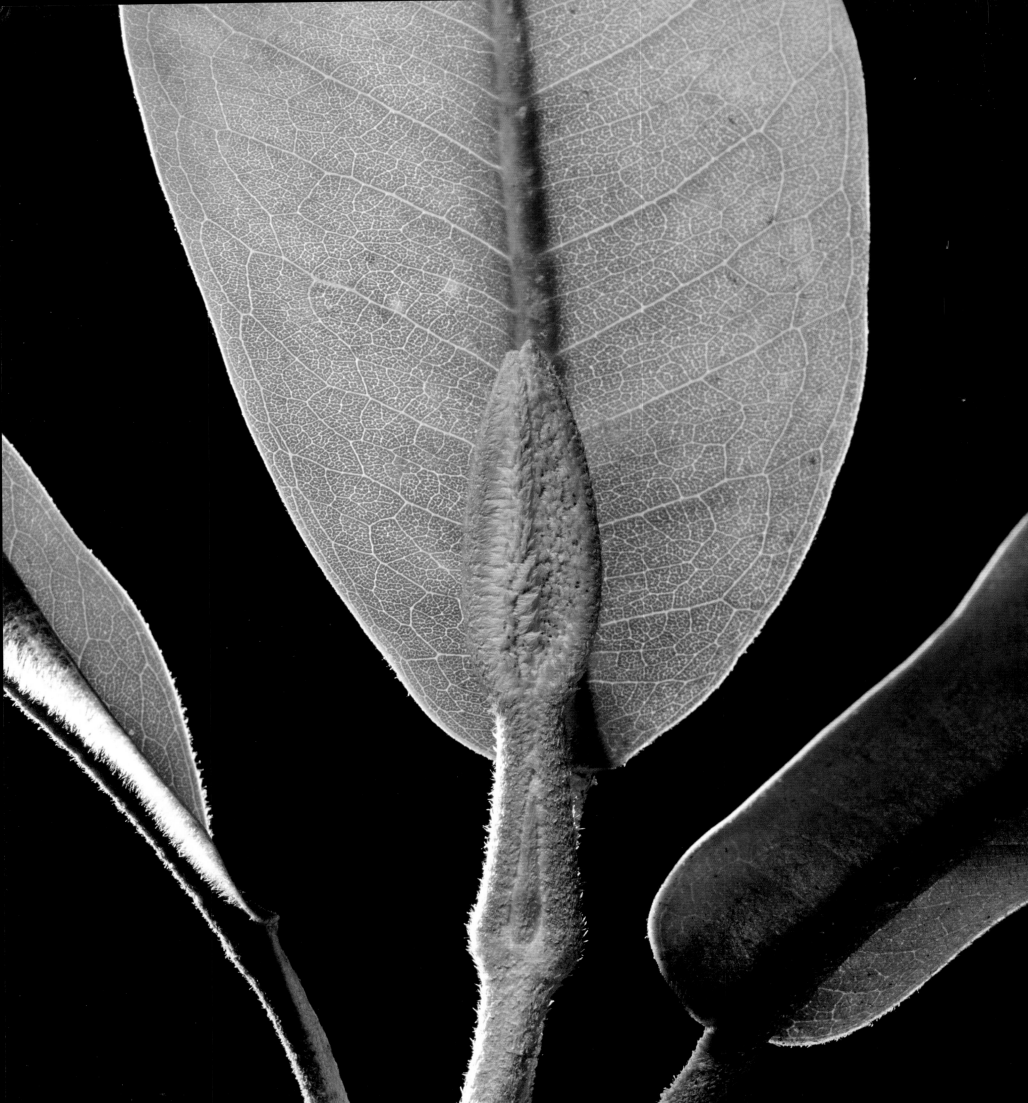

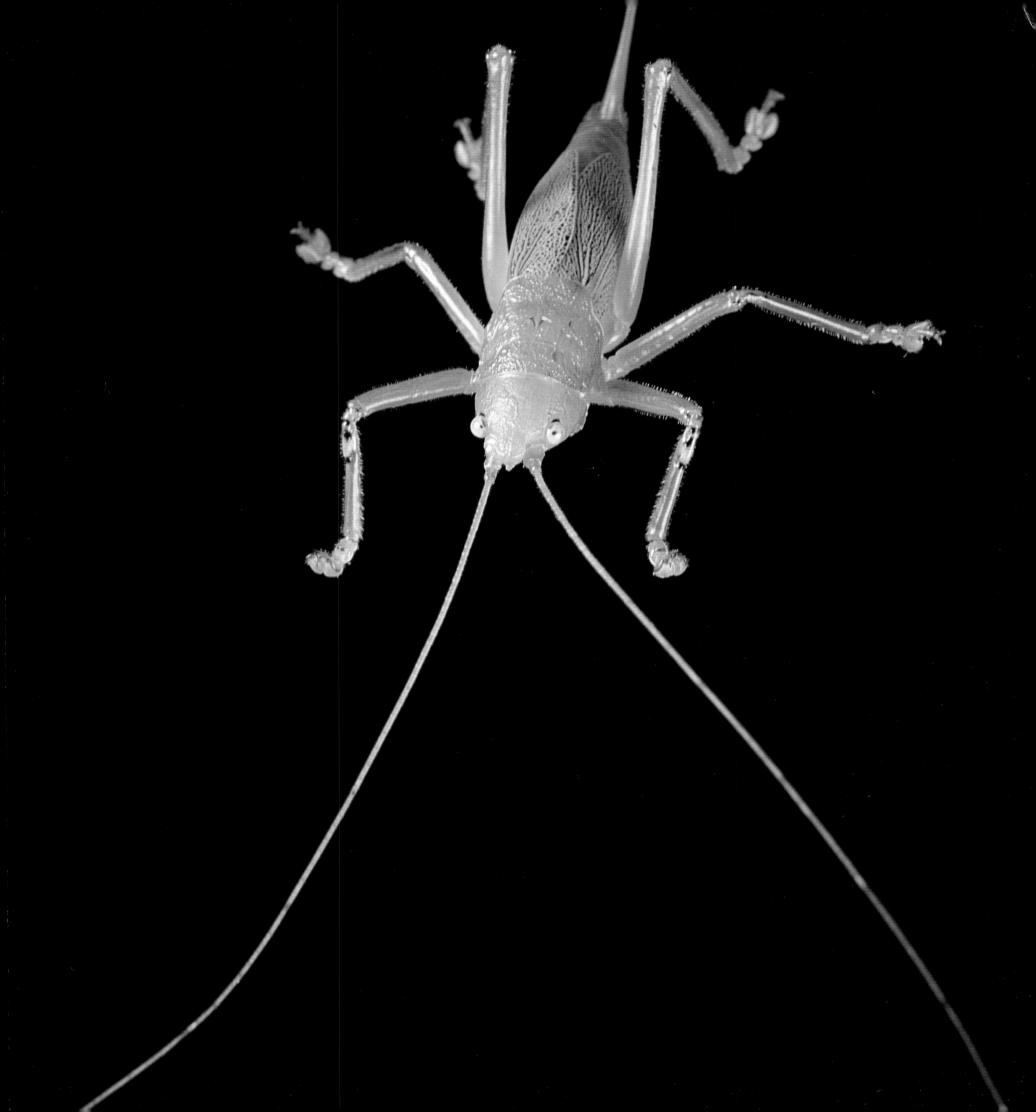

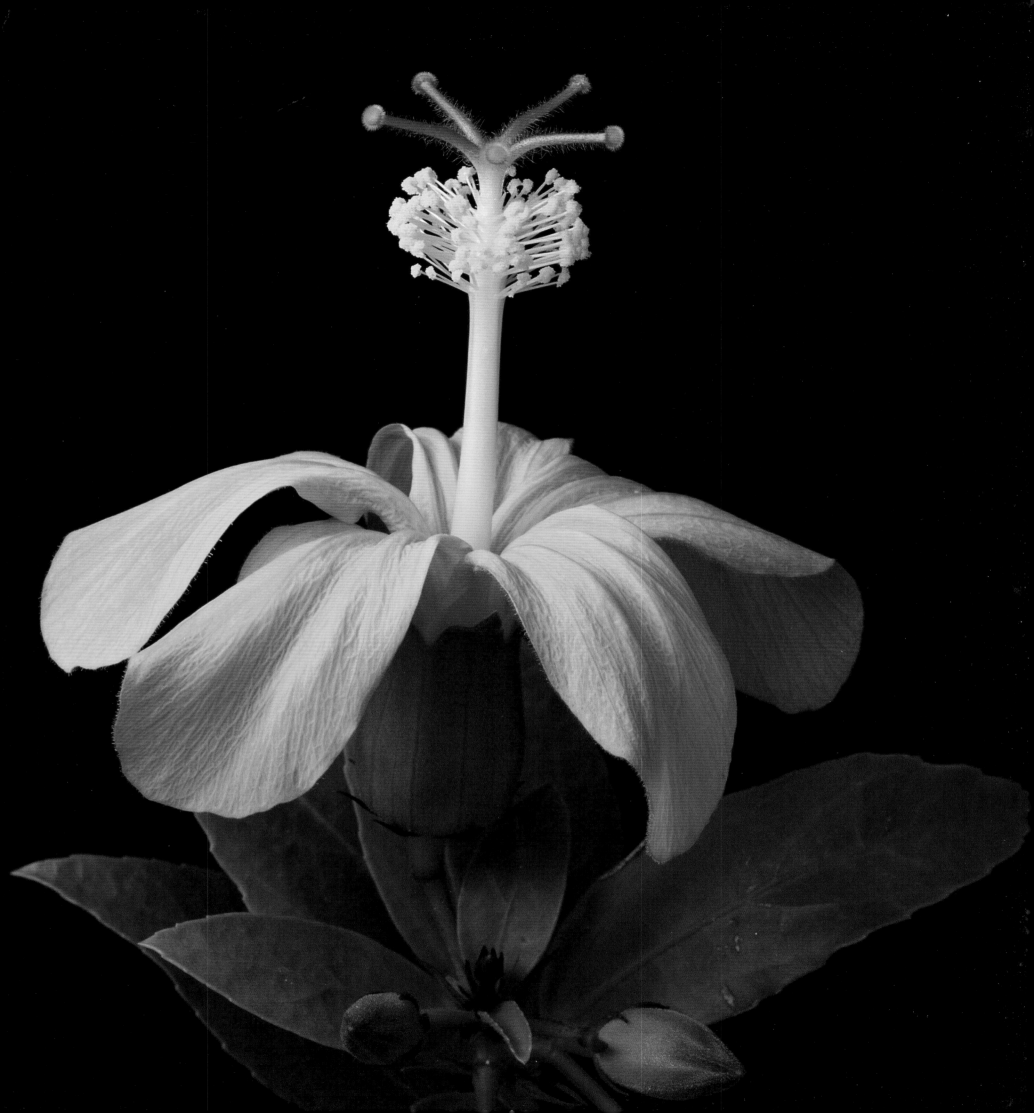

REMAINS OF A RAINBOW

RARE PLANTS AND ANIMALS OF HAWAI'I

DAVID LIITTSCHWAGER & SUSAN MIDDLETON

FOREWORD BY
W. S. MERWIN

IN ASSOCIATION WITH
ENVIRONMENTAL DEFENSE

WITH THE ASSISTANCE OF
NATIONAL TROPICAL BOTANICAL GARDEN
&
THE NATURE CONSERVANCY OF HAWAI'I

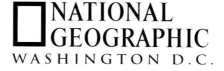

NATIONAL
GEOGRAPHIC
WASHINGTON D.C.

Produced by David Liittschwager and Susan Middleton
Designed by Jennifer Barry Design, Sausalito, CA

Published by the National Geographic Society
John M. Fahey, Jr., President and Chief Executive Officer
Gilbert M. Grosvenor, Chairman of the Board
Nina D. Hoffman, Executive Vice President

Prepared by the Book Division
Kevin Mulroy, Vice President and Editor-in-Chief
Charles Kogod, Illustrations Director
Barbara A. Payne, Editorial Director
Marianne Koszorus, Design Director

Staff for this Book
Lisa Lytton, Project Editor
Jennifer Barry, Designer
Kristen Wurz, Layout Production
Melissa Stein, Text Editor
Gary Colbert, Production Director
Holly Zimmerman and Barbara King, Proof Readers
Barbara King, Indexer

Manufacturing and Quality Control
George V. White, Director
John T. Dunn, Manager

The world's largest nonprofit scientific and educational organization, the National Geographic Society
was founded in 1888 "for the increase and diffusion of geographic knowledge." Since then it has supported
scientific exploration and spread information to its more than eight million members worldwide.

The National Geographic Society educates and inspires millions every day through magazines, books,
television programs, videos, maps and atlases, research grants, the National Geographic Bee, teacher
workshops, and innovative classroom materials.

The Society is supported through membership dues, charitable gifts, and income from the sale of its
educational products.

Members receive NATIONAL GEOGRAPHIC magazine—the Society's official journal—discounts on Society
products, and other benefits.

For more information about the National Geographic Society, its educational programs, publications, or
ways to support its work, please call 1-800-NGS-LINE (647-5463), or write to the following address:

National Geographic Society
1145 17th Street, N.W.
Washington, D.C. 20036-4688 U.S.A.
Visit the Society's Web site at www.nationalgeographic.com

Library of Congress Cataloging-in-Publication Data

Liittschwager, David.
Remains of a rainbow : rare plants and animals of Hawai'i / David Liittschwager &
Susan Middleton ; foreword by W.S. Merwin
    p.   cm.
ISBN 0-7922-6412-6 (hc.) -- ISBN 0-7922-6413-4 (pbk.)
1. Endangered species--Hawaii. 2. Rare animals--Hawaii. 3. Rare plants--Hawaii. I. Middleton, Susan.
II. Environmental Defense (Organization) III. National Tropical Botanical Garden. IV. Nature Conservancy
of Hawaii. V. Title.

QH76.5.H3 L55 2001
578.68'0969--dc21   2001030988

Printed in Italy

In the photograph captions in this book, English common names appear first, then Hawaiian names, then
scientific names. If a type of name does not appear, it is not known to the authors.

Photo captions for preceding pages: End of Waikamoi Flume (page 1); 'Ōhi'a Lehua (page 2); Rainbow-Eye
Damselfly (page 3); Stenogyne kealiae (page 4); Geranium arboreum (page 5); Moloka'i Tree Snail (page 6);
Nēnē (page 7); Silversword Bog (pages 8–9); Melicope degeneri (page 10); Kaua'i Flightless Cone Head
Katydid (page 11); Hibiscus kokio subsp. saintjohnianus (page 12). Following pages: Hawaiian Crow
(page 16); Lobelia gloria-montis in flower (pages 18–19).

FOR THOMAS EISNER
DEAR FRIEND, MENTOR, AND MUSE
D.L./S.M.

FOR MY PARENTS, AND FOR SUZIE RASHKIS
D.L.

TO THE MEMORY OF MY MOTHER, JEAN HINER MIDDLETON,
WHO WILL ALWAYS BE MY INSPIRATION
S.M.

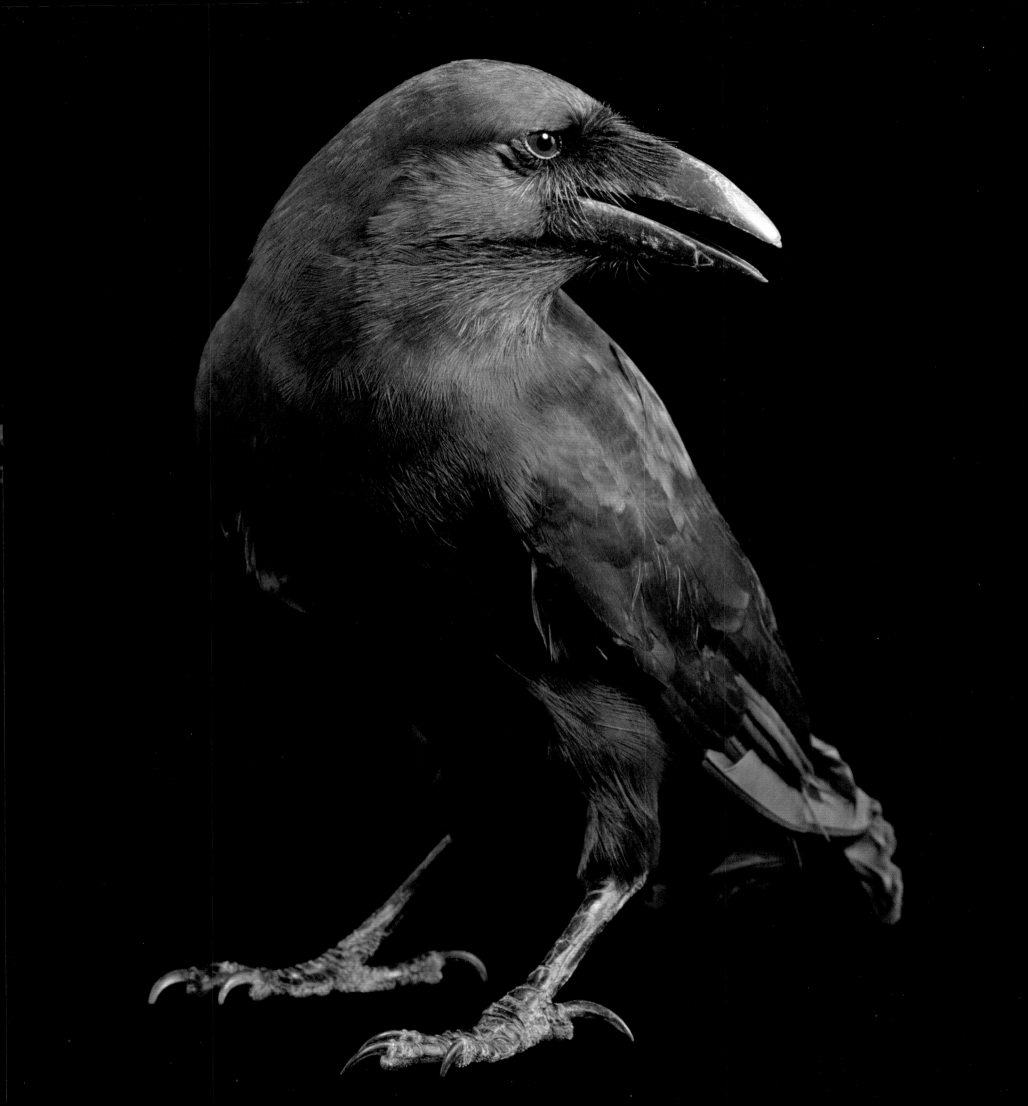

CONTENTS

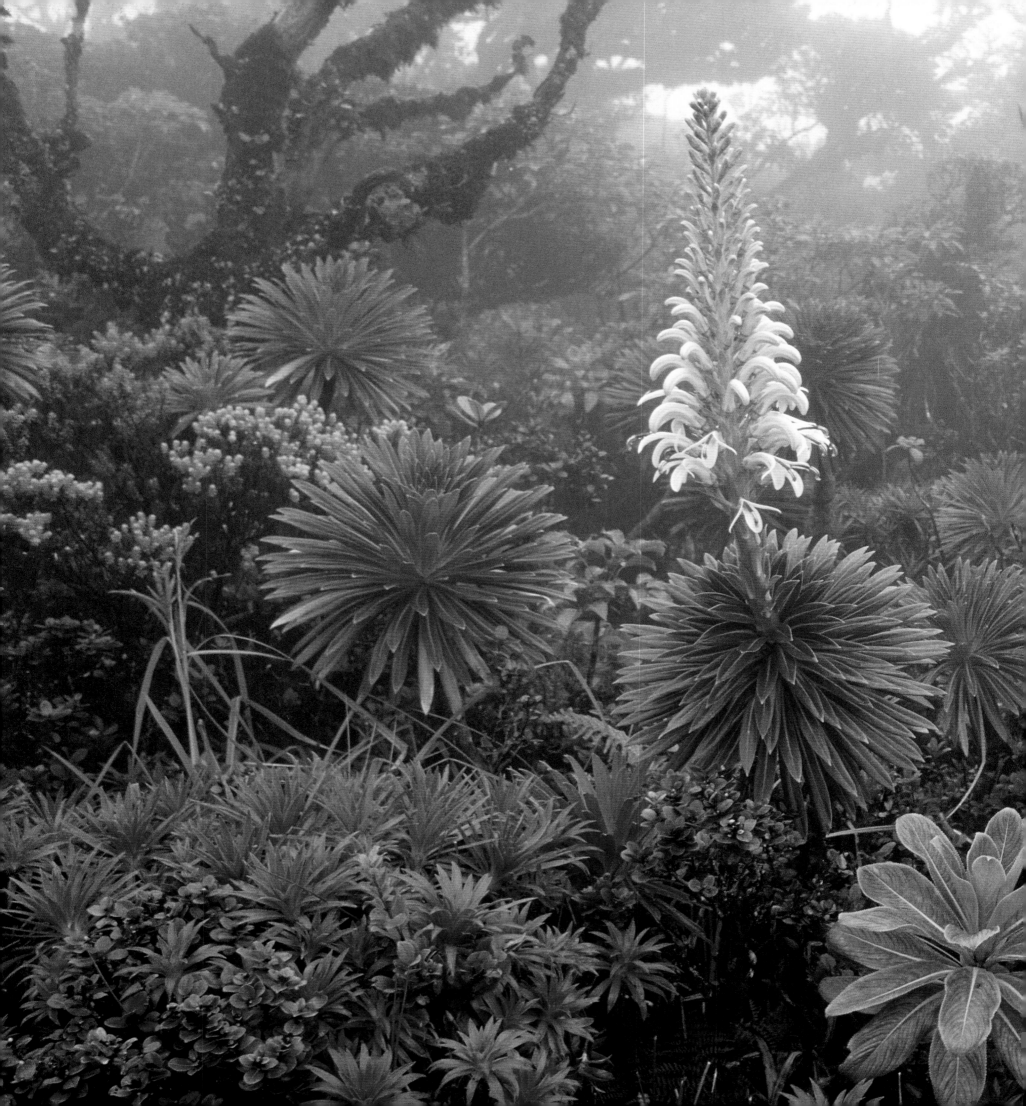

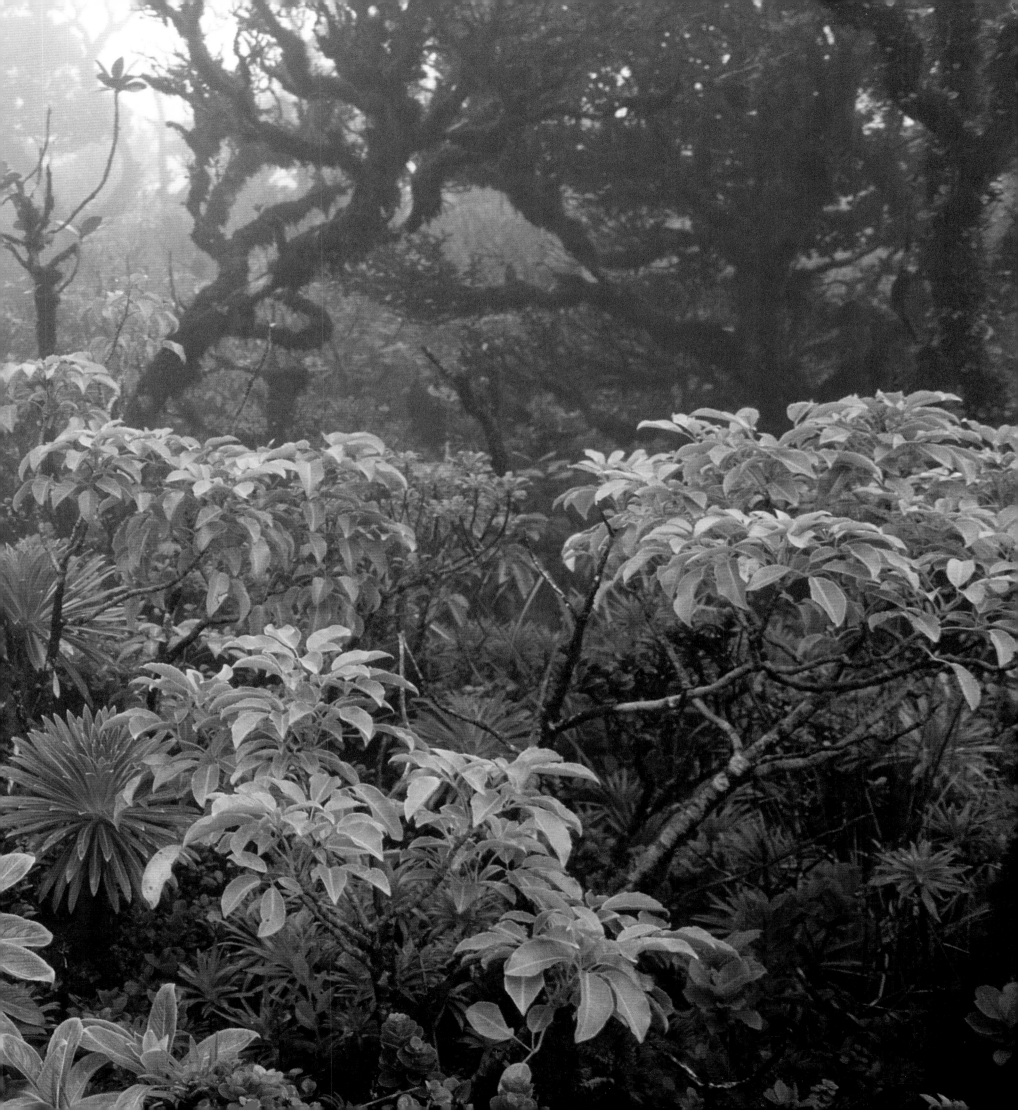

FOREWORD

Youth seems to be a constant element of the chain of volcanic islands that we call Hawai'i. It continues in them as a presence even though the summits of the older islands of the archipelago as we know it have eroded thousands of feet since their blazing origins, and vast sections of their cliff faces fell into the sea causing tidal waves that circled the globe, long before the emergence of the human species.

This feeling of the constancy of youth in the islands themselves suggests that their relation to age too may not be quite the same as that of the rest of the earth. In the mountains and deep valleys of Hawai'i we may be surprised by a feeling of being close to the barely imaginable beginning, and may discover an awareness of the evolution of the place and of its life as a single unbroken span.

We may even be able to understand some of the sources of these intimations. The island chain as a whole is ancient enough for the earliest craters, moving at a fraction of an inch a year, to have travelled most of the distance from their origin at the center of the Pacific to far in the northwest, worn down on the way to atolls, sandbars, shoals below sea level. Yet the entire procession, measured against the geological history of the earth, is of recent tenure. And over the ancestral well of molten lava itself, at the southeastern edge of the island of Hawai'i, the archipelago is still being formed. The flow from the recurring eruption of the volcano of Kilauea has added many square miles to the coast of the island in the past few years, and several miles to the southeast of the coast undersea wellings of lava are lifting seamounts—the embryos of islands yet to be born—nearer and nearer to the surface. All the stages of the islands from their rising to their disappearance are present in the chain at the same time.

And the site of the spring of lava out of which each island has been formed in turn is farther from other landmasses than any other spot on the planet. So that when the first lava cooled, in the sunlight above sea level, not only was there no life on it but there must have been none, or almost none, in the air above it. Life, in whatever form it found its way to the first island, began much more recently there than elsewhere on earth, and when it started to evolve it did so with a unique continuity and self-reference, less obviously affected by some of the cyclical cataclysms, such as massive glaciations, that punctuated the course of biological development on the continents. The means by which life reached the new shores as they rose into mountains—

spores and seeds borne by the wind and sea and eventually by birds and insects—can only be deduced. But once the progenitors reached the lava slopes they began an evolution of their own, independent of life elsewhere except for the sequence of subsequent arrivals, at long intervals, over millennia. Lichens, fungi, mosses, flowering plants, trees, freshwater life, insects, birds, in successions of their own, arrived, adapted themselves to specific areas and conditions aboveground and underground, and multiplied. As the island chain grew longer, forms of life found their way from older islands to younger ones, and then back to the older ones again, and as they developed they evolved an ecosystem distinct from any other on earth.

The islands began as mountains, with summits high enough to influence weather conditions, wet sides facing the prevailing northeast winds, dry sides to leeward, toward the south and west, and the developing life-forms changed in response to highly specific conditions of humidity, altitude, cloud cover, sunlight. Because there were no land mammals and no land snakes, and although there was predation from one-celled life to sea eagles, the environment of the islands must have remained, for millennia, gentler than that of most places on the planet. Several species of birds abandoned the ability to fly. Some plants stopped producing protective oils and odors. The climate was benign, with seasons but without extremes. The lava flows that periodically burned away swaths of forest on the younger islands were soon covered over with woodlands beginning again, another youth maturing into a biotope of enormous diversity and particularity.

This was the condition of the islands when the first humans found them, whoever they may have been, whenever they arrived, wherever they came from. The evidence at present indicates that the first who arrived in any numbers and stayed for any length of time, and took back word so that others followed them, were Polynesians from the crowded society of the Marquesas. They may have had predecessors—that remains uncertain—but in any case their appearance on the islands was as recent in human time as the islands were in geological time and as the islands' biotope was in the evolution of life as a whole. In the frame of history in which we view them now, the Polynesians must have reached the shores of the islands at about the time of the fall of Rome.

The real dangers to Hawaiian species began with the arrival of humans, with their alien talents.

It would be pleasant to be able to say that the early arrivals, overwhelmed by the innocent abundance of this unsuspecting world, allowed themselves to become part of its fabric, discovering in themselves an innocence of their own. In fact, the flightless birds were only too easy to catch and several species of them were soon completely exterminated. Besides such predation, the humans brought with them other exotic species including the Polynesian rat, which at once began to take its own toll. The Polynesian treatment of the natural world in Hawai'i over the next centuries was not quite as harmless, respectful, and benign as we might like to believe. The shorelines and valleys of the main islands were brought into cultivation, a process of inevitable disturbance. Featherwork certainly claimed the lives of many birds in the forests. But the Polynesian damage to the environment of the islands was dwarfed by the devastation inaugurated by European contact toward the end of the eighteenth century.

All the early writings about Hawai'i were set down either by persons of European ancestry or by Hawaiians educated—after conversion—by the missionaries, which has helped to maintain an illusion that post-European-contact history is the whole story of humankind in the islands. In fact James Cook, and the rest of the first Europeans to arrive, came at a crucial and unstable moment in the history of the Hawaiians, when several generations of warfare among feuding chiefs had weakened the farming populace and killed off entire dynasties of the ruling class. The Europeans' demands and imports (including their diseases) came ashore in the midst of Hawaiian factions and sufferings, and though Kamehameha himself managed to make use of the newcomers and retain his hegemony during his lifetime, he too contributed to the imbalance of his world.

The sandalwood trade, which began and reached its height during Kamehameha's rule, and from which he was one of those who profited most, was a major disaster to the structure of Hawaiian rural life, and to the forests of the main islands. The men of the farming class were forced to cut and load sandalwood, first on the lower slopes and then farther and farther up into the forests, to pay for the chiefs' acquisitions of weapons, warships, and European imports (porcelains, clothes, carriages, and liquor) and for the chiefs' increasing debts. It was, as far as we know, the first large-scale incursion of humans into the upper forests, and along with the unchecked spread of free-ranging cattle, it was irreparably destructive. The forced laborers are said to have destroyed sandalwood seedlings wherever they could, in order to root out the source of the traffic. Hawaiian sandalwood, of which at one time there were many species growing at various altitudes, was all but wiped out.

In the same years, with the rapid increase of European and American shipping—first traders, then whalers—the demand for firewood, and then for grazing land for cattle, sheep, goats, and pigs that the newcomers had brought and were raising, steadily shrank the forests. Fifty years after Cook's arrival the forests of Nuʻuanu Valley above Honolulu were all but gone. By that time clearance of forests for grazing, and then for sugar planting, was well under way, and the flaying and erosion of the islands continued unbroken, except for designated forest reserves, into the barely checked development of the present day.

Rats, hoofed animals, and invasive weeds were not the only environmentally ruinous imports: After quarreling with a chief, one of the early captains deliberately released mosquito larvae into Hawaiian freshwater, thus bringing avian malaria to the birds of Hawaiʻi, none of which had any resistance to it, so that they were eliminated from the lower slopes of all the islands. Habitat destruction and the spread of aggressive aliens represent the double assault by humans upon the intricate, unique, delicate biotope that had once inhabited Hawaiʻi.

By the mid-nineteenth century, forest destruction above Honolulu had altered the climate until there was concern for the city's water supply. In the long run there was an attempt to "reforest" the area—with imported species. But it was not until well into the latter half of the twentieth century that there was much general awareness of the extent of the damage that had been done to the Hawaiian environment. In recent years that has been described in various ways. It has been said that more species have been lost in Hawaiʻi during the past two hundred years than in the whole of North America since Columbus. The number of Hawaiian species that have become extinct in that time, combined with those that are vulnerable or on the verge of extinction now, whether or not they are officially "endangered" or protected in any way, is so large that it is scarcely an exaggeration to say that there are few indigenous Hawaiian species that are *not* in danger in the face of human presence, assumptions, and enterprise. And this is happening in a scene of biological splendor without parallel in the history of the earth.

Besides the islands' haunting reminder of youth, an observer of contemporary Hawaiʻi may notice its way of appearing (perhaps because of its relative isolation, and a surviving illusion of self-containment) to be a kind of hologram, an image on a small scale of the world at large. So that when we see the human threat to the irreplaceable treasures of the Hawaiian environment we may recognize that we are looking at the similar menace to the natural world everywhere.

The effect of humanity upon the rest of life has been there, no doubt, since the domestication of fire. But through most of history it went unnoticed, or was justified, advocated, and sanctified by religions, and was incorporated into the image of humanity as though it were an achievement.

It was probably not until after the work of Wallace and Darwin in the mid-nineteenth century that Europeans and Americans began to realize that the survival of our species depended upon a fabric of other kinds of life, and then that our species survived and multiplied at the expense of the rest of the living environment. And it was not until the latter part of the twentieth century, with our exploding population, proliferation of poisons both chemical and radioactive, and accelerating obliteration of other species, that the gravity of our role and the peril of our course dawned upon more than a few of humankind. The majority of humans, and the assumptions that underlie most human enterprise, consider the survival of other species to be relatively unimportant. It is a daunting realization, at odds with much that we have tried to believe about ourselves. Humans as a whole (if such a thing can be imagined) are still far from recognizing that what we do to the life in which we are privileged to have a place we are doing to ourselves, in every sense, and irrevocably. And so, as the devastation (and the justification of it) continues and accelerates, if we look beyond the advertisements we may come to wonder whether there is any hope.

We have never known the answer to that. But hope, I suspect, is not a matter of knowledge but a way of looking at life, and so we come to this book, to these extraordinary portraits and the point of view they present. Somewhere in the twentieth century our species reached the point where we were able to destroy life, singly or generally, anywhere on earth, and at that moment wilderness, in a sense, ceased to exist. After that, when some humans felt impelled to protect and preserve what was left of the natural world if they were able to, their relation to it became, suddenly, that of gardener to a garden. One of relative knowledge, endless ignorance, dubious and provisional control, and an effort at responsibility for the continuing welfare of life in the place.

At least in the Western world, we have persisted in defining our species in terms of intelligence—human intelligence, which is certainly distinct—and the distinction, we have maintained, confers upon us a superiority over any other kind of life. Whether indeed our intelligence exceeds that of any other form of life depends upon criteria devised only by ourselves, for our own interest. But our intelligence, in any case, has enabled us to do two things that have magnified it. One is the articulation of language, effecting the communication of feeling, information, and varieties of order. And then the recording of what has been expressed and thought and felt, allowing us to refer to the past intelligence and language of others.

But if we are to define and exclude ourselves from the rest of life on the basis of intelligence alone I can see no grounds for hope. Intelligence itself is morally indifferent, and as we see daily it can be bought and sold and used to advance any enterprise—including the most ruthless and ruinous.

I believe that our real superiority as a species is not our intelligence itself but the quality of imagination and compassion (in itself, perhaps, one of the blessings of language) that allows us to care about the welfare, suffering, and survival of lives far from our own, and not immediately or obviously related to our comforts, our prospects, or our acquisitions. Whatever we may call the sympathy that involves us with the fate of victims in war zones half a world away, the sonar torture of whales, the mutilation of women and the tortures of bears in Pakistan, or the last members of a species of rain forest honeycreeper, this regard for life apart from our own is something that, so far as I know, is unique to our species. We can glimpse ancestral forms of it in the family and group behavior of other animals, but its broader emergence is a mark of humanity. It is our talent and we have developed it in our own way. It is something that we cannot altogether account for. But if we do not live up to our gifts they do us no good. And what this gift demands of us constantly is a change of heart. What hope there may be depends upon whether or not we can believe in such a possibility.

But the photographs in this book are testaments to the real human talent that I have spoken of. The danger facing each of the lives portrayed here is something that talent recognizes. Most of the portraits have been made, deliberately and dramatically, in isolation (though a few, of montane tropical bogs, for instance, display the dazzling richness of interrelated life in a surviving place). This striking solitude again and again allows us to see each life as unique, a single appearance in all of time and existence, something that, paradoxically, it shares with every other life, and with the entire web of the waking world. As we see these images, these moments, it may be apparent to us that the value of each of them is beyond our ability to measure or to understand, and that, whether or not we know anything else about them, their present danger is something that we share.

—W. S. Merwin

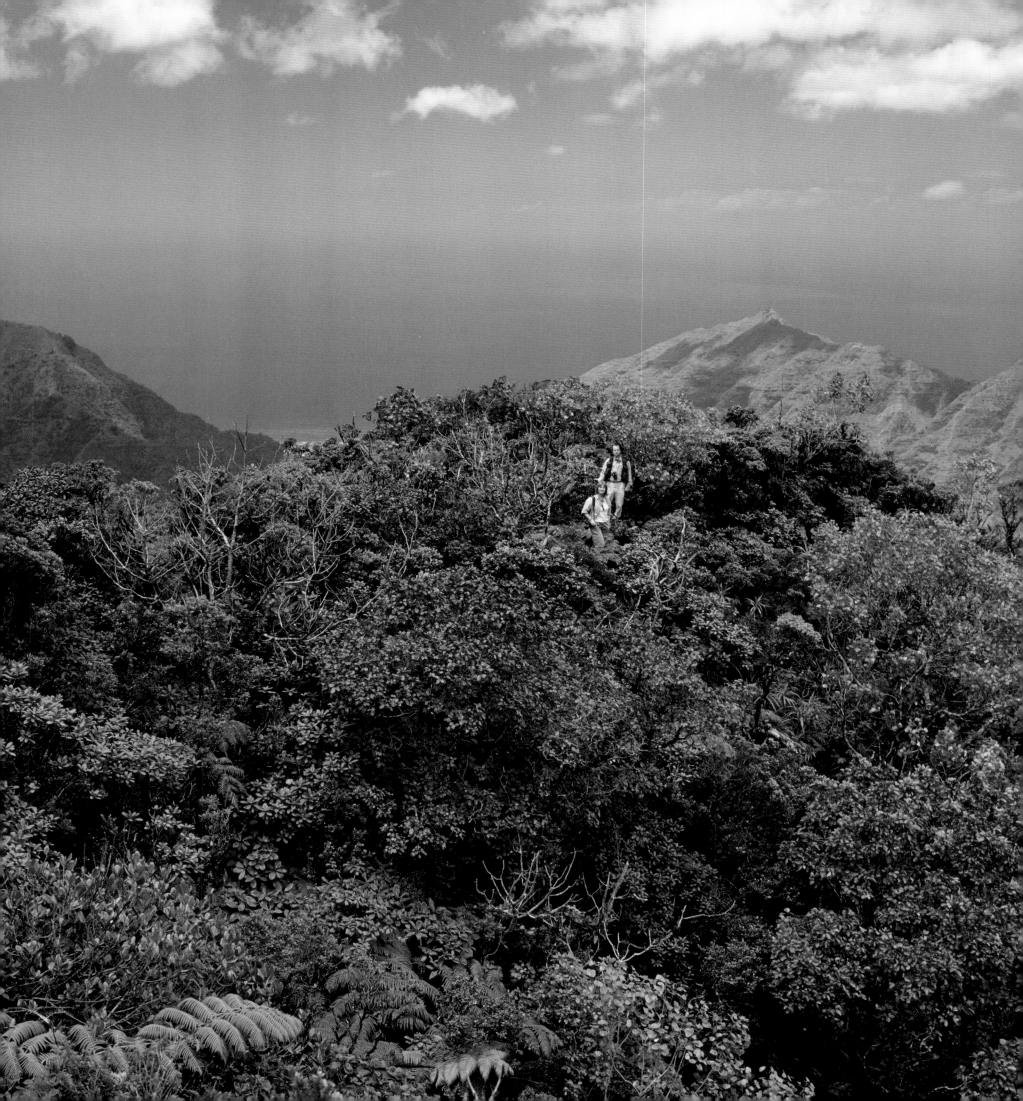

He aliʻi ka ʻāina; he kauwāke kanaka.
The land is a chief; man is its servant.
—from ʻŌlelo Noʻeau

INTRODUCTION

As I look back, it was when we were photographing a fragile tree named Cooke's *kokiʻo*, trying hard to light the ridge circling its narrow trunk so that it would show in the photograph, that we knew where our eyes would turn next.

We visited Hawaiʻi in February of 1993 to complete fieldwork for our book *Witness*, which was to be a representation of endangered species throughout the United States. We were introduced to an extremely rare plant, Cooke's *kokiʻo*, or *Kokia cookei*, by Robert Hobdy, an expert in native Hawaiian flora and chief forester with the Division of Forestry and Wildlife on Maui. We had met and photographed many endangered plants and animals by then, but the story of *Kokia cookei* was unlike anything we had heard or seen, and it changed our lives.

This plant was hanging on by a thread. The ridge on its narrow trunk was a graft scar. *Kokia cookei* lived above the scar; below was *Kokia drynarioides,* a related species that is also endangered, but not as endangered as *cookei.* We learned that this plant had become so rare that it could only live grafted onto another species—it was incapable of existing on its own roots.

These trees, which evolved over millennia and were once abundant in the lowland forests, are nearly gone due to free-ranging cattle and goats, which have chewed up their leaves and trampled their roots, and rats and insects, which have eaten their seeds. Without the devotion of a few people who cared, these trees wouldn't be with us at all.

Kokia cookei was discovered in the 1860s by a rancher on Molokaʻi. The Hawaiians had known this plant much earlier; they used the flowers and bark for medicine and crushed the bark to make a red dye for fishing nets. *Kokia* trees, a kind of Hibiscus, are spectacular in bloom, with hundreds of fleshy orange red flowers that can reach nine inches in diameter. Each flower carries an impressive load of nutrient-rich nectar that very likely was sipped by a now-extinct Hawaiian honeycreeper, which probably returned the favor by pollinating the plant.

The three known trees in the 1860s were eventually reduced to one lonesome tree on the west end of Molokaʻi around the turn of the century. This area had been a dryland forest but from the early 1800s had been denuded by free-ranging cattle and goats. Flowers and fruit were collected from this last wild tree and it was propagated on Moloka'i by a plantation manager, George P. Cooke. The next year the wild tree died, and for over sixty years the tree in Cooke's backyard, and progeny from this tree, were the very last of *Kokia cookei*.

In the 1970s Keith Woolliams from the Waimea Arboretum on O'ahu took an interest in *Kokia cookei* and felt something needed to be done to bring it back from the edge. He went to Moloka'i and collected seeds from the tree in Cooke's backyard. Just a few months later a brushfire swept through, killing Cooke's tree. Keith Woolliams got one seedling to grow at Waimea Arboretum and when it flowered he collected seed and tried to propagate it, only to discover that the plant wouldn't grow from the seed, which was not fertile. He tried cuttings and air layering, with no success, and finally tried grafting it onto a related species from the Big Island. He was able to get a few of the grafts to work before the mature tree that grew from seedling from Cooke's backyard died that same year. From those few grafts other grafts were made from the top cuttings of the trees, but the seeds have never germinated.

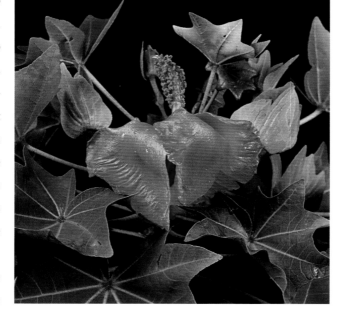

Consequently, all of the *Kokia cookei* plants are clones with no genetic variability. Some of the grafted trees were planted back on Moloka'i within fenced-off areas that protect them from grazing animals. Here they are maintained, watered, and monitored. If the seeds ever germinate, there might be a little variation expressed in the seed even though there is only one parent; with a graft, there is no variability. Presently there are only 15 individuals in the world—all grafts.

The tree we photographed in 1993 never flowered and eventually died. It wasn't until 1998, when we returned to Waimea Botanical Garden, that we were finally able to see and photograph the explosive red blossoms of *Kokia cookei*.

The story of *Kokia cookei* shows how precarious life can be for native Hawaiian species. We have learned that all too many Hawaiian plants and animals have a tenuous hold on life, like the *Kokia*. As Robert Hobdy said, "All it takes is for a few people to drop the ball for a little while and it's over."

We were so moved by what we saw during that first trip to Hawai'i in 1993 that we pursued our fieldwork with a kind of relentless enthusiasm until we realized we could never do justice to Hawai'i within the context of a project focusing upon endangered species of the United States. We would include Hawai'i in *Witness*, but we made a vow to return to Hawai'i and to create a project specifically focusing on rare plants, animals, and habitats of these islands. I realized then that Hawai'i is not generally understood or appreciated for the treasure that it is. A visitor may arrive and be immediately engulfed by the warmth of the soothing trade winds and overwhelmed by the steep volcanic cliffs cloaked in lush velvet green vegetation, perhaps even witness the primeval drama of an erupting volcano, and will likely experience the pleasure of immersion in the warm blue-green sea. It is an alluring place, and even the Hawaiian language sounds buttery and lyrical. But few visitors will ever see a native plant, animal, or place. The natives are shy, hard to see, and mostly hide out in inaccessible places, which contributes to why they still survive. Yet they are what most eloquently and authentically defines the real Hawai'i.

After 15 years of personal encounters with endangered species, we have turned our eyes toward Hawai'i, one of the richest natural environments on earth, and one of the most threatened. All of the plants and animals in this book are native to Hawai'i; that is, they came on their own, with the help of wind, water, or the wings of birds. The Hawaiian Islands are the most isolated archipelago in the world, more than 2,000 miles from the closest continental landmass. The chance of a plant or animal reaching one of the islands, especially in shape to grow and reproduce, was exceedingly slim. It is estimated that on average, only once in every 10,000 years was a plant or animal able to successfully establish itself on the Hawaiian Islands.

Susan Middleton and David Liittschwager,
Mount Ka'ala, O'ahu (page 26)

This process of evolution began over 70 million years ago, when the islands first emerged from the sea as volcanoes. Their isolation created the opportunity for an astonishing assemblage of plants and animals to evolve, most of them found nowhere else on earth. It is possible to observe the splendor of creation, both geological and biological, in Hawai'i.

A variety of habitats and climates, rich volcanic soils, perpetual spring and summer weather, the caressing trade winds, and the "isolation within isolation"—that is, the islands themselves as an isolated archipelago, and then the individual islands isolated from one another, and within each island a great variety of "microhabitats" separated and isolated from each other, often delineated by high mountain ridges and deep valleys—set the stage for the early colonizers to thrive and flourish. They found a great variety of rich, unoccupied habitats to settle into, and once settled tended to stay. Many became restricted to small localities with highly specialized requirements. Their energy went into becoming finely tuned to a particular habitat and set of conditions, growing and changing and developing into new forms, making them the quintessential expression of those places.

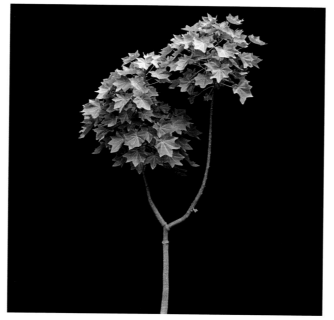

These native plants and animals are exceptionally vulnerable to changes in their environment. It doesn't mean they are weak. When I saw the silversword growing on the barren slopes and enduring the harsh climate of Haleakalā, Maui, I could not help but respect its toughness. Or when I observed the 'o'opu, the native freshwater goby, using its specially adapted suction device to navigate upstream and scale 1,000-foot waterfalls, I could not help but be impressed with this little fish's skill and tenacity. Yet the mighty silversword cannot defend itself against unleashed goats in Haleakalā and the hardy goby has no defense against agricultural pesticides that run off into the freshwater streams of Hawai'i.

During our time in Hawai'i we have experienced the euphoria of Eden and witnessed the devastation of its loss. Hawai'i has the unfortunate distinction of being the endangered species capital of the world. It comprises only one-fifth of one percent of the total U.S. land area, yet over 25 percent of the species on the U.S. endangered species list are Hawaiian, and 90 percent of those are plants. It can also be said that Hawai'i is the evolutionary capital of the world, the crown jewel of our national natural heritage.

The native plants and animals were the first Hawaiians, and the ancestral Hawaiian people were the first people to know them and live with them. Hawaiians named their plants and animals long before white people arrived and naturalists and biologists began assigning scientific names and descriptions in the Linnaean system. So, as plants and animals are described as "new discoveries," we refer to their being new to science, not necessarily new to humanity. Where the original Hawaiian names are known, we have included them.

Hawaiians understood that they were completely dependent upon the land and consequently they respected it and developed a relationship with it that is deeply spiritual. The Hawaiian word for land, 'āina, literally means "that which feeds." The early Hawaiians saw themselves as part of nature, and their interactions with it were oriented toward maintaining a unity and balance with the natural world. In traditional Hawaiian belief, the psychic and spiritual realm is embodied in the physical realm, so spirits inhabited everything in the natural world, animate and inanimate—even stones. In Hawai'i stones have volcanic origins, as the earth continues to re-create itself. The close proximity to erupting volcanoes must have led the early Hawaiians toward an intimate connection with and reverence for the earth. In Hawai'i one can see the beginnings and endings of nature with a particular, vivid clarity.

When I asked a Hawaiian friend about the link between native Hawaiian

Koki'o (left and right)
Kokia cookei

flora and fauna and the Hawaiian people, he replied, "As they go, we go." I understood this as a heartfelt testimonial to the connection Hawaiian people feel with their native land, combined with the recognition that the loss of native plants and animals is closely tied to the loss of the Hawaiian culture itself. The preservation of the unique Hawaiian heritage is both cultural and environmental: For the culture to authentically survive, the natural environment in which it evolved must also survive.

Over the last five years we have researched and photographed rare native species and habitats in Hawai'i. We have continued our portraiture of Hawaiian native plants and animals, including not only species on the endangered species list but also those that have not made it through the listing process and are known to be equally threatened, particularly terrestrial invertebrates. We have also highlighted species that are new discoveries (previously unknown to science) or rediscoveries (thought to be extinct), working closely with field biologists.

We show these plants and animals isolated, out of context with their natural environment, partly because their lives now are fractured and threatened and more vulnerable than ever, as their homes are degraded and destroyed and they are assaulted by alien forces over which they are powerless. But even more than this, we present them in isolation to reveal their natural splendor and aching beauty. Our process has been to practice a reverence for the innate value of each one of these animals and plants, which is rooted deeper than any system of economics. We wish to express that we are connected to them, and to suggest that they are our cousins in the larger community of life on earth. We want to shine a light on them, show them for who they are, and help to give them the attention they deserve.

Beyond the portraiture of individual species, we have illustrated rare native habitats—intact ecosystems—where plants and animals still live in healthy relationship to one another. Those places are like magic gardens, tapestries, mosaics, which appear as if they were designed by a master landscape architect. And in fact, they were—life unfolding over millions of years in splendid isolation. These natural communities, the only safe harbors for their inhabitants, are as fragile as they are remote, often situated high in the mountains on razorback ridges, on steep cliffs, and isolated, densely vegetated valleys. Their inaccessibility and the need to protect them from damage mean that few people will ever have the opportunity to experience them directly.

In many ways, the story of life in Hawai'i is the greatest story ever told. Because so many native species have gone extinct and those that remain are being pressured by alien species, we know we can no longer see and enjoy the complete picture—we cannot hear the symphony with all the players. But we can glimpse what it must have been like and we can observe specific places where all the members of the assembly of life are present. In this book we have attempted to show some of these intact native places, where diversity and harmony converge.

We did not undertake this work to memorialize plants and animals that are destined to go extinct. Quite the opposite. We have done it to call attention to their plight, with the hope that for most of them, it is not too late.

Often, I sense that many of us have fallen out of love with the natural world, and that it has become more and more difficult for us to feel at home here on earth. What drove me to embark on this project was a desire to connect with the unique and precarious life that has emerged in Hawai'i, and to express that connection. These bits of creation, each a masterpiece, have made me a believer in the world, a world inhabited by power and spirit—what Hawaiians call *mana*. And for me, this spiritual power is nowhere more perfectly embodied than in native plants and animals living together in a healthy home, where the artistry of existence is most coherent. These plants and animals are the real revelations, the living truths that have sustained us physically, mentally, and spiritually throughout our own evolution.

As native plants, animals, and natural communities have disappeared, so have we lost many of the subtle hues of that once-brilliant rainbow, but what remains bears witness to the beauty of the full spectrum. While we grieve the loss, we can find hope and inspiration in what remains. What evolved in Hawai'i was paradise, and these plants and animals, rare and vulnerable, are the truest expression of that paradise. We must devote all of our human ingenuity toward saving it. Without our direct acts of preservation, this masterpiece of creation will perish. I believe we need it as much as it needs us.

—Susan Middleton

There are 142 species portrayed in this book. The first picture we made in Hawai'i was of a Hawaiian hoary bat at the Honolulu Zoo in January 1993 (see page 65). The last picture made for this volume was of a pair of *Plagithmysus* beetles (see page 215). This final picture was made in November 2000 in a small dorm room at the University of Hawai'i in the middle of the night, a few months after what was supposed to be our deadline and several hours after the bags should have been packed for an early morning departure—just because we couldn't stop, because the bugs were so lively, and because we have developed a great affection for the creatures of Hawai'i.

While working on our book *Witness,* we became aware of the significance of Hawai'i to any survey of endangered species. We continued to work in Hawai'i at every opportunity, aided by many people and organizations, such as Maui Land & Pineapple Company, Inc., which supported several field trips to Pu'u Kukui; Waimea Arboretum and Botanical Garden, which gave access to and assistance with their Hawaiian endangered plants; and Maile Sakamoto and Peter Shannon, who arranged a visit with a Hawaiian Crow. In March 1998, after discussions with Fred Krupp, executive director of Environmental Defense, we entered into the partnership with Environmental Defense that, fueled by a grant from the MacArthur Foundation, enabled us to produce this book.

More than half of all of the plants on the United States endangered species list are Hawaiian, so we knew that plants would figure largely, if not predominantly, in our work. We approached Steve Perlman, a National Tropical Botanical Garden field botanist with over 30 years of experience in working with Hawaiian native flora, about our work with plants. Steve was enthusiastic about our project and offered to prepare a plan for our fieldwork and then accompany us in the field and guide us to the places where these rare plants live.

Over an eight-year period we made 20 trips to the islands. The shortest trip was three days; the longest was three months. Together they add up to more than one year on the ground in Hawai'i, Maui, Lāna'i, Moloka'i, O'ahu, Kaua'i, and Laysan.

Working out of a backpack was something new to us. For most of our work on the mainland we have had the luxury of a large truck filled with some 4,000 pounds of cameras, lights, stands, sandbags, backgrounds, lumber, aquarium tanks, filters, pumps, and generators. In 1993, the first time we traveled to Hawai'i, we considered shipping the truck so that we would have all of our tools (toys), but in the end, we arrived with 37 equipment cases and rented a U-Haul truck. On the second trip we pared down. Toward the end of the project, the maximum number of equipment and supply cases we brought was 10.

Fieldwork in Hawai'i often requires a long walk over steep terrain, so everything we thought we might need had to go into a backpack. My backpack held two and sometimes three Hasselblad cameras, three film magazines, a Polaroid film magazine, three or sometimes four lenses, two light meters, extension tubes, two 200-watt/second battery-operated electronic flashes, sync cords, two small soft boxes (a kind of lighting equipment), reflector cards, backgrounds (white, gray, and black), tripod, gaffer's tape, Super clamps, two articulating arms, armature wire, large garbage bags (for the rain), sash cord, clothespins, color film, black-and-white film, Polaroid film, one video camera, extra batteries for everything (these are heavy), sunblock, mosquito repellent, cell phone, compass, a GPS unit, two flashlights, a notebook, a tape measure, a small first-aid kit, and a small set of tools such as tweezers, makeup brushes, small scissors, pliers, screwdrivers, and needle and thread. Of all the tools, the one that was probably used most was a little makeup brush—Susan has spent many an hour dusting off a flower and spiffing up a leaf so that we can show it to you at its best.

Susan's backpack contained the 35mm equipment: two Nikon F4s, 20–35mm zoom lens, 105mm Macro lens, SB 24 flash, polarizing filter, a Contax snapshot camera, film, sunblock, mosquito repellent, more garbage bags for the rain, flashlight, notebook, and batteries as well as our water, lunch, and snacks.

The longest walk I can remember was about 11 miles round trip. This doesn't sound too bad, but because the trail gains and then loses several hundred feet in elevation many times along its course, and the backpack with the cameras and lights in it weighs close to 70 pounds, it made for a very long day. This walk produced the picture on page 118.

In Hawai'i rain is almost always a possibility so rain gear is part of the regular package. The steep and often slippery terrain makes proper footwear important. After a rough day rock-hopping up and down the Wailuku River, where our ordinary hiking boots provided only unsure footing on the wet slick rocks, we were instructed to acquire some spiked *tabis*. Spikes, as we affection-ately now call them, are a kind of Japanese fisherman's shoe made of canvas and rubber with steel spikes on the soles. They are slippers for the forest. These shoes feel a bit odd at first but it is amazing how much energy is saved by being certain of one's step. Many times over the past 15 years people have asked us which animal was the most dangerous to work with. The answer to this is prob-ably the wood bison—in the situation in which we photographed this animal, he could have knocked me down and crushed me. But in our experience in Hawai'i we have learned that gravity, the force behind every fall, is to be taken even more seriously. We were lucky—a couple of minor spills on slippery rocks were our only mishaps before we bought our spikes.

Many of the areas where the very rare plants still live are accessible only by helicopter. Sometimes we were dropped off on razorback ridges no wider than two feet or in the middle of riverbeds where there was no even ground. In these circumstances the helicopter pilot didn't actually land; he simply put one skid on a big rock and held it there while everybody stepped off carefully and quickly, *never* traveling immediately uphill or to the rear, where the rotor blades are. (Follow-ing these rules is absolutely essential to one's life and to the safety of one's colleagues.) There are some helicopter pilots who will not fly in the clouds. There are others that know the mountains of Hawai'i so well that they simply fly to where a familiar ridge meets the base of the clouds and then just follow the treetops straight up the mountain, through the fog and the rain to the exact spot they want to reach.

Flying from sea level in Hawai'i—where the temperature is 90 degrees, the skies are blue, and almost every plant and animal you see is a recent transplant from somewhere else in the world—and then, seven minutes later,

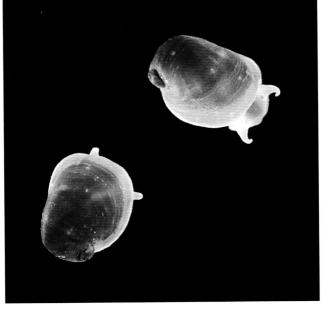

landing in the mountains and stepping out into a million-year-old native forest where the temperature is 50 degrees and it is raining (350 inches a year) can truly be called a mind-altering experience.

We photographed many of the plants in the wild and therefore had the great privilege of seeing these creatures in nature—in their evolutionary cradle. When it was not possible to get the camera to the subject, for reasons of safety (either the plants' or ours) we photographed specimens that were en route to the botanical garden for documentation or to be used as propagation material. Steve Perlman and Ken Wood provided us with important guidance, by their example, about how to behave around a plant that is the last of its kind: Do not do further damage; pay attention; do something to help.

In addition to taking photographs in the wild, we worked extensively in botanical gardens and nurseries, including the National Tropical Botanical Gardens, Waimea Arboretum and Botanical Garden, Pahole Rare Plant Facility, and Volcano Rare Plant Facility. Both situations have their virtues. In a botanical garden or nursery the technical options are more varied (bigger and more lights; shelter from the weather), but the opportunity to see the plants in their natural places is what I truly love.

Most of the photographs in this book were made using a Hasselblad 553 ELX camera with a Zeiss 135mm Makro-Planar and auto-bellows. For the small birds in aviaries we used a 250mm or a 500mm lens. For the extreme close-ups (magnification greater than life-size) we used a variety of lenses. To photo-graph moving insects at around two times life-size we used an 80mm Planar lens with its automatic f-stop on the auto-bellows. For increased sharpness at about twice life-size we used a 75mm Apo-Rodagon-D lens, and for subjects requiring four times life-size we used a 50mm Apo-Rodagon-N enlarging lens.

Newcomb's Snail (left)
Pūpū Wai Lani
Erinna newcombi

The transparency film we used for the portraits was primarily Kodak Ekatachrome E100 SW, and the 35mm transparency film was Fuji Provia RDP100. We used some high-speed Fuji color negative film, and the black-and-white film was Agfapan 100. All told, we exposed more than 2,000 rolls of film.

The black background was usually a piece of black velvet inserted behind the subject. The white background was, most often, a piece of plastic. For the insects and spiders we made small enclosures from plastic, glass, foam-core board, and tape, leaving the creature enough room to assume a natural or interesting posture while placing some limits on its movement to make the framing, lighting, and focus possible.

Time and distance have made Hawai'i a singular example of extraordinary biological diversity. The variety of life proliferating in such isolation produces creatures such as happyface spiders; the only known predacious caterpillars; 75 percent of the world's known pomace flies (the famed picture-wing *Drosophila* of which there are over 1,000 native Hawaiian species); and 75 percent of the world's long-legged flies (which include the greatest number of flightless fly species known from any one place). The mechanism that generates this diversity is called adaptive radiation, the diversification into different ecological niches by species derived from a common ancestor. It is a fascinating story of life begetting more life, constantly refining itself to better fit its habitat.

Over time, in response to their environment, species can become bigger, stronger, smaller, faster, or better hidden. The opportunities are so vast that one finds tree crickets that eventually have lost their ability to fly because they don't need to escape the kinds of predators that were present in the place from which their ancestors came. A more present danger is that of being blown out to sea while airborne. Wings become a liability when one lives on a single mountaintop sticking into the sky in the middle of the Pacific, surrounded by thousands of miles of open ocean. It is better to de-evolve one's wings over thousands of generations than to have to learn to be a fish in the next 30 seconds.

Every one of these creatures has a story that is millions of years in the making. These stories are surprising—and, in the face of extinction, they are heartbreaking. In 1973 the Congress of the United States had the wisdom to create the Endangered Species Act. Simply put, it forbids the unnecessary destruction of a race of beings. The definition of an endangered species is an organism that is likely to become extinct in the foreseeable future, given the current trend. Implicit in this definition are a couple of things that one can interpret as hopeful: One, the plant or animal is still alive; and two, this is an observed trend and not a foregone conclusion. The world is damaged but it is not used up. In most cases, we still have an opportunity to influence the outcome.

The law protects not only such familiar creatures as the Bald Eagle and the grizzly bear but also hundreds of Hawaiian plants and animals, including a small snail known as *Erinna newcombi* that lives in Makaleha Springs on the island of Kaua'i. A very small place, a sort of island within an island, this spring is the only home for the snail. The law will protect this creature by protecting its home. On the day we photographed *Erinna newcombi* another creature was discovered by Adam Asquith, the U.S. Fish and Wildlife Service biologist who had introduced us to the snail. He found an amphipod, a small aquatic crustacean, in the spring with the snail. This amphipod is new to us, new to science. We did not know of its kind. It had not yet been given a name. How many more creatures are there to know?

—David Liittschwager

Makaleha Spring Amphipod (right)
'Uku Wai
(unnamed new species)

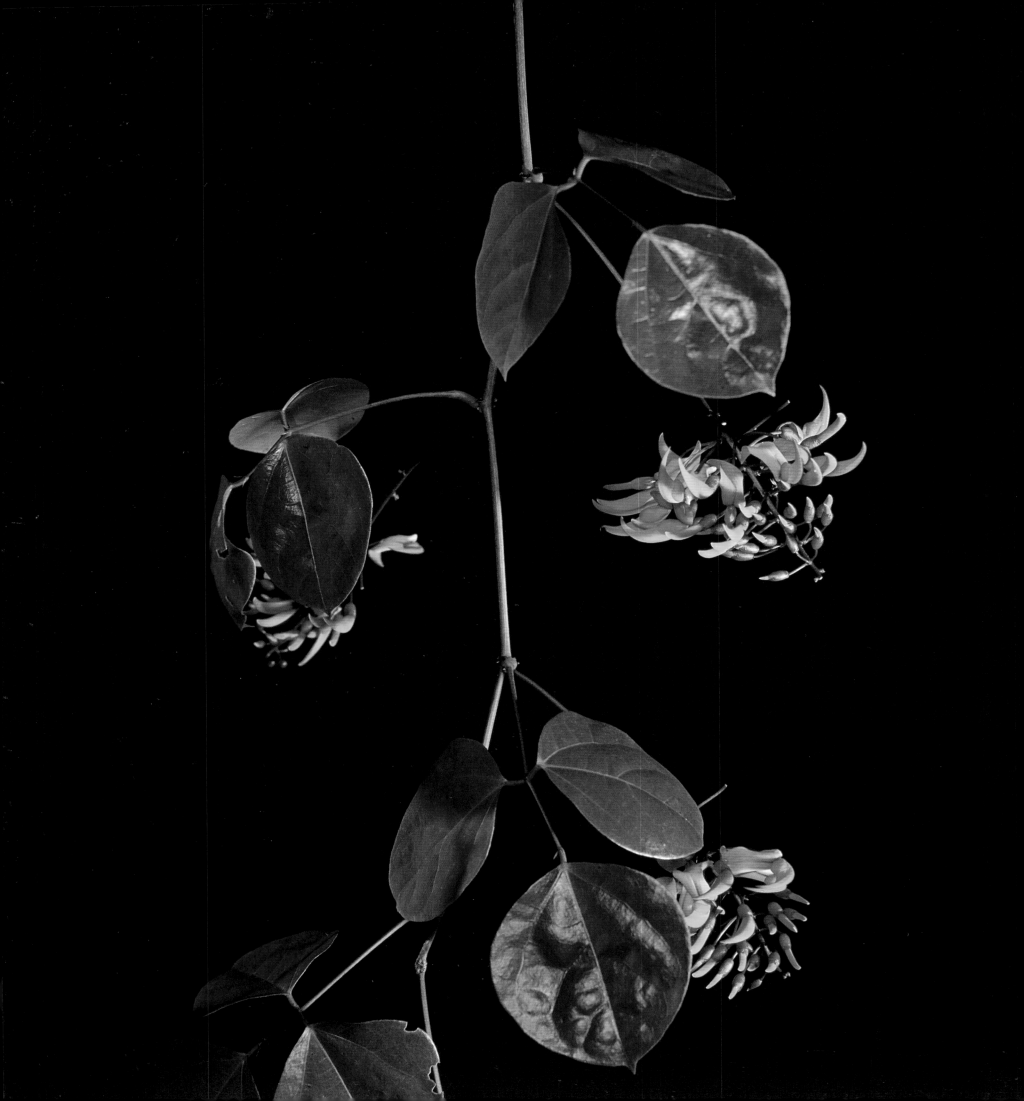

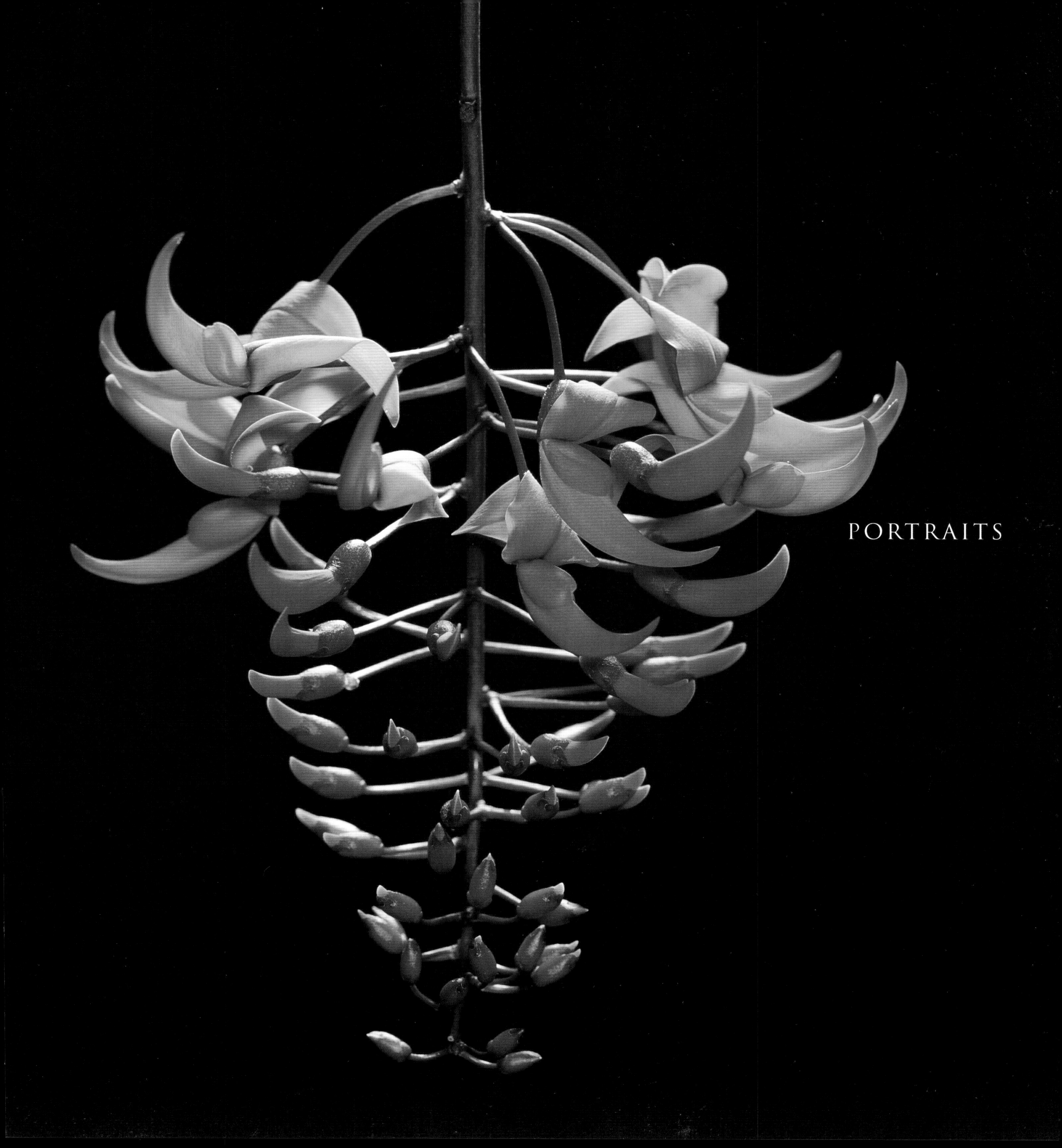

PORTRAITS

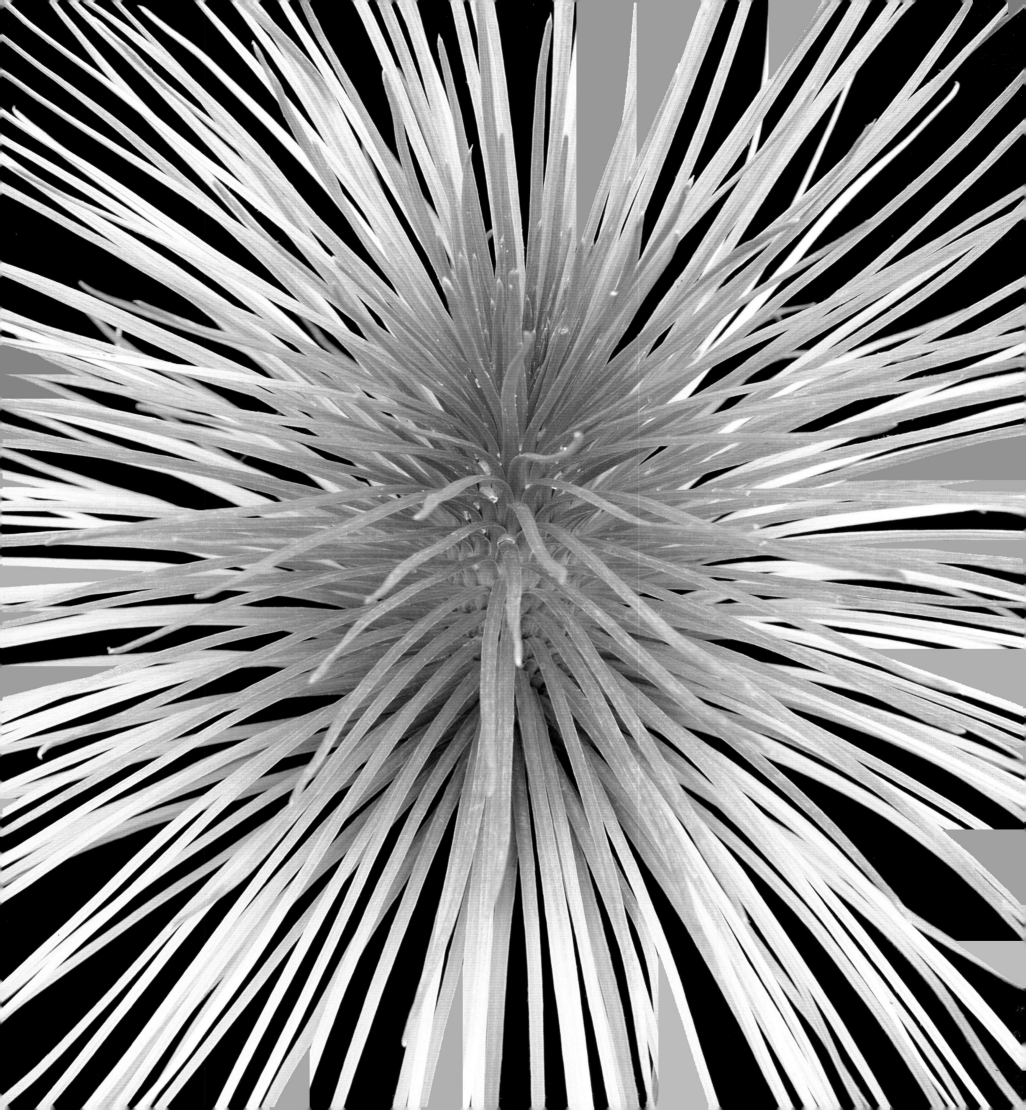

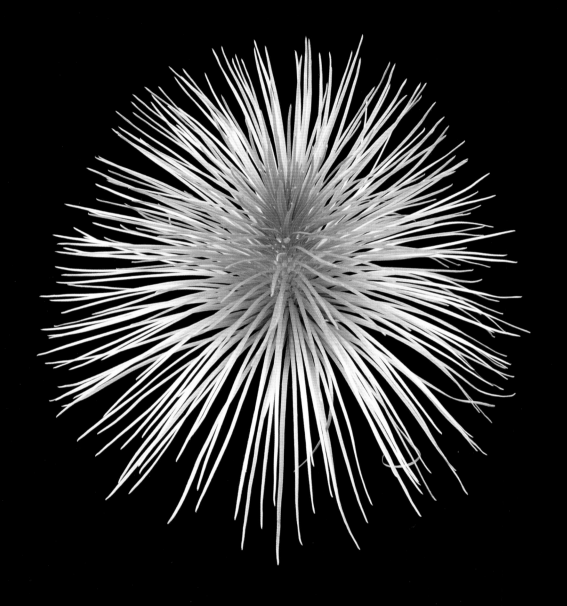

Ka'ū Silversword (left and right)
Argyroxiphium kauense

Nuku 'I'iwi; Ka 'I'iwi; Nuku (pages 34–35)
Strongylodon ruber

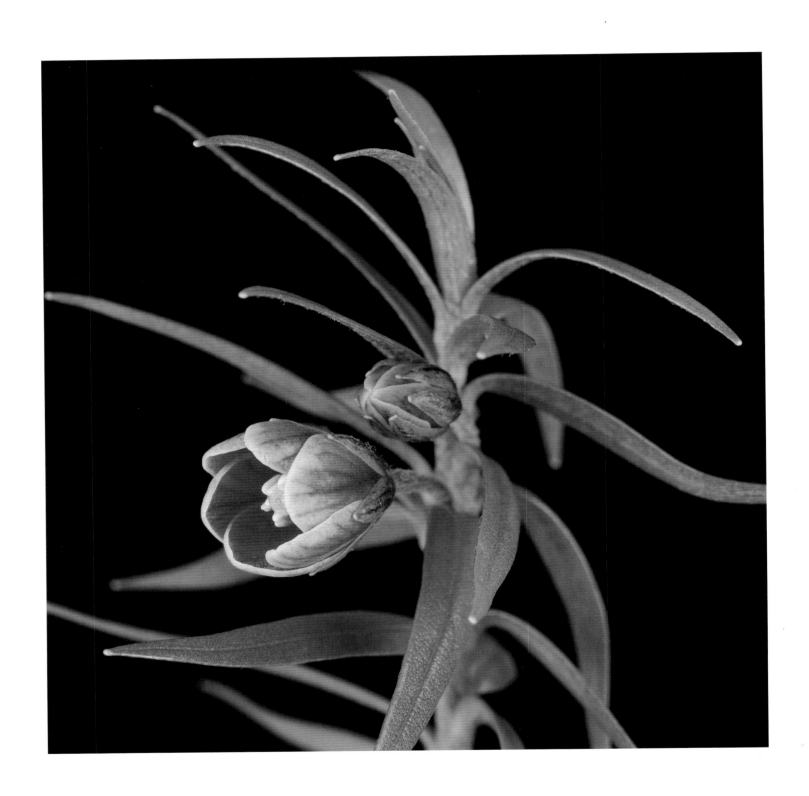

Lysimachia pendens (left)

Lehua Maka Noe; Kolokolo Kuahiwi;
Kolokolo Lehua; Kolekole Lehua (right)
Lysimachia daphnoides

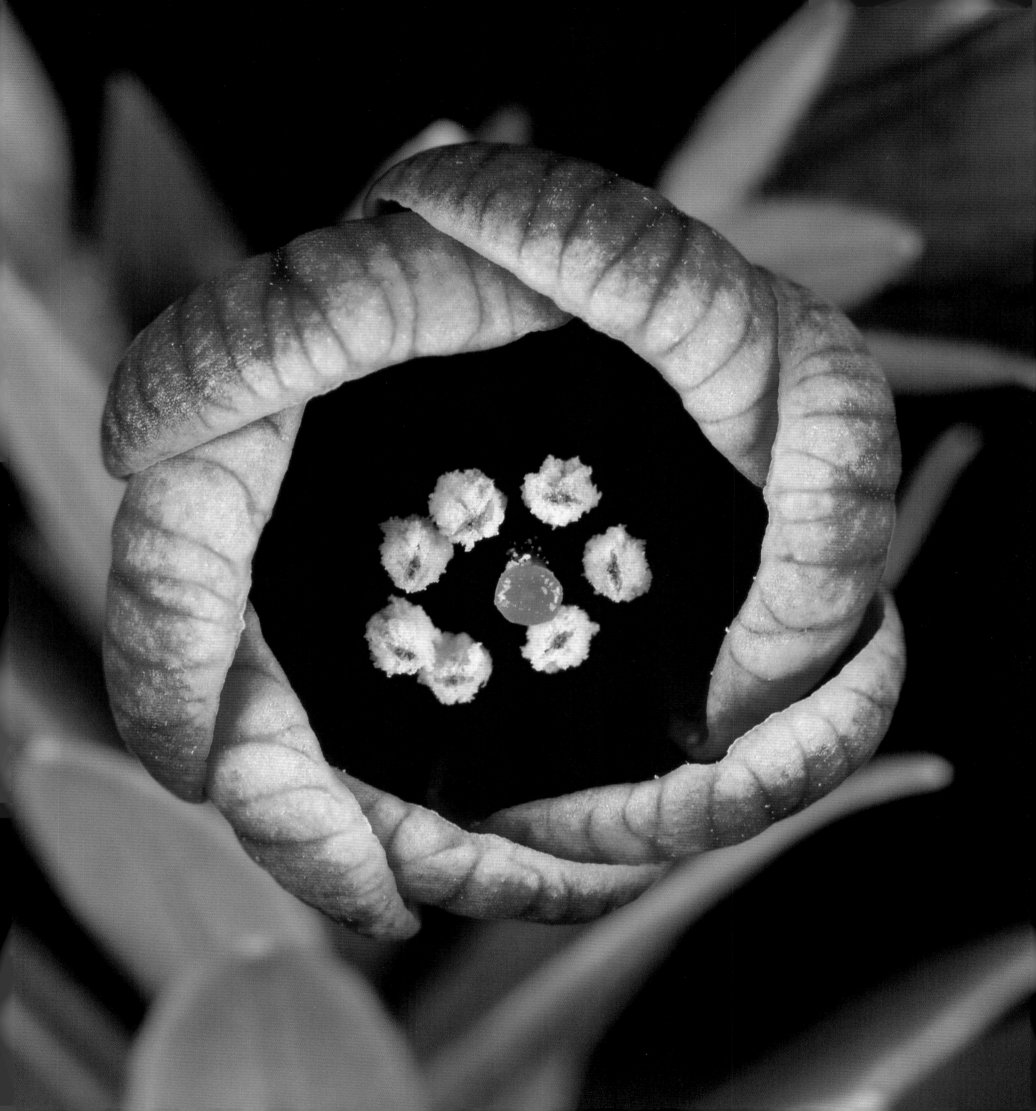

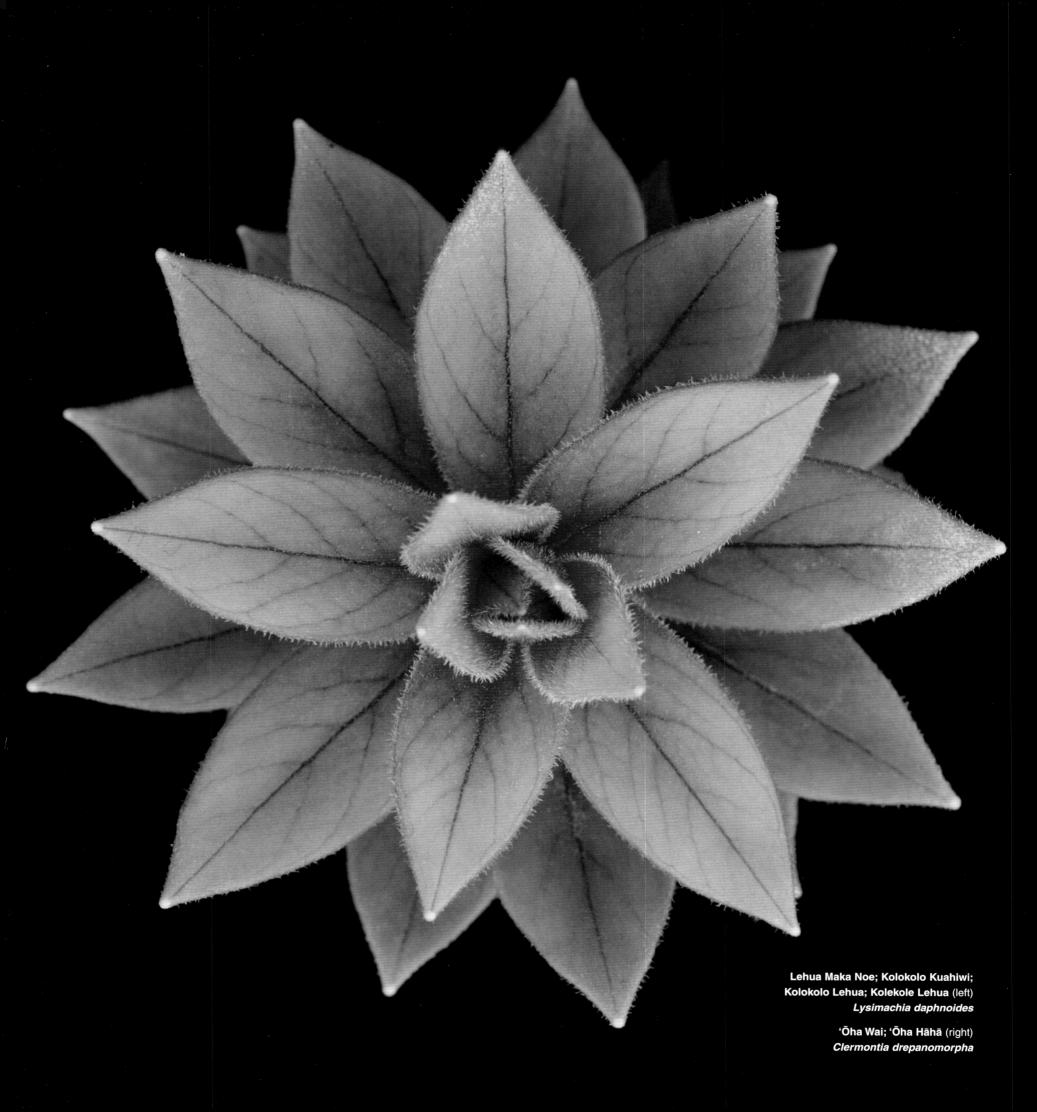

Lehua Maka Noe; Kolokolo Kuahiwi;
Kolokolo Lehua; Kolekole Lehua (left)
Lysimachia daphnoides

'Ōha Wai; 'Ōha Hāhā (right)
Clermontia drepanomorpha

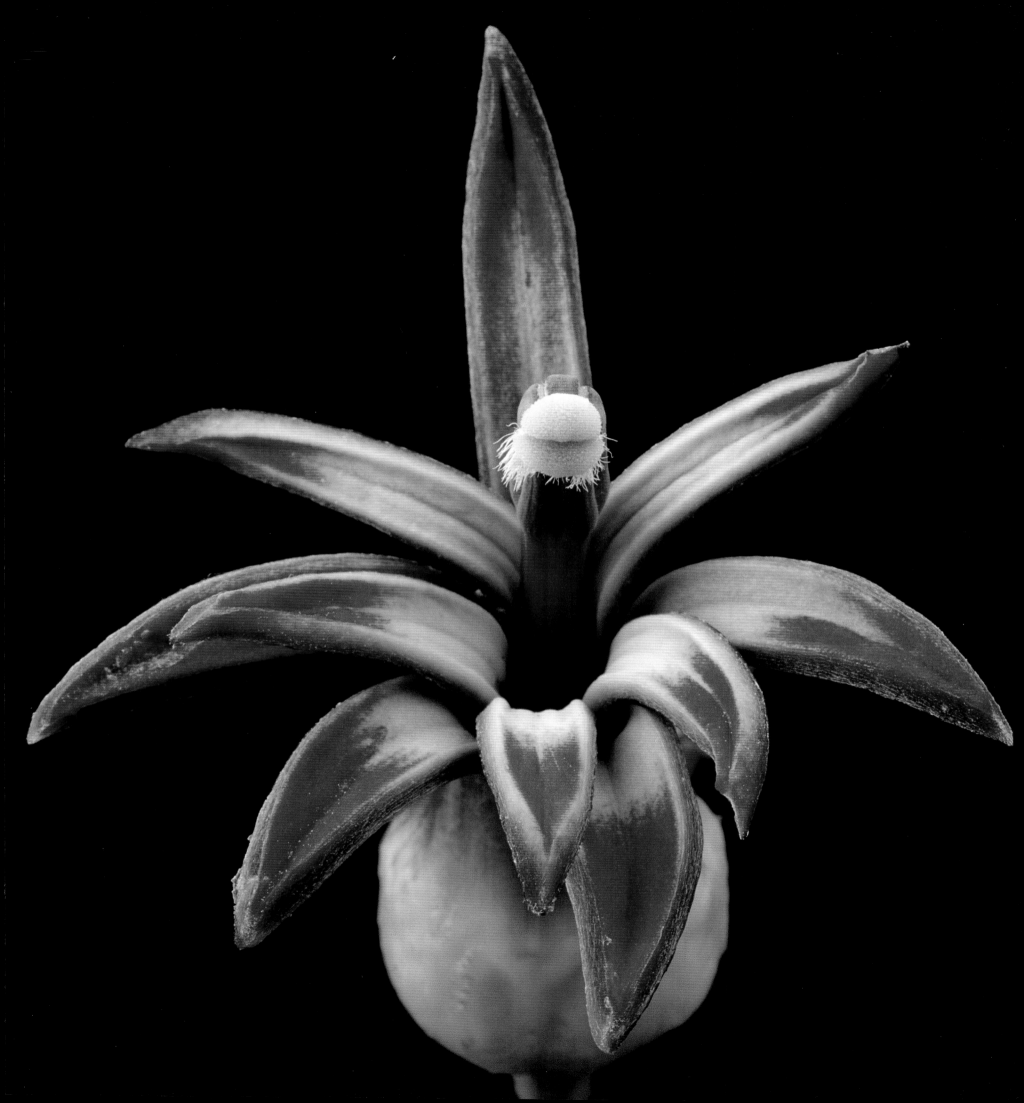

E nā akua,
Hoʻokumu, hoʻokawowo, hoʻoulu, hoʻohua
I nā lāhui kanaka,
A me nā mea ulu o uka a me ke kai.

May the gods
Establish, cause to thrive, sprout and bring to fruit
All mankind as well as
All living things from the uplands to the sea.

—from an ancient Hawaiian healing prayer,
translated by Nathan Napoka

Hesperomannia arbuscula

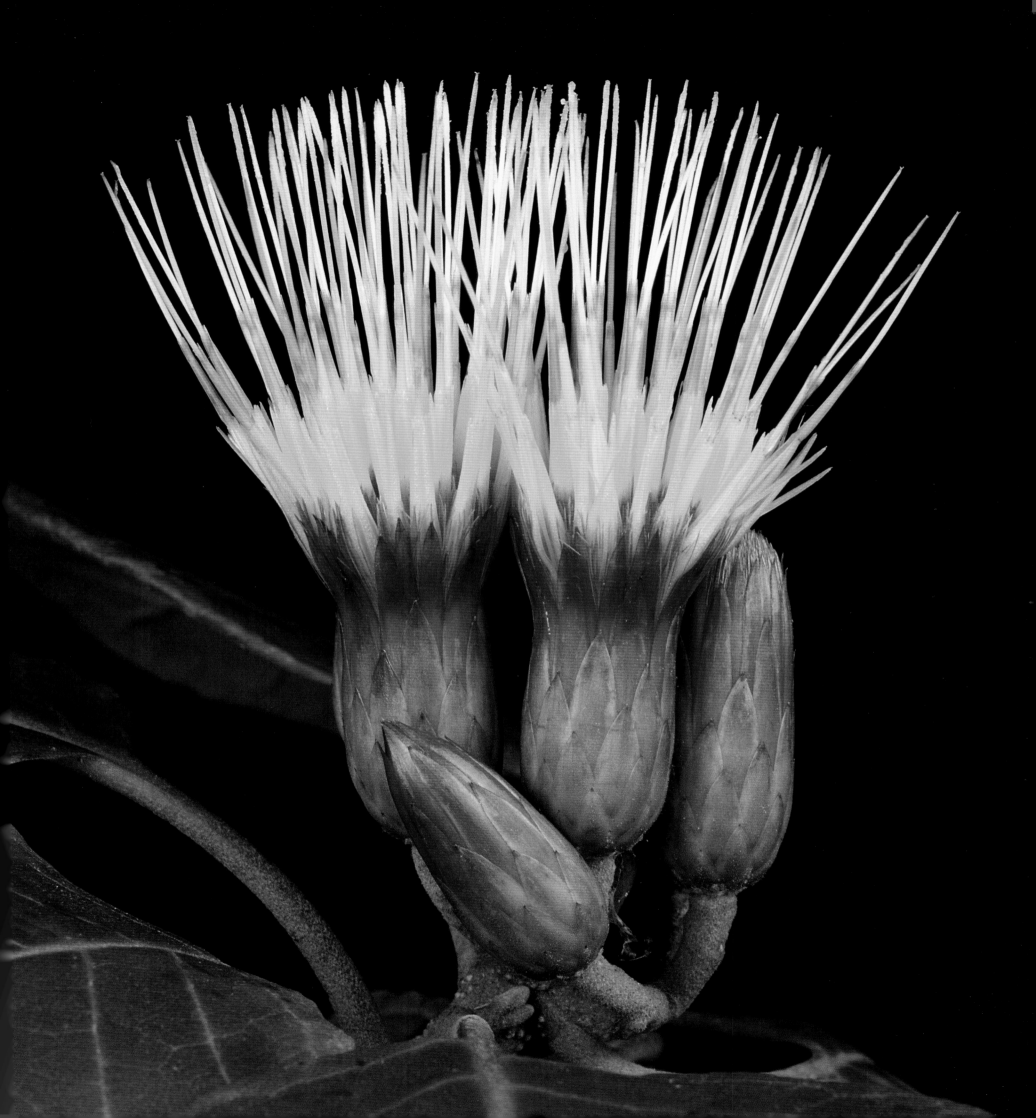

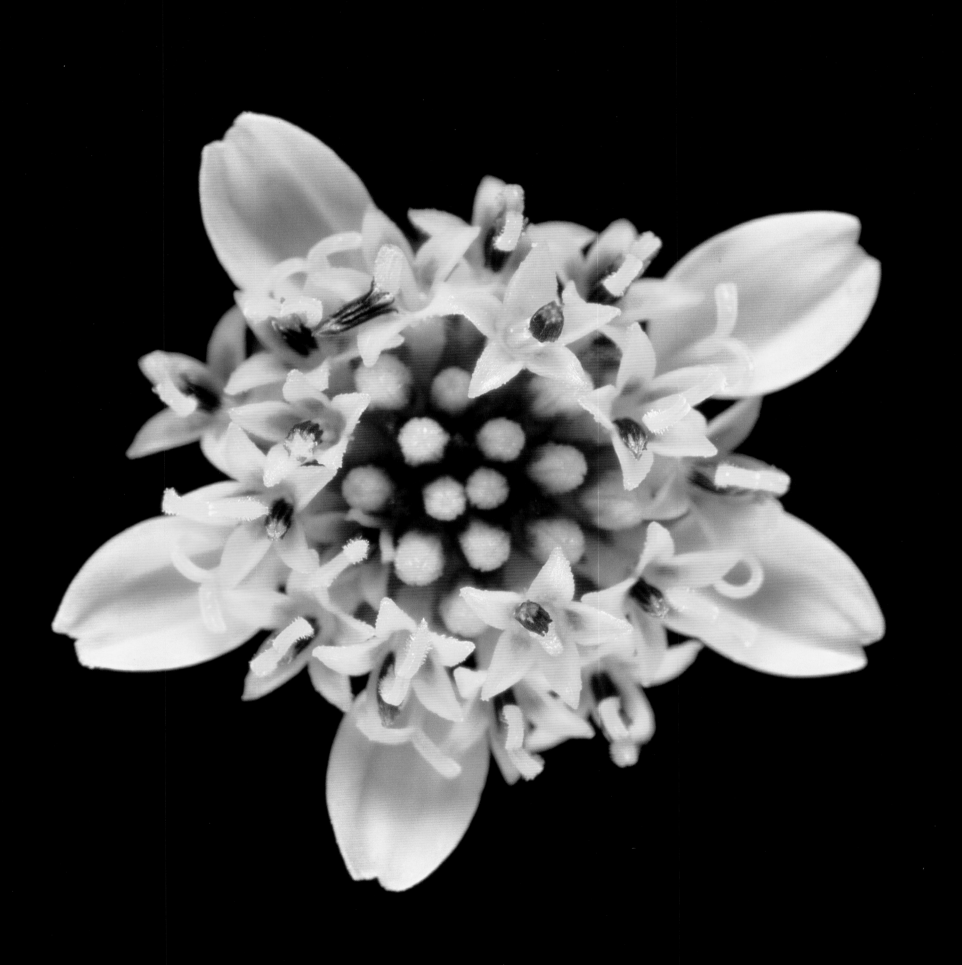

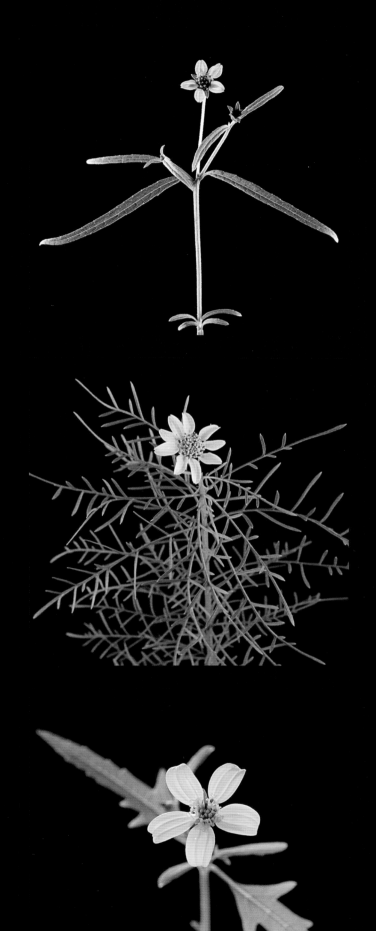

Nehe (left and right top)
Melanthera waimeaensis

Nehe (right center)
Melanthera tenuifolia

Nehe (right bottom)
Melanthera kamolensis

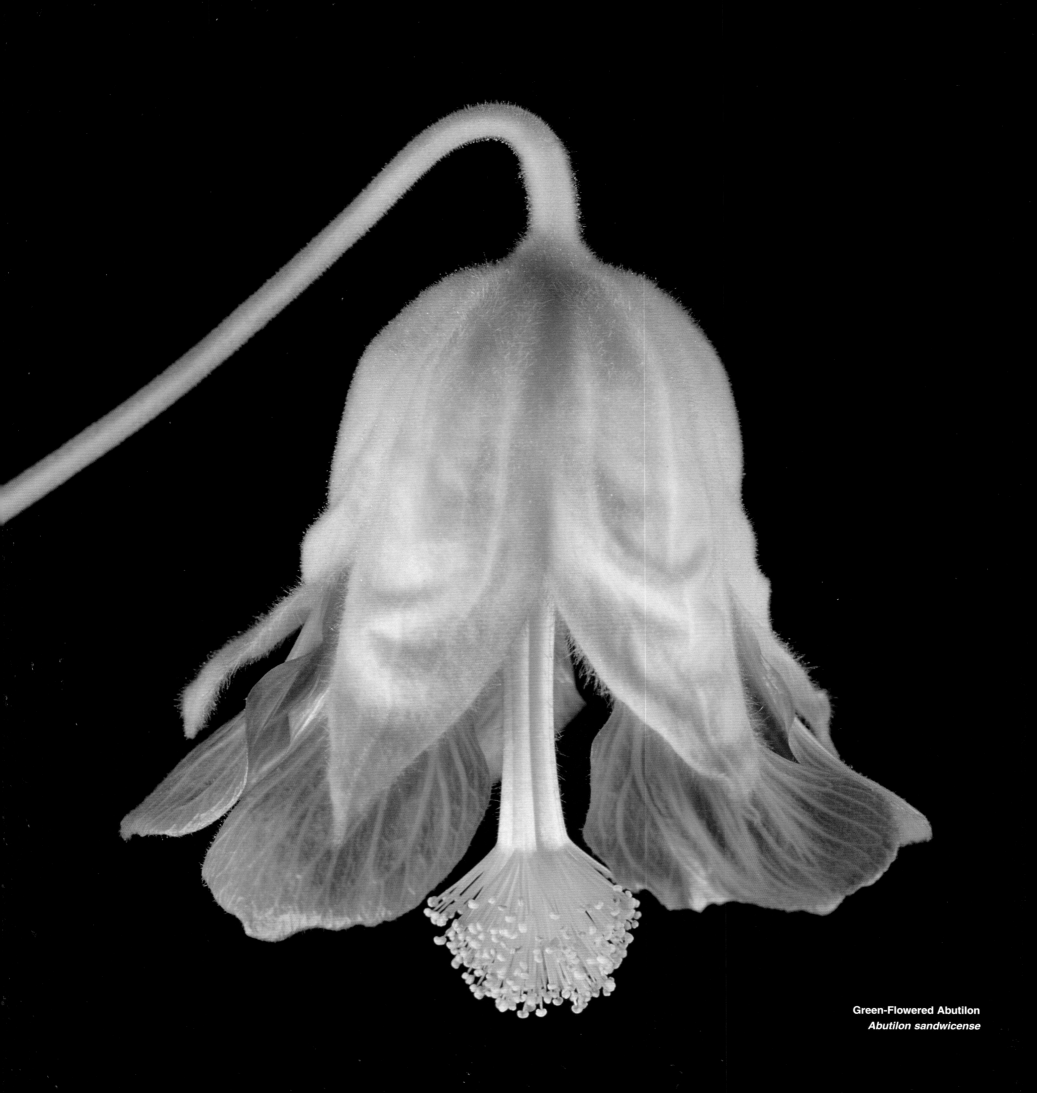

Green-Flowered Abutilon
Abutilon sandwicense

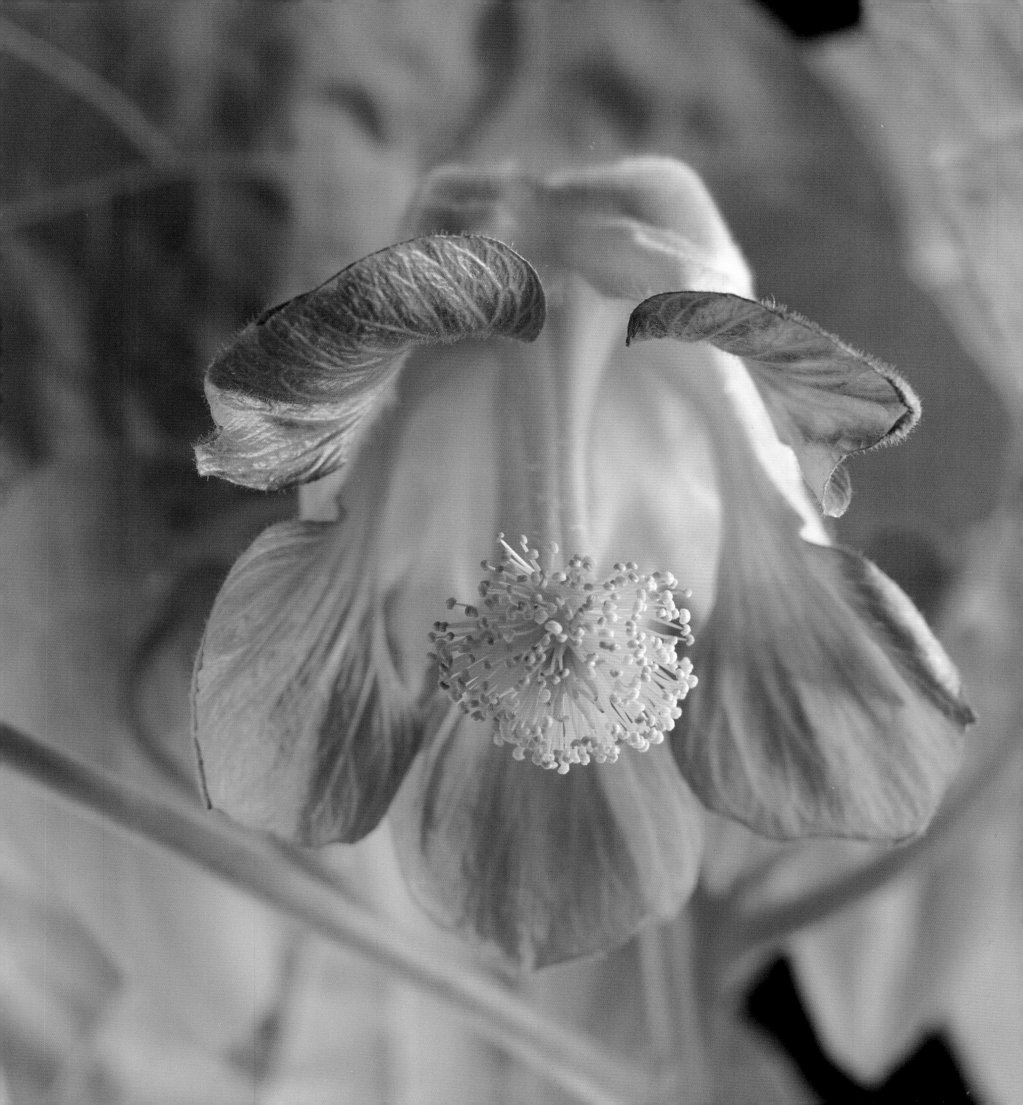

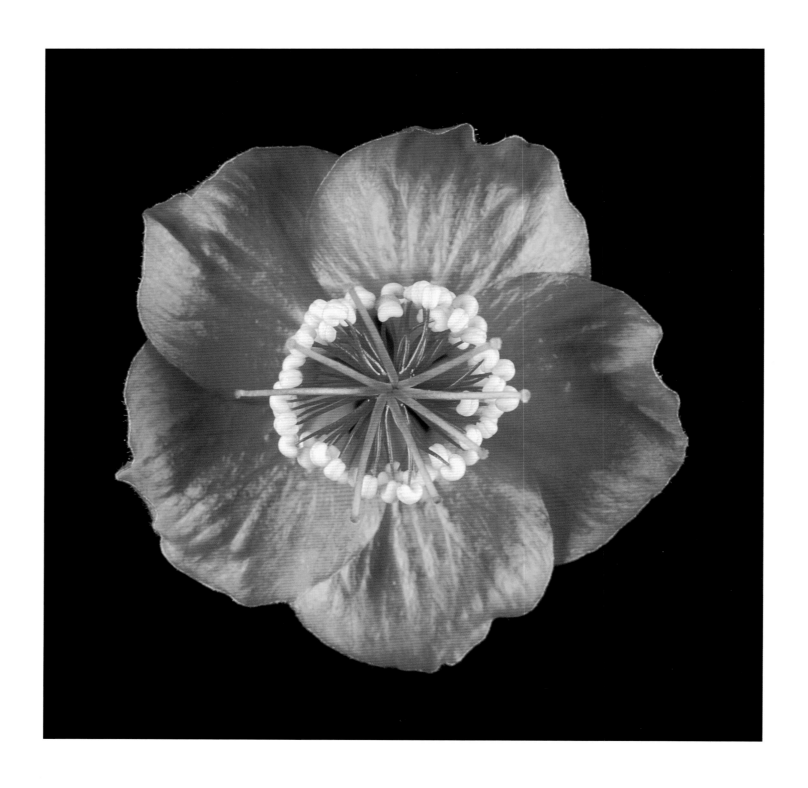

Koʻoloa ʻUla (left)
Abutilon menziesii

Hidden-Petaled Abutilon (right)
Abutilon eremitopetalum

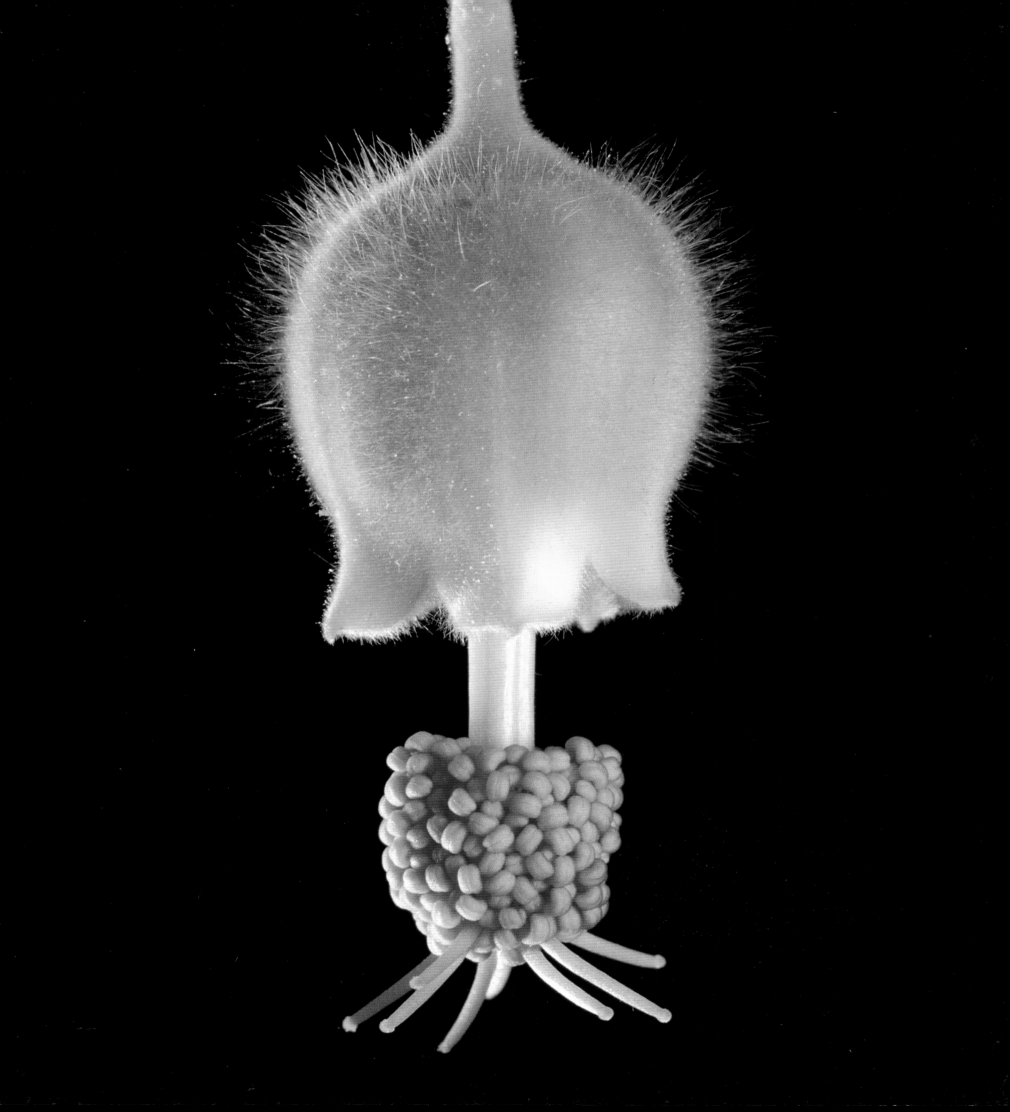

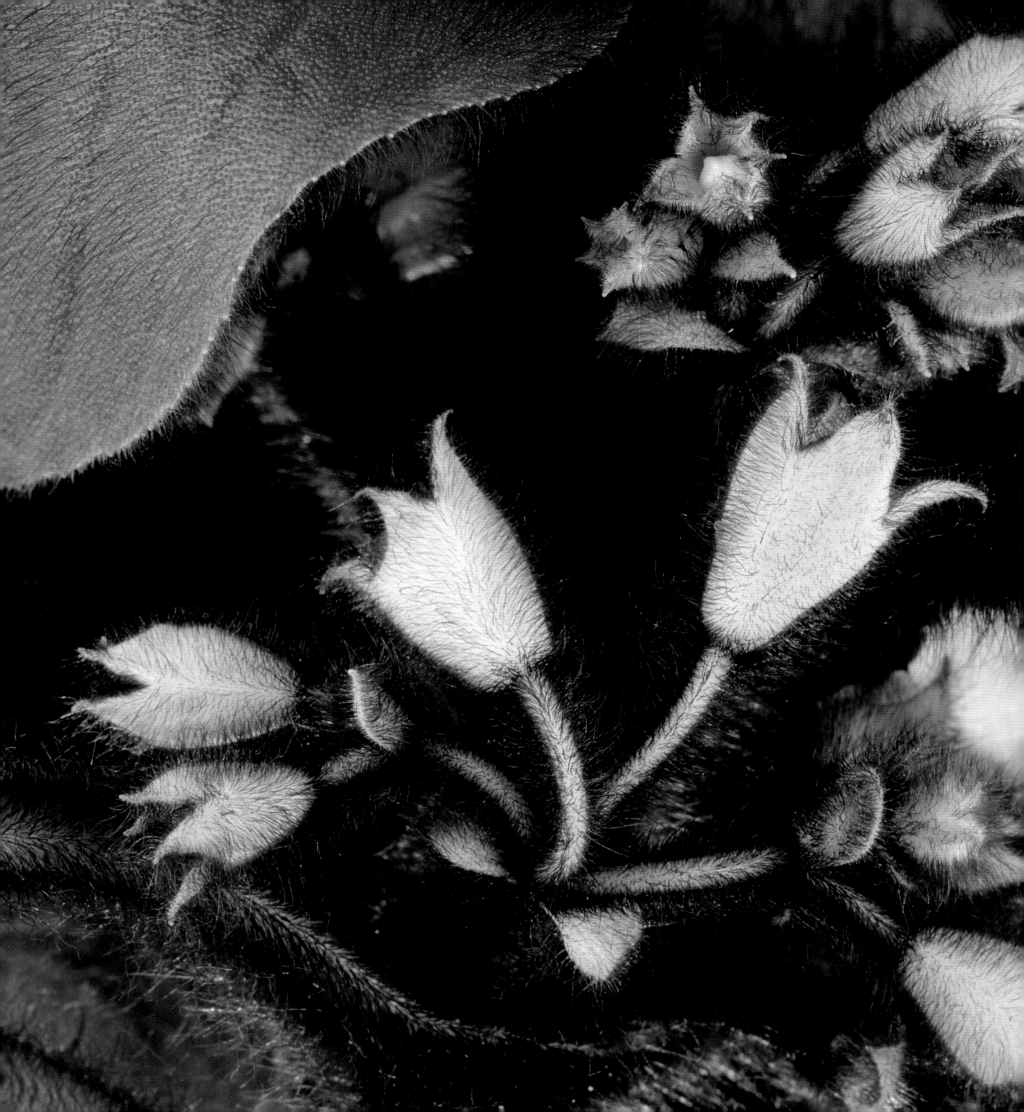

NEW DISCOVERIES

by Susan Middleton

New species and even new habitats are still being discovered in Hawai'i with surprising frequency. Hawai'i is home to the richest and most diverse variety of flora and fauna of any comparably sized island group on earth and it has the highest proportion of endemic plants and animals—that is, they exist only in Hawai'i. Approximately 90 percent of the native plants in Hawai'i are endemic. Though the early Hawaiians had a detailed knowledge of their natural environment, it wasn't until the arrival of European explorer naturalists that the uniqueness of the Hawaiian biota began to be understood. Even Darwin, who never visited the Hawaiian Islands, recognized their importance when, in 1850, he pleaded for a comprehensive account of Hawaiian flora. "Of all places in the world I should like to see a good flora of the Sandwich Islands," he wrote. At that time only brief, incomplete lists existed.

Considered by biologists to be a showcase of evolution, Hawai'i still promises new scientific discoveries, making it a particularly exciting place for biologists to do their work—and for photographers to tag along with them.

When we began our plant fieldwork, we worked closely with Steve Perlman and Ken Wood, botanists from the National Tropical Botanical Garden on Kaua'i. They have distinguished themselves by venturing to places never before visited by botanists, including vertical cliff faces, which they reach by rappelling down the sides of cliffs. Thus they have discovered many species previously unknown to science, and have even saved others from extinction—most notably *Brighamia insignis* (see page 80), which makes its home on the steep cliffs of the Nā Pali coast in Kaua'i. *Brighamia insignis*, a beautifully bizarre plant that resembles a cabbage perched on a bowling pin, seems to have lost its pollinator. So Steve and Ken, while dangling from ropes, carefully hand-pollinated the *Brighamia* and collected seed for propagating the plants in botanical gardens. *Cyrtandra paliku*, one of the first plants that Ken and Steve urged us to photograph, was a recent discovery. Describing one of these, Ken recalls, "I was astounded by the beauty of it—the long reddish black hairs, the soft texture of the leaf, the white flowers—and my first thought when looking at the stems was that they looked like the legs of a tarantula." This conjured up an image of something part plant and part animal. Of course, we were intrigued.

Palikū means "vertical cliff," and the logistics of getting to the plant were complicated. It lives on the north side of Kekoiki, the summit peak of Mount Nāmāhana, and one of the highest peaks of the Makaleha range on Kaua'i. The only way to get there is by helicopter, and the landing area at the summit is about the size of a small bedroom. The weather is often cloudy and windy, making a helicopter approach potentially dangerous.

Ken and Steve planned a trip to collect a specimen of the new plant for propagation and arranged for us to come along. We set up our equipment on the top of the mountain while Ken tied his rope to a sturdy tree and rappelled down the cliff. We fashioned a photo studio for the plant, made some test Polaroids to get the exposure right, and waited for Ken to return. The clouds engulfed us and rain began pouring down. We scurried to find plastic garbage bags to protect our equipment, hoping the storm would soon pass.

By the time the rain subsided, we heard Ken's voice and then saw him climb up over the rim, carrying a plastic bag. He carefully took the furry plant out of the bag. It was an exciting moment. The descriptions of its beauty had not been exaggerated. David and I had never seen anything like it. Working intensely to capture the essence of the plant while it was fresh, we looked at it from every conceivable angle and photographed it several different ways. We wanted to arrange the lights so that the furry surface would reveal its vibrant copper color.

In telling us about his discovery of the plant, Ken explained that for years when he traveled around the windward side of Kaua'i, he would look up at the isolated Makaleha range and daydream about working there. He had noticed that it appeared rich in native vegetation. In February 1993 he finally had the opportunity to go there, and he rappelled off the cliff to the site he had daydreamed about. There he found a population of what he identified as plants of the genus *Cyrtandra*, which are native to Hawai'i and related to African violets. But he perceived these were very different from previously documented Hawaiian *Cyrtandra* plants. Further surveys have indicated that this newly discovered species is restricted to this single mountain range at a particular elevation and requires certain types of winds and misty clouds. It is extremely rare, probably numbering fewer than one hundred plants.

While we were photographing, Ken surveyed the surrounding area, and after a while he called to us: "Do you want to see the most beautiful cricket I have ever seen? It just jumped on my sleeve." Naturally we were curious, and when he brought

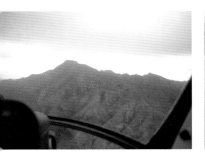 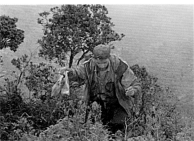 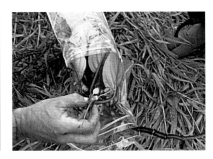 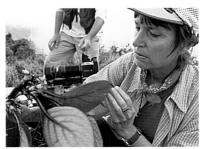 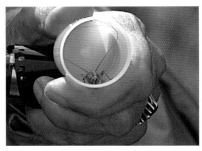

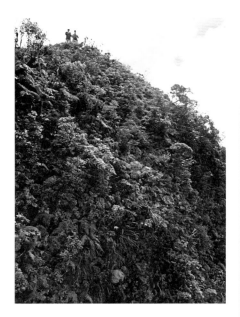

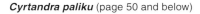

Cyrtandra paliku (page 50 and below)

Photographing *Cyrtandra paliku* and *Prognathogryllus* (new species of cricket) on Mount Kekoiki, Kaua'i (page 52)

Searching for insects and spiders on the summit of Mauna Kea, Hawai'i (page 53)

Big-Eyed Hunting Spider
(page 53, top row, far right)
Pe'epe'e Maka Nui
Lycosa new species

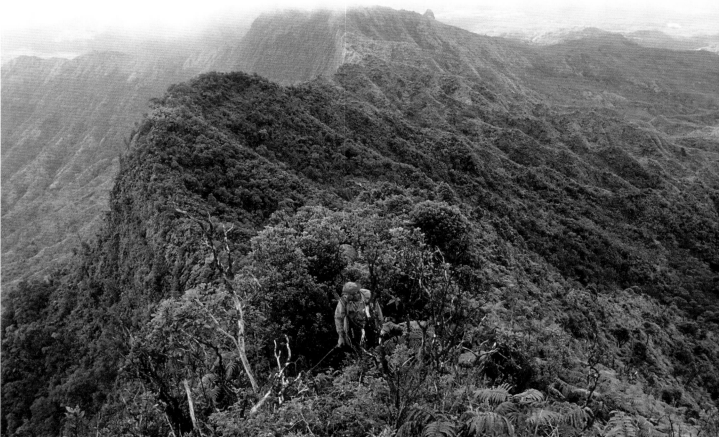

it to us we knew we had to photograph it (see page 214). It was an exquisite little creature, with extremely long antennae and small wing pads that were handsome but not functional for flying. When we showed our pictures to entomologists, they recognized that our little cricket, too, was a new discovery to science. We learned then that this was a flightless cricket, probably restricted to this particular mountain, and exquisitely adapted to it, just like the *Cyrtandra paliku*.

Our trip to the summit of Mauna Kea, which at 13,800 feet is the highest peak in Hawai'i, was an unexpected adventure. Our guide, Dr. Steven L. Montgomery, warned us that it would be cold, the air would be very thin, we might become sick or giddy, and we might experience temporary lapses in judgment. He suggested

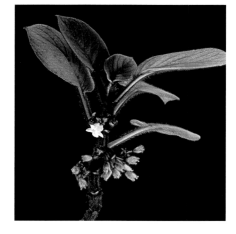 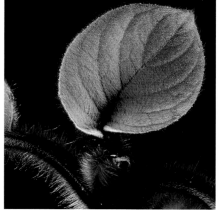

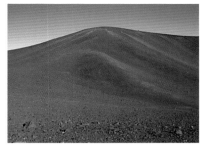
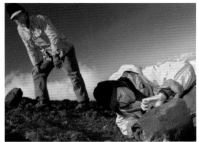
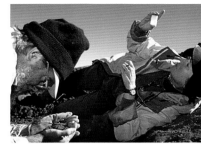
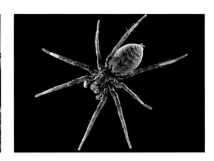

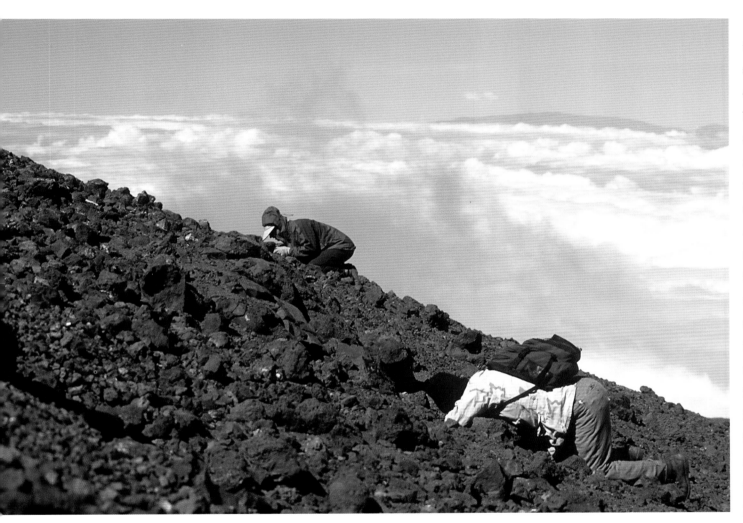

Steve trained us in the search technique. Very carefully, we would lift stone after stone, often exposing hundreds of mummified insects that had been carried there by the wind, and occasionally we would find a live insect or spider. Although we never found a wēkiu bug, we did find a beautiful big-eyed hunting spider (see page 58). At this point no one in the scientific community has studied the spider thoroughly enough to definitively declare it a new species, but it is strongly suspected that it is. Steve explains that there is a backlog of undescribed species and unanswered questions about them, especially concerning Hawaiian invertebrates, like the spider we photographed. There is also a shortage of specialists who can describe these species. But he adds, "Not knowing is part of it. The process of determining

that we wear lots of layers of warm clothing, bring aspirin for headaches, and stop for half an hour at 9,000 feet elevation to help us acclimate to the change in atmosphere.

We were on a mission to find insects that make this austere landscape their home. The area was deemed a lifeless desert when astronomy observatories were built here in the early 1960s. Curious and persistent entomologists, however, have made exciting discoveries that reveal that this alpine habitat is anything but lifeless. The flightless wēkiu bug, discovered in the 1970s, makes the summit its home. It scavenges on dying or dead insects blown up the mountainside by wind. Against the cold climate it has developed a chemical defense that works like antifreeze.

what is a species is part of the adventure and excitement."

Dr. David Lorence, a botanist specializing in Pacific flora, regards a new discovery as an exciting bonus that helps offset the tedium of descriptive work, which is the process of describing species according to the Linnaean system and code of botanical nomenclature. "Finding something new makes it all worthwhile," he says enthusiastically, referring to his experience with newly discovered plants, such as the *Lysimachia pendens*.

Guided by Steve Perlman, we helicoptered to the Blue Hole on Kaua'i to photograph rare plants, several of them endemic to this place. The Blue Hole is an extraordinary craterlike area at the base of Mount Wai'ale'ale, surrounded on three sides by steep waterfall-laced cliffs towering over 2,000 feet and opening into a lush valley. It is the embodiment of grandeur, overwhelming in its physical scale. When the three of us stepped out of the helicopter, we suddenly felt like tiny creatures making our way through the bottom of this enormous cauldron.

The plant we came to see had been discovered here by David Lorence in 1987 on his second or third helicopter trip ever—a rare opportunity to document the vegetation and flora of this pristine valley. David recalls that in over nine hours he collected ninety plants, more than he had ever collected in a single day. One of the most interesting plants was a delicate herb with beautiful bell-shaped

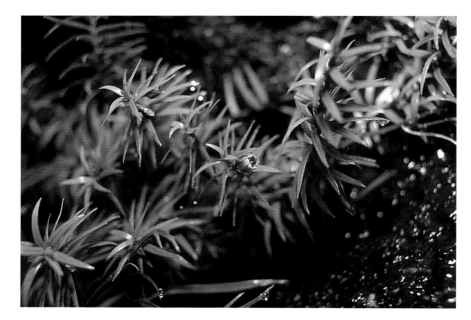

purple flowers, which he found growing on saturated mossy rocks near a waterfall under the cover of ferns. After several botanists examined the herb, it was declared a new species and given the name *Lysimachia pendens*, meaning "hanging," in reference to its pendulous stems. In the wild this lovely plant can only be found at the base of Mount Wai`ale`ale, although plants are now being propagated in native plant nurseries.

Also memorable was our encounter with the *Tetraplasandra flynnii* (see page 55) while accompanying Ken Wood and Steve Perlman on a seed-collecting expedition. We had been told that the only three known trees of this species lived just below the rim of Kalalau Valley in Kaua'i. Steve and Ken led us away from the trail, through dense forest on steep terrain, until we broke through into a clearing covered with non-native weedy grasses and exposed, eroded earth. Browsing goats were responsible for this damage. Goats, like all feral ungulates, are not native to Hawai'i, and they are a serious threat to the native vegetation in the area, including this extremely rare, recently discovered tree.

Ken, a skilled arborist and field botanist, slowly worked his way up one of the trees, careful not to bruise the bark or break branches, and collected a small amount of material for study and propagation. We were able to photograph what

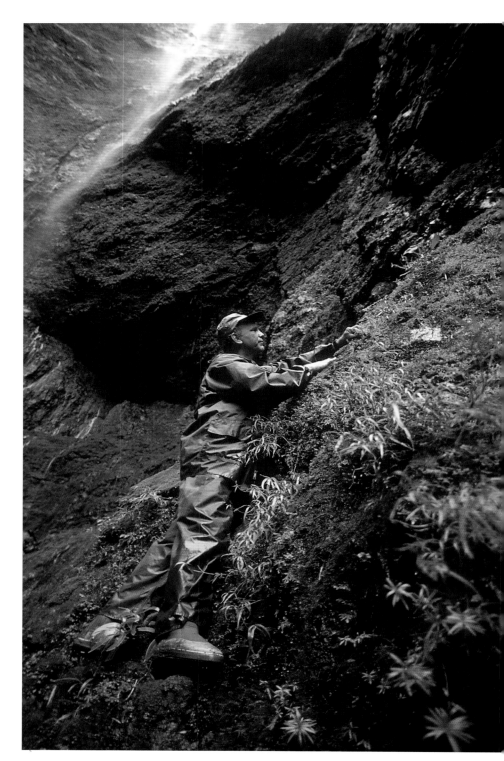

he collected, including close-ups of the flower, fruit, and the newly emerging leaves, which startled us with their resemblance to folded hands.

Tetraplasandra flynnii was named after botanist Tim Flynn, who discovered it in 1986 while on a field trip to see several rare plants in Kalalau Valley. As he hiked down a steep slope, approaching what was almost a sheer drop, he spotted a tree that had fallen over. He recognized it as a member of the genus *Tetraplasandra*. *Tetraplasandra* trees are often very tall, but as this one had fallen, its usually hard-to-reach flowers and fruit were now accessible, so Tim decided to collect material from it. He recalls, "Maybe I thought it looked a little different, but I really think it's

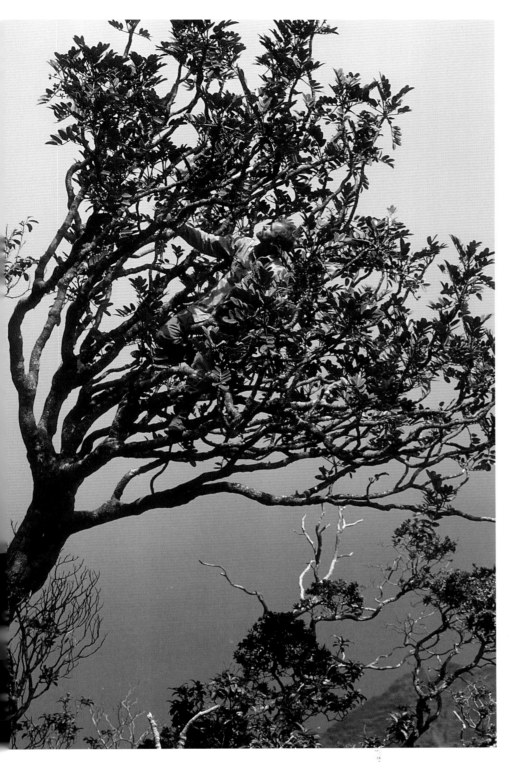

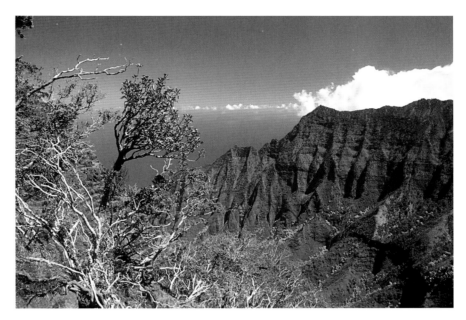

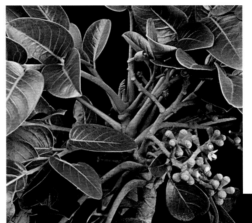

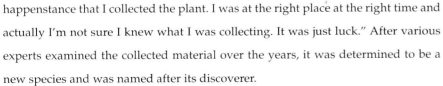

Lysimachia pendens (page 54, left)

Steve Perlman with *Lysimachia pendens* at Blue Hole, Kauaʻi (page 54, right)

Kalalau Valley, Kauaʻi (page 55, top right)

Ken Wood collecting seed in the *Tetraplasandra flynnii* tree (left)

Tetraplasandra flynnii (above and right)

happenstance that I collected the plant. I was at the right place at the right time and actually I'm not sure I knew what I was collecting. It was just luck." After various experts examined the collected material over the years, it was determined to be a new species and was named after its discoverer.

It is a common assumption that our natural world has been thoroughly explored and is well documented. In Hawaiʻi much has been lost, but because the Hawaiian biota is so rich, much still remains—and as we have seen, there is much still to be discovered. It represents a kind of biological frontier. We must come to know it so that we can learn how to preserve it.

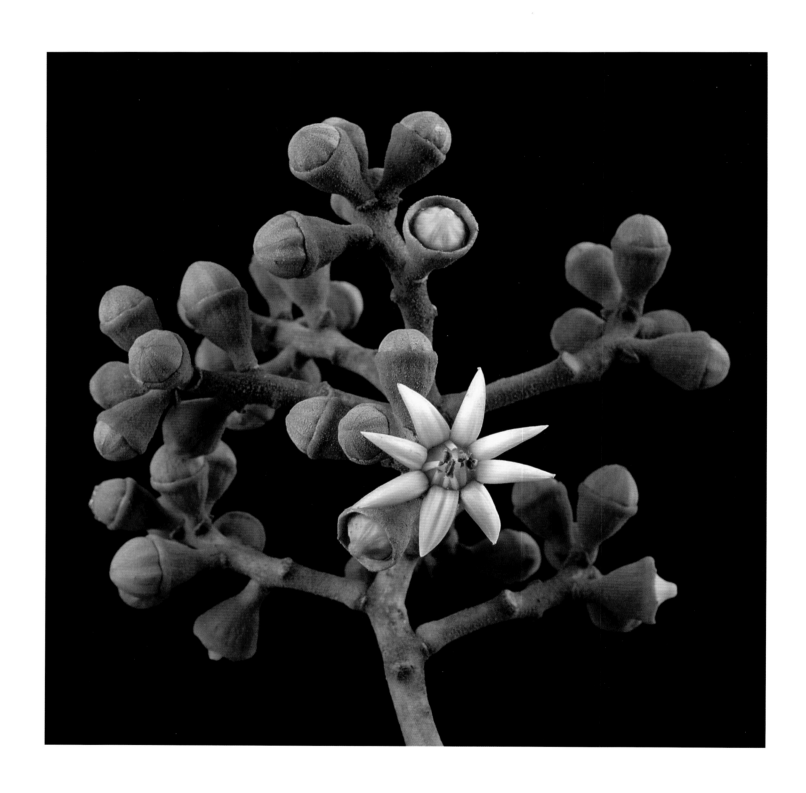

Tetraplasandra flynnii
(left, flower; right, new leaves)

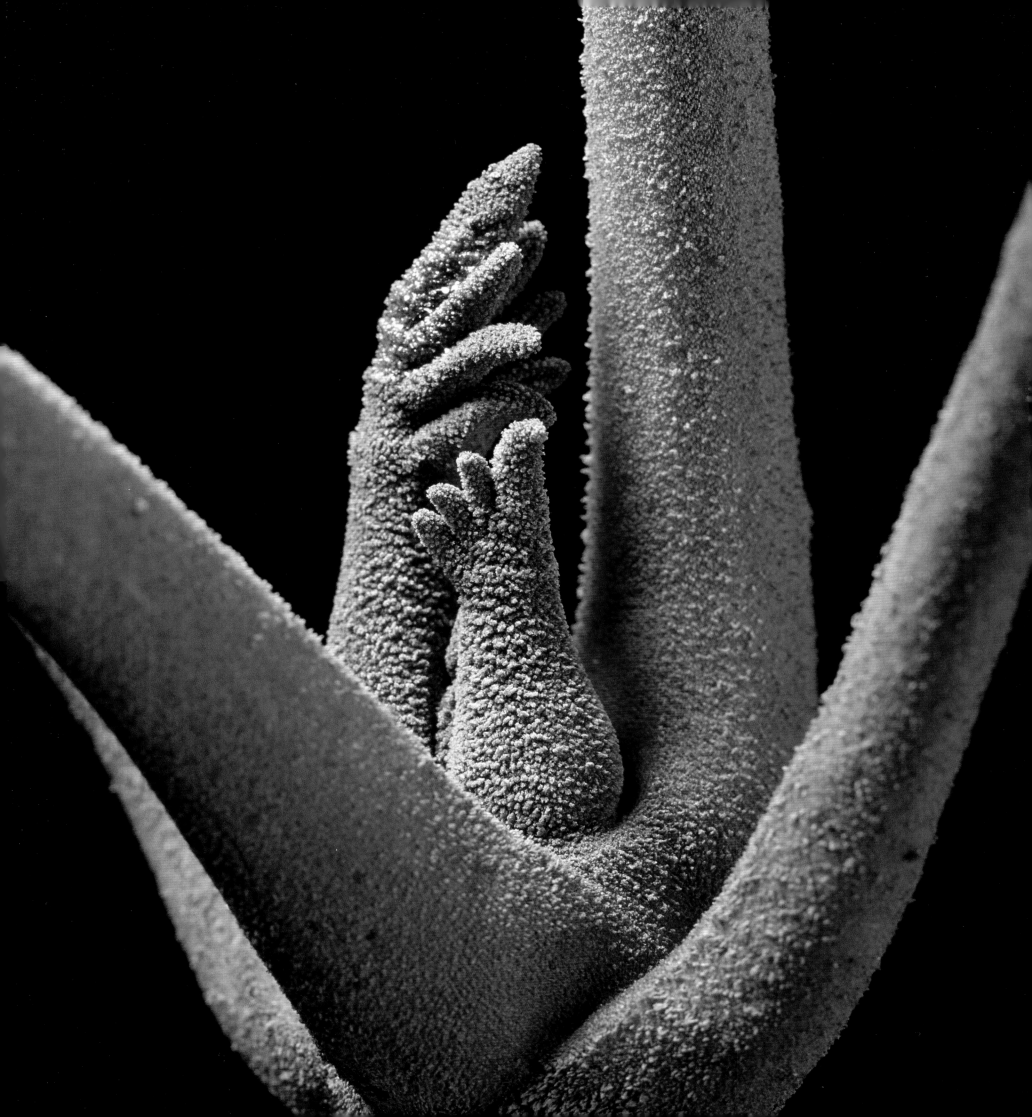

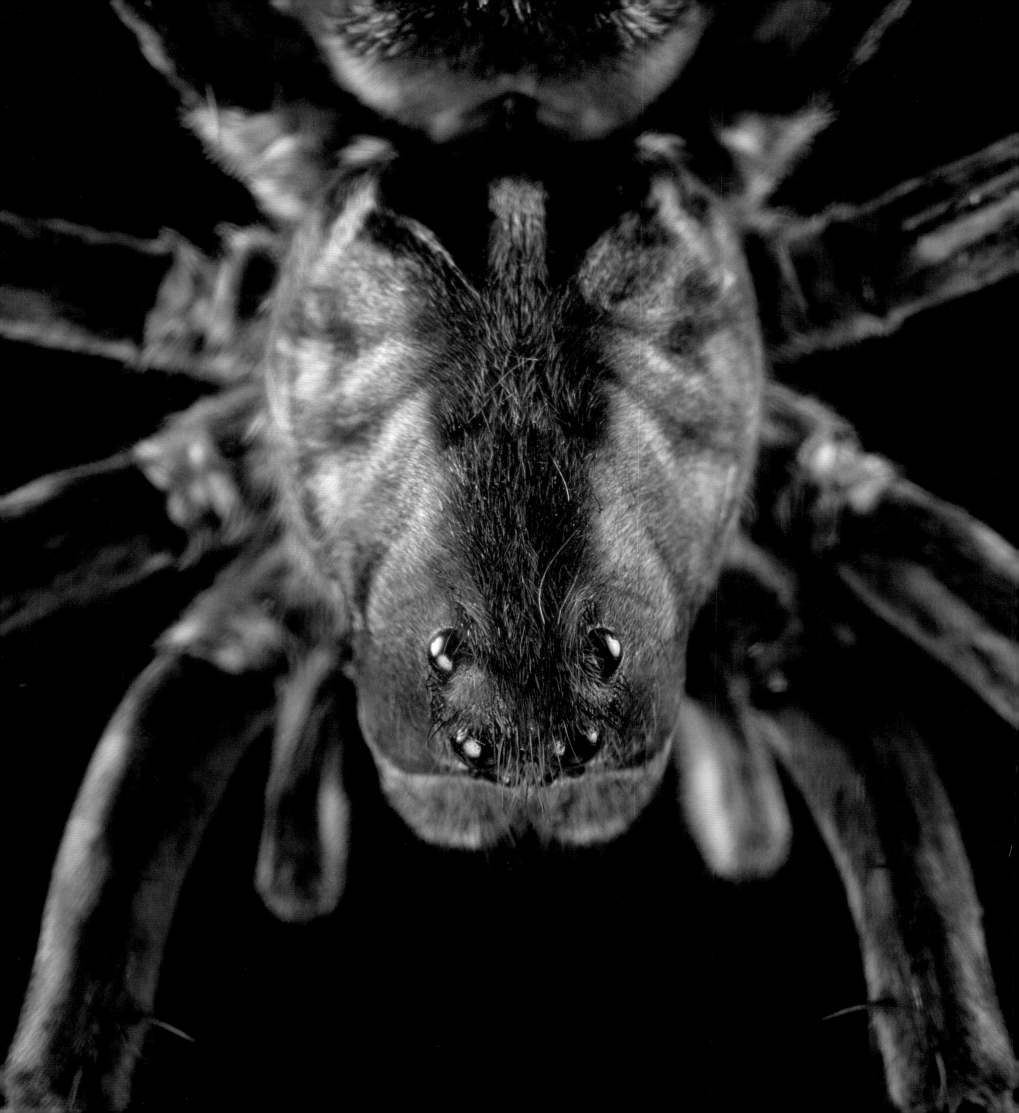

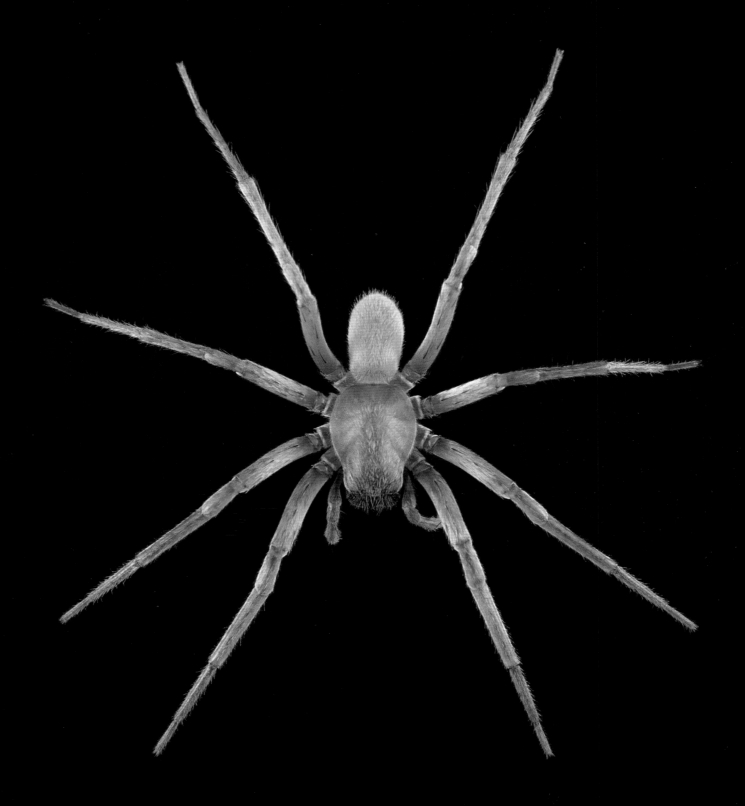

Wēkiu Wolf Spider; Big-Eyed Hunting Spider (left)
Pe'epe'e Maka Nui
Lycosa **new species**

Kaua'i Cave Wolf Spider; No-Eyed, Big-Eyed Hunting Spider (right)
Pe'epe'e Maka'ole
Adelocosa anops

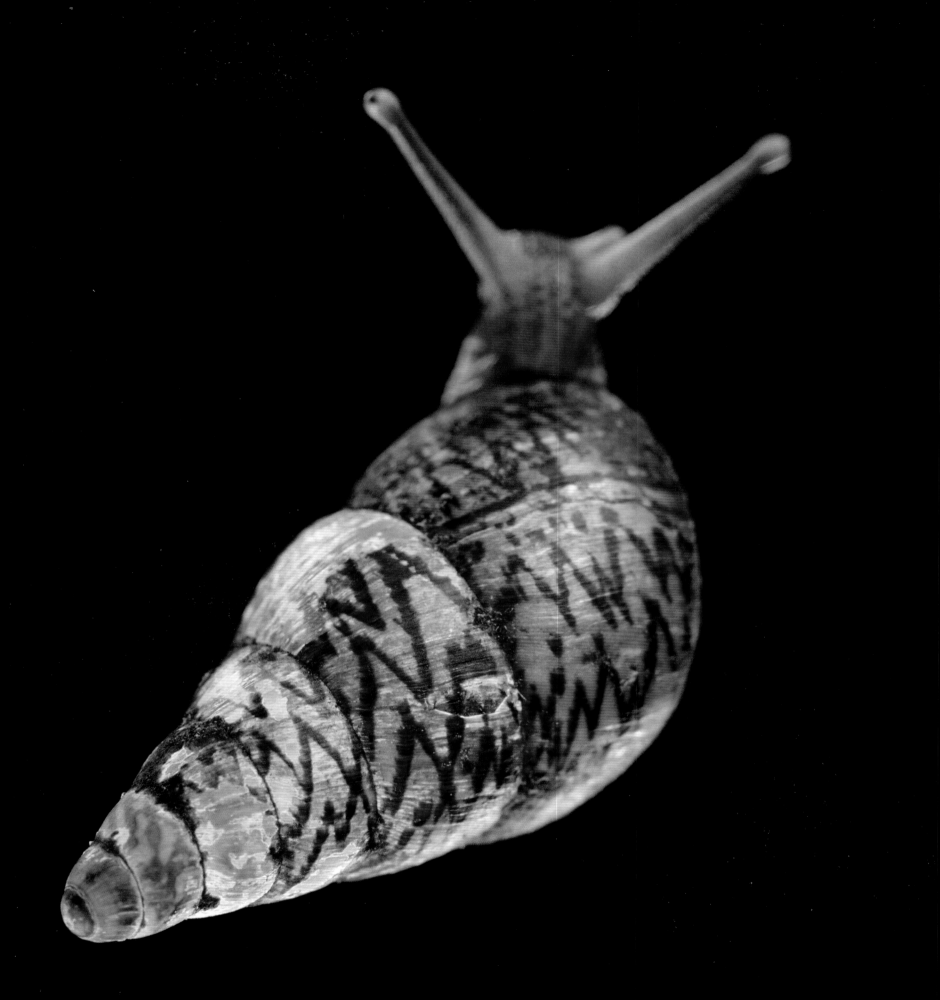

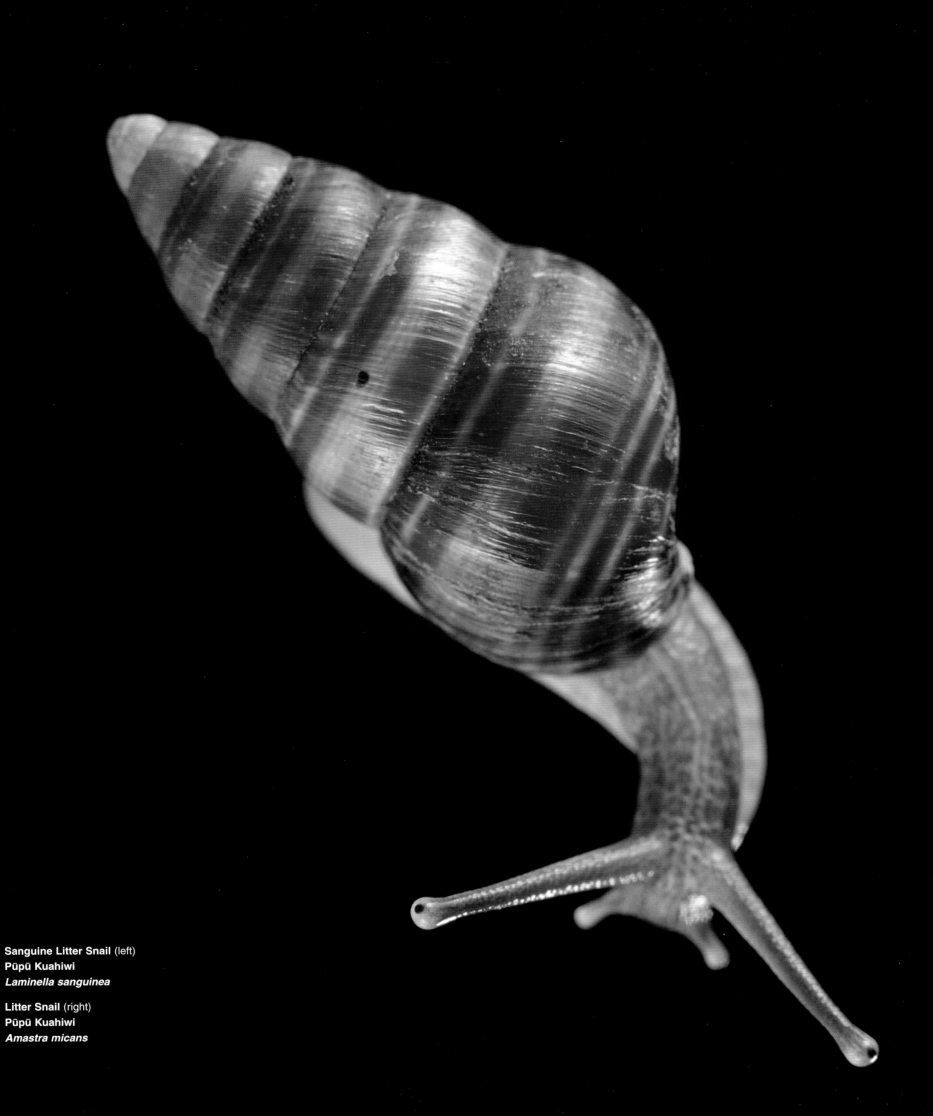

Sanguine Litter Snail (left)
Pūpū Kuahiwi
Laminella sanguinea

Litter Snail (right)
Pūpū Kuahiwi
Amastra micans

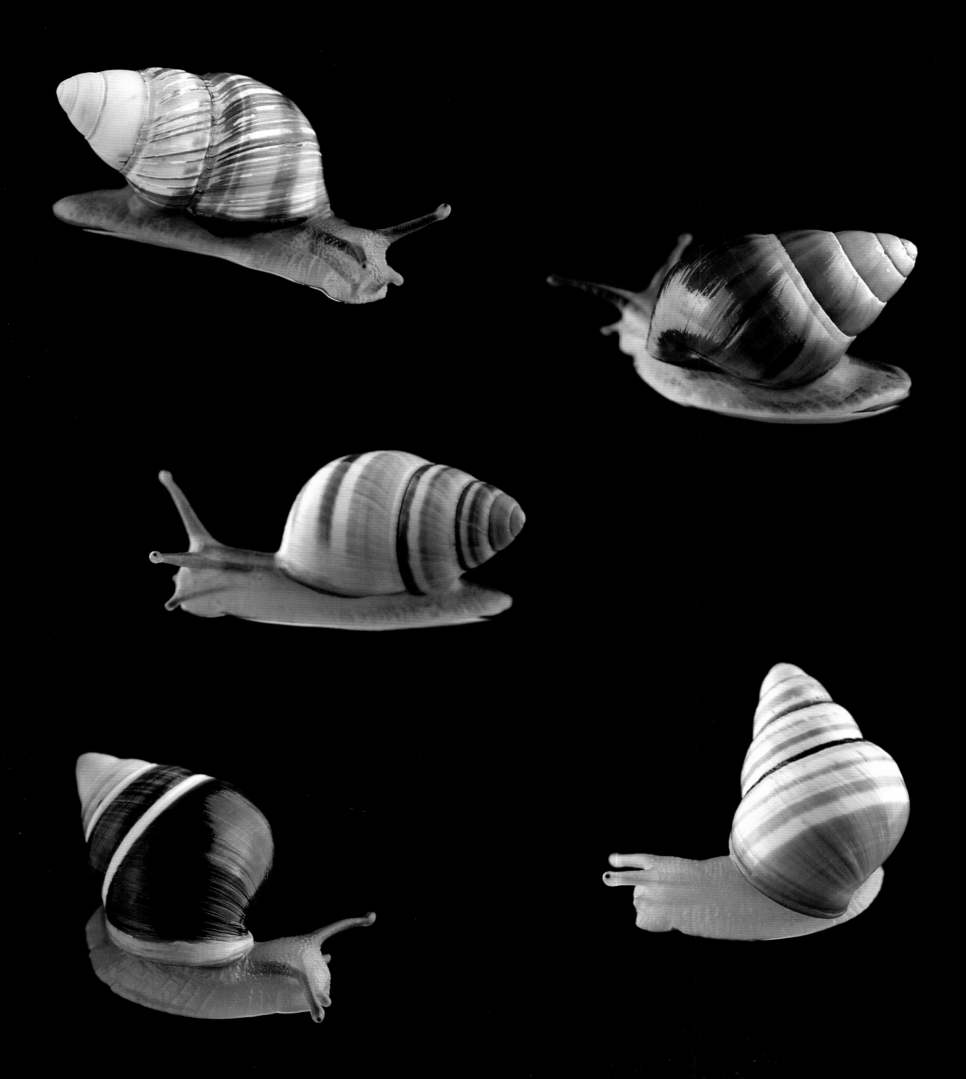

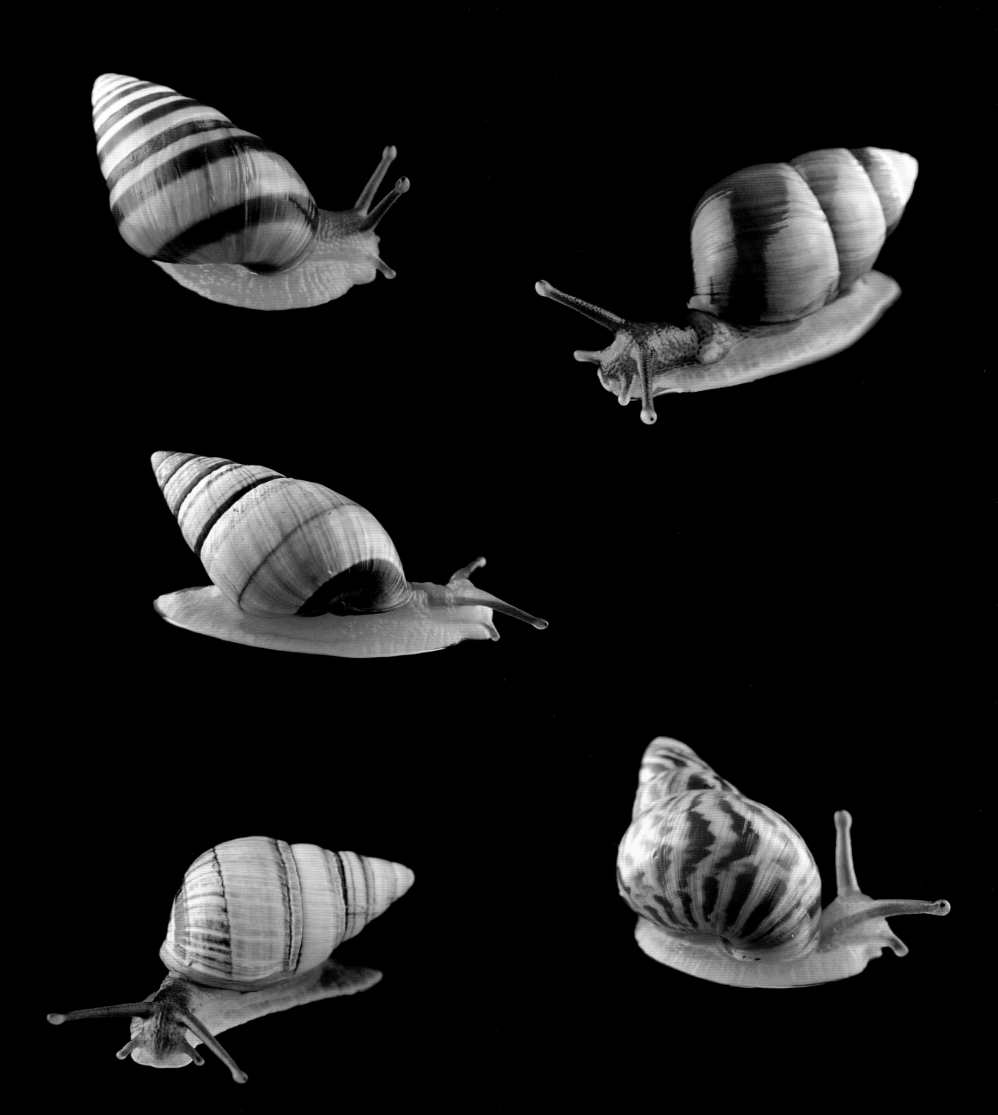

Page 62 (clockwise from top left):
O'ahu Tree Snail
Kāhuli; Pūpū
Achatinella decipiens

O'ahu Tree Snail
Kāhuli; Pūpū
Achatinella sowerbyana

Moloka'i Tree Snail
Kāhuli; Pūpū
Partulina mighelsiana

O'ahu Tree Snail
Kāhuli; Pūpū
Achatinella apexfulva

O'ahu Tree Snail
Kāhuli; Pūpū
Achatinella fuscobasis

Page 63 (clockwise from top left):
O'ahu Tree Snail
Kāhuli; Pūpū
Achatinella livida

O'ahu Tree Snail
Kāhuli; Pūpū
Achatinella lila

Moloka'i Tree Snail
Kāhuli; Pūpū
Partulina proxima

O'ahu Tree Snail
Kāhuli; Pūpū
Achatinella mustelina

Moloka'i Tree Snail
Kāhuli; Pūpū
Partulina redfieldi

Hawaiian Hoary Bat (right)
'Ōpe'ape'a
Lasiurus cinereus semotus

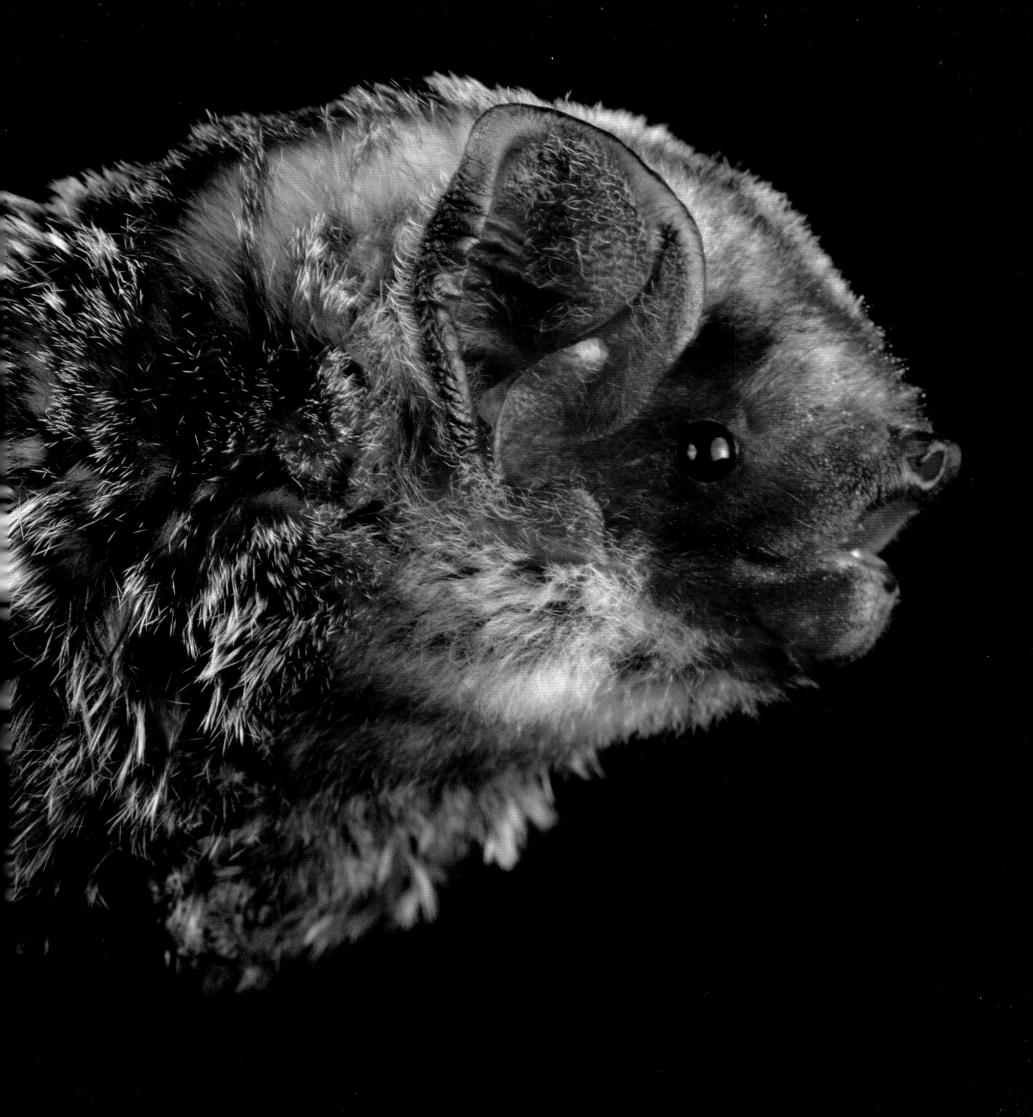

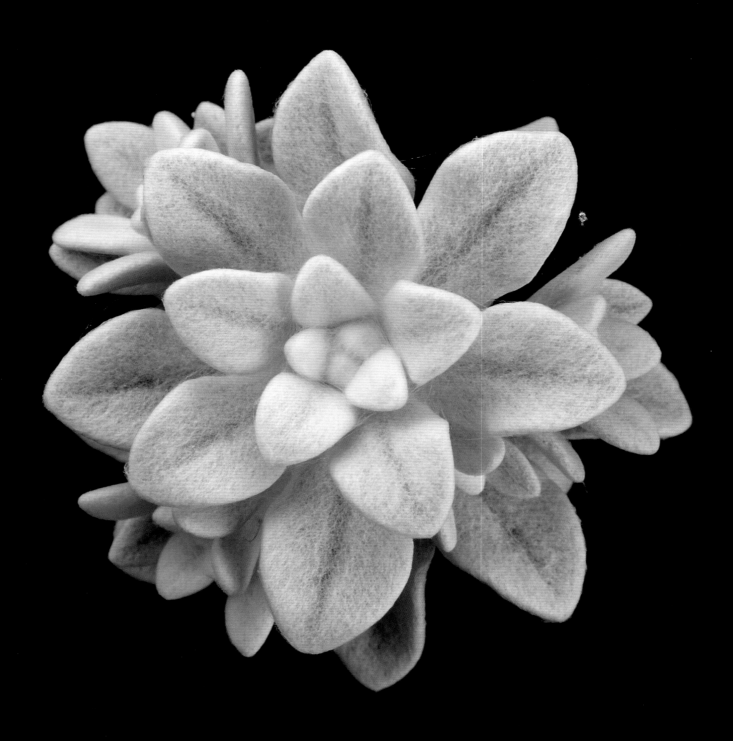

Cudweed (left)
'Ena'ena
Pseudognaphalium sandwicensium var. *molokaiense*

Cudweed growing at Moʻomomi Preserve, Molokaʻi (right)

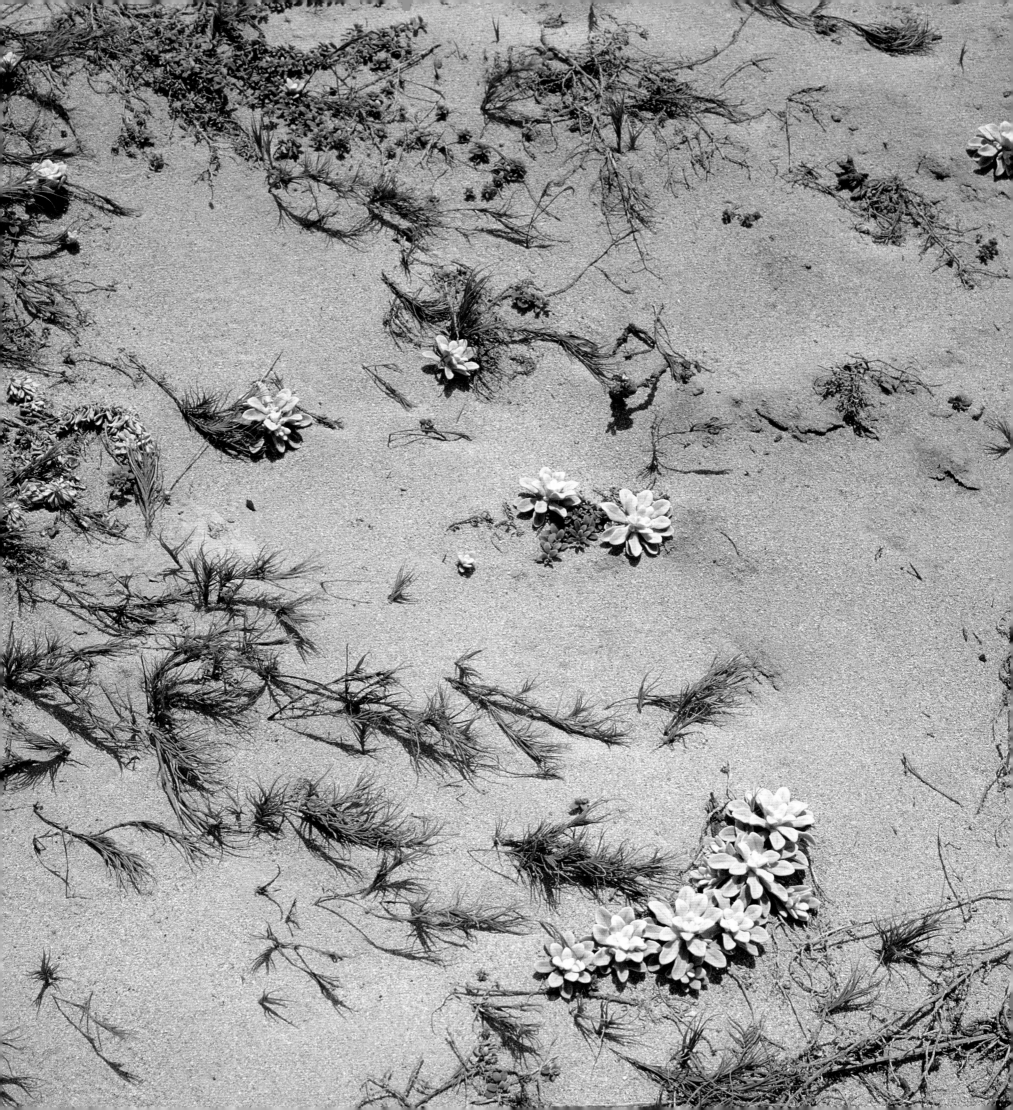

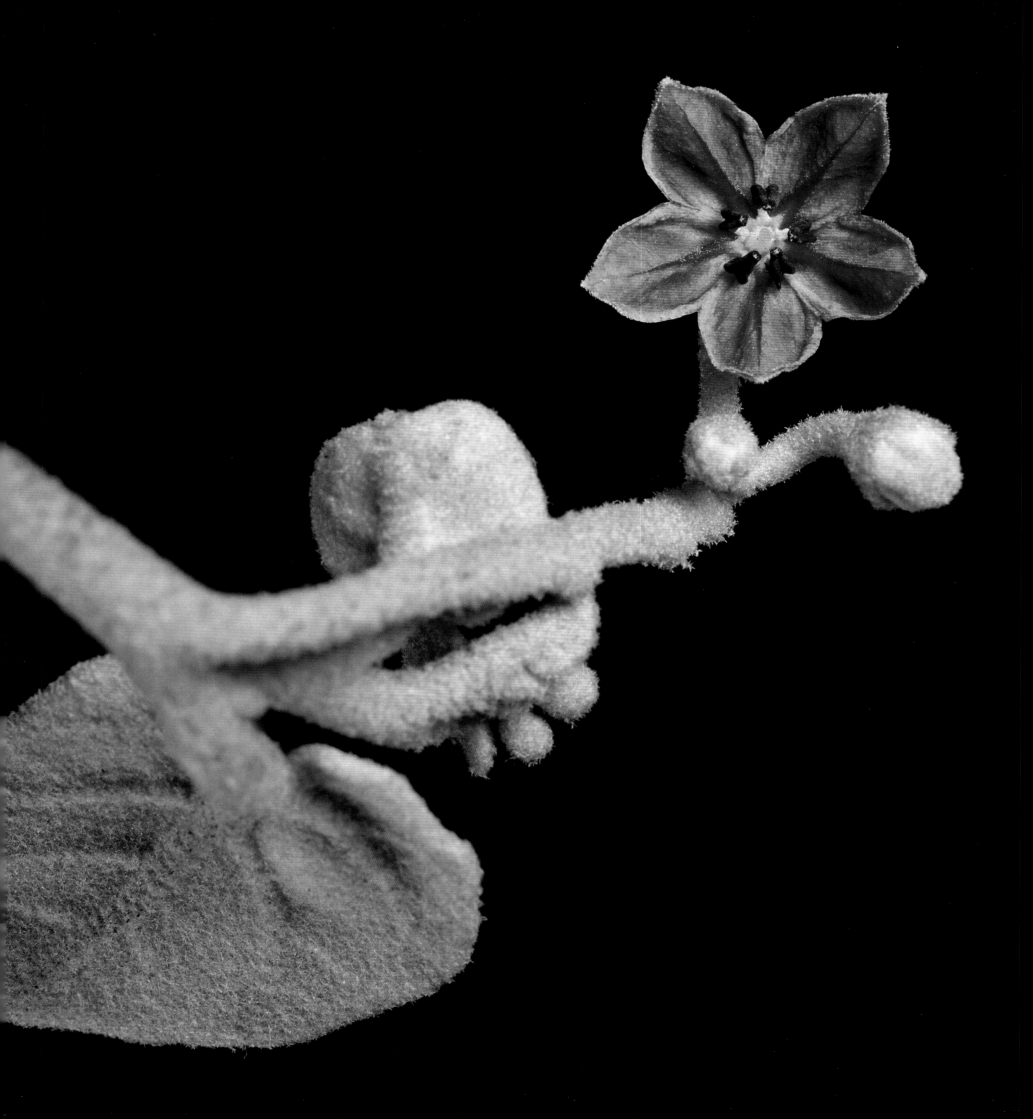

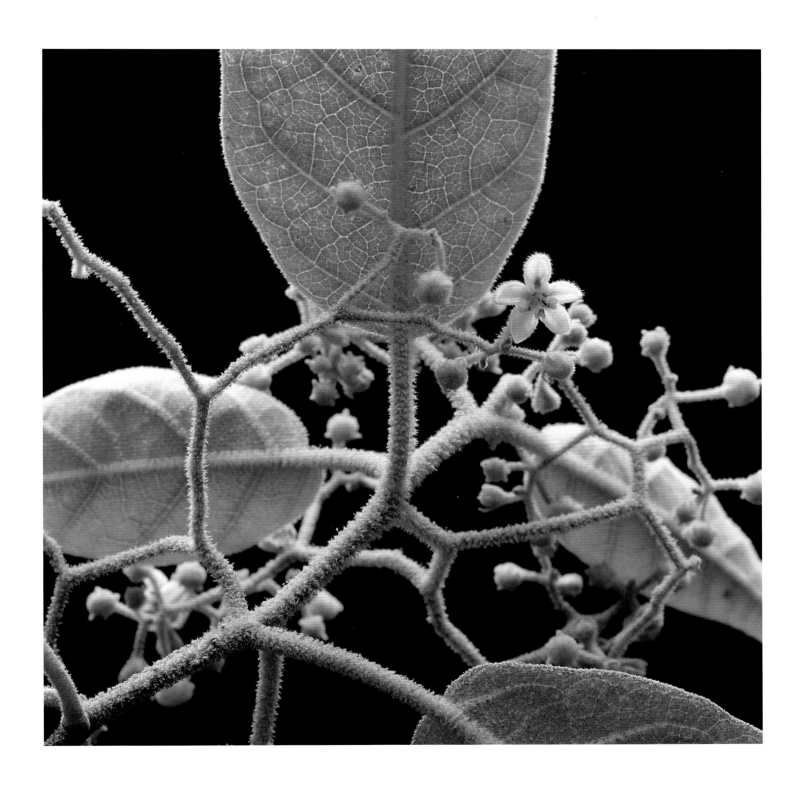

Nightshade (left)
ʻĀkia (Niʻihau); Pōpolo
Solanum nelsonii

Nightshade (right)
Pōpolo ʻAiakeakua; Pōpolo
Solanum sandwicense

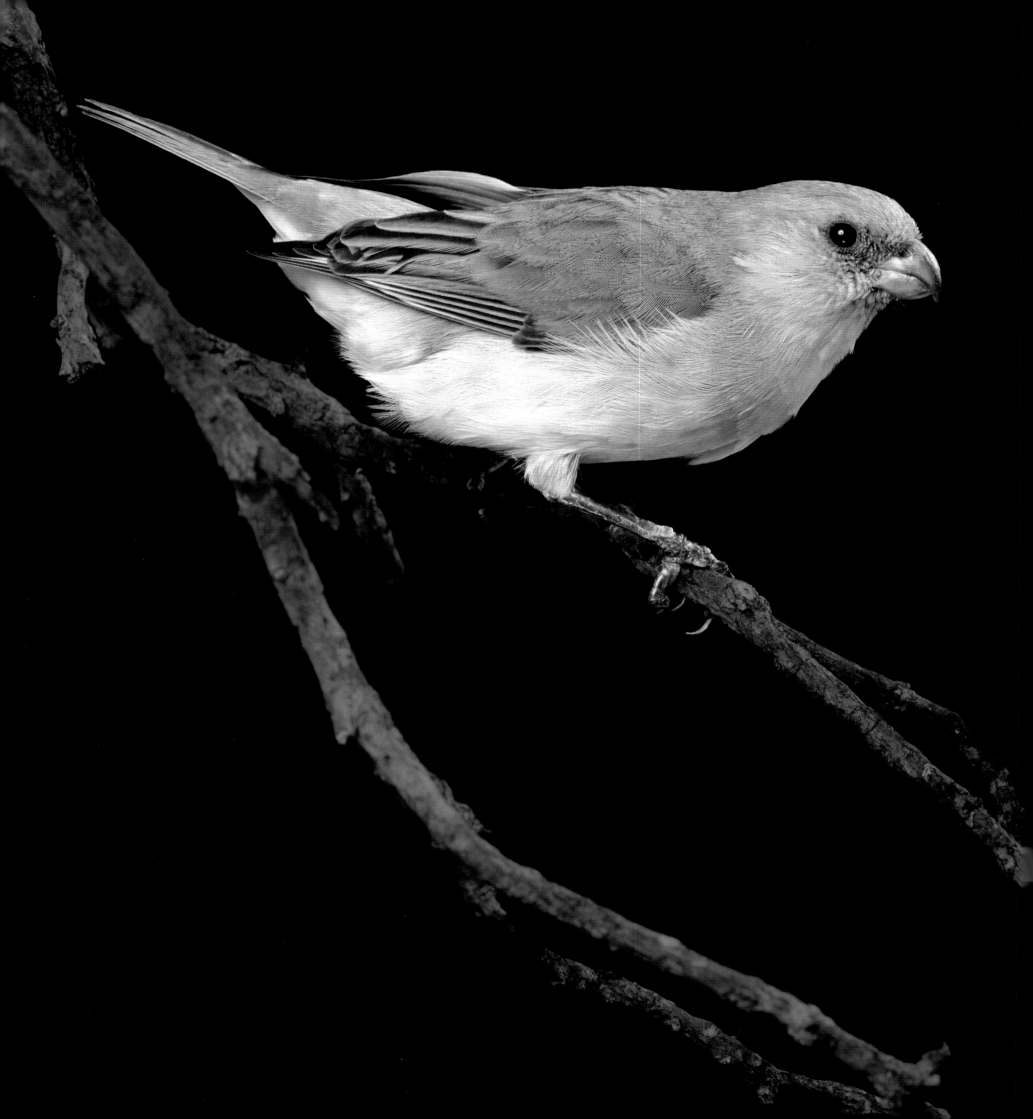

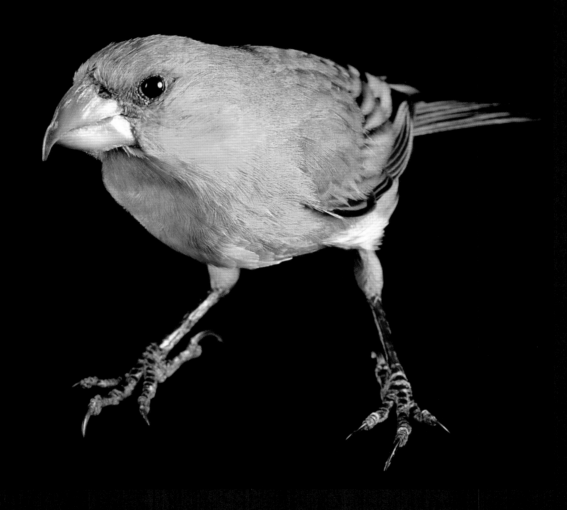

Palila (left)
Loxioides bailleui

Laysan Finch (right)
Telespiza cantans

'Ākepa (pages 72–73)
Loxops coccineus coccineus

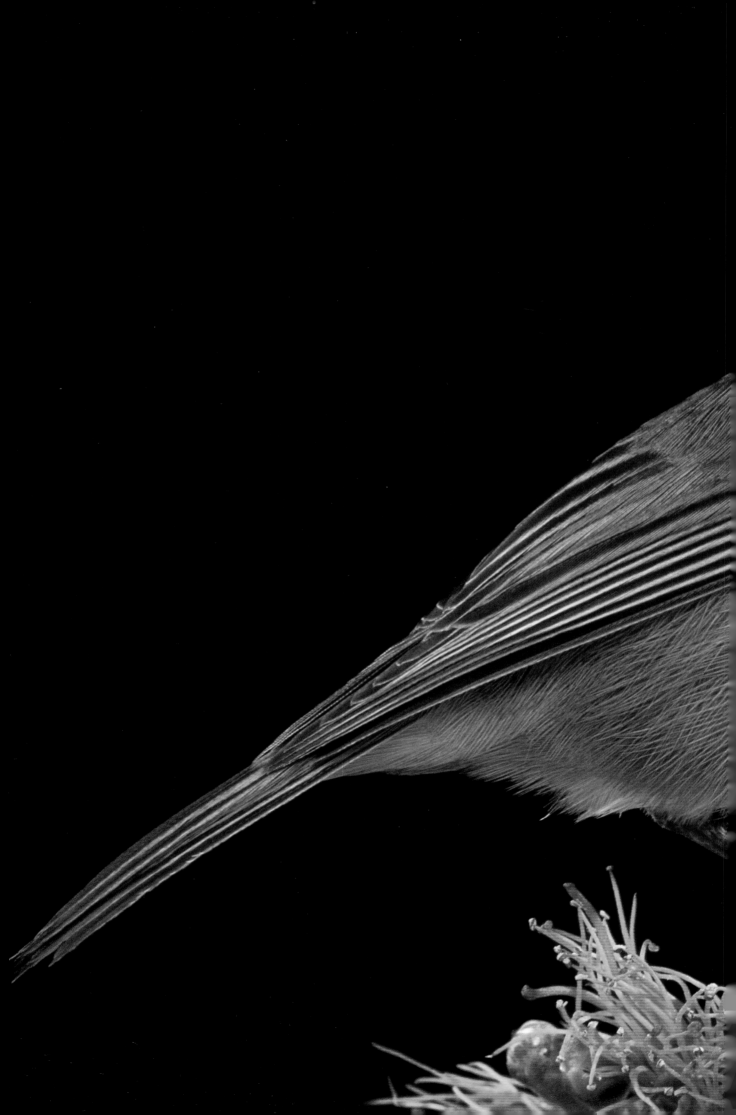

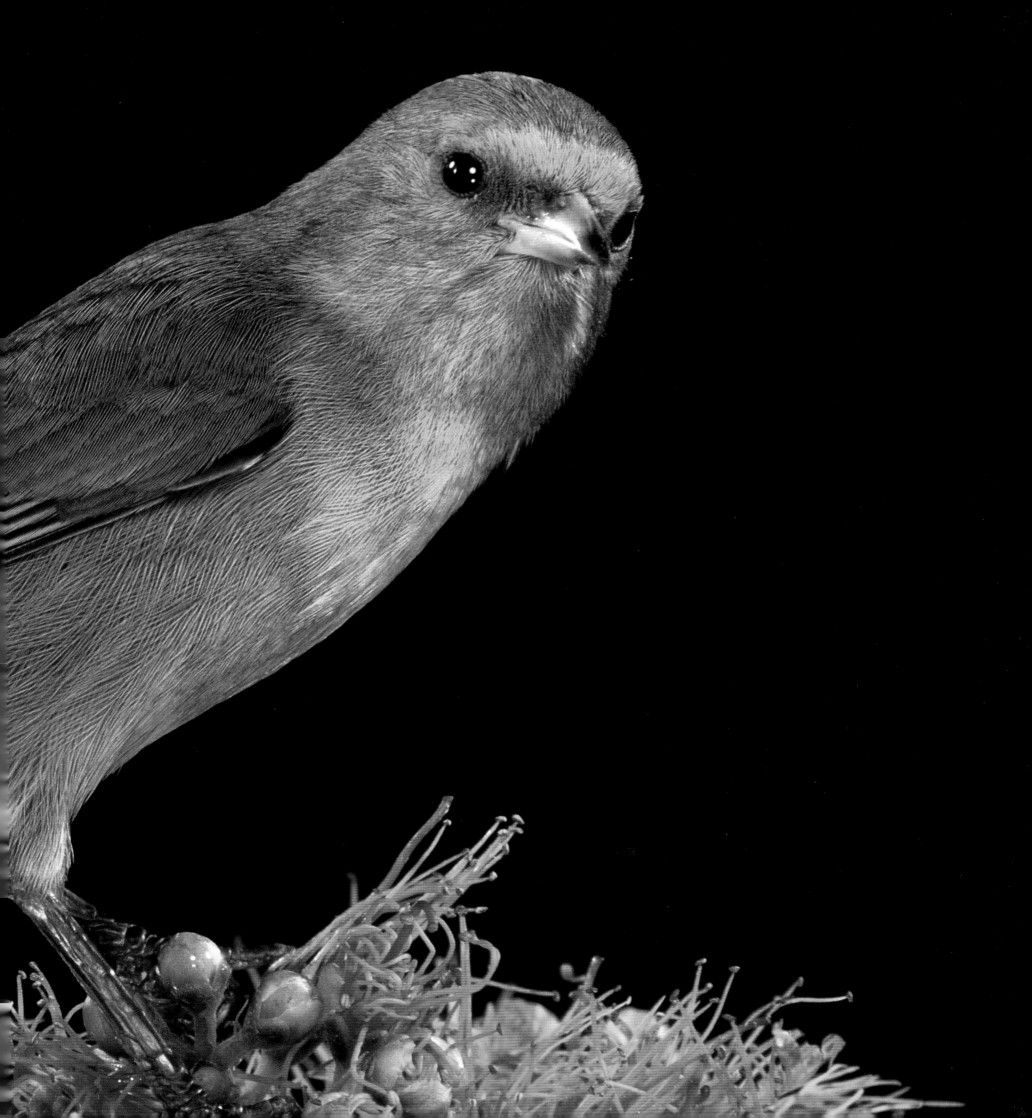

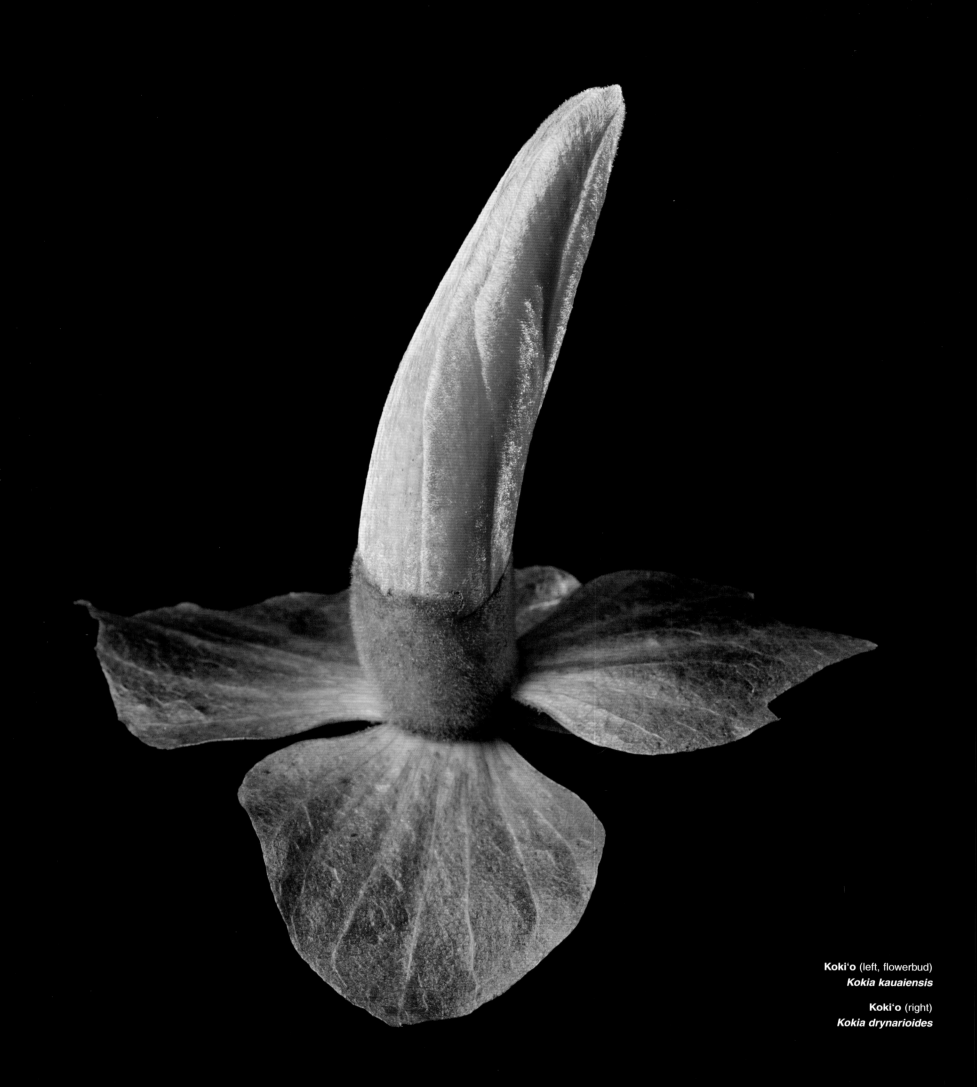

Koki'o (left, flowerbud)
Kokia kauaiensis

Koki'o (right)
Kokia drynarioides

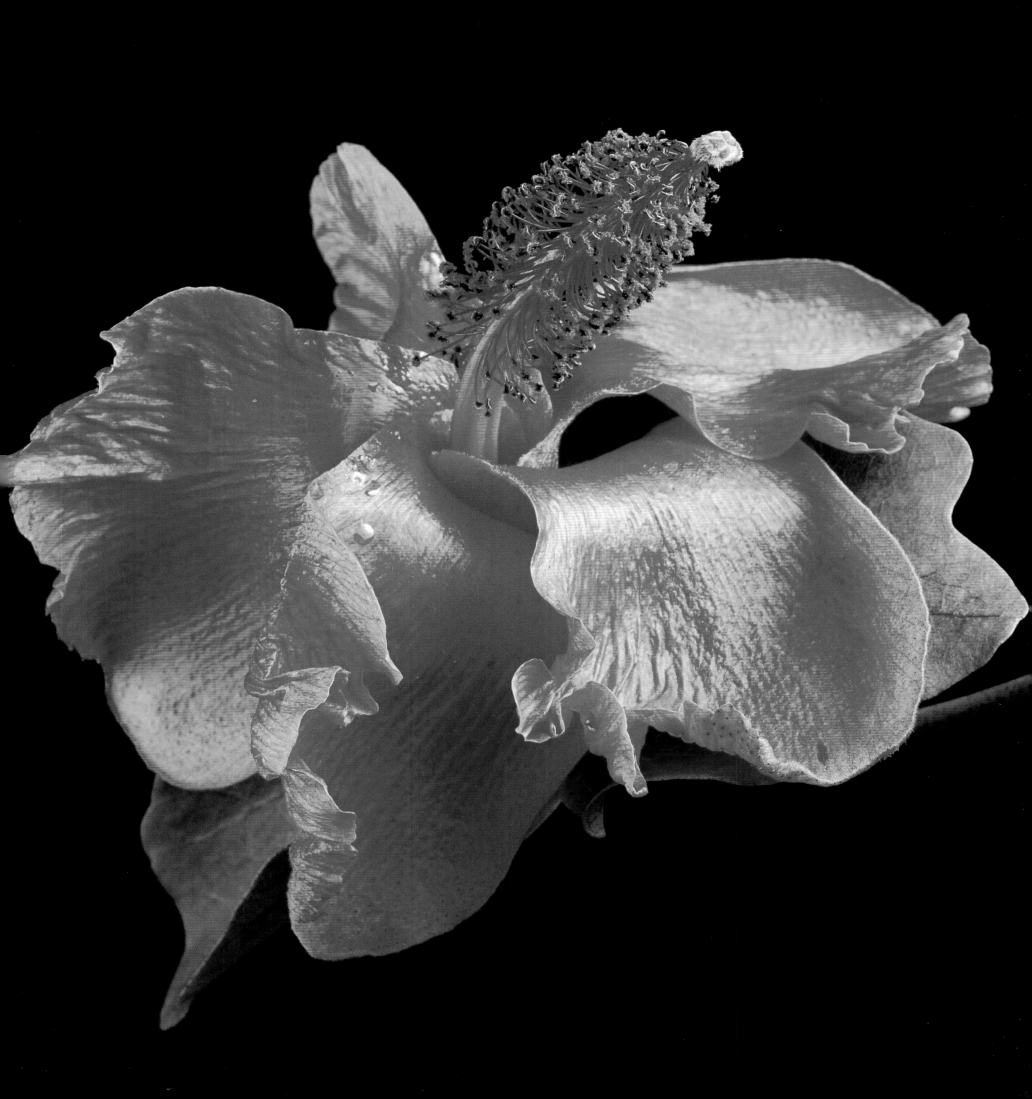

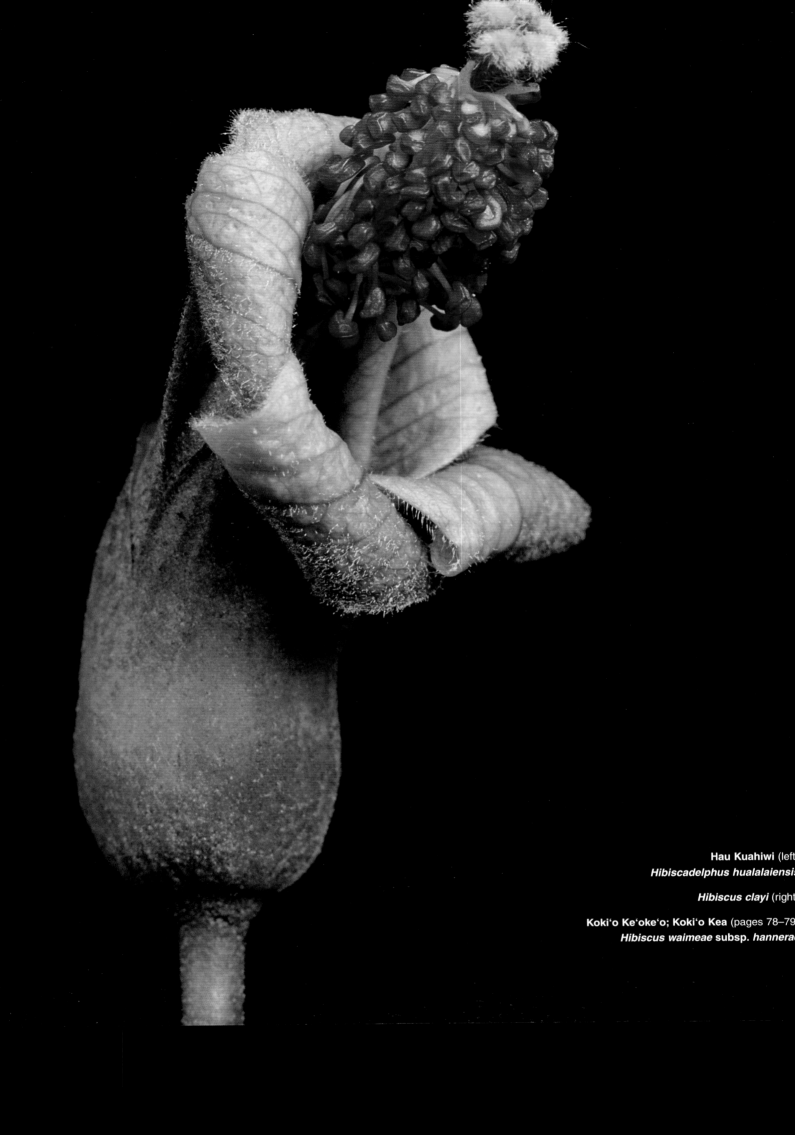

Hau Kuahiwi (left)
Hibiscadelphus hualalaiensis

Hibiscus clayi (right)

Kokiʻo Keʻokeʻo; Kokiʻo Kea (pages 78–79)
Hibiscus waimeae subsp. *hannerae*

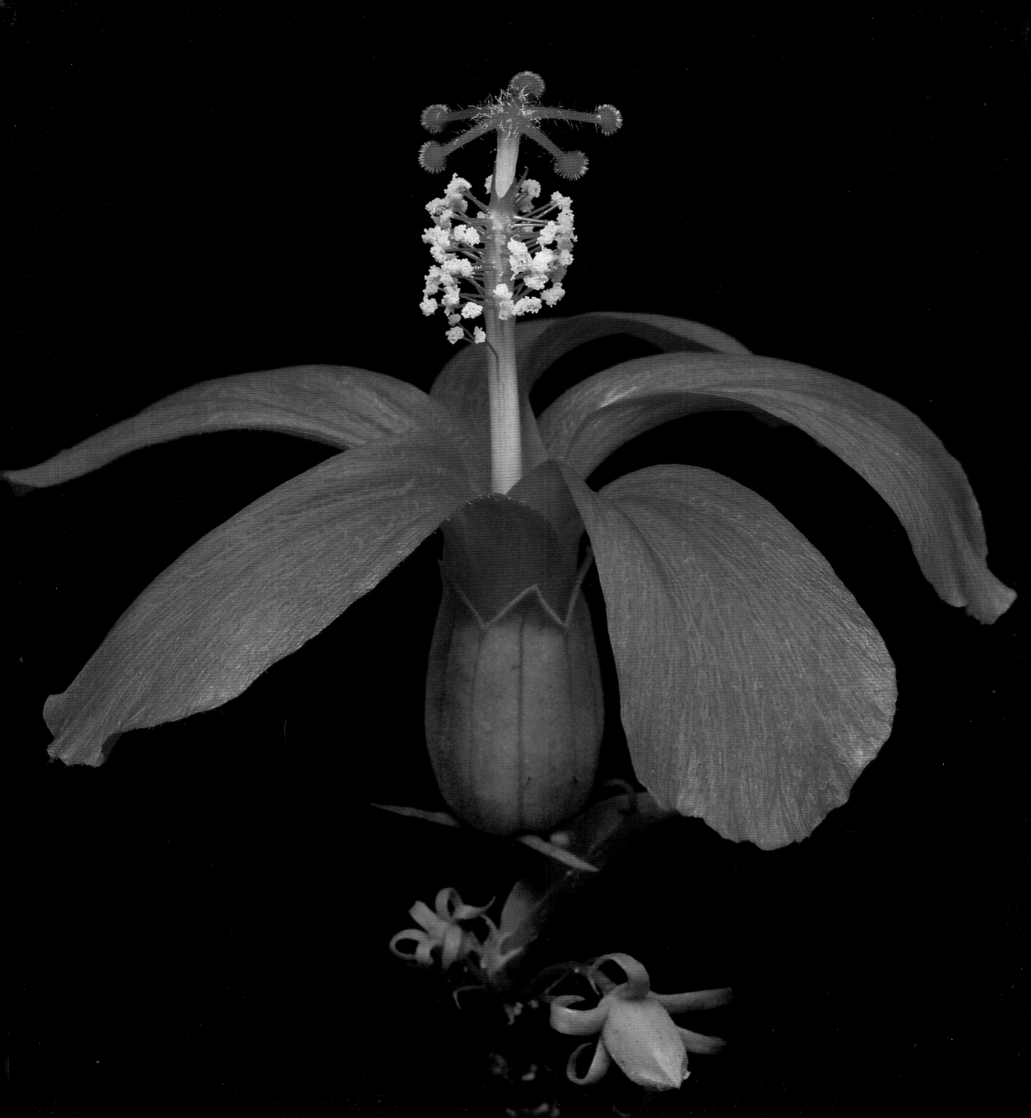

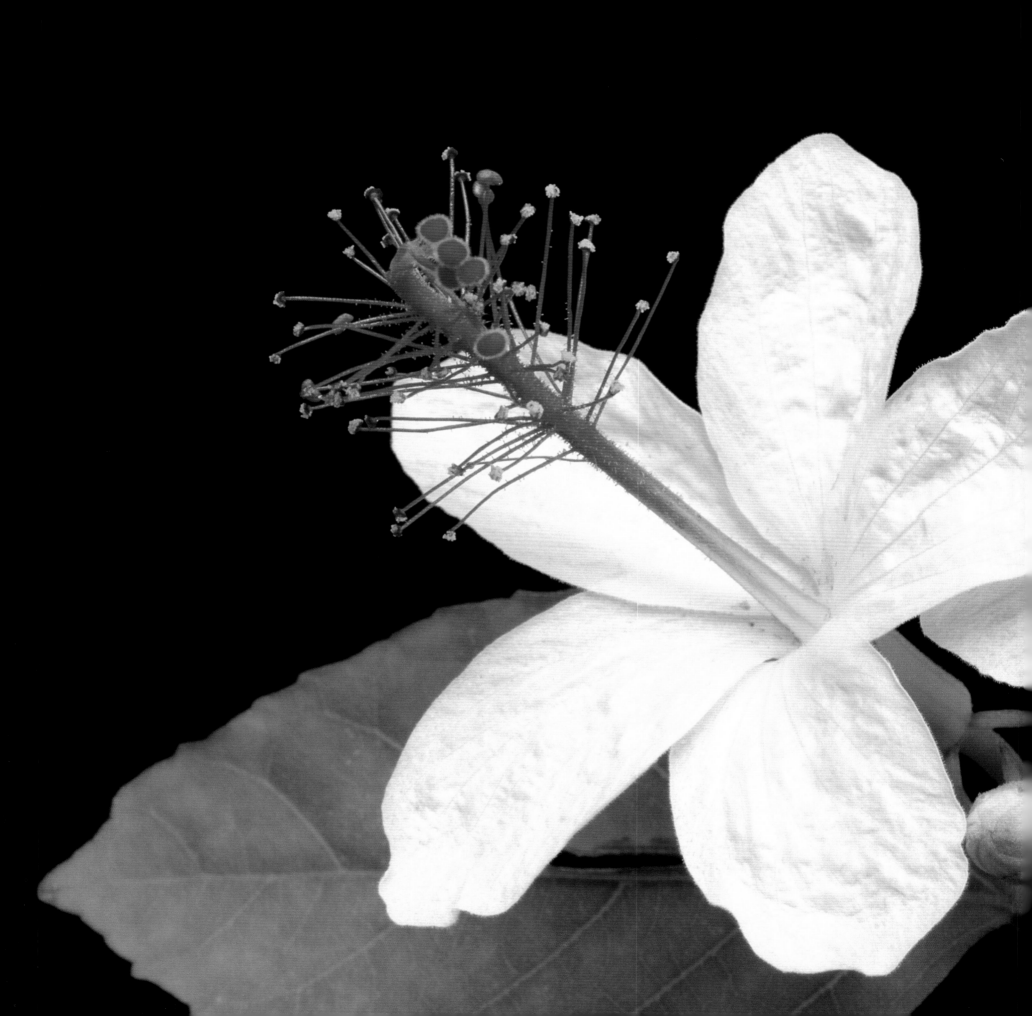

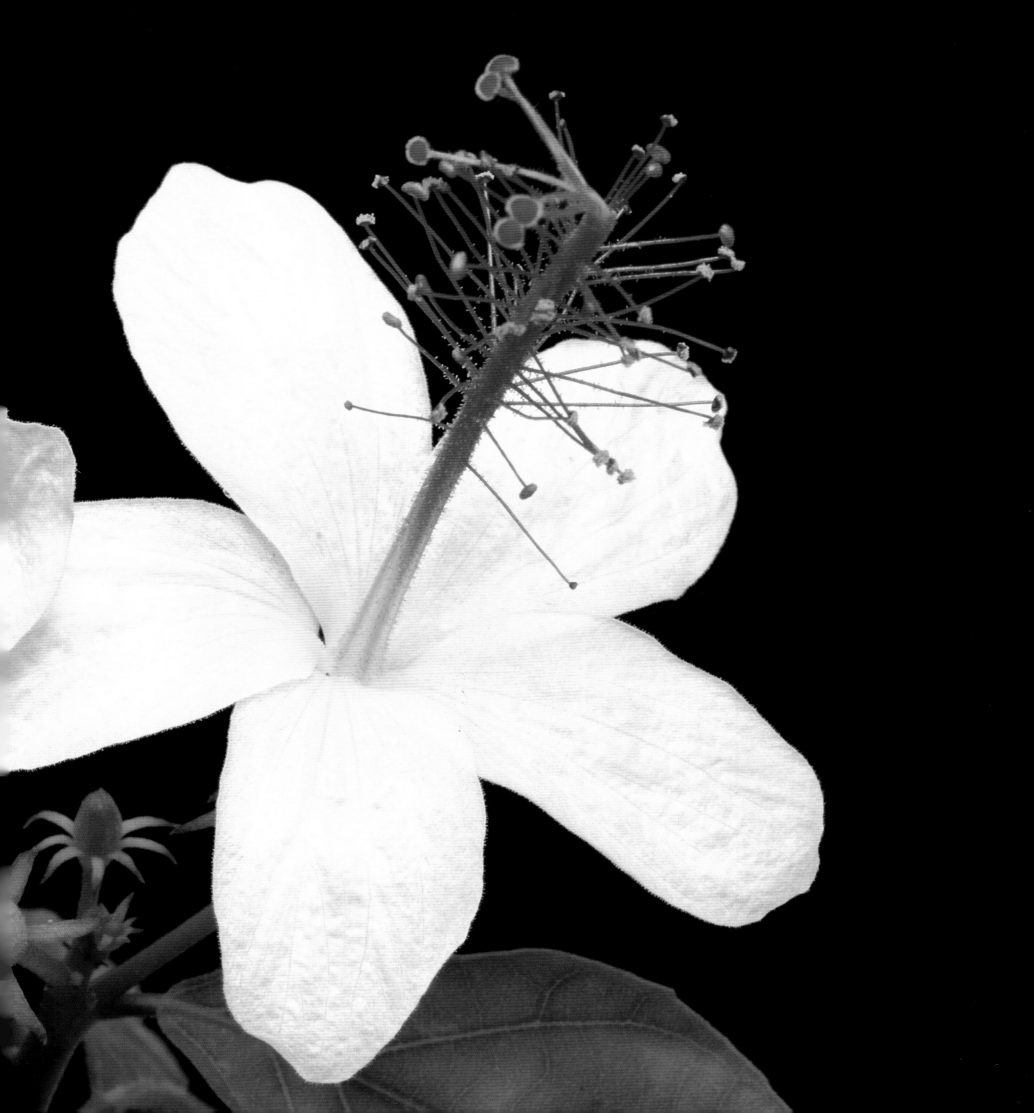

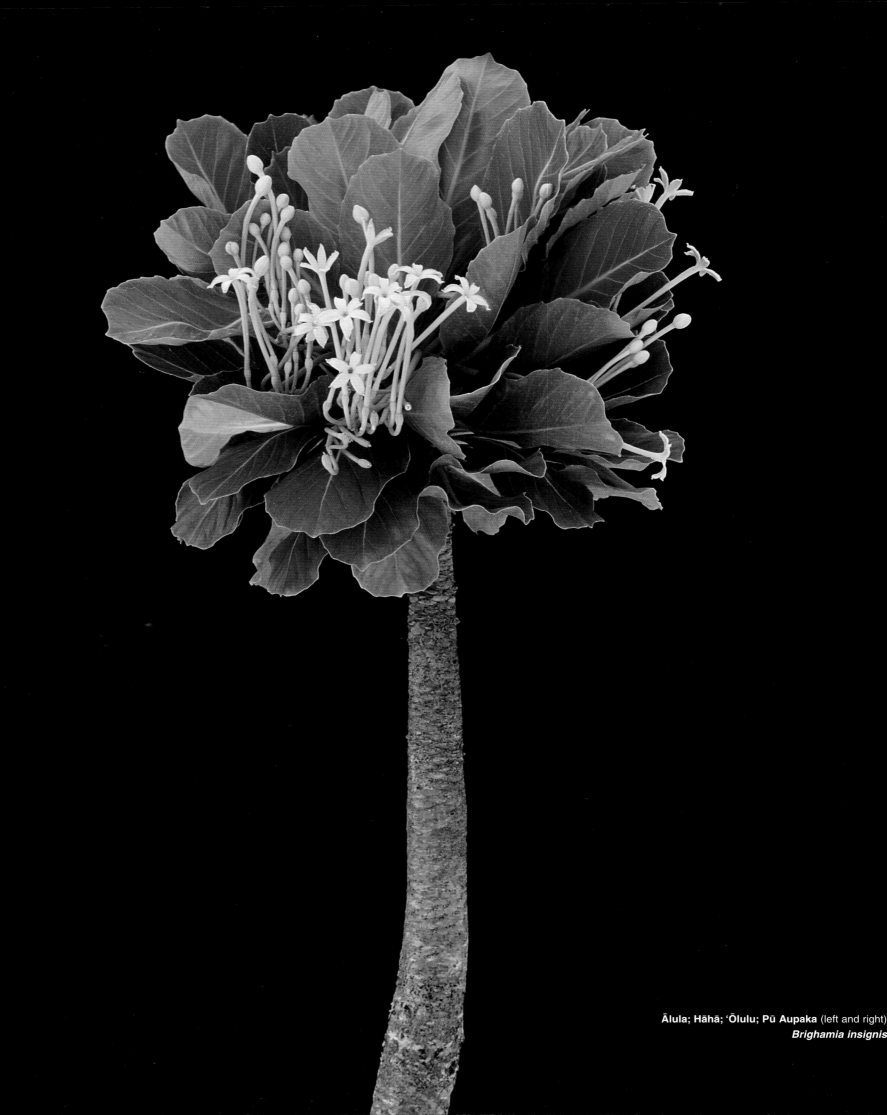

Ālula; Hāhā; ʻŌlulu; Pū Aupaka (left and right)
Brighamia insignis

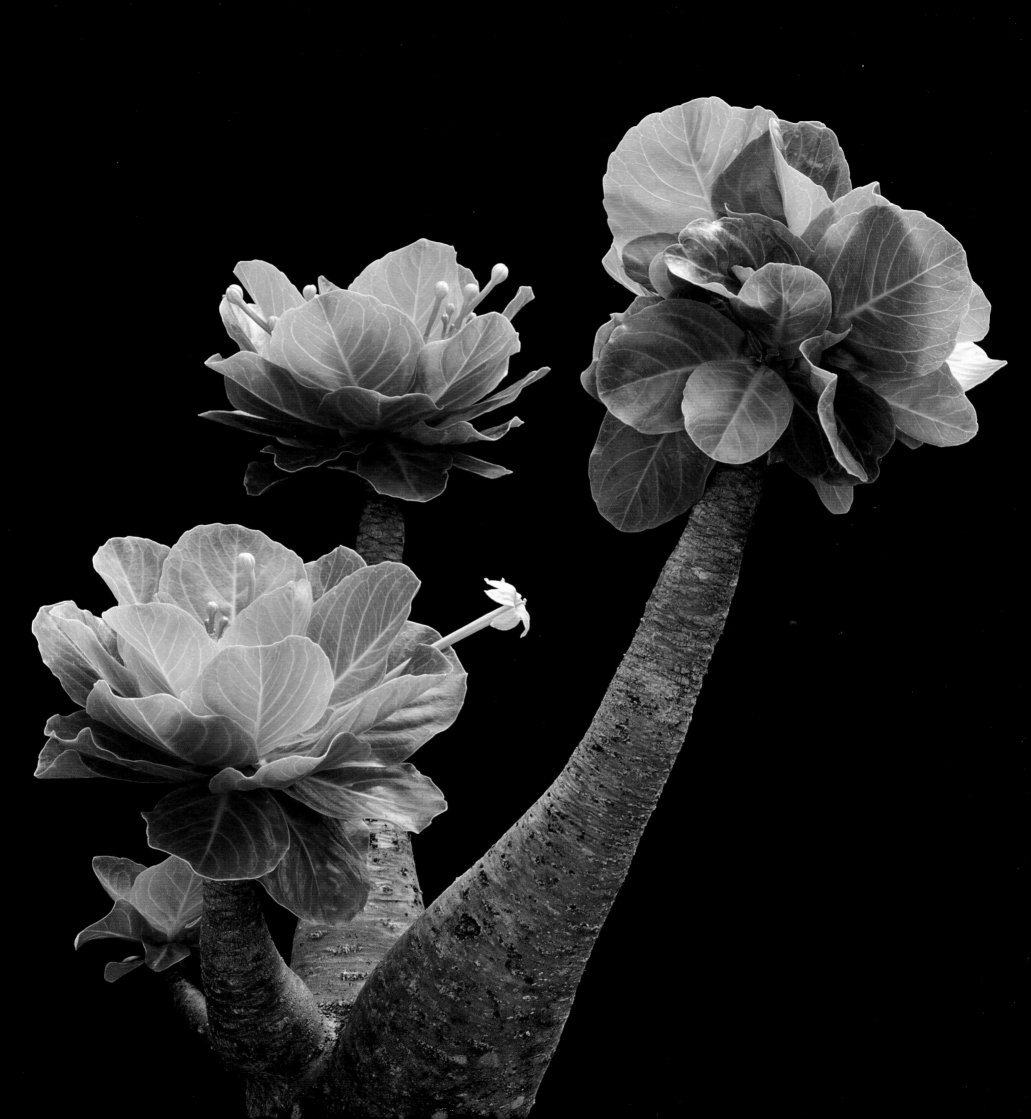

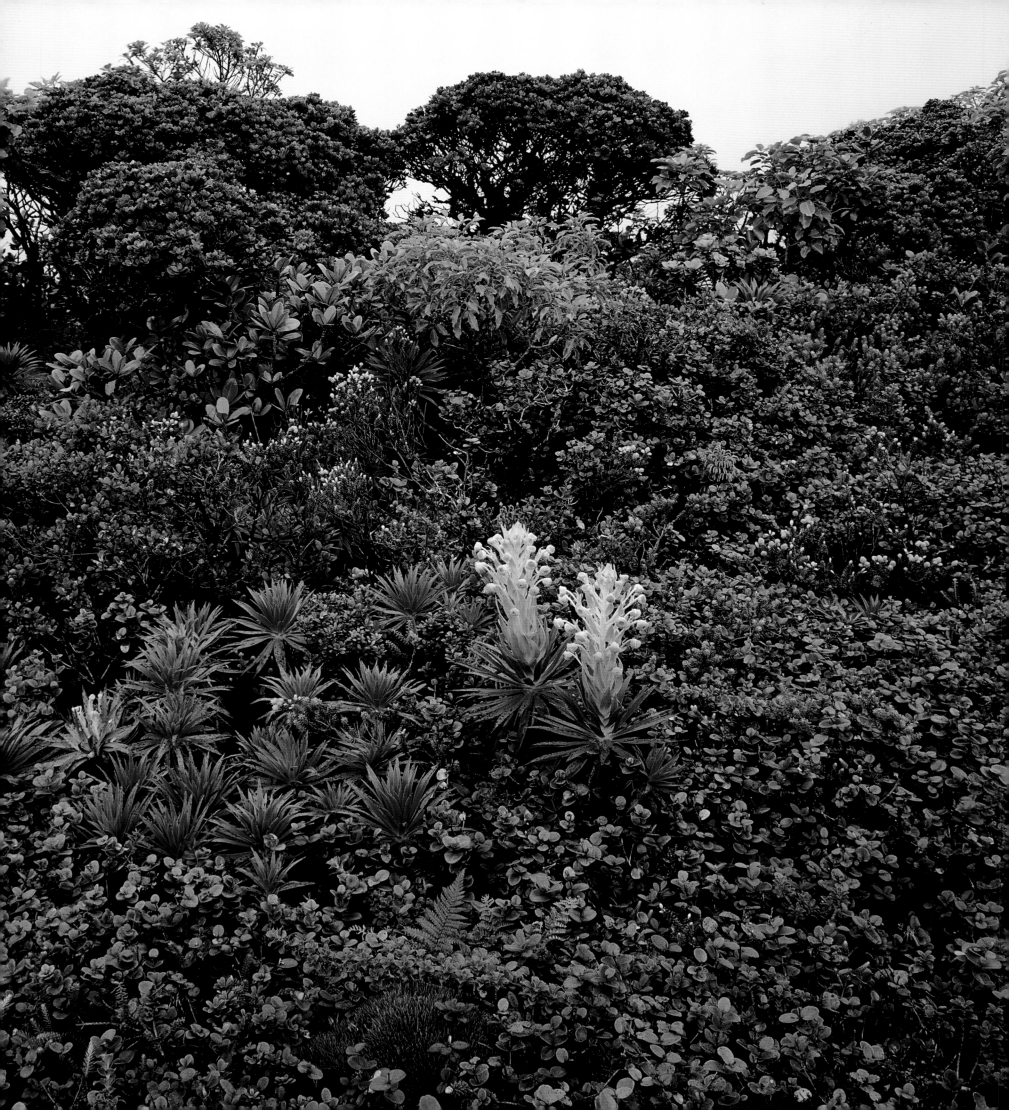

PU'U KUKUI: HILL OF ENLIGHTENMENT

by David Liittschwager

Pu'u Kukui, the summit of Mauna Kahalawai, West Maui, was the first native Hawaiian forest I have had the privilege to see. We were given a tour of Pu'u Kukui in 1995 as part of the planning for a conservation conference (the Earth Maui Nature Summit) to be sponsored by the Kapalua Nature Society. Although I've only seen a fraction of the Hawai'i that was known to the noted contemporary naturalist Sherwin Carlquist, I would have to agree with his description of the Pu'u Kukui bogs as "perhaps the loveliest in all the Islands."

Mauna Kahalawai is a giant mountain if measured from its base on the ocean floor. When the island was born the mountain was even more massive, but due to subsidence and erosion over 1.4 million years, the summit of Mauna Kahalawai is now 5,788 feet above sea level. The bogs of Pu'u Kukui are considered one of the jewels of Hawaiian biological diversity. In the bog, every foot of accumulated organic material represents 10,000 years of growth. Core samples have revealed that some bogs began forming at least 140,000 years ago. Pu'u Kukui Watershed has 279 vascular plant species (flowering plants, ferns, and fern allies); one mammal; nine birds; at least 11 terrestrial snail species; at least three fish species; other invertebrate species, many undescribed; and probably hundreds of cryptogam species (nonvascular plants such as mosses, liverworts, lichens, algae, and fungi).

Pu'u Kukui embodies the upper sections of several *ahupua'a,* a traditional Hawaiian land division once managed by practices that recognize the importance of holistic and sustainable land management. During our fieldwork in Hawai'i, I learned that *ahupua'a* is typically a slice of land that often originates at the summit of a mountain and follows a perennial stream all the way down to the ocean and beyond the outer reefs. The result is a triangular area that includes both land and sea, and all of the earth, freshwater, and marine resources to be found therein. *Ahupua'a* is an example of the environmental philosophy of the Hawaiians who lived on and managed these portions of land for centuries before Captain James Cook arrived. These special land designations provided the basis for a well-organized, long-lasting system of government for the early Hawaiians. Many of the ancient *ahupua'a* boundaries still stand, and this is a testament to the wisdom and practicality of this Hawaiian system.

The name *Pu'u Kukui,* which means "Hill of Light" or "Hill of Enlightenment," has been passed down through the ages. Pu'u Kukui, along with all the mountain peaks in

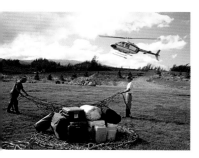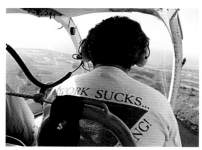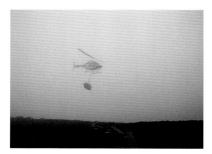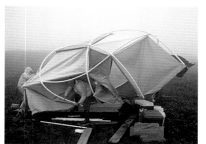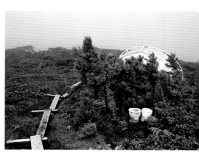

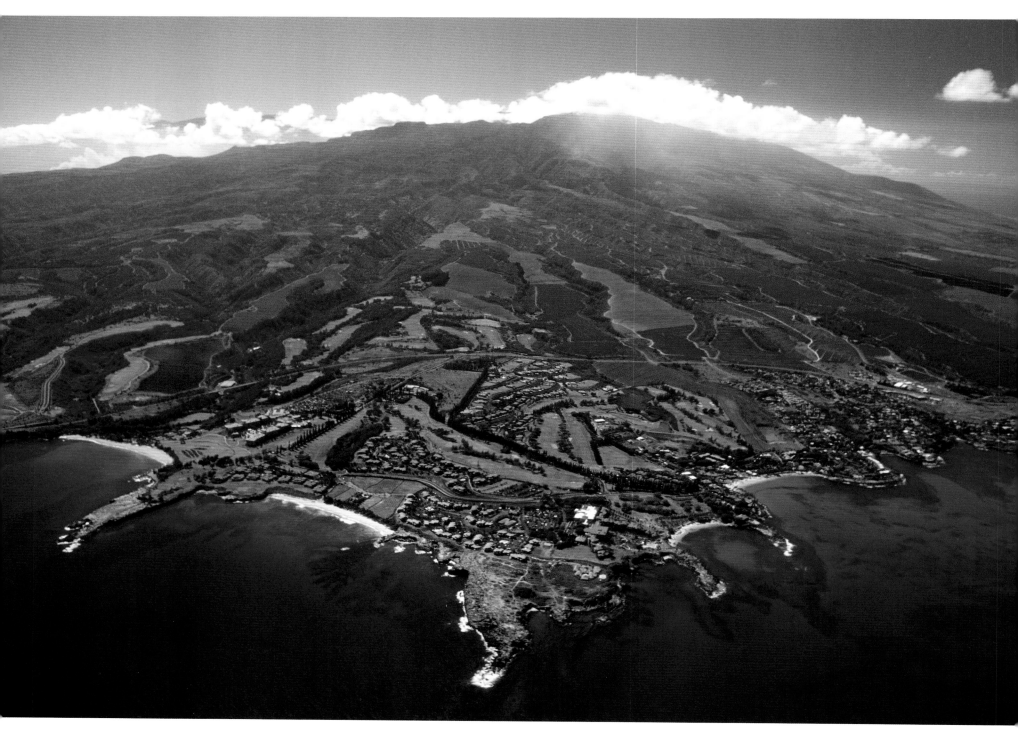

**Greenswords in flower, Puʻu Kukui
Preserve, West Maui** (page 82)

View of Puʻu Kukui Summit (left)

Puʻu Kukui Boardwalk (right)

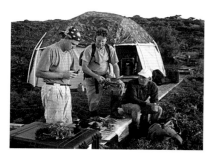 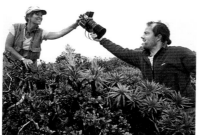 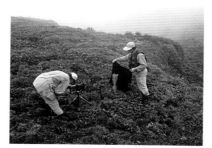 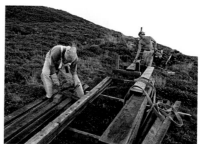 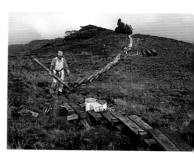

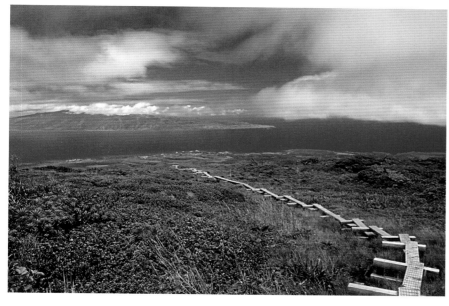

the Hawaiian Islands, exists in the inland/upland regions that Hawaiians call the *wao akua*—literally "the realm of spirit-beings"—and is therefore a sacred place. We were able to go there as guests of the current landowners, the Maui Land & Pineapple Company, Inc., at the invitation of the Kapalua Nature Society, one of the company's educational programs. In order to ensure the long-term protection of the area, the Pu'u Kukui Preserve was created by Maui Land & Pineapple Company, Inc. in 1988; the conservation easement for the preserve is due to a contractual arrangement with The Nature Conservancy of Hawai'i and the Natural Area Partnership Program of the State of Hawai'i—a conservation arrangement unique in the entire nation. Pu'u Kukui Preserve, at 8,661 acres the largest privately owned nature reserve in Hawai'i, contains 15 native plant communities.

The first time we were taken to Pu'u Kukui, it was a spectacular day. Early in the morning we joined our guides: Randy Bartlett, the Pu'u Kukui Watershed manager, and Scott Meidell and Hank Oppenheimer, the preserve's field technicians. We waited in a ball field for a helicopter to pick us up. The skies were clear all the way to the summit, which I later learned is not the norm. Eight minutes later we were dropped off at a place called Silversword Bog, eight miles from and 4,500 feet above the ball field. We climbed out and the magic carpet left. All was silent. The

wind was soft and cool. I could see Lāna'i and Moloka'i across the channel. Everything looked new and ancient at the same time, sparkling.

I will never forget my first glimpse of Pu'u Kukui. I grew up in the Pacific Northwest of North America, and the nature of the forests there is such that one can only see parts at a time. The canopy is hundreds of feet above you; to "see" the shape of the forest you have to get so far back that you can no longer pick out individual flora. At Pu'u Kukui I could see the forest surrounding me and comprehend its shape and texture much more immediately. The arrangement seemed the work of a master landscape architect. Evolution has worked nearly 1.5 million years to reach this apparent perfection.

In Silversword Bog, acidic soil conditions dwarf the *'ōhi'a* trees—fully mature plants are four to six inches tall, while at lower, warmer elevations out of the wind they can reach 100 feet with trunks eight feet in diameter. These conditions create what feels like a bonsai forest. When I looked carefully at the plants in the bog, at their structure and organization, they appeared, from a distance, to lie on a single plane. They made a fine tapestry, harmonious, perfectly ordered, nothing crowding anything else out. Each shape nested elegantly within the next. When the community is healthy and undamaged, there are no blank spots.

Lower down in the forest, below the bogs, I saw more colors of green in a single view than I had imagined possible: deep blue-greens in the moss of the shaded areas lit only by the blue sky and bright yellow-greens of the *'ōlapa* leaves sparkling in the sun. The range of color was far beyond what we could hope to record on a single piece of film.

This first experience in a native Hawaiian forest and montane bogs changed the way I thought about the work we had been doing. While we had been creating portraits of individuals for years, we now felt that to portray just the individual would be stripping away too much. Ninety percent of the Hawaiian species we had photographed lived in some captive situation—either a zoo, a botanical garden, or a university lab. Endangered species find themselves in these places because their homes are gone and they have no healthy places to live. But at Pu'u Kukui they're still whole; they still have their associations with the life around them. To portray

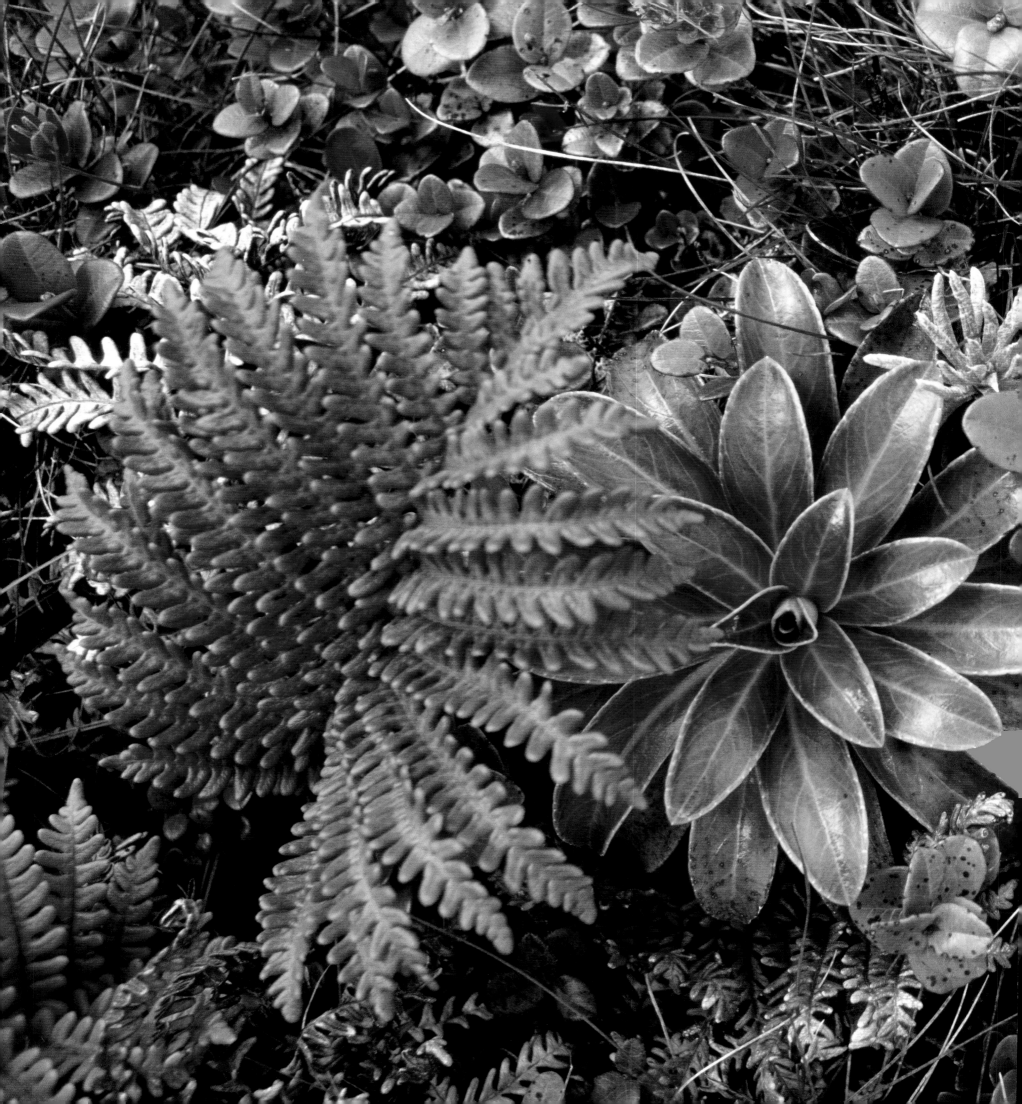

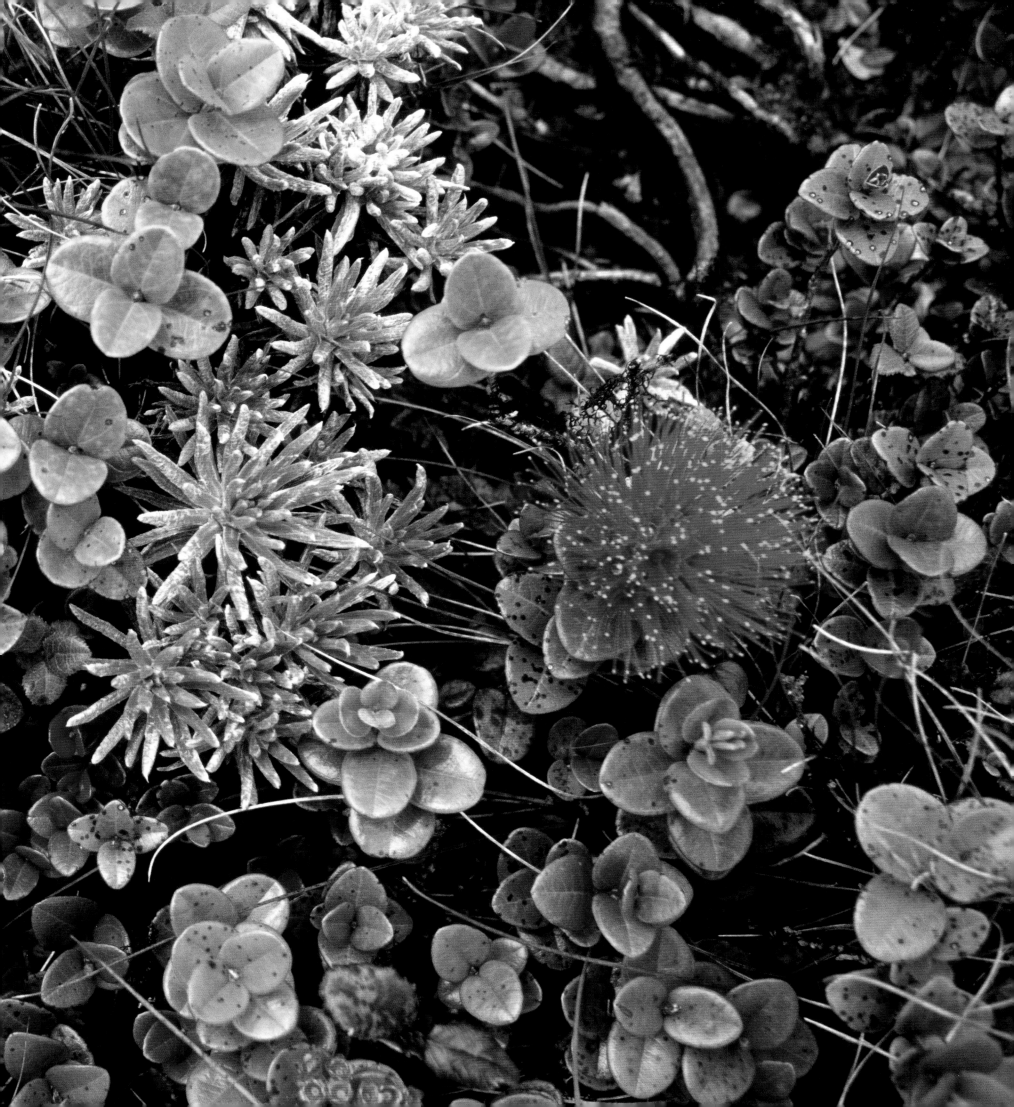

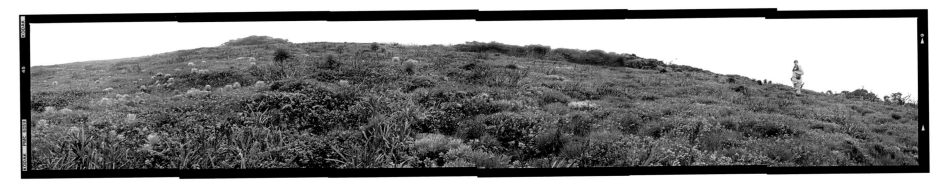

them with only a black background behind them and completely exclude their context seemed inappropriate. It was time to try to portray their place in the world.

Working in this new way presented many challenges. It's much easier—a lot of work, but still easier—to do a portrait. We like the graphic simplicity possible with a plain background. It is always more difficult to make a family portrait. How do you photograph something that's a foot or two across on a scale that's physically intimate? How do you find miniature, cohesive communities and get close enough to really see how everything is made and how it is relating to what's around it—all in a shape that will fit into a frame?

In the Silversword Bog, these challenges were compounded by the fact that we needed to stay on the one-foot-across boardwalk built over the bog to protect it, and after seeing how badly the bog can be damaged by repeated foot traffic, we understood why. The boardwalk, under construction while we were shooting but completed in December of 2000, is more than two miles long. Built and maintained in cooperation with the State of Hawai'i, it allows managers and visiting researchers access to the area while preventing trampling and degradation of the fragile peat and substrate. Keeping the native-plant community intact prevents erosion and the invasion of aggressive alien plants.

When we returned to Hawai'i about six months later to give a slide show at the Earth Maui Nature Summit, arrangements were made for us to spend a couple of days on Pu'u Kukui taking photographs of the bogs and forest while Scott and Hank continued their construction of the boardwalk. Randy picked us up and took us to the ball field to meet up with Hank and Scott. That morning things had a very different look than the first time we were there. I saw several large stacks of lumber, bundles of steel, and other paraphernalia. Also laid out were two large net slings: one was being filled with tools and building supplies and the other held camping gear. Everything was being parceled out into 650-pound groups to be lifted to the top of the mountain by helicopter. Building a boardwalk is very hard work— even building and maintaining a fence in the steep, wet conditions of a Hawaiian rain forest is not for the faint of heart. Keeping this place whole has required a commitment and vigilance that is to be admired and can be used as an example of what is possible.

Any person entering a forest has an effect on the place. The night before, following Randy's directions, I had spent a couple of hours cleaning all of the bags, shaking the dirt out, emptying pockets, removing little bits of dander from Velcro, cleaning boots, picking through everything in search of seeds. This has since become a regular practice before entering any native forest in order to minimize the extent to which I am a "weed-dispersal mechanism." Without knowing why, I followed Scott's and Hank's example and put on raingear even though it was 80 degrees and the sun shone brightly. We brushed off our boots and boarded the helicopter.

The weather was very different this time around—there was no clear view to the summit, and we were told it was going to be wet up top. We were dropped off on a platform about a quarter mile uphill from Silversword Bog. The pilot flew the last mile uphill, following the boardwalk because the visibility was well under 500 feet. The wind was blowing at about 20 miles per hour and there was a heavy mist. It felt like a completely different place from our first trip.

Mauna Kahalawai rises right into the trade winds—at the summit it is common for the wind to reach 50 miles per hour. The wind is part of what shapes the landscape of Pu'u Kukui. An interesting characteristic of a Hawaiian rain forest or cloud forest is that most of the diversity is on the ground, not in the canopy. This is because the 'ōhi'a, the most numerous trees in this forest, are so battered by the wind that the forest canopy never completely closes. This partially sheltered place with its abundance of light and water creates a magnificent variety of life.

Pu'u Kukui is also made by the rain. The Pu'u Kukui summit, the second-wettest spot on the Hawaiian Islands (after Mount Wai'ale'ale on Kaua'i), has received up to 600 inches of rain in one year—that's 50 feet of water! The annual average recorded rainfall at Pu'u Kukui is 350 inches. To get a real sense of the wetness you also have to add about 30 percent for the fog drip caused by condensation on the plants. In the area of Oregon in which I was raised, known for its rain, 65 inches is considered a wet year.

Strong forces make Pu'u Kukui what it is. The wind and the rain are brutal. We were able to visit there in semi-comfort because of nylon, Gore-Tex, and other artificial things we brought with us via helicopter. It was sobering to realize that technology was the only reason we had access to this extraordinary place.

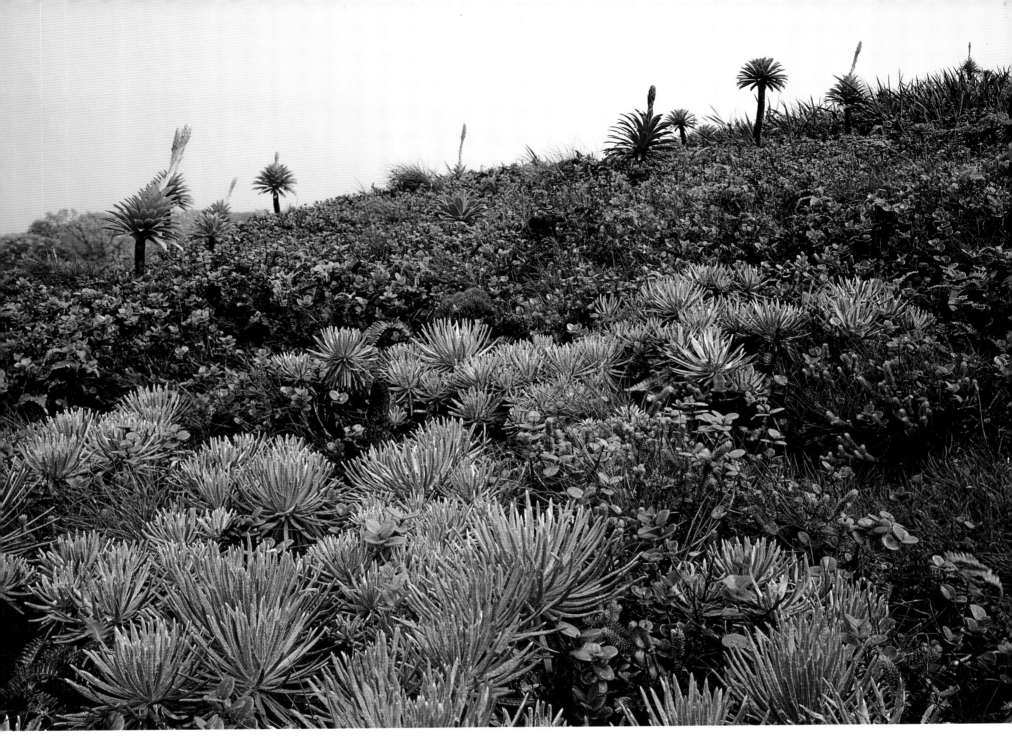

Silversword Bog, Pu'u Kukui Preserve,
West Maui (pages 86–87)

Silversword Bog (left and above)

Hōwaiaula (near right)
Lagenifera maviensis

Kolea (center right)
Myrsine vaccinioides

Viola maviensis (far right)

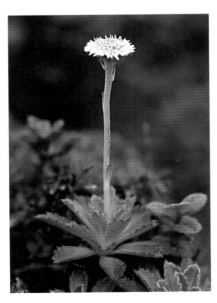

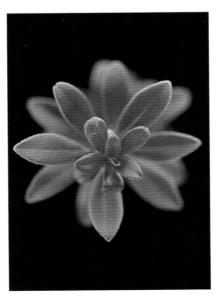

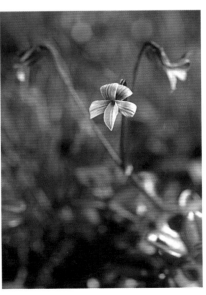

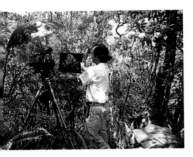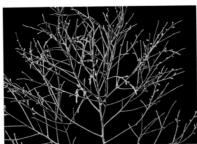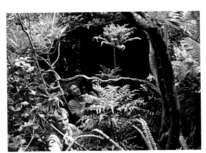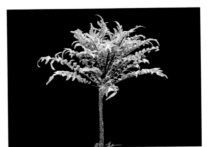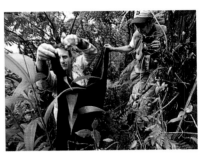

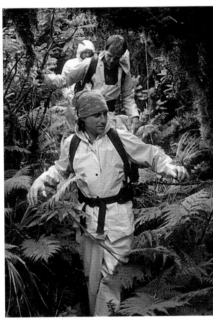

When we began to set up camp on the mountain, what was to become our shelter was a three-foot-by-five-foot bundle of PVC pipes and nylon material that, when assembled, makes a dome that is seven feet high and 15 feet across. The tent is designed to withstand wind of up to 46 miles per hour. On one trip we had the experience of what happens to the dome when the wind reaches 47 miles per hour. It collapsed on top of us in the middle of the night and we all had to put our feet up and push quite hard to get it to pop back into place. After that, frequent, hasty repairs kept us dry until dawn. When daylight came, it was time to leave; the weather was not improving. This time the mountain dismissed us. Short of a life-threatening situation, which this was not, no one would ask the helicopter to come get us. We packed up our gear, abandoned it on the platform, and walked a long, rough path down the mountain to the road. Two days later our equipment was brought down the mountain. It took two more days to dry everything out.

While a deluge halts all work, a little rain is a wonderful thing for photography. Film can't see into the shadows of a bright, sunny day—all it can see is the highlights, so it misses half the scene. In a photograph of a plant, for example, all you'll see is the tops of the flowers. When it's cloudy and things are wet, it raises the contrast but not in a harsh way. When it rains, things look fresh and open in the bog. The first time we went there the place was not in character (that is, very, very wet), although it was lovely and vibrant. Now, in the light mist, with the sun popping in and out of the clouds, it *really* sparkled.

Our fourth trip to the bog was the most productive. We had perfect weather for two and a half days: light mist, but it wasn't a storm, and the wind wasn't howling. In a 20-mile-an-hour wind the camera doesn't hold still. The wind vibrates the tripod and the camera, and it makes all the flowers shake, so close-ups aren't possible. On this trip, aided by good weather, we photographed the perennial herb *Sanicula purpurea* (snakeroot), which grows nestled atop the diminutive ʻōhiʻa toward the bog margins. Vines seven to nine feet long wind through the surrounding vegetation, their leaves (and from time to time, flowers and fruit) poking up here and there. *Sanicula purpurea* is well hidden, and I might have walked right by it if Steve Perlman hadn't pointed out this exceedingly rare plant as one that we should include in our portrayal of this place.

This plant's ancestors are believed to have dispersed to Hawaiʻi from the Americas. How could they possibly have crossed 2,400 ocean miles against prevailing winds? It is likely that the plant's burrlike fruits hitchhiked on shore birds, which flew back and forth quite readily across the Pacific. Though hardy enough to have survived this journey and flourished, at least initially, today only about 150 plants exist in the wild.

We set up for a picture from the boardwalk to show the plant in situ. (The *Sanicula* is in the very center of the frame on page 92). Upon closer inspection with a hand lens Steve told us that the plant was in flower. Yet how could we get ourselves and our camera, tripod, and lights close enough for a photo without trampling the area in which this endangered plant lived? We decided not to risk harming the plant by damaging the surrounding area. In order to make a photograph of the flowers, Steve took a very small specimen—fewer than two inches from one tip. The photograph—24 times life size—appears on page 93.

The flowers of *Sanicula purpurea* are so small that they can't be seen with the naked eye; the flower clusters appear to be little brown nubs. Yet magnification reveals a profusion of reds, greens, and yellows. Even the tiniest elements of the bog reflect its primeval, sublime beauty.

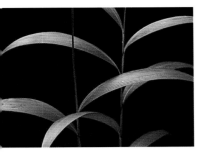
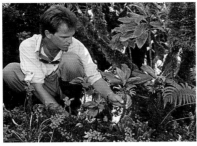
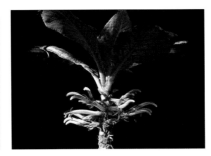
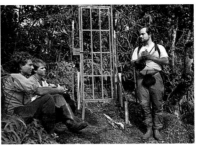
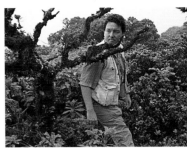

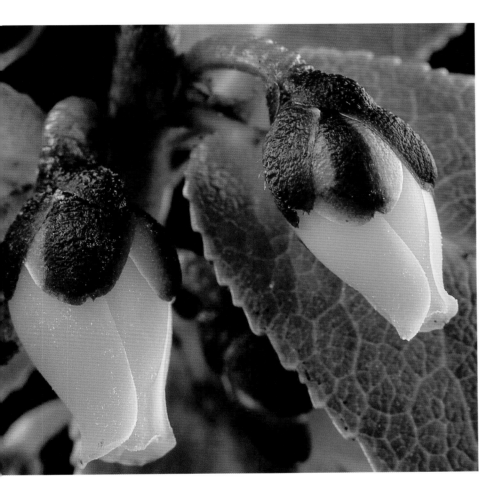

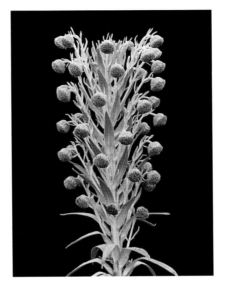

Ānini; Wānini (far left)
Eurya sandwicensis

Greensword (near left)
Argyroxiphium grayanum

Pauoa (below right)
Ctenitis squamigera

Laukahi (below left)
Elaphoglossum crassifolium

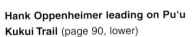

Hank Oppenheimer leading on Puʻu Kukui Trail (page 90, lower)

At Puʻu Kukui, we were shown many rare plants by the preserve staff, who assisted us with the photography (top row, pages 90 and 91).

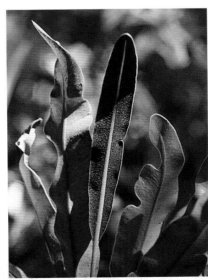

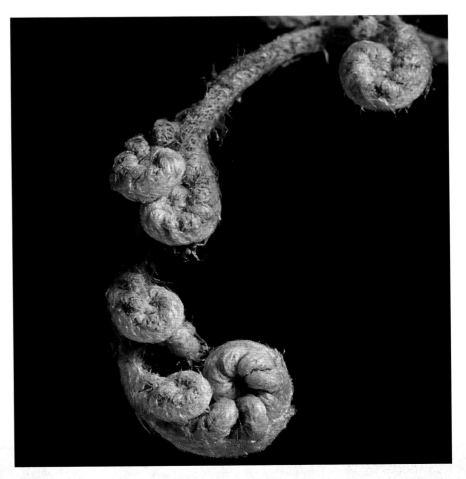

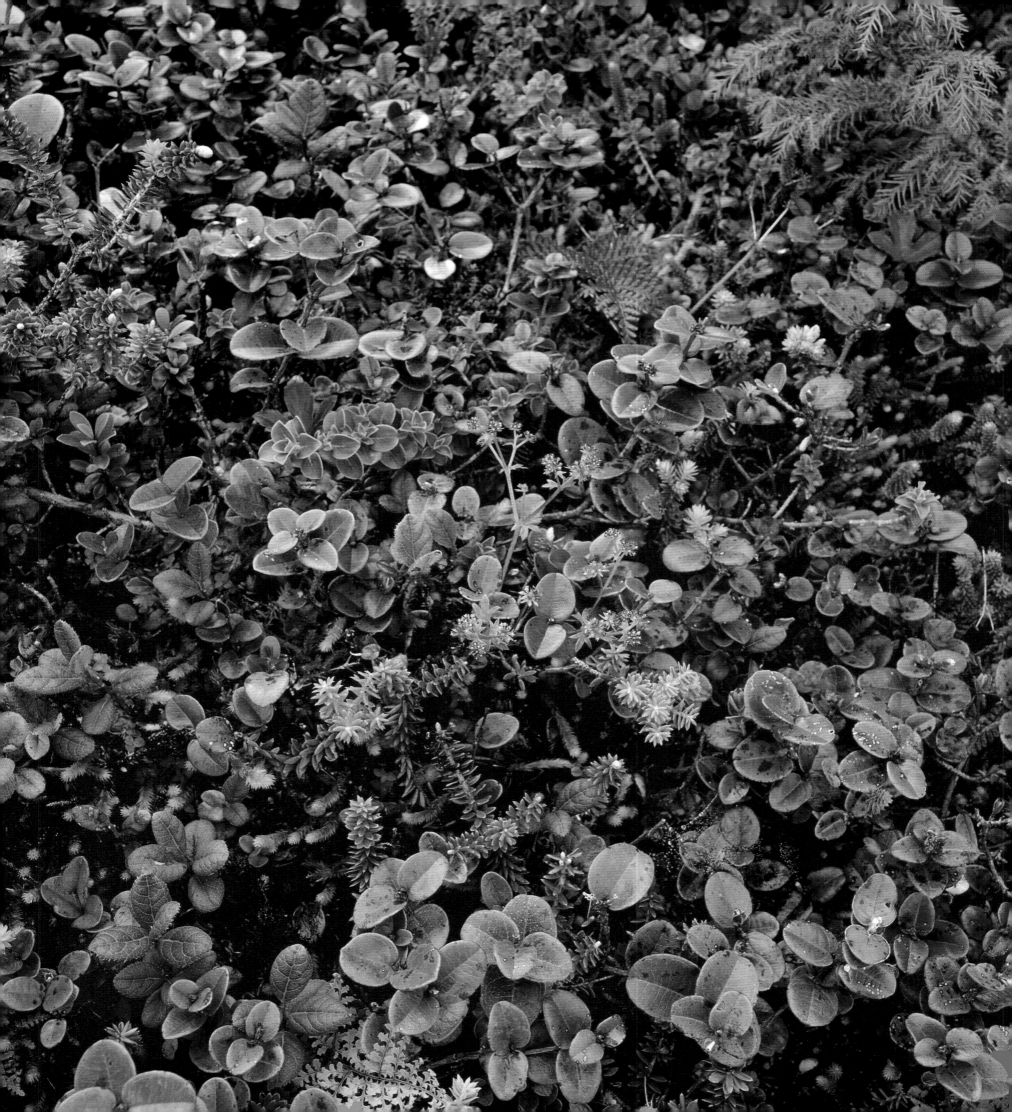

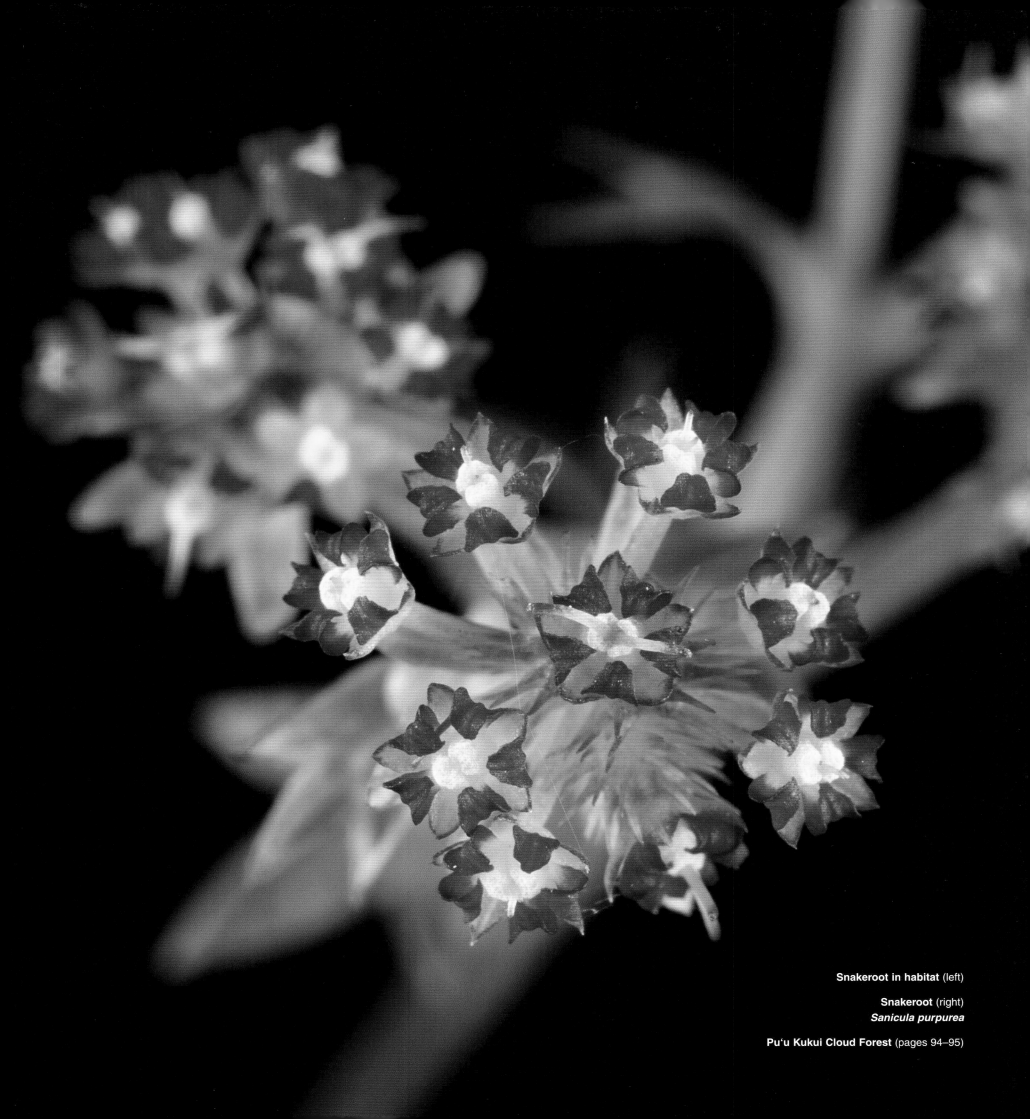

Snakeroot in habitat (left)

Snakeroot (right)
Sanicula purpurea

Puʻu Kukui Cloud Forest (pages 94–95)

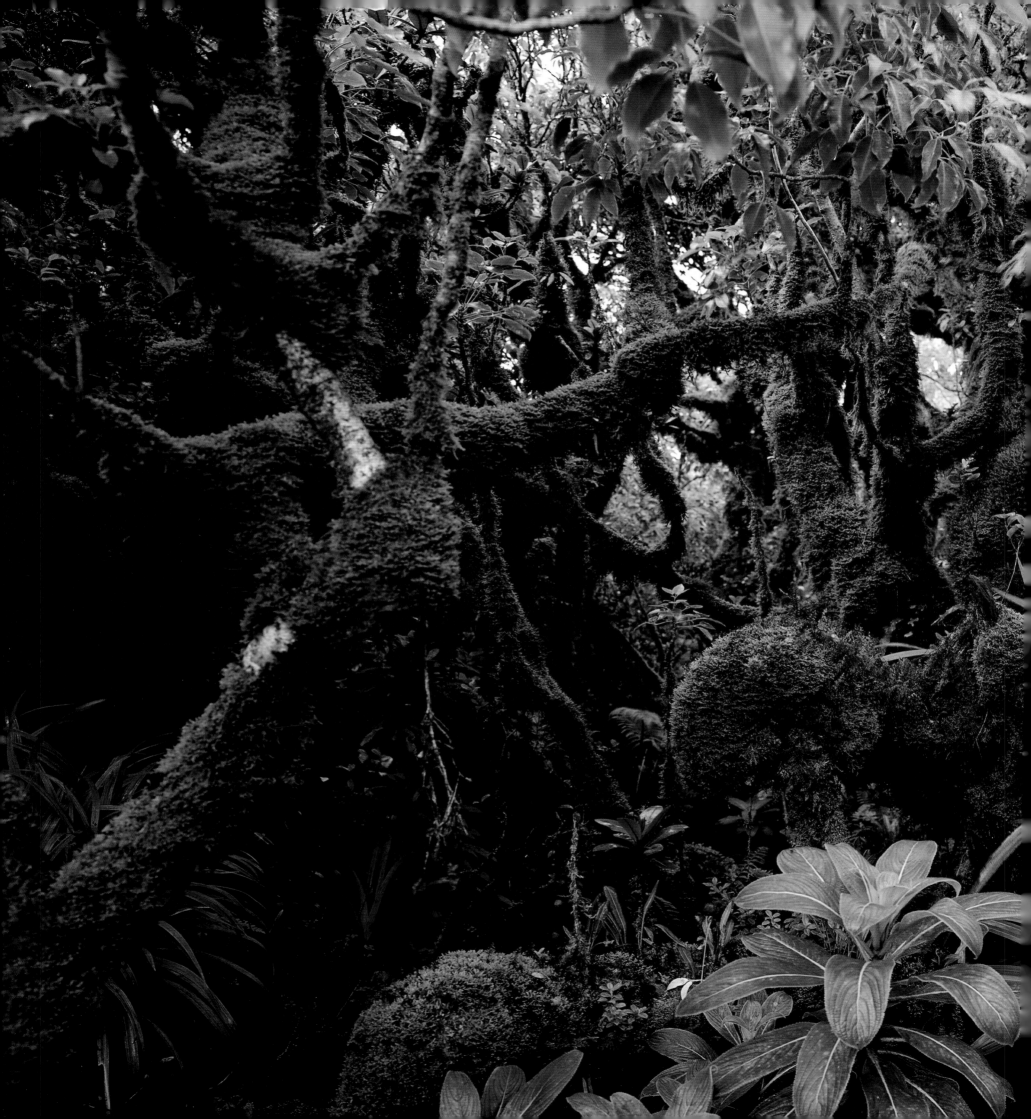

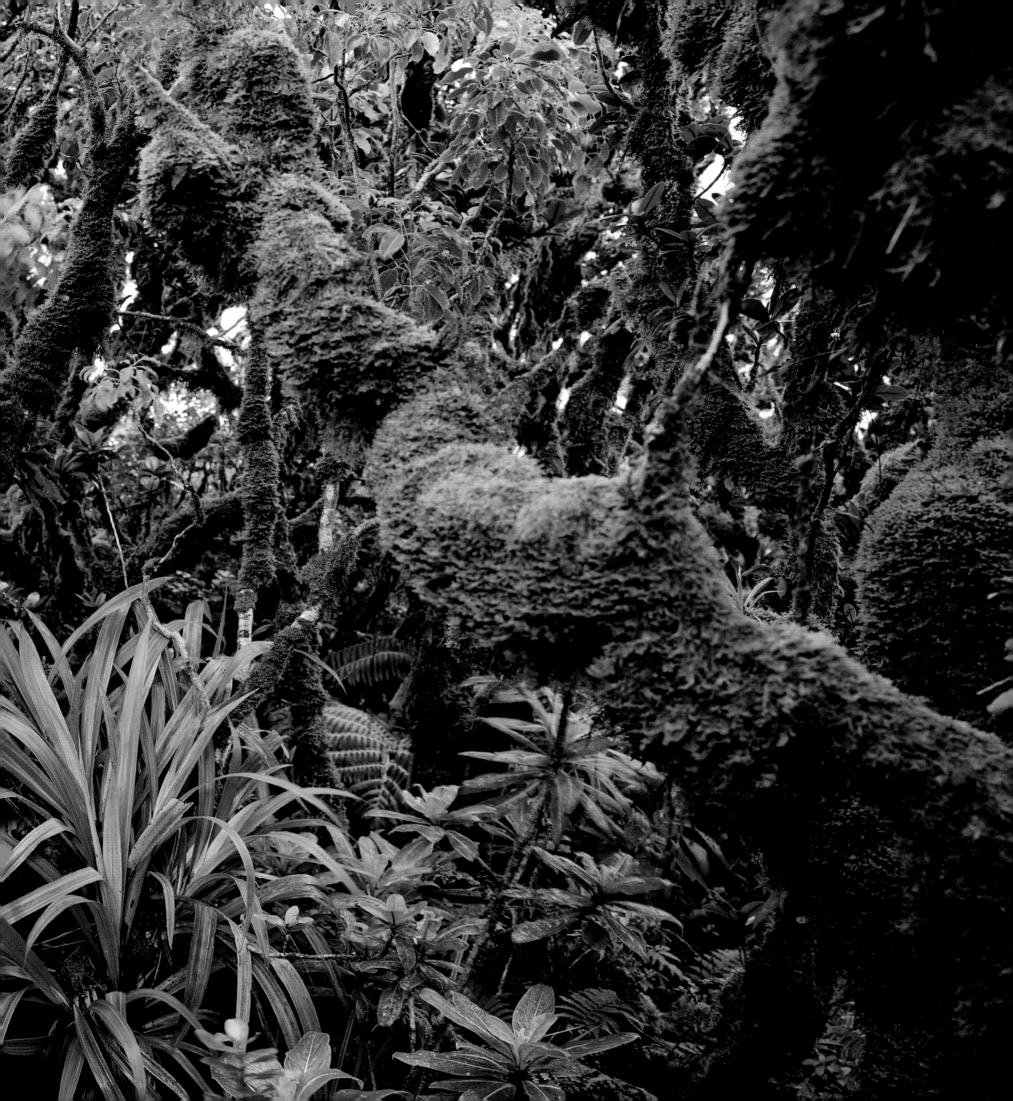

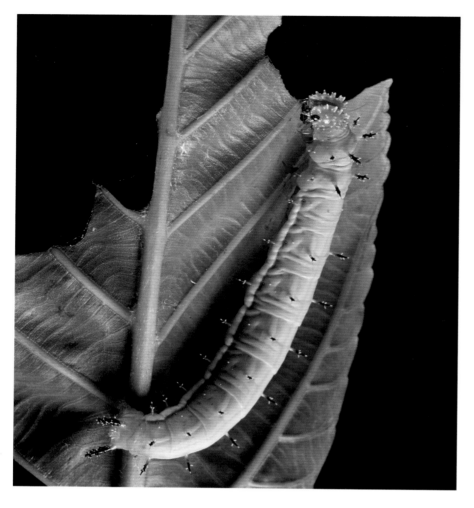
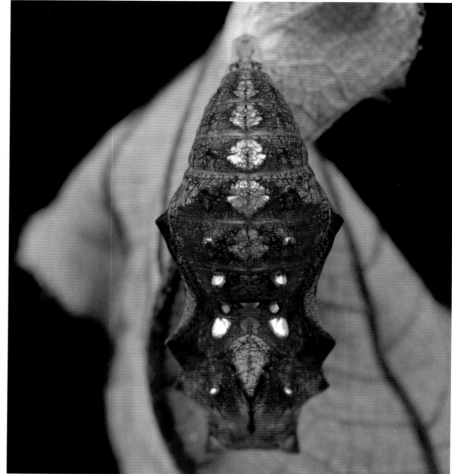
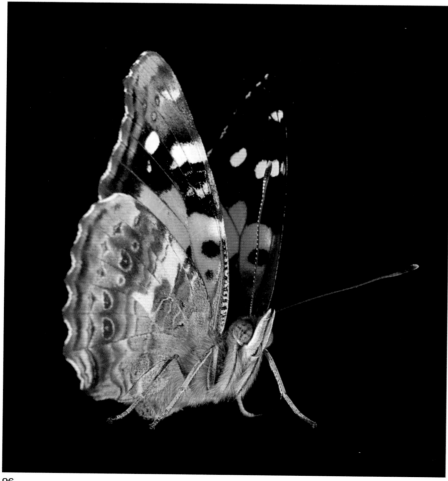
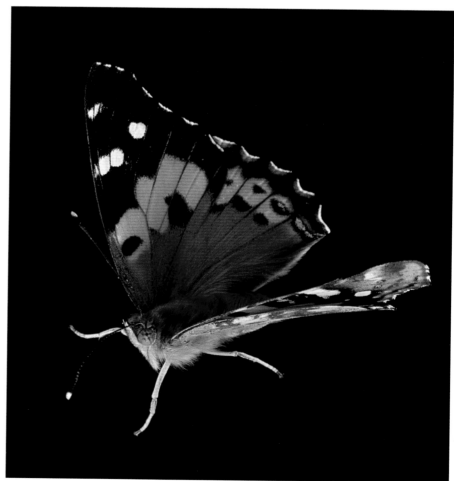

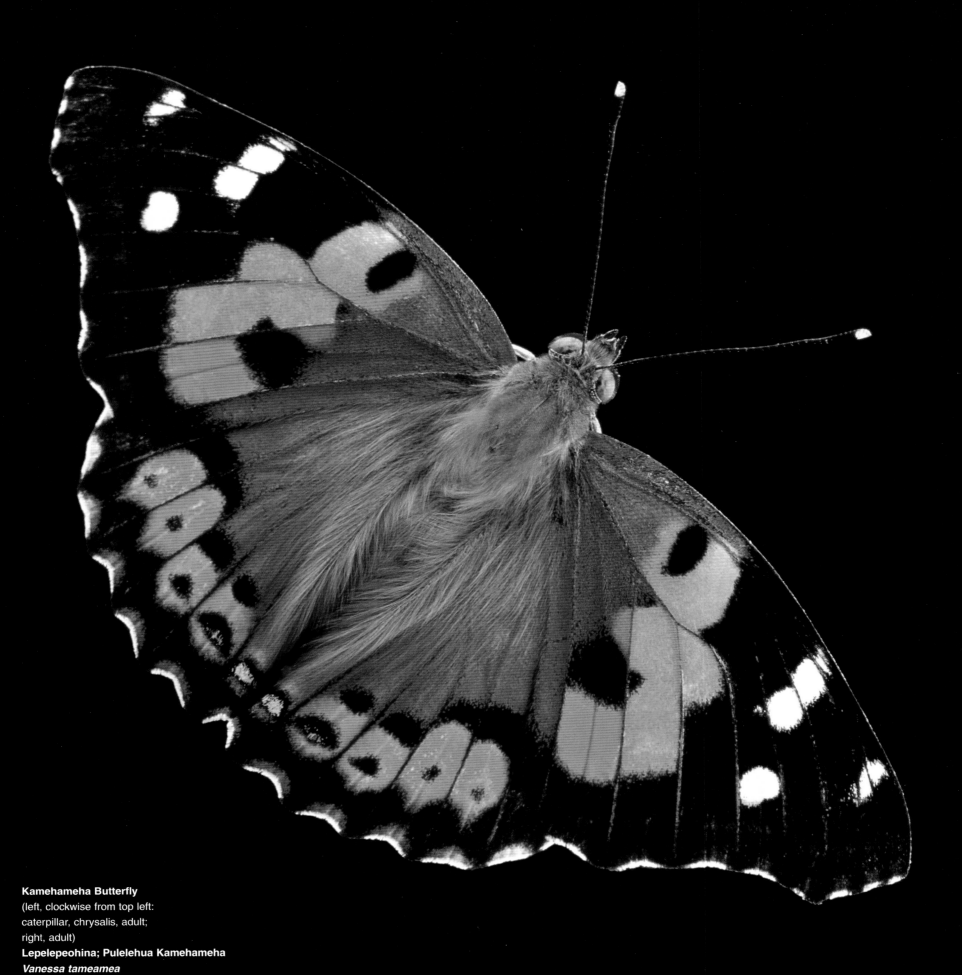

Kamehameha Butterfly
(left, clockwise from top left:
caterpillar, chrysalis, adult;
right, adult)
Lepelepeohina; Pulelehua Kamehameha
Vanessa tameamea

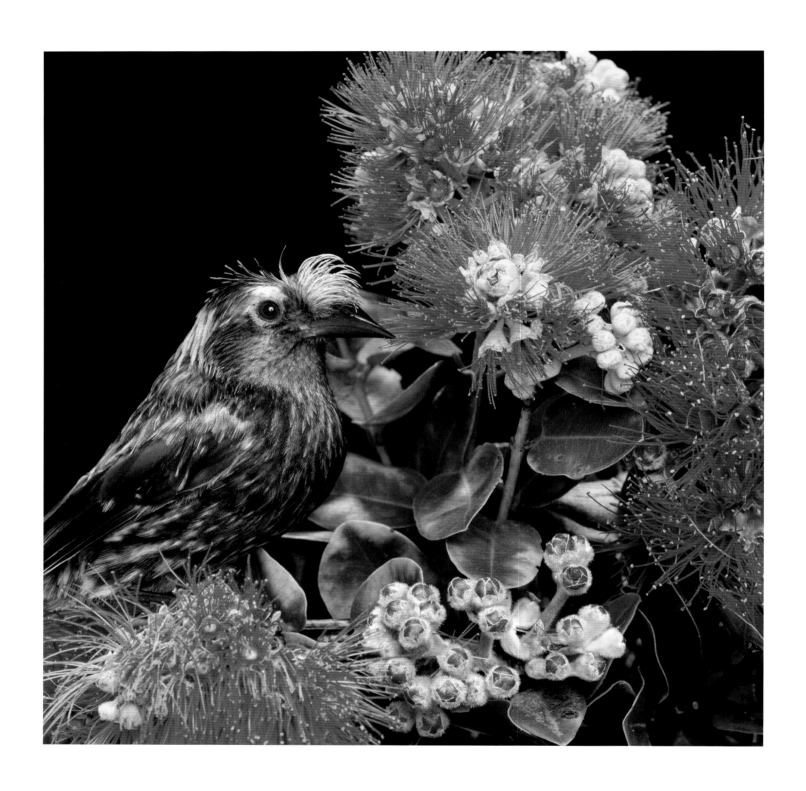

Crested Honeycreeper
with ʻŌhiʻa Lehua (left)

Crested Honeycreeper (right)
ʻĀkohekohe
Palmeria dolei

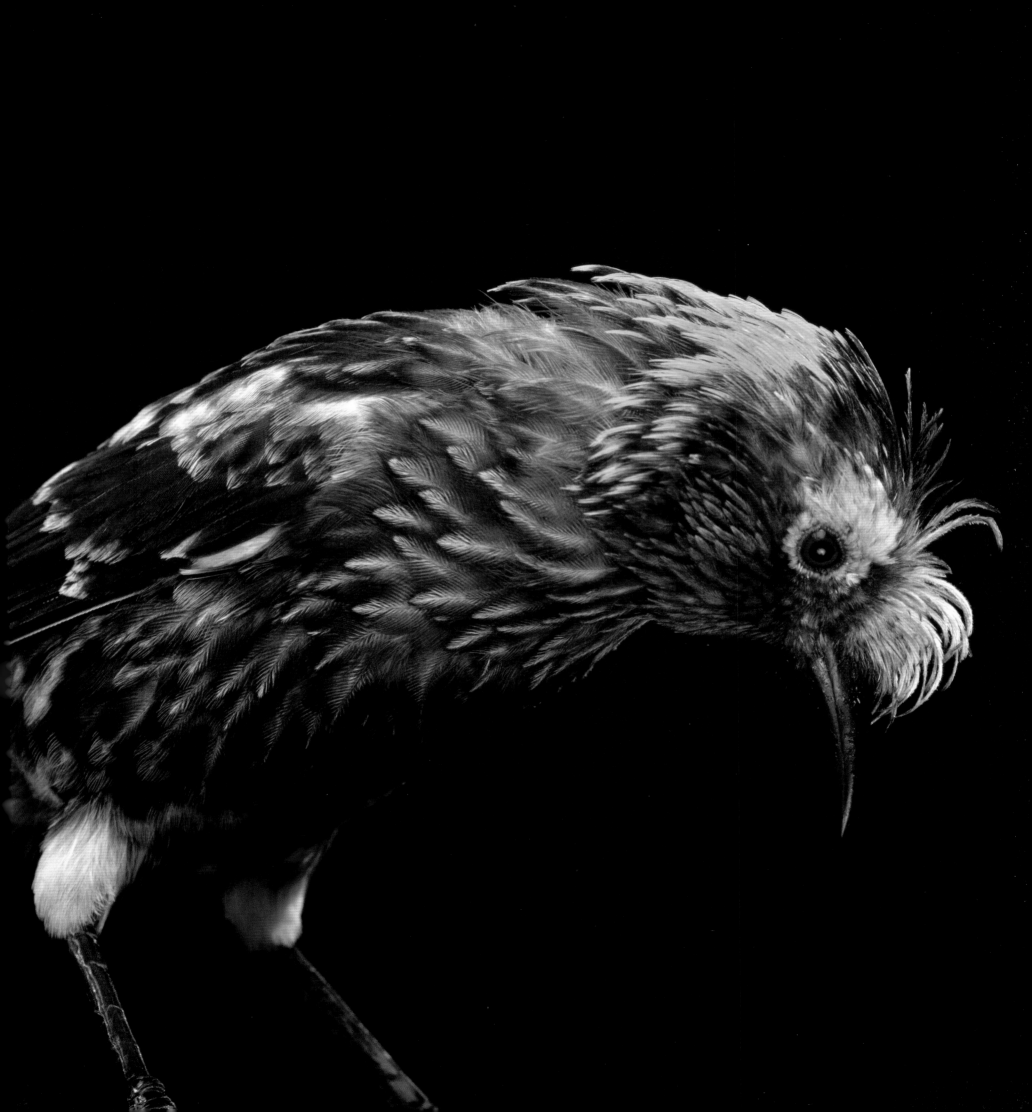

Crested Honeycreeper
ʻĀkohekohe
Palmeria dolei

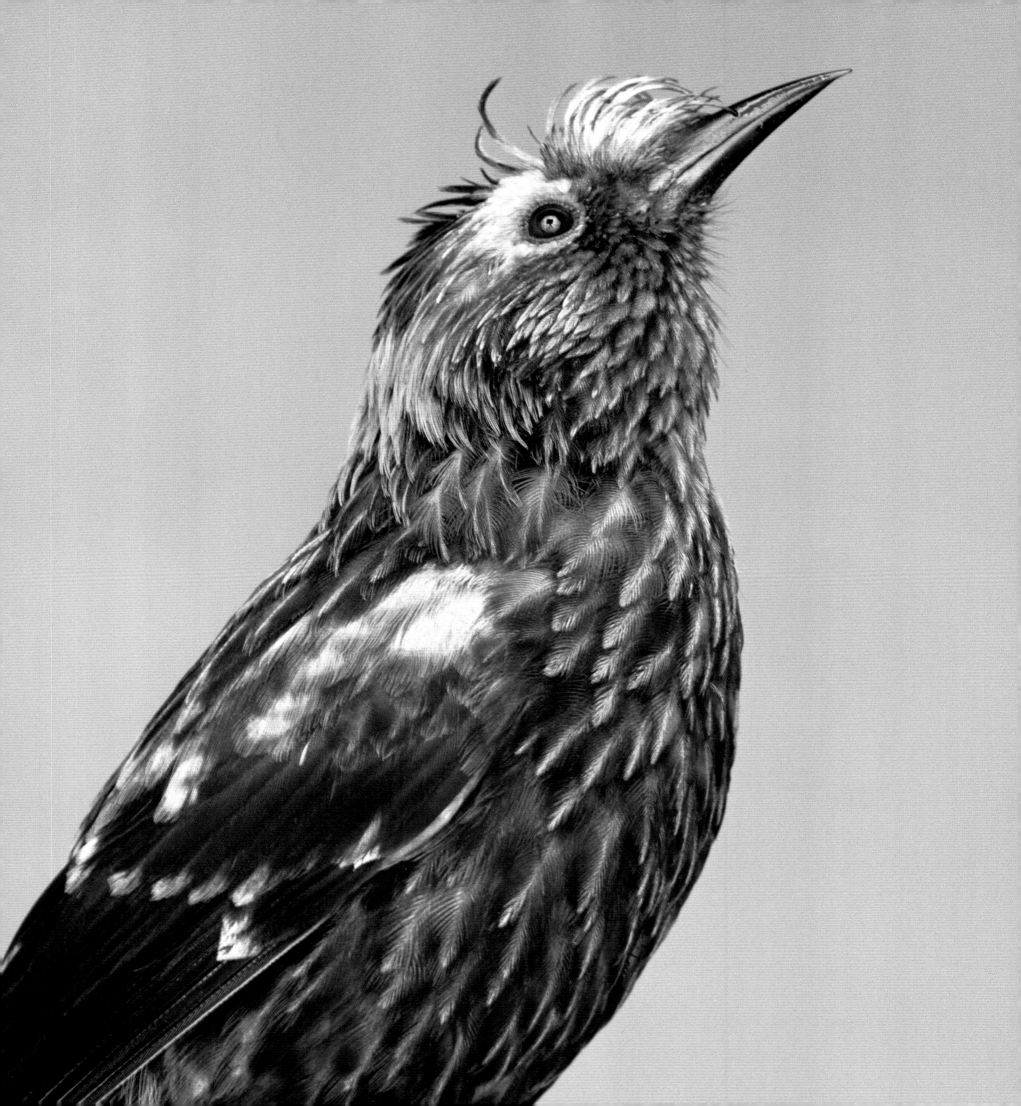

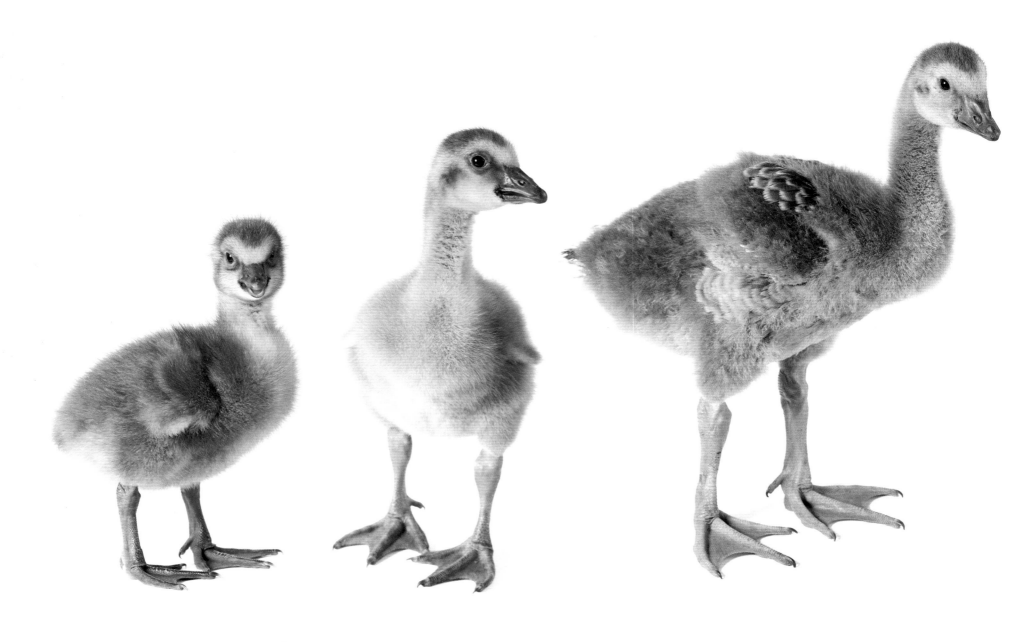

Hawaiian Goose
(from left to right: 3 days old,
16 days old, 33 days old, adult)
Nēnē
Branta sandvicensis

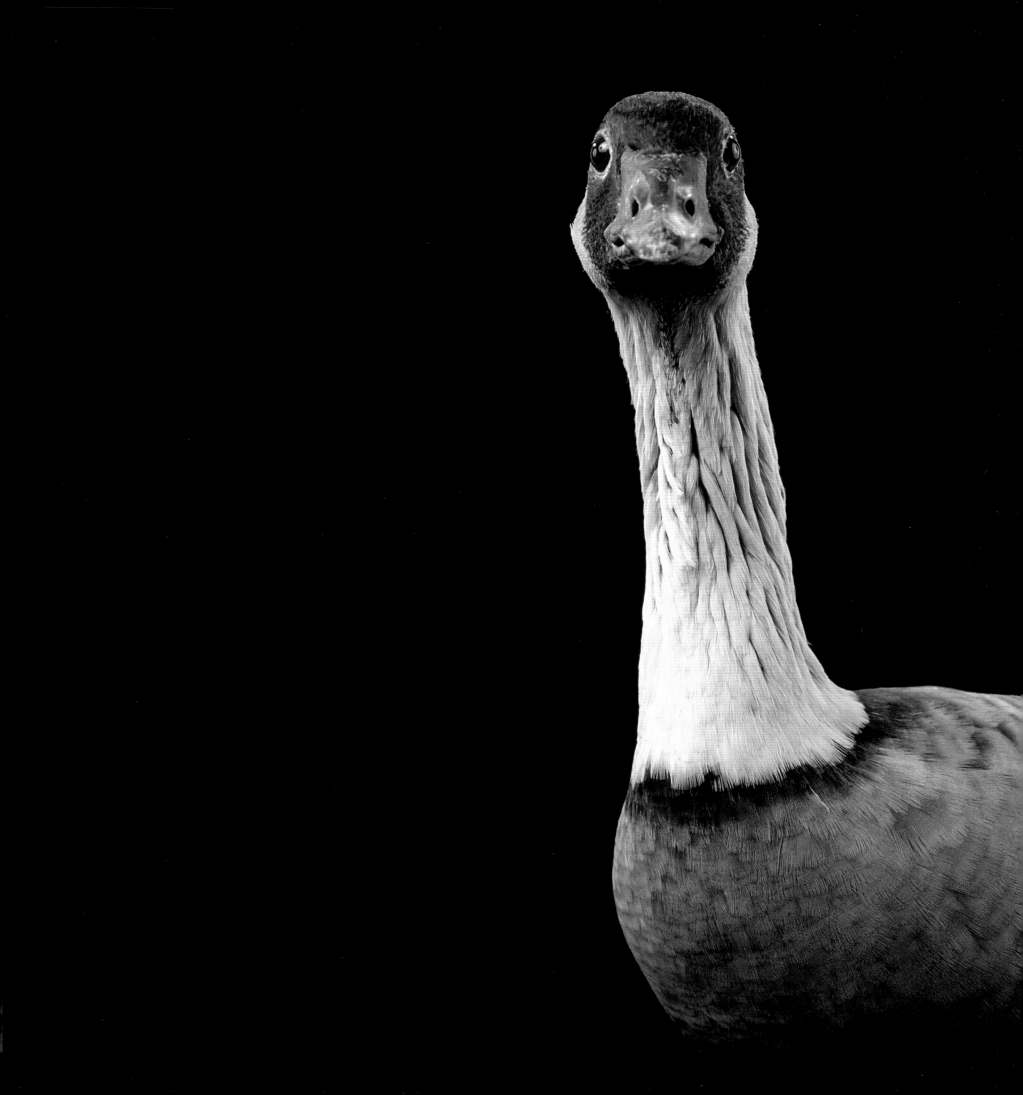

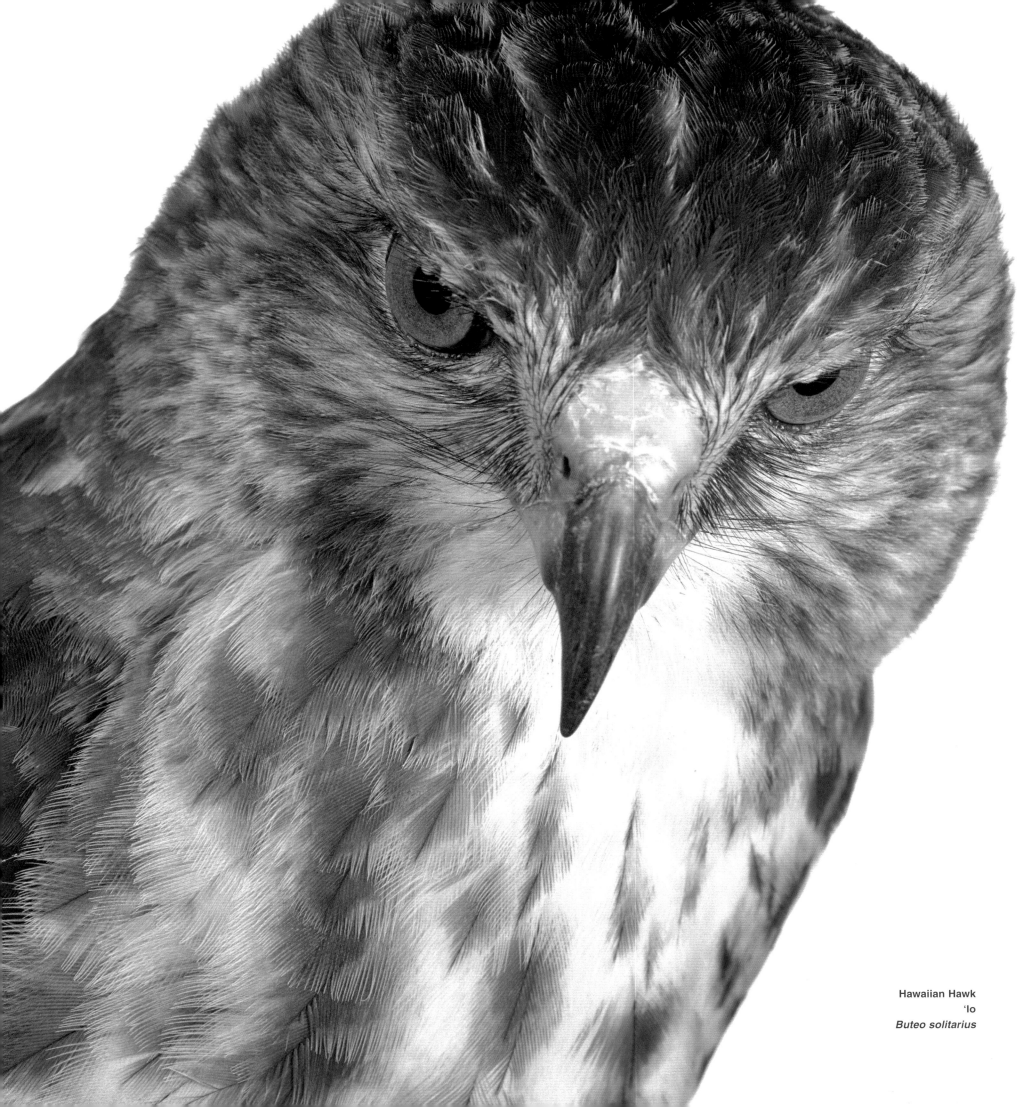

Hawaiian Hawk
'Io
Buteo solitarius

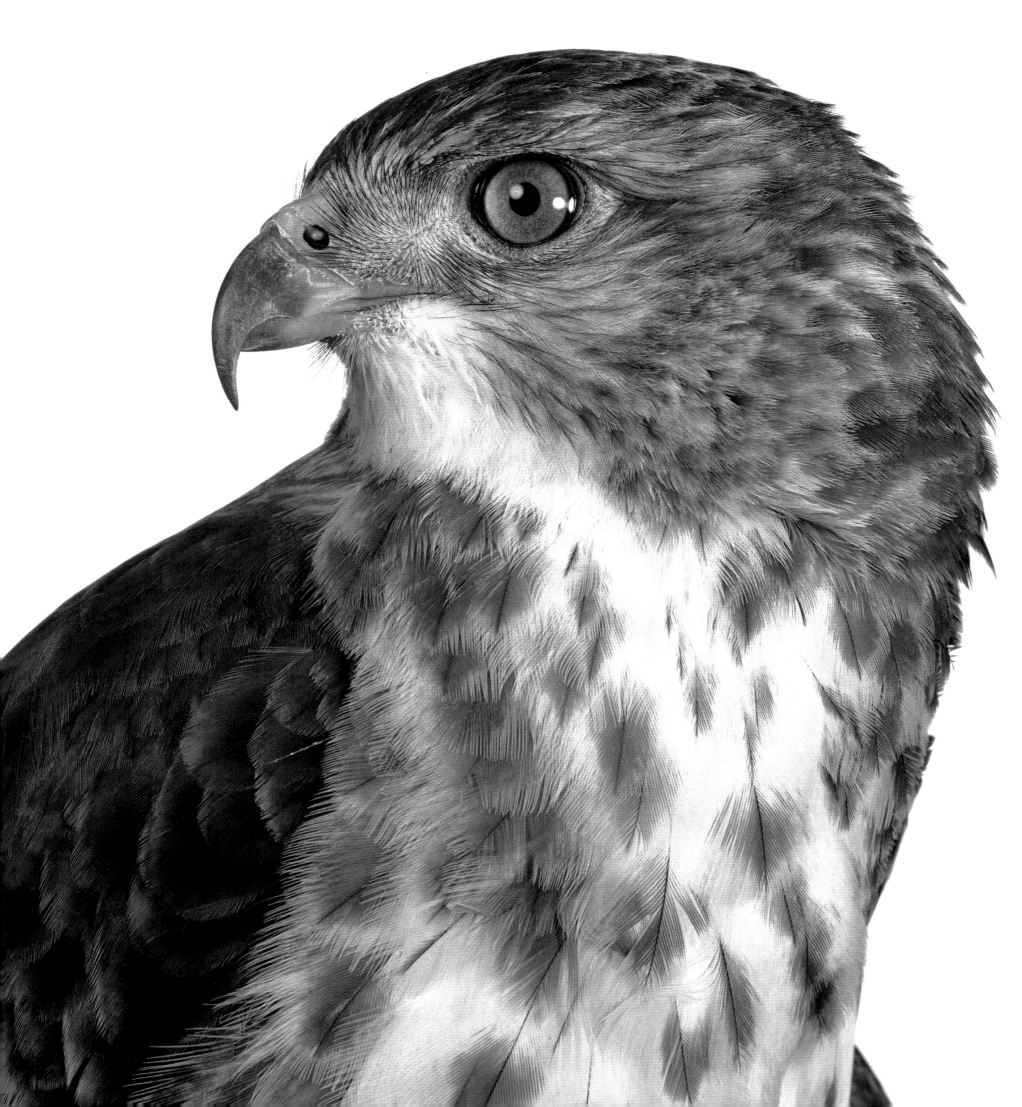

Nohoanu; Hinahina
Geranium kauaiense

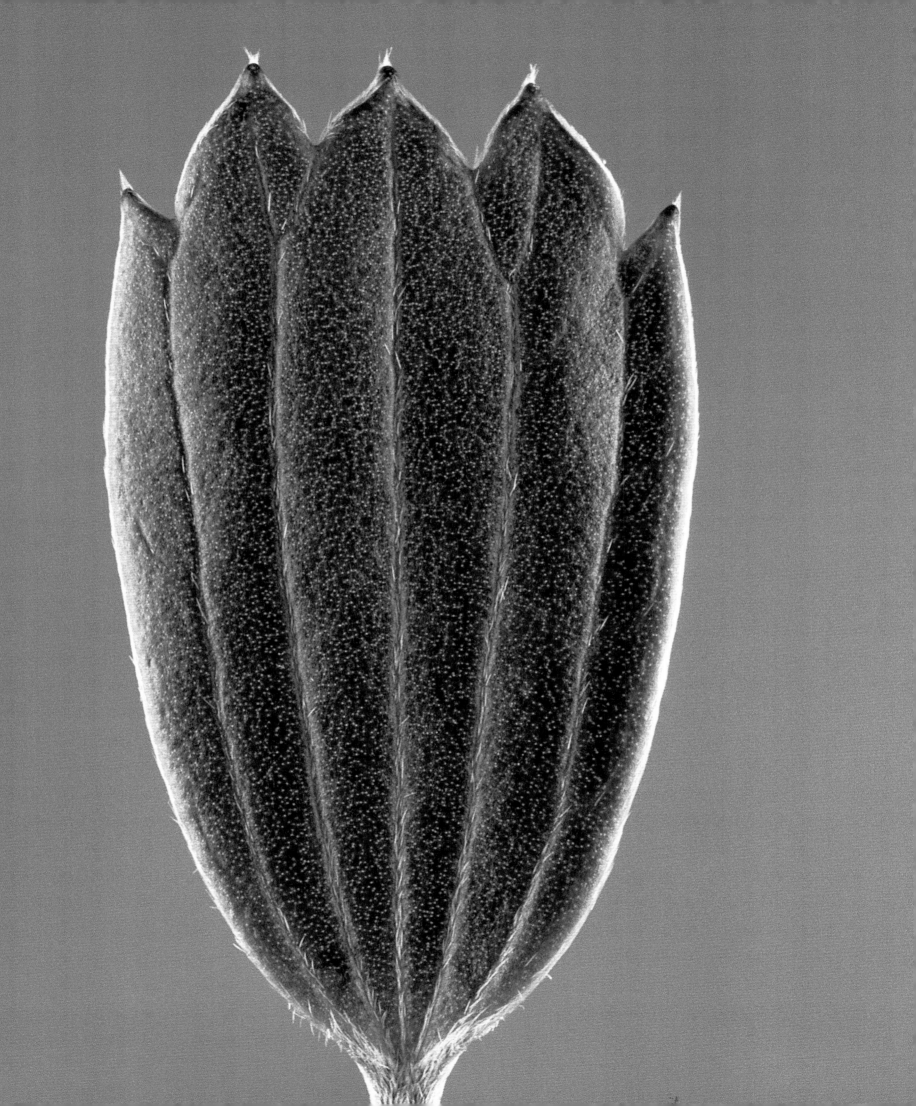

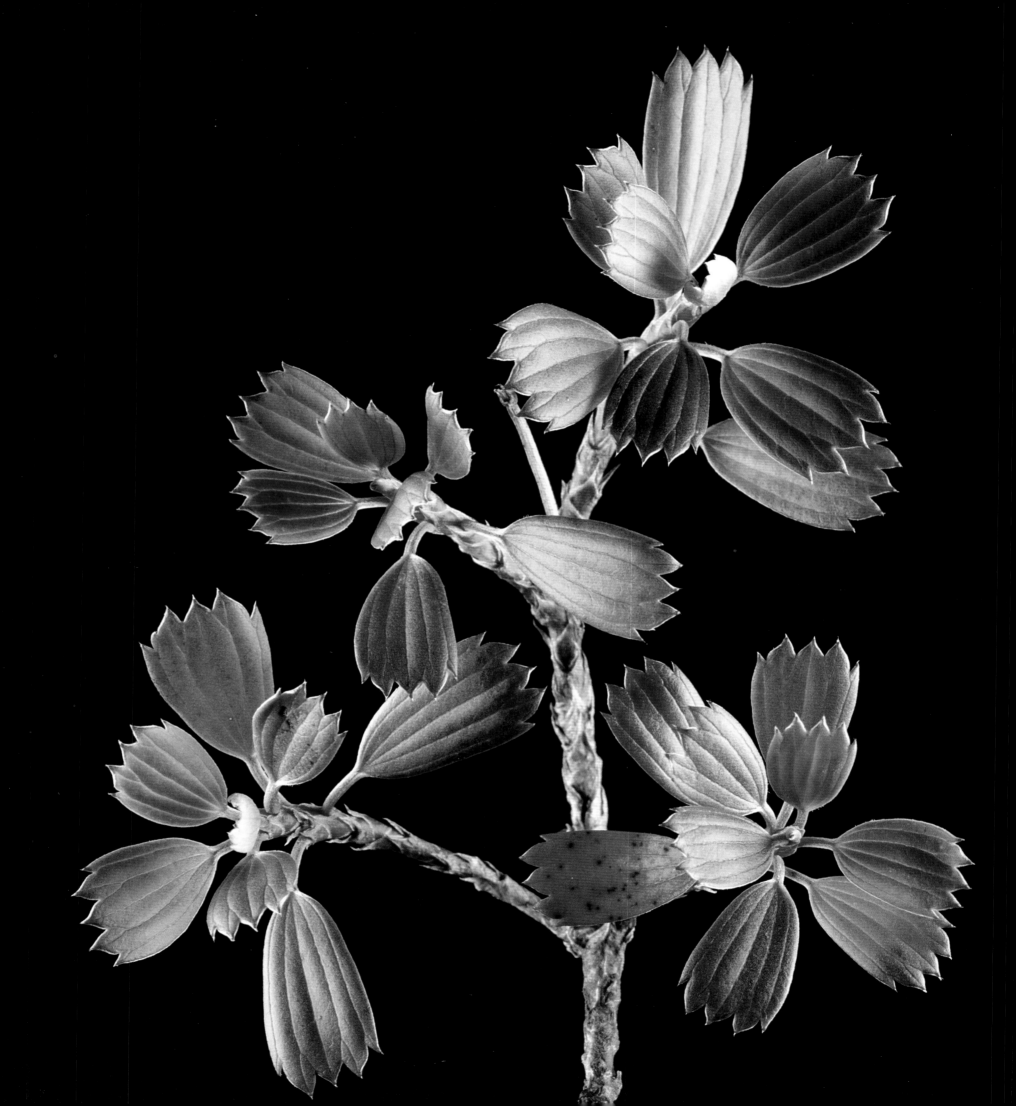

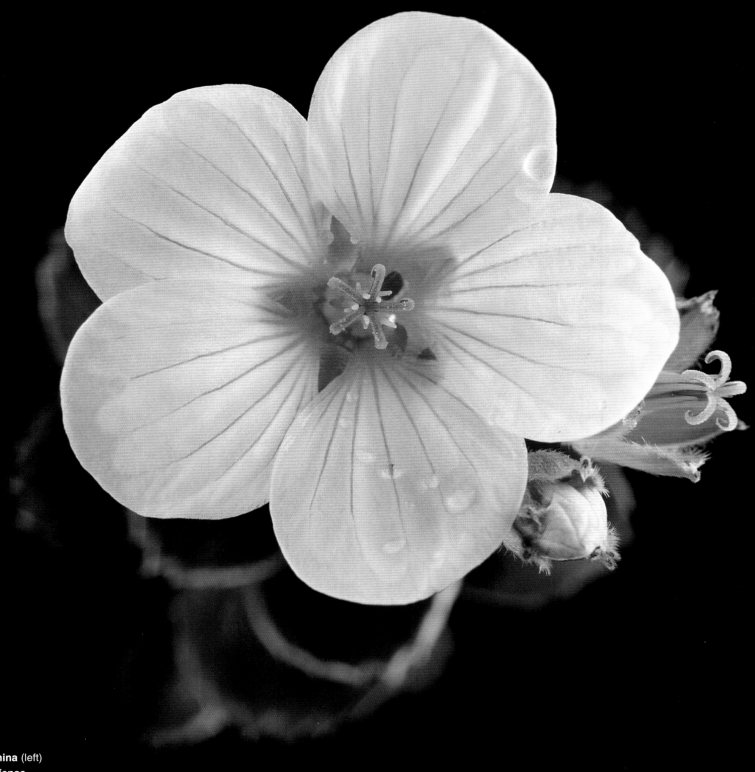

Nohoanu; Hinahina (left)
Geranium kauaiense

Nohoanu; Hinahina; Nohuanu (right)
Geranium hillebrandii

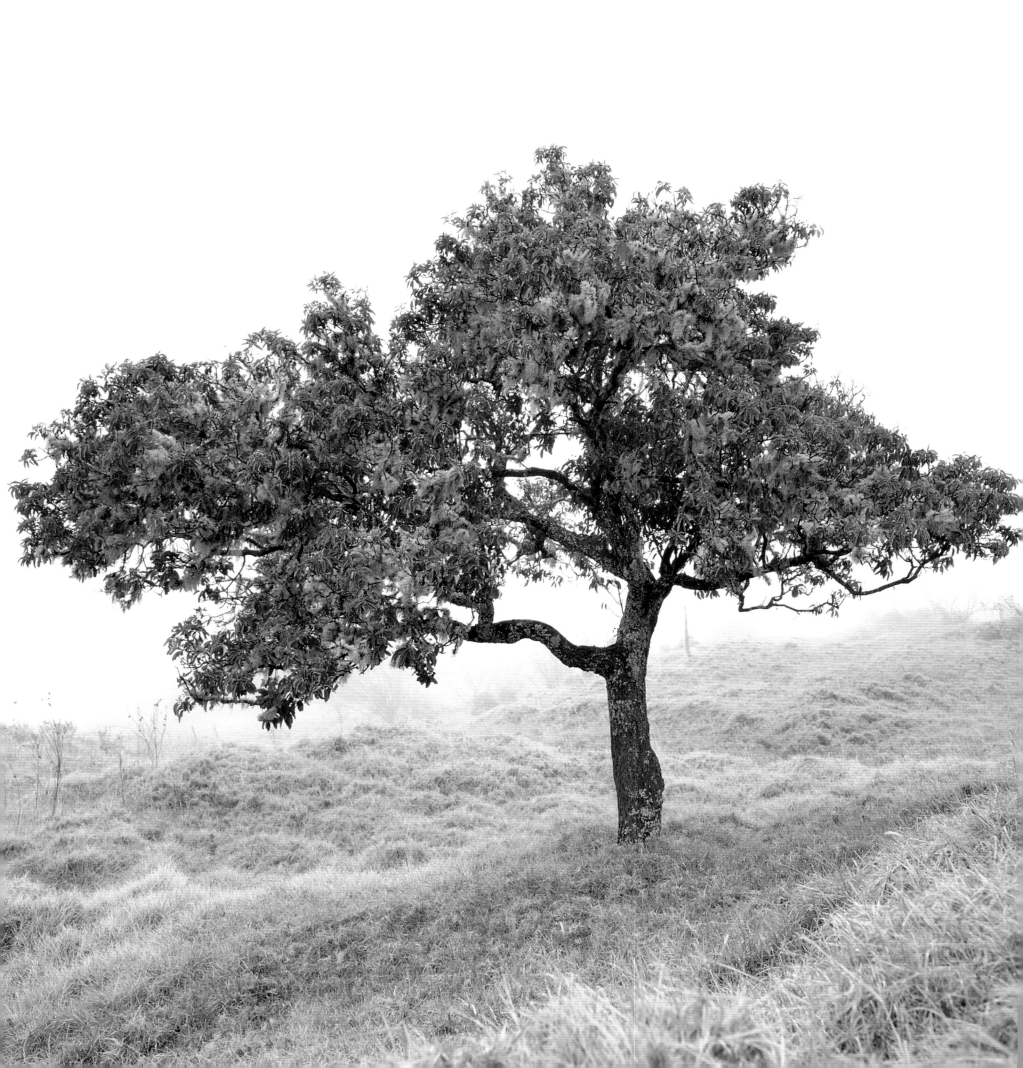

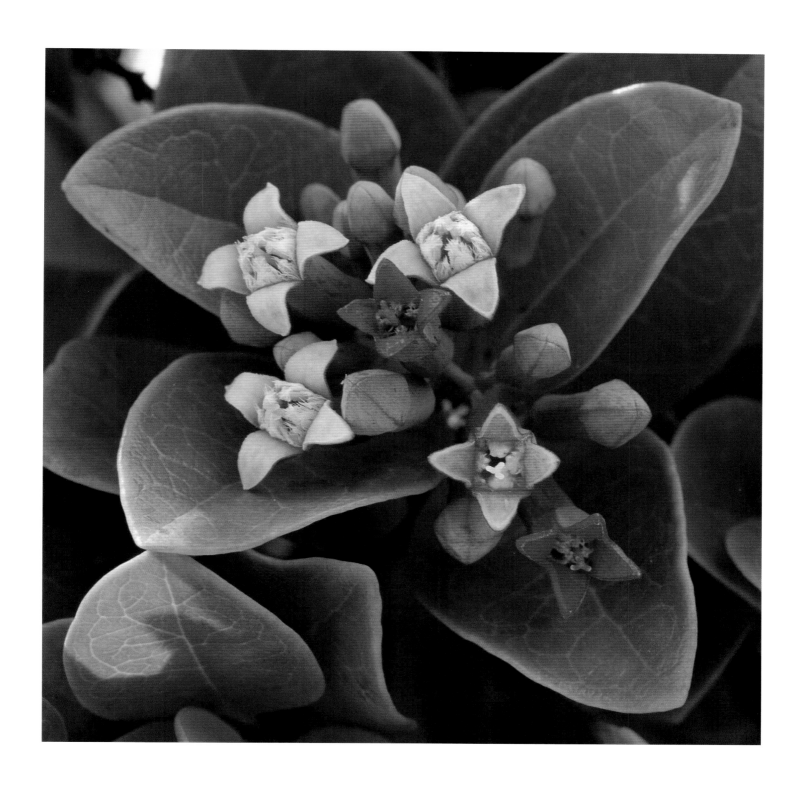

Sandalwood Tree (left; right, flower)
'Iliahi
Santalum freycinetianum **var.** *lanaiense*

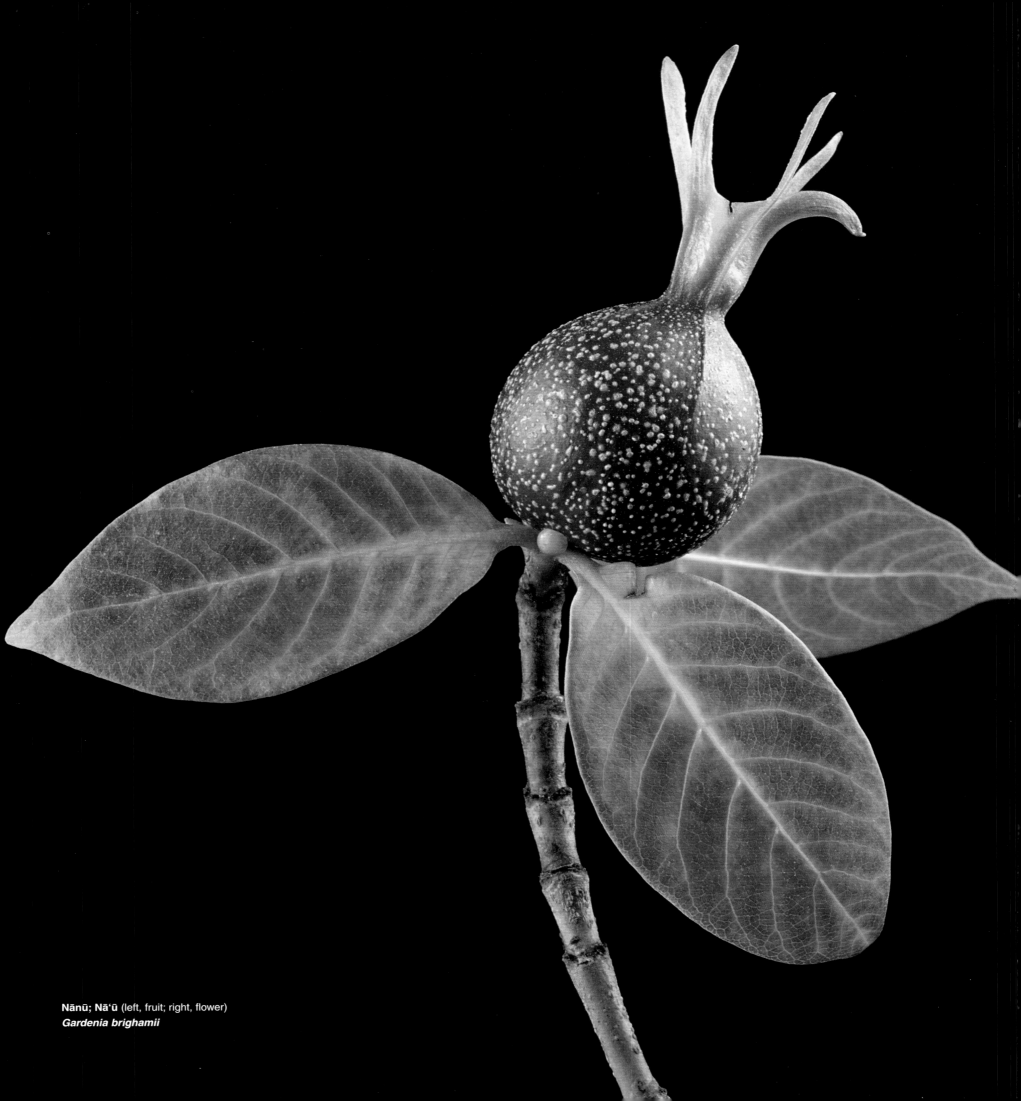

Nānū; Nāʻū (left, fruit; right, flower)
Gardenia brighamii

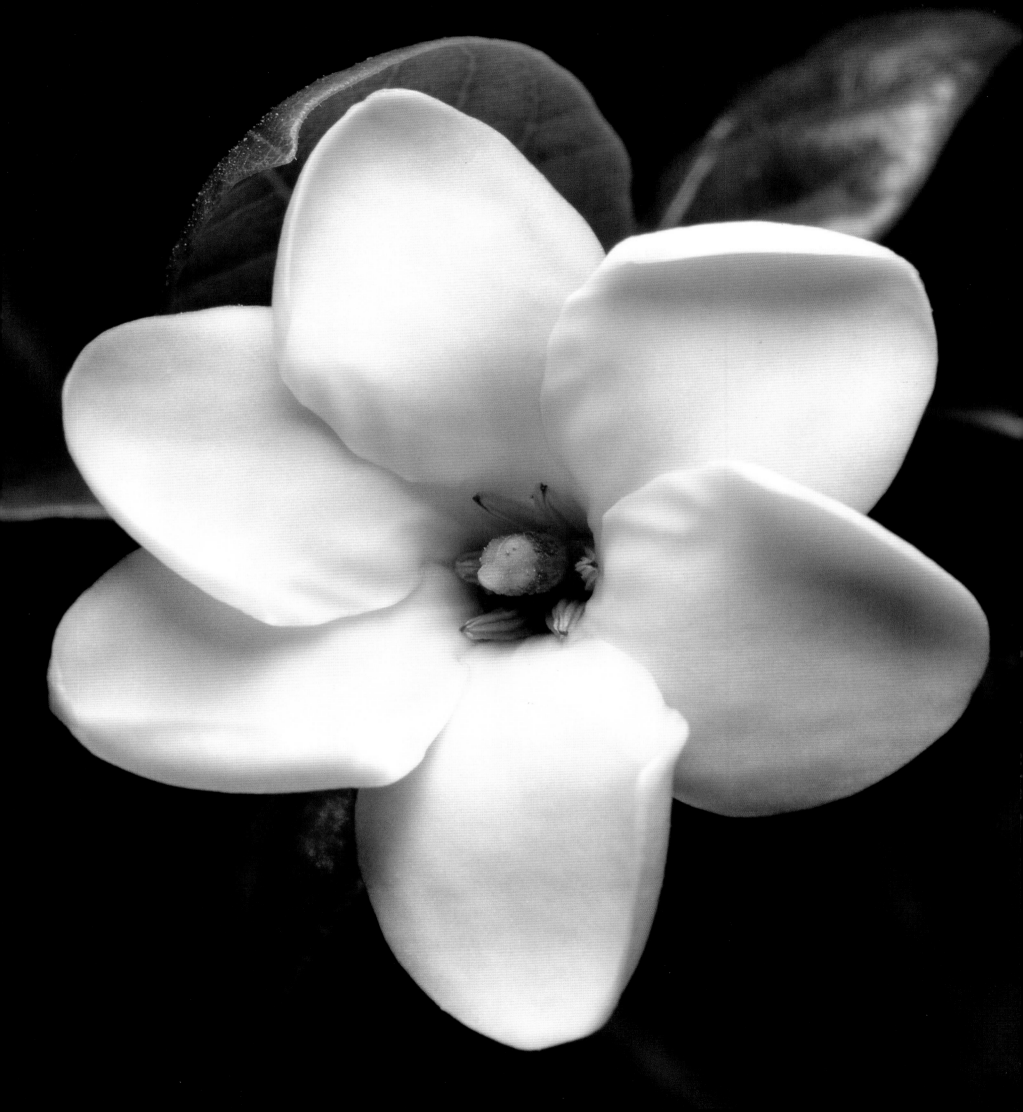

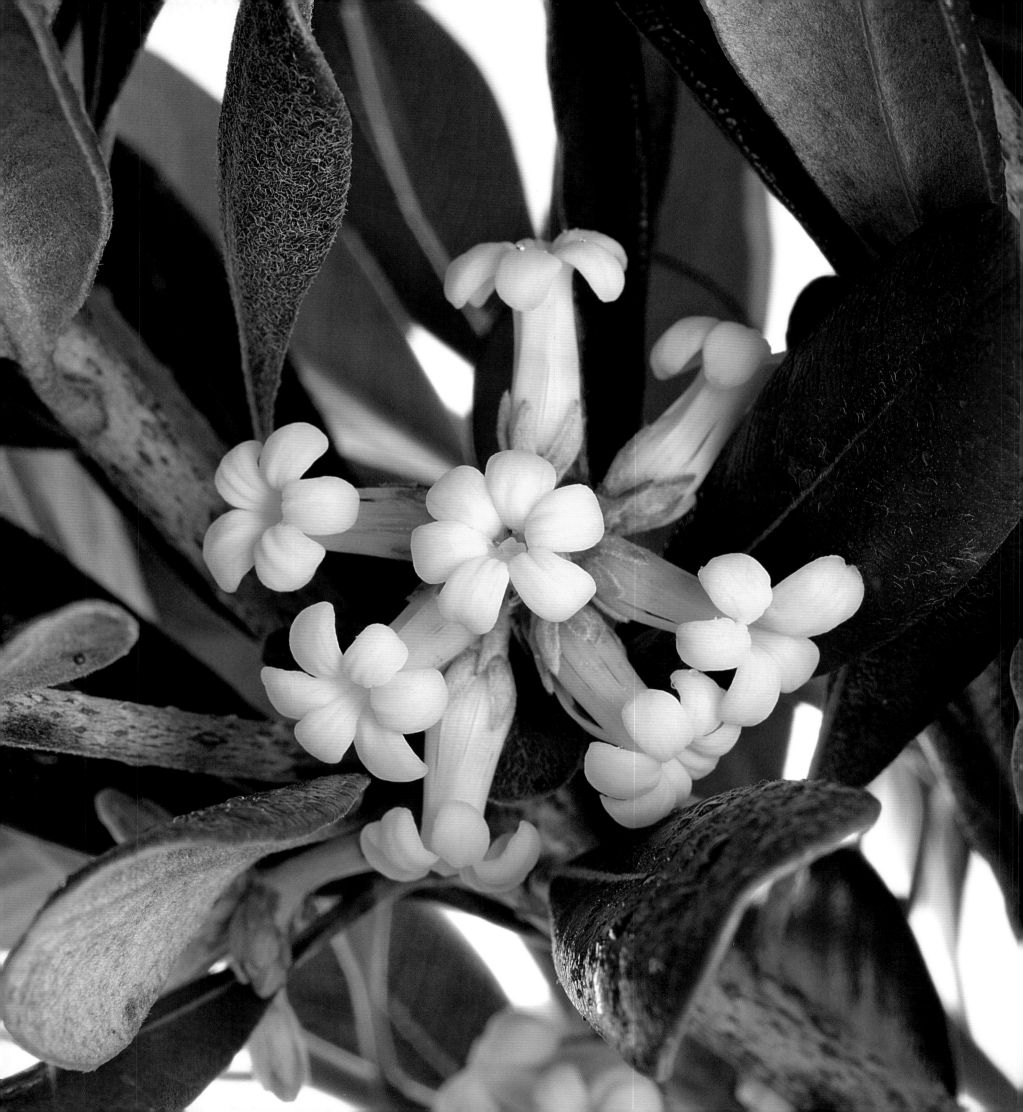

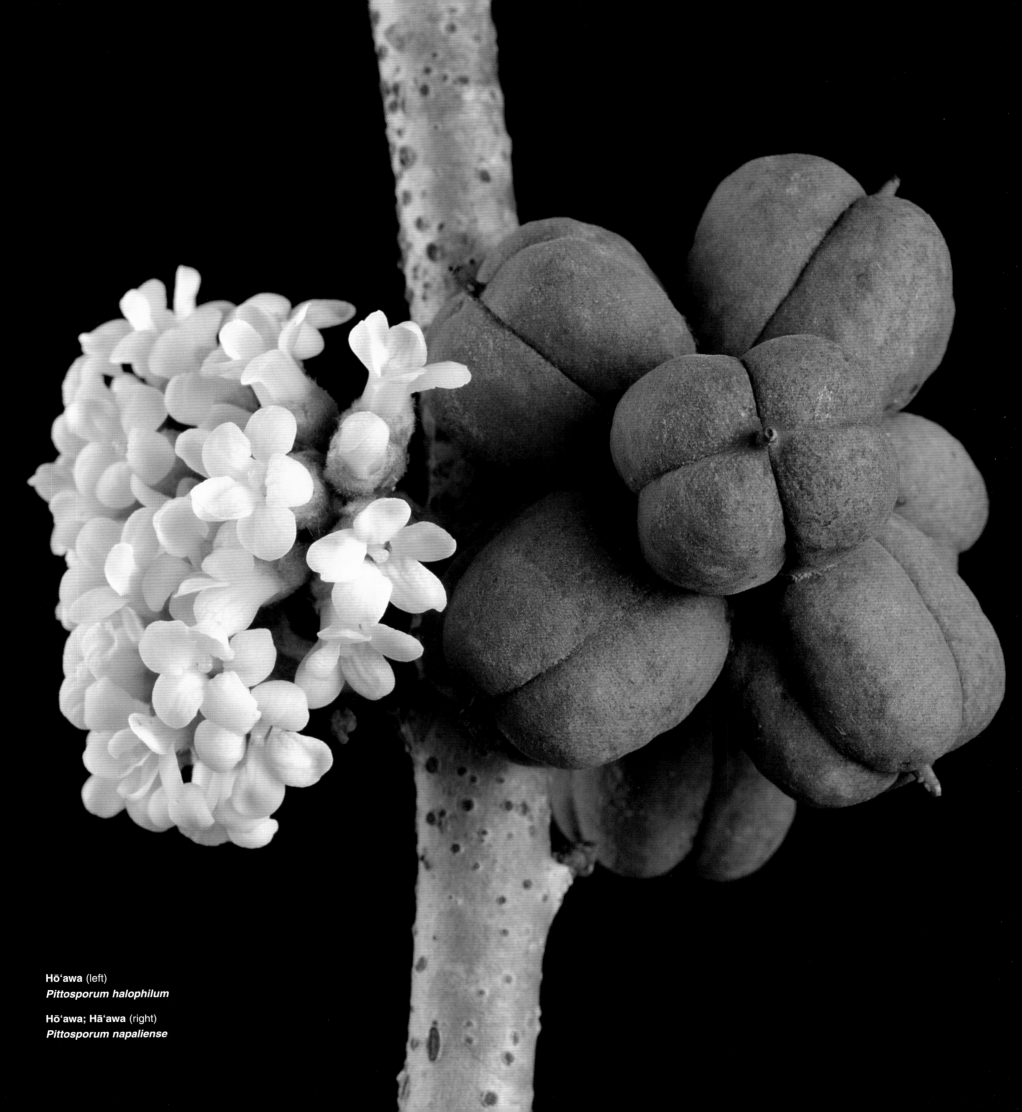

Hōʻawa (left)
Pittosporum halophilum

Hōʻawa; Hāʻawa (right)
Pittosporum napaliense

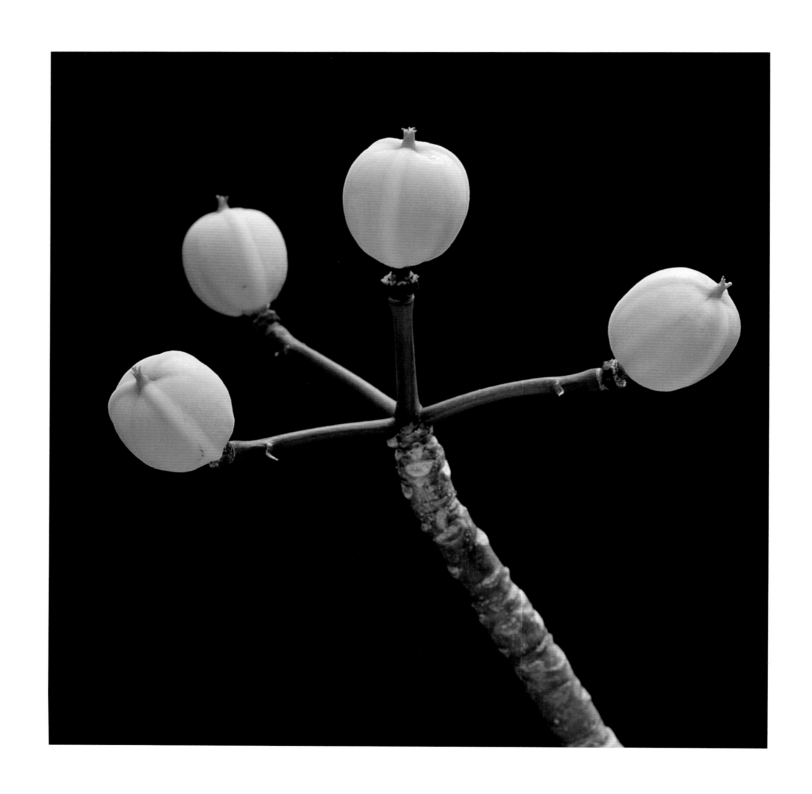

Euphorbia haeleeleana
(left, fruit; right, in flower)

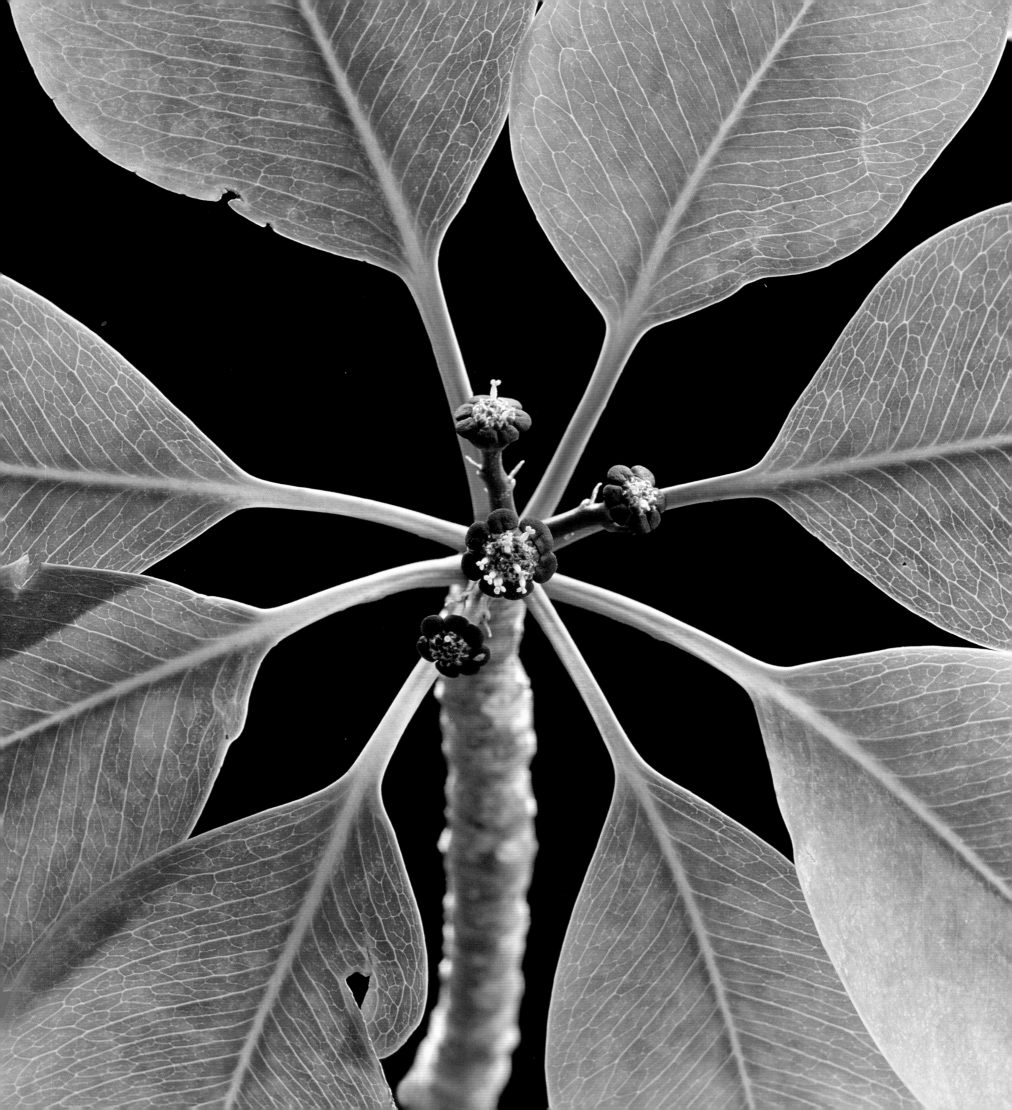

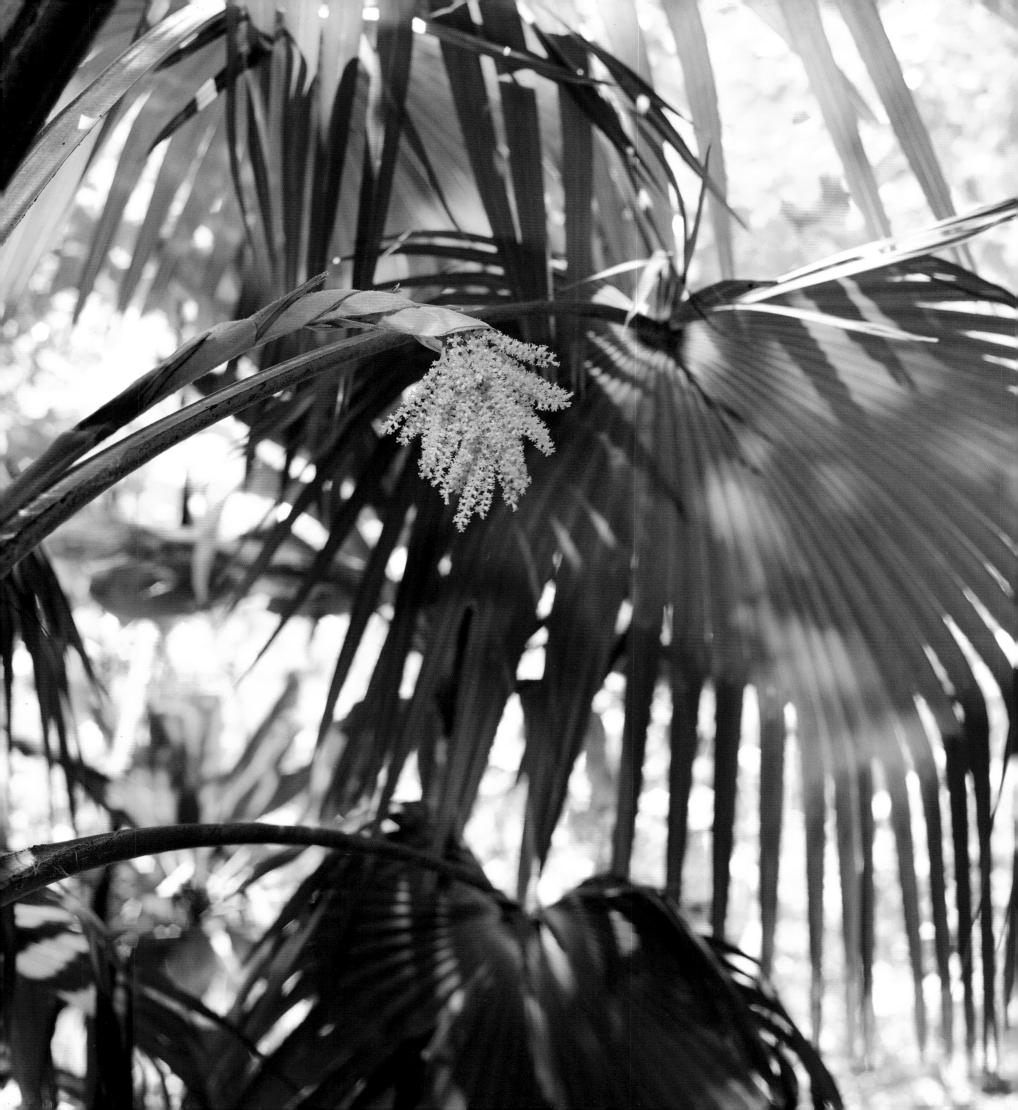

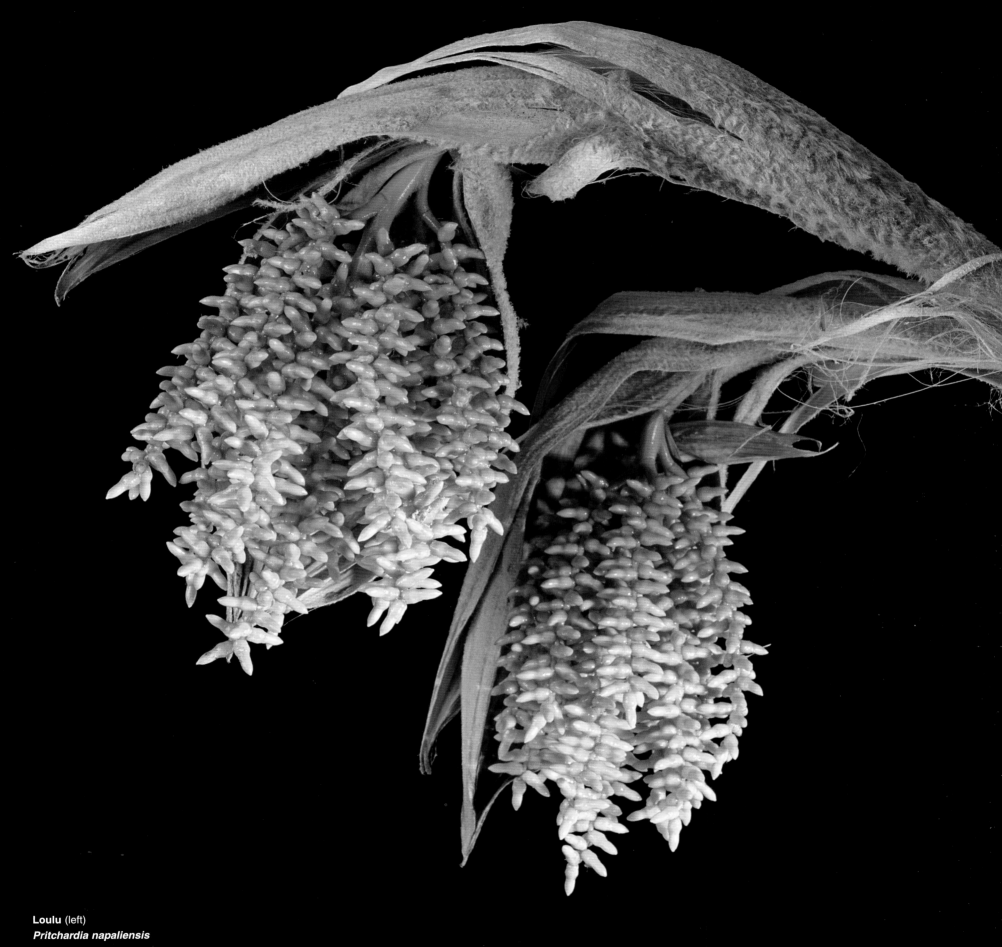

Loulu (left)
Pritchardia napaliensis

Loulu (right, flower bud)
Pritchardia viscosa

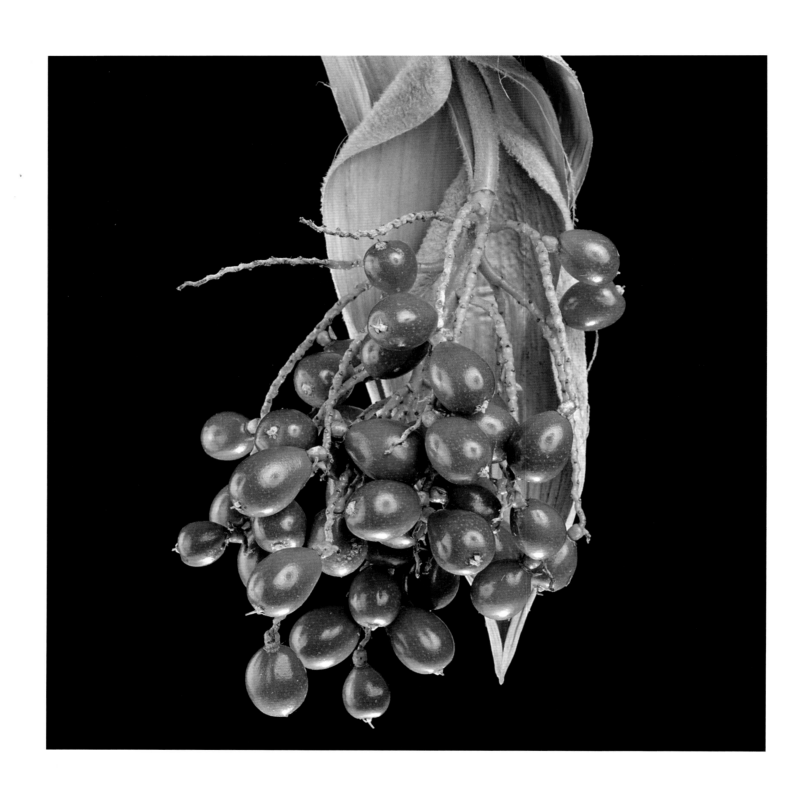

Loulu (left, fruit)
Pritchardia viscosa

Loulu (right)
Pritchardia schattaueri

Munroidendron racemosum
(pages 122–125, left to right:
leaves, bud, flower, fruit)

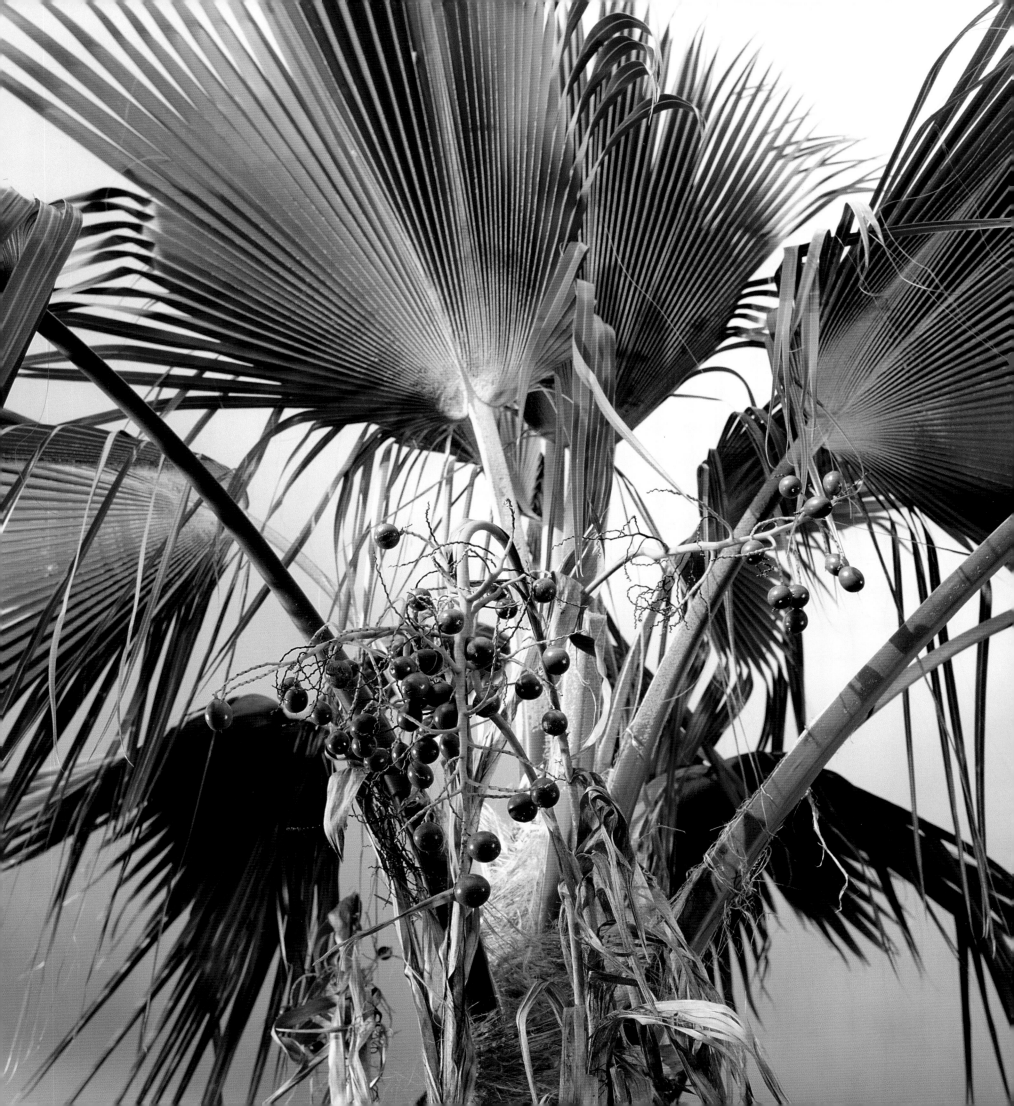

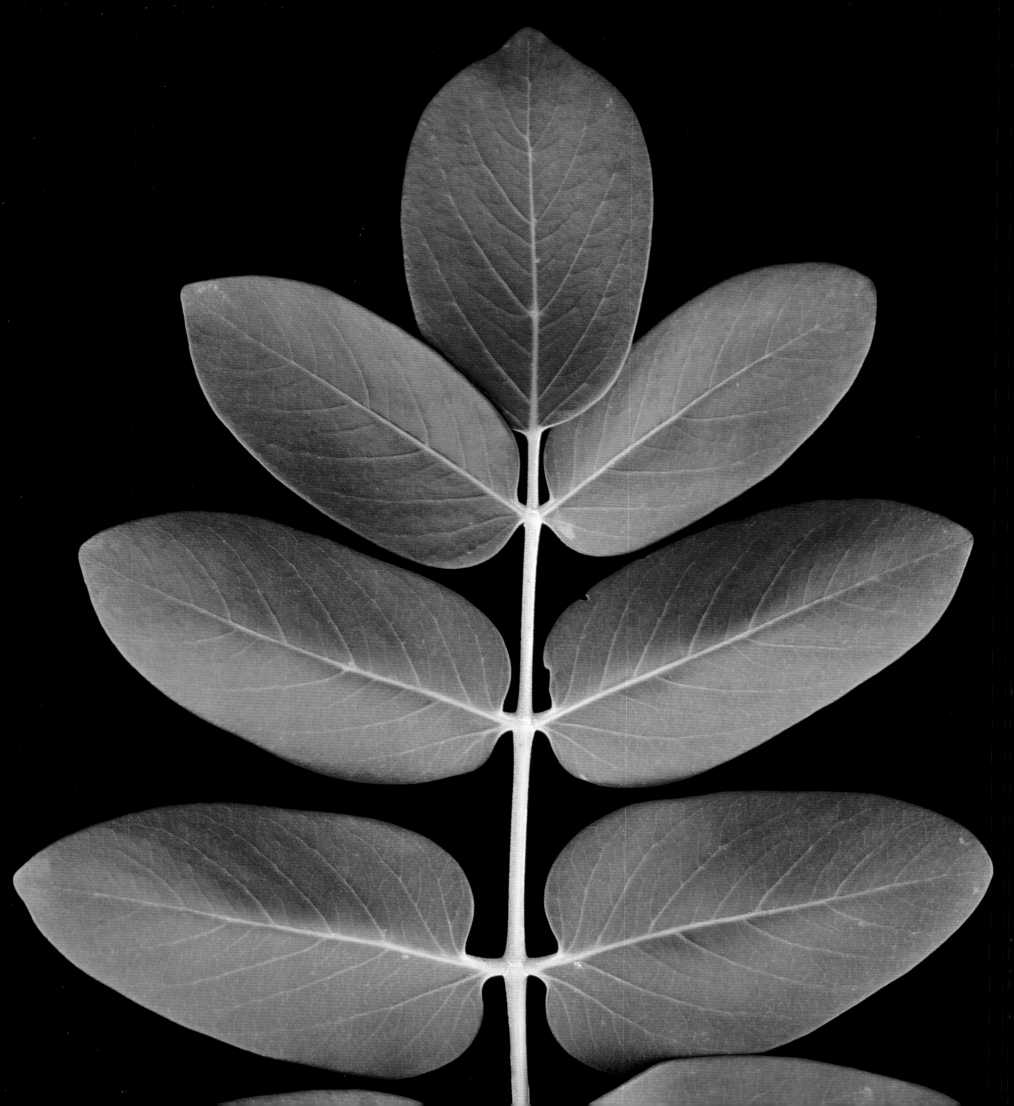

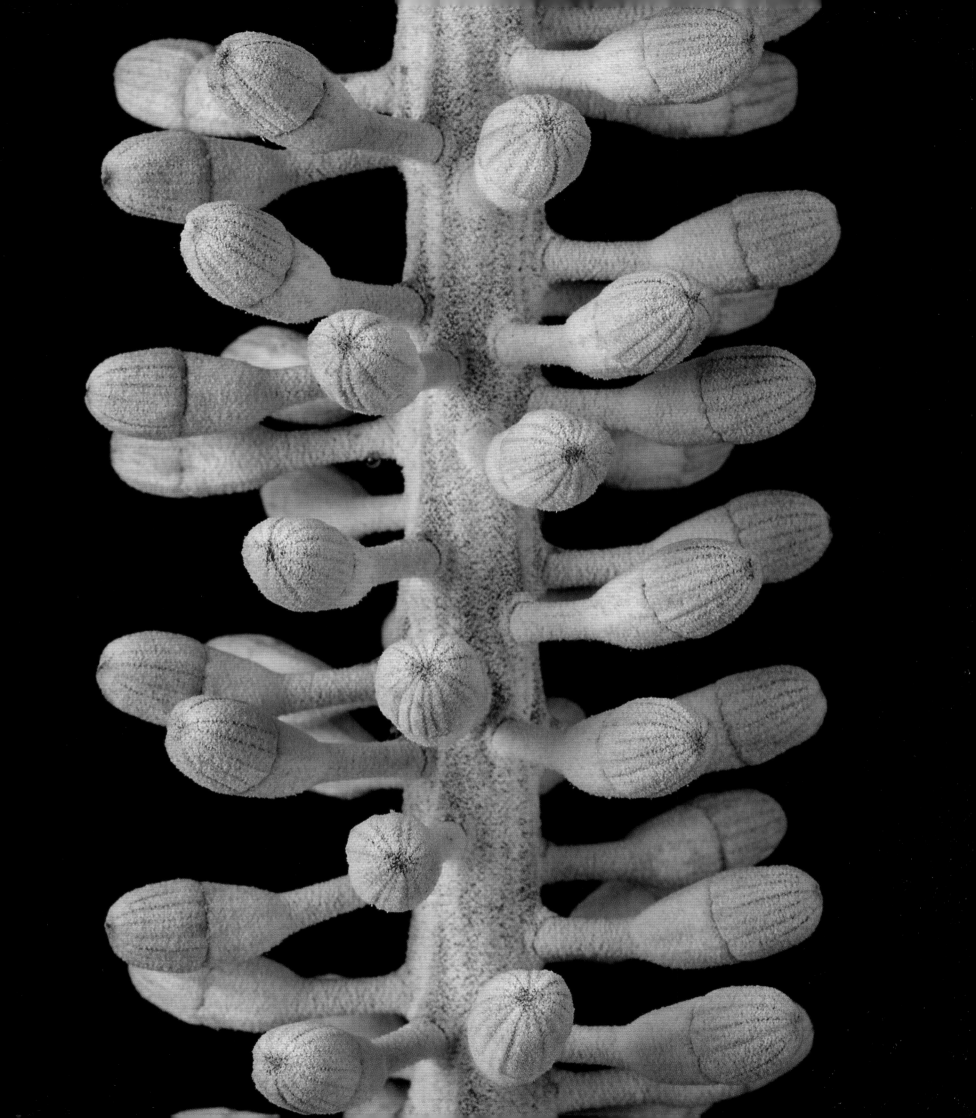

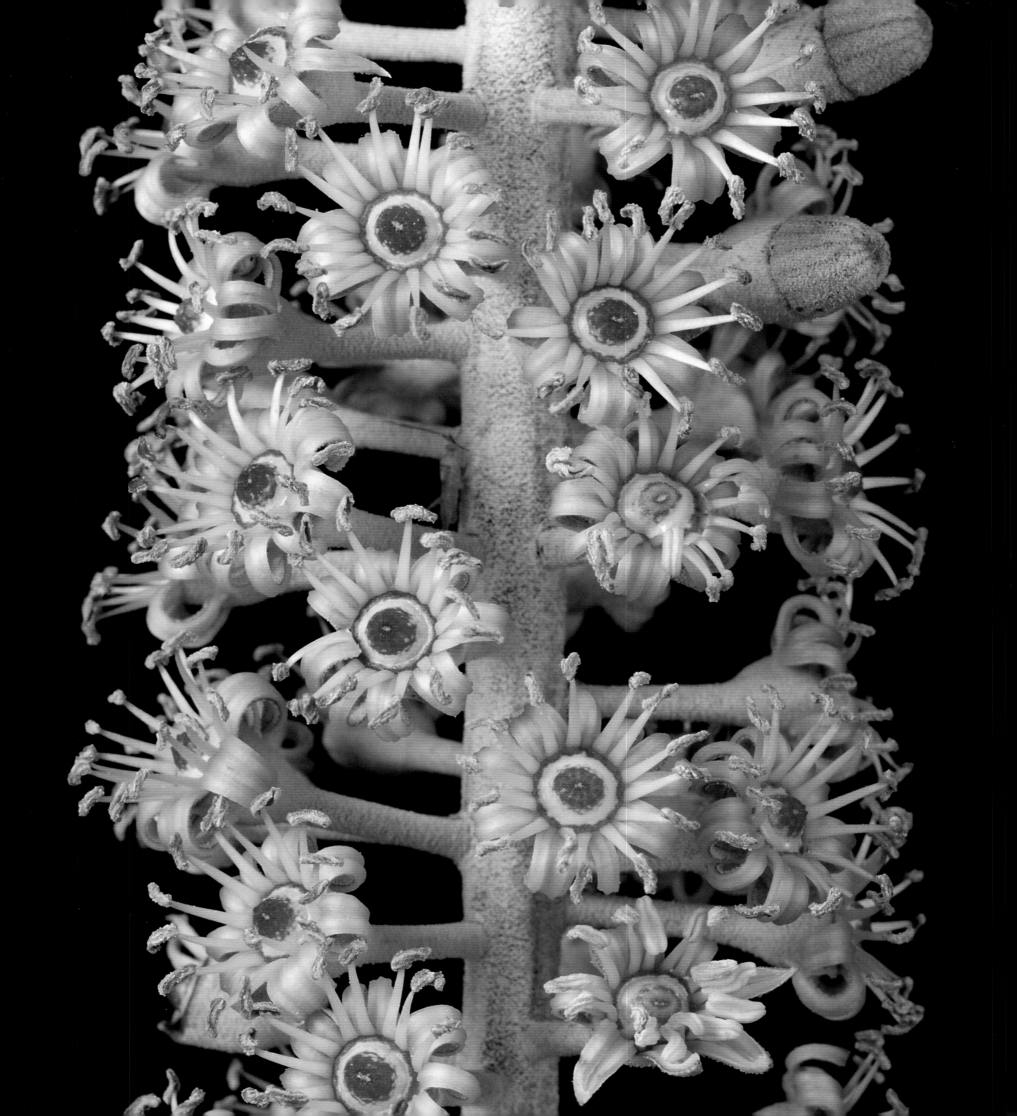

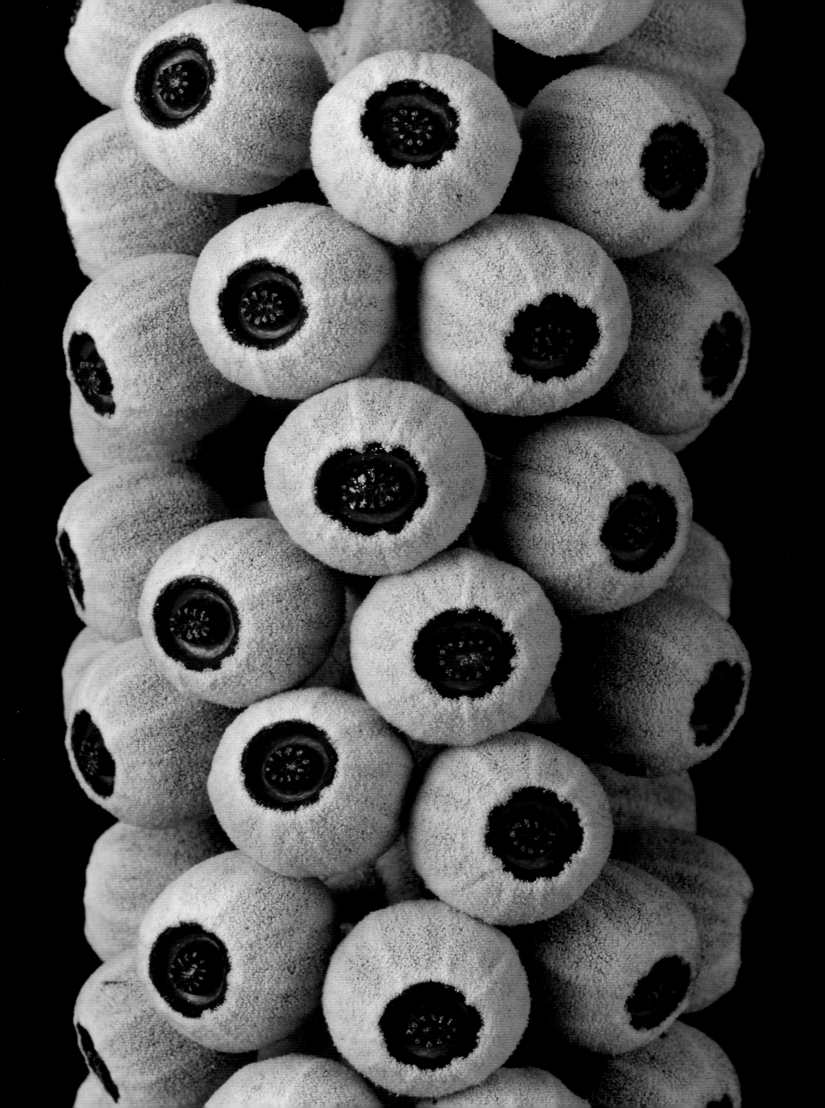

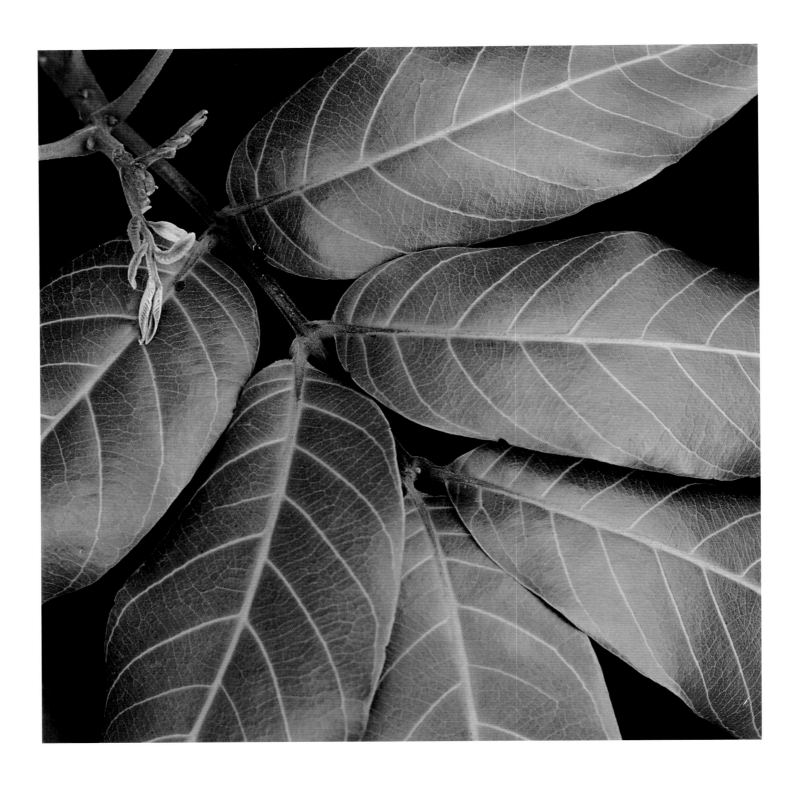

Māhoe; ʻAlaʻalahua (left, leaves; right, fruit)
Alectryon macrococcus* var. *auwahiensis

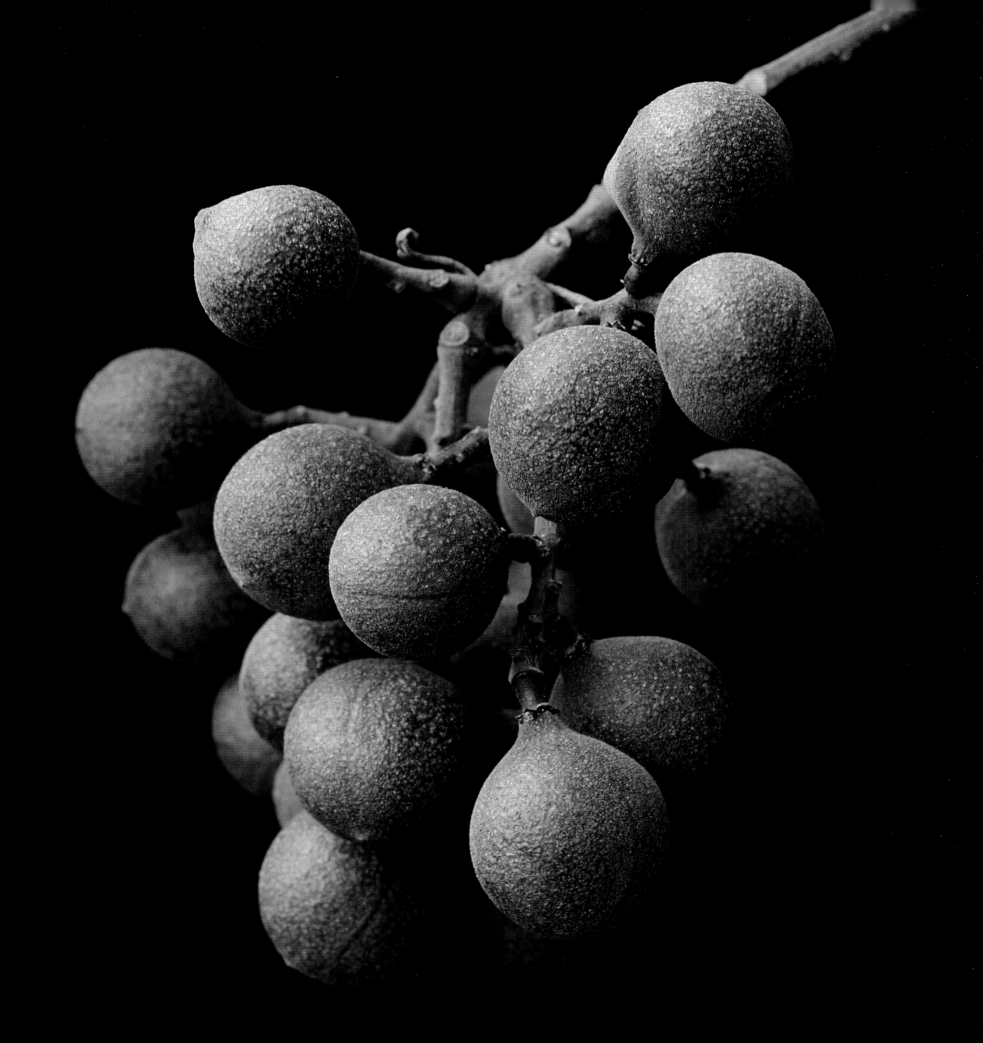

Lahaina Foliar Snout Beetle
Ponu ʻAi Lau
Rhyncogonus lahainae

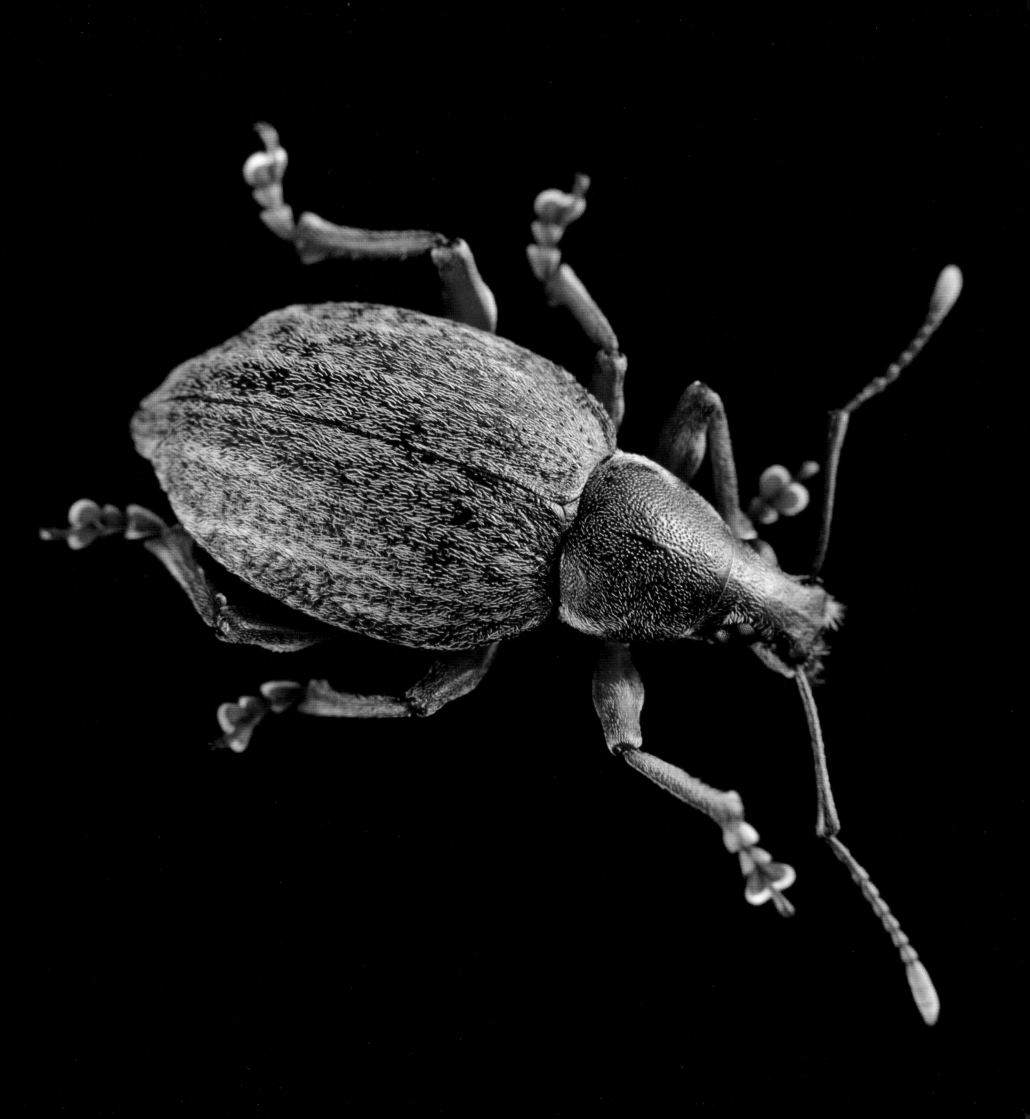

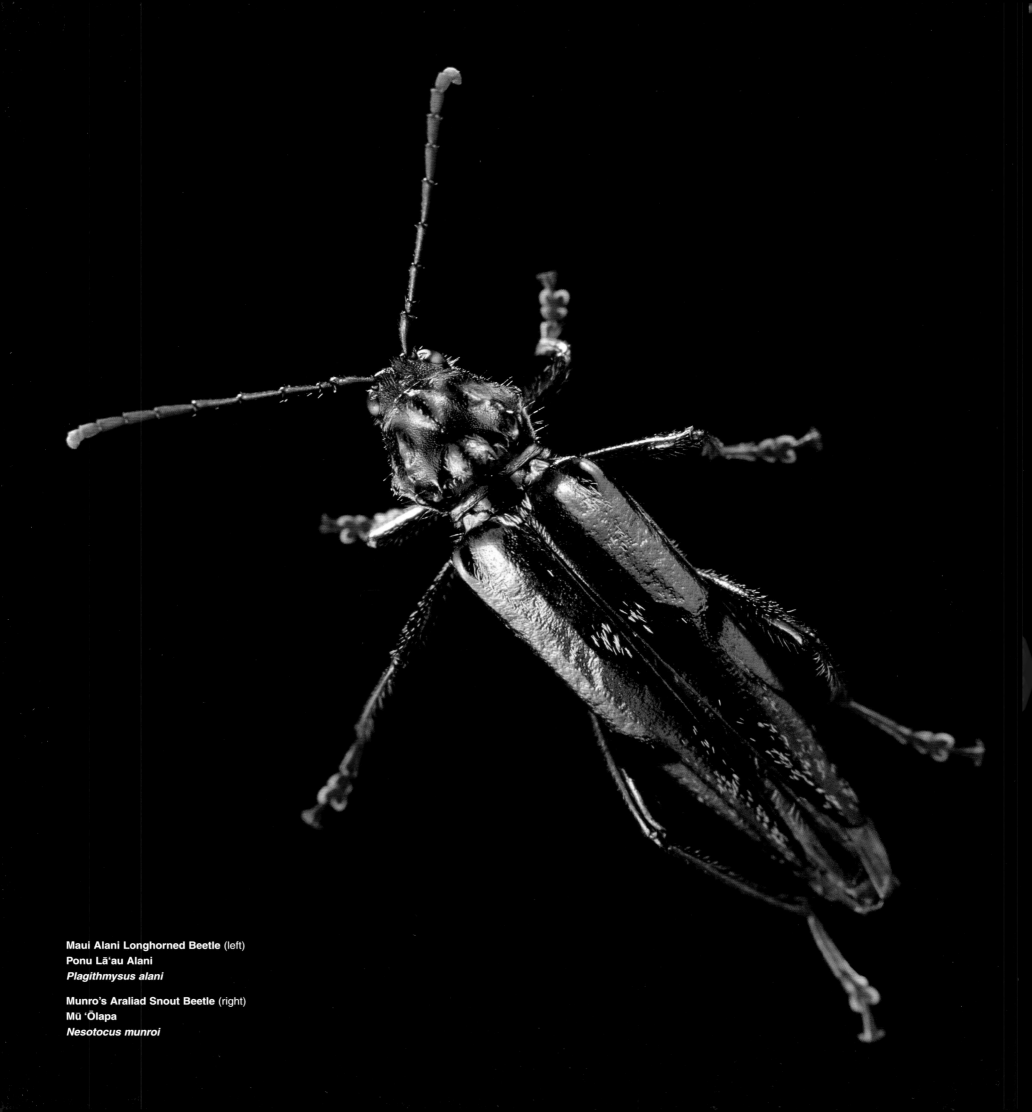

Maui Alani Longhorned Beetle (left)
Ponu Lāʻau Alani
Plagithmysus alani

Munro's Araliad Snout Beetle (right)
Mū ʻŌlapa
Nesotocus munroi

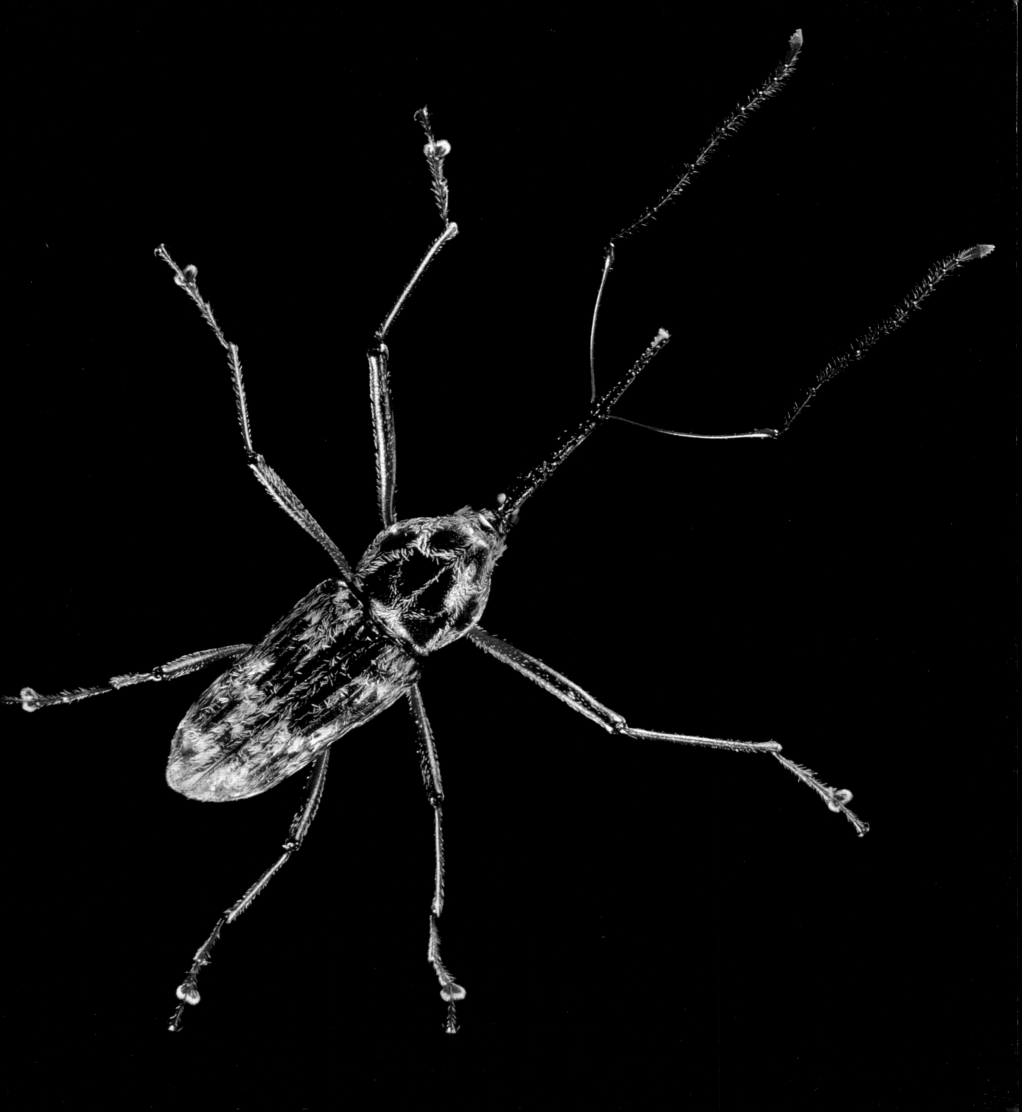

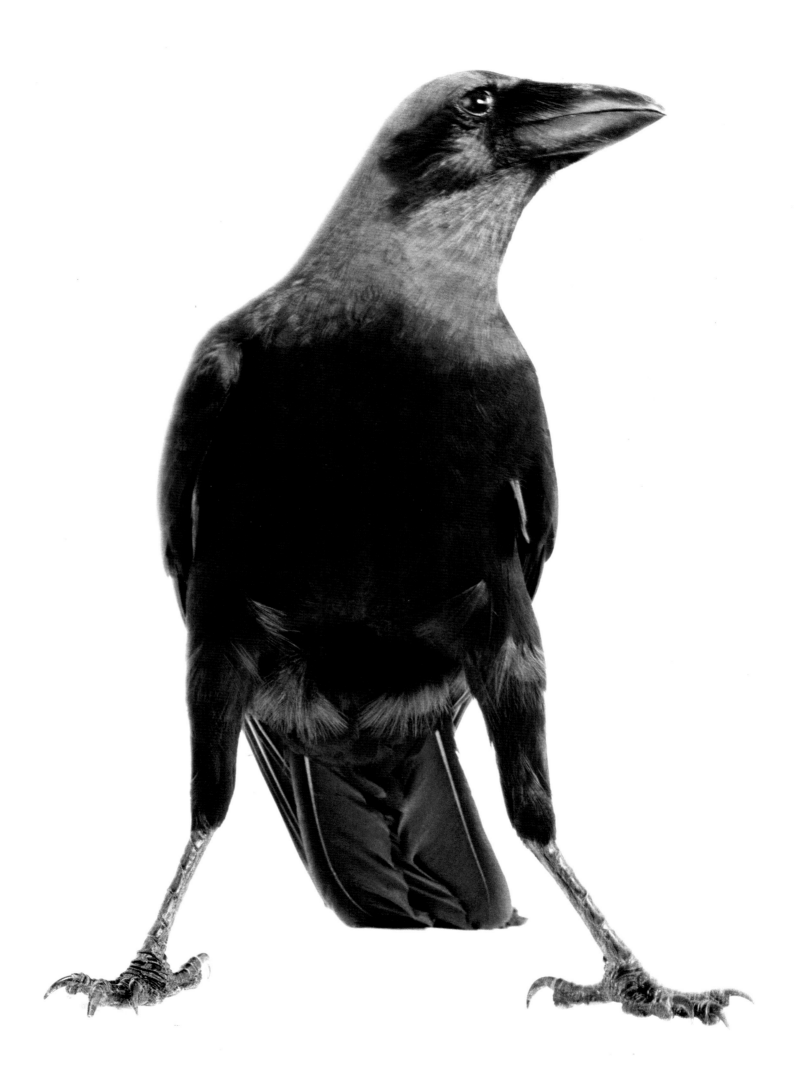

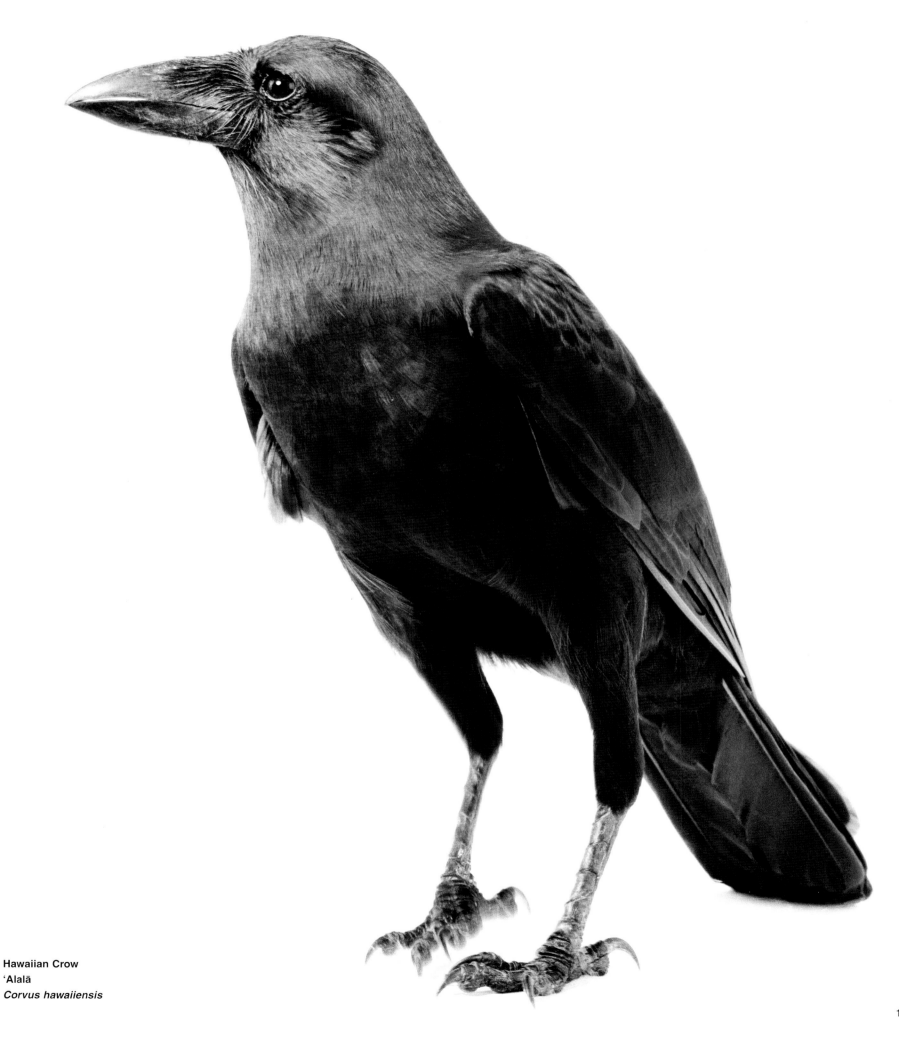

Hawaiian Crow
'Alalā
Corvus hawaiiensis

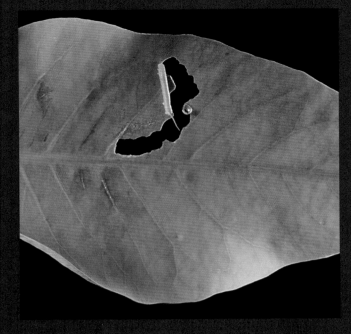

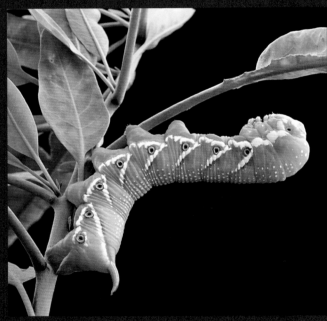

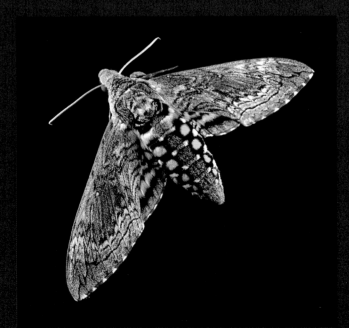

Blackburn's Hawk Moth
(left, from top to bottom: day old caterpillar,
mature caterpillar, adult; right, pupa)
'Ōka'i
Manduca blackburni

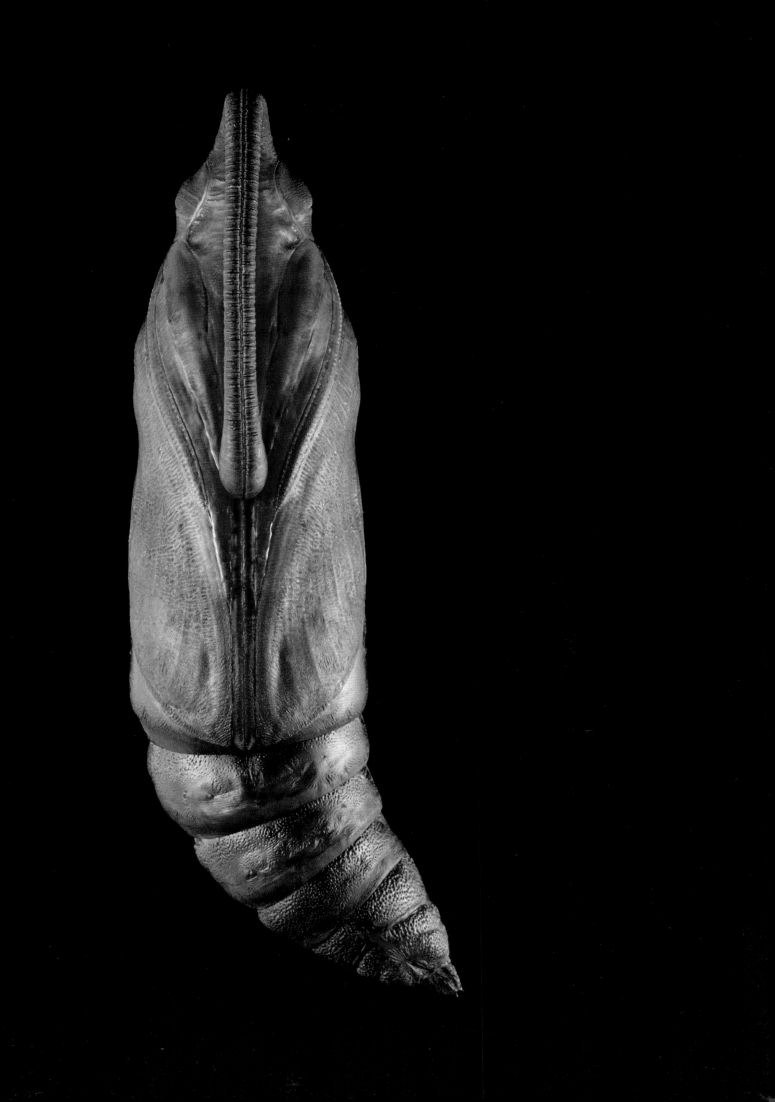

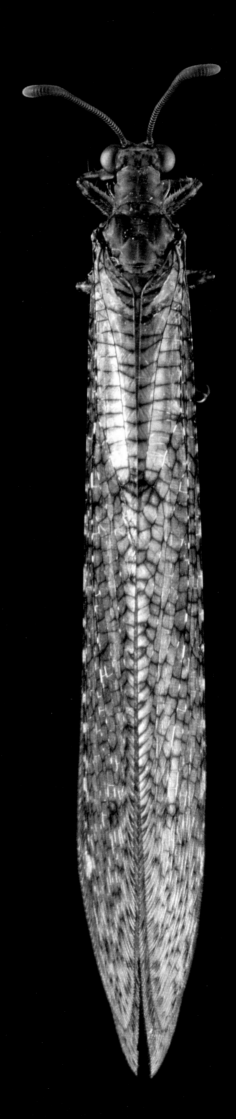

Wilson's Hawaiian Antlion
Pinao Huna
Distoleon wilsoni

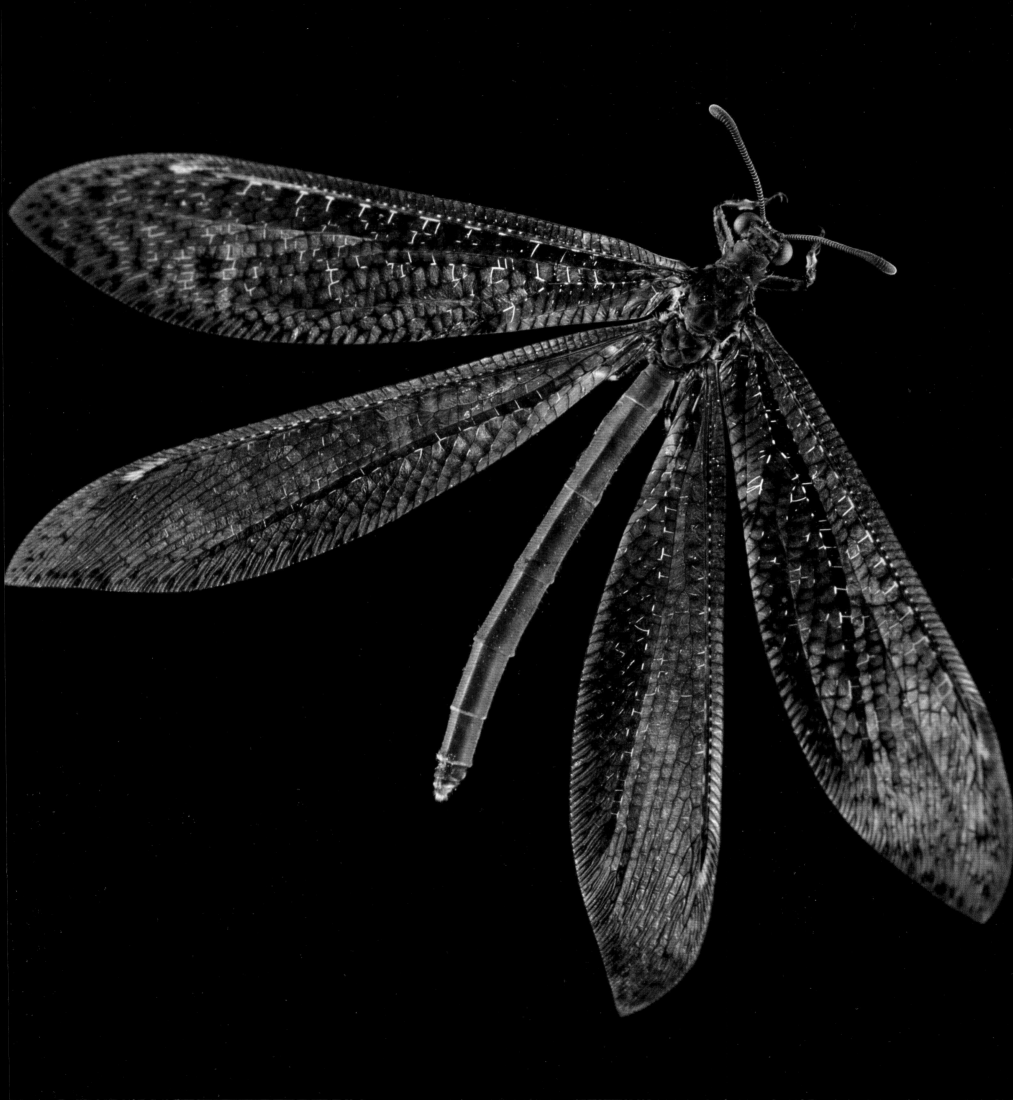

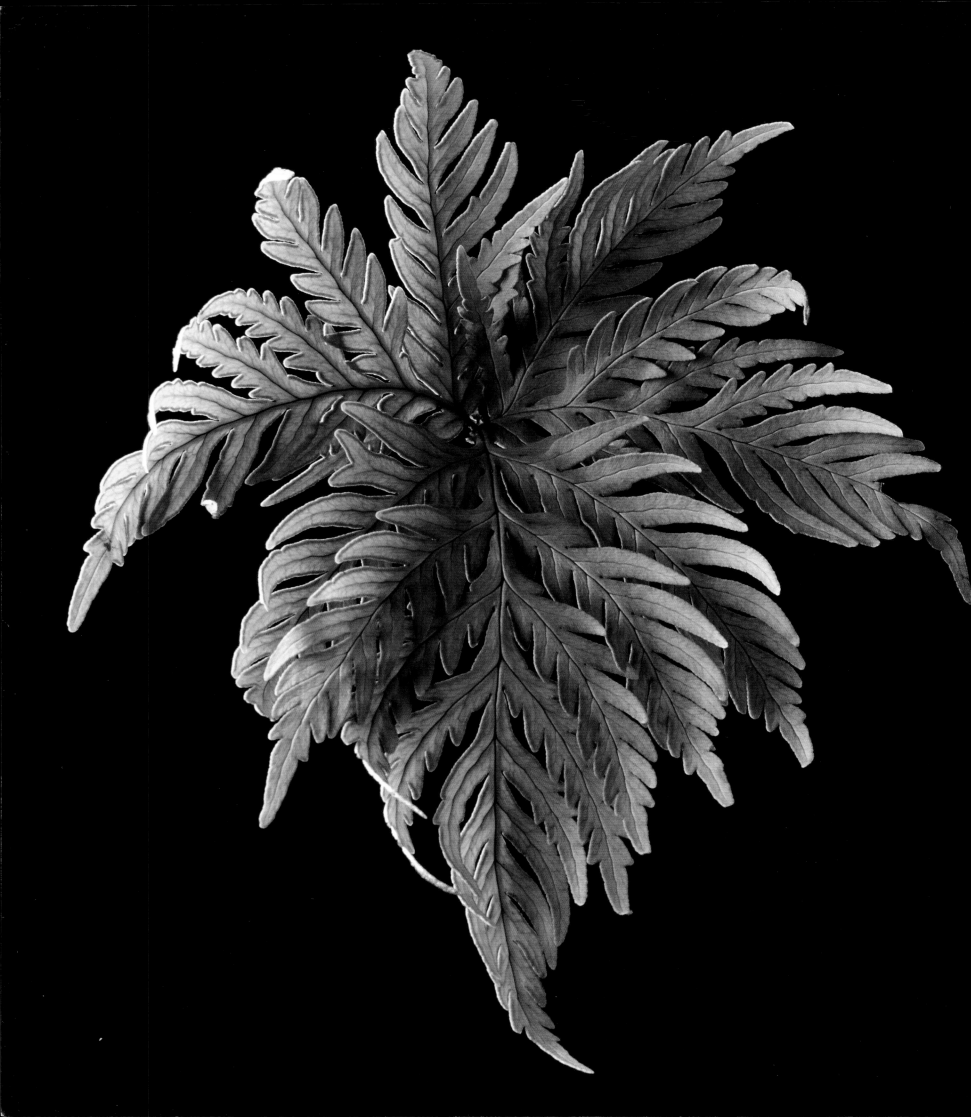

LOOKING AT DIVERSITY

by David Liittschwager

One in six Hawaiian native plants is a fern. There are 139 species, subspecies, varieties, and forms of native ferns. We first learned of their abundance from Hank Oppenheimer when we were working on Puʻu Kukui. While stuck inside the dome tent because of heavy rain, I asked Hank how many different species of ferns he might be able to collect from, say, 50 feet of the boardwalk—sort of a miniature survey of one group of plants. Hank thought for a minute and answered, "Maybe 15 or 20." Our musing became a plan. Later he went out to collect the plants and Susan and I made a set in which to photograph them. Hank returned several times throughout the day, bringing many specimens that were very surprising. Some of the plants were not recognizable to us as ferns; they resembled pom-poms, belt straps, or ribbons—even a tiny toothbrush! The length of their fronds ranged from one inch to almost nine feet. So many sizes and textures required numerous adjustments to the photographic set. Hank continued collecting into the night, and somewhere around midnight our species count was over 50. We have included 19 in these pages.

Hawaiʻi in general (and Puʻu Kukui specifically) is a very ferny place. Ferns, unlike flowering plants, reproduce with spores—single-celled reproductive bodies—rather than seeds. Spores are highly portable in the wind, and compared to other colonizers (for instance, seeds too heavy to stay aloft the entire way to Hawaiʻi, or seeds that must hitch-hike on a migratory bird) it is relatively easy, over millions of years, for ferns to colonize remote islands. The diversity of ferns in Hawaiʻi is a testament to the variety of habitat types that are present: coastal to alpine, desert conditions to the wettest place known on Earth—almost every combination of elevation and moisture that is conducive to life is available in Hawaiʻi.

Doryopteris angelica (left) is a new discovery. No one yet knows exactly where it came from or how long it has been in Hawaiʻi. It may be of recent origin, or this rare plant may be from the last extant population of an old species. We photographed this fern in a nursery about two hours after it was collected for propagation. Its home in the wild was far too steep for us to reach with our equipment.

Although ferns, some of our oldest known plants, have flourished and endured for more than 350 million years throughout the world, in recent time five species of native Hawaiian ferns have been lost and 31 have become imperiled. Fortunately, only five of the ferns on these pages have become scarce. We have included the others simply for their range of form and their beauty.

Angel Wing Fern (page 138)
Doryopteris angelica

Page 140:
Palapalai 'Aumakua (1)
Dryopteris crinalis

Adder's Tongue (2)
Moa; Puapua Moa; Laukahi
Ophioderma pendulum subsp. *pendulum*

Hō'o'o Kula (3)
Pneumatopteris sandwicensis

Māku'e (4)
Elaphoglossum paleaceum

Mule's Foot Fern (5)
Pala; Kapua'i Lio
Marrattia douglasii

'Ōhi'a Kū (6)
Mecodium recurvum

Page 141:
Uluhe (1)
Dicranopteris linearis

'Ākōlea (2)
Athyrium microphyllum

Ctenitis squamigera (3)

Hoe A Māui; 'Ēkaha (4)
Elaphoglossum wawrae

'Apu'u (5)
Sadleria squarrosa

Adenophorus periens (6)

Doodia lyonii (7)

Nothoperanema rubiginosa (8)

'Ama'u (9)
Sadleria pallida

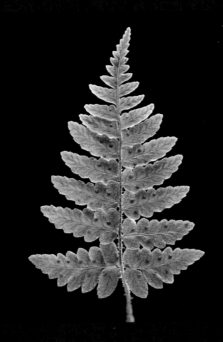

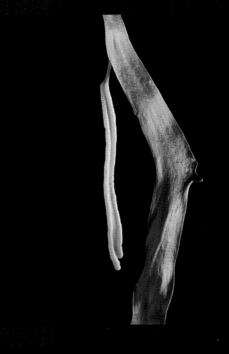

1

2

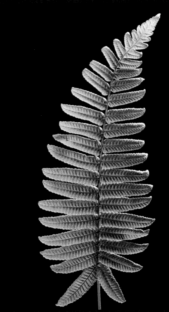

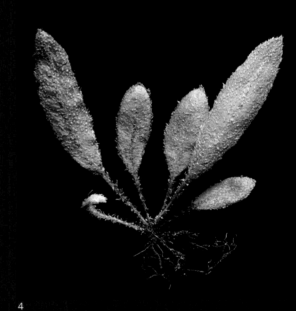

3

4

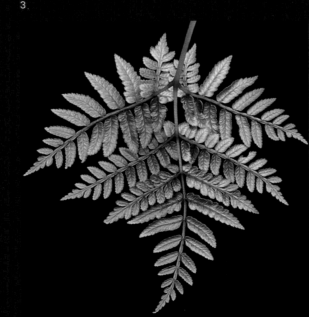

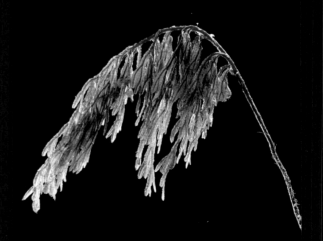

5

6

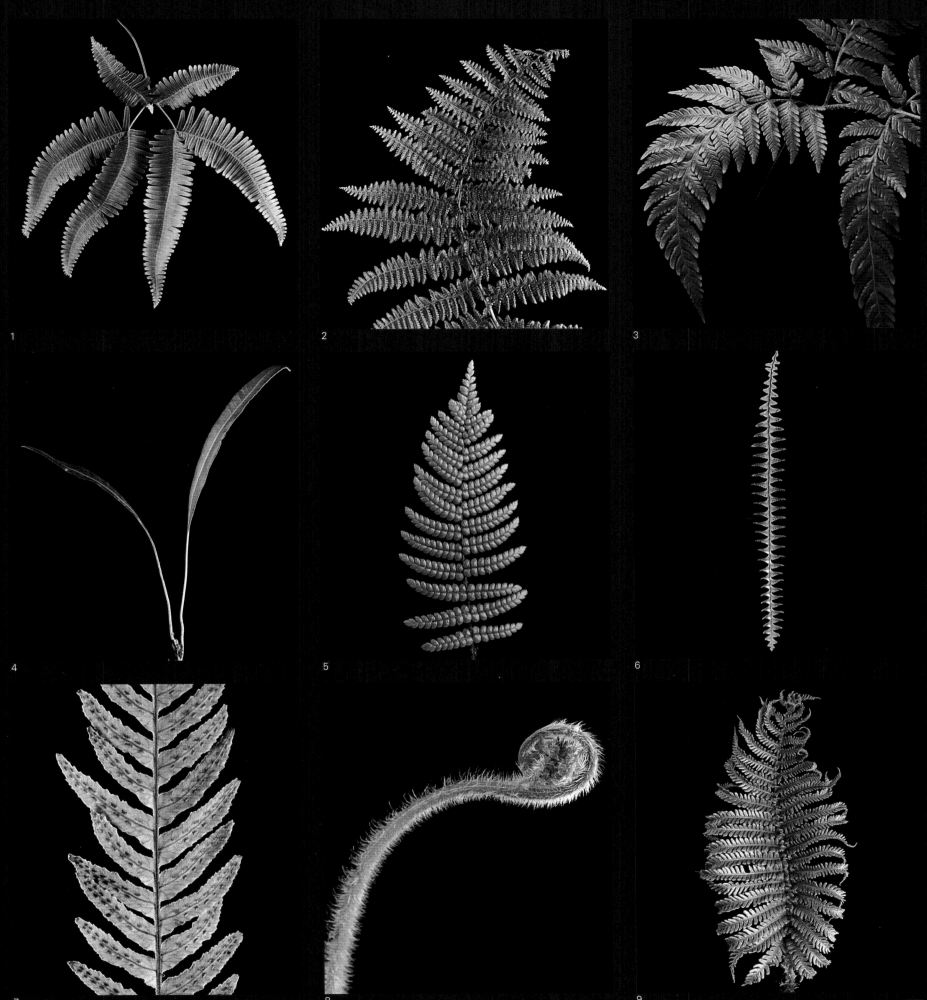

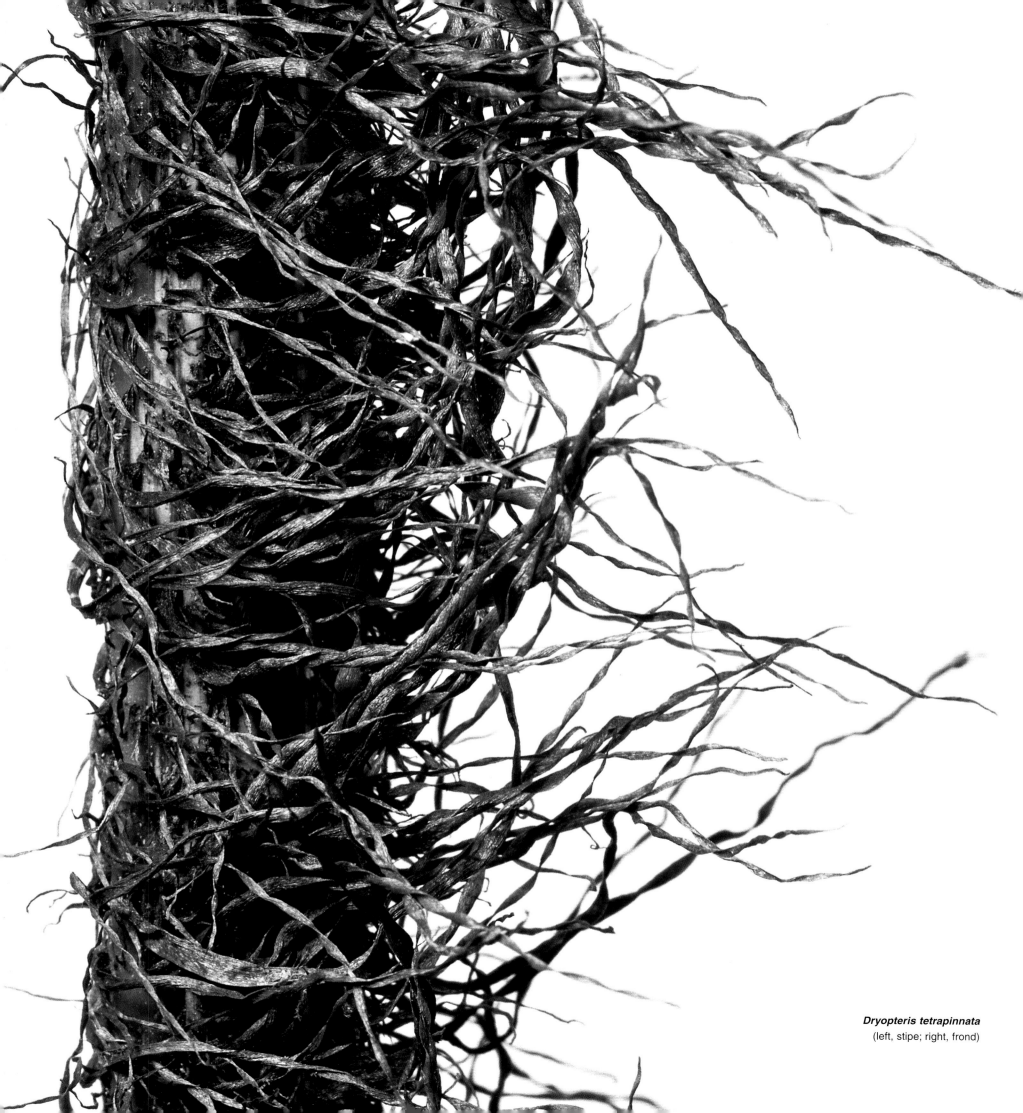

Dryopteris tetrapinnata
(left, stipe; right, frond)

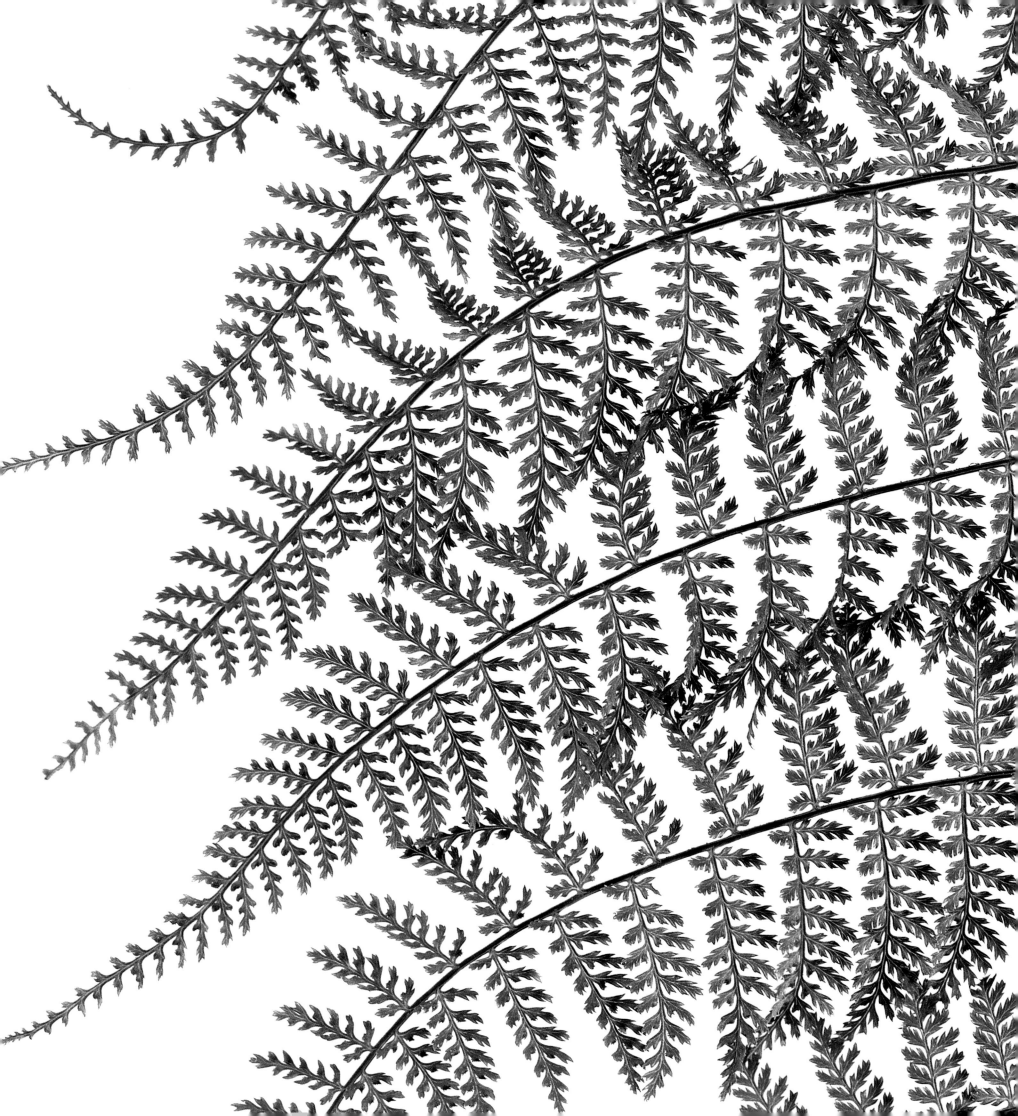

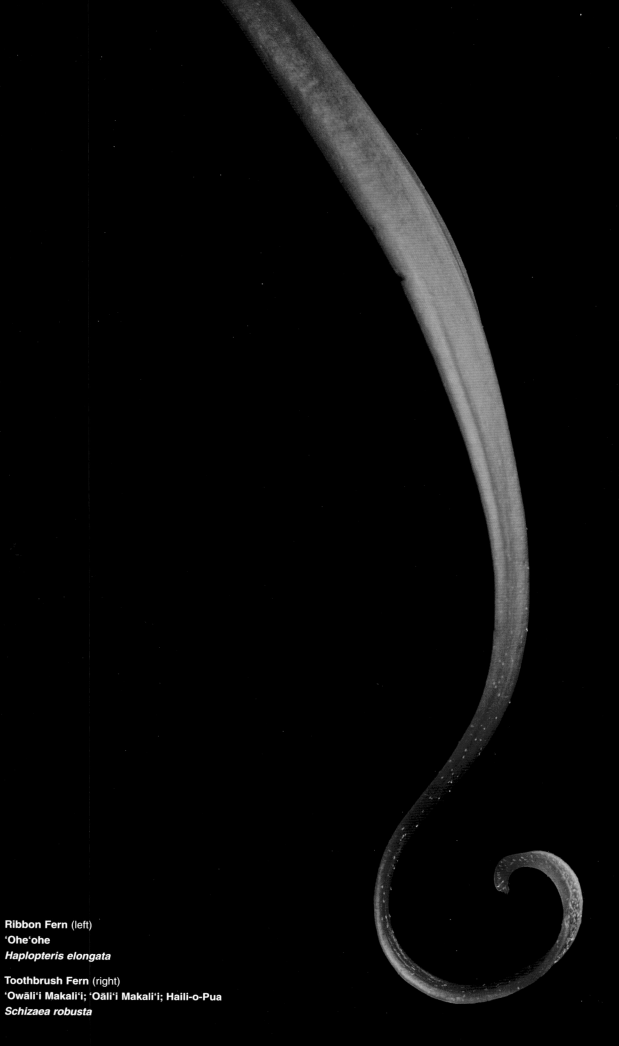

Ribbon Fern (left)
ʻOheʻohe
Haplopteris elongata

Toothbrush Fern (right)
ʻOwāliʻi Makaliʻi; ʻOāliʻi Makaliʻi; Haili-o-Pua
Schizaea robusta

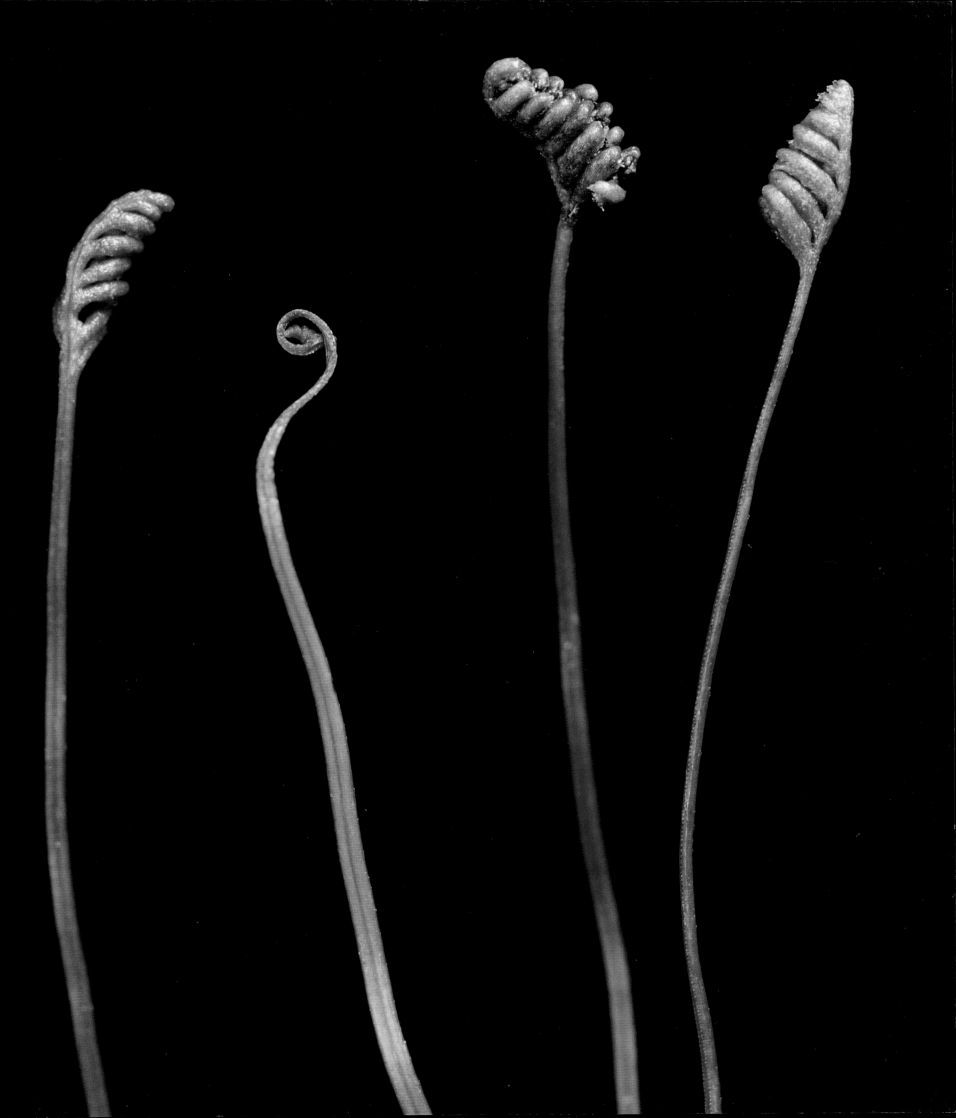

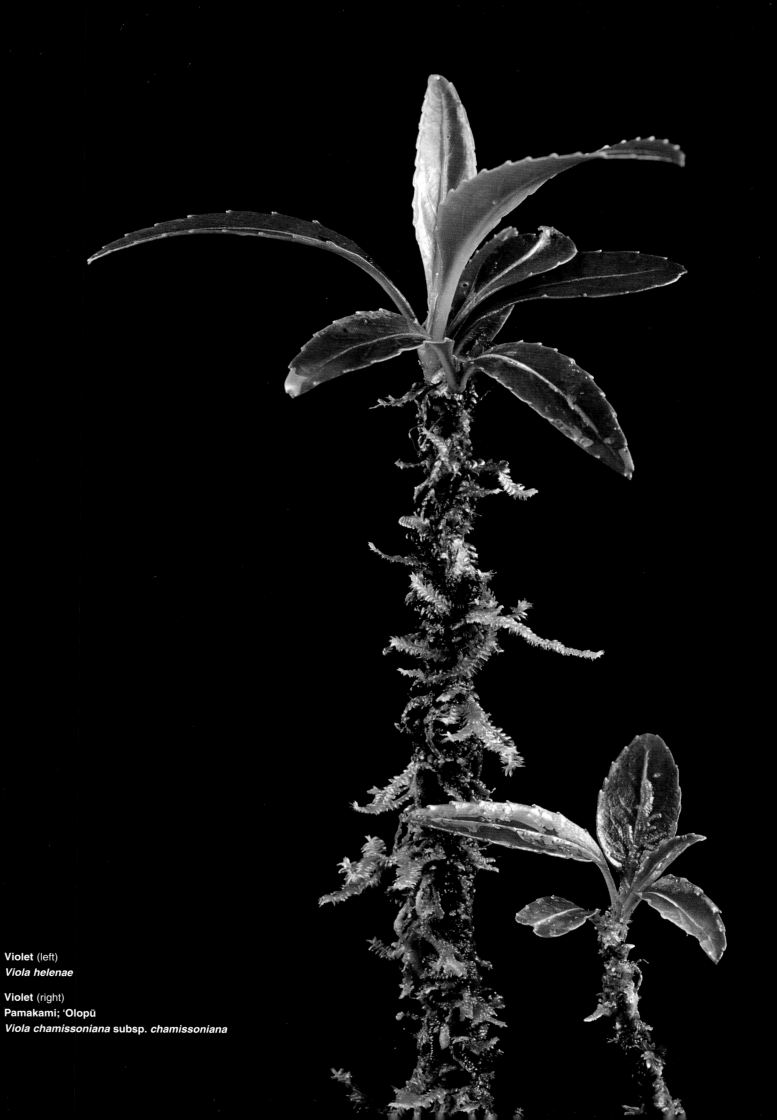

Violet (left)
Viola helenae

Violet (right)
Pamakami; ʻOlopū
Viola chamissoniana subsp. *chamissoniana*

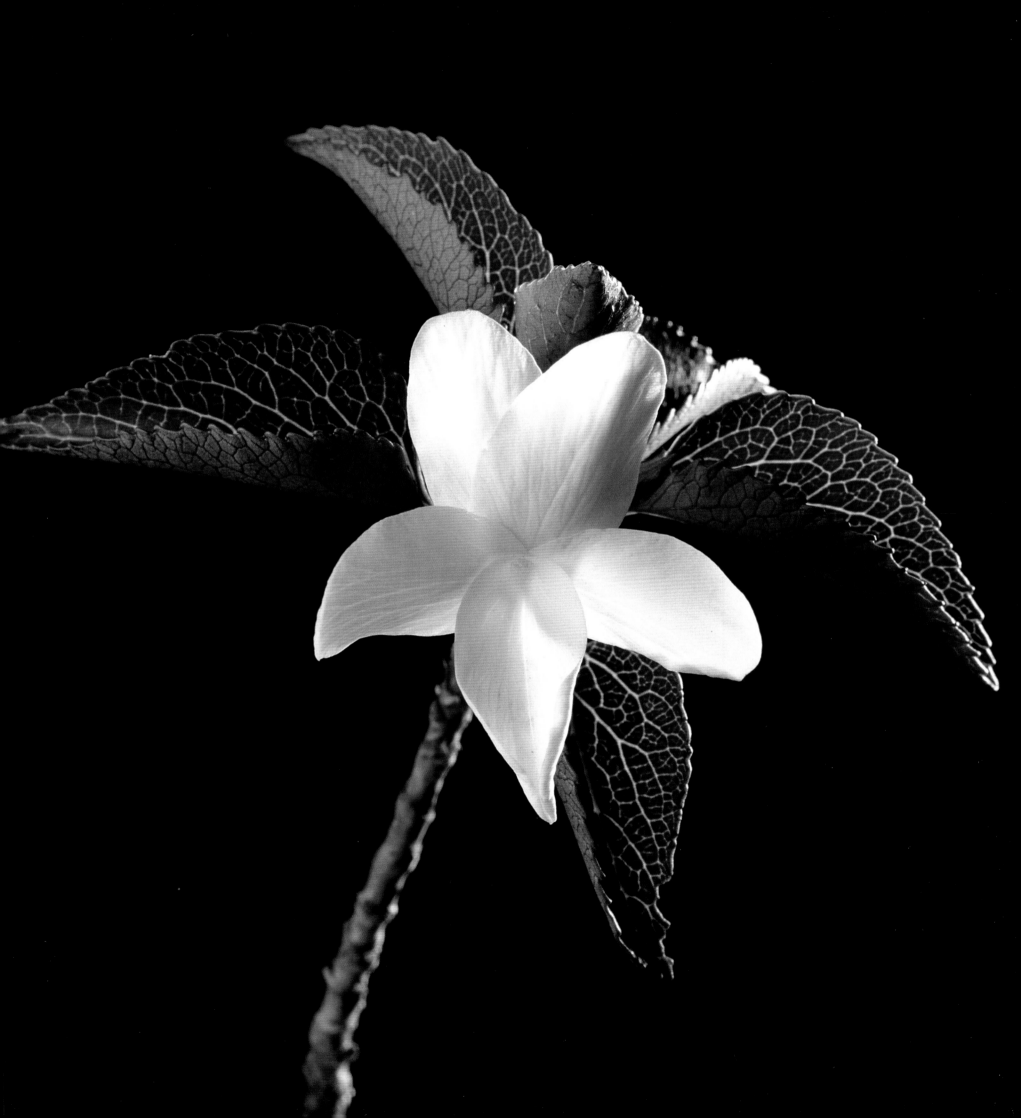

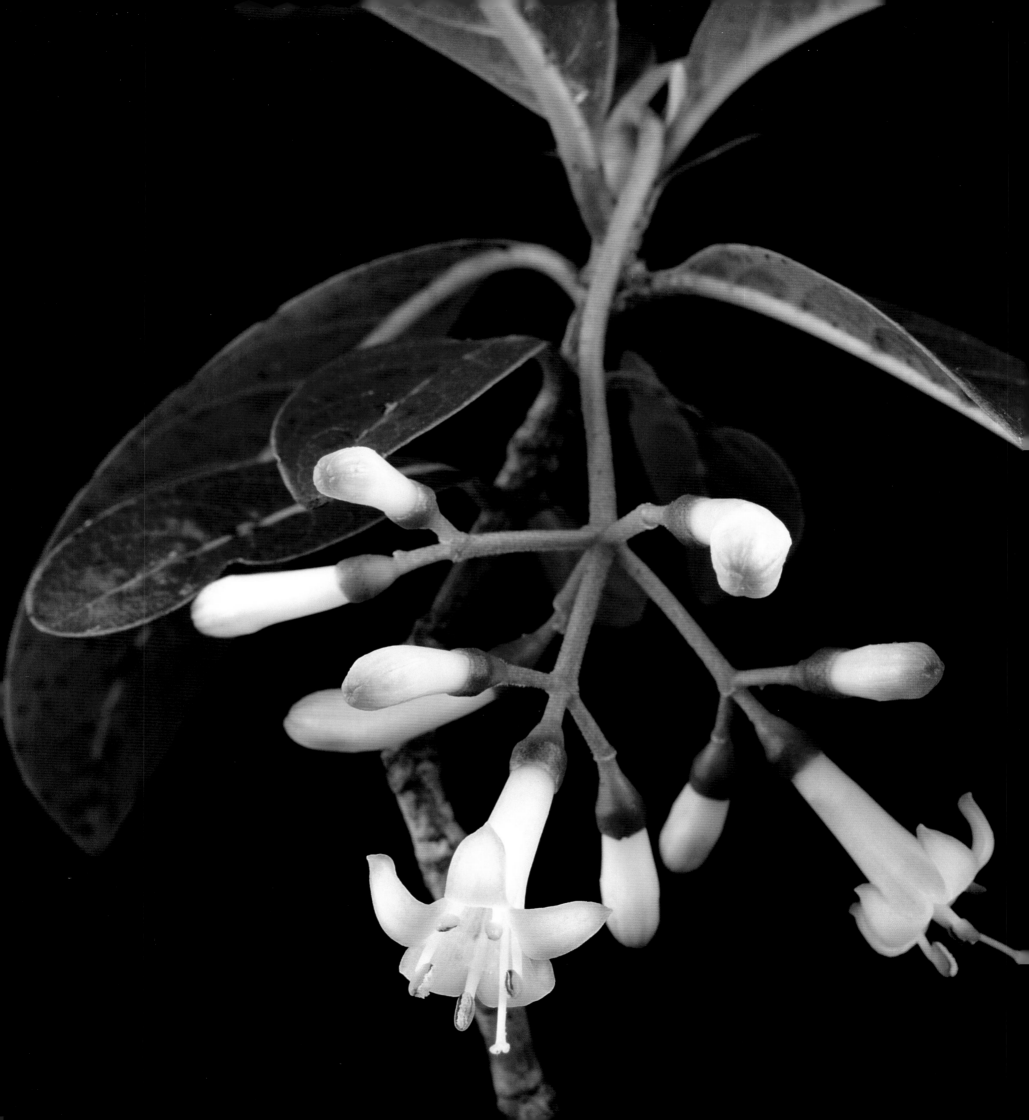

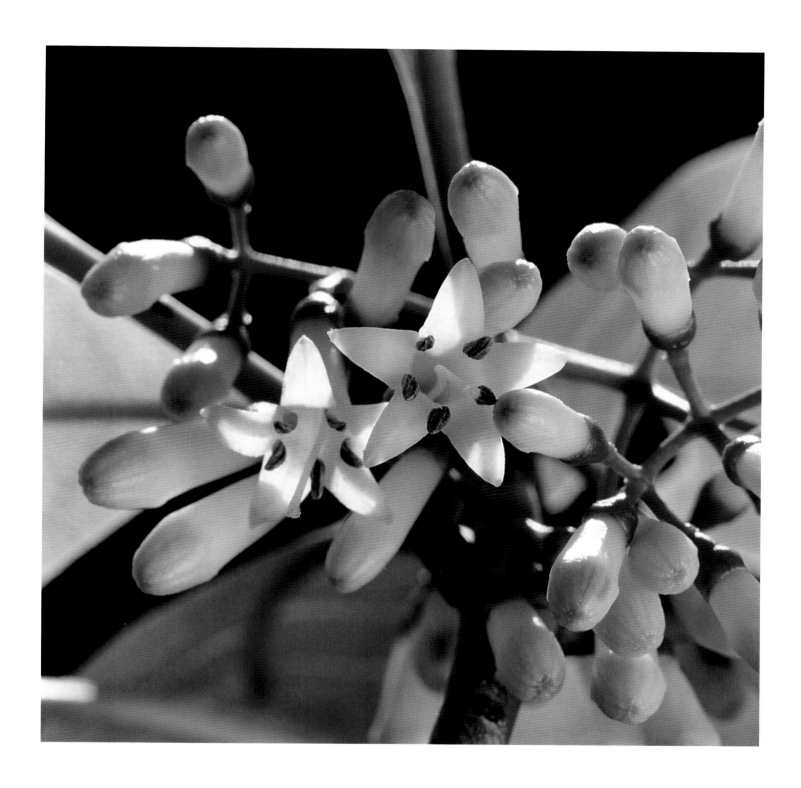

Kōpiko (left)
Psychotria grandiflora

Psychotria hobdyi (right)

Phyllostegia bracteata (page 150)

Phyllostegia warshaueri (page 151)

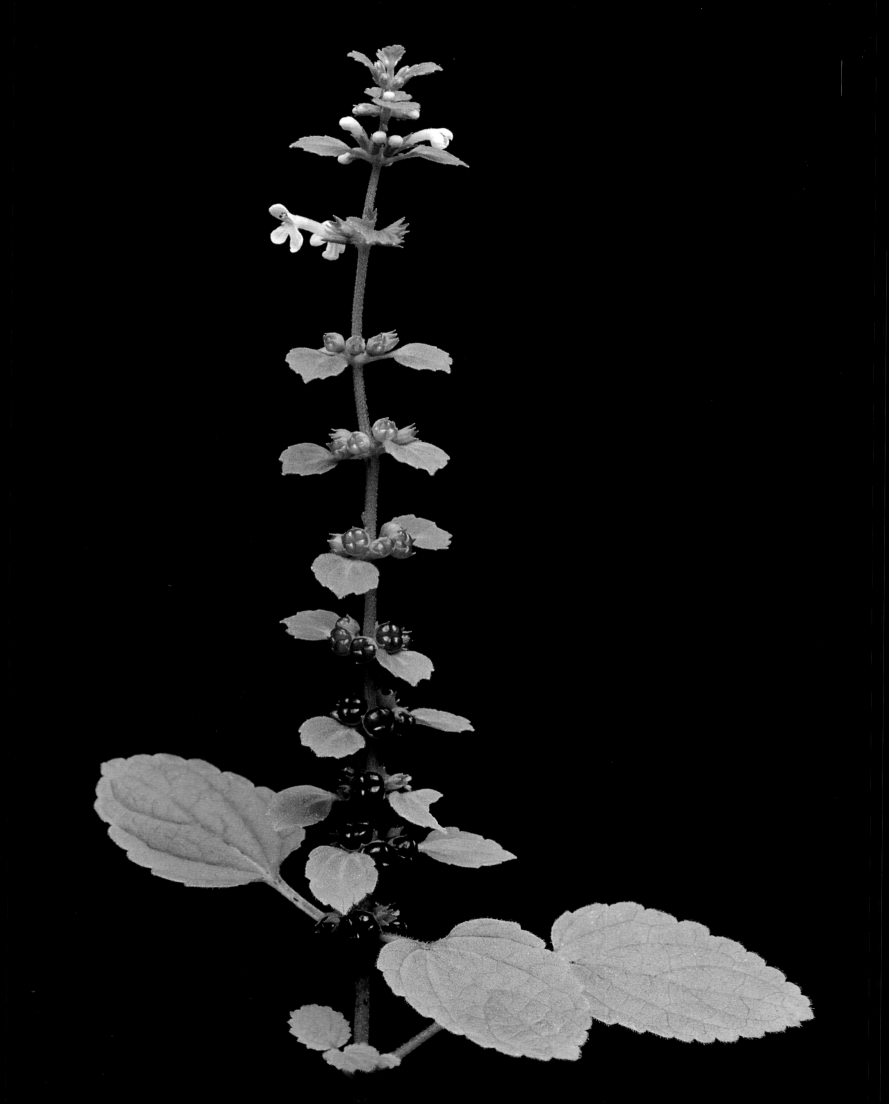

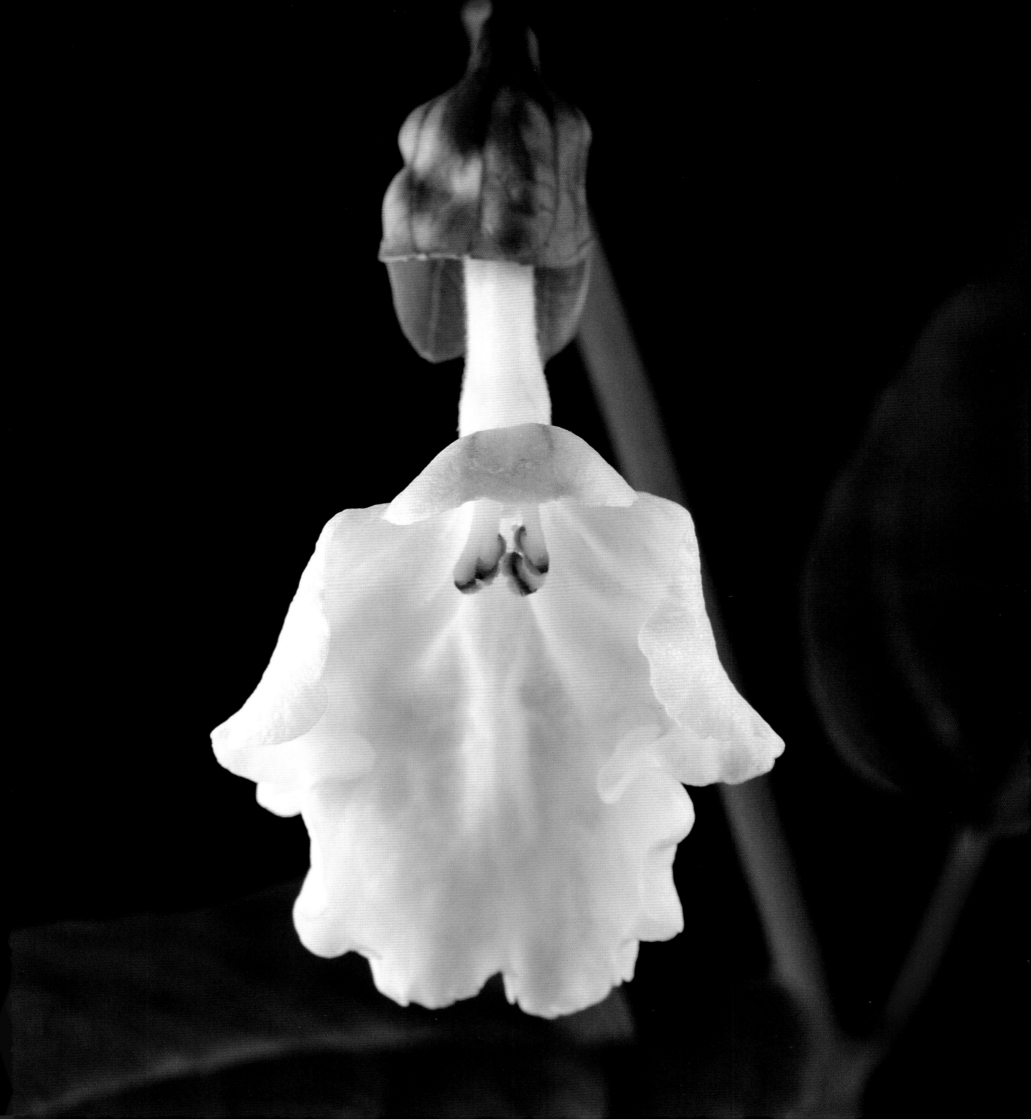

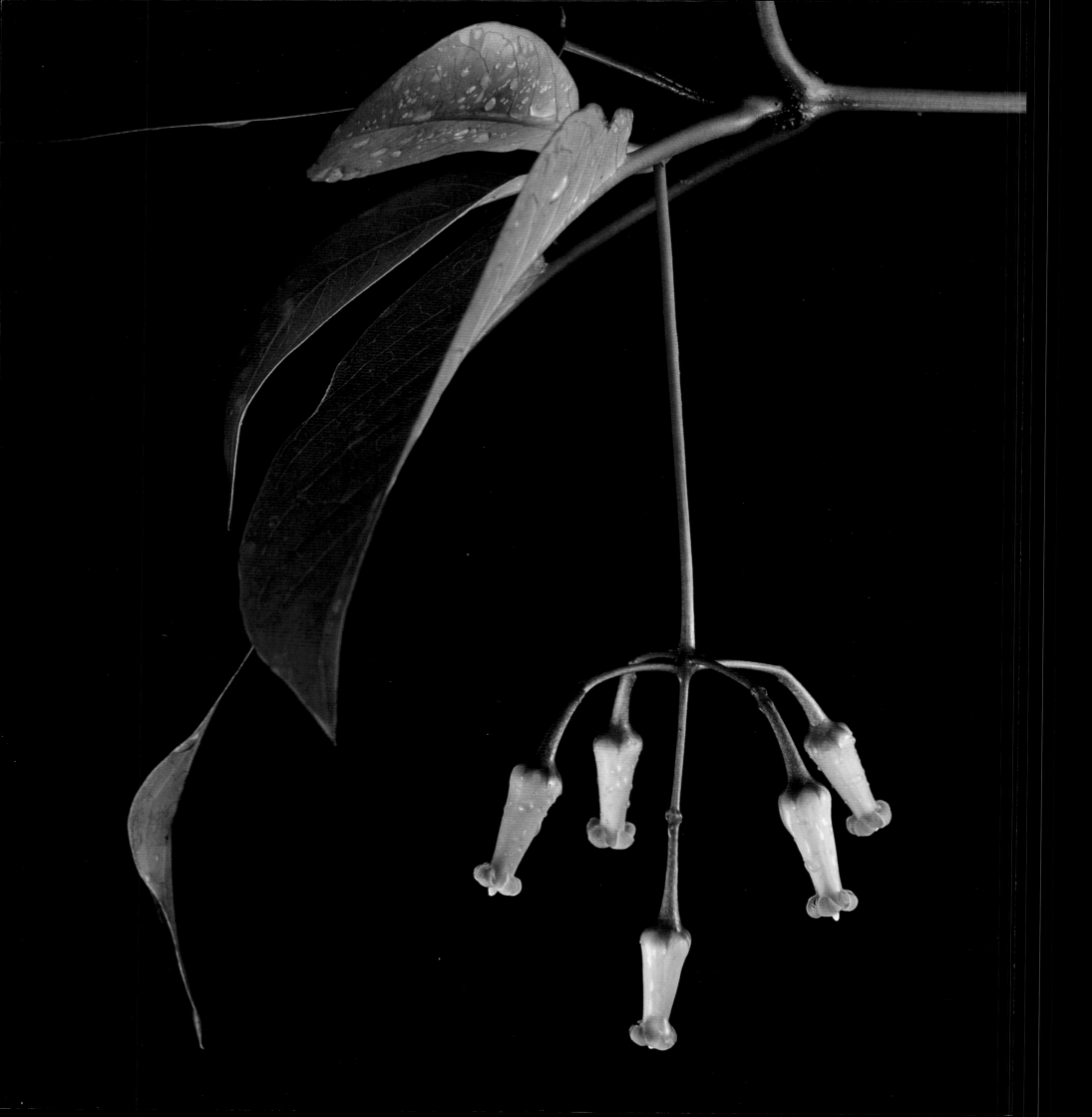

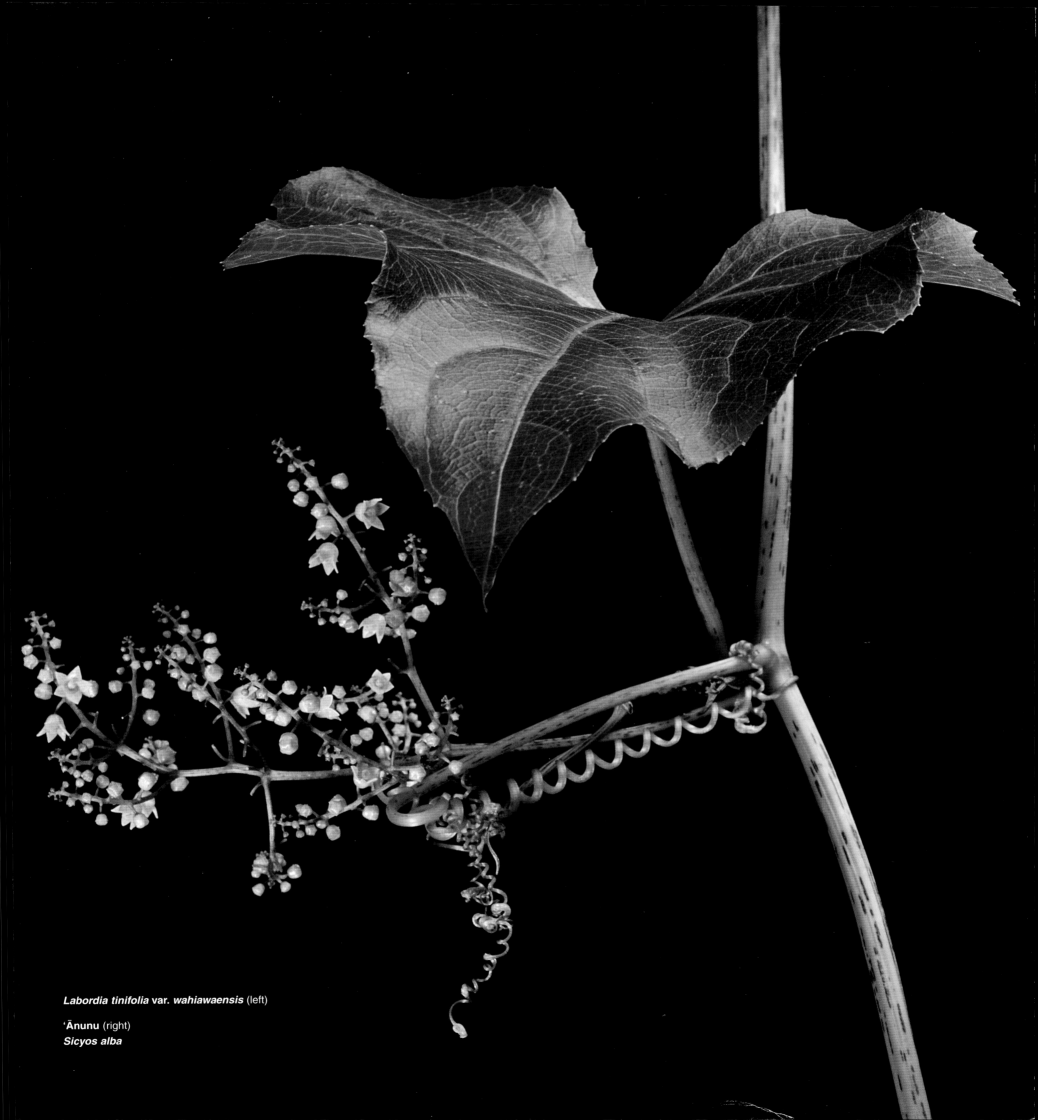

Labordia tinifolia var. wahiawaensis (left)

'Ānunu (right)
Sicyos alba

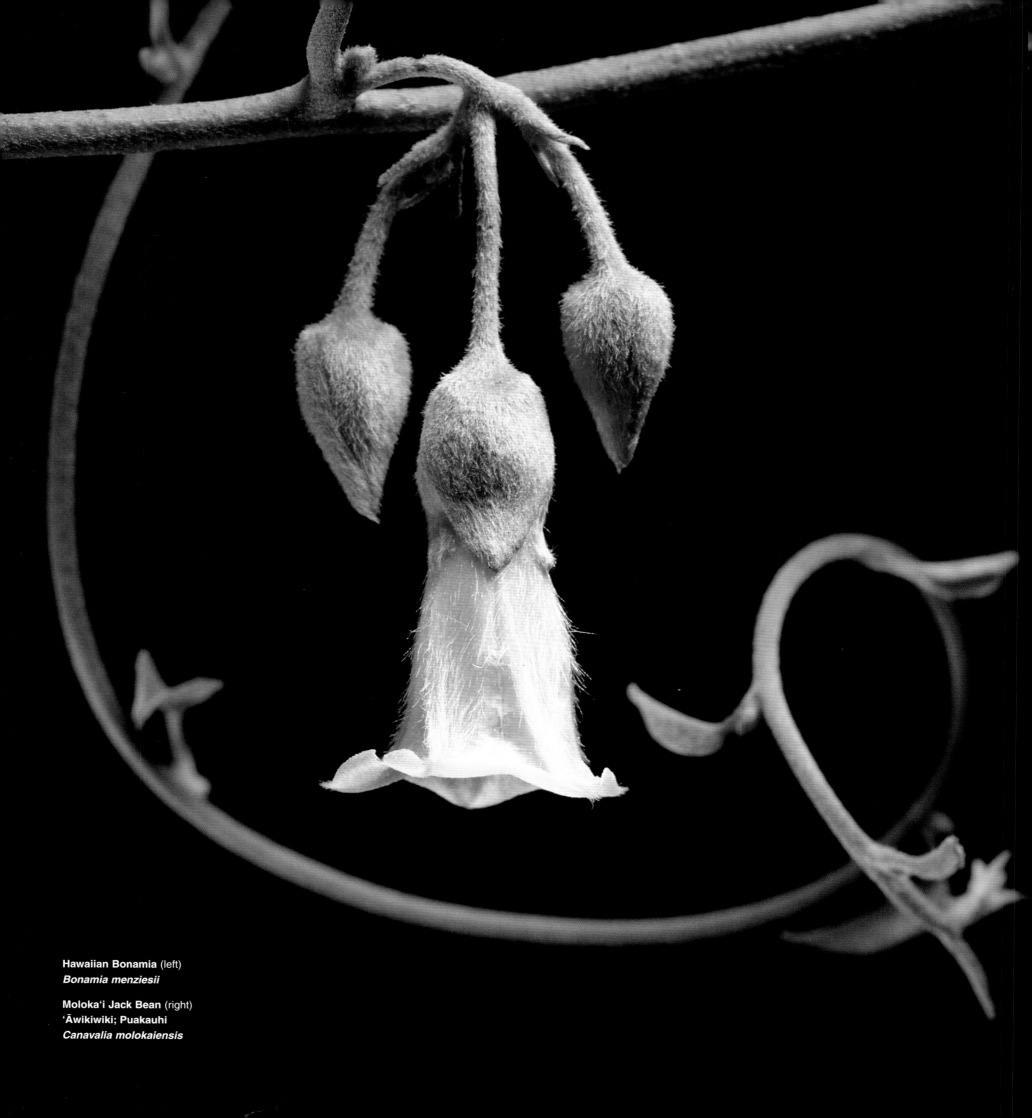

Hawaiian Bonamia (left)
Bonamia menziesii

Moloka'i Jack Bean (right)
'Āwikiwiki; Puakauhi
Canavalia molokaiensis

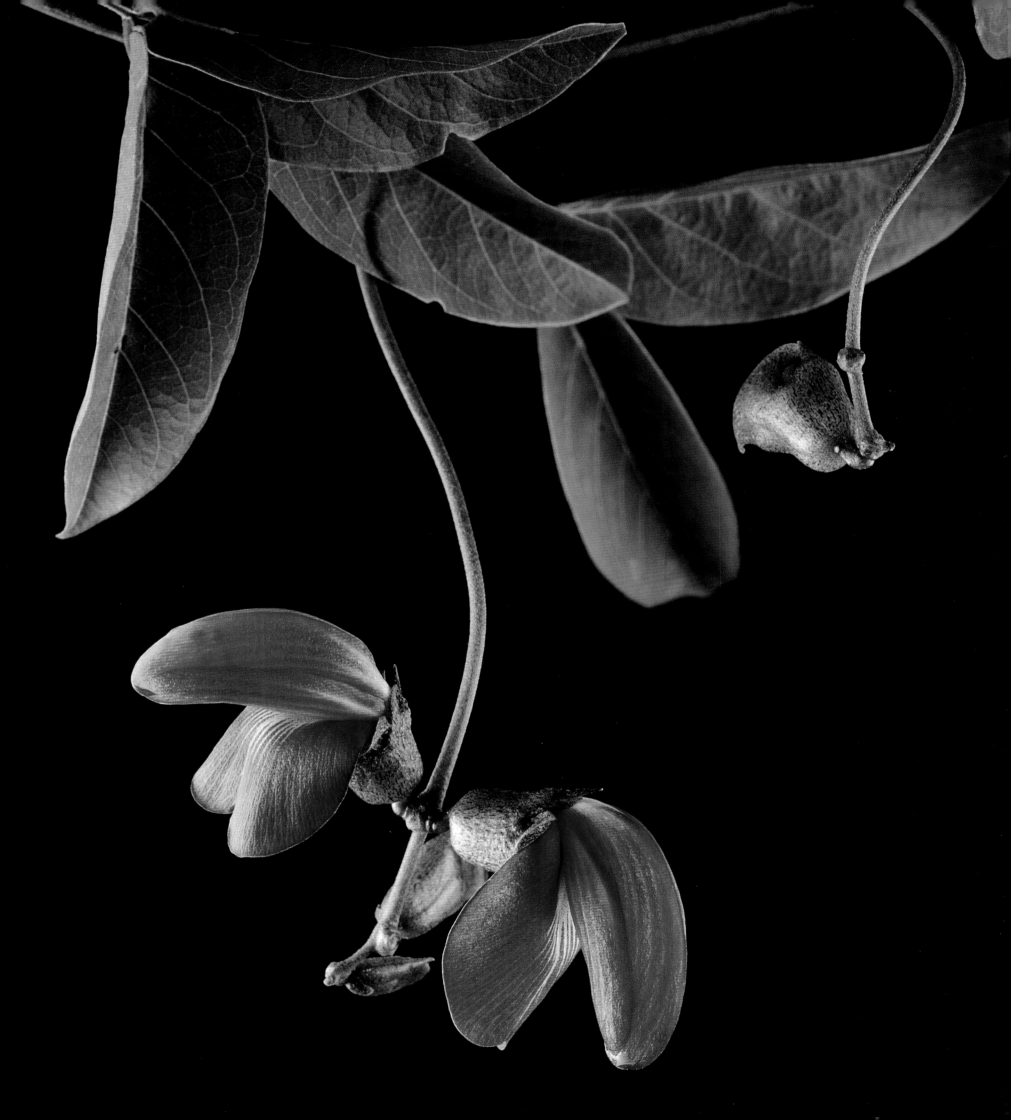

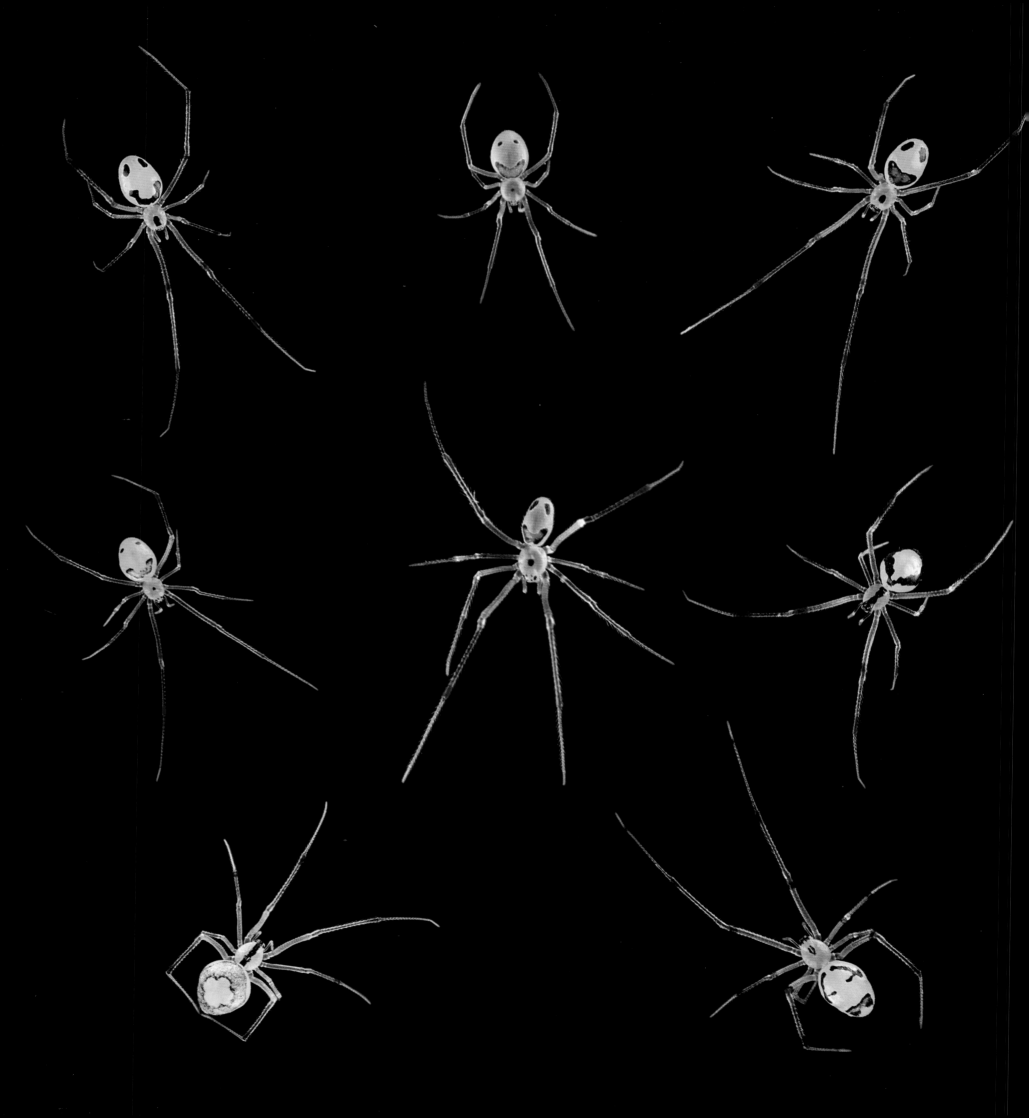

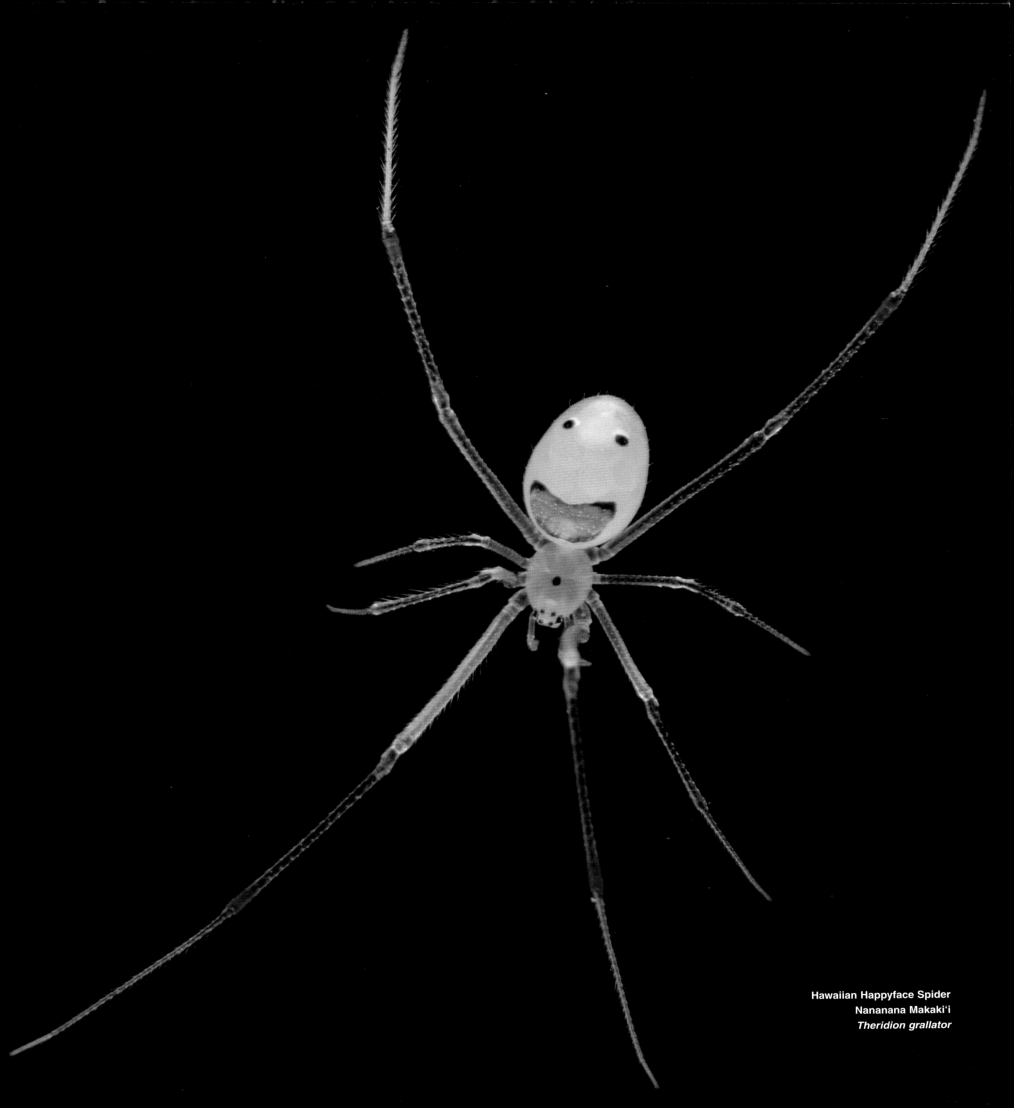

Hawaiian Happyface Spider
Nananana Makaki'i
Theridion grallator

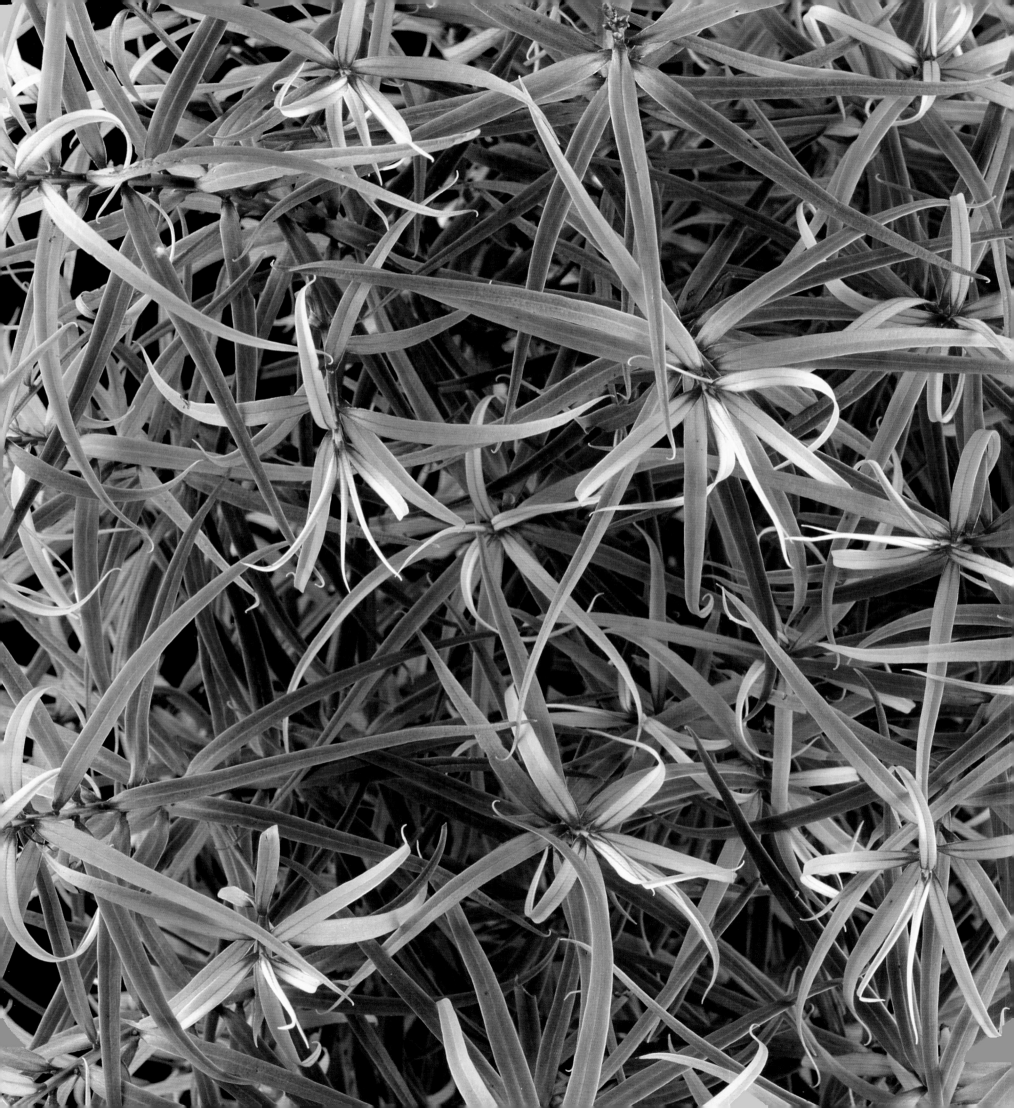

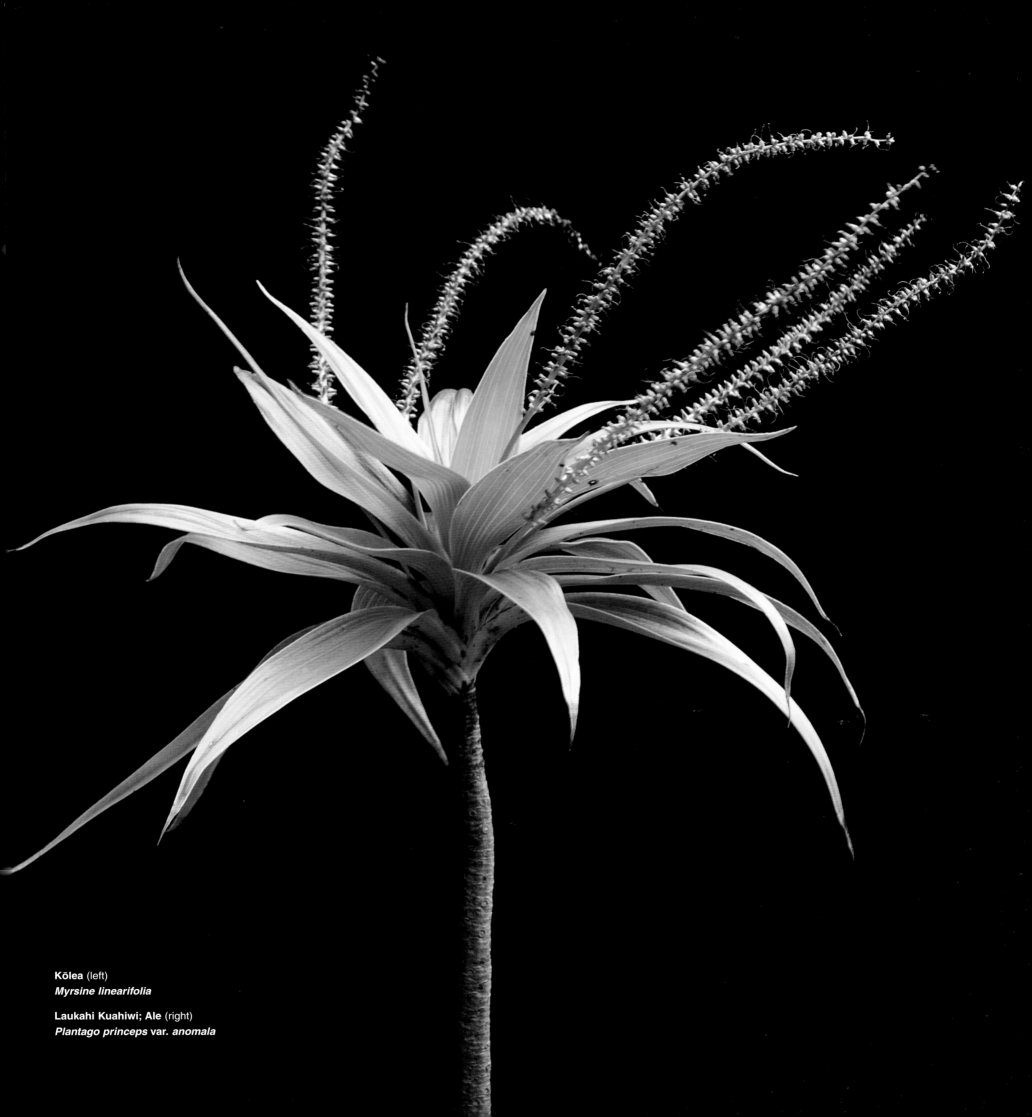

Kōlea (left)
Myrsine linearifolia

Laukahi Kuahiwi; Ale (right)
Plantago princeps var. *anomala*

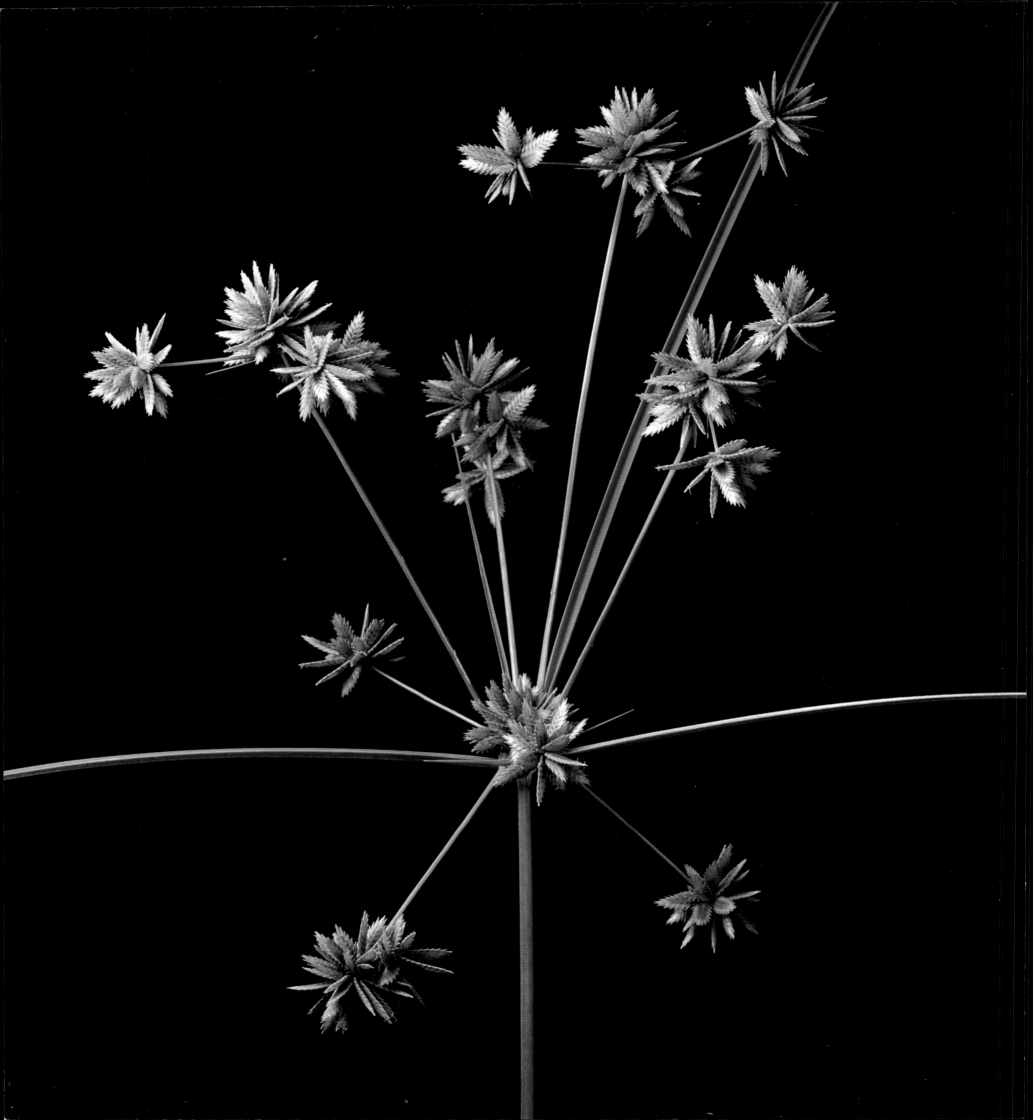

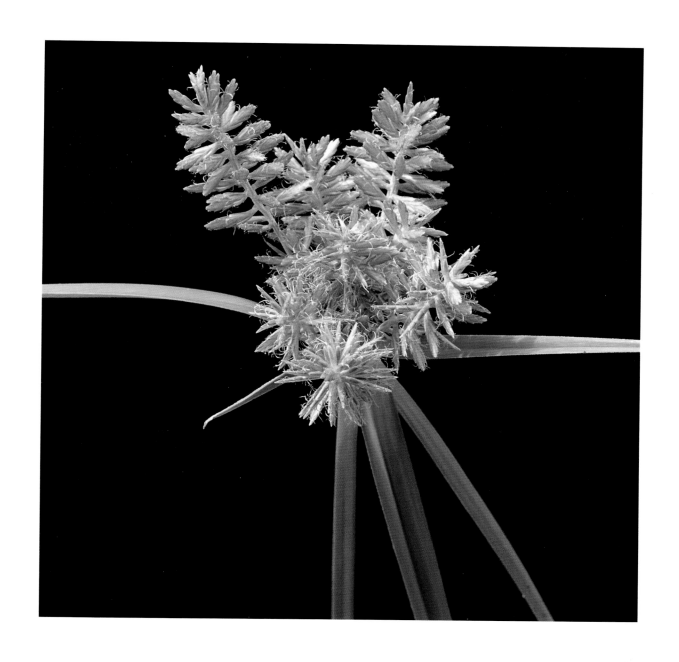

Puʻukaʻa (left)
Cyperus trachysanthos

Puʻukaʻa (right)
Cyperus pennatiformis **var.** *bryanii*

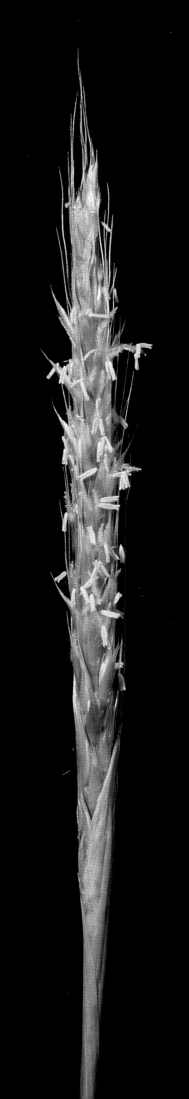

Hilo Ischaemum (left)
Ischaemum byrone

Pa'iniu (right)
Astelia waialealae

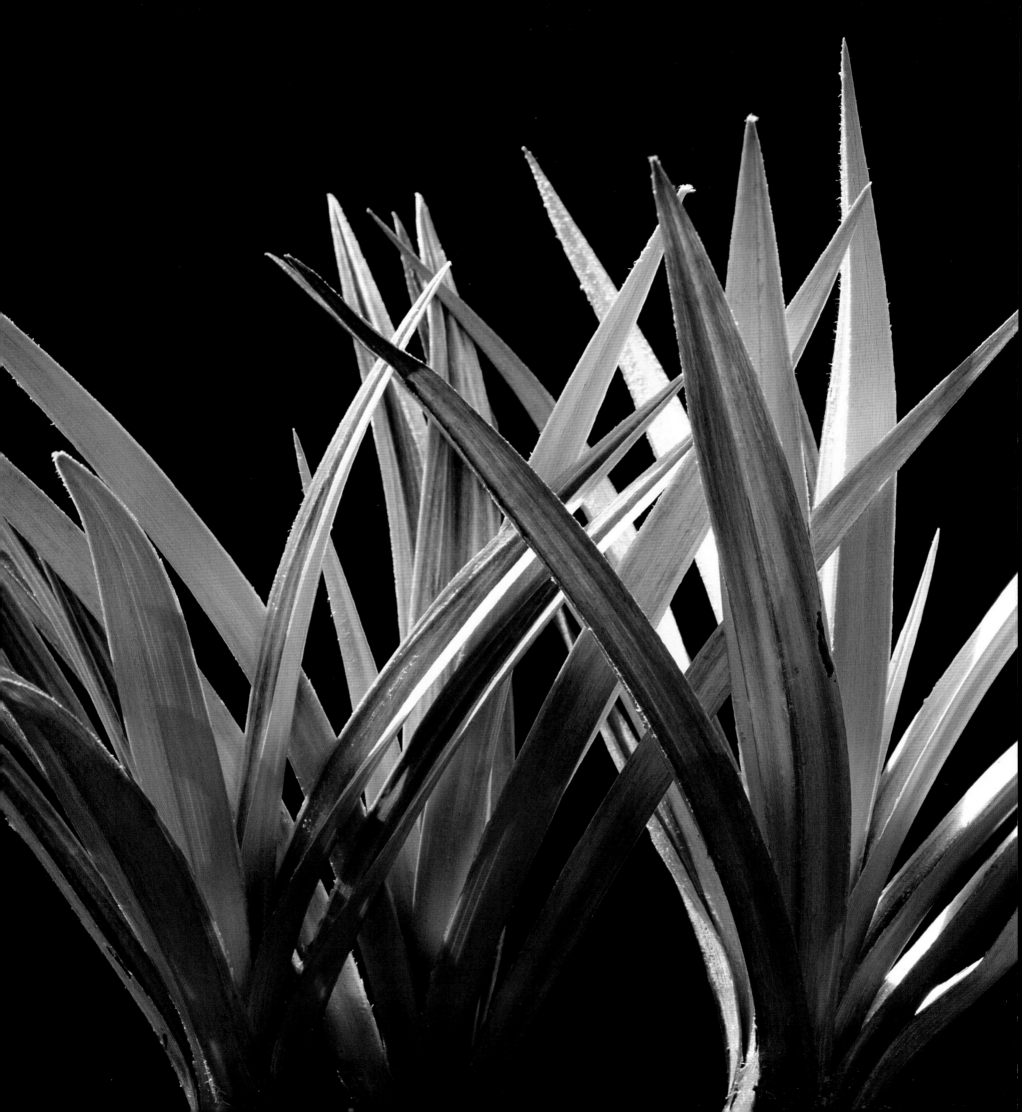

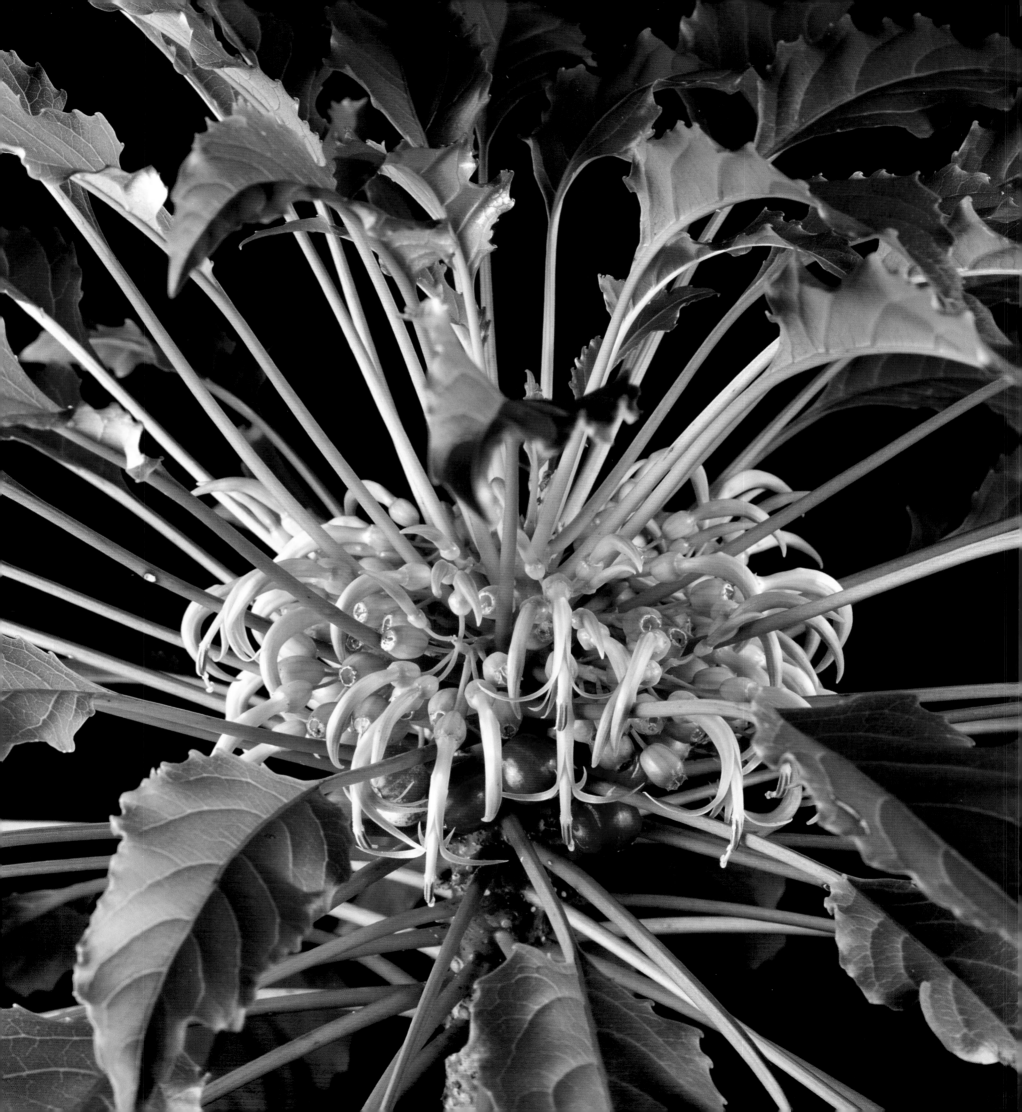

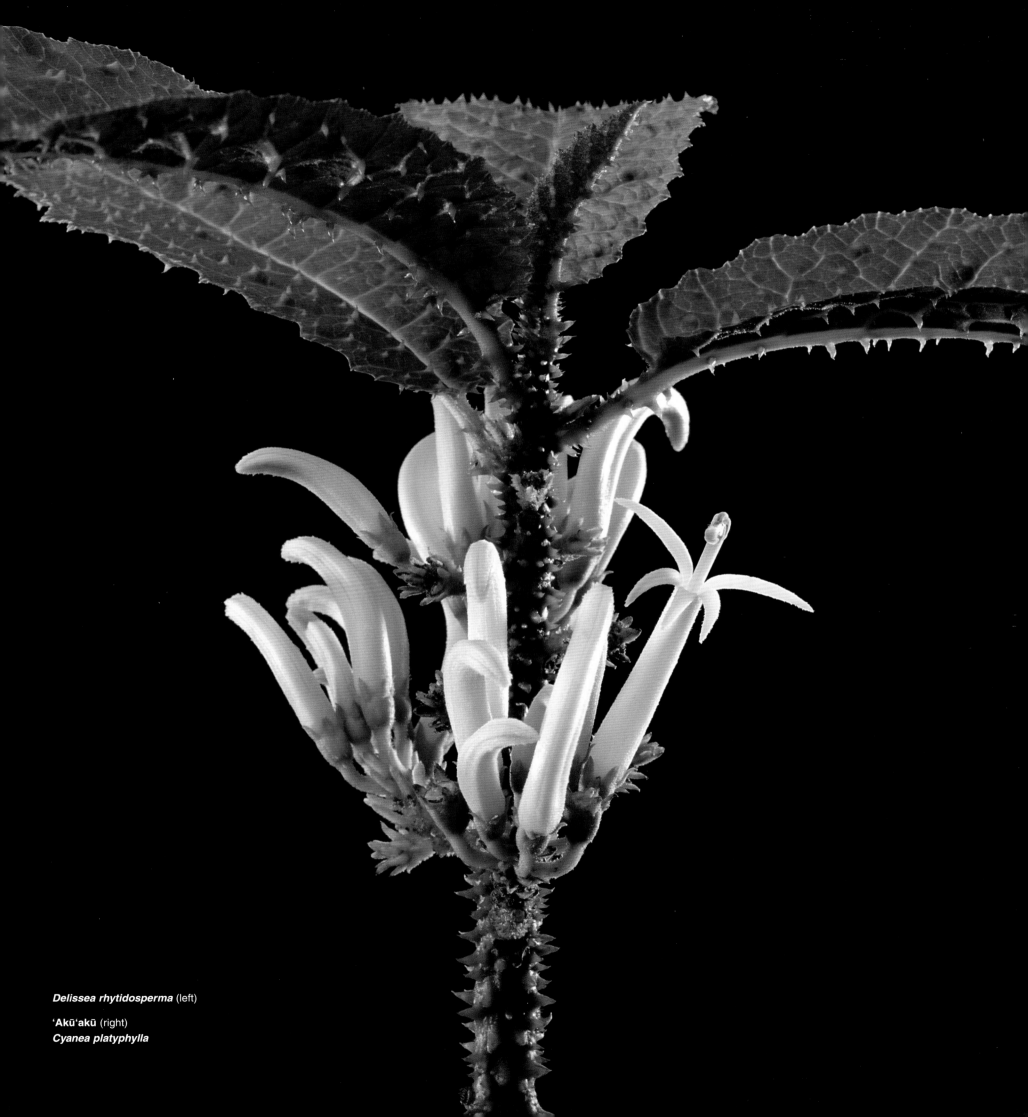

Delissea rhytidosperma (left)

'Akū'akū (right)
Cyanea platyphylla

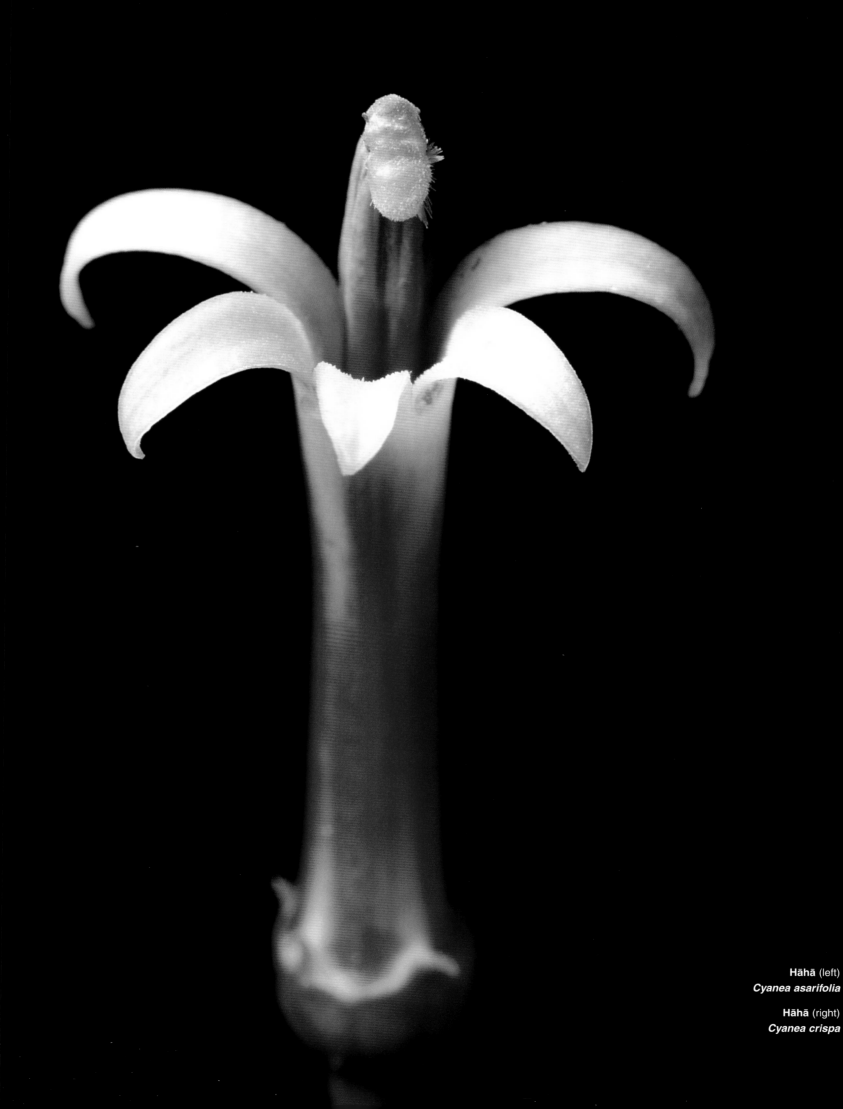

Hāhā (left)
Cyanea asarifolia

Hāhā (right)
Cyanea crispa

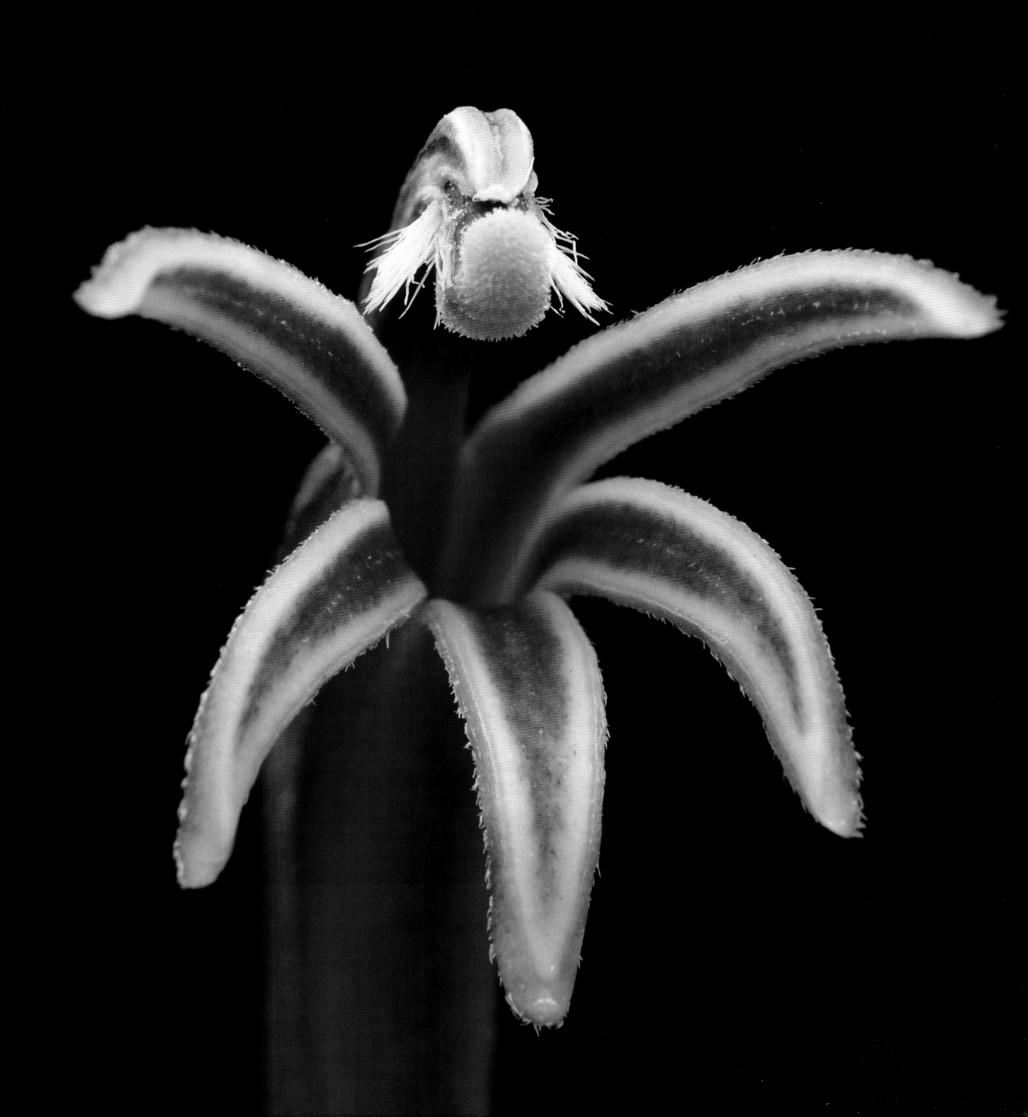

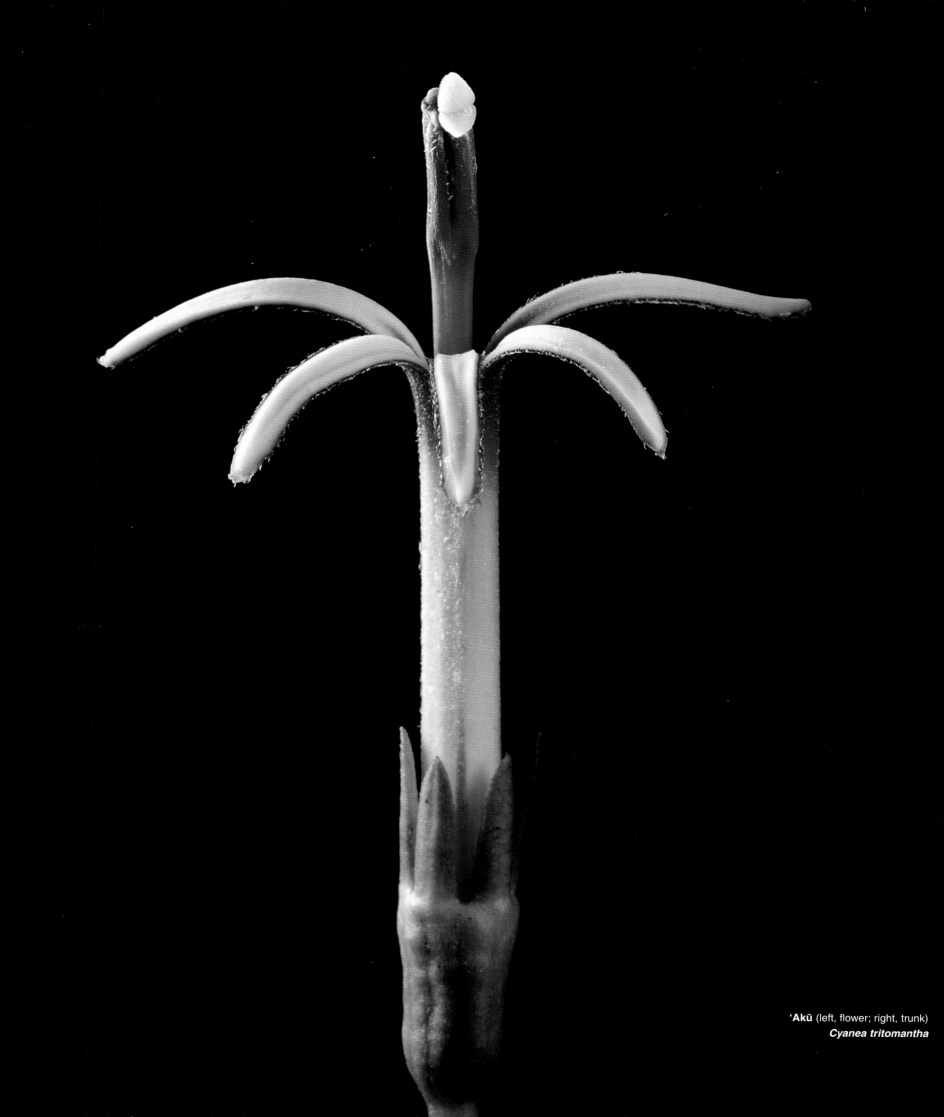

'Akū (left, flower; right, trunk)
Cyanea tritomantha

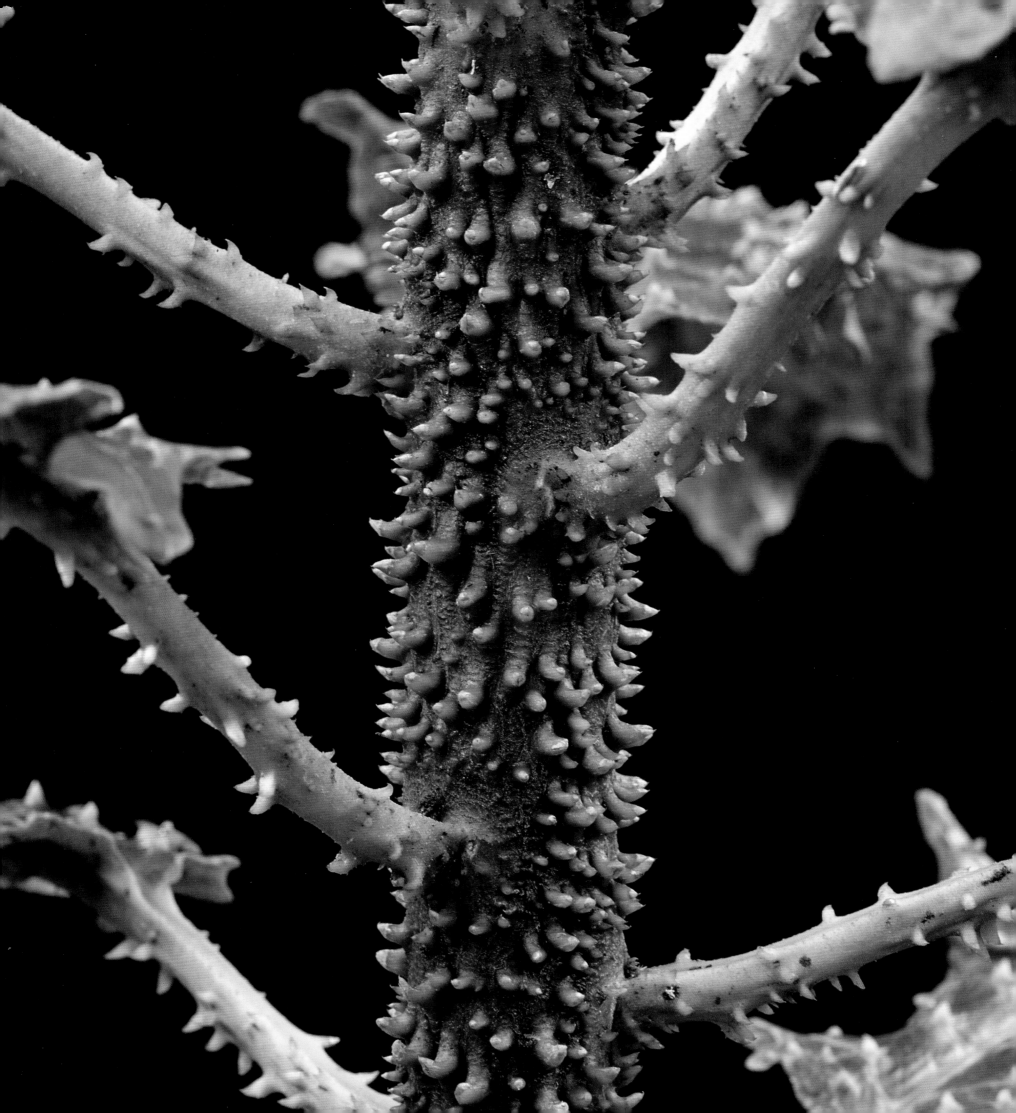

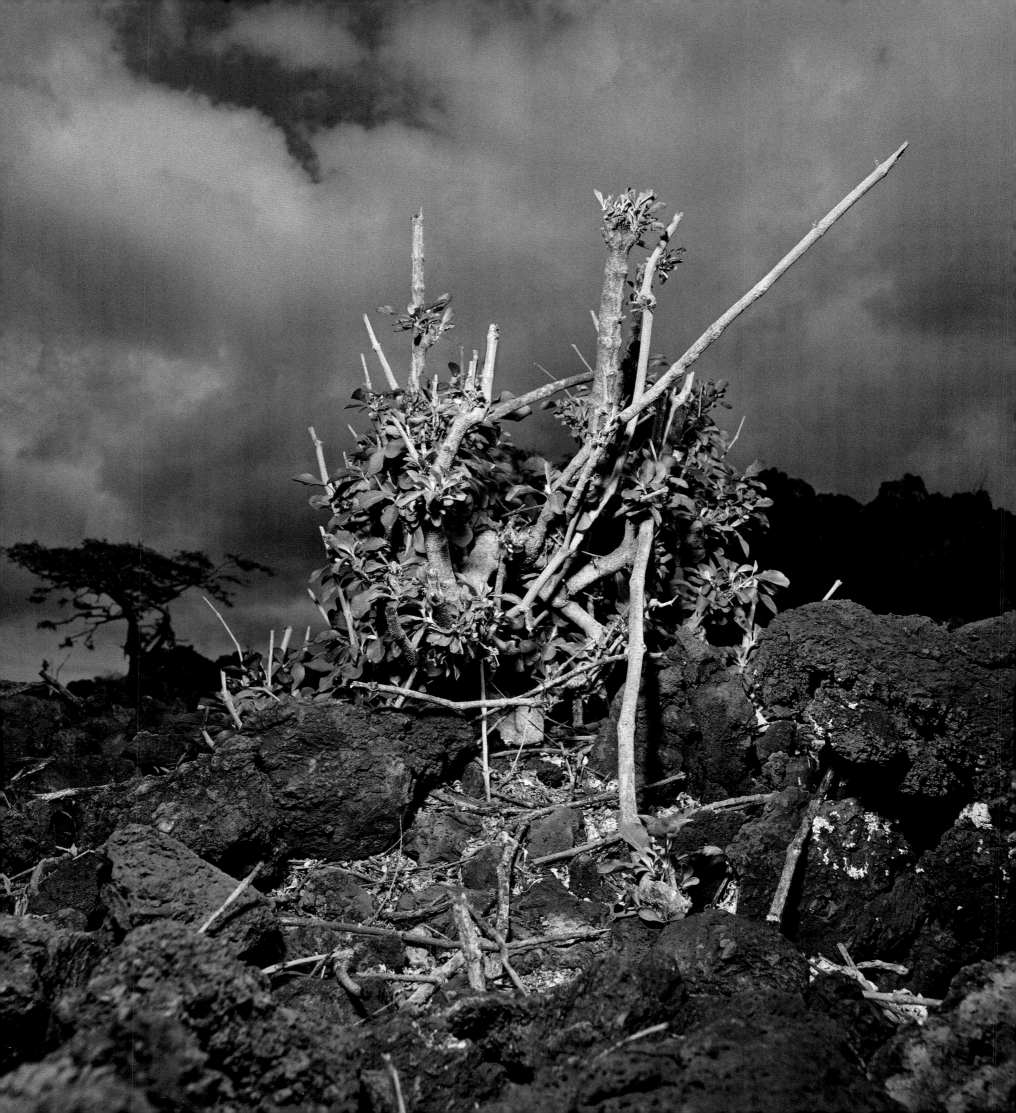

O kau ke anoano ia'u kualono Fear falls upon me on the mountain top
He ano no ka pō hāne'e aku Fear of the passing night
He ano no ka pō hāne'e mai Fear of the night approaching
He ano no ka pō pihapiha Fear of the pregnant night
He ano no ka ha'iha'i Fear of the breach of the law
—from *The Kumulipo*

INVASION/PRESERVATION

by David Liittschwager

I have grown to love the native forests of Hawai'i and am appalled by the extent to which they have been damaged. Of all the destruction we have witnessed in the Hawaiian native forest, the most graphic example is damage done by feral animals. On the facing page is a photograph of an *Achyranthes splendens* var. *splendens* (a kind of amaranth) that has been chewed up by deer. Neither deer nor any other mammalian herbivore are native to Hawai'i. The native plants of Hawai'i have evolved in the absence of this kind of assault, and they lack the ability to protect themselves or recover from such continued and extreme pressure. This *Achyranthes* is trying to grow in a place called Pu'u o Kali, which is on the dry side of East Maui just above the town of Kīhei. A pioneer of bare lava, this *Achyranthes* found a refuge where almost nothing else can grow and made itself a home. Now it is being lost to an invasion entirely of our own making, a result of our careless importation of thousands of plants and animals from other parts of the world.

The most harmful agents of destruction are quieter, and, in the earliest stages of their rampage, less obvious: the proliferation of habitat-altering species of non-native plants poses the biggest threat to the native forests of Hawai'i. These plants change the very structure of the ecosystem. Some of these plants were brought to Hawai'i purposely— as garden ornamentals, for example. Others came in a manner that seems rather innocent, such as on the sole of a hiker's boot. Once they begin to take hold in Hawai'i, they obliterate the native diversity. The aggressive alien plants exploit disturbed habitats and thrive in the absence of limiting factors such as harsh seasons, certain predators, and competition for resources. An aggressive alien that arrives from another place has left behind the other members and circumstances of its community that keep it in balance with its surroundings.

Feral animals and the spread of aggressive alien plants are not separate problems. A pig that gorges on the fruit of the non-native strawberry guava will spend the next twenty-four hours disturbing the native vegetation and spreading an immense quantity of viable seed throughout the forest. Non-native birds are also an excellent dispersal mechanism for non-native plants. The same deer that are chewing the *Achyranthes* promote the growth of non-native grasses by breaking up the lava with their hooves and adding nutrients through their droppings, thereby creating a medium that supports the growth of non-native grasses. Next will come the cows, which will do more trampling and add more

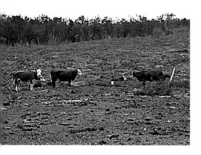 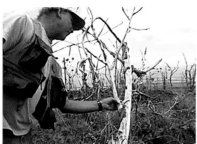 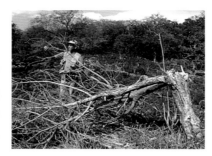 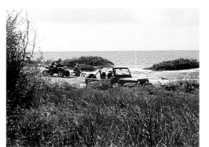 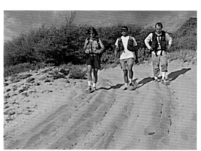

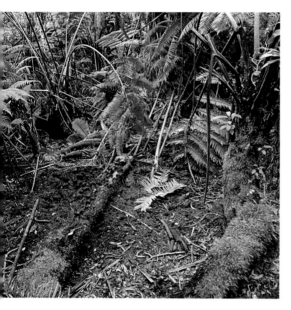

nutrients. Unless we intervene, this pattern will create the circumstances for the extinction of this *Achyranthes*.

The photographs above and left show damage to the native environment, past and present, by cattle, deer, pigs, and off-road vehicles. We were told that 10 percent of the dryland forest still remains. But after seeing many "dryland forests" that looked little like forests, as the understory had been lost and trees were few and far between, this estimate seems optimistic. The dryland forest is considered the most diverse of all Hawaiian forest types. We observed that it is also the most damaged.

Cattle in the lands of Puʻu Waʻawaʻa District on the island of Hawaiʻi have eaten most of the understory, preventing the forest from recovering on its own. This area has also been overrun by fire-adapted non-native grasses (especially the nefarious fountain grass, the death of the dryland forest), which are fast-growing annuals that bear large amounts of seed. When the grass has dried out, the fuel load builds. The dead grass burns quickly and fire sweeps across the forest, destroying much in its path—yet the grass itself flourishes, for its seed, scattered in the soil, has been protected. These grasses may be the nail in the coffin for this area's rare plants and animals because the grasses' presence almost guarantees the obliteration of the remaining forest by wildfire.

Steve Perlman is shown in Puʻu Waʻawaʻa (top, second from left) with the skeleton of the last known wild *hau kuahiwi (Hibiscadelphus hualalaiensis)*, which died in 1992. This species, whose small, elegant flowers mature from light green to burnt orange, was lost to cattle grazing. The last tree was within a small fenced area and was not eaten, but the protection came too late—there were not enough of these trees to sustain the species in the wild. Today, *hau kuahiwi* only exists in botanical gardens. (A photograph of a botanical garden specimen appears on page 76.) In the next picture Steve is standing with the remains of a *maʻo hau hele (Hibiscus*

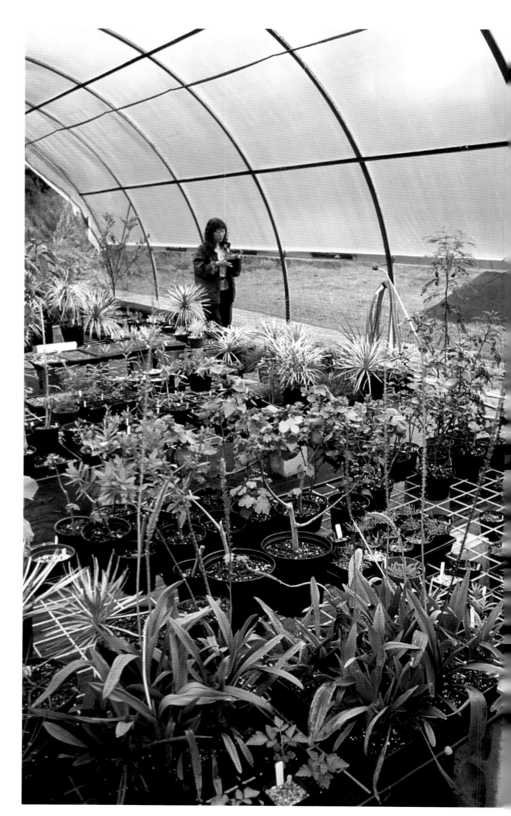

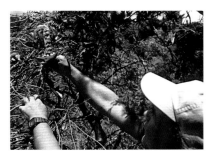 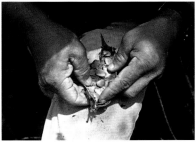 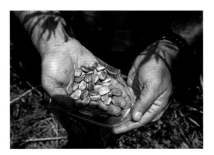 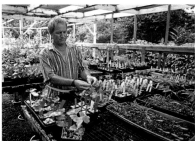 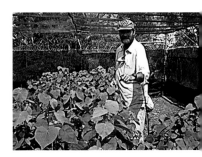

brackenridgei subsp. *brackenridgei)*, the Hawaiian state flower, which has been knocked over by deer. Fewer than 100 plants remain in the wild.

Recreational off-road-vehicle use is very harmful to the plants and animals of the coast. Above (top, fourth from left) is a scene from Ka'ena Point, a conservation area on O'ahu. The next photograph shows deep ruts in the sand dunes of Polihale on Kaua'i. Both of these areas are home to the different color variations of the 'ohai (*Sesbania tomentosa;* see page 177), a bush or small tree with bright blooms. The place where the 'ohai grows at South Point on the island of Hawai'i is suffering the same fate.

In our time in Hawai'i one of the most disturbing sights we witnessed was that of pig damage in the native forest. It looked as if a rototiller had churned everything up. The pigs had been rooting for earthworms and knocking down and eating the hearts of native tree ferns, creating mud puddles in which mosquitoes can breed (despite the prolific rainfall, Hawaiian rainforests have little or no standing water). Their snuffling had exposed bare ground in which non-native species of aggressive weeds can take hold and cause serious erosion on steep slopes that receive 100 or more inches of rainfall annually.

Because of the great number of plants that have become extremely rare, any hope of recovery depends upon the collection of genetic material, propagation, and reintroduction. In an effort to stave off extinction and provide plants for reintroduction to protected areas, several greenhouses specializing in rare and endangered plants are in operation, such as the Volcano Rare Plant Facility on Hawai'i where Patty Moriyasu specializes in cultivating the Mauna Loa Silversword (left).

The photographs above show Steve Perlman collecting seed from a wild 'āwikiwiki (*Canavalia molokaiensis)*, also known as *puakauhi* or Moloka'i jack bean. He is splitting open the pods and separating the seeds so that they can be grown in the nursery at the National Tropical Botanical Garden on Kaua'i. The collected seeds can then be shared with others working to preserve the native plants of Hawai'i.

Many plants have elevation and temperature preferences. A plant from the uplands may not thrive in a greenhouse at sea level. To meet the needs of particular plants from O'ahu, Bill Garnett (top right) oversees a mid-elevation nursery at Pahole in the Wai'anae Mountains, operated by the Department of Land and Natural Resources of the Division of Forestry and Wildlife.

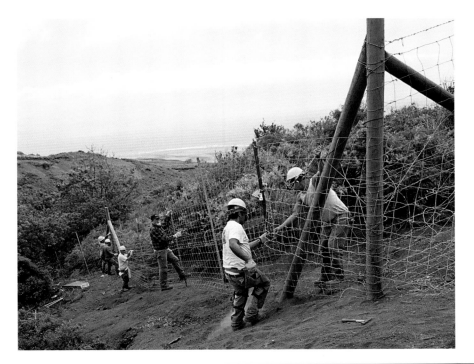

Robert Hobdy and Department of Forestry and Wildlife team construct fenced exclosure to protect native *Gardenia brighamii* (above).

Endangered plant seedlings at National Tropical Botanical Garden (right)

Dave Bender and Susan Middleton planting out endangered species at Limahuli Preserve, Kaua'i (below)

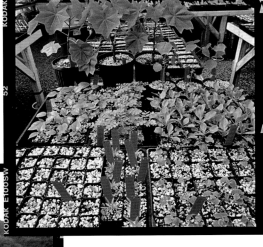

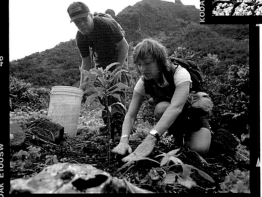

173

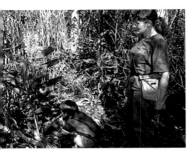 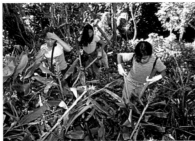 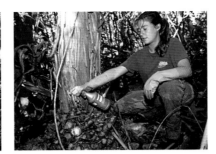 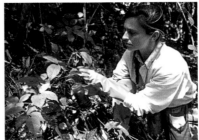 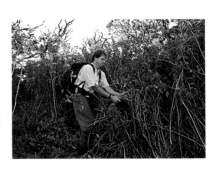

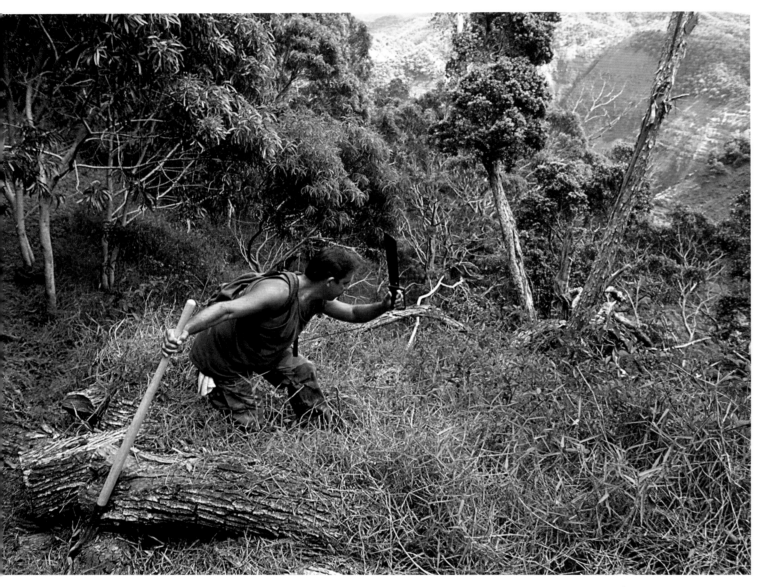

In the wild, fences are the most effective tool to protect the native forest and its rarest components from the ravages of feral mammals. Pigs, goats, sheep, and deer can be completely excluded from an area by the construction and maintenance of an appropriate fence. It is essential that the fence be placed, if not with the complete blessing of the human community in the immediate area, at least with its tolerance and participation—otherwise the goal may be compromised by a resentful citizen, such as a hunter who feels restricted by the fences. The fence in the photograph on page 173 is being built to protect over 200 plantings of the Lāna'i variety of the *nānū* or *nā'ū* (*Gardenia brighamii*). This native Hawaiian gardenia has a rich scent, more subtle and complex than that of most florist-shop flowers I have smelled. The flower we photographed (see page 113) smelled slightly of cinnamon.

Early in our work in Hawai'i we had the opportunity to visit and work in the nursery at the National Tropical Botanical Garden on Kaua'i. There were more endangered species in that nursery than in any other single place I had seen. Eight years later it was still true. It is a living plant collection and seed bank, a genetic safety net, for most of the endangered and rare plants of Hawai'i.

Katie Cassel and the Kōke'e Resource Conservation Program's volunteers and staff help control the growth of non-native plants, Kaua'i; Scott Meidell pulling *Tibouchina***, Maui** (top row).

Zachary Simao removing invasive blackberry (above).

Kay Kokie protecting a native Koa tree seedling from alien weeds (right).

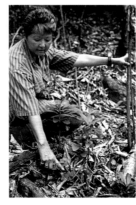 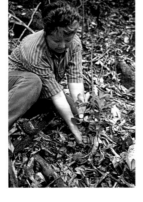

There are several ways to deal with weeds—all of them a great deal of work if one is to be selective about what one removes. There is the mechanical approach (cut it or pull it), the chemical method (spray it or paint it), and the magic bullet—an insect or other organism that can be used as a biological control to limit or eliminate the unwanted species. The latter option has had the least success in Hawai'i. The

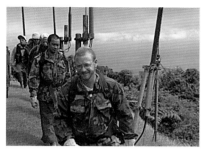 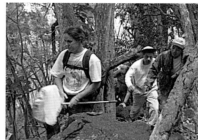 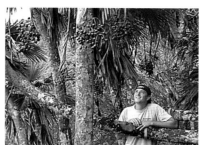 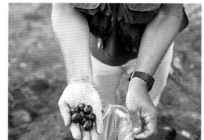

Kapua Kawelo and Army environmental team protecting endangered species on Army land, Oʻahu (page 175, top row)

Cyanea dunbarii **in Mokomoko Gulch, Molokaʻi, being crowded out by alien ginger plants** (below)

Cyanea dunbarii (below right)

history of the use of biological control agents in Hawaiʻi is full of folly and disaster, and goes something like the tale of the old lady that swallowed a fly. For example, mongooses were brought to Hawaiʻi in an effort to control rats, but the mongooses ate many native birds and very few rats because mongooses are diurnal and rats are nocturnal. (This strategy was already known to have failed in Jamaica, but was tried in Hawaiʻi anyway.) A species of carnivorous snail was imported to control an alien snail that was an agricultural pest, yet the imported snail did not solve the pest problem, choosing instead to dine on native snails, which it is now driving toward extinction. In Hawaiʻi, happy endings are not assured. So for the most part the tools of the trade are the old-fashioned ones, with many hands to help.

It does no good to give up in the face of the storm of destruction by aggressive alien plants. Ginger plants, for instance, are used ornamentally in some gardens, but loose in the native forest they become a devastating biological wave, eliminating diversity and smothering all of the native plants in their path. To prevent non-native plants from taking over, a small, spirited contingent goes into battle on a daily basis, armed with pruning shears, machetes, herbicide, and muscle. They are gardeners of the forest. One such gardener is Scott Meidell (page 174, top right), who is doing the only thing known to control *Tibouchina*—pulling it out by hand.

The U.S. Army may seem an unlikely ally in the effort to protect endangered species. However, because of the way the Endangered Species Act is written, the Army is responsible for the continued existence and future well-being of some 80 federally listed endangered species in Hawaiʻi that live on Army land. The Army owns about 20 percent of the island of Oʻahu, on which it carries out training exercises. Training for war damages land that is the habitat of endangered species.

Kapua Kawelo of the U.S. Army's Directorate of Public Works Environmental Division heads the Natural Resources Center on Oʻahu. Kapua and her crew of six have a job description that includes finding, protecting, and collecting seed and/or other genetic material, as well as propagating and outplanting more than 50 endangered plant species. On a trip to ʻŌhikilolo Ridge, part of the Mākua Military Reservation, to photograph the *pamakami* or *ʻolopū*, a rare native violet (*Viola chamissoniana* subsp. *chamissoniana;* see page 147), we saw how effective the Army's efforts at restoration and recovery can be. A fence recently constructed to exclude goats has allowed the native *ʻieʻie (Freycinetia arborea),* a plant that is home to rare damselflies and endangered snails, to flourish once again. The success of baiting for rats was

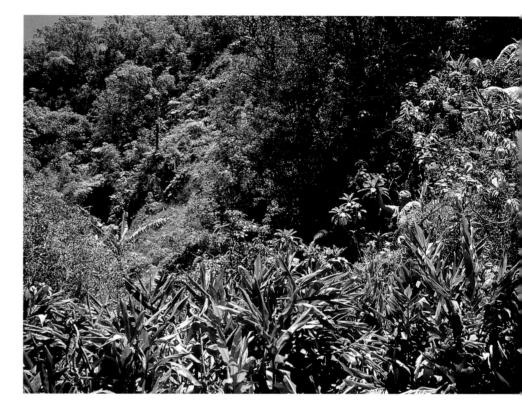

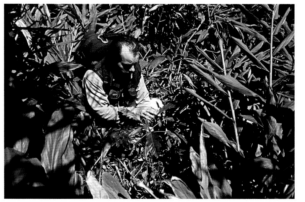 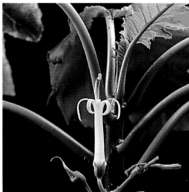

visible in a bumper crop of fruit, the likes of which had not been seen in decades, on the *loulu (Pritchardia kaalae),* an endangered palm.

The tide of destruction can be stopped by halting the importation of new destructive organisms, nurturing native plants and animals, and removing disruptive non-native species. This work can only accomplished by an educated, supportive, and involved community. I continue to be inspired by the enthusiastic efforts of the people I have met in Hawaiʻi. Their affection—their aloha—for the native plants and animals is enormous.

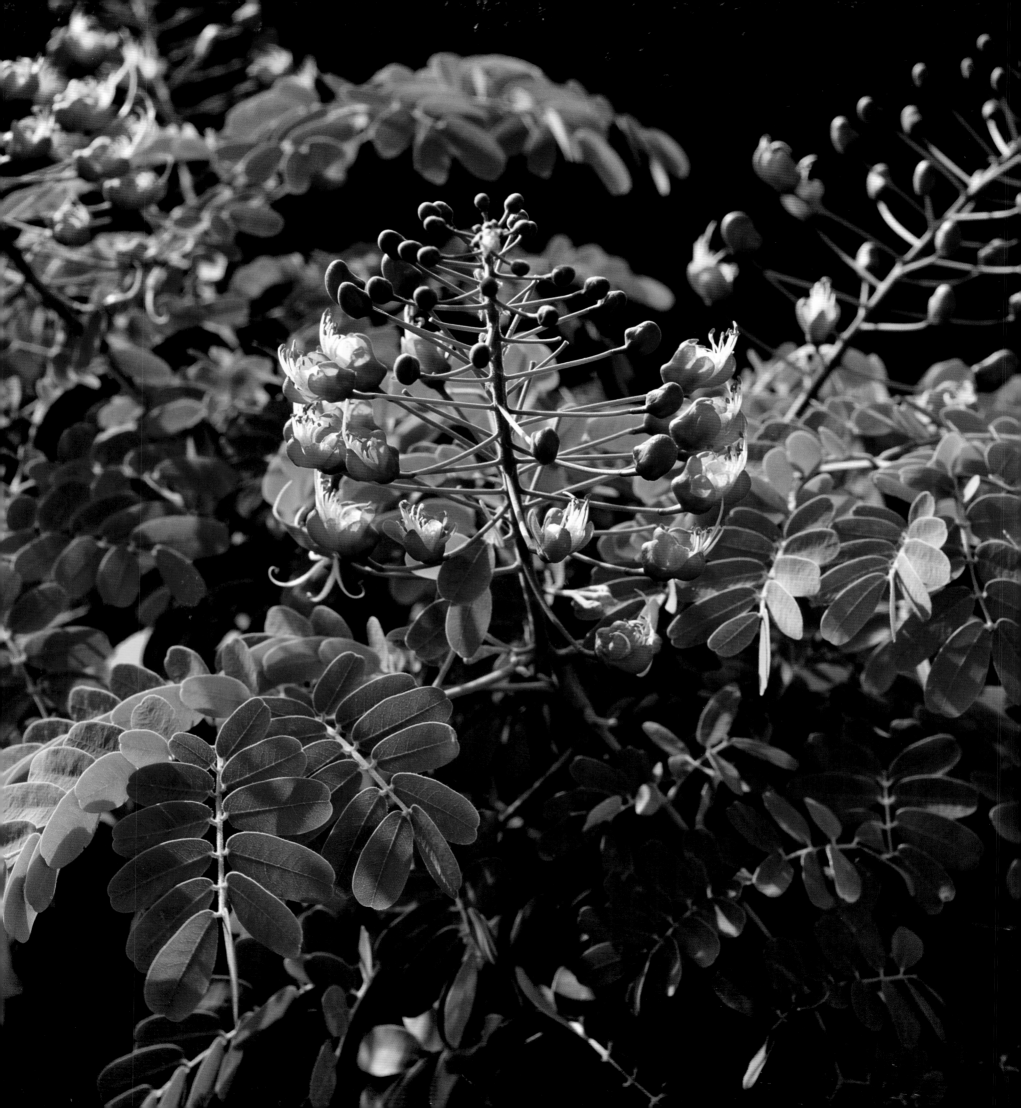

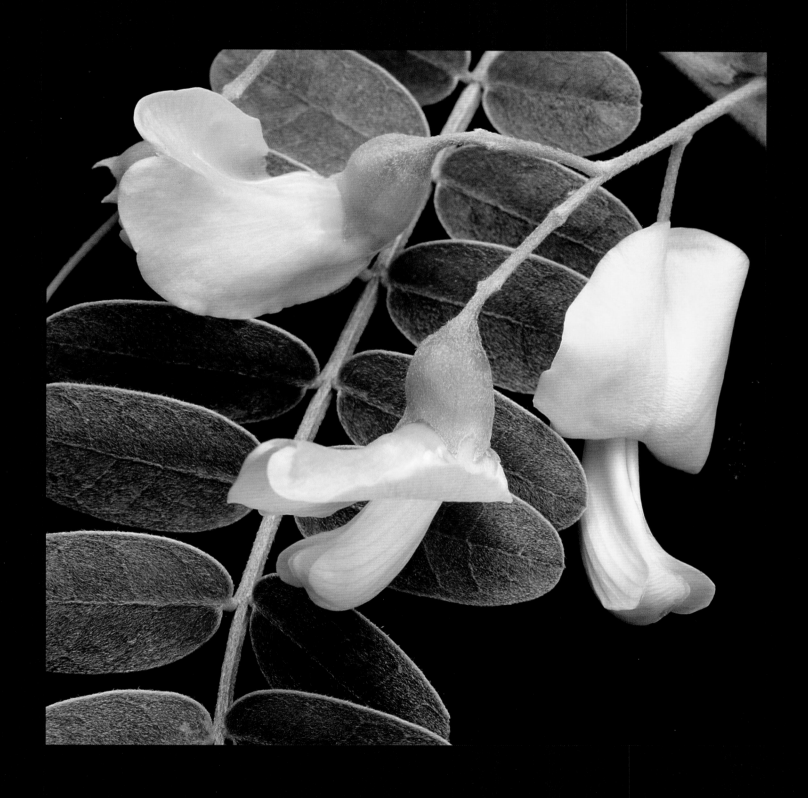

Uhiuhi; Kāwaʻu Kea (left)
Caesalpinia kavaiensis

ʻOhai (right)
Sesbania tomentosa

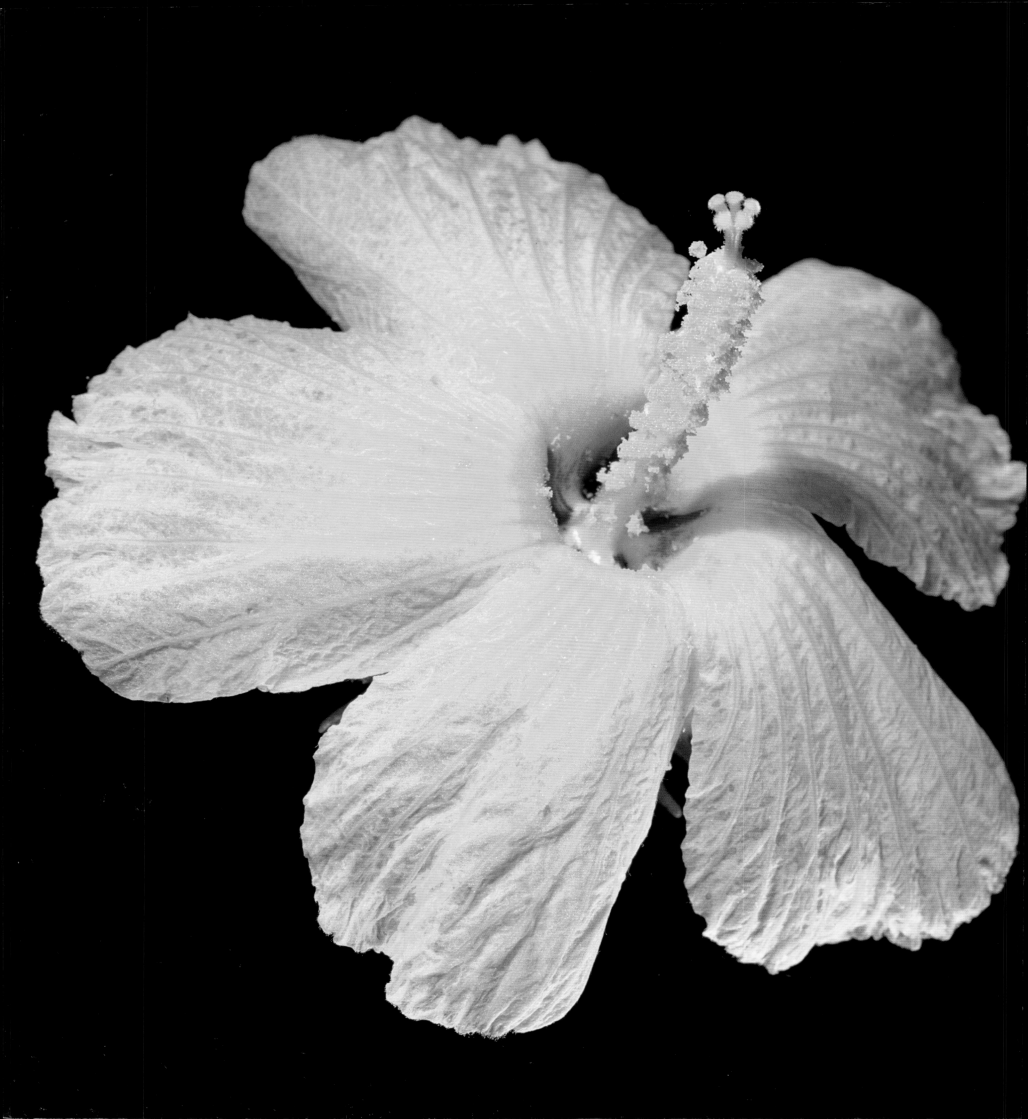

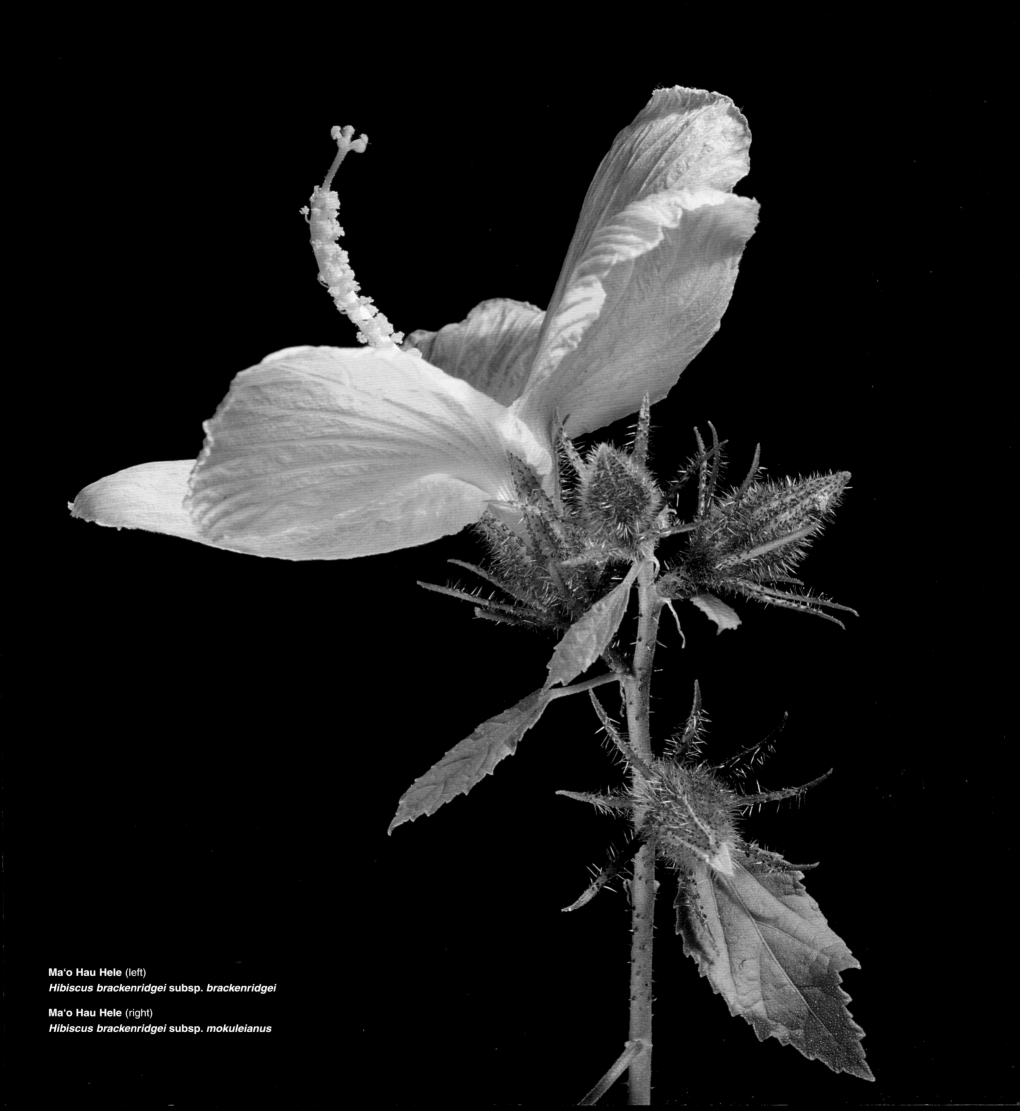

Maʻo Hau Hele (left)
Hibiscus brackenridgei subsp. *brackenridgei*

Maʻo Hau Hele (right)
Hibiscus brackenridgei subsp. *mokuleianus*

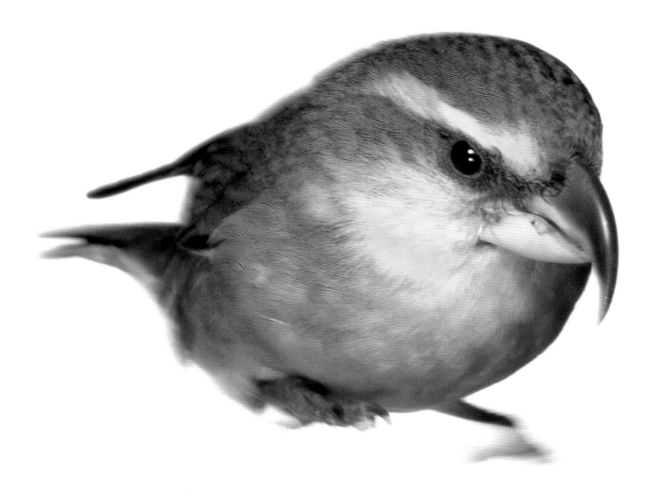

Maui Parrotbill
Pseudonestor xanthophrys

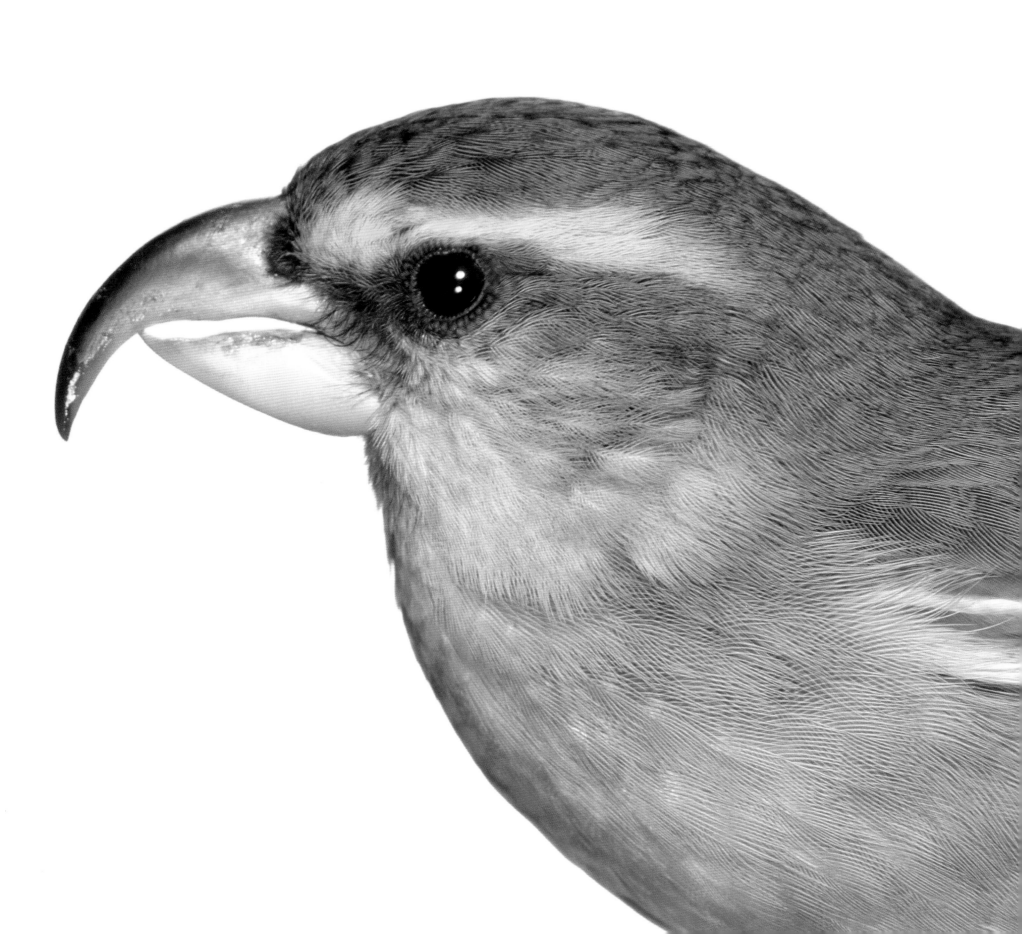

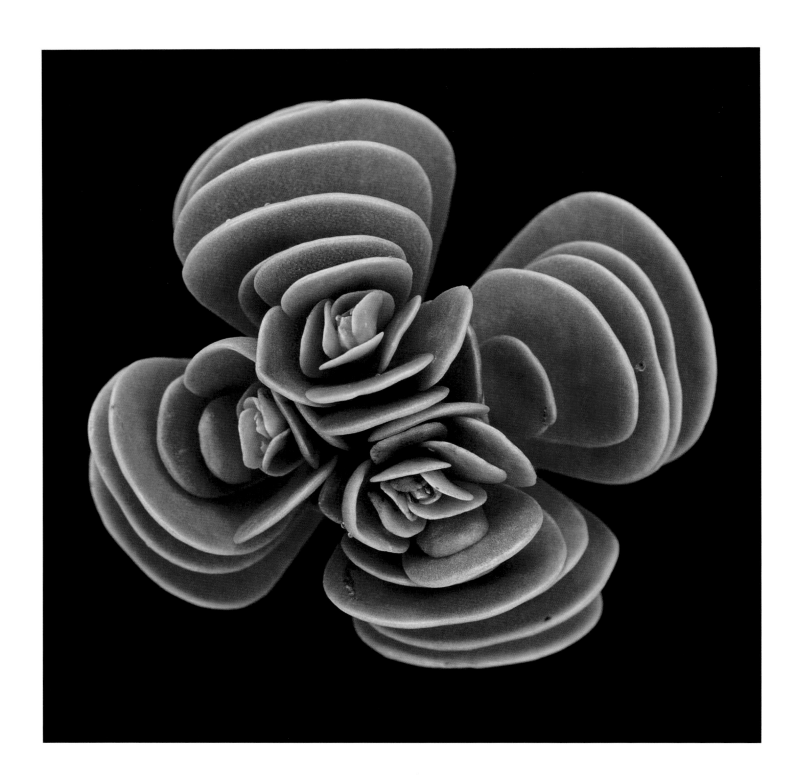

Purslane
ʻIhi
Portulaca molokiniensis

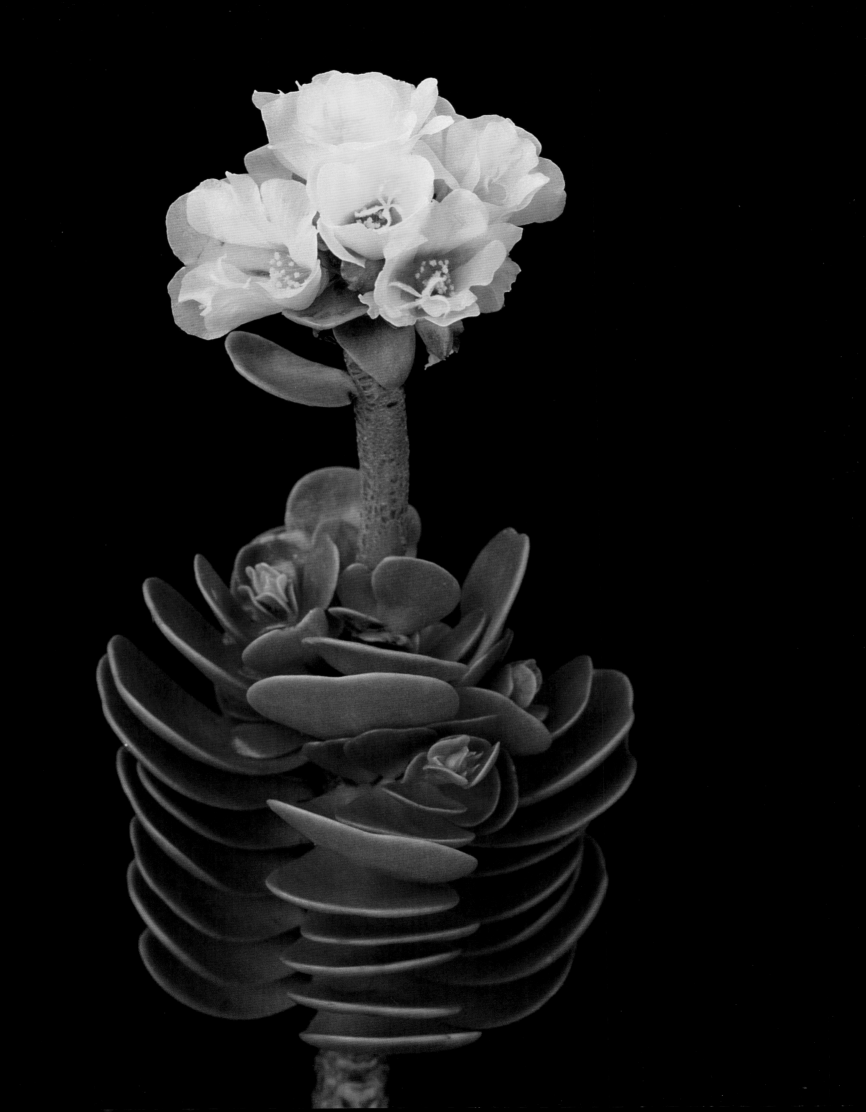

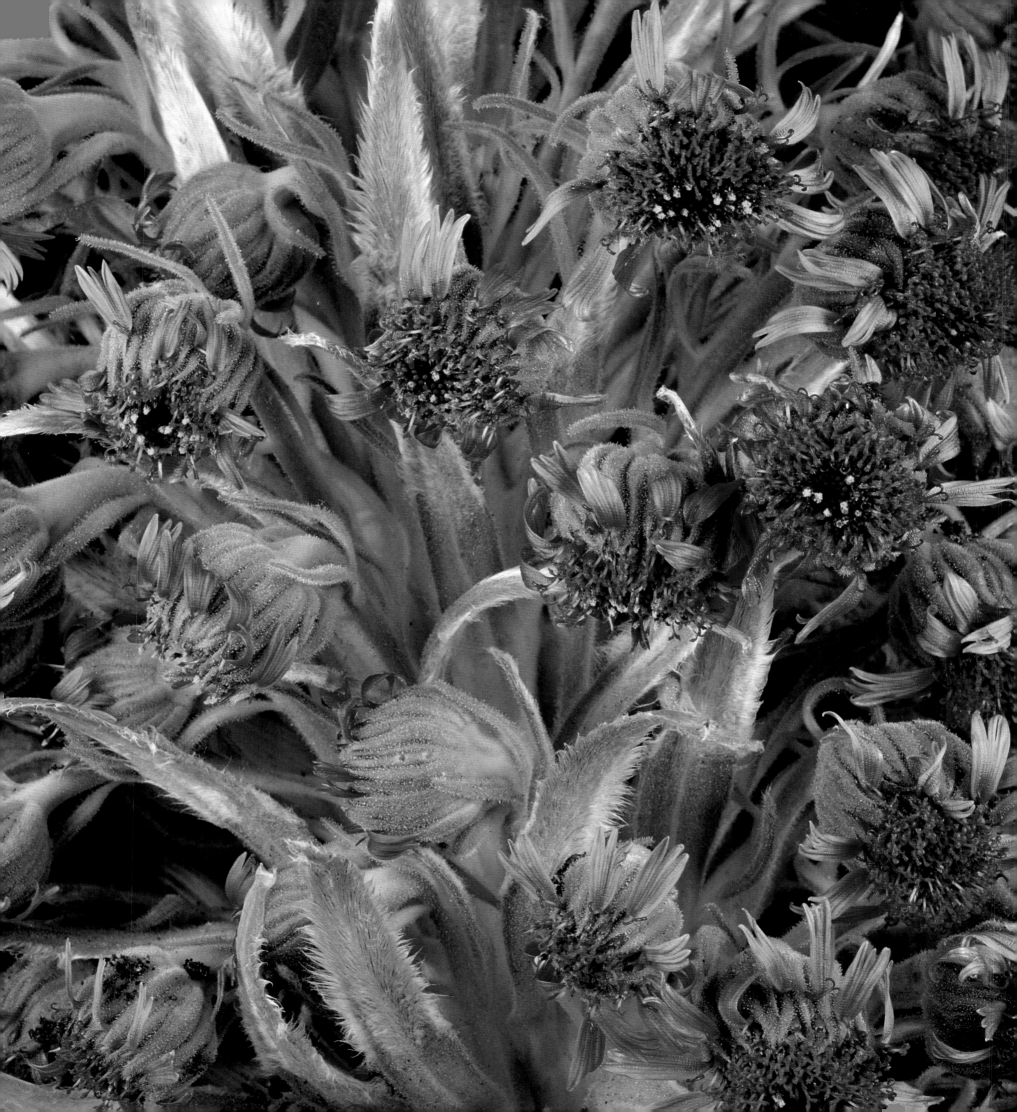

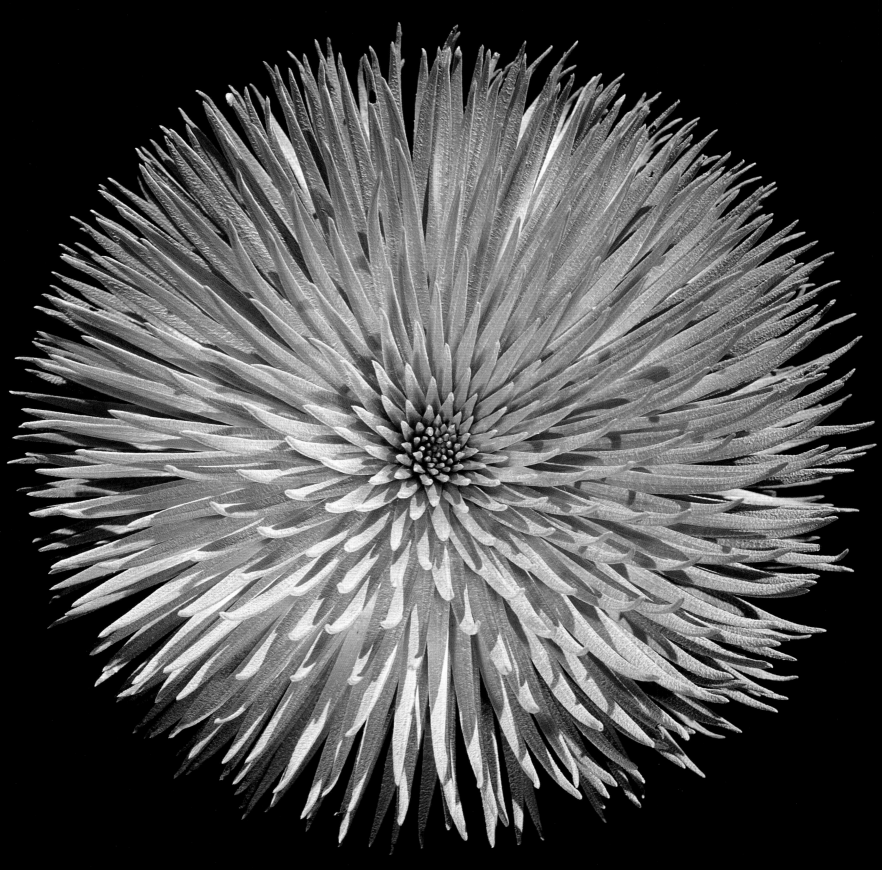

Haleakalā Silversword
(left, flowers; right, whole plant before flowering)
ʻĀhinahina
Argyroxiphium sandwicense* subsp. *macrocephalum

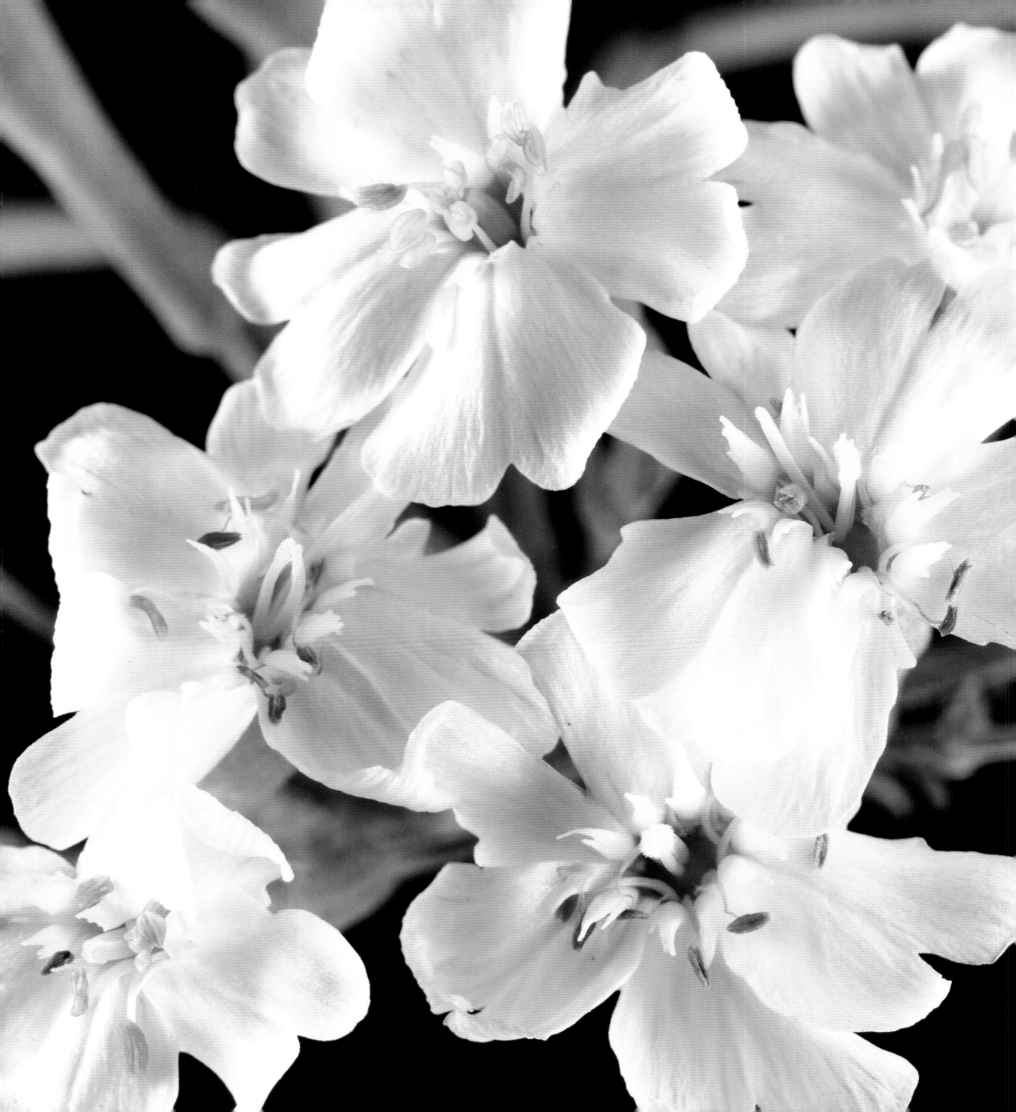

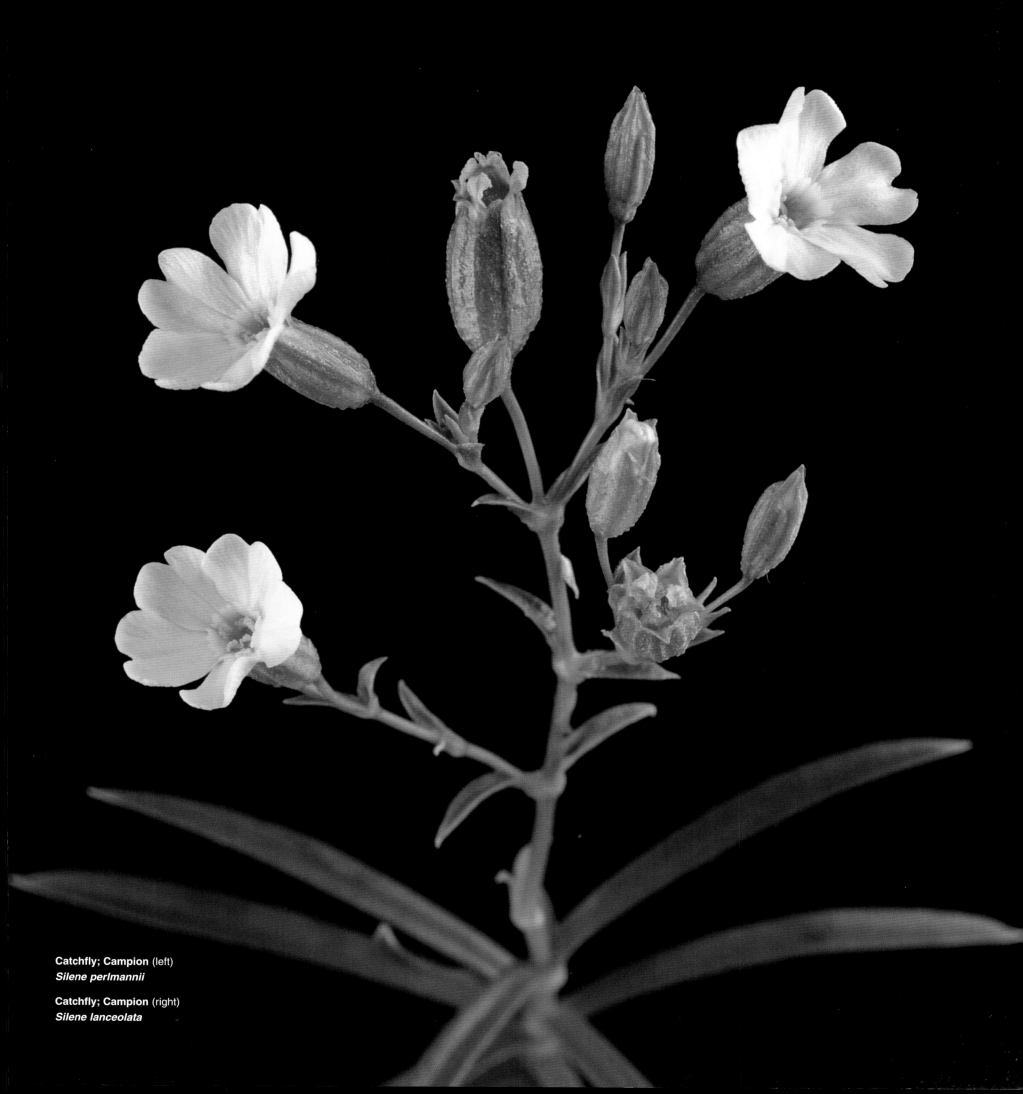

Catchfly; Campion (left)
Silene perlmannii

Catchfly; Campion (right)
Silene lanceolata

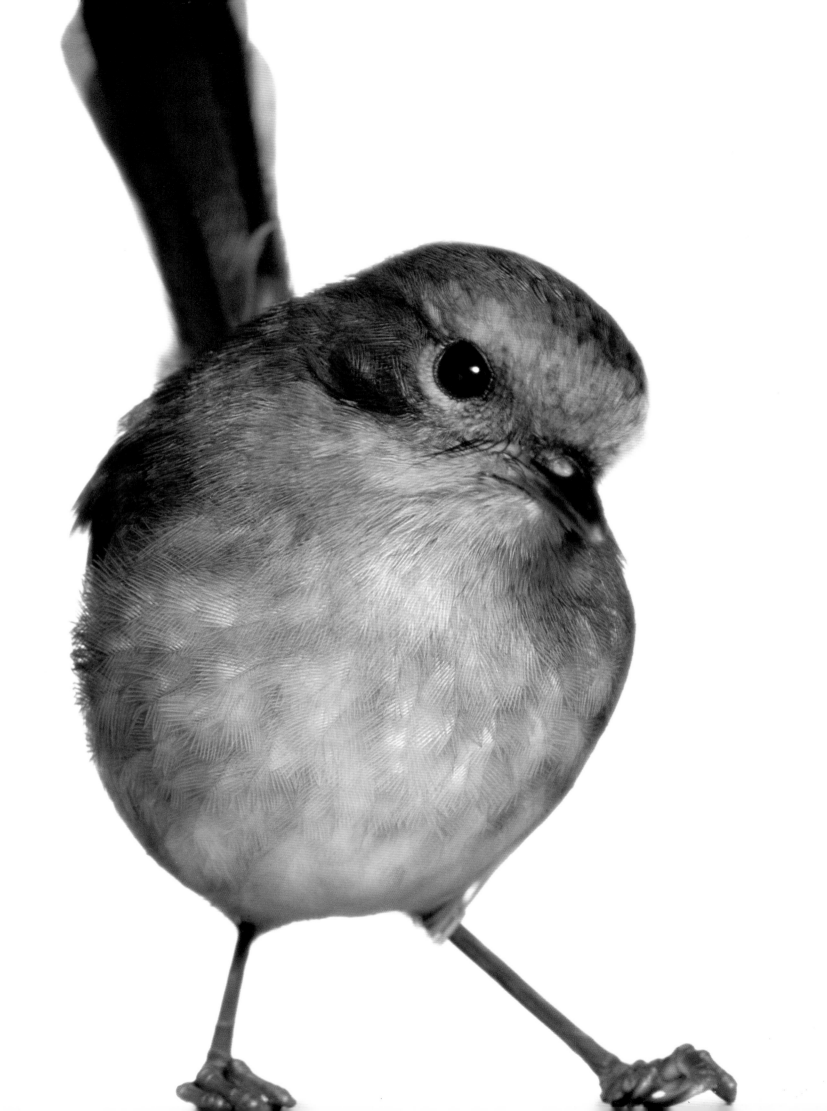

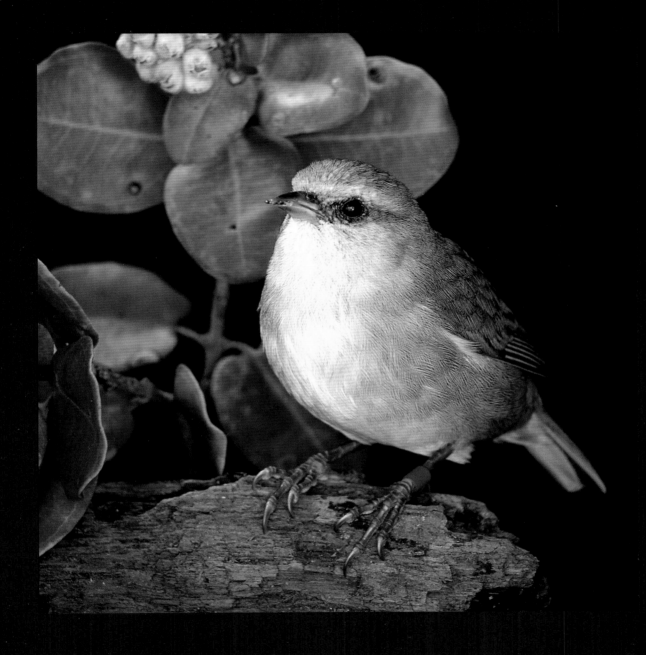

'Elepaio (left)
Chasiempis sandwichensis

Hawai'i Creeper (right)
Oreomystis mana

Small Kaua'i Thrush;
Palmer's Thrush (pages 190–191)
Puaiohi
Myadestes palmeri

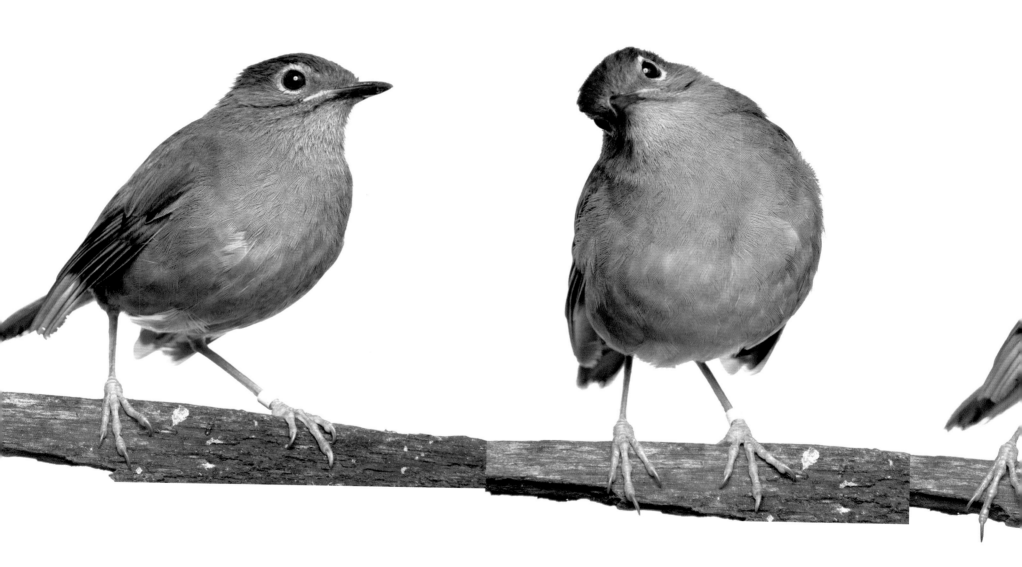

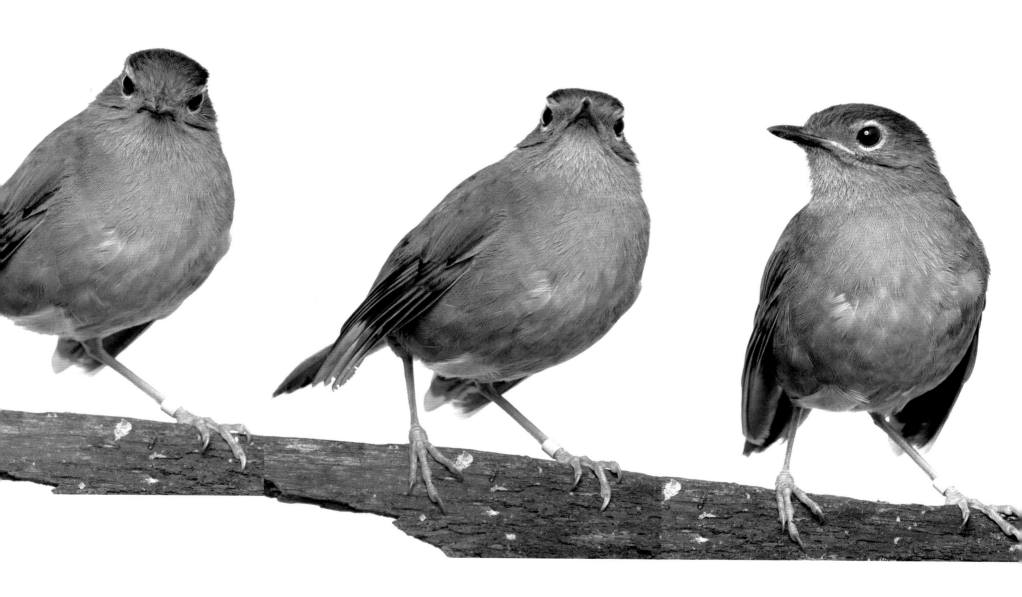

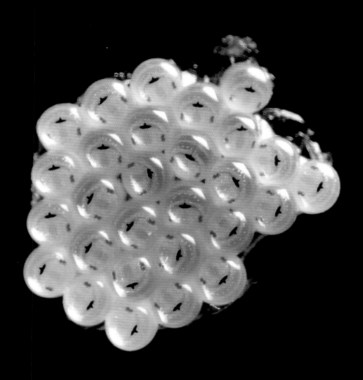
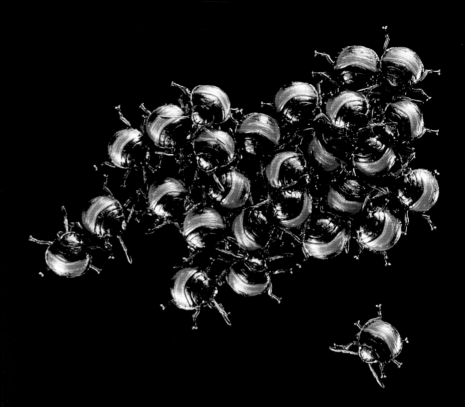
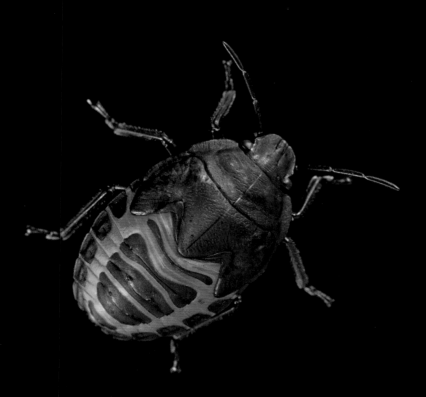
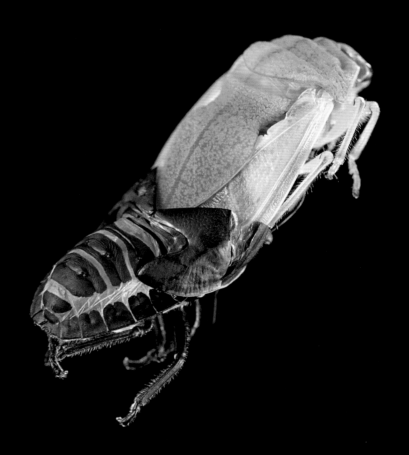

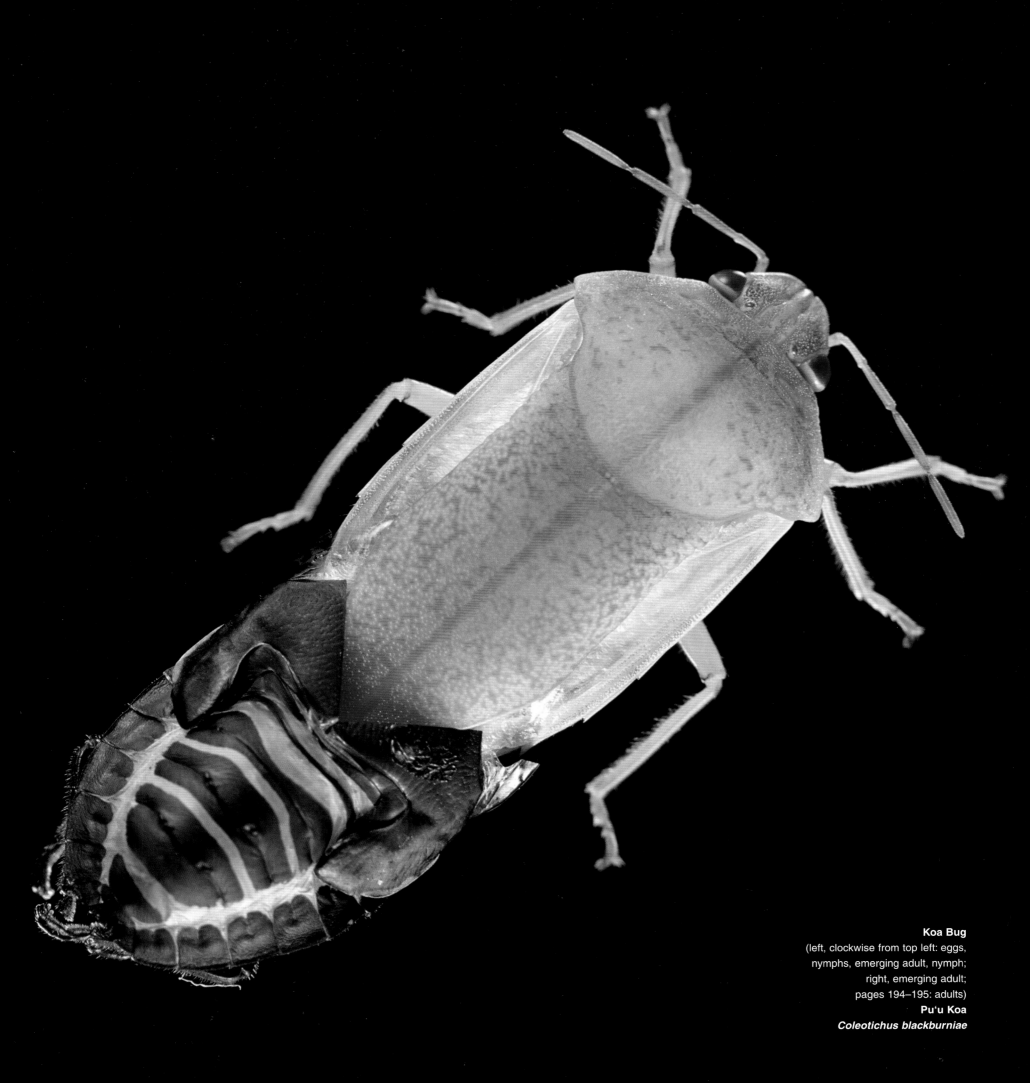

Koa Bug
(left, clockwise from top left: eggs,
nymphs, emerging adult, nymph;
right, emerging adult;
pages 194–195: adults)
Puʻu Koa
Coleotichus blackburniae

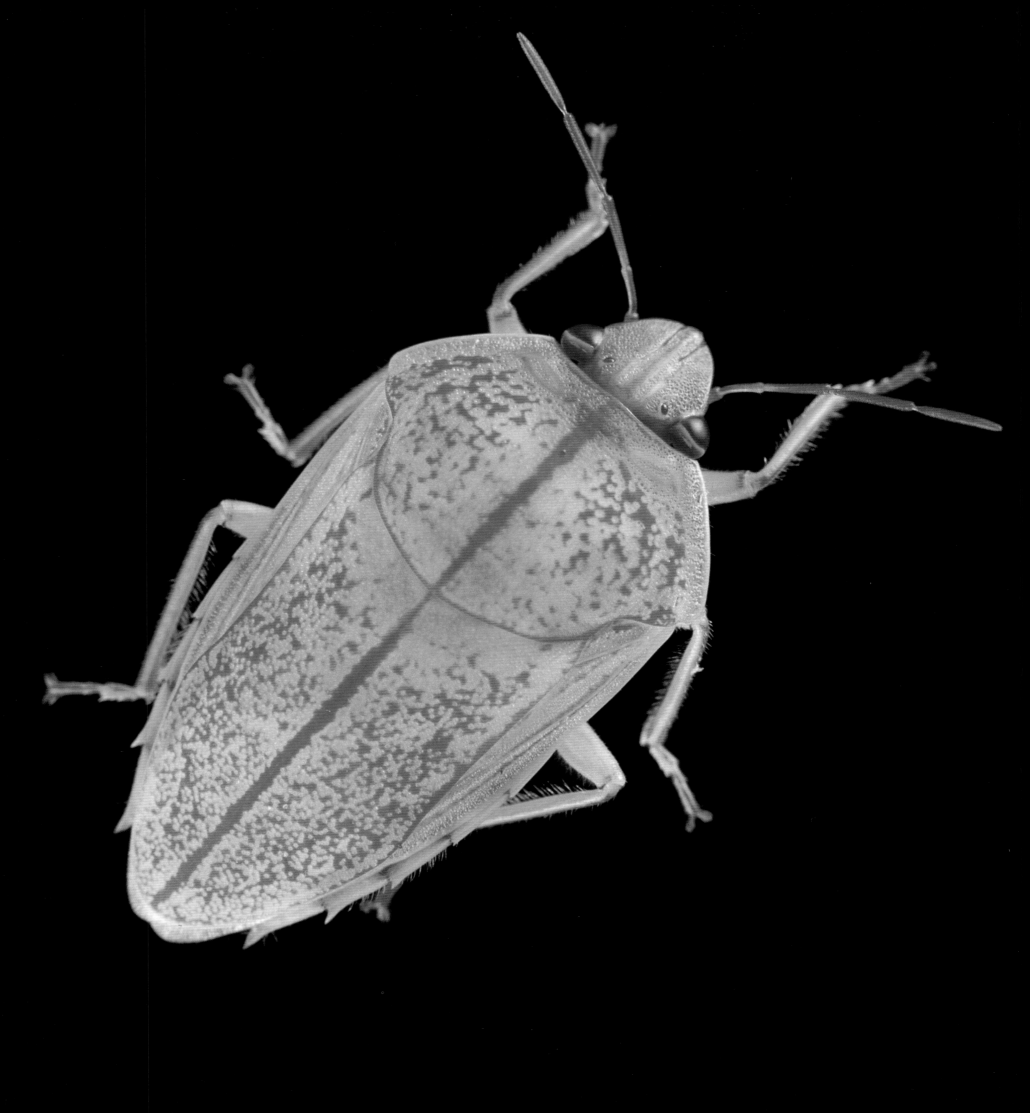

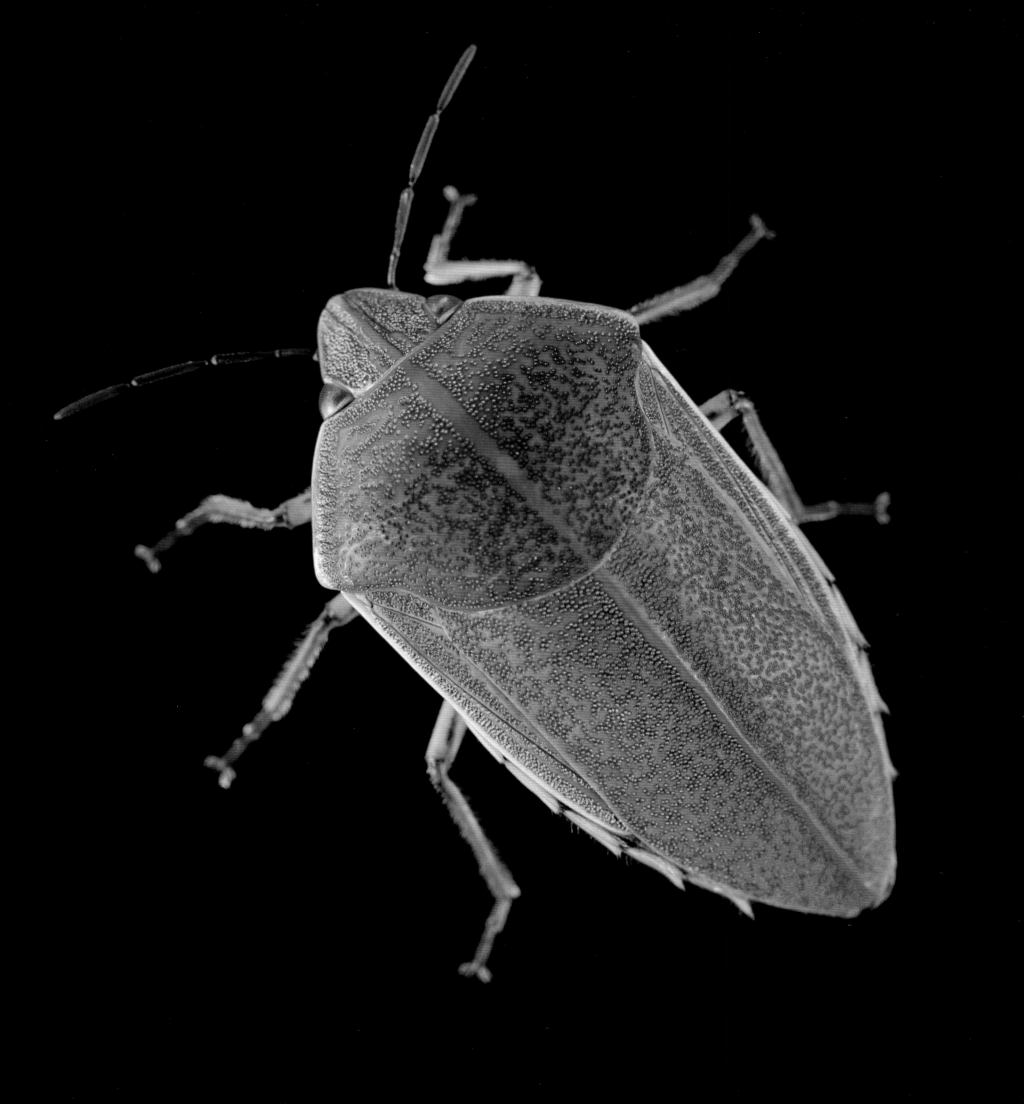

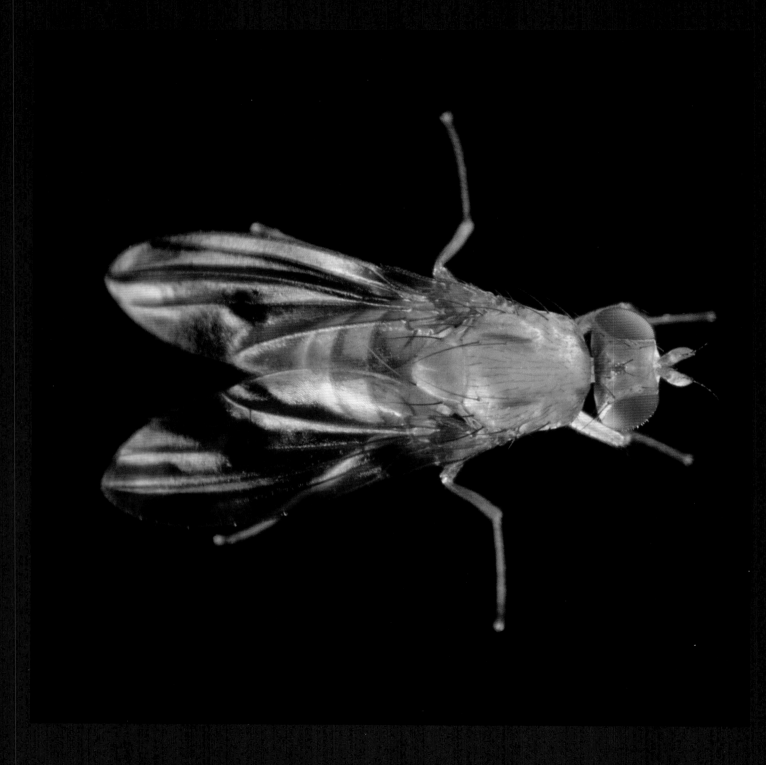

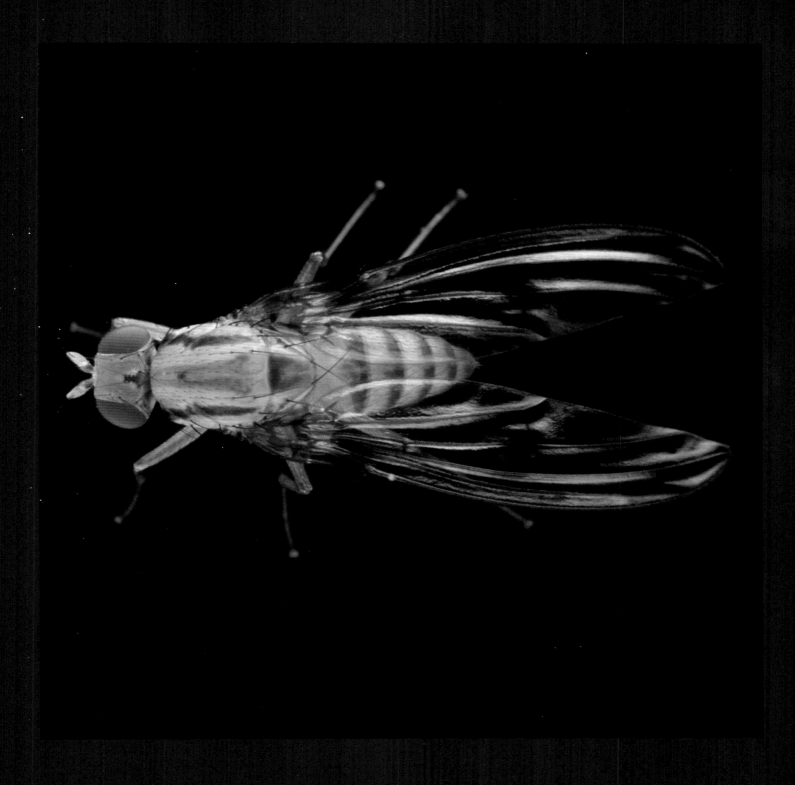

Golden Picture-Wing Bird Lime Tree Fly (left)
Ponalo Pāpala Kēpau
Drosophila ambochila

Pointed Wing Pāpala Picture-Wing Fly (right)
Ponalo Pāpala
Drosophila lanaiensis or relative

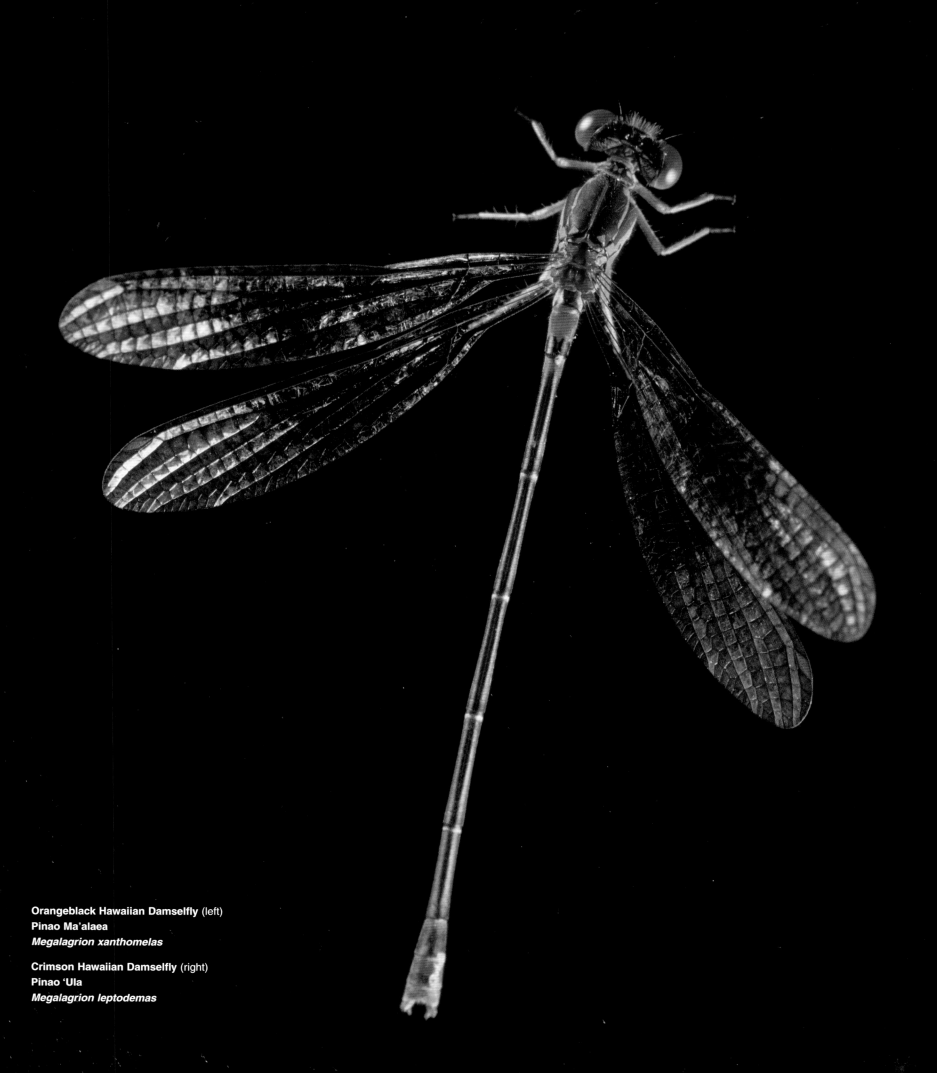

Orangeblack Hawaiian Damselfly (left)
Pinao Ma'alaea
Megalagrion xanthomelas

Crimson Hawaiian Damselfly (right)
Pinao ʻUla
Megalagrion leptodemas

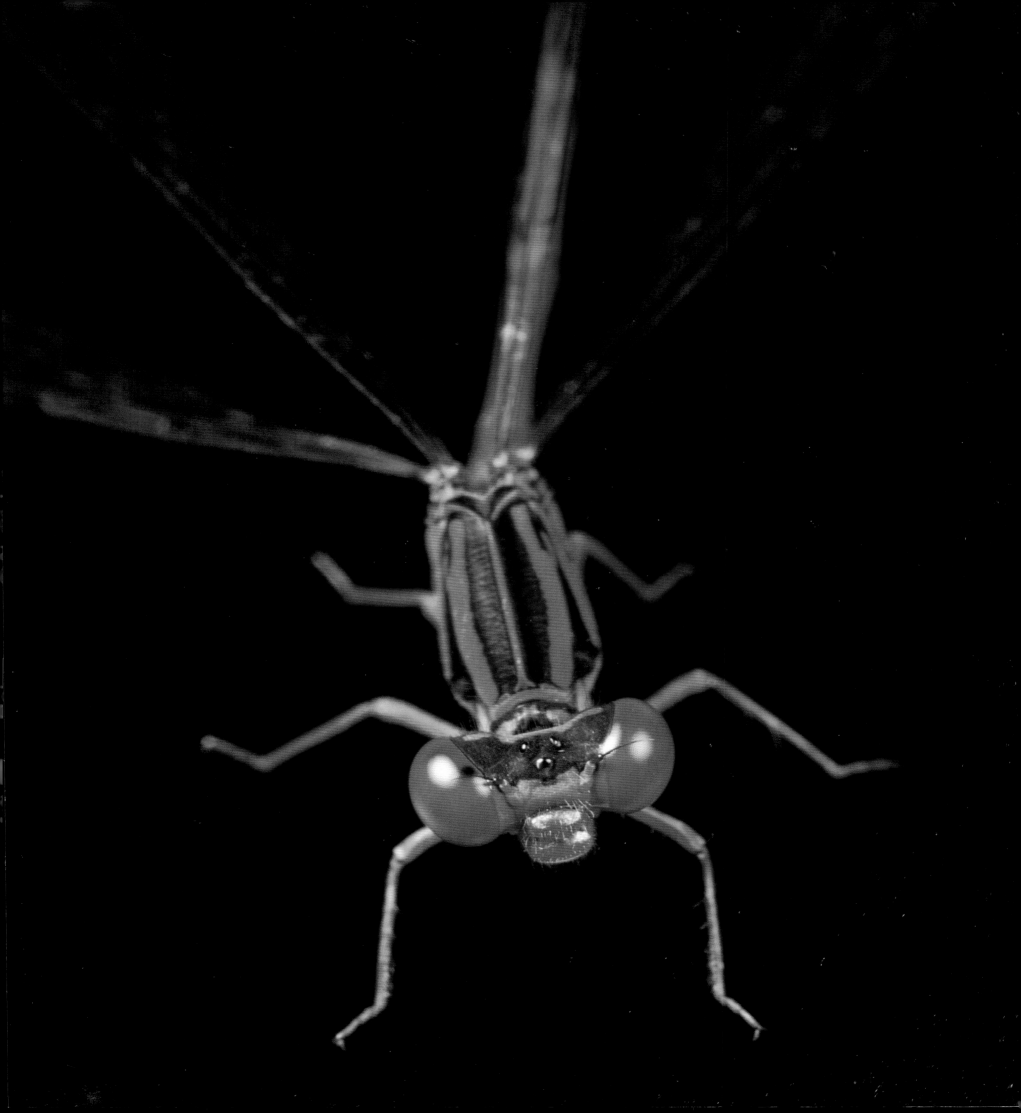

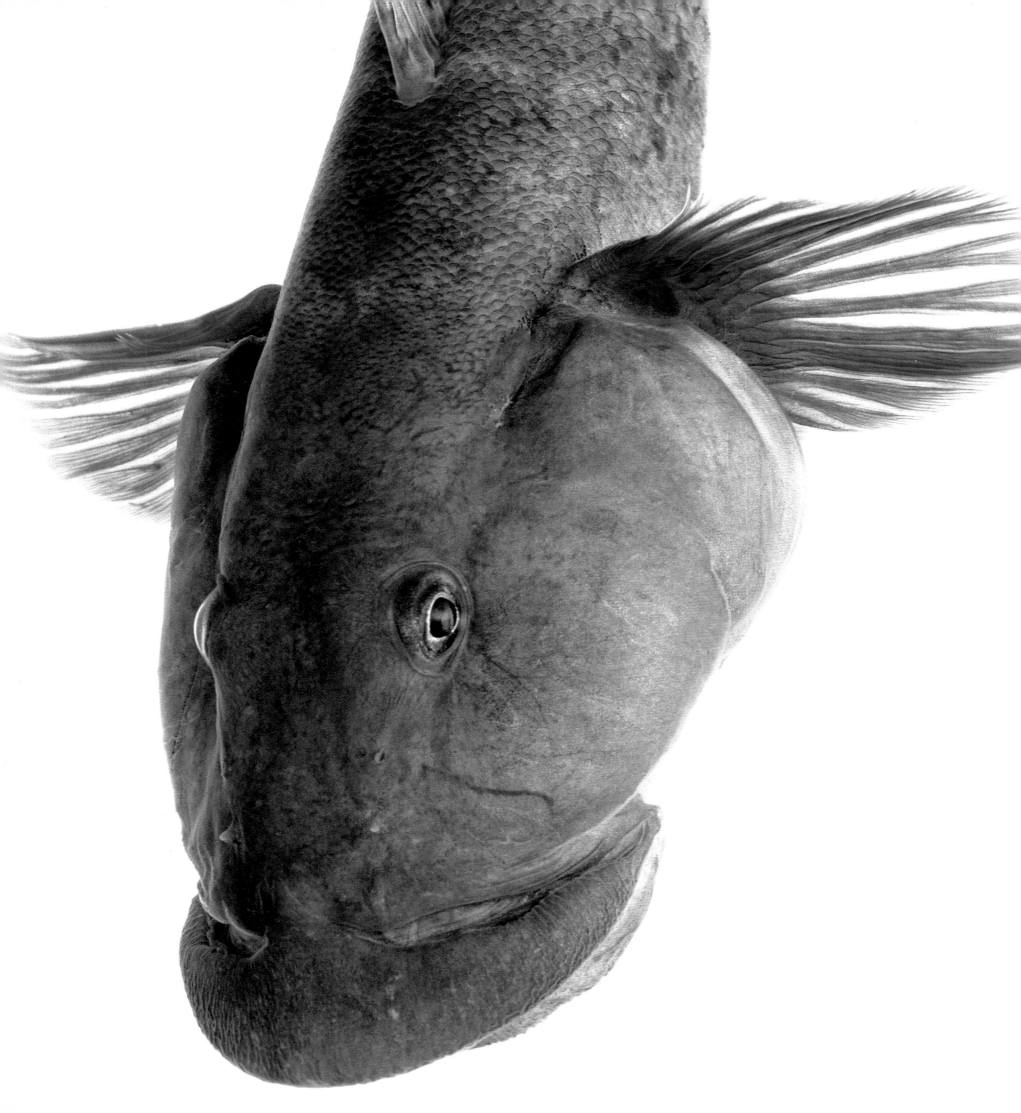

O kāne iā Wai'ololī, o ka wahine iā Wai'ololā

Hānau ka 'O'opukai noho i kai

Kia'i iā e ka 'O'opuwai noho i uka

Man for the narrow stream, woman for the broad stream

Born is the *'O'opu* living in the sea

Guarded by the *'O'opu* living in the fresh water

—from *The Kumulipo*

NATIVE STREAM FISH

by Susan Middleton

We had heard many tales about the *'o'opu,* the name given by the early Hawaiians to all five species of native stream fish. These fish begin their lives in the ocean as their larval phases are washed down from the mountains, and then work their way up the freshwater streams that will be their homes. To accomplish this formidable task, the fish have evolved a suction device on their undersides from what was originally a ventral fin, so that they can brace themselves on rocks along the stream bottom during their swim against the current. Hawaiian rivers usually originate high in the mountains and are swift and steep, often including waterfalls. The ability of these fish to navigate these streams—even climbing up 1,000-foot waterfalls—fascinated us. We had heard of the beautiful two-tone orange and black coloration of one of the fish, the *Lentipes concolor*. And we had been told that the stream fish are extremely difficult to catch.

We contacted Mike Kido, the expert in Hawaiian freshwater stream ecology—who, ironically, was the first to point out how little is actually known about the ecosystem of the *o'o'pu*. He explained that four out of the five stream fishes are believed to be endemic, meaning they are found nowhere else in the world. He suggested we work with two people who assist him at the Hawai'i Stream Research Center, Charlie McDonald and Jeff Koppel. We made arrangements to do the fieldwork next to Limahuli Stream, one of the few remaining healthy Hawaiian streams, where studies have been conducted on freshwater ecology over the last several years.

Having photographed fish and other aquatic creatures for our last book, *Witness,* we are familiar with the challenges of setting up a fish "photo studio." We use aquariums of various sizes, water filters, oxygenators, and lots of Plexiglas and black velvet, which must be cut to the appropriate sizes. We have to worry about reflections, keeping the water clean, making the background black or white, getting the exposure right, and keeping the fish happy.

We begin by collecting water from the stream, filling aquariums, and filtering the water for clarity. Meanwhile Charlie dons a wet suit and dive mask and searches for fish, carrying several kinds of nets and a white plastic holding bucket. He discovers that the fish are easier to see than to catch, masterfully eluding his attempts. He succeeds in catching one fish that first day, an *'o'opu nōpili,* who becomes our first subject. Charlie helps us set up a holding aquarium with stream stones and algae (the fish's primary food source) to make the fish feel at home. From the holding aquarium the fish will be

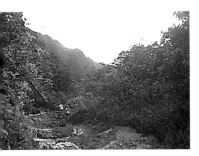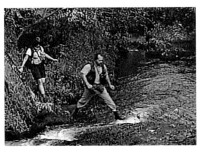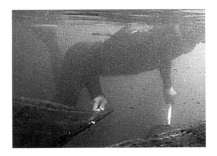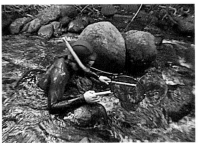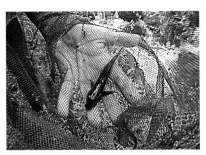

transferred to the "photo aquarium" or "photarium," as we call it, for the photo sessions. The photarium is completely clear with either a black or white background, thereby eliminating all visual distractions. As soon as we feel we have good pictures, the fish are returned to their stream.

After lots of looking we decide to try to make a portrait of this fish—that is, a close-up picture of a fish face! Not so easy, we discover. Our fish liked to move around continuously or stay hunkered down on the tank bottom, neither activity being optimal for portrait making. When we crouch low for a "fish-eye" view of our subject, we observe a wonderful gesture that the fish performs from time to time, unfortunately not on cue: It faces the camera, bright-eyed, and props itself up on its suction cup like a little pedestal, shifting attentive eyes around its new environment. It is as curious as we are. Eventually we manage to capture this position on film. Though not spectacularly showy like Hawaiian reef fishes, this resourceful little stream creature possesses a character all its own, and we want to show that.

Jeff Koppel soon joins Charlie to help locate and capture fish. Jeff has observed the stream fish for the last three years while working with the Limahuli Stream

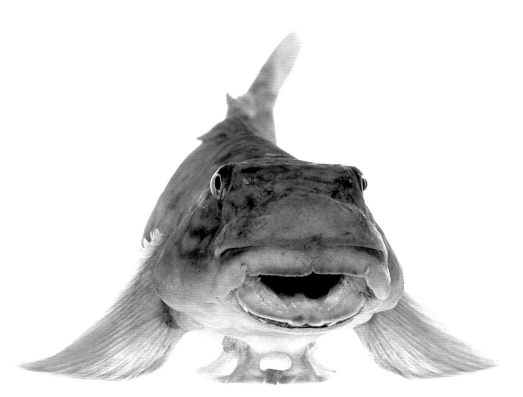

Research Center and is a master fish catcher. We accompany Charlie and Jeff on several of their fish field trips, hiking up the stream to learn about and photograph the habitat, which we can show along with the individual portraits of our fish heroes. The water is cold and even with wet suits Jeff and Charlie emerge shivering. We help by bringing the bucket to them when they've made a catch. Heavy rain delays the process, causing the water to become murky and making the fish harder to see.

Finding and capturing all five species of fish and then successfully photographing them proves to be a bigger challenge than we anticipated. We've been at it for over a week now, and we have photographed four of the five species: ʻoʻopu nōpili (Sicyopterus stimpsoni), ʻoʻopu nākea (Awaous guamensis), ʻoʻopu ʻakupa (Eleotris sandwicensis), and ʻoʻopu ʻalamoʻo (Lentipes concolor). The ʻoʻopu ʻakupa is the only one that is carnivorous—the others are vegetarian and eat algae. It is also the only one without a suction device. In our photographs it appears to have a big smile. The ʻoʻopu ʻalamoʻo is the two-tone fish. It is a sleek little animal with a deep black front that changes to a vivid orange on the back half of its body. After capture the brilliance of the color faded in the white bucket and in the holding aquarium, only to reappear mysteriously after entering the dark photarium. Charlie just returned from a trip to another stream with the fifth and most difficult to find species, the ʻoʻopu naniha (Stenogobius hawaiiensis). We will undoubtedly photograph it late into the night.

Even in Limahuli Stream, where the fish thrive, they are difficult to see. Their coloration and movements provide effective camouflage in the dark, rocky, fast-flowing stream. Finding them and photographing them tested our collective patience, but it was all worthwhile once we saw them close-up on the first test Polaroids!

Though we have been unable to incorporate marine ecosystems into our Hawaiian project, we always hoped we could include these highly specialized native fish that inhabit the healthy freshwater streams of Hawaiʻi. They are rare because their habitats are at risk from alien-species introductions, water withdrawal, and agricultural and hydropower development.

Limahuli Stream is protected by National Tropical Botanical Garden and is part of a mountain forest preserve and botanical garden that features native Hawaiian plants as well as Polynesian-introduced plants that were culturally significant, including taro terraces. Limahuli Garden and Preserve is managed according to the concept of ahupuaʻa, which is a traditional Hawaiian unit of land extending from mountaintop into the sea. In Hawaiʻi, fresh water comes from the

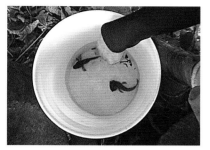
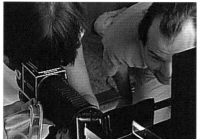
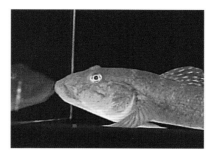

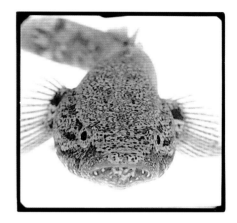

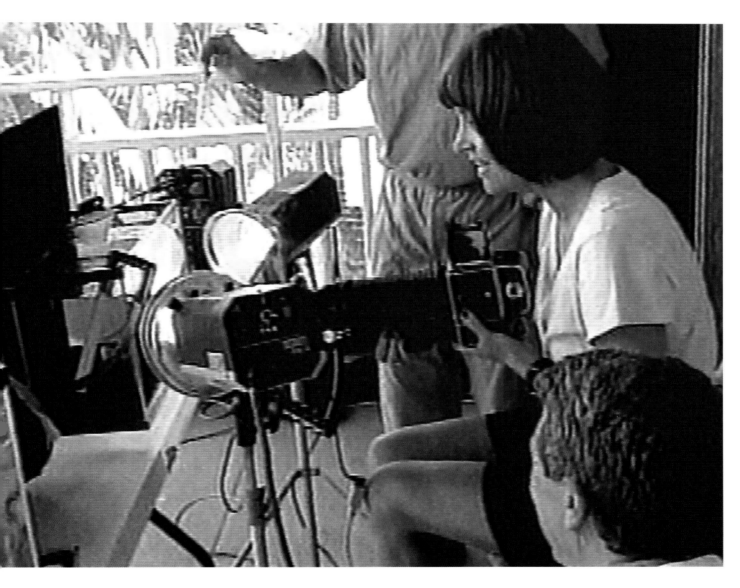

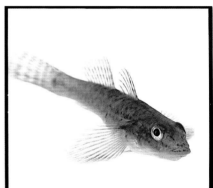

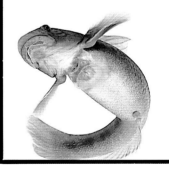

mountains and flows down to the sea. The early Hawaiians recognized that water, land, and sea are vitally connected and that these resources are most effectively managed as an integrated system. Today it is unusual for land to be managed in this holistic way, largely because the original large, pie-shaped segments of land extending from mountain to sea have been subdivided, and the caretaking of those divisions has become fractured or no longer exists. Fortunately for these fish and the other creatures who make it their home, Limahuli Stream has its source high in the mountains, which are part of the preserve, and flows down through the botanical garden toward the sea, protected all the way, as it was in ancient times.

'Oʻopu Nākea (page 200)
Awaous guamensis

Finding, capturing, and photographing fish at Limahuli Stream, Kauaʻi (top row, pages 202–203 and above)

'Oʻopu Nōpili (left)
Sicyopterus stimpsoni

From top right:
'Oʻopu ʻAkupa
Eleotris sandwicensis

'Oʻopu Nākea
Awaous guamensis

'Oʻopu Nōpili
Sicyopterus stimpsoni

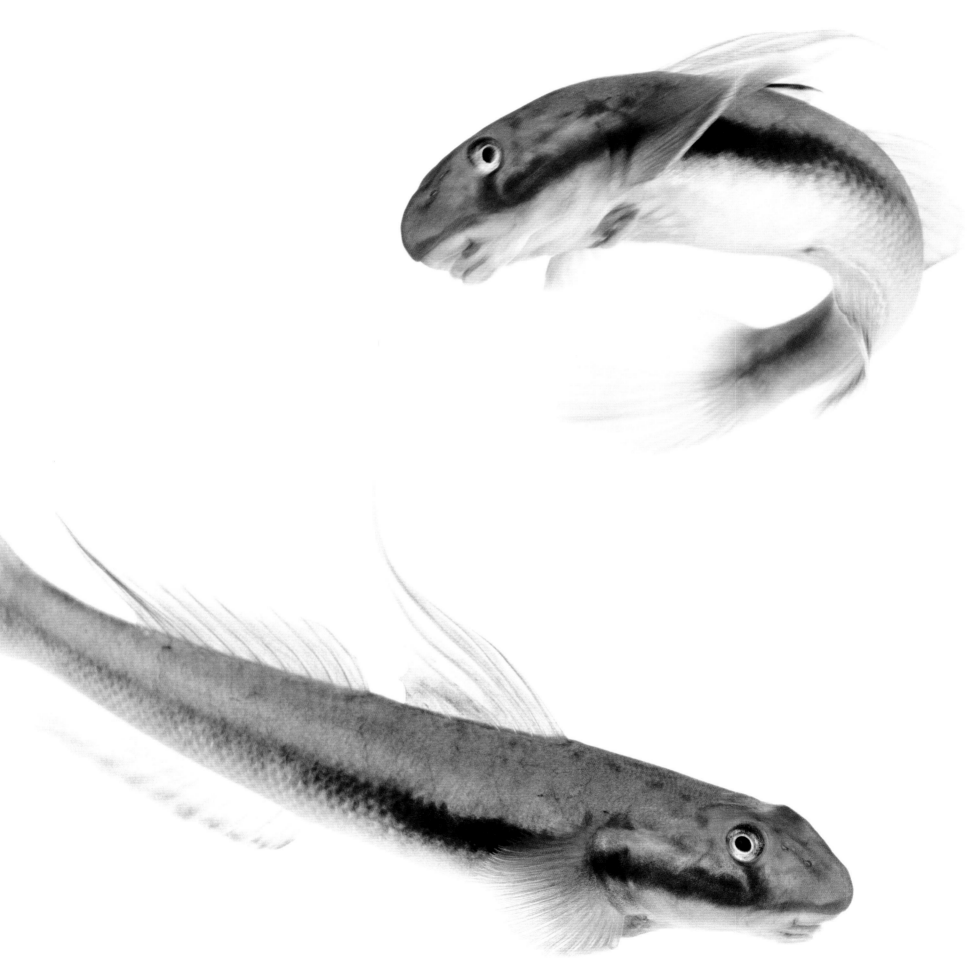

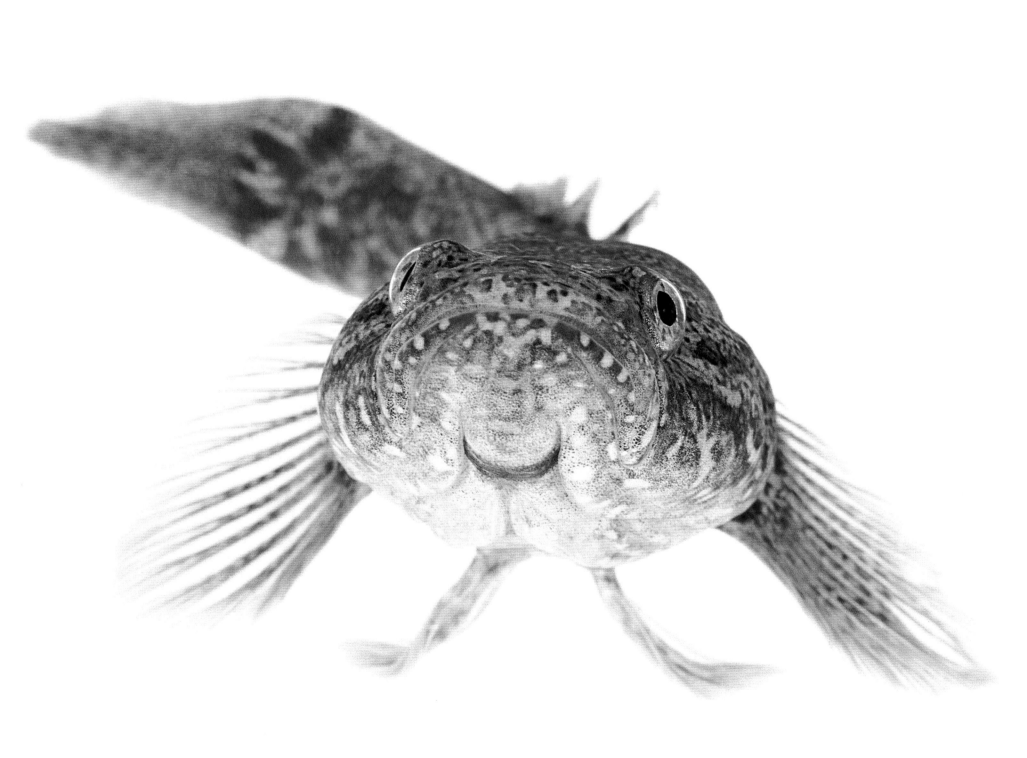

'O'opu Nōpili (left)
Sicyopterus stimpsoni

'O'opu 'Akupa (right)
Eleotris sandwicensis

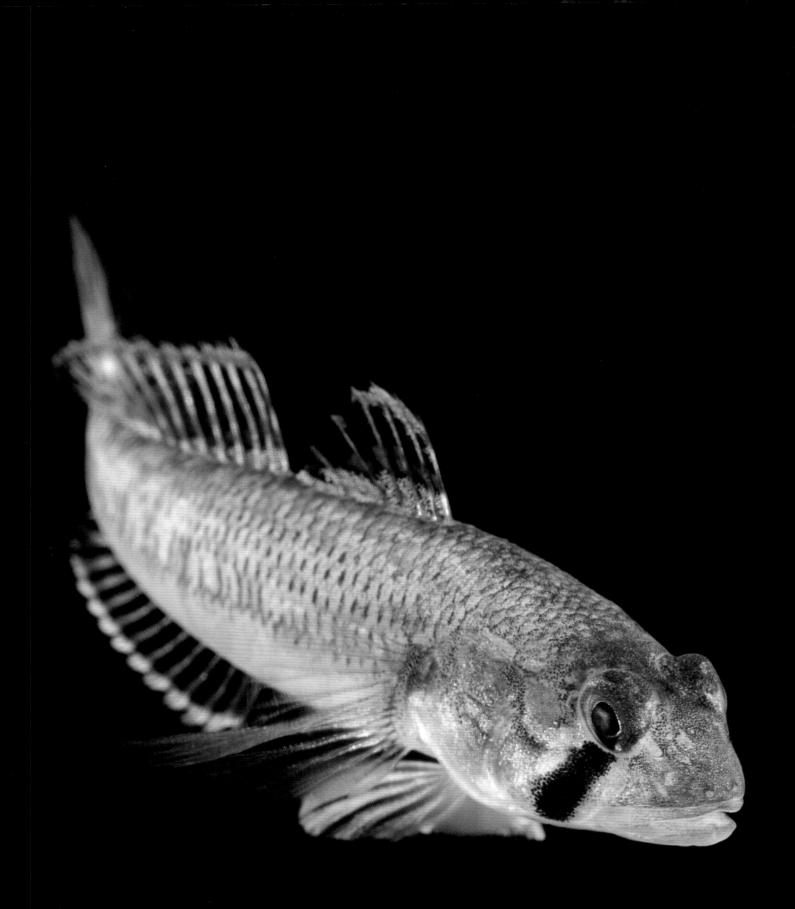

‘O‘opu Naniha (left)
Stenogobius hawaiiensis

‘O‘opu ‘Alamo‘o (right)
Lentipes concolor

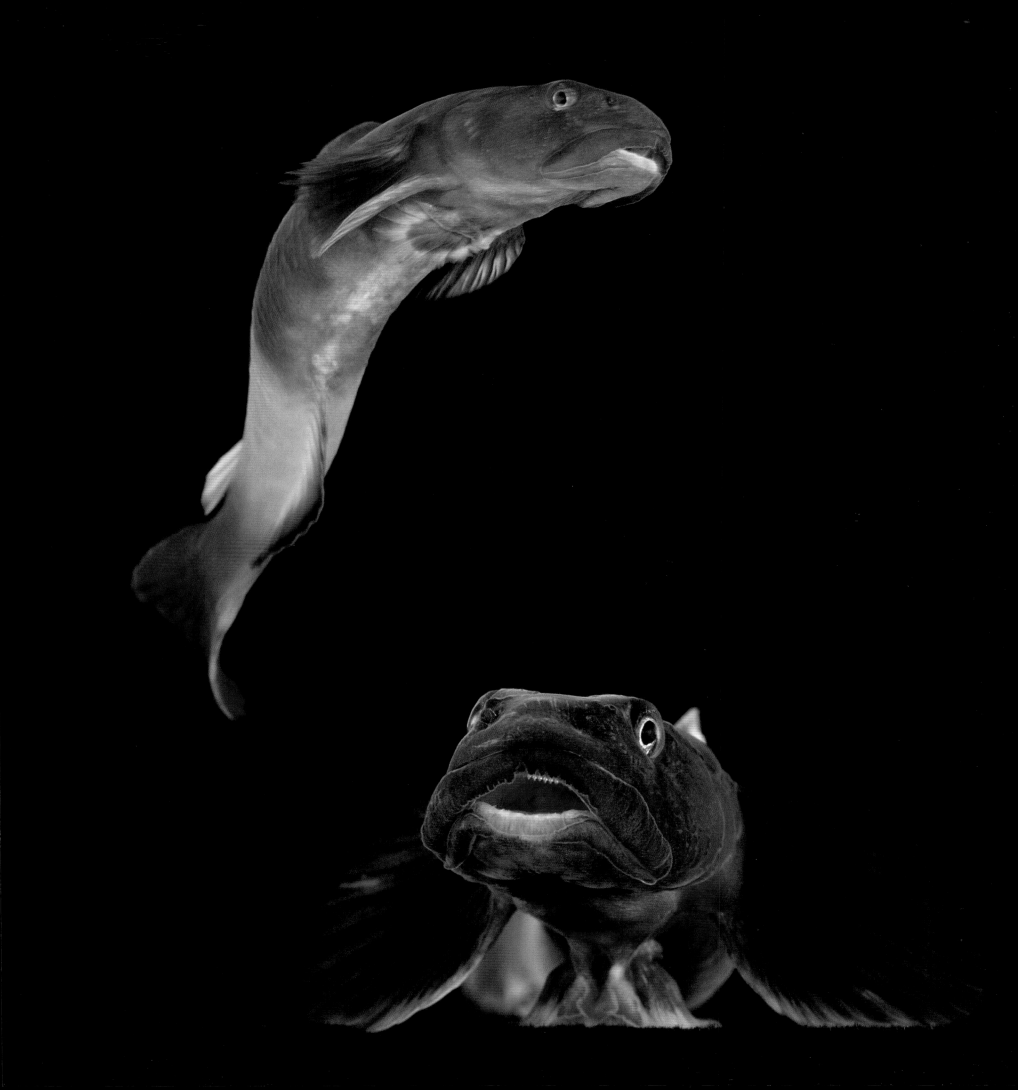

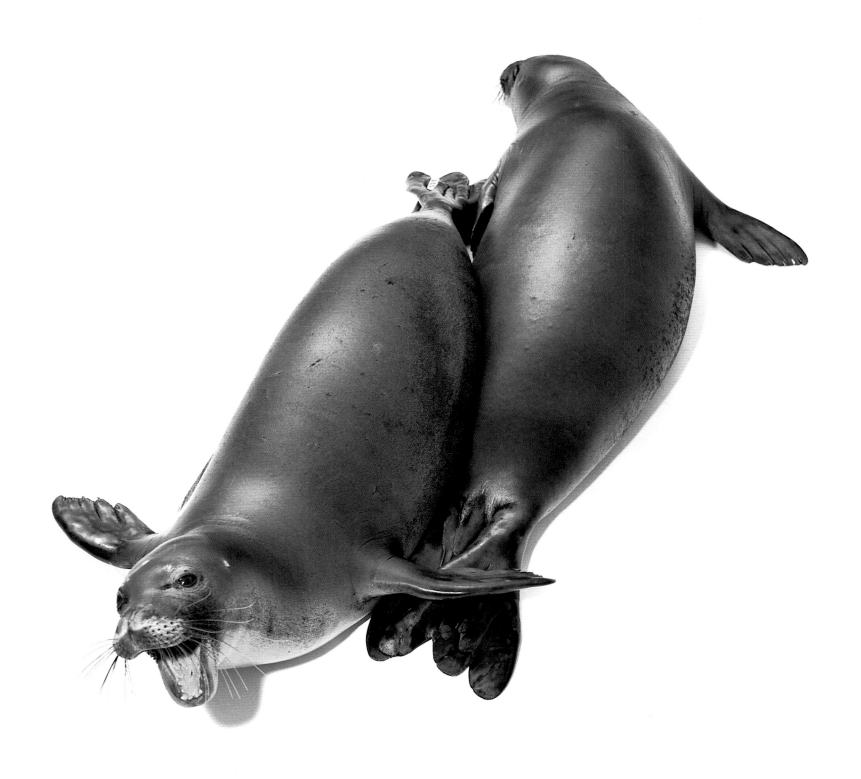

Hawaiian Monk Seal
(left, juveniles; right, adult)
ʻĪlioholoikauaua
Monachus schauinslandi

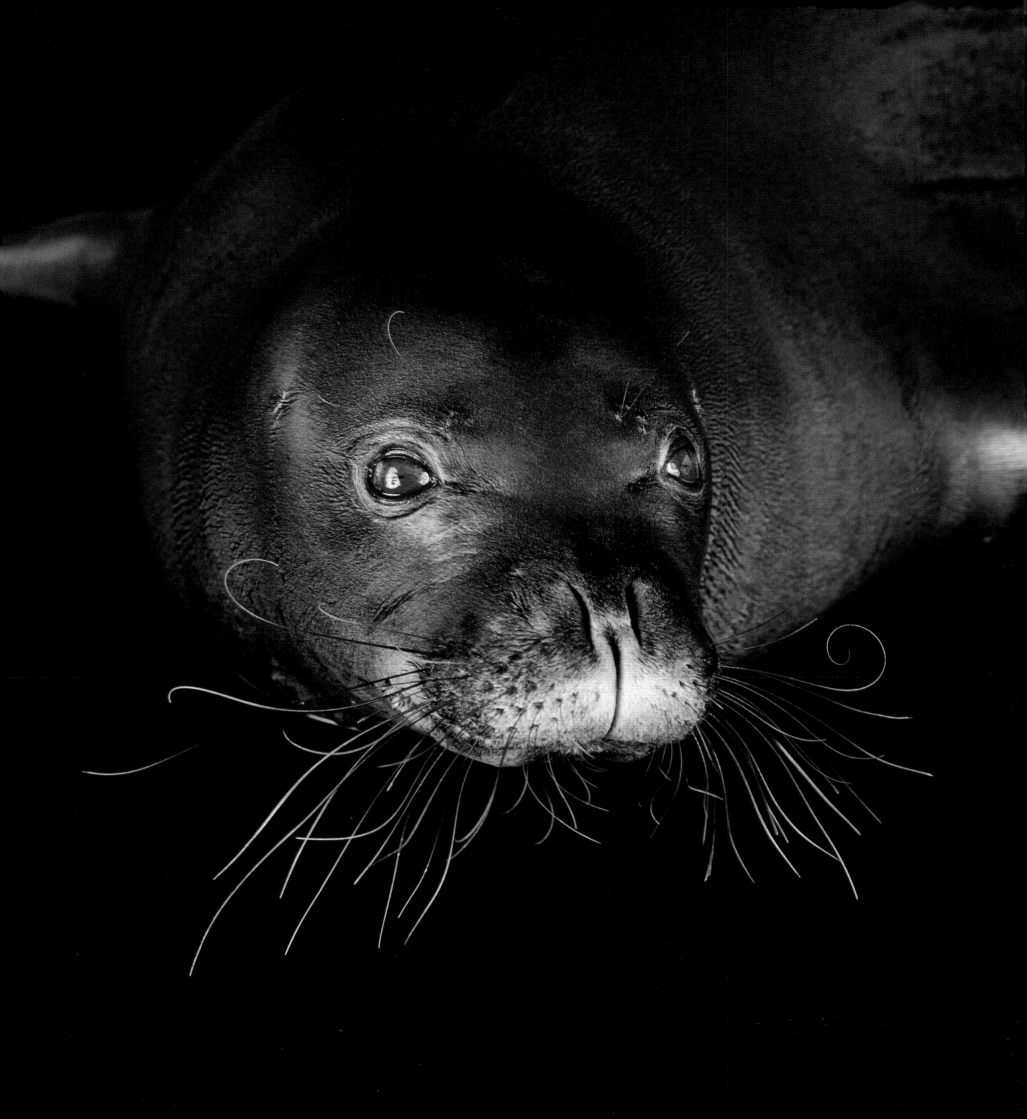

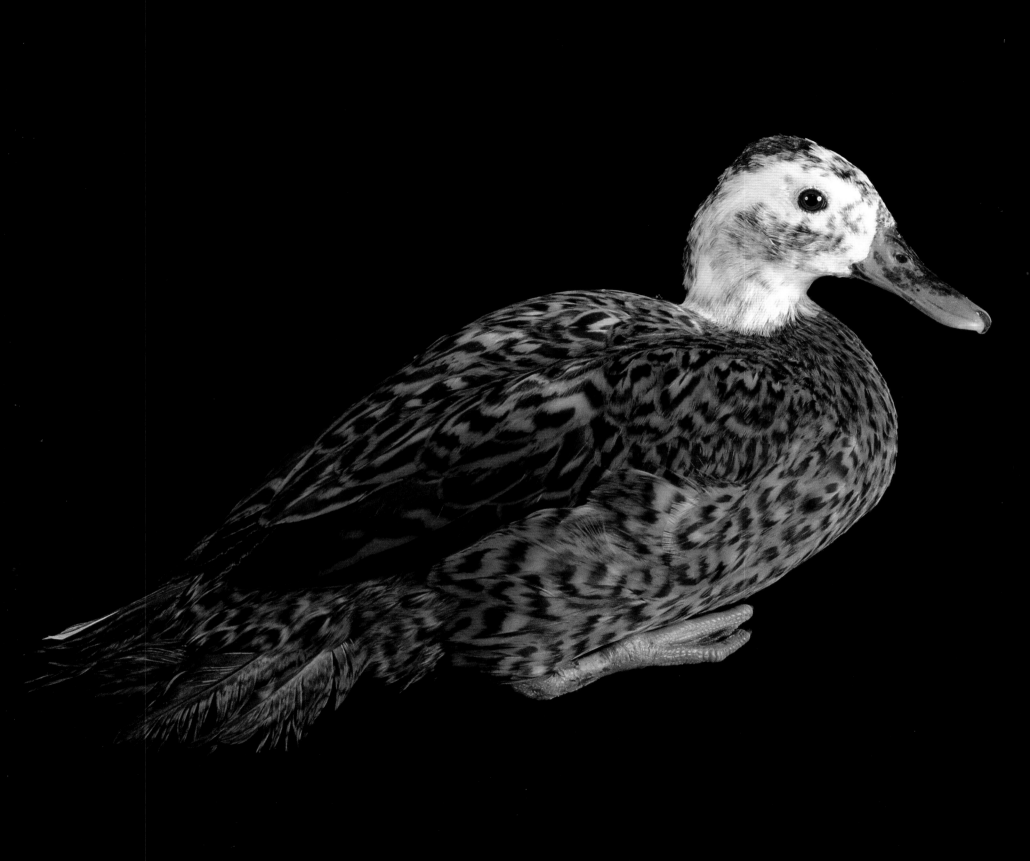

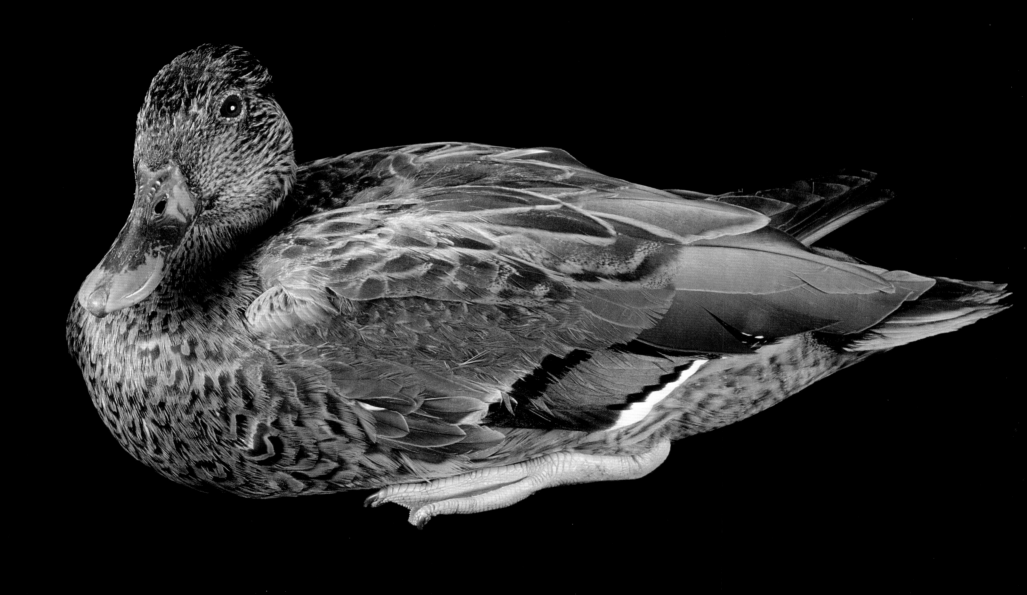

Laysan Duck (left)
Anas laysanensis

Hawaiian Duck (right)
Koloa Maoli
Anas wyvilliana

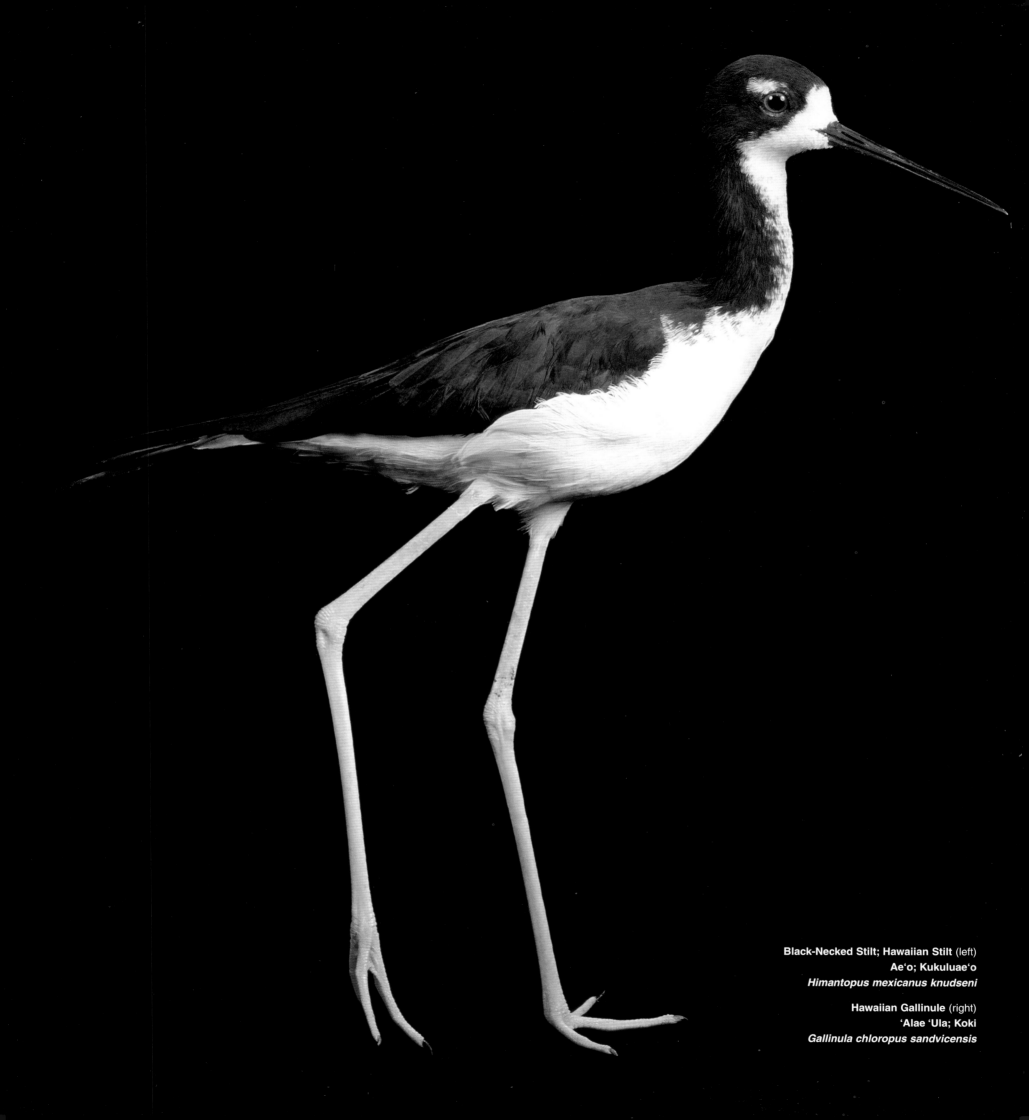

Black-Necked Stilt; Hawaiian Stilt (left)
Aeʻo; Kukuluaeʻo
Himantopus mexicanus knudseni

Hawaiian Gallinule (right)
ʻAlae ʻUla; Koki
Gallinula chloropus sandvicensis

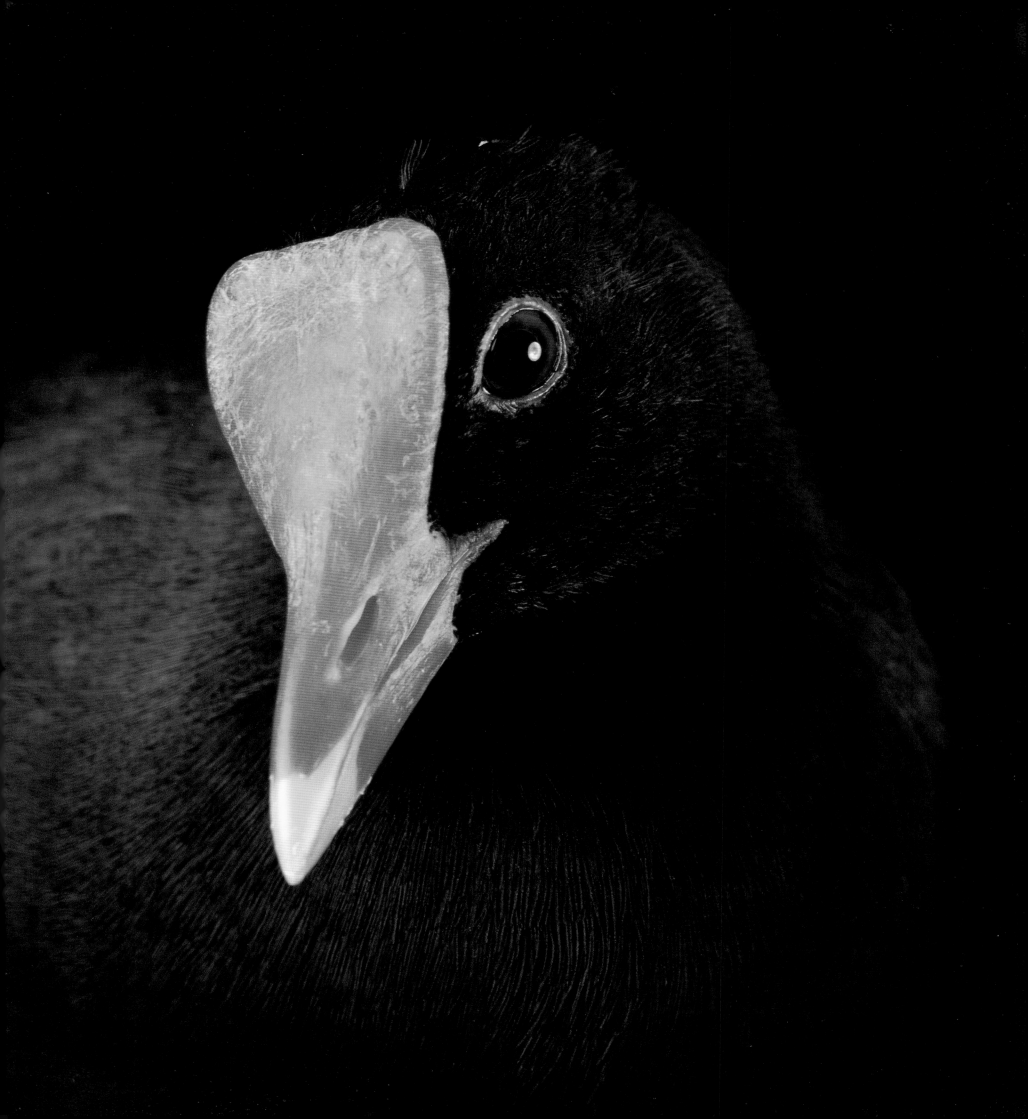

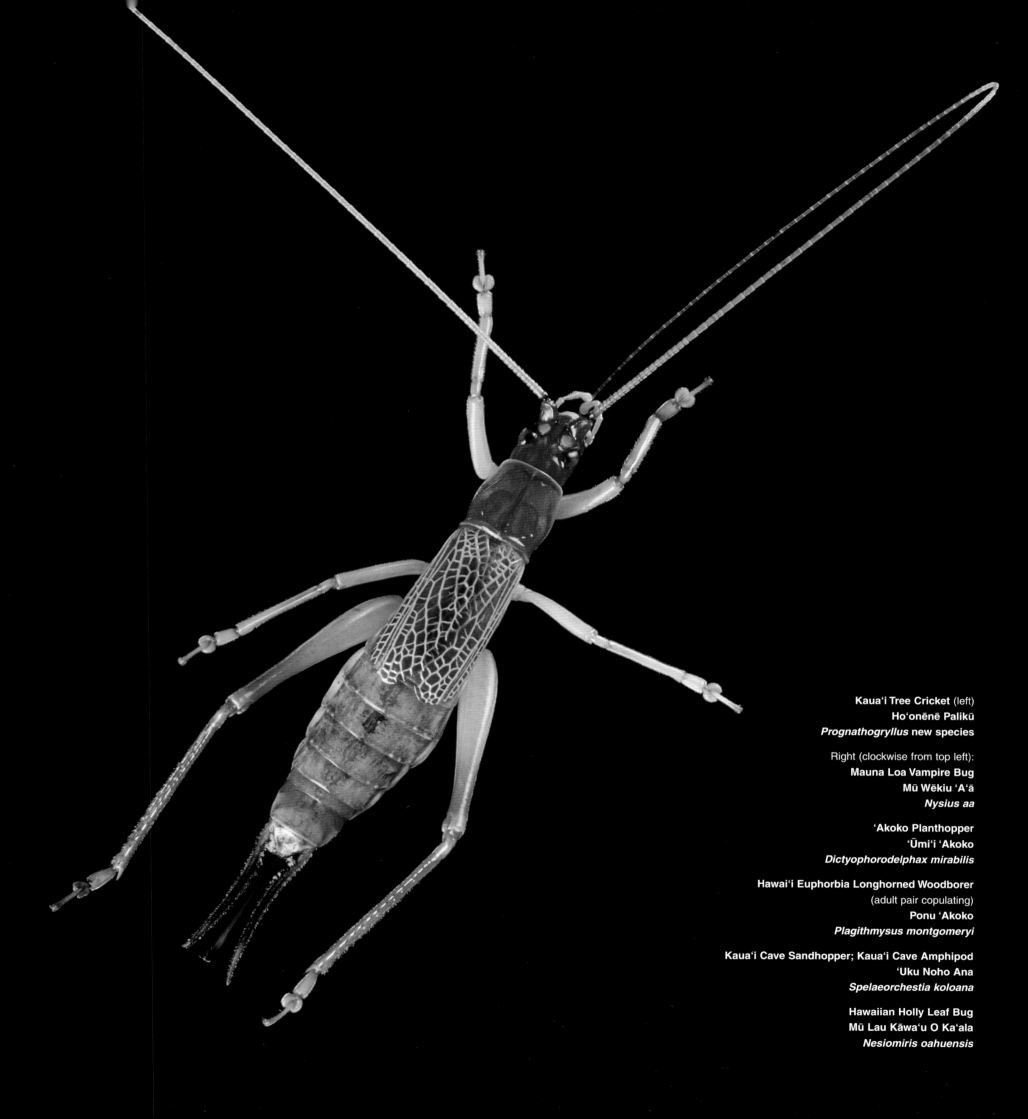

Kaua'i Tree Cricket (left)
Hoʻonēnē Palikū
Prognathogryllus **new species**

Right (clockwise from top left):
Mauna Loa Vampire Bug
Mū Wēkiu ʻAʻā
Nysius aa

ʻAkoko Planthopper
ʻŪmiʻi ʻAkoko
Dictyophorodelphax mirabilis

Hawaiʻi Euphorbia Longhorned Woodborer
(adult pair copulating)
Ponu ʻAkoko
Plagithmysus montgomeryi

Kauaʻi Cave Sandhopper; Kauaʻi Cave Amphipod
ʻUku Noho Ana
Spelaeorchestia koloana

Hawaiian Holly Leaf Bug
Mū Lau Kāwaʻu O Kaʻala
Nesiomiris oahuensis

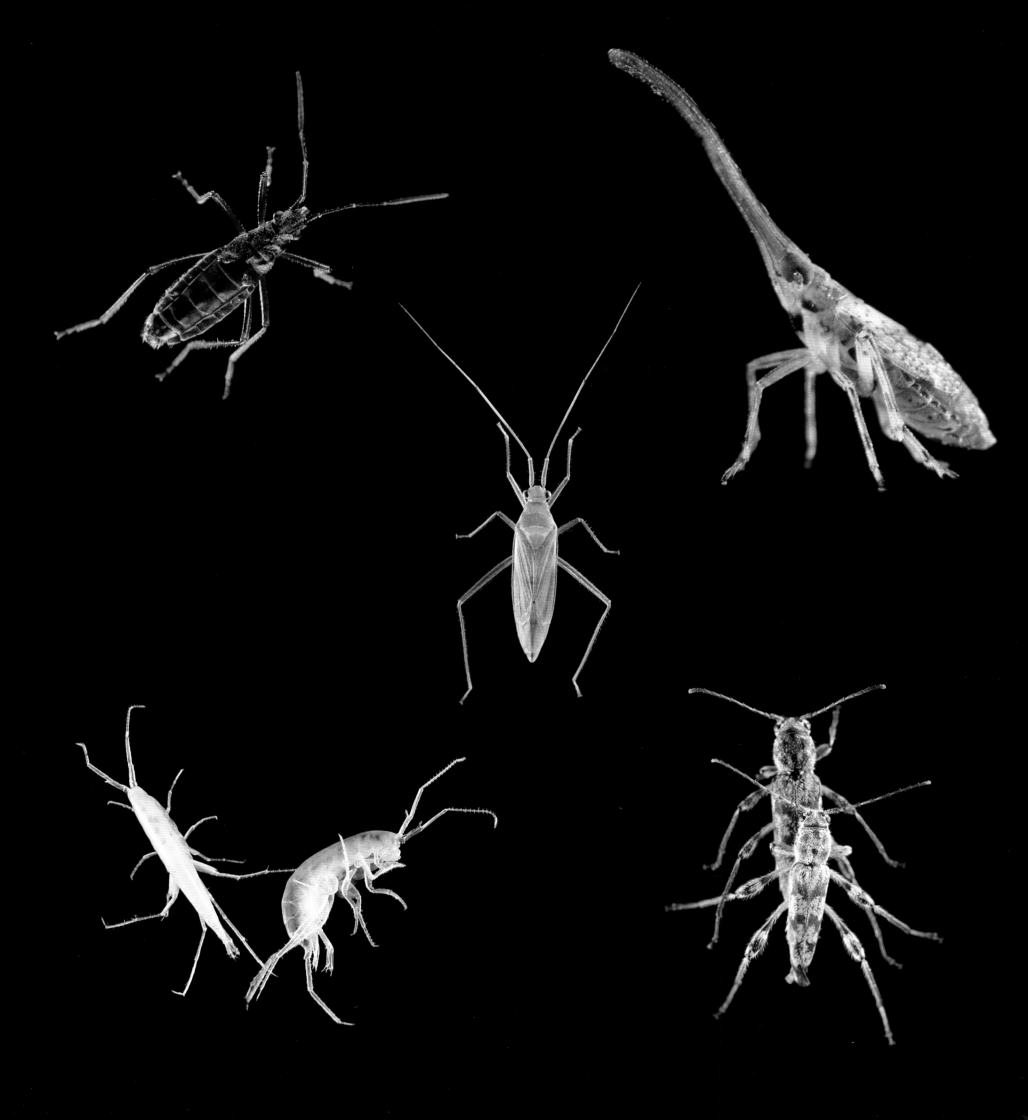

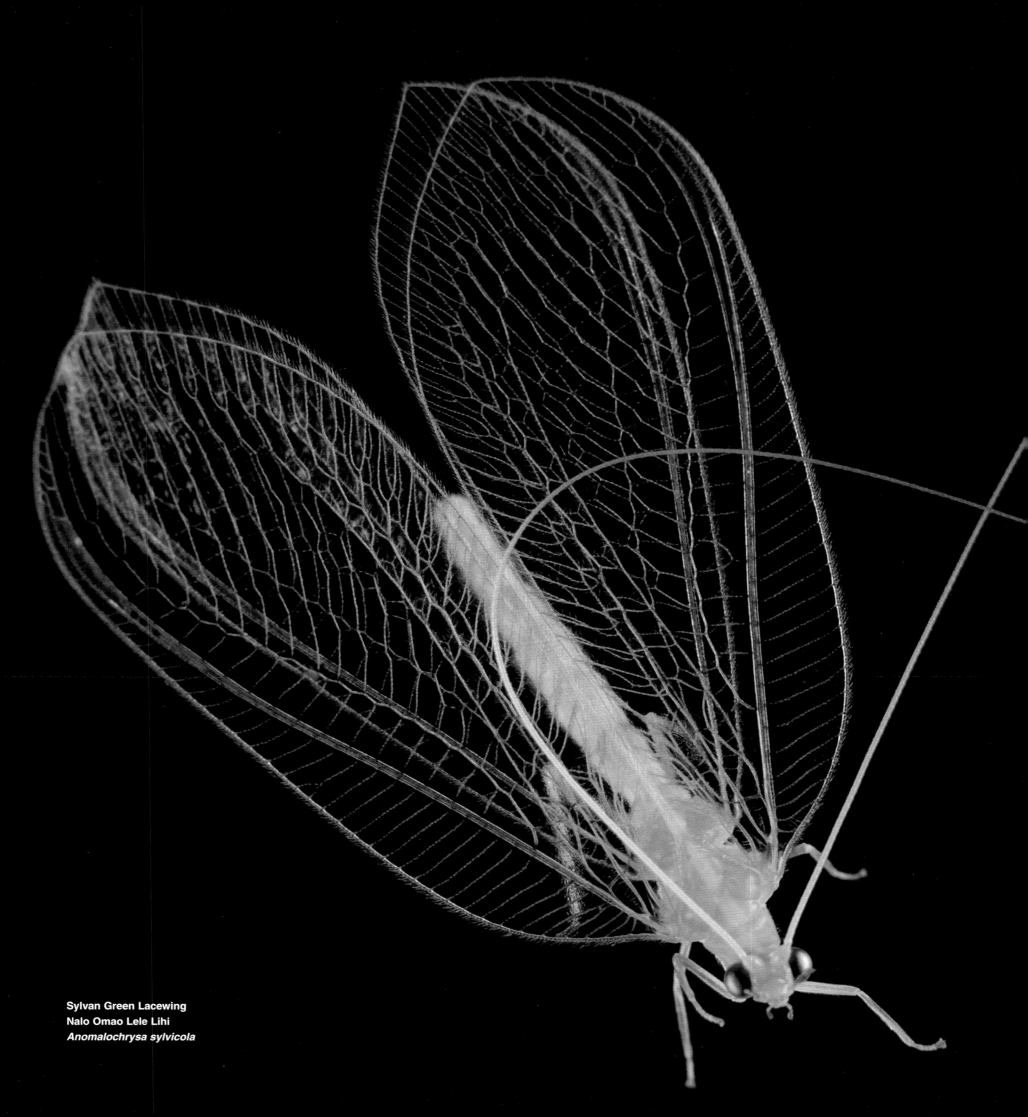

Sylvan Green Lacewing
Nalo Omao Lele Lihi
Anomalochrysa sylvicola

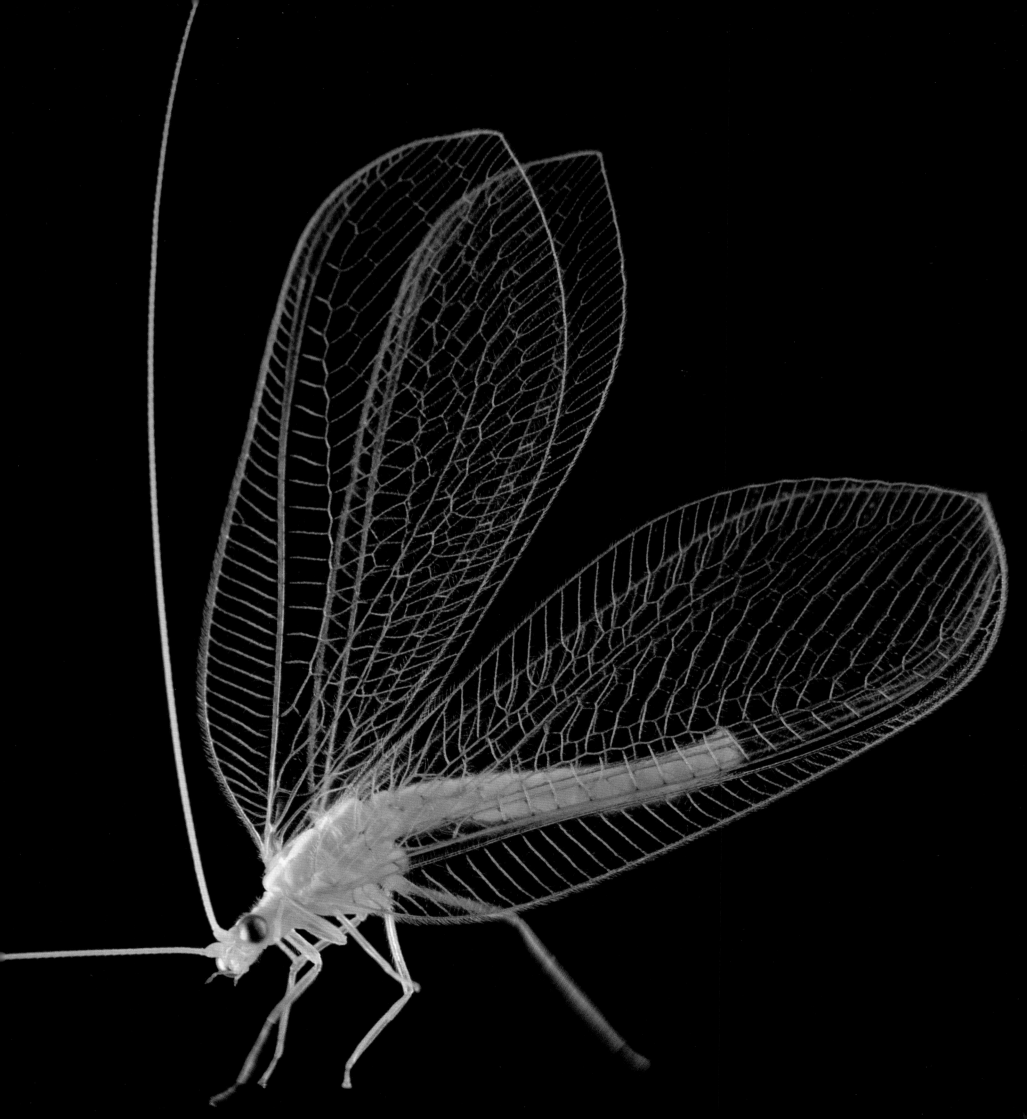

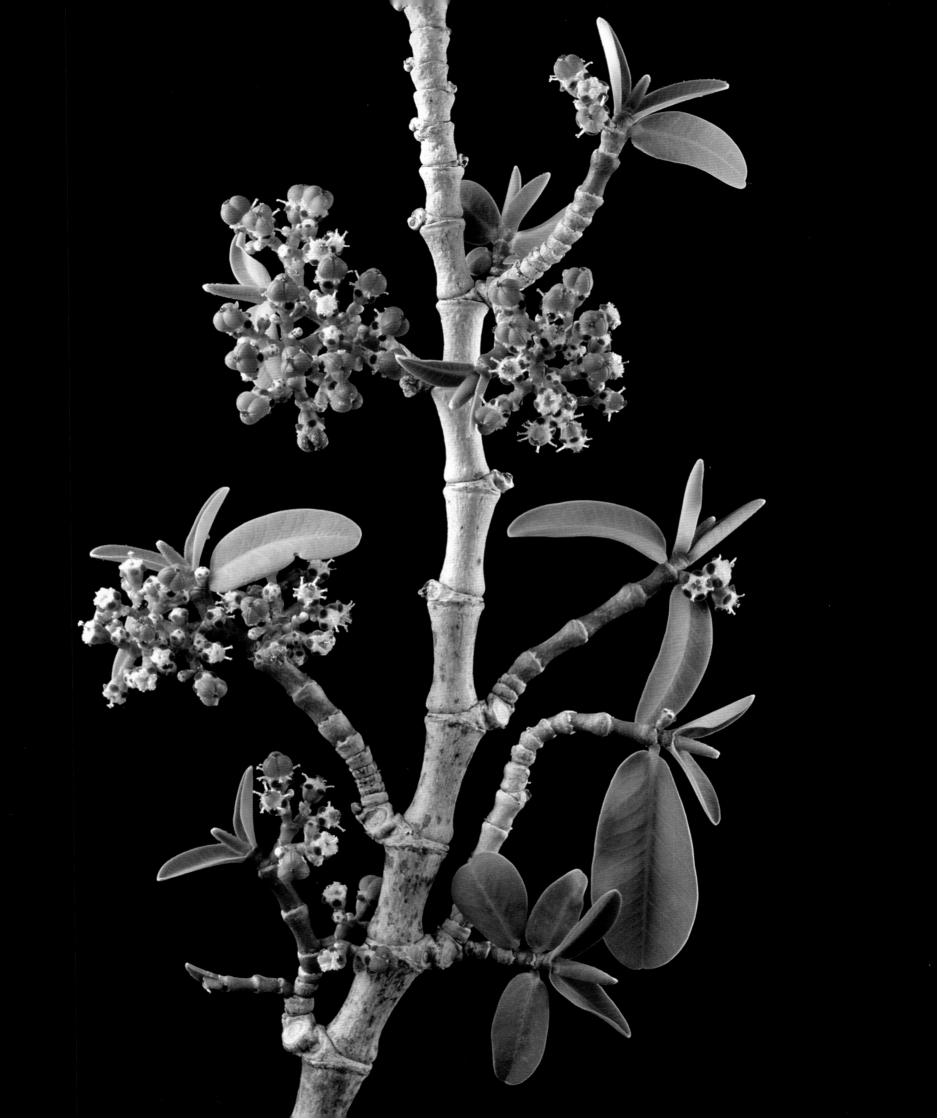

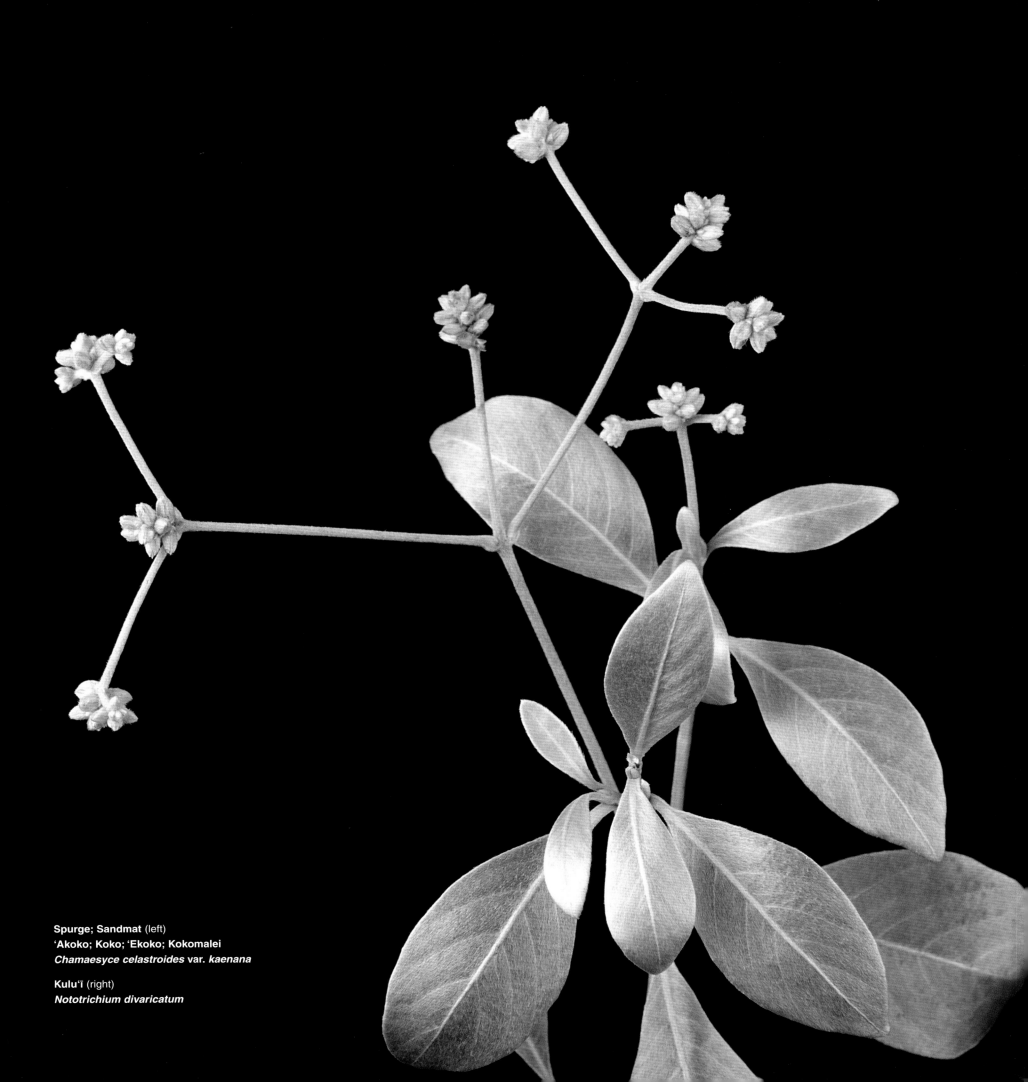

Spurge; Sandmat (left)
'Akoko; Koko; 'Ekoko; Kokomalei
Chamaesyce celastroides **var.** *kaenana*

Kulu'ī (right)
Nototrichium divaricatum

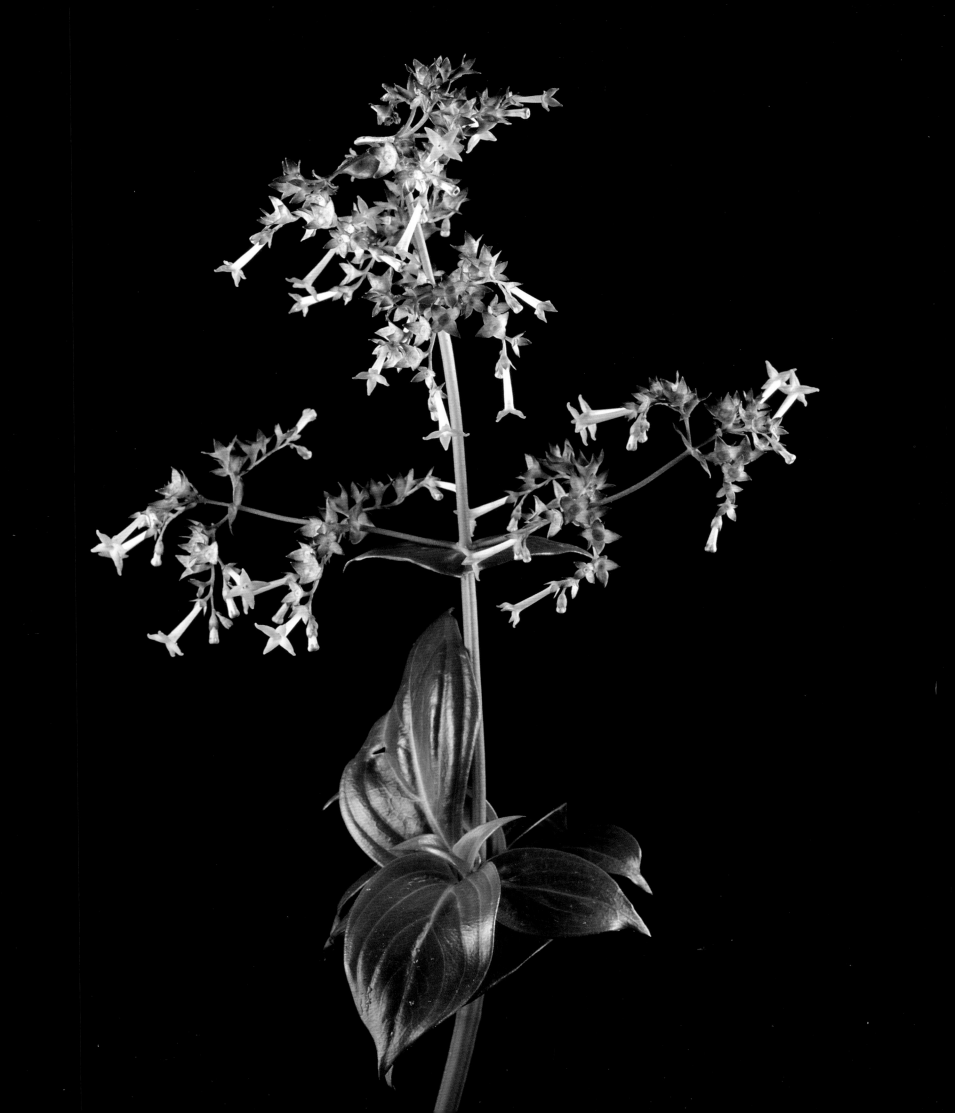

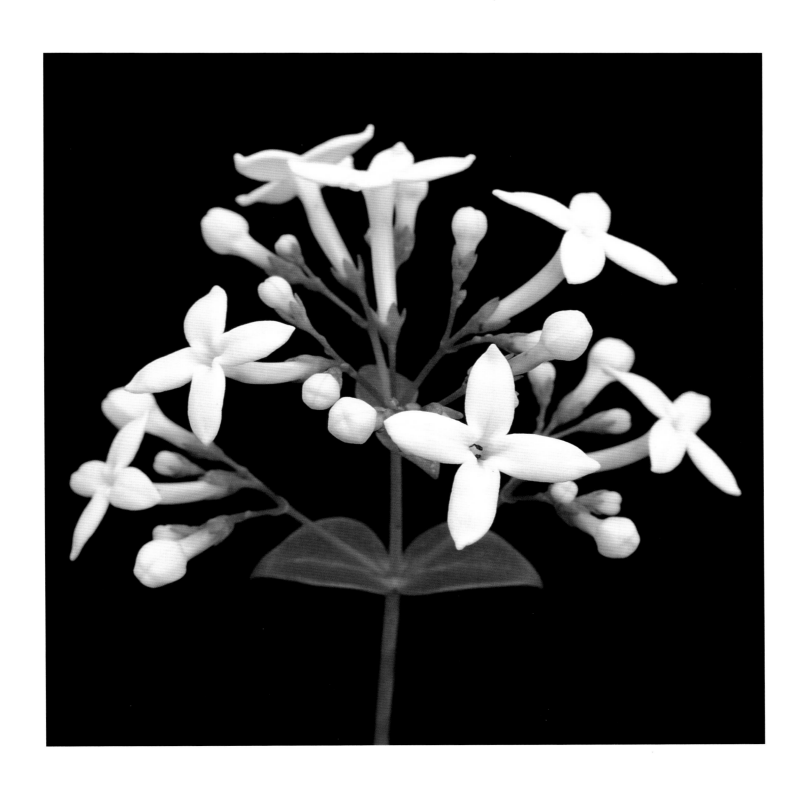

Pilo (left)
Hedyotis mannii

Pilo (right)
Hedyotis parvula

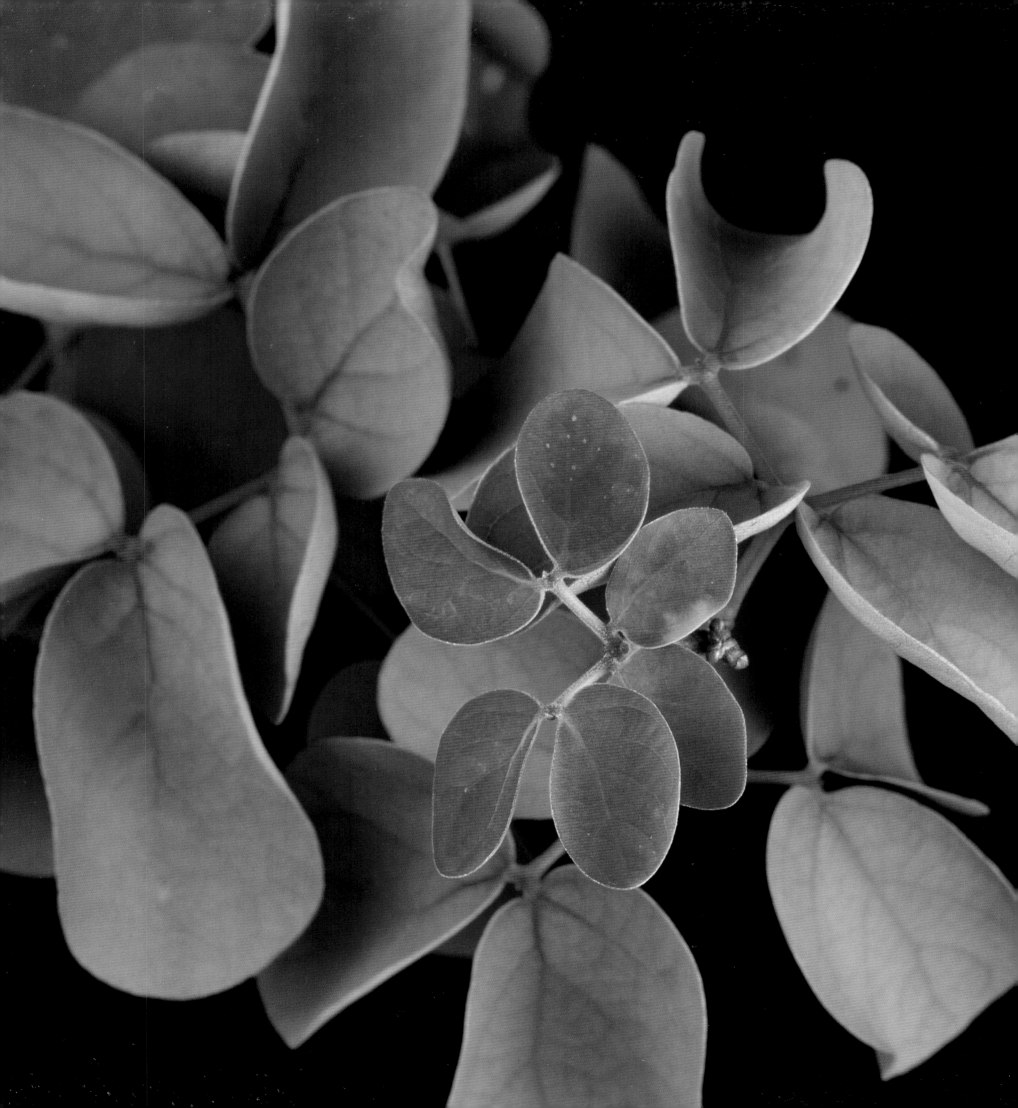

'Anihinihi ke ola.

Life is in a precarious position.

—from *'Ōlelo No'eau*

RAREST OF THE RARE

by Susan Middleton

Rarity comes with island existence. Islands are isolated landmasses with limited area available to maintain the unique biota that evolved on them, making native plants and animals particularly vulnerable to extinction. More plants and animals have gone extinct in Hawai'i than in all of North America, and there are more than 100 native Hawaiian plant species with fewer than 20 known individuals remaining.

I have been shocked, saddened, and compelled by what I have seen in Hawai'i. Never before have I experienced such a richness in nature, nor have I been exposed to such extreme loss. Almost every person we worked with has witnessed an animal or plant become extinct. This has no parallel on the mainland. Botanist Steve Perlman describes it as terminal patient syndrome. "When you work with terminal patients, you know you are going to come back and find them gone."

People working in conservation in Hawai'i carry a heavy burden of grief, and at the same time they are passionately devoted to the preservation of these disappearing plants and animals. The loss of diversity is extreme in Hawai'i, and it represents a fast-forward view of declining biodiversity worldwide. Correspondingly, it is on the cutting edge of conservation. We can hope that the lessons learned will be applied toward continents as they go through their own extinction crises.

Kanaloa kahoolawensis—a recent discovery—is exceedingly rare and distinctive in several ways. There are only two known wild plants (one of which is dying), and three plants in cultivation, grown from seed collected from the wild plants. Despite intensive efforts at grafting, air layering, and tissue culture, the only way this plant has been able to reproduce thus far is from seed, and the cultivated plants have yet to set seed. Since the plants were discovered in 1992, the heart-shaped seeds have only been seen a few times.

Not only is this a new species, it represents a unique genus in Hawaiian flora. When the pollen was examined by experts it was found to match a mysterious unidentified legume pollen from a plant in the fossil record that was thought to be extinct, and which was once a common component of lowland forests throughout the islands before the Polynesians arrived.

In 1992 Ken Wood and Steve Perlman were involved in surveying the cliffs of Kaho'olawe. Although these cliffs are not rich in native vegetation, Ken and Steve had noticed that two small islets offshore, Pu'u Koa'e and a sea stack just next to it named 'Ale-'ale, looked as if they might have native shrubland. Access to 'Ale-'ale, a steep rocky spine, is tricky, and there was no record of anyone ever having visited it. On a trip to Pu'u Koa'e, Steve, Ken, and a survey team wanted to explore 'Ale-'ale, but it required descending a 700-foot cliff, which was eroded and dangerous, then climbing up the other side onto 'Ale-'ale. Using ropes, Steve and Ken managed to get down over 600 feet of the cliff when they reached a 75-foot straight drop into the ocean. At that point they tied Ken's rope onto the only available tree, an unhealthy, weak *kiawe* shrub. Ken descended while Steve watched the rope, ready to grab it if the tree gave way. Ken made it down to the ocean onto some rocks that formed a little bridge to 'Ale-'ale. He carefully ascended to the top of the sea stack and found himself in the middle of a seabird colony, surrounded by an intact native shrubland, totally pristine, with no weeds. Many native plants were growing out of purple, yellow, brown, and red basalt, thriving on their tiny island home.

Ken recognized all the native plants he was seeing—until he saw the *kanaloa*. "Time totally stopped when I saw it. It was like nothing I had ever seen before. It was so radiant and beautiful, with a strange compound leaf form." He made a small collection of it, including flowers and fruit, and then made his way back to show the rest of the team. Everyone was excited, and botanist Joel Lau expressed a hunch that it could be a new genus.

Life is tenuous for the *kanaloa* because thus far it only grows from seed, and seed is hard to come by. A reliable propagation strategy has yet to be worked out, and meanwhile the two wild plants on 'Ale-'ale have suffered the effects of a severe drought. Many of the other native plants have died. Subsequent visits have been by helicopter, and water has been taken in for the two *kanaloa* plants, keeping at least one alive. The smaller of the two is not doing well and probably will not survive.

We first saw an *Alectryon macrococcus* var. *auwahiensis* at Waimea Botanical Garden in 1993. It was a sad-looking tree, lacking vigor. We photographed it because there were fewer than 10 wild individuals known and the cultivated *Alectryon,* weak as it was, represented an attempt to conserve a species that was on

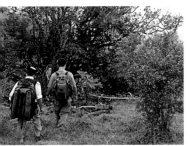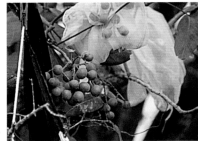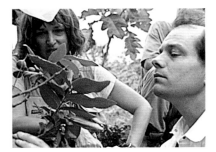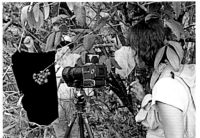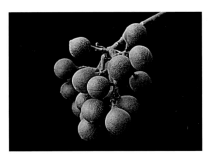

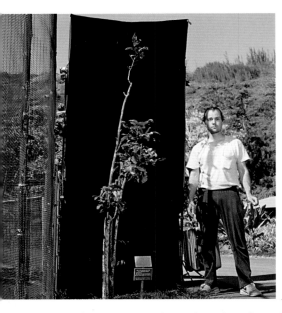

the critical list. We learned that its natural home is an area on the south slope of Haleakalā, Maui, a dryland forest known as Auwahi that bears little resemblance to what it was in healthier days.

We wanted to see the wild trees then but were informed that they were in bad shape and would not be photogenic. In 2000 we finally visited Auwahi with botanist Chuck Chimera as guide. It felt like a pilgrimage. This forest has been in jeopardy throughout the last century, severely damaged by grazing cattle and invasive weeds. We have heard it referred to as a "geriatric forest" because the remaining native trees are all old and there is no regeneration. Seedlings can't make it through the thick, weedy grass. Roughly 90 percent of Hawaiian dryland forests, once the most diverse habitats in Hawai'i, are gone.

As we approached the *Alectryon* we noticed that it was festooned with white net bags tied around the clusters of seeds. The netting is to protect the seeds from being eaten by insects and to discourage rats, both threats to the plants' production of viable seeds. Chuck removed the netting from one of the seed clusters so we could photograph it. Resembling a bronze cluster of grapes, the seeds are large and smooth and round. Though difficult to germinate, young seedlings are being cultivated with the intention of planting them in an area protected from cattle and managed for weeds as part of a larger dryland forest restoration project.

There is only one known wild *Cyanea pinnatifida*. It grows out of the side of a vertical wall just underneath a large rock that could dislodge and crush the roots of the plant at any moment. This species was thought to be extinct when Steve Perlman rediscovered it in 1987 at Honouliuli, a Nature Conservancy preserve in the southern Wai'anae

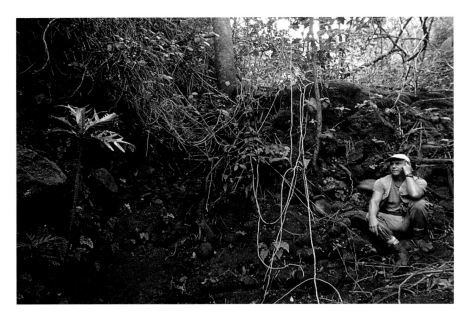

Mountains on O'ahu. He could find only one plant, and there were no seeds or flowers. Concerned about its precarious state, Steve Perlman and Greg Koob collected pieces of tissue from the base of the plant and took it into the tissue-culture lab at Lyon Arboretum in O'ahu. After Greg got the material to grow successfully in test tubes, he was able to divide it and to grow many plants to maturity. These plants flower and produce seed, and now plants can be cultivated from seed. This provides some limited opportunity for genetic variability to be expressed even though the plants are from a single parent.

The *Cyanea pinnatifida* was reduced to one plant and was saved. Many of these plants are now being cultivated and the opportunity exists for them to be returned to protected outplanting sites in their natural habitat.

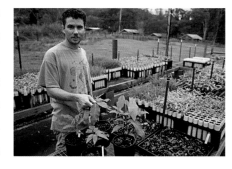

Kanaloa (page 222)
Palupalu O Kanaloa
Kanaloa kahoolawensis

Photographing one of the last *māhoe*, *Alectryon macrococcus*, in Auwahi, Maui (top row)

David with *māhoe*, Waimea Arboretum and Botanical Garden (above left)

Steve Perlman with last known *Cyanea pinnatifida* (above right)

Chuck Chimera with *māhoe* seedlings, Ulu Pala Kua, Maui (left)

Opposite page, clockwise from top left:
Last known wild *Cyanea pinnatifida*;
Tissue culture of *Cyanea pinnatifida* (second test tube from left), Lyon Arboretum; *Cyanea pinnatifida* in propagation at National Tropical Botanical Garden; Young *Cyanea pinnatifida* ready to plant

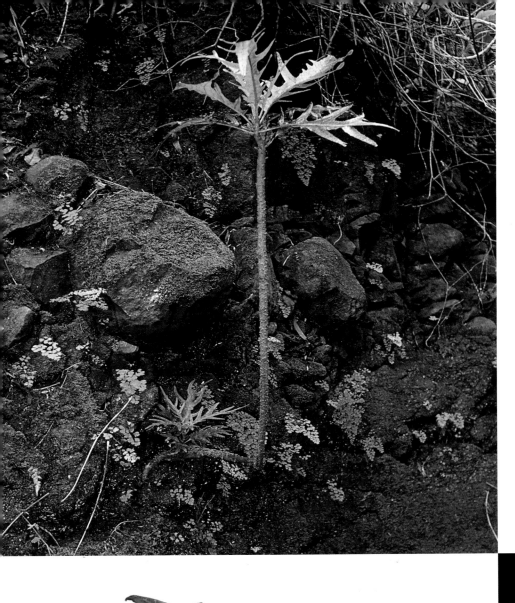
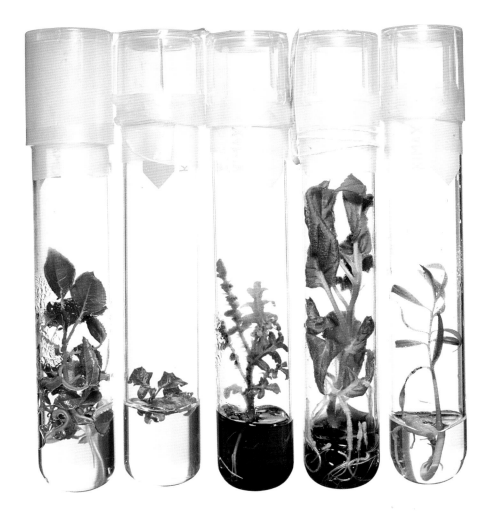
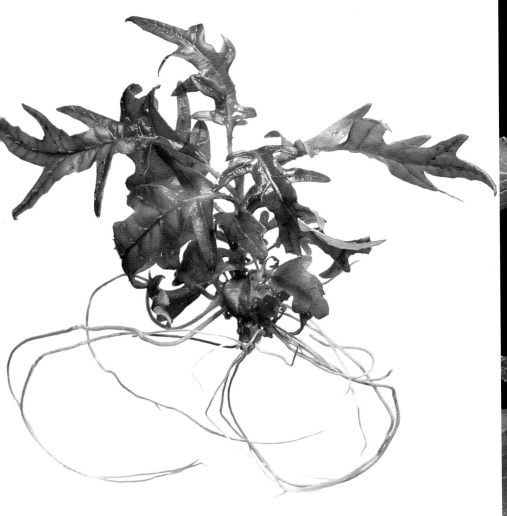
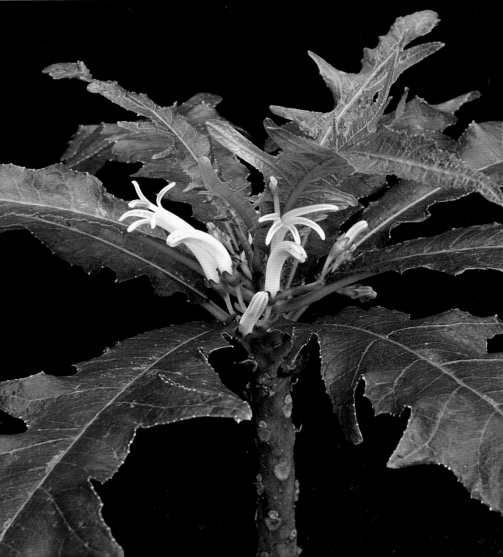

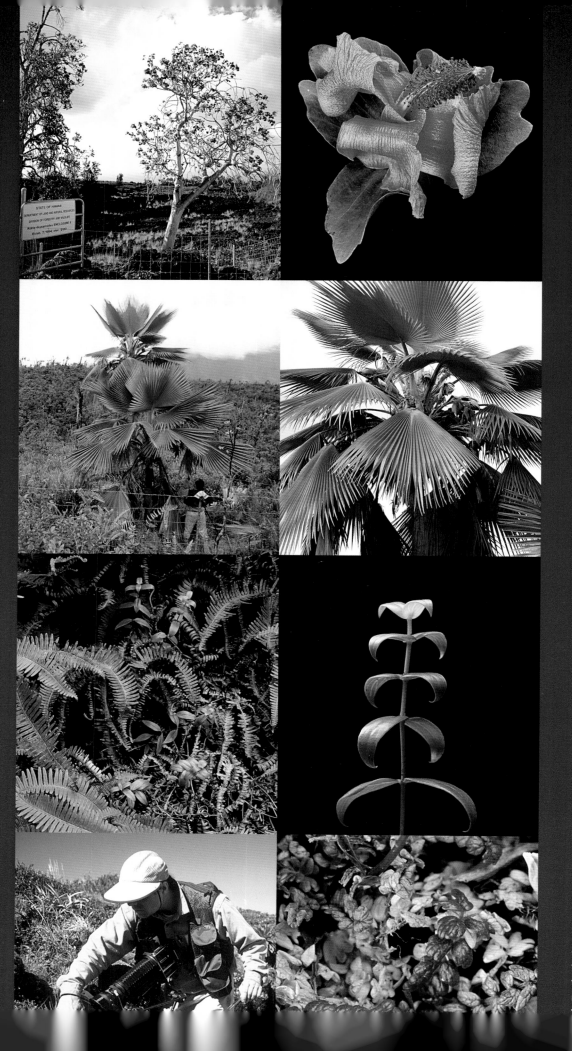

1) *Kokia drynarioides*—There are fewer than five wild *Kokia drynarioides* trees. They live on the Big Island of Hawai'i, and were once abundant in dryland forests. Most dryland forests have been lost due to human development, cattle grazing, alien weeds, and fires. The remaining trees are protected by fenced exclosures to exclude cattle and goats. The wild trees do flower and produce seed and they are relatively easy to grow, so trees can be seen in several botanical gardens.

2) *Pritchardia viscosa*—These native palms are restricted to Kaua'i, and prior to Hurricane 'Iniki in 1992 there were no more than twelve plants. The hurricane destroyed all but four adult plants, and two of these are protected by a fenced exclosure. Rats love to eat the tasty seeds, so metal guards have been placed around the trunks of the trees to prevent rats from climbing to the seed clusters. There is no regeneration, however, because once the seeds drop the rats quickly consume them. Seeds are periodically collected from these trees, and young trees are growing in botanical gardens.

3) *Hedyotis schlectendahliana*—This plant is only known from Lāna'i, and historically there were three documented populations. Grazing animals—deer, goats, sheep, and cattle—have destroyed most of the native forest on Lāna'i, and consequently there remains only one population of *Hedyotis schlectendahliana* with two known plants, nestled among ferns on the rim of a gulch. Deer are abundant in this area and are a serious threat to the remaining plants. Seeds have never been seen on the wild individuals, and there are no plants in cultivation.

4) *Acaena exigua*—A member of the rose family, this tiny plant was thought to be extinct when it was rediscovered in 1997 in the bogs at the summit of Pu'u Kukui Preserve on West Maui. Extensive surveys resulted in only one known individual, which died within two years. There are no plants in cultivation and there may be none left in the wild.

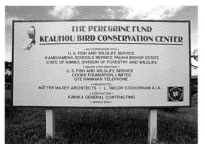 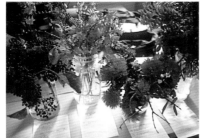 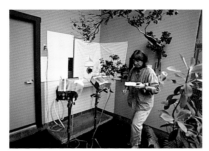 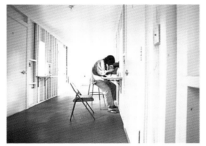 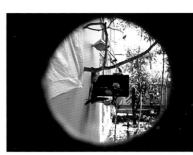

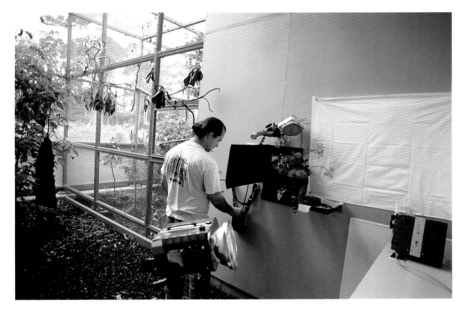

We deliberated about how to photograph rare Hawaiian forest birds, and concluded that there was only one way: to plead with Alan Lieberman and Cyndi Keuhler at Keauhou Bird Conservation Center in Volcano, Hawai'i, to allow us to come and work in their aviaries. After lengthy discussions they agreed to let us try. They set a lot of limits, most having to do with not disturbing the birds in any way. Together we devised a working process.

Birds thrive on predictability. In their natural environment life is predictable, except for weather, for which they seem to have a built-in adaptability. Anything new to the birds is suspect and usually avoided. Before we arrived to photograph, Alan placed black construction paper on the walls of the aviary to help habituate birds to our black backgrounds. A small sprig of 'ōhi'a was placed in the center of each piece of black paper to serve as a landing place. Weeks later, we positioned ourselves and the camera equipment inside the interior hallway just outside the areas where the birds live, and aimed our cameras through small doors that are used as food ports. Next to each food port was a small mirrored glass window that let us observe the birds without being seen. Perches made of 'ōhi'a branches were bracketed to the walls at a strategic distance, and black velvet-covered foam-core panels were affixed perpendicular to the aviary walls and behind the perches to create our black backgrounds. Inside each aviary we placed our studio lights and attached a white shower curtain to the walls so that light could reflect off it, creating a soft glow on the bird. Of course this plan depended completely on the birds coming to these new perches, when they had many other wonderful places they could be within the large aviaries. The perches were placed near feeding platforms, which would theoretically lure the birds toward our perches. Alan collected native plants that the birds love to feed on: *māmane, 'ōhi'a, 'ōlapa*. We positioned the most attractive sprigs on the perches to further entice our subjects. The birds needed time to adjust to the new things we placed in their aviaries, and we needed time to wait for those rare, fleeting windows of opportunity when a bird would land on our perch and we could expose film. It reminded me of fishing: quietly waiting with your line out for whole mornings or afternoons, anticipating the strike. We worked for hours and then days, and then weeks, during which we were able to observe the birds over long stretches of time, watching every movement and gesture, getting to know them. There was one day on which I was able to expose only two frames of film.

The building, containing 19 aviaries, is an intensive-care unit for the most critically endangered forest birds of Hawai'i. Here the birds are lovingly and expertly cared for and monitored. The goal is to breed the birds and build up a healthy captive population that can be reintroduced into protected habitats. For many of these birds, their numbers in the wild are declining so quickly that without this kind of intervention they could perish.

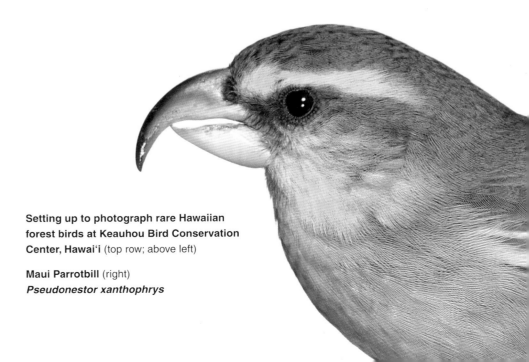

Setting up to photograph rare Hawaiian forest birds at Keauhou Bird Conservation Center, Hawai'i (top row; above left)

Maui Parrotbill (right)
Pseudonestor xanthophrys

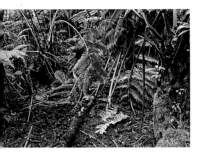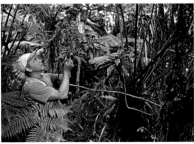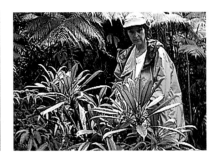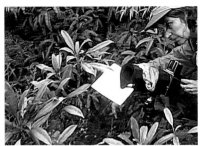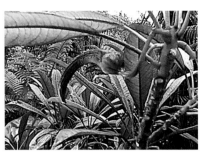

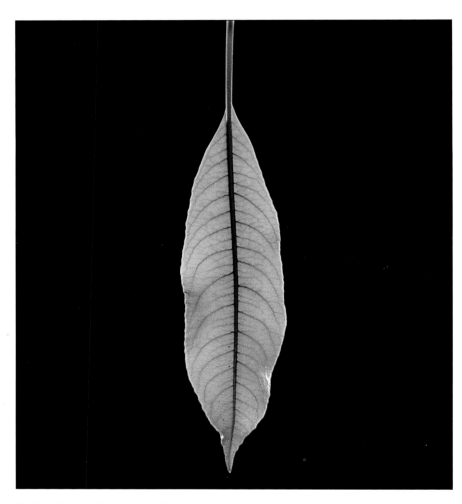

On the trips to photograph *Clermontia peleana*, **we saw one healthy-looking specimen and significant pig damage in the surrounding area** (top row).

Clermontia peleana subsp. *peleana*, **single leaf** (left)

Last known wild *Clermontia peleana* subsp. *peleana*, **now extinct in the wild** (right)

After 15 years working with endangered species we've always expected that within our lifetime some animal or plant that we had photographed would go extinct. We hoped that it would not happen and thought it would be a few years ahead, or maybe even many years. We were wrong.

We visited *Clermontia peleana* with Steve Perlman in 1998 near the Wailuku River on the island of Hawai'i. Three years earlier he had counted six plants at this site; now there were only two. One of them was dying and the other, a younger plant, looked like it was struggling: Many of its leaves were yellow. The area was torn up by pigs and several different alien weeds were aggressively moving in and choking the native forest. We did not have much to work with, so we chose to photograph a single leaf, feeling that it best represented the inherent beauty of the plant.

The next year a single *Clermontia peleana* plant was found at another site and was reported to be healthy and in flower. We made a one-day trip to the Big Island, and Ken Wood led us to the site. The forest was wet and soggy, and it was raining hard. The plant was past being in full flower but there were a few deep purple flowers just about to open, showing the graceful curvilinear form typical of many of the lobelioids. We set up to photograph, careful not to step too close to the roots. Plastic garbage bags protected our camera and lights as we persevered, waiting for opportunities between downpours when we could photograph. At the time we thought that the *Clermontia peleana* might not be included in the final edit for the book since it was not in prime condition either time we visited it. In August of 2000 we attended a conservation conference in Hawai'i and were informed that the plants we had visited, which were the only known wild individuals of the species, had died. My heart sank. We had spent two days with this plant, concentrating on it intensely for the many hours of photography, developing an affection for it and an appreciation for its unique qualities. It is now presumed to be extinct in the wild. We learned that there is a single plant in cultivation and a small collection of seeds taken from the last wild plants. Maybe with a lot of work and attention, it can be brought back.

As soon as we returned to our studio, we pulled out the pictures of *Clermontia peleana*. We looked at the single leaf and the graceful arc of the soon-to-open flower holding a raindrop, which suddenly resembled a tear.

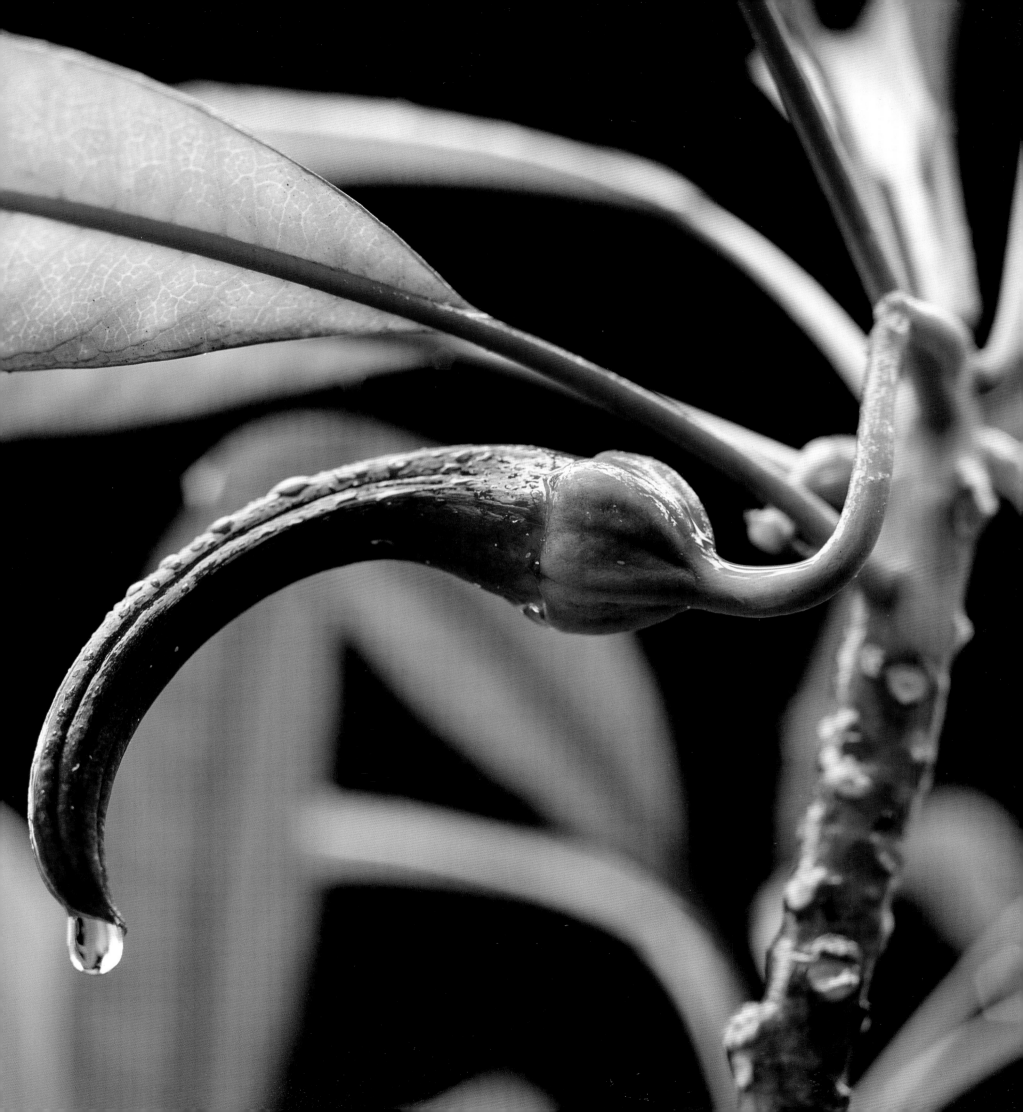

AFTERWORD

Life in Hawai'i is defined by improbable events. Every plant and animal that has managed to gain a foothold there, unassisted by humans, has done so against extraordinary odds. Because the Hawaiian Islands began as lifeless extrusions of lava from the earth's gut, every species on those islands had to originate from someplace else. That "someplace else" was typically the nearest mainland or large archipelago, such as North America, some 2,500 miles to the east, the Marquesas Islands some 2,000 miles to the south, or Asia, some 3,500 miles to the west. In any case, an immense expanse of inhospitable ocean separated the Hawaiian Islands from the nearest sources of life.

Different species employed different methods to cross the seas. Birds, bats, and certain insects flew. Marine fishes and the ancestors of the Hawaiian monk seal swam. The seeds of certain plants may have floated to the islands, while other insects may have arrived on board life rafts of flotsam set adrift from the mainland. And still other plants and animals hitchhiked to Hawai'i as burrs or parasites attached to the skin and feathers of migratory birds.

Regardless of the means of transport, the odds were wildly against the colonists. The winds or currents had to be just right, lest the floating seed, spider, or insect sail past the Hawaiian Islands and vanish in the ocean. Wandering birds, bats, or butterflies had to have the good fortune to stumble upon the islands before they died of exhaustion. Once safely ashore, a given plant or animal could not survive unless the plants and animals *it* needed for survival had preceded it; thus, the order in which the species arrived proved critically important. Finally, for the species as a whole to persist over time, the colonist must have been either a gravid female or lucky enough to have one or more members of the opposite sex show up more or less contemporaneously. By such strokes of extraordinary luck was produced what biologist John L. Culliney has called "one of the rarest and most improbable living assemblages on the earth."

Unfortunately, the geographical isolation that gave rise to such a remarkable flora and fauna also made many of those same species vulnerable to extinction. First, the vast majority of native plants and animals living in the Hawaiian Islands occur nowhere else on earth. Many, in fact, are restricted to a single island. If their habitats in Hawai'i are destroyed, they will become extinct, simply because there are no "backup" populations in other parts of the world. Second, the isolation of the Hawaiian archipelago ensured that a variety of widespread mainland species never gained a foothold there. Native Hawaiian mammals, for example, consist of a bat and a seal, but no large grazers, such as bison or deer, and no predators, such as cats, stoats, or foxes. Over time, therefore, many Hawaiian species lost their defenses against these nonexistent threats. For example, a number of geese, ibises, and rails became flightless, and the native nettle, or *mamaki,* lost its prickers. From an evolutionary perspective, these changes made sense: Why should a bird invest precious resources in growing strong wings if there are no predators to ambush it on the ground and if it has no reason to wander off the island on which it lives? And why should a plant expend energy in growing prickers if no deer or goat is likely to nibble it?

All of this changed when humans began arriving some 1,500 years ago. The Polynesians brought a handful of plants and animals with them, including pigs, dogs, chickens, and Pacific rats, while the white settlers subsequently unleashed a menagerie featuring goats, sheep, cattle, cats, mongooses, ship rats, and thousands of other species. In the blink of an eye in evolutionary time, the Hawaiian Islands were filled with species that would never have gotten there without human assistance, much to the detriment of the native flora and fauna.

Along with the alien plants and animals came new diseases to which some native species lacked immunity. People, of course, began clearing the native vegetation to make room for croplands, pastures, and (eventually) cities, thereby adding the impact of habitat destruction to that of alien species.

The result has been a one-two punch that has devastated the native flora and fauna. At least half and perhaps more than two-thirds of the native land birds of Hawai'i vanished during the Polynesian era. Of those that survived the Polynesian era, approximately half were subsequently eradicated by white settlers via habitat destruction and the spread of alien species and diseases. Nor have the losses been confined to birds. Virtually every group of organisms native to Hawai'i—from plants to snails to insects—has suffered high losses. According to The Nature Conservancy, 60 percent of the native fauna and flora of Hawai'i is imperiled, by far the highest percentage of vulnerable species of any state in the Union.

Yet to a casual observer (and, indeed, to many longtime residents), Hawai'i still seems like a remarkably unspoiled place. On Maui, O'ahu, or Kaua'i, for example, one can drive or hike for miles through verdant forests filled with interesting species. Yet almost every one of the trees or birds one sees, especially in the lowlands, are nonnative species, interlopers from other lands that were brought to Hawai'i by humans. What little is left of the native Hawaiian flora and fauna clings to existence in the nooks and crannies that time forgot—on steep mountain slopes or atop inaccessible plateaus, or on the leeward islands, where people and alien species have not taken over.

In those few special places where the native wildlife hangs on, a small band of dedicated professionals and volunteers is waging a heroic battle on its behalf. The frontline troops include intrepid botanists who rappel down cliffs to manually pollinate rare plants whose native pollinators have long since disappeared, ornithologists who spend days slogging through some of the steepest, muddiest, and wettest forests on earth to count rare songbirds, volunteers who devote their weekends to pulling up weeds that are outcompeting the native plants, and men and women who take on the deeply unpleasant but essential task of eradicating pigs, goats, cats, and other alien animals that threaten the natives. All of these people are racing against the clock, saving lives on a shoestring budget.

The future of conservation in Hawai'i is clear. A growing roster of imperiled species and damaged ecosystems will require ever more vigilant management against a growing roster of harmful alien species. And increasingly expensive and risky steps, such as captive propagation, will have to be taken to save the rarest species. But make no mistake about it—species can be saved and ecosystems can be repaired, even in this battered and bruised corner of the earth, provided we have the will and the resources to do so. The keys to success include strong environmental laws like the Endangered Species Act, adequate funding for conservation programs, cooperation with landowners, and, above all, public education.

Behind each of David Liittschwager's and Susan Middleton's stunning portraits is the story of a survivor, a plant or animal that beat the odds and flourished in the Hawaiian Islands, only to have its world turned upside down by humans. In the final analysis, of course, it will be people who determine how many and which of the imperiled species of Hawai'i make it through this decade or this century. Having overcome great obstacles to get to Hawai'i, these remarkable plants and animals must now surmount one last hurdle—human indifference—to stay there.

—David S. Wilcove, Senior Ecologist, Environmental Defense

SPECIES PROFILES

Flora by Dr. David Lorence (D.L.) and Dr. Warren L. Wagner (W.L.W.)
Fauna by Anita Manning and Dr. Steven Lee Montgomery (A.M./S.L.M.)

In these profiles, English common names are listed first, then Hawaiian names, then scientific names. Not all names exist for all species.

Scale information contains the size range of a species and/or the size of the individual(s) shown in the photograph.

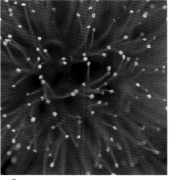

p. 2

'Ōhi'a; 'Ōhi'a Lehua; Lehua
Metrosideros polymorpha

Photograph: Pu'u Kukui Preserve, West Maui
Range: all of the main islands except Ni'ihau and Kaho'olawe
Habitat: near sea level to over 8,000 feet; from barren lava flows to montane bogs
Population: probably the most common Hawaiian native plant
Threats: habitat degradation and destruction
Legal status: none
Scale: small trailing shrub in bogs to giant forest trees 80 feet or more tall; flower portion shown 1 inch

More than any other plant, the *'ōhi'a, Metrosideros polymorpha,* is the icon of the Hawaiian environment. It is nearly ubiquitous in the myriad of habitats from the coast to the wettest environment in the world, the montane Hawaiian bog. It is often a tree, but can be a shrub on arid lava fields or a small trailing shrub in the water-soaked bogs. This extremely variable species has bottlebrush-like heads of flowers that are usually vivid red but sometimes pale red, orange, white, or yellow. The leaves are even more variable. They can be round or narrow, have rounded or pointed tips, have smooth hairless surfaces, or can be clothed in a dense wool, and young leaves can be pale green or red. The species, currently subdivided into eight varieties, occurs in or dominates numerous habitats from young lavas to mature wet forest and even bogs. The seeds are minute and are believed to have been dispersed over the ocean by high-elevation winds. The abundant flowers are a major source of nectar for many Hawaiian birds; feeding birds follow "waves" of flowering in different parts of the forest. The *'ōhi'a* was an important plant to the Hawaiians, who used the heavy, hard, and strong wood in construction and for carved images, household implements, and canoe seats and gunwales. The flowers and leaves were used to weave *lei.—W.L.W.*

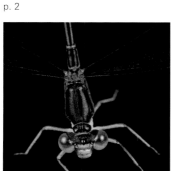

p. 3

Blackline Damselfly; Rainbow-Eye Damselfly
Pinao Ānuenue
Megalagrion nigrohamatum nigrolineatum

Photograph: temporary studio, East–West Center, O'ahu
Range: sea level to 2,400 feet, Ko'olau Mountains, O'ahu; historic: Wai'anae Mountains, O'ahu
Habitat: naiads prefer midland streamsides in standing pools, under stones and algae
Population: rare
Threats: predation on naiads by alien fish
Legal status: species of concern
Scale: 2 inches long

Most remarkable for luminous eyes compounded of thousands of tiny lens facets arrayed in a spectrum from lime to turquoise to red, this rainbow-eye damselfly is a beauty to observe. Its large wraparound eyes give panoramic vision for easy detection of prey movements. • Of all 25 native damselfly species, amazingly, one (*M. oahuense*) was proven not to be aquatic. In a ferny rain forest five miles inland from Waikiki Beach, on a volcanic slope so steep there is no standing or flowing water, dwell three commonly seen and resident damselflies. Two species place eggs in wet leaf axils of lilies and climbing screwpine vines, where progeny will always have prey. Sugar entomologist Francis Williams, devoting weekends to finding nymphs of the third species, made seven hikes to search low vegetation, where the damsels so often rested to avoid being eaten by the hawking giant Hawaiian dragonfly, and to devour mites and myriads of midges. Encouraged to search the ground by spotting freshly emerged adults in low ferns, finally upon Williams's eighth visit to the same site, he triumphantly discovered a woolly nymph under a fern thicket. This terrestrial existence is a singular life in the world's ancient order of dragonfly. Williams wrote a masterful and exciting report on water-loving insects, ending it with the "extra-aquatic" naiad that spurned water.—*A.M./S.L.M.*

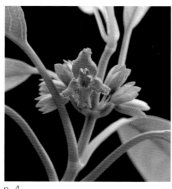

p. 4

Stenogyne kealiae

Photograph: National Tropical Botanical Garden Nursery, Lāwa'i, Kaua'i
Range: Kōke'e State Park, Kaua'i, from Awa'awapuhi to Kalalau Valleys
Habitat: 3,570 to 4,100 feet; rain forest
Population: five populations with about 100–200 individuals total
Threats: habitat destruction and trampling by feral animals, especially goats and pigs; competition from alien plants; land-use practices
Legal status: candidate for endangered status
Scale: vine up to 10 feet or more in length; flower ¹⁄₂ inch across

Stenogyne is one of the more interesting genera in the mint family (Lamiaceae) because the species are mostly perennial vines that send long stems up into the rain forest trees, such as *S. càlaminthoides,* or sprawl along the ground or on shrubs, such as *S. purpurea.* Field studies on Kaua'i showed that thick-leaved plants identified as the widespread Kaua'i species *S. purpurea* actually represent a distinct species. The distinctive leaves, coupled with occurrence at the same location of plants of the typical *S. purpurea* without hybridization, provided the evidence to show it represented a separate species rather than an ecological form. Tim Flynn's discovery of a population of these plants provided crucial evidence for botanists Steve Weller (University of California) and Warren Wagner to understand the nature of the distinction between these closely related species. It turns out that the botanist Heinrich Wawra, a member of the Austrian East Asiatic Exploring Expedition in 1870, collected this thick-leaved plant and later described it as *S. kealiae,* the name it now goes by. • The reduced lower lip of the flower, exserted stamens, abundant nectar production, lack of floral odor, and long curved flowers of some *Stenogyne* species, as well as many observations of visitations by Hawaiian honeycreepers, provide circumstantial evidence for pollination of *Stenogyne* by honeycreepers. It is not known what pollinates the smaller reddish purple flowers of *S. kealiae.*—*W.L.W.*

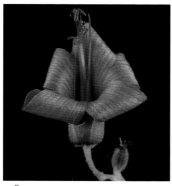

p. 5

Nohoanu; Hinahina
Geranium arboreum

Photograph: Polipoli State Park, Maui
Range: north and west slopes of Haleakalā; formerly Luala'ilua Hills, East Maui
Habitat: steep narrow gulches in subalpine woodland
Population: four populations with fewer than 300 individuals total
Threats: past threats include cattle grazing and rooting activities of pigs; competition from alien plants; fire
Legal status: endangered
Scale: 6–13 feet tall; flower ³⁄₄ inch across

Unique in the Geranium family, *Geranium arboreum,* which is endemic to East Maui, is the only bird-pollinated member of this worldwide family of some 700 species. The bright red flowers of *G. arboreum* bear a striking resemblance to those of *Kokia* in the Hibiscus family. This resemblance is related to the evolution of both of these plants from insect to bird pollination. Both genera have somewhat asymmetrical twisted flower parts that form a tube into which a visiting bird inserts its curved bill to drink nectar. To date the only published observation of visits to *G. arboreum* by Hawaiian birds was that made by Sherwin Carlquist, a renowned biologist who wrote *Island Biology,* an influential book on island evolution. He observed the *'Apapane,* one of the Hawaiian honeycreepers, taking nectar from the flowers. Unfortunately there has been no detailed study of pollination of *G. arboreum,* but reduction in numbers of Hawaiian birds since humans arrived in the islands centuries ago must be a factor in the rarity of *G. arboreum, Kokia,* and many other Hawaiian plants pollinated by birds. The other five species of Hawaiian *Geranium* have flowers more typical for the genus. They have flat, spreading, symmetrical flowers that are white or pinkish with usually purple veins. It is not known what pollinates the other species, but it is most likely small insects.—*W.L.W.*

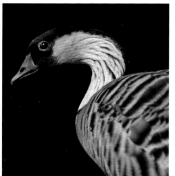

Hawaiian Goose
Nēnē
Branta sandvicensis

Photograph: Honolulu Zoo, Honolulu, Oʻahu (adult); Olinda Endangered Species Facility, Maui (goslings)
Range: Kauaʻi lowlands; Haleakalā National Park, Maui; Hawaiʻi Volcanoes National Park, Hawaiʻi
Habitat: sea level to 10,000 feet; shrubland and grassy areas
Population: about 850 wild birds
Threats: low-protein alien grasses; dogs, cats, mongoose; competition from goats; habitat loss
Legal status: endangered
Scale: about 5 pounds

Nēnē are related to the continental Canada goose, but have longer legs, smaller wing-to-body mass ratio, and no long-distance migration. Partially webbed feet are an adaptation to long residence on land; *Nēnē* are rarely seen on water. • *Nēnē*, the state bird of Hawaiʻi, are the charismatic native wildlife everyone wants to save. They are carried home as plush toys. They appear on logo merchandise, holiday greeting cards, mugs, puzzles, and T-shirts. They are easily the most photographed bird in Hawaiʻi. Tolerant of humans, they are sometimes hassled by visitors wanting to get that special photo. Birds are vigorously protected inside national parks, but some mooch food in parking lots and are occasionally run over. • Originally, people viewed *Nēnē* as food, not fad. First Polynesians then Westerners hunted them. Following continental tradition, as late as 1904 government-sanctioned hunting seasons overlapped the *Nēnē* breeding time. Human lowland expansion forced the species into upslope locales where winters are too cold for good gosling health. In 1952 the wild population numbered about 30 birds. *Nēnē* were saved by 1950s private captive-breeding programs administered by Herbert Shipman of Hawaiʻi and Wildfowl Trust of England, followed by 1960s state programs using federal funds. Today government-private cooperation reintroduces the birds to lowland habitat while studying nutritional needs and controlling predators. The *Nēnē's* future looks encouraging but isn't assured.—*A.M./S.L.M.*

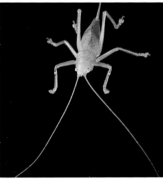

Alani; Alani Kuahiwi
Melicope degeneri

Photograph: Kōkeʻe State Park, Kauaʻi
Range: Kauaʻi
Habitat: wet forest
Population: two populations with 11 individuals total
Threats: goats and weeds; black twig borer poses potential threat
Legal status: candidate for endangered status
Scale: tree up to 20 feet tall; leaf 1¾ inches across

Melicope degeneri was known from a single collection made in 1926 along Kōkeʻe Stream on Kauaʻi. Despite numerous botanists collecting over the past 75 years, it has never been found in this area again. In 1995 Ken Wood of the National Tropical Botanical Garden (NTBG) discovered a new population of this species north of Kōkeʻe Stream in Hanakoa Valley. He has been studying this rare species and many other *Melicope* species for the past five years and has learned a great deal about their population and conservation status. His work resulted in discovery of yet another population of *M. degeneri* in Koaiʻe Valley. • *Melicope* is one of the largest genera of Hawaiian plants, containing about 50 species. The species are often a conspicuous component of the forests. Until recently they were classified as the genus *Pelea*, named in honor of the volcano goddess Pele, but new studies on a global scale showed them to be best considered part of the large Australasian genus *Melicope*. The crushed leaves of many of the species have a strong anise odor, but there is variation in the exact nature of the odor and its intensity. Another species from Kauaʻi, *M. anisata*, has the strongest odor and is known as *mokihana*. Fruits of this species, which were strung into fragrant *lei* for the head or around the neck, provided one of the Hawaiians' favorite perfumes.—*W.L.W.*

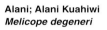

Kauaʻi Flightless Cone Head Katydid
ʻŪhini
Banza kauaiensis

Photograph: Kapalua Golf Villas, Kapalua, Maui
Range: Kauaʻi
Habitat: 3,000–4,500 feet; mountain moist and wet forests
Population: rare
Threats: predation by alien rats, Common Mynas, ants; alien wasp (parasites of eggs)
Legal status: none
Scale: body 1 inch long

From a single type of winged katydid that crossed the ocean to arrive in primordial Hawaiʻi, a dozen species evolved. They are recognizable by their cone-shaped heads. Very short wings make them flightless. Although discovered by explorers in the 1860s, this cluster of endemic creatures has only recently been studied. John Strazanac, who knows these insects intimately from a thorough field survey for his thesis, says, "They hop if alarmed and project themselves into the air to avoid capture. This looks neat, as they are spread-eagle, with open wings to slow down the drop, legs out to grab any twig or leaf." • Days are for hiding. Evening is for eating and romance. Males court females with a faint, very high-pitched, irresistible song made by rasping their wings' edges. The female body ends in a swordlike ovipositor for placing eggs. *Banza* do not chew on leaves; rather they are scavengers and predators. They readily munch dead flies and crush beetles with powerful jaws, which for defensive displays can be flashed open with sharp-clawed, spiny legs raised. • Known today only from the highest forest on Kauaʻi, why these interesting creatures do not occupy other suitable habitat is unknown. Lab-raised *Banza* from Oʻahu displayed a highly unusual color change: A few green nymphs (immatures) molted into brown just before the adult stage, then became brown adults with black faces.—*A.M./S.L.M.*

Kokiʻo; Kokiʻo ʻUla; Kokiʻo ʻUlaʻula; Mākū
Hibiscus kokio subsp. saintjohnianus

Photograph: National Tropical Botanical Garden, Limahuli Garden, Kauaʻi
Range: Kauaʻi
Habitat: mesic forests and cliff shrublands
Population: 20 or more populations with several thousand individuals total
Threats: competition from alien weeds; disturbance by feral goats and pigs
Legal status: species of concern
Scale: petal 1⅘–2⅖ inches long

The five Hawaiian endemic *Hibiscus* species are highly attractive and easily cultivated for their white, yellow, orange, or red colored flowers. Pictured here is *Hibiscus kokio* subspecies *saintjohnianus*, a compact shrub with many erect branches. This *kokiʻo* is found only in the rugged mountains of northwestern Kauaʻi, where plants are confined to pockets of mesic forest and shrubland on steep cliff walls along the Nā Pali coast from Limahuli Valley westward to Nuʻalolo Valley. • Cornell University specialist Dr. David Bates separates *Hibiscus kokio* into two subspecies. The more common and widespread subspecies *kokio* is always red flowered. Flower color in subspecies *saintjohnianus* is variable, ranging from deep yellow to orange or orange-red. The name honors the late Dr. Harold St. John, a prolific collector and botanist who studied and published extensively on Hawaiian plants for much of his long career. • Field botanists estimate that up to 20 populations of subspecies *saintjohnianus* exist in the wild, largely in areas such as the Nā Pali–Kona State Park. In spite of a relatively high number of plants, this subspecies is threatened by large feral goat populations and aggressive alien weeds that prevent growth of young plants and regeneration in the wild. Fortunately, this attractive *kokiʻo* thrives in cultivation by seeds or cuttings, thus helping ensure its survival.—*D.L.*

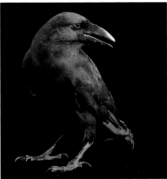

Hawaiian Crow
ʻAlalā
Corvus hawaiiensis

Photograph: Dept. of Land and Natural Resources, Olinda Endangered Species Facility, Olinda, Maui
Range: Hawaiʻi Island, very limited; historic: larger areas, but still restricted
Habitat: 1,000–8,000 feet; dry forest and open country
Population: 30 birds: 27 in a captive breeding program and 3 known in wild
Threats: habitat loss; disease; small gene pool
Legal status: endangered
Scale: about 21 inches head to tail

"Why worry about *crows?*" Conservationists confront this reaction to the *ʻAlalā's* precarious hold on life. The *ʻAlalā*, a distinct species, suffers under the bad-boy reputation of continental relatives. While *ʻAlalā* eat an omnivorous diet of fruits, nectar, and invertebrates, they feed and act more like parrots. They stay in the upper canopy, jumping and climbing from branch to branch, not flying, as first choice. *ʻAlalā* means "to bawl, cry, or bleat." A loud person might be chided as an *ʻAlalā: He ʻalalā, he manu leo nui* ("It is the crow, a loud-voiced bird").[1] Seventy distinct calls are known including a terrifying yowl comparable to a cougar's cry. *ʻAlalā* formed flocks, using calls for cohesion. • Hawaiians hunted *ʻAlalā* for decorative feathers and food. In the 1890s the continental crow's reputation led to shooting *ʻAlalā* as pests. *ʻAlalā* are also vulnerable to disease: One rancher recalls, as a boy in the 1920s, hearing "a baby crying in the forest." The sound led him to a grounded, dying *ʻAlalā* flock, faces and feet covered in disabling avian pox lesions. • A federally funded, state-led propagation program conducted by a private zoological society aims to save this species from extinction. *ʻAlalā* captive breeding programs are handicapped because the few wild-collected birds are mostly related, resulting in inbreeding effects. Breeding success with such a small group of individual birds is problematic, but possible.—*A.M./S.L.M.*

1. M. K. Pukui, *ʻŌlelo Noʻeau: Hawaiian Proverbs and Poetical Sayings*, Special Publication 71 (Honolulu: Bishop Museum Press, 1983), p. 62.

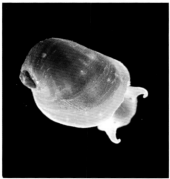

Newcomb's Snail
Pūpū Wai Lani
Erinna newcombi

Photograph: National Tropical Botanical Garden, Ulu Ali'i Research Apartment, Lāwa'i, Kaua'i
Range: six streams on Kaua'i
Habitat: fast-flowing perennial freshwater streams with rocky waterfalls, seeps, and springs
Population: 6,000–7,000; very rare
Threats: rosy wolf snail *(Euglandina rosea)*, two species of marsh flies, and other alien species; stream flow reduction
Legal status: threatened
Scale: 1/4 inch long

Erinna newcombi honors 1850s Honolulu physician Dr. Wesley Newcomb, a land-snail enthusiast whose discoveries were recognized internationally. Although intensive surveys in the early 1990s located four previously unknown locations, the number of populations has declined by up to 60 percent since 1925. Newcomb's snail is extremely vulnerable to local disasters or predation. Most Hawaiian freshwater stream life spends part of its life in the ocean and then returns to any available stream. With no dispersing larval stage, Newcomb's snail completes its entire life cycle in its parental stream. Additionally, 90 percent of the population lives in only two locations. • Intentional and accidental introductions of alien fish, snails, flies, and frogs threaten this lovely snail's survival. The rosy wolf snail, introduced in 1955, is the most serious threat. This usually terrestrial predator can fully submerge itself to eat. The green swordtail fish, a 1922 mosquito-control introduction, and two accidental introductions, the American bullfrog, in 1867, and the wrinkled frog, in 1896, all prey on Newcomb's snail. Two nonnative marsh flies, introduced in 1958 and 1966 as controls on an alien snail hosting the cattle liver fluke, are significant parasites. Since February 2000, federal threatened status has provided significant protection to Newcomb's snail and its habitat.—*A.M./S.L.M.*

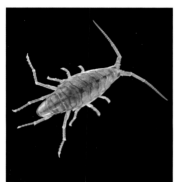

Makaleha Spring Amphipod
'Uku Wai
(Unnamed new species)

Photograph: National Tropical Botanical Garden, Ulu Ali'i Research Apartment, Lāwa'i, Kaua'i
Range: Makaleha Spring on Makaleha Stream, Kaua'i
Habitat: 800 feet; on moss in the splash zone of a perennial freshwater spring
Population: unknown
Threats: stream flow reduction
Legal status: none
Scale: 1/2 inch long

Over 100 years ago British exploratory biologist R. C. L. Perkins predicted the Hawaiian mini-wildlife would "always yield new things." Since Perkins's prediction, the list of Hawaiian insects, spiders, snails, and other invertebrates has grown by thousands. Many other plants and animals are yet undiscovered and await curious and adventurous future biologists. Those willing to tramp through wet forests, hot lowlands, or cold mountaintops to collect, compare, and classify may experience the "aha!" of discovery, the reward of finding something previously hidden. • Laws offer protection only to named flora and fauna. A scientific name, with its description, gives scientists, government, and landowners a shared definition and vocabulary. In 1994 a proposed water development project threatened to degrade Makaleha Spring. The project was rejected to preserve Newcomb's snail (*Erinna newcombi*, p. 32). This then-unknown creature, and others still unknown, benefited. Officially designated as threatened years later, the snail's presence in Makaleha Spring also protects this amphipod. Habitat destruction is the single largest cause of extinction in Hawai'i. Saving habitat saves many creatures and plants beyond those few for which a place is designated "critical habitat." • Makaleha's literal translation is "eyes looking about in wonder and admiration": a prophetically apt name for the place of discovery of a new and tiny creature.—*A.M./S.L.M.*

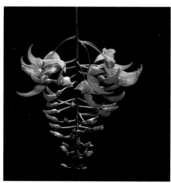

Nuku 'I'iwi; Ka 'I'iwi; Nuku
Strongylodon ruber

Photograph: Pu'u Kukui Preserve, West Maui
Range: Kaua'i, O'ahu, Moloka'i, Maui, Hawai'i
Habitat: lowland to mid-elevation mesic to wet forests
Population: possibly several thousand plants; number of populations unknown
Threats: damage from feral pigs; competition from alien weeds; rat and insect predation on seeds; landslides; fire
Legal status: species of concern
Scale: flower 1 1/3–1 2/3 inches long

Although lianas or truly woody vines are common in many tropical areas, there are only a few species in Hawai'i. One such liana is *Strongylodon ruber,* one of the most strikingly beautiful flowering plants of Hawai'i, with clusters of bright scarlet flowers dangling from supporting tree branches. It was known to the Hawaiians as *nuku 'i'iwi, kā 'i'iwi,* or *nuku,* signifying the flowers' resemblance to the curved red beak *(nuku)* of the *'i'iwi,* a bright vermilion native bird. After flowering, large dangling pods develop with one or two black seeds about an inch in diameter. A genus of about 15 to 20 species ranging from Madagascar to Polynesia, *Strongylodon* contains a number of showy species. Some, like *Strongylodon ruber,* have red flowers pollinated by birds. Others produce bluish green flowers that are pollinated by bats, including *S. macrobotrys,* a favorite horticultural species in Hawai'i known as the jade vine. Because of its high-climbing habit, *Strongylodon ruber* is inconspicuous except in flower. Consequently, it is difficult to estimate the actual number and size of its populations. Until additional field surveys yield more accurate information on its populations, the *nuku 'i'iwi* will remain classified as a Species of Concern.—*D.L.*

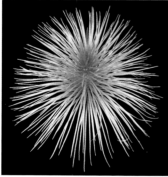

Ka'ū Silversword
Argyroxiphium kauense

Photograph: Volcano Rare Plant Facility, Center for Conservation Research and Training, University of Hawai'i, Volcano, Hawai'i
Range: Mauna Loa and Hualālai, Hawai'i
Habitat: 5,300–7,600 feet; bogs and wet forest on lava flows
Population: three populations with fewer than 500 individuals total
Threats: habitat degradation by mouflon sheep and goats; rooting by pigs; small population size
Legal status: endangered
Scale: 2 1/2–10 feet tall in flower

The most common of the five silversword species is *Argyroxiphium sandwicense* from East Maui and Hawai'i. Another lesser-known species is *A. kauense,* which, until recently, was thought to be nearly extinct. This species is of extremely localized distribution on the island of Hawai'i, on Mauna Loa and formerly on Hualālai. It is now restricted to upper Waiākea Forest Reserve, Keāpōhina on Kahuku Ranch, and 'Āinapō Trail. • Gerald Carr (University of Hawai'i) has been studying the classification, hybridization, and evolution of the silverswords and their other Hawaiian relatives, *Dubautia* and *Wilkesia,* for over 20 years. He and numerous colleagues including Sherwin Carlquist (Santa Barbara), Bruce Baldwin (University of California), and Robert Robichaux (University of Arizona) have made the silversword alliance among the best understood organisms in the Hawaiian Islands through intensive study of their molecular biology, physiology, and other biological aspects. For example, they determined that this unique and extraordinarily diverse group of plants arose from a single long-distance colonist from a hybrid between two California tarweed genera at least five million years ago.—*W.L.W.*

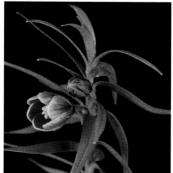

Lysimachia pendens

Photograph: National Tropical Botanical Garden, Ulu Ali'i Research Apartment, Lāwa'i, Kaua'i
Range: Kaua'i
Habitat: wet cliff faces, lowland wet forest
Population: one population of fewer than 100 plants
Threats: rockslides; possible competition from alien weeds
Legal status: species of concern
Scale: leaf 3/4–1 3/4 inches long; flower 3/8 inch diameter

This small, delicately pendulous shrub typically grows on seeping, moss-covered rock walls and cliff faces near waterfalls where the constant spray maintains the high humidity it requires. Slender tapering leaves and small, purplish red bell-shaped flowers resemble those of *Lysimachia filifolia,* a related species from Kaua'i and O'ahu for which it was at first mistaken. However, studies of Hawaiian *Lysimachia* by Dr. Kendrick L. Marr revealed that this population of Kaua'i plants represented a new species, which he named *Lysimachia pendens.* The species name signifies "pendent," alluding to its hanging growth form, presumably an adaptation to minimize resistance to water cascading down the cliff faces during heavy rains. *Lysimachia pendens* is currently known from a single locality near the base of Mount Wai'ale'ale on the northern Wailua River. Due to its small population size, *Lysimachia pendens* is particularly vulnerable to rockslides that constantly erode these cliffs. In 1992 Hurricane 'Iniki caused damage to this population. Several alien plants able to successfully colonize wet rock faces may compete with *Lysimachia pendens.* • Because of its specialized habitat requirements, this species is difficult to maintain in cultivation. Nevertheless, several plants have been propagated and grown at NTBG and Lyon Arboretum. Conservation efforts for this fragile species clearly need to focus primarily on habitat preservation.—*D.L.*

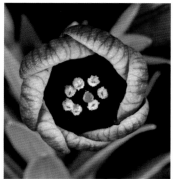

Lehua Maka Noe; Kolokolo Kuahiwi; Kolokolo Lehua; Kolekole Lehua
Lysimachia daphnoides

Photograph: Sincock Bog, Kaua'i; Alaka'i Wilderness Area, Kaua'i
Range: Kaua'i
Habitat: bog vegetation
Population: nine populations with 180–300 plants total
Threats: pigs; competition from alien plants
Legal status: candidate for endangered status
Scale: leaf 4/5–2 inches long; flower 1/2 inch across

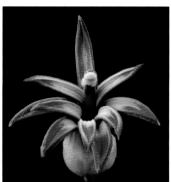

p. 41

'Ōha Wai; 'Ōha Hāhā
Clermontia drepanomorpha

Photograph: Volcano Rare Plant Facility, Center for Conservation Research and Training, University of Hawai'i, Volcano, Hawai'i
Range: Kohala Mountains, Hawai'i
Habitat: wet and low-stature boggy forest along edges of gorges of the plateau and near summit
Population: six populations with fewer than 300 individuals
Threats: alien plants; habitat destruction (natural events, humans, animals); small population size
Legal status: endangered
Scale: flower 2 1/2 inches across

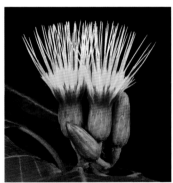

p. 43

Hesperomannia arbuscula

Photograph: Wai'anae Kai, O'ahu
Range: Wai'anae Kai, O'ahu, and 'Īao Valley, West Maui; historically known from central and southern Wai'anae Mountains, O'ahu; West Maui
Habitat: slopes and ridges in mesic to wet forest
Population: five populations with about 90 individuals total
Threats: pigs and rats; competition from alien plants such as blackberry, Christmasberry, and Koster's curse; small population size
Legal status: endangered
Scale: plant 6 1/2–11 feet tall; flower 1 3/4 inches long

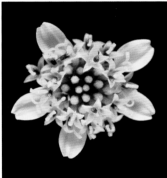

pp. 44, 45

Nehe
Melanthera waimeaensis

Photograph: National Tropical Botanical Garden, Native Hawaiian Plant Section, Lāwa'i, Kaua'i
Range: north-facing slopes of Waimea Canyon, Kaua'i
Habitat: 1,150 to 1,300 feet; steep slopes in dry shrubland
Population: one population with about 50 individuals total
Threats: habitat destruction by feral animals; competition from alien plants; fire; erosion
Legal status: endangered
Scale: flower 1/2 inch across

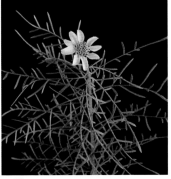

p. 45

Nehe
Melanthera tenuifolia

Photograph: Makua Military Reservation, O'ahu
Range: northern portion of Wai'anae Mountains, O'ahu
Habitat: ridgetops and bluffs in mesic forest
Population: six populations with about 4,000 individuals total
Threats: habitat destruction by feral animals, especially goats and pigs; competition for light and space with alien plants; fire
Legal status: endangered
Scale: stem up to 10 feet long; flower 3/4 inch across

Observant hikers along the remote Alaka'i Swamp Trail in Kaua'i may notice small, compact shrubs scattered on vegetation islands in the misty bogs. A closer look reveals clumped, upright stems symmetrically clad with pale mint green leaves embellished with purple veination. Delicately beautiful nodding bell-like flowers are produced singly among the upper leaves. Six or seven dark purple petals shade to deep burgundy or almost black within, contrasting with the yellow stamens. This lovely plant is known to botanists as *Lysimachia daphnoides,* and the Hawaiians were also familiar with it, judging by its four Hawaiian names. • Existing populations of *Lysimachia daphnoides* are known only from the Alaka'i Swamp; a second population from the lower elevation Wahiawa Bog is probably now extirpated. Bogs form only on level montane areas where rainfall exceeds drainage, and water pools over the impermeable lava. The vegetation is characterized by hummocks of low herbs, grasses, sedges, and mosses, with scattered dwarf shrubs. The largest bog in Hawai'i is found in the Alaka'i Swamp on Kaua'i, and a few smaller ones exist on Moloka'i, O'ahu, and Maui. Hawaiian bog vegetation is slow growing, sensitive to rooting and trampling by pigs, and extremely slow to recover from damage. Invasion by several alien plant species adapted to bog life is another concern, but few weeds can grow in the waterlogged, oxygen deprived soil conditions.—*D.L.*

Joseph F. Rock, a prominent botanist who contributed greatly to the description and understanding of the Hawaiian lobelioids, named *Clermontia drepanomorpha* based on specimens he and A. S. Hitchcock of the Smithsonian Institution collected in the Kohala Mountains, Hawai'i, in the early 1900s. *Clermontia drepanomorpha,* a terrestrial or epiphytic (not rooted in the soil) tree, has clusters of leaves nearly a foot long near the end of the branches, and has two to four flowers open at a time. The flowers are a deep wine color and have a tube up to two inches long with widely spreading lobes. The flower parts, which are typically differentiated into two dissimilar series, giving the flower a double appearance, are very similar in size and appearance in this and several other species of *Clermontia.* • Rock wrote that *Clermontia drepanomorpha* occurred in stands of thousands of trees. Since that time the population has been reduced to somewhat fewer than 300 individuals. In general, species of *Clermontia* tend to occupy more open habitats than other members of the Hawaiian lobelioids such as *Cyanea,* and thus often occur in larger numbers than these other genera. Because of this ecological attribute, fewer *Clermontia* species are at risk of extinction. Currently, about 60 percent of *Clermontia* species are a conservation concern, compared to 88 percent of *Cyanea* species.—*W.L.W.*

The three species of the Hawaiian genus *Hesperomannia* are highly distinctive in the sunflower family. When the genus was first described in 1865 by Asa Gray at Harvard University, one of the leading botanists of his day, it was considered to be the only Pacific Island member of the tribe Mutisiae, which are primarily from South America and Asia. The three species have large wine red heads of more than 30 to 40 golden yellow flowers either held erect as in *H. arbuscula* and the very closely related *H. arborescens,* or pendent as in the rare Kaua'i endemic *H. lydgatei.* This interesting genus was thought to be related to South American plants despite several odd features such as differently shaped pollen. Yet a recent study of the DNA sequences of *Hesperomannia* and numerous other members of the family led to a surprising conclusion: *Hesperomannia* is actually related to a completely different tribe, the ironweeds, which occur worldwide. The study showed that *Hesperomannia* is related to African or Asian members of the genus *Vernonia,* demonstrating that evolution in the remote Hawaiian Islands often leads to very different-appearing organisms than their continental ancestors, making it difficult to trace their ancestry. One aspect of this divergence is seen in the large heads of *Hesperomannia,* which have evolved from pollination by insects to pollination by birds such as the Hawaiian honeycreepers.—*W.L.W.*

Melanthera waimeaensis was collected for the first time in 1967. It had been overlooked by scientists for many decades because of its steep, inaccessible (at least to humans) habitat and its extreme rarity. It was discovered by Robert Hobdy, one of Hawai'i's eminent natural historians, at the time a Hawai'i State Forester working on Kaua'i. Like many of the species of the genus it is a sprawling or climbing perennial with fragile stems that can root at the nodes and thus spread without producing seeds. This type of reproduction is found in many plants and can be very useful in plants occurring in such unstable habitats as the steep, easily eroding slopes of Waimea Canyon. Plants like *Melanthera waimeaensis* that occur in inaccessible habitat may actually be more common than the known populations, although this can be true for any species because it is nearly impossible for biologists to survey every possible habitat for populations. To discover any new populations that exist would be essentially serendipitous. Therefore, we must act to conserve the only known population. —*W.L.W.*

The name of *Melanthera tenuifolia,* a sprawling or climbing perennial with fragile stems, is derived from the Latin for "slender leaves." The leaves—the strangest among all 35 species of the genus worldwide—are indeed the unique feature of this species. They are formally referred to as *ternately compound.* This means that each leaf is divided into three separate lobes so deep as to appear that it is actually three leaves. There are two leaves at a node, so *M. tenuifolia,* with its three-lobed leaves unlike any other species in the genus, appears to have a whorl of six leaves at each node. This makes for a rather attractive foliage. The leaves of many other Hawaiian species of *Melanthera* are also lobed or divided. It is not clear why lobed or divided leaves would evolve and be more suited to their particular Hawaiian environment. It may have something to do with light and/ or moisture levels.—*W.L.W.*

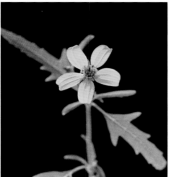

Nehe
Melanthera kamolensis

Photograph: National Tropical Botanical Garden, Kahanu Garden, Maui
Range: Kamole Gulch, leeward East Maui
Habitat: lowland dry forest
Population: one population with about 500 individuals total
Threats: habitat destruction by feral animals, including cattle and goats; natural or human disturbance such as a fire could eliminate the population due to its extremely narrow distribution
Legal status: endangered
Scale: flower 3/4 inch across

Melanthera kamolensis is a sprawling or climbing perennial with fragile stems. Typical of many members of the sunflower family, it has heads of tiny yellow flowers. It was named for Kamole Gulch, the only place it grows, and was originally described as a member of the Hawaiian genus *Lipochaeta*. With the advent of easy jet travel there was a great increase in the number of scientists studying Hawaiian plants. One of these was Robert Gardner, a graduate student from Ohio State University who discovered that one group of *Lipochaeta* species, including what was then referred to as *L. kamolenis,* had 30 chromosomes and another smaller group of six Hawaiian *Lipochaeta* species had 52 chromosomes. This discovery—along with experimental study of hybrids between species, DNA sequencing, and study of the structures of the fruits by several other scientists—has contributed to a revised classification that represents the genealogy of these Hawaiian species more accurately. All of the Hawaiian species with 30 chromosomes share this and many other features with a worldwide group, *Melanthera*. Recently, the formal process of proposing a new classification was completed. Thus the completely Hawaiian genus *Lipochaeta* is now restricted to only six of the species, those with 52 chromosomes, and the remainder have been transferred into *Melanthera.—W.L.W.*

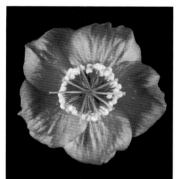

Green-Flowered Abutilon
Abutilon sandwicense

Photograph: Waimea Arboretum and Botanical Garden, O'ahu
Range: O'ahu
Habitat: 1,000–2,000 feet; dry to mesic lowland forest
Population: 12 populations with fewer than 300 individuals
Threats: competition from alien weeds; fire; drought; trampling by goats, pigs, and cattle
Legal status: endangered
Scale: petal 1 3/4–2 inches long

Of the seven *Abutilon* species known from the Hawaiian Islands, three are endemic and rare enough to be federally listed as endangered species. Of these, *Abutilon sandwicense* produces the largest flowers. It is a sprawling shrub with softly hairy, pale green leaves. The solitary flowers display a downy, greenish white bell-like calyx surrounding five large petals that enclose a brushlike cluster of yellow stamens. Generally the petals are bright green, but in some plants they may be reddish maroon shading to green basally. At first nodding and pendulous, the flowers become upright as the capsules mature and eventually split to release their seeds in a shakerlike fashion. • *Abutilon sandwicense* is known only from western O'ahu where it occurs on steep lower slopes and gulches in dry to mesic lowland forest. Historically this species grew along much of O'ahu's western Wai'anae Mountain range, but fewer than 300 plants remain. Although plants flower and fruit profusely, few seedlings survive to maturity. Two introduced beetles, the black twig borer and Chinese rose beetle, attack plants in cultivation and may also harm them in the wild. Conservation strategies for this species include alien weed control and outplanting. • *Abutilon sandwicense* also thrives in cultivation and is being successfully grown at several botanical gardens in Hawai'i. It tolerates dry conditions and makes an attractive horticultural and display plant.—*D.L.*

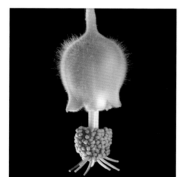

Ko'oloa 'Ula
Abutilon menziesii

Photograph: Keone, Lāna'i
Range: O'ahu, Lāna'i, Maui, Hawai'i
Habitat: dry to mesic lowland forest
Population: 10 populations ranging in size from one to several hundred plants; 450–500 total
Threats: human disturbance; competition from alien weeds; browsing and trampling by deer, goats, mouflon, pigs, cattle; fire
Legal status: endangered
Scale: flower 1 inch across

Resembling miniature hibiscus blossoms with flaring petals, flowers of *Abutilon menziesii* come in rich shades of maroon, deep red, or occasionally pale pink. Bell-shaped and lustrous, the flowers contrast with the velvety, grayish green foliage of this attractive shrub. *Abutilon* is a large genus belonging to the mallow family, with approximately 150 species in the tropics and subtropics. Of the seven species from the Hawaiian Islands, three are endemic and rare enough to be federally listed as endangered. Widely regarded as the most beautiful of these, *Abutilon menziesii* was known to the Hawaiians as *ko'oloa 'ula,* which means "red *ko'oloa*." *Abutilon menziesii* was declared endangered in 1986 and today is known only from scattered plants in remnants of dry forest and shrubland on O'ahu, Lāna'i, East Maui, and the Big Island of Hawai'i. Easily grown from seed and cuttings, this handsome plant thrives and blooms regularly under cultivation, tolerating dry, sunny conditions quite well. Genetic stock collected from populations on various islands is represented in the living collections at various Hawaiian botanical gardens. • The species name commemorates Archibald Menzies, British surgeon and naturalist under Captain George Vancouver on the HMS *Discovery,* which stopped in Hawai'i in 1792, 1793, and 1794.—*D.L.*

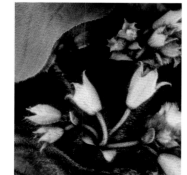

Hidden-Petaled Abutilon
Abutilon eremitopetalum

Photograph: Waimea Arboretum and Botanical Garden, O'ahu
Range: Lāna'i
Habitat: dry forest
Population: one population of nearly 100 plants
Threats: browsing from feral deer; competition from alien weeds; landslides; possibly fire
Legal status: endangered
Scale: flower 1 inch long

Flowers of the hidden-petaled abutilon are among the most unusual of the numerous Hawaiian members of the mallow (hibiscus) family. At first glance, hanging from the branches singly or in pairs, the flowers appear somehow abnormal because they seem to lack petals. Looking more like a Japanese lantern than a flower, the pale green calyx covered with fuzzy, stiff white hairs actually conceals five small green petals, invisible without peering directly inside. Hanging like a bell clapper, the showy staminal column bears a cluster of coral-colored anthers and yellow-to-pink style branches typical of its mallow relatives. • A small shrub six to eight feet high with softly downy, heart-shaped leaves, *Abutilon eremitopetalum* is now known from only a single population on Lāna'i. First discovered in the 1930s, the hidden-petaled abutilon was formerly more widespread, but cattle grazing and loss of habitat contributed to its decline and presumed extinction. A population of about 60 to 70 plants discovered by Steve Perlman in 1987 declined to 7 plants six years later, having been eaten by feral deer. The population was fenced and a crop of new seedlings is now growing in the exclosure, offering hope for the future. Fortunately, seeds of the hidden-petaled abutilon retain their viability in storage. This species is easily cultivated and conservation collections exist in a number of botanical gardens and other collections in the state.—*D.L.*

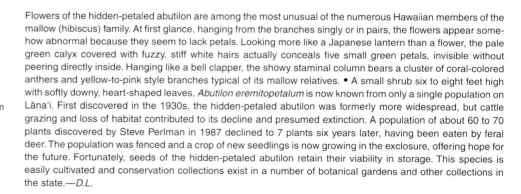

Cyrtandra paliku

Photograph: Mount Kekoiki, Kaua'i
Range: Kaua'i
Habitat: mist-shrouded cliff face in lowland wet forest
Population: about 70 plants (50 adults and 20 juveniles)
Threats: rockslides; competition from alien plants
Legal status: none
Scale: 1–3 feet high; leaf 1 3/4–3 1/2 inches wide

The rarity of certain endemic Hawaiian plant species is not always due to habitat loss, disturbance, or competition; rather, these organisms have evolved to occupy extremely specialized habitats, a process known to biologists as adaptive radiation. *Cyrtandra paliku,* a member of the African violet family, is just such a specialist. It was first discovered in 1993 by field botanist Ken Wood while rappelling down a cliff face during a botanical survey of the Makaleha Mountains in Kaua'i. His were likely the first human eyes to gaze upon the herb's marvelously velvety leaves and pure white flowers. Its strikingly hairy stems and leaves, evocative of the legs of some weird botanical tarantula, probably represent an adaptation to the moist, shady habitat. In Hawaiian *pali kū* means "vertical cliff." • Despite searches of similar cliff habitats on Kaua'i, only a single population comprising about 70 plants is known to exist on vertical saturated basalt walls, rooting in nearly pure stands of delicate, mosslike *Selaginella*. Although the plant is extremely rare and localized, threats are minimal: Few alien weeds can find a foothold on the sheer rock face, although landslides could pose a serious threat. Animals other than the skilled field botanist are unable to reach its isolated refuge. This is fortunate, as this fragile beauty is extremely difficult to propagate and grow *ex situ*. Only a single plant is known in cultivation, at the NTBG.—*D.L.*

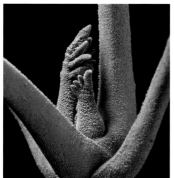

Tetraplasandra flynnii

Photograph: Kōke'e State Park, Kaua'i
Range: Kaua'i
Habitat: montane *Metrosideros* wet forest
Population: one population of three plants in an area of less than 2/5 square mile
Threats: feral goats; competition from alien weeds; vandalism
Legal status: species of concern
Scale: leaflet 1–1 1/2 inches long

Foliage of glossy leaflets conceals flower and fruit clusters. Look closer: New developing leaves resemble tiny hands reaching upward. All are covered with scurfy brown fuzz for protection. These features belong to the rarest of the 'ohe species, *Tetraplasandra flynnii*. This newly described and published species is named for Tim Flynn, botanist and curator of the herbarium at the NTBG, who first collected it and pointed out its uniqueness. • *Tetraplasandra* is a Hawaiian endemic genus belonging to the same family as ginseng and English ivy. Unlike their herbaceous relatives from temperate climates, however, *Tetraplasandra* species are majestic forest trees. The only known population of *T. flynnii* is restricted to a small area on the steep, north-facing slopes of the spectacular, cloud-shrouded Kalalau Valley in Kaua'i. Constant browsing by feral goats has severely impacted the native vegetation in Kalalau, resulting in little or no regeneration of most native species for many years now. Scoring a direct hit on Kaua'i in 1992, Hurricane 'Iniki decimated the population of *Tetraplasandra flynnii*, leaving only three trees. The bark of one unfortunate tree was girdled in a senseless act of vandalism. Propagation of this species using both seeds and embryo culture shows promise, and it may still be possible to save this beautiful endemic tree, a masterpiece of evolution that hovers precariously close to extinction.—D.L.

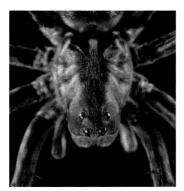

Wēkiu Wolf Spider; Big-Eyed Hunting Spider
Pe'epe'e Maka Nui
Lycosa new species

Photograph: Center for Conservation Research and Training Lab, University of Hawai'i, Mānoa, O'ahu
Range: Mauna Kea summit zone, Hawai'i
Habitat: treeless, dry alpine cinder and lava fields
Population: unknown
Threats: alien species
Legal status: none
Scale: portion shown 1 inch

Mauna Kea's alpine wolf spiders are top carnivores—large and fleet. They prey upon insects blown up from warmer habitats. Using keen sight and ambidextrous legs, this black spider swiftly runs down prey, like a wolf or cat. On the 13,800-foot tropical summit, each night is a cold winter, and each noon is a baking summer. One strategy to survive daily extreme fluctuations of cold or heat is building tunnels under stones. Cold tolerance allows this amazing spider to survive freezing to 23°F, a University of Notre Dame cryobiologist discovered. • Many females become widows, eating the male after mating. This hearty meal sustains them during a month of egg-sac carrying. The mother-to-be spins a silk mat, then a fine, silken bowl in which she lays a heap of pearly eggs. She deftly wraps this silk napkin around the eggs and glues it to her spinnerets. Upon hatching, 200 spiderlings scramble out to climb upon her back. • When spiderlings leave their mother, they run up on high points, raise their abdomens, and squirt a silk thread into a passing breeze. Lifted by this silk kite, they soar a yard—or miles—to new hunting grounds away from siblings. Similarly, their continental ancestor probably rode up into the jet stream to be dropped out over Hawai'i. The newly landed spiderlings may live up to seven years.—A.M./S.L.M.

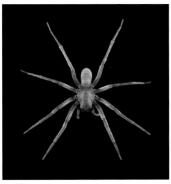

Kaua'i Cave Wolf Spider; No-Eyed, Big-Eyed Hunting Spider
Pe'epe'e Maka'ole
Adelocosa anops

Photograph: Kōloa Cave #2, Kaua'i
Range: Kōloa District, Kaua'i
Habitat: dark, moist subterranean caverns or tubes of lava rock
Population: extremely rare
Threats: habitat loss; predation on young by introduced alien spiders; prey reduction
Legal status: endangered
Scale: shown left, life size; body 1/2 inch long

In the perpetual darkness of a deep, damp Kaua'i lava tube lives the world's only eyeless wolf spider. Whereas cousin wolf spiders wear four large and four small eyes, this fellow has none. Hunting cues come from sounds received by an extra pair of sensory hairs on the front legs. Their egg sacs carry fewer eggs than cousins' (only 1/12th as many), but each egg is far larger. Spiderlings ride atop their mother's back only half as long before departing to hunt solo. These wolf spiders prey mostly on cave amphipods or landhoppers (see p. 215), also endangered. • Experts had assumed cave-adapted creatures were not present in Hawaiian lava tubes, thought too young to harbor such animals. In 1971, questioning assumptions, spelunker and Bishop Museum scientist Dr. Francis Howarth discovered many interdependent species in a simple food chain. Many creatures lack pigment or eyes. In young caves on Hawai'i Island, the small-eyed, big-eyed hunting spider, *Lycosa howarthi*, was discovered. The arachnophile who named both species found anatomical proof that they evolved independently from different surface-living ancestors. Although individual tubes are young, cave-adapted creatures apparently migrate from more ancient tubes to newly formed ones via underground cracks. • Spider populations are known in three Kaua'i caves, all under private ownership. The U.S. Fish & Wildlife Service is working with the owners to restore and protect caves that provide essential habitat.—A.M./S.L.M.

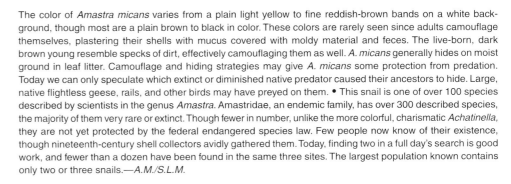

Sanguine Litter Snail
Pūpū Kuahiwi
Laminella sanguinea

Photograph: temporary studio, East–West Center, O'ahu
Range: Wai'anae Mountains, O'ahu; parts of Ko'olau Mountains above 1,800 feet
Habitat: native moist forest
Population: unknown
Threats: alien rats, rosy wolf snail, flatworms; pigs and goats; introduced weeds; drought; fierce storms
Legal status: species of concern
Scale: adult 4/5 inch long; at birth 1/5 inch

This species is particularly attractive, and usually the adult shell is very flashy: scarlet with black zigzag stripes. This design is rarely seen since this snail, like others in the genus, camouflages itself by hiding its beautiful color and taking on the appearance of bird droppings. Among the predators *L. sanguinea* needed to evade are native blow flies recorded as parasitizing some native snails. • Like many of the native land snails in recent decades, this species apparently has disappeared from drying forest areas. They persist precariously in small patches of moister native forest amid ever-encroaching weeds and alien predators. Very small populations are restricted to mountainous microhabitats with fallen *Urera* leaves in the wetter and cooler areas. Unlike most near relatives, this land-snail group prefers living epiphytically on plants like climbing screw pine and *ōpuhe* instead of on the ground. Like many island animals it is so dependent on native flora that preservation of habitat against conversion to a continental flora by mammals is vital. • Since 1980 fewer than 30 *L. sanguinea* individuals have been observed; as of 2000 the largest colony contained fewer than 20 individuals. *L. sanguinea* is one of 14 *Laminella* species described by scientists, and is the only one now found on O'ahu. Two have been driven to extinction since 1950. Shells of freshly dead snails are often found on the ground, victims of *Euglandina rosea* attacks.—A.M./S.L.M.

Litter Snail
Pūpū Kuahiwi
Amastra micans

Photograph: temporary studio, East–West Center, O'ahu
Range: Wai'anae Mountains, O'ahu
Habitat: mesic forest above 2,000 feet on the ground or lower stems and leaves of native shrubs
Population: unknown, but since 1970 fewer than 10 individuals seen
Threats: alien rats, rosy wolf snail, flatworms; pigs and goats; alien weeds; drought; storms
Legal status: species of concern
Scale: adult 3/5–9/10 inch long

The color of *Amastra micans* varies from a plain light yellow to fine reddish-brown bands on a white background, though most are a plain brown to black in color. These colors are rarely seen since adults camouflage themselves, plastering their shells with mucus covered with moldy material and feces. The live-born, dark brown young resemble specks of dirt, effectively camouflaging them as well. *A. micans* generally hides on moist ground in leaf litter. Camouflage and hiding strategies may give *A. micans* some protection from predation. Today we can only speculate which extinct or diminished native predator caused their ancestors to hide. Large, native flightless geese, rails, and other birds may have preyed on them. • This snail is one of over 100 species described by scientists in the genus *Amastra*. Amastridae, an endemic family, has over 300 described species, the majority of them very rare or extinct. Though fewer in number, unlike the more colorful, charismatic *Achatinella*, they are not yet protected by the federal endangered species law. Few people now know of their existence, though nineteenth-century shell collectors avidly gathered them. Today, finding two in a full day's search is good work, and fewer than a dozen have been found in the same three sites. The largest population known contains only two or three snails.—A.M./S.L.M.

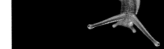

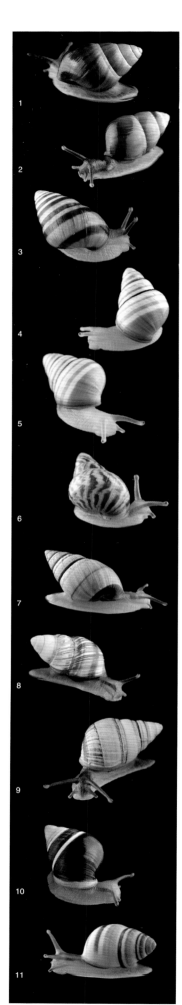

O'ahu Tree Snail
Achatinella sowerbyana (1); ***Achatinella lila*** (2); ***Achatinella livida*** (3)

Range: Ko'olau Mountains, O'ahu
Habitat: 2,000–3,000 feet; mixed wet forest with mostly native vegetation, near the summit
Population: small groups of 5 to 12 individuals in a few isolated pockets; small population in lab
Threats: predation by rosy wolf snail and black rats; habitat alteration by pigs
Legal status: endangered
Scale: adult 7/10–9/10 inch long; at birth 1/5 inch

Moloka'i Tree Snail
Partulina mighelsiana (4 & 5); ***Partulina proxima*** (6); ***Partulina redfieldi*** (7)

Range: Moloka'i
Habitat: 2,500–4,000 feet; wet forest with mixed native trees dominated by 'ōhi'a lehua
Population: thinly distributed over wide areas in mountains; small population in lab
Threats: predation by rosy wolf snail and black rats; habitat alteration by pigs and feral goats
Legal status: species of concern
Scale: adult 4/5–9/10 inch long; at birth 1/5 inch

O'ahu Tree Snail
Achatinella decipiens (8)

Range: Ko'olau Mountains, O'ahu
Habitat: 2,000–3,000 feet; mixed wet forest with mostly native vegetation, near the summit
Population: small groups of 5 to 12 individuals in a few isolated pockets; about 30 in lab
Threats: predation by rosy wolf snail and black rats; habitat alteration by pigs
Legal status: endangered
Scale: adult 7/10–9/10 inch long; at birth 1/5 inch

O'ahu Tree Snail
Achatinella mustelina (9)

Range: isolated patches above 1,800 feet, Wai'anae Mountains, O'ahu; historic: continuous forest above 1,150 feet
Habitat: dense, moderately wet forests; native host plants include *olopua, manono,* and *'ōhi'a lehua*
Population: rare, but most abundant of the living land snails
Threats: predation by rosy wolf snail and black rats; habitat alteration by feral goats and pigs
Legal status: endangered
Scale: adult 7/10–4/5 inch long; at birth 1/5 inch

O'ahu Tree Snail
Achatinella apexfulva (10); ***Achatinella fuscobasis*** (11)

Range: Ko'olau Mountains, O'ahu (extinct in the wild)
Habitat: mid-elevation, wet forests based on *'ōhi'a* and *koa* trees
Population: *Achatinella apexfulva,* eight animals in lab; *Achatinella fuscobasis,* more than 200 animals in lab and increasing
Threats: predation by rosy wolf snail and black rats; habitat alteration by pigs
Legal status: endangered
Scale: adult 7/10–4/5 inch long; at birth 1/5 inch

Tree Snail
Kāhuli; Pūpū

Photographs: temporary studio, Endangered Tree Snails Conservation Lab, University of Hawai'i, O'ahu

Since their arrival several million years ago, the tree snails of Hawai'i expanded in record time to occupy habitats high and low, wet and dry on every island. The life style included impregnation late in life, bearing live young one at a time, and growing slowly while staying lifelong in small ranges. The approach worked well with the predator-free microenvironments of Hawai'i, where a mile distant is a new temperature and humidity. Since first Western contact in 1778 the snails have faced drastic habitat destruction and efficient alien predators. High rates of extinction are predictable.

For over 100 years Hawaiian land snails have fueled speciation studies. So little land (6,400 sq. miles), so short a time and so far away (2,400 miles from anywhere) added up to so much variation. How did this happen? Predation was not a major cause; mutation and genetic drift within diverse habitats appear to be the engines of change. Snail collector Rev. John Thomas Gulick, son of missionaries, suggested a theory he termed "divergent evolution through cumulative segregation." In 1891 the Boston Society of Natural History "caught the snails in the very act of evoluting" by placing Gulick's snails at their origin on a model of O'ahu "so as to illustrate his views."[1] Gulick wasn't too far off, says University of Hawai'i zoology professor Dr. Michael Hadfield, who has studied the snails for decades.

Common garden (*Helix* species) and giant African snails (*Achatina fulica*) mature sexually at one year, repeatedly lay 40 to 50 egg clutches, and are short-lived. In contrast, the tree snails of Hawai'i reach sexual maturity slowly (five to seven years), bear fully formed, live single young four to six times annually, and live 18 to 20 years. Tree snails typically exchange genetic material, but some apparently reproduce in isolation. One snail gave birth after four years alone; an isolated, lab-born snail gave birth after reaching maturity. The mechanism used (self-fertilization, long-term sperm/egg storage, or parthenogenesis) has not been determined.

Mature snails brood one to three embryos at a time. At birth, baby leaves the uterus and emerges from under the parent's shell. The birth size is large, about a quarter of the adult's. Live birth gives the new snail a strong start in life, equal to safely completing a whole growth stage, but this strategy requires a larger (older) parent. If predators or human collectors select the largest shells, they are removing the breeding snails.

Hawaiian tree snails are very polite; they do not harm their host trees. Snails emerge at night to eat epiphytic fungi, with a dash of algae, growing on slick-leaved native trees. A few nonnative plants will support snails, but not consistently. Snails cruise the leaves, using the tiniest teeth in the animal kingdom to graze on a very thin, usually invisible layer of food. A belt of 50 sandpapery teeth rubs back and forth over the leaf, scraping off dinner.

Studies show that availability of food appears to control growth rates toward breeding maturity. Wild food sources are erratic. Humidity necessary for fungi growth will be reduced by drought or by cattle or goats eating the forest understory, resulting in an overall drying of the forest. Habitat protection and restoration would contribute to a healthier diet and earlier breeding ages.

Two major predators attack snail populations, even exterminating isolated colonies.

The alien black rat is a visually oriented predator that easily finds the larger, reproductively active snails. Smaller snails, hidden in the foliage, often escape foraging rats. Rats bite into the snail's shell and devour the living animal. Although a colony is severely reduced by the death of breeders, gorged rats do move on—with the young remaining, the population can bounce back eventually.

A more destructive predator is the rosy wolf snail (*Euglandina rosea*), which was introduced by the Hawai'i Department of Agriculture in 1955–56 in a misguided attempt to control the pest giant African snail (*Achatina fulica*). *Euglandina* feeding leaves no hole in the snail's shell, so observers easily distinguish between predators. Field studies show that *E. rosea* eats all snails regardless of size. A colony can be annihilated with no chance of recovery.

The Endangered Species Act controls collection of *Achatinella* by humans. Rat and *Euglandina* predation must be controlled by wildlife agencies and volunteers at preserves such as those in The Nature Conservancy and state Natural Area Reserves System.

One person *can* make a difference. Alan Hart, an artist and scientific illustrator, is responsible for placement of *Achatinella* on the endangered species list. Alan became enchanted with these "little agates" as others had, but he went a step further. He asked, "What can I do?" He had hiked the forest trails and knew *Achatinella*'s rapidly declining numbers and habitat. The Endangered Species Act offered protection through a petition process that required time, knowledge, and effort. Alan assumed the task of nominating not just one or two species but the entire genus *Achatinella* for endangered status. Starting in the early 1970s, he began compiling the data and statistics to support the nomination. The initiative took time but was successful. On January 13, 1981, the *Achatinella* were officially listed as endangered, the first time an entire genus was listed.—*A.M./S.L.M.*

1. David Sharp to R. C. L. Perkins, 21 May 1892, Bishop Museum Archives, Ms Grp. 141, box.

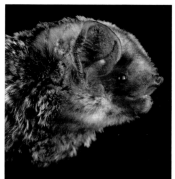

p. 65

Hawaiian Hoary Bat
ʻŌpeʻapeʻa
Lasiurus cinereus semotus

Photograph: Honolulu Zoo, Oʻahu
Range: Kauaʻi, Maui, Hawaiʻi; possibly Niʻihau, Oʻahu, Molokaʻi, and Lānaʻi
Habitat: wide range from sea level to summit of highest mountains
Population: estimated in thousands, locally rare; most abundant on Hawaiʻi
Threats: destruction of feeding and roosting sites; pesticide poisoning of insect prey
Legal status: endangered
Scale: 3 1/2 inches long; wing spread 10–13 inches

A flying insect-vacuum-cleaner: That's the only native Hawaiian land mammal. ʻŌpeʻapeʻa uses many different habitats, resting by day in alien or native trees or in lava tubes. Hawaiian bats rarely feed in groups. Individuals fly out at dusk to dine on both alien and native insects. They hunt by echolocation over open grasslands and even near-shore ocean. Moths and beetles are favored prey, but any flying insect, including termites, will be taken on the wing. Enterprising bats may feed on light-attracted insects at the edges of forests. • The English common name "hoary" refers to the frosted tips of body hair (clearly seen in the photo). Their Hawaiian name may refer to the roosting bat's crossed arms. Hawaiians grouped bats with other flying things such as dragonflies and butterflies, and considered them inedible. Practically, the bats' small size and solitary habits made them an unlikely food source. Western visitors to Hawaiʻi did not report the bat until 1816. Kotzebue, chronicler for a Russian expedition, noted seeing a feeding group on Oʻahu, but U.S. Exploring Expedition naturalist T. R. Peale provided the first published record in 1840. • Solitary roosting Hawaiian bats never evoked human fears and resulting eradication programs. ʻŌpeʻapeʻa can make a solid recovery if humans are able to protect essential habitat and prey.—*A.M./S.L.M.*

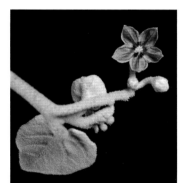

pp. 66, 67

Cudweed
ʻEnaʻena
Pseudognaphalium sandwicensium var. *molokaiense*

Photograph: Kaiehu Point, The Nature Conservancy Moʻomomi Preserve, Molokaʻi
Range: Oʻahu, Molokaʻi, Lānaʻi, Maui
Habitat: strand and consolidated dunes
Population: unknown number of populations; fewer than 100 individuals
Threats: potential development of coastal areas; deer and weeds
Legal status: none
Scale: 2 inches across

Pseudognaphalium sandwicensium is an extremely variable perennial herb. It occurs throughout nearly all the Hawaiian chain from Kure and Midway atolls and all of the main islands, and ranges from sea level to more than 9,800 feet. It is subdivided into four intergrading varieties. All four have very densely woolly stems and leaves as well as small heads of yellow flowers. The rarest of the varieties is var. *molokaiense*. It is very densely white-woolly-pubescent over the entire plant, stems prostrate to sometimes erect, and leaves usually wider than in the other varieties. Populations somewhat intermediate between var. *molokaiense* and var. *sandwicensium* are known from dry, bare, or coastal habitats from Waimanalo and Diamond Head on Oʻahu, Hālawa Valley on Molokaʻi, Lānaʻi, and between Waiehu and Wailuku on Maui. In a recent reevaluation of these plants, they were considered better referred to *P. sandwicensium* var. *molokaiense* as they are a closer match morphologically to var. *molokaiense* than var. *sandwicensium*, and probably represent past Pleistocene direct connections among the islands of the Maui complex (Maui, Molokaʻi, Lānaʻi, and Kahoʻolawe, known collectively as Maui Nui) and the thin land connection between Oʻahu and Molokaʻi.—*W.L.W.*

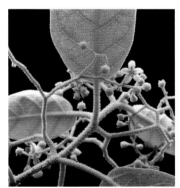

p. 68

Nightshade
ʻĀkia (Niʻihau); Pōpolo
Solanum nelsonii

Photograph: Kaiehu Point, The Nature Conservancy Moʻomomi Preserve, Molokaʻi
Range: Kure, Midway, Pearl and Hermes atolls, Laysan, Nihoa, Niʻihau, Kauaʻi, Oʻahu, Molokaʻi, Maui, Hawaiʻi
Habitat: coastal sites, in coral rubble or sand
Population: 10 populations, fewer than 300 individuals
Threats: goats, deer, cattle; alien plants
Legal status: none
Scale: flower 1/2 inch diameter

Solanum nelsonii, named in honor of David Nelson, the first person to collect botanical specimens in Hawaiʻi, is a sprawling shrub, sometimes forming clumps up to 4 to 5 feet in diameter. The stems and leaves are densely covered with gray to golden star-shaped hairs. It has attractive purple flowers with unique purple anthers. This species is rather variable, and in different parts of its wide range it exhibits different leaf size and shape and flower colors. Most of these variants have been named as varieties. Coastal dune ecosystems, like those inhabited by *S. nelsonii*, were once common in the Hawaiian Islands, but now nearly all have been lost to coastal development, sand mining, or conversion to pasture. Within the main Hawaiian Islands, there is still one large area of native coastal ecosystem that has been preserved, the Moʻomomi Preserve. Local residents consider this land sacred and continue to rely on Moʻomomi for gathering fish, seaweed, and salt. The preserve harbors more than 22 native Hawaiian plant species, 4 of which are endangered, as well as an important nesting site for the endangered green sea turtle. Deposits of bird bones studied by Smithsonian scientists Storrs Olson and Helen James reveal that the dunes were once home to at least 30 bird species, of which about one-third have since become extinct.—*W.L.W.*

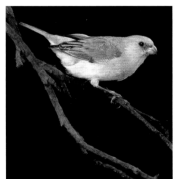

p. 69

Nightshade
Pōpolo ʻAiakeakua; Pōpolo
Solanum sandwicense

Photograph: Nualolo Trail, Kōkeʻe State Park, Kauaʻi
Range: Kōkeʻe and Nā Pali Coast State Parks; Kauaʻi Honouliuli Preserve, Oʻahu
Habitat: open sunny areas in diverse mesic forest
Population: five populations with about 14 individuals total
Threats: feral pigs; fire; urban development; alien plants; overcollecting; small population size
Legal status: endangered
Scale: flower 1/2 inch diameter

Solanum sandwicense or *pōpolo ʻaiakeakua* ("pōpolo eaten by the god") is a large sprawling shrub. These shrubs are easy to distinguish from most other Hawaiian plants by the dense covering of yellowish brown star-shaped hairs. The flowers are up to an inch in diameter and up to 40 are arranged in a complex branching inflorescence. At one time the Oʻahu populations were recognized as *Solanum sandwicense* while the Kauaʻi plants were separated as *Solanum kavaiense*. But because they are only slightly distinctive in having a thicker mat of pubescence on the inflorescences and young growth, and the hairs are more yellowish brown, they were not considered to represent a separate species. *Solanum sandwicense* is one of three Hawaiian species and considered to be of American origin. The genus *Solanum*, with over 1,700 species, is one of the largest flowering-plant genera. The best-known species of *Solanum* are the tomato (*S. lycopersicum*), the potato (*S. tuberosum*), and the eggplant (*S. melongena* var. *esculentum*). Nearly all species have poisonous alkaloids in the fruits and seeds (such as solasodine, which is extracted from several species of *Solanum*) that have been used in Europe to produce contraceptives. Many species are also very weedy, particularly in overgrazed lands. Several species introduced into Hawaiʻi, such as *S. linnaeanum*, the apple of Sodom, are problems in pastures.—*W.L.W.*

Palila
Loxioides bailleui

Photograph: Keauhou Bird Conservation Center, Volcano, Hawaiʻi
Range: Mauna Kea slopes, Hawaiʻi
Habitat: 6,600–9,200-foot slopes; relatively dry, cool, stony *māmane–naio* forests
Population: 8,000
Threats: grazing by alien sheep and goats; fire spread by alien grasses; feral cats and rats
Legal status: endangered
Scale: 6 inches head to tail

A yellow head gives camouflage in yellow-flowered *māmane* trees, aiding evasion of the Hawaiian Hawk, *ʻIo*, and perhaps the extinct native eagle. While other honeycreepers evolved beaks to feed on flower nectar, the *Palila* stayed a seedeater, retaining its finch beak. Green *māmane* pods, held in the feet, are ripped open with the bill to extract seeds. A balanced *Palila* diet, founded on seeds, includes insects, *naio* berries, and a salad of tender *māmane* shoots and flowers. • Sport-hunted feral goats and sheep, and mouflon were eating seedlings and new growth and browsing mature trees. In defense the *Palila* sued the state; EarthJustice represented coplaintiffs Sierra Club, Hawaiʻi and National Audubon Societies, and Dr. A. Ziegler. In a precedent-setting lawsuit the U.S. Supreme Court ruled that habitat destruction was "taking" the bird, and was prohibited under the Endangered Species Act. After several defeated challenges to the ruling and despite complaints from hunters, most sheep and goats were removed. • Today, *Palila* are increasing on Mauna Kea's western slopes as *māmane* saplings mature, but are not expanding in range; 96 percent of the population occurs in 11 1/2 square miles of habitat. The small eastern and southern populations may be declining. Successful fledging of young, resulting from improved food sources, will take time. Recovery depends on pod-bearing maturity of trees growing slowly at dry, cool, high elevations. Vigilance against browsers and fire must continue.—*A.M./S.L.M.*

p. 70

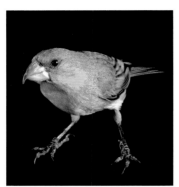

Laysan Finch
Telespiza cantans

Photograph: Honolulu Zoo, O'ahu
Range: Northwestern Hawaiian Islands, Laysan, and introduced to Pearl and Hermes atoll
Habitat: 1,000 acres of low coral-sand island with a central depression and briny lagoon
Population: rare; 10,000 on Laysan; very low number on Pearl and Hermes
Threats: habitat alteration by human impact (alien plants, animals); natural disasters; disease
Legal status: endangered
Scale: 7 1/2 inches long head to tail

p. 71

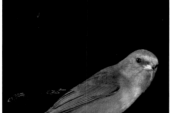

'Ākepa
Loxops coccineus coccineus

Photograph: Keauhou Bird Conservation Center, Volcano, Hawai'i
Range: Hawai'i Island
Habitat: *'ōhi'a, koa* forests above 3,000 feet
Population: 14,000 in three populations ca. 1980; fairly common in upper elevations
Threats: habitat loss and destruction of old-growth forest; rat predation; avian disease
Legal status: endangered
Scale: 4–5 inches head to tail

pp. 72–73

Koki'o
Kokia kauaiensis

Photograph: Paiki Valley, Kaua'i
Range: western and central Kaua'i
Habitat: mesic forest
Population: six populations with fewer than 100 individuals total
Threats: alien weeds; fire; trampling and browsing of seedlings by goats and deer; rooting by pigs; seed predation by insects and rats
Legal status: endangered
Scale: tree 30 feet tall; flower bud 3 inches long

p. 74

Koki'o
Kokia drynarioides

Photograph: Bishop Museum, Amy B. H. Greenwell Ethnobotanical Garden, Captain Cook, Hawai'i
Range: leeward Hawai'i Island
Habitat: dry lowland forest
Population: two populations with about five individuals total
Threats: alien weeds; fire; trampling by goats and cattle; seed predation by insects and rats
Legal status: endangered
Scale: tree 35 feet tall; flower 4 inches across

p. 75

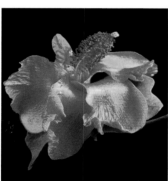

Hau Kuahiwi
Hibiscadelphus hualalaiensis

Photograph: Bishop Museum, Amy B. H. Greenwell Ethnobotanical Garden, Captain Cook, Hawai'i
Range: formerly Hawai'i Island
Habitat: dry forest
Population: extinct in the wild; exist only as cultivated plants
Threats: grazing by cattle and feral goats; agriculture; fire; alien weeds
Legal status: endangered
Scale: flower 1 3/4 inches long

p. 76

What to eat is never a question for the Laysan Finch, whose strategy is "eat everything." Seeds, flower buds, insects, other birds' eggs, and ripe carrion are all options. Described as "curious," the birds are likely surveying the dinner prospects. This flexible diet kept the birds alive when rabbits, introduced in 1903, denuded the island of essentially all vegetation. A honeycreeper, millerbird, and rail, all found only on Laysan, became extinct during the rabbit-induced famine. The Laysan Finch has recovered from a low of 100 birds in 1923. • One event can cause the extinction of a species when the population lives in a single vulnerable location. Attempts at insurance were made in 1891 and 1905 by releasing Laysan Finches and Laysan Rails on Midway atoll, but the accidental arrival of rats during World War II caused the extermination of both. Rats continued to prey on Midway's seabirds' eggs and chicks until exterminated by the U.S. Fish and Wildlife Service in the late 1990s. A 1967 introduction of the finch to tiny Pearl and Hermes atoll, located between Laysan and Midway, has been more successful. Today both locations are protected in the Hawaiian Islands National Wildlife Refuge, established in 1909. The Coral Reef Ecosystem Reserve federally designated in December 2000 provides further protection. Vigilance against the accidental introduction of weeds or introduction of rats by shipwreck remains essential.—*A.M./S.L.M.*

The Hawaiian name of this bird, 'Ākepa or "quick and nimble," is well chosen. With its bill, 'Ākepa pries open flowers, seedpods, and galls to look for insects. The dependable nectar of *'ōhi'a* makes this red-flowered tree a buffet of insects. • Hawai'i 'Ākepa populations are fragmented and believed to be declining. The Kaua'i species is strong only in the Alaka'i Wilderness Preserve. The O'ahu subspecies is extinct; the Maui subspecies has not been seen in 10 years and may be extinct. Captive breeding and release programs can help, but a wild population needs reproductive success in safe nest sites. The birds nest only in cavities in large, old-growth *'ōhi'a* and *koa* trees. Cavities form mostly in single-trunked trees. Old trees fall faster than new cavities develop. One hundred years of forest disturbance, especially understory removal by browsers, means that more sunlight reaches young trees, allowing development of more multiple-trunked trees with fewer cavities for 'Ākepa nesting. • Humans cannot create old-growth forest, but can imitate it. At Hakalau Forest National Wildlife Refuge, University of Hawai'i zoologist Dr. Leonard Freed and his students are coming to the rescue with substitutes. Short lengths of plastic pipe are fitted with a removable cap for monitoring nesting. The pipes, clamped on *'ōhi'a* trees, have been offered to 'Ākepa as nest sites with some success. Long-term breeding success will require habitat improvement and protection.—*A.M./S.L.M.*

Kokia kauaiensis trees are a conspicuous element of the mesic forest when in flower. In most respects this species is very similar to the Hawai'i Island species *K. drynarioides,* but it has the largest flowers in the genus, up to six inches long. Molecular studies have suggested that the Hawaiian genus *Kokia* is closely related to an African genus, *Gossypioides,* and two cosmopolitan genera, cotton *(Gossypium)* and *Thespesia.* One species, *Thespesia populnea,* is widely distributed worldwide, including the Hawaiian Islands, where it is known as *milo.* How did the ancestor of *Kokia* colonize the Hawaiian Islands and the related groups achieve such wide distributions? The answer appears to be ocean dispersal. All of these genera have very hairy seeds, which in *Gossypium* is the source of commercial cotton fiber. The hairs, along with an impermeable seed coat, act to protect the seed from damage by seawater during long periods in the ocean. • The species of *Kokia* with the largest numbers is *K. kauaiensis,* now restricted to western and central Kaua'i. Subfossilized fruits of *K. kauaiensis* were recently discovered in eastern Kaua'i, suggesting that these once majestic trees were a common part of the lowland mesic forests of Kaua'i before human settlement.—*W.L.W.*

There are only four species of the Hawaiian tree genus *Kokia.* They are distinguished from other members of the Hibiscus family by their large orange to brick red flowers, which are twisted into a curved tube with widely spreading tips. This unique flower type has evolved as an adaptation to pollination by birds. *Kokia drynariodes* is known only from remnant dryland forest in North Kona on Hawai'i Island. First collected for scientific study by David Nelson in 1779 during Cook's third voyage to the Hawaiian Islands, it was described as a species of cotton *(Gossypium).* Joseph Rock (1884–1962), who rediscovered populations of this species in the early 1900s, noted that it could continue to thrive only if protected from the ravages of wild cattle. Soon the area was fenced by the landowner and a regulation was posted to prevent further collection of its bark for dye, but in 1919 Rock observed that the wall had already fallen down. Today the only known wild populations are scattered on state and private land in Ka'ūpūlehu and Pu'u Wa'awa'a in severely degraded dryland forest. Current surveys suggest that just five individuals remain. Wildfires threaten the remaining trees, a problem greatly exacerbated by introduced fountain grass *(Pennisetum setaceum)* that covers the once-barren lava, fueling intense wildfires.—*W.L.W.*

A small tree with a long, tongue-twisting name, *Hibiscadelphus hualalaiensis* once grew on the slopes of Mount Hualalai in the North Kona District of the Big Island of Hawai'i. Broadly rounded, light green leaves conceal curved, tubular flowers with yellow-green, recurved petals supporting a cluster of maroon stamens. As of 1973 only three plants survived in the wild on Pu'u Wa'awa'a Ranch. Although the last plant was fenced to protect it from grazing cattle, it died in 1992. For field botanist Steve Perlman, who has witnessed too many Hawaiian plants go extinct during his 30-year career, visiting this last dead plant was painful. After bowing his head in silence to reflect on the loss of yet another unique species, he gathered the plant's remaining dry capsules and brought them back to the NTBG for propagation. Progeny from this last survivor now grow in living collections at NTBG, other Hawaiian gardens, and outplanting sites in dry forest near Ka'ūpūlehu on the Big Island. • Closely related to *Hibiscus, Hibiscadelphus* ("brother of *Hibiscus*") is endemic to the Hawaiian Islands. The flowers were presumably adapted to pollination by the Hawaiian honeyeaters and honeycreepers. Loss of dry and mesic forest habitat, decline of the Hawaiian honeycreepers, and extinction of the honeyeaters have driven five of the seven *Hibiscadelphus* species to extinction in the wild.—*D.L.*

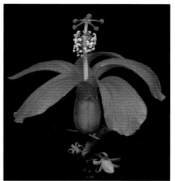

Hibiscus clayi

Photograph: Waimea Arboretum and Botanical Garden, Oʻahu
Range: Kauaʻi
Habitat: lowland mesic forest
Population: one population of four plants
Threats: alien plants; alteration of habitat; human disturbance; feral pigs
Legal status: endangered
Scale: petal 1 3/4–2 1/4 inches long

While I was hiking along a mountain trail on Kauaʻi, a tree with intensely red blossoms caught my eye. Upon closer examination it turned out to be *Hibiscus,* probably a native species, but which one? • The plant I spotted was *Hibiscus clayi,* a small tree reaching 26 feet high with deep red, recurved petals. All red-flowered hibiscus were called *koki'o 'ula* by the Hawaiians. This rare beauty is found only in eastern Kauaʻi where one population of four plants is confined to weedy, degraded mountain forest. Its rarity and endangered status are due to a number of factors, including past cattle grazing and degradation of its original habitat. The Kauaʻi District Division of Forestry and Wildlife (DOFAW) and community groups have augmented this population with plants grown from wild collected seed. • An attractive plant that thrives in cultivation, *Hibiscus clayi* is widely grown in conservation collections at NTBG and other botanical gardens. The late horticulturist and college instructor Dr. Horace F. Clay noticed this red hibiscus growing in Ala Moana Park on Oʻahu, grown from cuttings gathered on Kauaʻi by forester Al Duvel. It turned out to be a new species named in honor of Dr. Clay by Otto and Isa Degener.—*D.L.*

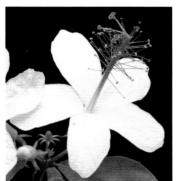

Koki'o Ke'oke'o; Koki'o Kea
Hibiscus waimeae subsp. hannerae

Photograph: Waimea Arboretum and Botanical Garden, Oʻahu
Range: Kauaʻi
Habitat: lowland wet forest
Population: two populations comprising 150–200 plants
Threats: competition from alien plants; habitat degradation by feral pigs and goats; landslides; hurricanes
Legal status: endangered
Scale: petal 1 3/5–2 2/5 inches long

A crimson column of slender, yellow-tipped stamens and fuzzy red stigmas rises, brushlike, above the five pure white petals. The petals' texture is softly creped, and a sweet, heady perfume emanates from the flowers. This and other species of native white-flowered hibiscus are called *koki'o ke'oke'o,* meaning "white hibiscus" in Hawaiian. • *Hibiscus waimeae* subspecies *hannerae* differs from typical subspecies *waimeae* in having larger leaves but smaller flowers with shorter, more spreading or even recurved petals. It is currently known only from two valleys, Limahuli and Hanakāpiʻai, on northwestern Kauaʻi. Although choking by alien weeds often prevents establishment of seedlings, subspecies *hannerae* is easily propagated by cuttings and seeds. On a visit to Limahuli Preserve we collected pencil-sized cuttings from many *koki'o ke'oke'o* and brought them back to the NTBG for propagation. After they had grown sufficiently, restoration biologist David Bender at NTBG's Limahuli Garden planted these new young recruits in the preserve to bolster the natural population of this rare and elegant Kauaʻi native. Additional plants are in cultivation at NTBG gardens and at Waimea Arboretum. • First collected by the Rev. John M. Lydgate in 1913, this plant was later named by Otto and Isa Degener as a variety in honor of Mrs. Ruth Knudsen Hanner, a supporter of their work on Kauaʻi.—*D.L.*

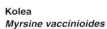

Ālula; Hāhā; ʻŌlulu; Pū Aupaka
Brighamia insignis

Photograph: National Tropical Botanical Garden Nursery, Lāwaʻi, Kauaʻi; National Tropical Botanical Garden, Limahuli Garden
Range: Kaʻali Cliff, Niʻihau; Nā Pali coast and Hāʻupu Ridge, Kauaʻi
Habitat: sea cliffs
Population: four populations with 20 individuals
Threats: alien plants; alien carmine spider mite; habitat destruction by feral goats and hikers; small population size
Legal status: endangered
Scale: 3–16 feet tall

Brighamia insignis commemorates the first director of the Bishop Museum in Honolulu, William Tufts Brigham (1841–1926). The specific name means "outstanding," which refers to the plant's peculiar appearance. *Brighamia insignis* is certainly among the most unusual Hawaiian plants, resembling a cabbage head stuck on a pole. The stem is succulent, broad at the base, and tapering to the top. The yellow, aromatic flowers are arranged in clusters, each with a tube nearly six inches long. Tom Lammers of the University of Wisconsin showed that the nectar of *Brighamia* flowers is sucrose-dominated, which characteristically attracts hawk moths for pollination. Despite this expectation, the moths have never been observed pollinating *Brighamia.* There is considerable concern that the pollinators have gone extinct, yet a possible pollinator, the Blackburn's Hawk Moth, is still extant on Kauaʻi. In the windy coastal habitat of *Brighamia,* pollination by these moths is likely an occasional event. Moreover, *Brighamia* may have occurred in a wider array of habitats than just windy ridges before mammal browsers eliminated populations in all but inaccessible sites. If so, then pollination may have been more regular in less windy sites. • Several organizations are attempting to reestablish *Brighamia insignis* in the wild. The Lyon Arboretum, NTBG, and the Waimea Arboretum have already begun to grow plants successfully. The easy-to-grow *Brighamia* has become a popular cultivated succulent.—*W.L.W.*

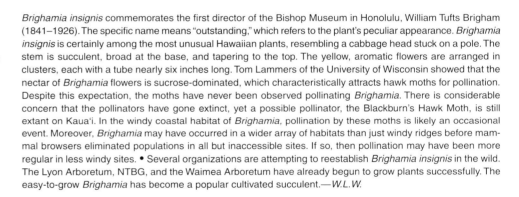

Kolea
Myrsine vaccinioides

Photograph: Puʻu Kukui Preserve, West Maui
Range: near Violet Lake, Puʻu Kukui, West Maui
Habitat: shrubby bogs
Population: two populations with about 250 individuals total
Threats: competition from alien weeds; feral pigs
Legal status: none
Scale: plant 1–3 feet tall; portion shown 2 inches across

Myrsine vaccinioides was discovered in 1980 by Robert Hobdy, a Maui forester, while collecting in the bogs around Violet Lake. A few years after this collection was made, Warren Wagner and Derral Herbst wrote an analysis of the 20 or so species of this complex genus for the *Manual of the Flowering Plants of Hawaiʻi,* the first new compilation of the Hawaiian flora in one hundred years. It became clear that the Hobdy collection represented a new species restricted to the bogs of that area. In fact, this new species had been collected once before in 1948 but was thought to represent a Kauaʻi species. *Myrsine vaccinioides* is a small shrub with distinctive raised reddish purple secretory lines on the lower leaf surface. All species have secretory ducts in the leaves, but only *M. vaccinioides* among the small-leaved Hawaiian species have such conspicuous ones. The flowers, minute and red, appear in small clusters along the upper stems. • *Myrsine* is a complex pantropical genus, occurring throughout most of the Pacific Basin, with perhaps 150 to 200 species. Most species of *Myrsine* differ from one another only in rather minute floral features and in vegetative characters such as size, shape, presence of marginal teeth, or venation of leaves. These features ordinarily would not be the only ones used to distinguish a majority of the species within a genus.—*W.L.W.*

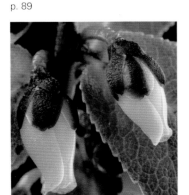

Ānini; Wānini
Eurya sandwicensis

Photograph: Puʻu Kukui Preserve, West Maui
Range: Kauaʻi, Oʻahu, Molokaʻi, Maui, Hawaiʻi
Habitat: wet forest and shrubland
Population: estimated to be over 50 populations with perhaps several thousand individuals
Threats: not adequately assessed yet; certainly competition from alien plants and damage from feral animals occur in some areas
Legal status: species of concern
Scale: flower 1/4–3/8 inch long

This unassuming plant may be encountered as a small, slender tree growing in wet forests or sometimes on windswept mountain ridges where its growth form is often shrubby and sprawling. The small, dark green leaves have a network of fine veins and finely toothed margins similar to its relatives, tea and garden camellias. Flowers of the *ānini* are much smaller and urn-shaped, though, with inconspicuous cream-colored or light yellow petals. Male and female flowers are produced on separate plants. As the pea-sized fruits ripen, their fleshy sepals turn a shiny purplish black color. • As *Eurya sandwicensis* is the only member of the tea family to occur in Hawaiʻi, its origins and affinities are somewhat perplexing to botanists. Its relationships seem to lie with relatives in the Indo-Pacific region, although it is distinctive enough from other *Eurya* species to merit placement in its own subgenus *(Ternstroemiopsis).* Though *ānini* is rare enough to be considered a species of concern, details of its population size and structure are nevertheless poorly known. It seems to be a naturally rare species, occurring as widely scattered populations or individuals growing in healthy native forest. Further studies are necessary to accurately determine population size and threats to *Eurya sandwicensis* and to develop propagation techniques.—*D.L.*

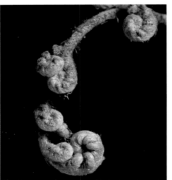

pp. 91, 141

Pauoa
Ctenitis squamigera

Photograph: Pu'u Kukui Preserve, West Maui
Range: Kaua'i (extinct), O'ahu, Moloka'i (extinct), Lāna'i, Maui
Habitat: mesic and diverse mesic forest
Population: seven populations on three islands totaling about 160 plants
Threats: rooting by feral pigs; browsing by goats and deer; competition from alien weeds
Legal status: endangered
Scale: leaf blade 16–32 inches long

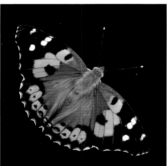

pp. 92, 93

Snakeroot
Sanicula purpurea

Photograph: Pu'u Kukui Preserve, West Maui
Range: Ko'olau Mountains, O'ahu; West Maui
Habitat: mossy precipitous slopes and open bogs, rarely in low elevation wet forests
Population: four populations with about 150 individuals total
Threats: habitat degradation by natural events and feral pigs; decreased reproductive vigor due to small population size
Legal status: endangered
Scale: 3 inches–1 foot tall; flower head 1/3 inch diameter

Kamehameha Butterfly
Lepelepeohina; Pulelehua Kamehameha
Vanessa tameamea

Photograph: Center for Conservation Research and Training Lab, Univ. of Hawai'i at Mānoa, O'ahu; Betty Alberts residence, Pā'ia, Maui
Range: all Hawaiian Islands
Habitat: open disturbed areas, damp valley bottoms, stream banks
Population: rare
Threats: introduced parasitic wasps, alien birds
Legal status: none
Scale: 2 1/2-inch wing spread

pp. 96, 97

Crested Honeycreeper
'Ākohekohe
Palmeria dolei

Photograph: Keauhou Bird Conservation Center, Volcano, Hawai'i
Range: only Mount Haleakalā, East Maui
Habitat: 4,500–6,500 feet on windward slopes; wet forests with 'ōhi'a and koa trees
Population: perhaps 3,500 birds
Threats: habitat loss; grazing animals; disease
Legal status: endangered
Scale: 6 1/2 to 7 inches head to tail

pp. 98, 99, 101

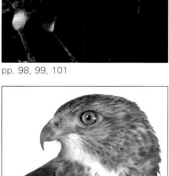

pp. 104, 105

Hawaiian Hawk
'Io
Buteo solitarius (male)

Photograph: Pana'ewa Rainforest Zoo, Hilo
Range: very rarely on Kaua'i, O'ahu, Maui; Hawai'i
Habitat: below 8,500 feet; forage in forests of all types, but nest in native forest
Population: 1,500–2,500
Threats: habitat conversion of forests to monoculture agriculture or urban uses; illegal shooting; vehicle collisions; poisoning; predation
Legal status: endangered
Scale: 16–18 inches long; female larger than male

Ferns and related plants known as fern allies may not be as colorful or conspicuous as the flowering plants featured in this work, but they are certainly important constituents of Hawaiian ecosystems. Ferns range in size from delicate, mosslike filmy ferns growing on rocks and trees to hardy colonizers of barren lava flows, and large tree ferns with trunks 10 to 15 feet tall that dominate the understory of many Hawaiian wet forests. Certain Hawaiian ferns are as rare and endangered as their flowering counterparts. Of the approximately 140 native ferns and fern allies of Hawai'i, 32 species are either considered candidates for listing, threatened, or endangered. Terrestrial ferns are particularly vulnerable to disturbances from feral animals and weeds. *Ctenitis squamigera* is restricted to the understory of low- to mid-elevation mesic and diverse mesic forests. *Squamigera* signifies "bearing scales," alluding to the dense covering of tan-colored scales on the tightly curled young fronds and also persistent on the leaf stalk and lower surface of mature fronds. When mature, the arching, lustrous green fronds may reach five feet in length. Now considered extinct on Kaua'i and Moloka'i, *Ctenitis squamigera* is known from seven populations comprising about 160 plants on Maui, Lāna'i, and O'ahu. Weed control and fencing to exclude feral animals would provide good protection for this and other endangered species, but *in situ* conservation measures await implementation.—*D.L.*

One of four Hawaiian snakeroots, *S. purpurea* is a stout perennial herb from a massive branching rootstock. It has three- to seven-lobed leaves, a mixture of male and hermaphroditic flowers in each cluster, and nearly spherical tiny fruits covered with prickles. The Hawaiian species of *Sanicula* are among a minority (about 20 percent) of ancestral Hawaiian plant colonists thought to have dispersed from the Americas, despite adverse prevailing winds and water currents. Plant dispersal across the unbroken 2,400-mile oceanic expanse between North America and the Hawaiian Islands appears to have been very rare, although recent molecular evidence for just this kind of origin has been provided for *Sanicula*. Moreover, the same study by Bruce Baldwin (University of California) and collaborators showed that there were two long-distance dispersals of *Sanicula* from North America to southern South America. How did these extraordinary dispersal events take place? Most likely, dispersal was bird-assisted. All species of the lineage to which the Hawaiian species and South American species belong have fruits covered with hooked prickles that may have promoted dispersal by sticking on the feathers of birds. Regular sightings of North American migratory birds and "accidentals" in the Hawaiian Islands as well as regular migration of various species of Charadriiformes (shore birds) between California and southern South America show the potential for long-distance dispersal of this type.—*W.L.W.*

One of only two native butterflies, the Kamehameha was the first Hawaiian insect named by Western science. It was initially collected in 1816 by Dr. Eschscholtz, naturalist on the voyage of the Russian ship *Rurick* under Capt. Kotzebue. Published in 1821, the name *Kamehameha* honors the first chief to unite the islands. • Now you see it, now you don't. A growing caterpillar's head resembles *māmaki* fruit on whose leaves it feeds. Young caterpillars shelter from birds under rolled leaves. Chrysalis mimics dried, rolled leaves. Adults combine upper-wing flashy color with closed-wing camouflage, which resembles the bark of *koa* and *naio*. On these trees adults suck nourishing sap, oozing at wounds or fluxes. • *Māmaki* grows easily on wet, disturbed, or open ground. Newly opened areas in the forests, such as home sites, often experience a flush of host-plant *māmaki* and Kamehamehas. In the 1890s naturalist R. C. L. Perkins saw the Kamehameha occasionally in Honolulu gardens. Unlikely today. As *māmaki* can survive trimming by road crews and resprout, the adult is sometimes seen at roadsides. Residents and visitors chance seeing this strong flier near Nu'uanu Pali and Akaka Falls State Parks. • Although most eggs hatch, many caterpillars do not survive the chrysalis stage. Instead, parasitizing wasps emerge. Introduced to control alien crop pests, the wasps do not distinguish native from pest.—*A.M./S.L.M.*

The *'Ākohekohe*'s crest makes it exceptional viewing for birders. The crest carries *'ōhi'a lehua* pollen from blossom to blossom as the bird sucks up nectar and nabs caterpillars for breakfast, lunch, and dinner. The crest seems an obvious feature separating this bird from other honeycreepers—if it weren't for one little problem. When Scott Wilson first discovered the bird in 1888 he collected a crestless, immature bird. Engaged in a running print battle with wealthy collector Sir Lionel Rothschild, Wilson rushed into print, naming his new species *Himatione dolei* (Sanford B. Dole: amateur ornithologist, future revolutionary, and eventual territorial governor). When Henry Palmer, Rothschild's collector, obtained the crested adult in 1892 Rothschild created a new genus, naming it *Palmeria*. Wilson's advocate, Cambridge University's Alfred Newton, referred to this "new" species as *Poach-eria*. • The birds require dense and damp forests. Experienced field biologist R. C. L. Perkins reported that *'Ākohekohe* deserted forests opened and dried out by browsing cattle. Last seen on Moloka'i in 1907 by W. Alanson Bryan, Bishop Museum ornithologist, the bird appears extinct there. In unaltered Maui habitat it is not rare, but the areas it claims are dwindling. Captive breeding programs can only provide higher population numbers for the *'Ākohekohe*. We must also provide suitable habitat. The future of Hawaiian species lies in preservation of habitat and control of alien predators.—*A.M./S.L.M.*

He 'io au, 'a'ohe lālā kau 'ole. / I am a hawk; there is no branch on which I cannot perch. / (I am the chief; I go where I please.)[1] • The Hawaiian Hawk, *'Io*, is master of island skies and is seen in flight wherever there are trees for perching. Hawaiians recognized majestic qualities in the *'Io*, making it a chiefly symbol. 'Iolani was among the royal names of both Kamehameha II and IV, comparing them to the all-seeing hawk, symbol of the heavens. • The hawk now nests only on Hawai'i Island, but fossil records, very rare sightings on older islands, and multi-island recognition of the hawk as a Hawaiian cultural symbol prove an archipelago-wide distribution before the present era. These hawks are rarely seen in arid, treeless areas, or even native shrublands, since trees provide required perches for spotting likely prey. Hawaiian Hawks forage in habitats as divergent as papaya and macadamia nut orchards and the primeval *'ōhi'a* and *koa* forests of Hawai'i Volcanoes National Park. They favor nesting in native forest. Adapting well to feeding in altered habitat, they eat whatever their claws can catch. Prey include mice, rats, small wild birds, moths, caterpillars and other insects, and even the occasional crayfish. Misinformed "chicken hawk" fears about birds of prey led to open shooting until the 1940s. Illegal shooting still occurs, though rarely.—*A.M./S.L.M.*

1. M. K. Pukui, *'Ōlelo No'eau: Hawaiian Proverbs and Poetical Sayings*, Special Publication 71 (Honolulu: Bishop Museum Press, 1983), p. 72.

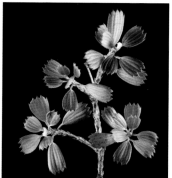

Nohoanu; Hinahina
Geranium kauaiense

Photograph: Sincock Bog, Kaua'i
Range: Alaka'i Swamp to Mount Wai'ale'ale, Kaua'i
Habitat: montane bogs
Population: three populations with about 100–200 individuals total
Threats: pigs; invasion by alien plants
Legal status: candidate for endangered status
Scale: stem 1 1/2–3 1/2 feet long; leaf 3/4 inch long

Most people know *Geranium* or cranesbill as annual or perennial herbs with white, purple, or pink flowers. The genus name is derived from the Greek word *Geranos* for "crane," in reference to the long sterile apical portion of the fruit, which resembles a crane's bill. The fruit of most species open explosively and may throw seeds several feet. All Hawaiian *Geranium* species have the characteristic fruit but are unique in many other ways— enough so that Otto Degener, a renowned Hawaiian botanist and collector, placed them in their own genus, *Neurophyllodes,* referring to the prominently nerved leaves. The Hawaiian species are all shrubs rather than perennial herbs, and have unlobed leaves with teeth along the upper half of the leaf and parallel nerves running the length of the leaf. Each Hawaiian species occupies a different ecological montane habitat, ranging from rain forest to dry subalpine and alpine shrubland to bogs. Like many Hawaiian bog plants, *Geranium kauaiense* has trailing woody stems that root along the nodes, making it and the closely related *G. hillebrandii* of West Maui the most specialized species among the Hawaiian group. A Hawaiian bog is a very difficult place for plants to grow. The waterlogged soils are poor in nitrogen and roots underwater are starved for oxygen.—*W.L.W.*

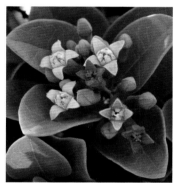

Nohoanu; Hinahina; Nohuanu
Geranium hillebrandii

Photograph: Pu'u Kukui Preserve, West Maui
Range: Pu'u Kukui and Mauna 'Eke, West Maui
Habitat: montane bogs
Population: two populations with about 500 individuals total
Threats: pigs; invasion by alien plants
Legal status: candidate for endangered status
Scale: stem 1 1/2–3 1/2 feet long; flower 7/8 inch diameter

Little is known of the origin of the Hawaiian geraniums, but a recent molecular study of DNA sequences suggests that the shrubby Hawaiian species, with their special adaptations for a woody habit and leaves, are related to quite typical members of the genus. Another study of patterns of colonization and diversification in Hawaiian plants and animals showed that most original colonizations from continental source areas occurred on older islands followed by short-distance colonization from the older to younger islands. New species often evolved on the new island or in new habitats on the same island. In a very few organisms the reverse pattern, a younger to older island colonization pattern, is found. The Hawaiian *Geranium* is one of these groups. • *Geranium* apparently first colonized on East Maui with dispersal (and speciation) in two directions, one to the island of Hawai'i and the other first to the bogs of West Maui (*G. hillebrandii*) then to the bogs of Kaua'i (*G. kauaiense*). Each of the four East Maui species occurs at or in a somewhat different elevation or habitat. Evolution proceeded in two directions: In one group there was a gradual shift into alpine habitats followed by dispersal to Hawai'i, while the other group moved into bogs. Species of *Geranium* grow in all available subalpine and alpine areas and bogs of substantial size and constancy in the archipelago.—*W.L.W.*

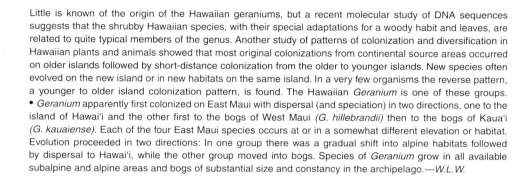

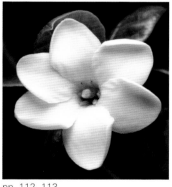

Sandalwood
'Iliahi
Santalum freycinetianum var. *lanaiense*

Photograph: Auwahi, Maui; Kahue unit of The Nature Conservancy Kanepu'u Preserve, Lāna'i
Range: Lāna'i, Maui
Habitat: mesic to wet forest, dry forest on Lāna'i
Population: four populations with over 275 individuals
Threats: fire; human activities; various ungulates; predation by rats; invasion of alien plants
Legal status: endangered
Scale: tree 20 feet tall; flower 3/8 inch across

Santalum freycinetianum is one of four Hawaiian species of sandalwood. This red-flowered species is the most widespread, occurring on five of the islands. It is also the most variable, and is subdivided into three varieties, one of which is restricted to dry to wet forests on the islands of Lāna'i and Maui. *Santalum freycinetianum* var. *lanaiense* is distinguished by its typically broad leaves and smooth fruit. • During the late 18th to early 19th centuries, the sandalwood trade was widespread in the Pacific. Ships from many countries scoured Pacific islands for sources and supply. In 1791 Captain John Kendrick, a Boston fur trader, initiated trade of sandalwood in the Hawaiian Islands, which reached its height between 1810 and 1820. The price of sandalwood ran upward of $125 per ton, and it is estimated that the total sales of the Hawaiian sandalwood reached $3 to $4 million. Hawaiian chiefs forced their people to labor in the forests, cutting the trees and transporting the wood to the harbors for export. However, the chiefs were so extravagant in their spending that they eventually went into debt purchasing ships and overpriced luxury goods. Overall, the sandalwood trade was so lucrative that supplies across the Pacific were soon exhausted, and the exports ended around 1840. The notorious exploits of the colorful individuals involved have been the subject of many popular books.—*W.L.W.*

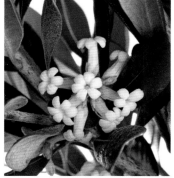

Nānū; Nā'ū
Gardenia brighamii

Photograph: National Tropical Botanical Garden Nursery, Lāwa'i, Kaua'i; Waimea Arboretum and Botanical Garden, O'ahu
Range: Moloka'i, O'ahu, and Lāna'i (one tree), Maui and Hawai'i (extirpated)
Habitat: dry forest
Population: six populations, 15–19 individuals
Threats: feral goats, sheep, deer; predation by rats; introduced insects; alien weeds; fire
Legal status: endangered
Scale: flower 1 1/4–1 1/2 inches across; fruit 1–1 3/8 inches across

Snowy white flowers with six overlapping lobes grace the twig tips of this compact, glossy-leaved shrub or small tree. Male and female flowers are borne on separate trees, the females developing into round, speckled green fruits topped by spurlike calyx lobes and filled with hundreds of seeds. Three *Gardenia* species are endemic to Hawai'i, and all are rare. *Gardenia brighamii* inhabits dry forest communities, whereas the other two are somewhat larger trees of mesic to wet forests. All three species produce delicately fragrant white flowers characteristic of many gardenias. Because most dry forests in the Hawaiian Islands have been destroyed or reduced to small patches, *Gardenia brighamii* has become rare and critically endangered. Historically known from Hawai'i and Maui, this *nā'u* is now extirpated on these islands. Factors contributing to its rarity are numerous, but habitat destruction for agriculture and other uses is paramount. Conservation efforts *in situ* include fencing to exclude feral animals, such as at The Nature Conservancy's site at Kānepu'u on Lāna'i. Attractive and relatively easy to grow from seed, *Gardenia brighamii* is cultivated in conservation collections at a number of botanical gardens in the state including Waimea Arboretum and the NTBG, which harbors several dozen plants.—*D.L.*

Hō'awa
Pittosporum halophilum

Photograph: National Tropical Botanical Garden, Native Hawaiian Plant Section, Lāwa'i, Kaua'i
Range: Moloka'i
Habitat: coastal forest
Population: three populations totaling 17 individuals
Threats: competition from alien plant species; rat predation on Mokapu islet; rockslides; low population numbers
Legal status: species of concern
Scale: leaf blade 1 1/2–2 1/2 inches long

During a 1994 botanical survey of rare coastal palm forest on Huelo Rock, a small volcanic islet located off the windward north shore of Moloka'i, NTBG field botanist Ken Wood came upon two compact shrubs with fragrant cream-colored flowers, knobby fruits, and shiny dark green leaves with undersides covered by silky tan hairs. He knew it was a type of *hō'awa* or *Pittosporum* but was uncertain which of the 10 endemic Hawaiian species it represented. Field observations and later careful study of his herbarium specimens showed it to be *Pittosporum halophilum,* a species whose name means "salt-loving" for the rugged coastal areas it inhabits. First described by botanist Joseph Rock in 1911, this rare *hō'awa* was later dismissed as a minor variant of the widespread *Pittosporum confertiflorum,* a variable species known from four of the Hawaiian Islands. Further fieldwork by NTBG staff on the adjacent islet of Mokapu revealed another population of 15 plants. *Pittosporum halophilum* is known only from 17 individuals on these two small islets, both bird sanctuaries, off the coast of Moloka'i. Seeds have germinated and are now represented by five plants at NTBG, several of which have flowered. An attractive native shrub that tolerates salt spray, *Pittosporum halophilum* holds promise as an ornamental and landscape plant for coastal areas.—*D.L.*

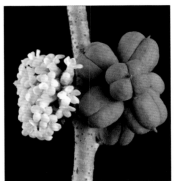

Hōʻawa; Hāʻawa
Pittosporum napaliense

Photograph: National Tropical Botanical Garden, Native Hawaiian Plant Section, Lāwaʻi, Kauaʻi
Range: northwestern Kauaʻi, along the Nā Pali coast from Limahuli to Hanakoa Valleys
Habitat: about 400–1,800 feet; coastal mesic *Pandanus* forest and lowland mixed mesic forest
Population: six populations with several hundred individuals
Threats: disturbance by feral pigs; competition from alien weeds
Legal status: candidate for listing
Scale: seed capsule 3/4–4/5 inch long

Approximately 150 species of *Pittosporum* occur in the Old World tropics and various Pacific islands, mainly in the Southern Hemisphere. Its generic name is derived from the Greek *pittos*, "pitch," and *sporos*, "seeds," referring to the sticky resin that coats the black seeds. The seeds contrast strongly with the orange or red inner surface of the split capsules, and their resinous coating presumably facilitates seed dispersal by sticking to feathers of the birds that eat them. *Pittosporum* is represented in Hawaiʻi by 11 endemic species of shrubs or small trees, several of which have large, knobby capsules several inches long with correspondingly large seeds. This is an example of fruit and seed gigantism in island plants resulting in a loss of dispersibility, as increased seed size reduces the likelihood of seed transport. *Pittosporum napaliense* is a small tree restricted to the northwestern shore of Kauaʻi along the Nā Pali coast and its adjacent valleys. The fragrant cream-colored flowers are produced in clusters along the twigs and branches. Separate trees bear either bisexual or female flowers. When ripe, the four-lobed capsules split in half to reveal the sticky black seeds. Conservation efforts include cultivation of about a dozen mature plants at NTBG's Limahuli and McBryde Gardens.—*D.L.*

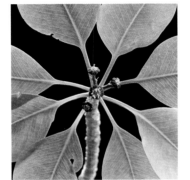

Euphorbia haeleeleana

Photograph: Makua Military Reservation, Oʻahu
Range: Kauaʻi, Oʻahu
Habitat: diverse mesic forest
Population: 13 populations comprising an estimated 450–625 individuals
Threats: rooting of young plants by pigs; browsing by feral deer; seed predation by rats; competition from alien weeds; landslides; fire
Legal status: endangered
Scale: leaf blade 1 3/4–2 1/5 inches wide; capsule 1/2–5/8 inch wide

This unusual tree was first discovered in 1970 in diverse mesic forest on western Kauaʻi. Named for one of its Kauaʻi localities, Hāʻeleʻele Valley, *Euphorbia haeleeleana* is endemic and the only member of the genus native to Hawaiʻi, as all its relatives are either introduced weedy herbs or cultivated shrubs, including the poinsettia. Recent DNA studies show that this species is most closely related to one ranging from Fiji to northern Australia, presumably its ancestor. • *Euphorbia haeleeleana* is a medium-sized tree with distinctive whorls of succulent branches, milky sap, and broad leaves. During dry periods the trees may shed their leaves. Separate male and female flowers are produced in cuplike dark purple or brown structures called cyathia. Tiny yellow and white male flowers consist of a single stamen. The solitary female flower later develops into a bright yellow, three-seeded capsule that explodes when ripe, scattering the seeds a short distance. Consequently, populations tend to be localized; 11 populations occur on western Kauaʻi and 2 more in the Waiʻanae Mountains of western Oʻahu. Some of the individuals in the Mahanaloa Valley population on Kauaʻi have been fenced to exclude feral deer and pigs, although rats continue to consume most of the seed crop, preventing regeneration. *Euphorbia haeleeleana* is in cultivation in several Hawaiian botanical gardens.—*D.L.*

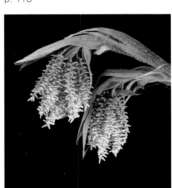

Loulu
Pritchardia napaliensis

Photograph: Nā Pali Coast State Park, Kauaʻi
Range: Kauaʻi
Habitat: coastal to lowland dry, mesic, and wet forests
Population: three populations comprising fewer than 90 plants
Threats: seed predation by rats; feral pigs and goats; competition from alien weeds; possible landslides
Legal status: endangered
Scale: palm 10–23 feet high

Many of the 23 endemic *loulu* species of Hawaiʻi are extremely rare and localized; several have only one or two individuals left in the wild. Kauaʻi is home to seven *loulu* species (including a new one not yet published). *Pritchardia napaliensis* is found only in three localities along the Nā Pali coast of Kauaʻi. It is a delicate palm with a small trunk, graceful fronds with drooping leaflet tips, and arching clusters of yellow flowers. Alien weeds and populations of feral goats and pigs thwart regeneration of seedlings for many *Pritchardia* species, while ubiquitous wild rats eat their fruits. Conservation methods for *Pritchardia* need to focus on exclusion of rats, allowing the fruits to ripen for collection and propagation, and of feral ungulates. Once ripe fruits are collected, they are usually easy to germinate and grow in cultivation. All of the Hawaiian *loulu* species are represented at various sites of the NTBG. A collaborative project between the Kauaʻi District DOFAW and NTBG involved planting 39 young plants of *Pritchardia napaliensis* to augment a wild population from which seeds were collected. Although this population was fenced to exclude feral animals, the fence was vandalized and all the young plants were stolen, senselessly thwarting efforts to conserve this endangered palm.—*D.L.*

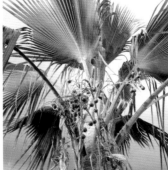

Loulu
Pritchardia viscosa

Photograph: National Tropical Botanical Garden, Lāwaʻi, Kauaʻi
Range: Kauaʻi
Habitat: wet forest
Population: one population of four mature plants, a juvenile, and a seedling
Threats: competition from alien plants; feral pigs; seed predation by rodents; human disturbance
Legal status: endangered
Scale: palm 10–26 feet high

Forming a dense crown atop the stout trunk, 20 or more rigid, circular leaves rattle in the brisk trade winds. Clear green above and silvery tan beneath, the leaf pleats radiate symmetrically to stiff daggerlike lobes fringing the blade. Arching clusters of flowers and fruits on wooly stalks nest within the leaf crown. The pointed flower buds and egg-shaped green fruits shine as if varnished, evoking the species name *viscosa* for this majestic palm. • Named in honor of William T. Pritchard, 19th-century British consul in the Fiji Islands, *Pritchardia* comprises 27 species restricted to the Hawaiian Islands, Fiji, Tonga, Cook Islands, and the Tuamotu Archipelago. All but four are endemic to the Hawaiian Islands, where they are known as *loulu* and *hāwane*. Some *loulu* have become critically endangered, including *Pritchardia viscosa*, whose unique surviving population is restricted to northwestern Kauaʻi. In 1992 Hurricane ʻIniki destroyed two adult trees, leaving only the current population. Two adults have been fenced by the Kauaʻi DOFAW, however the exclosure fails to prevent seed predation by rats and illegal pilfering of seeds—and even a young plant—by unscrupulous collectors. Conservationists continue to collect seeds from the mature trees and healthy young plants are now secure in cultivation at the NTBG, Lyon Arboretum, and Waimea Arboretum.—*D.L.*

Loulu
Pritchardia schattaueri

Photograph: Bishop Museum, Amy B. H. Greenwell Ethnobotanical Garden, Captain Cook, Hawaiʻi
Range: Hawaiʻi Island
Habitat: mesic forest
Population: three populations comprising 12–13 individuals
Threats: feral pigs; seed predation by rats; competition from alien plants; grazing and trampling by cattle; human development
Legal status: endangered
Scale: palm 90–100 feet high

Pritchardia schattaueri is among the largest of the Hawaiian *loulu*. A dozen large pleated leaves with drooping tips crown the stout trunk. Emerging from the fibrous leaf bases are branching clusters of tiny flowers and conspicuously large, round to egg-shaped fruits up to two inches in diameter. The species is named for George Schattauer, who discovered it in 1957. At two inches long, fruits of *Pritchardia schattaueri* and *P. lowreyana* from Molokaʻi are the largest in the genus. Most Hawaiian *Pritchardia* have fruits about an inch across, whereas they are pea-sized in some Pacific species. A phenomenon known as fruit or seed gigantism characterizes certain tropical island plants. Once established in a favorable habitat, these plants no longer require seeds that will disperse to distant locations. Instead they sometimes evolve large seeds that store abundant food reserves, enabling their seedlings to survive and grow in the forest understory near the mother plant. In the absence of threats and disturbance this strategy works well, but since the arrival of humans and the alien plants and animals they introduced, conditions have changed drastically. Now only about a dozen individuals of *Pritchardia schattaueri* remain on the Big Island in disturbed mesic forest partly cleared for ranching and agriculture. Young plants are in cultivation in botanical gardens, and exclosures on the Big Island are maintained by DOFAW.—*D.L.*

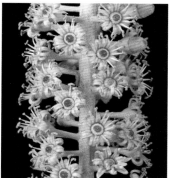

pp. 122, 123, 124, 125

Munroidendron racemosum

Photograph: National Tropical Botanical Garden, Medicinal Section, Lāwaʻi, Kauaʻi
Range: Kauaʻi
Habitat: low- to mid-elevation mesic forest
Population: eight populations with 75 plants total
Threats: feral goats; competition from alien plants; habitat alteration; introduced insects; seed predation by rats; fire
Legal status: endangered
Scale: flower and fruit cluster 1½–2 inches across

Munroidendron is one of only six monotypic plant genera endemic to Hawaiʻi. "Monotypic" signifies a genus comprising only a single species, often representing a unique evolutionary lineage. The single species *Munroidendron racemosum* is endemic to Kauaʻi. • This remarkable tree was named to commemorate eminent ornithologist, botanical explorer, and conservationist George C. Munro (1866–1963), who apparently first recognized it as a new taxon. The suffix *dendron* means "tree." It has a straight trunk, smooth gray bark, and rounded or umbrella-shaped canopy. Succulent branches bear attractive grayish green compound leaves that are softly whitish tan beneath. Often leafless when flowering, it produces long, dangling inflorescences crowded with pale yellow to cream-colored and purple flowers. Thick, cylindrical masses of ovoid fruits are at first cream-colored with purple tips and then become dark purple as they ripen. • *Munroidendron racemosum* is known from 75 individuals occurring in eight populations scattered in mesic forest remnants around Kauaʻi. The largest population contains only 30 individuals and most others consist of 1 to several trees. *Munroidendron* is easily propagated from seed and thrives in cultivation. Unusual and attractive, it is drought-resistant and generally pest-free. Conservation collections of *Munroidendron racemosum* are grown at the NTBG's Limahuli and McBryde Gardens to ensure the survival and genetic diversity of this elegant plant.—*D.L.*

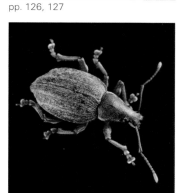

pp. 126, 127

Māhoe; ʻAlaʻalahua
Alectryon macrococcus var. *auwahiensis*

Photograph: Auwahi, Maui
Range: East Maui
Habitat: 2,600–3,500 feet; open dry forest
Population: one population of 12 individuals
Threats: cattle grazing; feral goats and pigs; rodents; alien weeds, especially pasture grasses; alien insects; fire; small population size; low seed viability
Legal status: endangered
Scale: leaflet 4–7 inches long; fruit 1–2 inches across

Hawaiʻi is home to a single *Alectryon* species, *A. macrococcus*, with two varieties: var. *macrococcus* occurs on Kauaʻi, Oʻahu, Molokaʻi, and West Maui; and var. *auwahiensis* only on East Maui. Both varieties are slow-growing, hard-wooded trees reaching 35 feet in height with compound leaves and leathery leaflets. The small flowers develop into fruits one to two inches across, resembling clusters of brown grapes. Mature fruits split open to reveal a single large seed enveloped in a bright red fleshy coating or aril; both have been used as food. In Latin the species name *macrococcus* refers to these large seeds. Its Hawaiian name *māhoe* signifies twins, as the fruits are often paired. • *Māhoe* has become increasingly rare; about 500 individuals of var. *macrococcus* are known from Kauaʻi, Oʻahu, Molokaʻi, and West Maui. The status of var. *auwahiensis* is much more precarious, as only 12 individuals occur in a single population on ranchland on the dry southern slopes of Haleakalā on leeward East Maui. The large seeds suffer predation by rats and boring insects, low viability and germination, and poor dispersal. Black-twig-borer infestations impact wild and cultivated plants, further hindering conservation and recovery efforts for the *māhoe*. Although rare in cultivation, seedlings are being grown by Bill Garnett at the DOFAW nursery at Pahole, Oʻahu.—*D.L.*

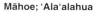

p. 129

Lahaina Foliar Snout Beetle
Ponu ʻAi Lau
Rhyncogonus lahainae

Photograph: temporary studio, East–West Center, Oʻahu
Range: West Maui Mountains, Maui
Habitat: 3,000 feet; mountainous cloud forest; annual rainfall of 98 inches
Population: rare
Threats: rat predation
Legal status: species of concern
Scale: ⅜ inch long

Think *tank:* stout bodied. Wing covers fused for protection, but power of flight lost. Wide foot pads for walking on leaves. This beetle eats from the edge of a leaf in deep scallops toward the midrib. To avoid bird predation, beetles hide in tree crotches and leaf litter during the day and feed nocturnally. Despite such secretive habits, entomologist R. C. L. Perkins noted that sister species are big on the bird buffet. He found the *Puaiohi* fed heavily, even exclusively, on these weevils. • In Hawaiʻi there are *Rhyncogonus* species on every island. How wingless beetles colonized every island is most perplexing. *Rhyncogonus* are on each major island, tiny Nihoa and Necker, even distant Wake Atoll. Older islands have more species, reflecting the time for differences to evolve new species. • In the 1890s Perkins observed a sister species swarming on beach vitex. Their hard, dry wing covers litter the ground even now under native dryland vegetation. Predator African big-headed ants brought lowland species to near extinction. The cloud forest habitat is yet safe from ants, although rats do eat *Rhyncogonus.* Maui Land & Pineapple Company, Inc. has established a West Maui Preserve where species such as this are given some protection from rats and pigs altering the habitat.—*A.M./S.L.M.*

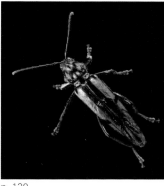

p. 130

Maui Alani Longhorned Beetle
Ponu Lāʻau Alani
Plagithmysus alani

Photograph: temporary studio, East–West Center, Oʻahu
Range: West Maui Mountains, Maui
Habitat: 3,000 feet; cloud forest
Population: very rare; only five collected since 1972 discovery
Threats: habitat alteration by alien pigs
Legal status: species of concern
Scale: 1 inch long

With an extremely narrow body and partly exposed wings, these beetles are easily mistaken for crickets, grasshoppers, or wasps. *Plagithmysus alani* is named for fragrant *alani*, the Hawaiian *Melicope* trees. Although there are 136 *Plagithmysus* species and 30 other host plants, each beetle keeps to its specific food plant by instinctive behaviors, ensuring species do not interbreed. The beetle attacks damaged, weakened, or dying trees, speeding decomposition and use by other forest creatures. The antennae sniff out rotting *alani* tree bark, where adults will lay eggs. Related species are gregarious, and large numbers appear on suitable trees to lay eggs. Massing promotes mating but allows birds to find the adults. For protection the larvae feed below the bark, leaving long flat grooves. Despite the beetles' evasive strategy, the Maui Parrotbill uses its strong bill to crush twigs and fill its stomach with this nutritious food. • Very early in the morning, beetles rise out of the understory and fly to tree trunks as the sun warms the forest. An intact ecosystem is important to survival. Saving only the host plant would not be enough; lower-growing plants are important for night security. Fortunately, Maui Land & Pineapple Company, Inc. continues a century of care of alani beetle habitat on their upland Maui property. Controlling alien pigs and stopping weed invasions have helped maintain habitat. Taking good care of the forest means a good water supply and good business.—*A.M./S.L.M.*

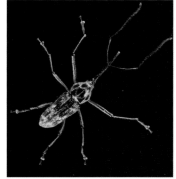

p. 131

Munro's Araliad Snout Beetle
Mū ʻŌlapa
Nesotocus munroi

Photograph: Betty Alberts residence, Pāʻia, Maui
Range: Hawaiʻi Island
Habitat: 3,000–5,000 feet; wet, mixed moist forest with ʻōlapa and ʻoheʻohe tree host plants
Population: rare
Threats: habitat alteration by cattle and feral pigs; habitat displacement by tree plantations
Legal status: species of concern
Scale: 1 inch long

Nesotocus munroi honors George C. Munro, who came to Hawaiʻi in the 1890s as a bird collector, stayed as a ranch manager, befriended biologist R. C. L. Perkins, and founded the Hawaiʻi Audubon Society. He literally "wrote the book" on Hawaiian birds. • In the thick rain forest, Perkins saw these snout beetles active all day, running rapidly over tree trunks, but in dry forests they were active at night. When disturbed they dropped to the ground, lying motionless. Disruptive patterns, mimicking lichens or bark, make them hard to detect. Why? Most likely they are hiding from hungry birds. • The araliad or ginseng family trees have well-developed secretory canals, so wounds flush a resinous sap, stopping beetles and decay. Only after the plant is seriously wounded can beetles lay eggs. The beetle's comical antennae sport sensory pits and bristles for smelling and feeling its way to damaged or rotting trees. The antennae are mounted on a long throat with a tiny, tip mounted mouth. Mother beetle smells a damaged tree where conditions are just right to raise a family. Using two tiny teeth in her snout-mounted jaws, she bores a hole and deposits her eggs. Her grubs will feed on the already rotting tree, form pupae, and emerge as adults to carry on the species.—*A.M./S.L.M.*

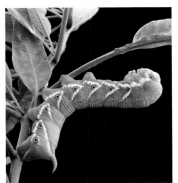

Blackburn's Hawk Moth
'Ōka'i
Manduca blackburni

Photograph: Ulupalakua Ranch, Maui; Betty Alberts residence, Pā'ia, Maui; Temporary studio, Kahalui, Maui
Range: restricted areas on Maui and Hawai'i; Kaho'olawe; believed extinct on other major islands
Habitat: sea level to 3,500 feet; dry side of island
Population: very rare
Threats: cattle and feral goats; alien wasps
Legal status: endangered
Scale: up to 6 inches long

Professional entomologists misidentified *Manduca* for 100 years. Fortunately, "amateurs" were more attentive to the largest insect of Hawai'i. Rev. Thomas Blackburn collected *Manduca* between 1877 and 1880, when the published description honored him. Almost 20 years later a survey of Hawaiian butterflies and moths erroneously lumped *Manduca* with continental hawk moths, and professionals lost interest. Confusion with tomato and tobacco hornworms continued into the 1950s. Economic entomologists undervalued *Manduca,* rarely found feeding on crops. Most native insects are so host-specific they never feed on alien plants. • In 1955 William Meinecke, accountant and naturalist, reared a *Manduca* caterpillar found in his Hawai'i Island garden, the first sighting in 30 years. A student found an adult at a light on Maui in 1975. A devoted amateur sphinx collector's 1984 visit to Maui inspired botanist Betsy Gagné to speculate on possible native host plants. Although she systematically searched Maui for *Manduca,* she was photographing a flower when she finally saw a caterpillar chomping on *'aiea*. Father Charles Riotte, a retired priest, studied the species and in 1986 published a review and revision confirming *Manduca* as endemic. • *Manduca* caterpillars presently dine mostly on alien tree tobacco. With tree tobacco naturalized near habitations and agriculture on all islands, *Manduca* reintroduction could eventually bring this showy moth to coexistence with admiring naturalists.—*A.M./S.L.M.*

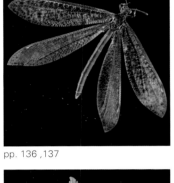

Wilson's Hawaiian Antlion
Pinao Huna
Distoleon wilsoni

Photograph: Betty Alberts residence, Pā'ia, Maui
Range: probably extinct on Lāna'i and Maui; Kaho'olawe; Hawai'i Island's central saddle, SW Mauna Loa
Habitat: 1,300 to 6,800 feet; young arid *'a'ā* lava flows
Population: rare on Hawai'i, maybe 1,000–3,000; extremely rare on Kaho'olawe
Threats: alien ants
Legal status: none
Scale: adult 2¹/₂ inches long; 4-inch wing spread

This visually and behaviorally interesting insect is a big puzzle in need of keen observation. Continental antlions or doodlebug larvae excavate conical sand pits to trap prey, especially ants. In the upper slopes, where island antlions once abounded, they could not prey on ants, for old Hawai'i was without ants. Virtually nothing is known of their diet or life history. Where the larvae set up their ambush is uncertain, but it may be under stones or in porous lava cavities, ashy soil, or ground litter. A few cocoons were found under stones in the dry, montane zone of Hawai'i Island, near Mauna Kea State Park. In the 1890s one suspected larva was found under a streamside stone on Maui. • Before 1883 the Rev. Thomas Blackburn, founder of Hawaiian entomology, resided six years in the Hawaiian Islands. He observed adult antlions only on Maui in a single, leeward ravine, and wrote that the antlion was too large and conspicuous to escape notice if occurring elsewhere. Antlions fly in an unusual way, rising very abruptly when startled, and settling cryptically 100 feet away after a rapid and well directed but ungainly flight. • This insect might be called a "lava-lion" since it only occurs in dry, barren lavascapes—which has a benefit, as its preferred habitat is unappealing for land developments.—*A.M./S.L.M.*

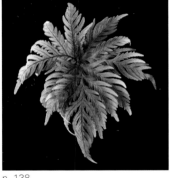

Angel Wing Fern
Doryopteris angelica

Photograph: National Tropical Botanical Garden Nursery, Lāwa'i, Kaua'i
Range: Kaua'i
Habitat: mesic forest
Population: three small populations of fewer than 50 plants
Threats: invasion by alien plants; rooting by feral pigs and browsing by black-tailed deer
Legal status: species of concern
Scale: leaf blade 5¹/₂–12 inches long

This intricately lobed fern is found only in the mesic forests of the western mountains of Kaua'i. First named and published in 1999, it was discovered just a few years earlier by NTBG botanist Ken Wood: "I was working with Joel Lau of The Nature Conservancy in the high mesic forest of Kaua'i and for no apparent reason stopped to open my plant press. I paused in silence for a moment because I had no plant to collect, and then I saw, no more than three meters away, an extraordinary new species of large fern. Perhaps there is a guardian angel of the forest." • Wood sent a specimen of the unusual fern to Warren H. "Herb" Wagner for identification. Wagner, a world authority on Hawaiian ferns, confirmed it was indeed a new species and subsequently coauthored it with Wood. The species name *angelica* describes the winglike appearance of the fern's leaves, and also alludes to the unique manner of its discovery. • *Doryopteris angelica* is among the largest and most elegant members of its genus. Its extreme rarity is likely due to slow growth and exacting habitat requirements. Three plants are in cultivation at the NTBG, where horticulturists are attempting to learn more about its growth and propagation requirements.—*D.L.*

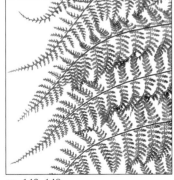

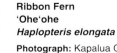

Dryopteris tetrapinnata

Photograph: Kapalua Golf Villa, Kapalua, Maui
Range: East Maui
Habitat: 4,600–6,000 feet; mesic and wet forest
Population: approximately 10 populations totaling approximately 1,000 plants
Threats: rooting by feral pigs; possible browsing by feral deer; competition from alien plants
Legal status: species of concern
Scale: frond 6–9 feet long

Dryopteris is a genus of approximately 200 species mostly from cooler temperate areas of the world, but 10 endemic species occur in Hawai'i. *Dryopteris tetrapinnata* is a spectacular ground fern with fronds reaching six to nine feet in length. Its huge frond size may make it the world's largest *Dryopteris* species. The stalks supporting the fronds are covered by narrow, twisted, dark brown scales. *Tetrapinnata* refers to the finely dissected fronds, which are divided up to four times and end in numerous small, delicately lobed leaflets. This impressive species is still locally abundant in cool undisturbed mesic and wet forests on the north, east, and southern slopes of Haleakalā on East Maui, where it forms healthy populations sometimes consisting of hundreds of plants. Although *Dryopteris tetrapinnata* is not in immediate danger and consequently has no legal status, preservation of healthy forest communities is essential for the continued survival of this and other species sharing the same habitat.—*D.L.*

Ribbon Fern
'Ohe'ohe
Haplopteris elongata

Photograph: Kapalua Golf Villa, Kapalua, Maui
Range: Kaua'i, O'ahu, Moloka'i, Lāna'i, Maui, Hawai'i
Habitat: about 50–4,000 feet; lowland to montane wet forests
Population: common and widespread
Threats: deforestation
Legal status: none
Scale: leaf blade ¹/₈–¹/₄ inch wide

While exploring Hawaiian forests you may notice a clump of narrow, dark green, ribbonlike leaves up to three feet long hanging from a mossy tree trunk. This peculiar plant is known as the ribbon fern. The Hawaiians called it *'ohe'ohe* in reference to its similarity to bamboo or reed leaves. Formerly known as *Vittaria elongata* (and mistakenly as *H. zosterifolia*), its correct name is *Haplopteris elongata*. The *'ohe'ohe* often occurs as an epiphyte on native trees such as the *koa* or *'ōhi'a* or, rarely, terrestrially on mossy hummocks. An epiphyte is a plant that derives its nutrients and moisture from the air and rainfall and usually perches on another plant to obtain more light or growing space. Epiphytes in Hawaiian forests generally consist of bryophytes (mosses and liverworts), ferns, and a few flowering plant species. In contrast, the epiphyte flora in tropical continental forests is generally more diverse and includes numerous flowering plant species such as orchids, bromeliads, and even cacti. *Haplopteris elongata* is the only ribbon fern species in Hawai'i, where it occurs on six of the main islands. Found in wet forests from the lowlands to montane areas, this highly adaptable fern is equally at home in native, disturbed, and secondary forests as long as the appropriate rough-barked trees are available for it.—*D.L.*

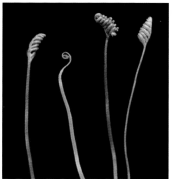

p. 145

Toothbrush Fern
'Owāli'i Makali'i; 'Oāli'i Makali'i; Haili-o-Pua
Schizaea robusta

Photograph: Pu'u Kukui Preserve, West Maui
Range: Kaua'i, O'ahu, Moloka'i, West Maui, Hawai'i
Habitat: about 2,100–5,000 feet; wet forest and shrubland, bogs and bog margins
Population: unknown but widespread
Threats: habitat destruction; rooting by feral pigs; invasion by alien plant species
Legal status: none
Scale: leaf 3–16 inches long, toothbrushlike portion ³/₁₀–³/₅ inch long

At first sight this small terrestrial herb appears grasslike. However, closer examination reveals that the dark green leaves—technically called fronds—5 to 18 inches tall actually belong to a fern, *Schizaea robusta*. Tips of most fronds are fertile and bear structures resembling miniature brown toothbrushes. These are actually dense, featherlike clusters of tiny capsules containing the spores by which this strange fern propagates itself. *Schizaea* is a peculiar fern genus comprising about 30 species occurring in tropical, subtropical, and even temperate zones, with a single species, *S. robusta*, endemic to the Hawaiian Islands. Some species have fronds that are divided or bifurcated several times into equal segments, a condition known as dichotomous branching. • Although not considered threatened or endangered, *Schizaea robusta* is not especially abundant on any of the five islands on which it occurs. This distinctive species grows on nutrient-poor soils, particularly in boggy areas on mossy hummocks and around tree bases, or sometimes on decaying wood. Habitat destruction including disturbances by feral animals, especially pigs that like to root in bogs, and competition from vigorous alien plant species are likely resulting in a decrease in its population numbers. Further field studies are required to determine the number, size, and extent of its populations in Hawai'i.—*D.L.*

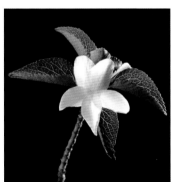

p. 146

Violet
Viola helenae

Photograph: Wahiawa Mountains, Kaua'i
Range: Wahiawa Stream, Kaua'i
Habitat: wet slope of stream
Population: one population with fewer than 100 individuals total
Threats: pigs and alien plants, which are moving up into the remote Wahiawa Stream area; small population size
Legal status: endangered
Scale: portion shown 5 inches tall

Viola helenae is one of the rarest species in the genus. Historically known from two of the branches of the upper Wahiawa Stream on Kaua'i, it was first collected in 1908 by the Rev. John M. Lydgate, a prominent civic leader on Kaua'i who went on a number of plant-collecting trips on most of the islands. The following year he and Charles Forbes, a botanist at Bishop Museum, described it as *Viola helenae* in honor of Lydgate's wife, Helen. This species is a knee-high unbranched shrub with tiny pale lavender to white flowers. • *Viola helenae*, like many species of Hawaiian plants, is highly restricted geographically. In the highly dissected terrain of a five-million-year-old island like Kaua'i, species either evolved in a small microclimate like the isolated rain forests at the base of the Wahiawa Mountains and were never able to colonize other areas, or they were more widespread at a much earlier geological stage of the island and sequentially were eliminated from all but one refuge. In either case this violet was probably already very rare by the time humans colonized the islands. A small disturbance to a population's birthplace or final refuge may lead to extinction.—*W.L.W.*

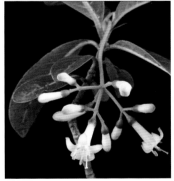

p. 147

Violet
Pamakami; 'Olopū
Viola chamissoniana subsp. *chamissoniana*

Photograph: Makua Military Reservation, Ohikilolo Ridge, O'ahu
Range: Wai'anae Mountains, O'ahu
Habitat: dry cliffs in mesic forest
Population: six populations with fewer than 400 individuals total
Threats: habitat destruction by feral animals; competition from alien plants; fire
Legal status: endangered
Scale: plant 2–3 feet tall; flower 1 inch across

Adaptive radiation on islands can yield dramatically different yet closely related species. This can make research difficult for evolutionary biologists who attempt to understand how island plants and animals achieved their novel forms. Even more arduous is investigating to which continental group the island species are most closely related. An excellent example of this is found in the Hawaiian violets. Violets are a large genus of annual to perennial herbs with 500 species primarily in temperate areas of the world. In the Hawaiian Islands there are seven species, only one of which is herbaceous. The others—woody spindly shrubs—are unique in the genus. *Viola chamissoniana* is one of the most specialized of the Hawaiian species and subspecies *tracheliifolia* has the largest stems, up to 10 feet high. In the high Andes of South America there are other somewhat woody violets. Among other features, this similarity of habit between the Hawaiian and Andean species has led botanists to suggest that the Hawaiian violets are an ancient group within the genus and are related to neotropical ancestors. It has come as a great surprise then that a recent molecular study by Harvey Ballard of Ohio University comparing the DNA sequences of numerous violets from around the world suggests that the ancestors are creeping herbaceous violets of the high Arctic.—*W.L.W.*

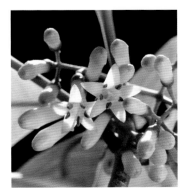

p. 148

Kōpiko
Psychotria grandiflora

Photograph: Kōke'e State Park, Kaua'i
Range: Kaua'i
Habitat: mesic to wet forest
Population: four populations totaling 9 or 10 plants
Threats: alien plants; pigs; black-tailed deer
Legal status: candidate for endangered status
Scale: corolla tube ²/₅–⁴/₅ inch long

Waxy white, tubular flowers hanging in clusters of 3 to 11 make *Psychotria grandiflora* one of the most ornamental Hawaiian members of its genus. The pale yellow margins and midrib of its leaves are also attractive, although when not in flower only a trained eye can distinguish this rare *kōpiko* from its relatives in the mesic and wet forests it inhabits. Kaua'i harbors 8 of the 11 endemic Hawaiian *Psychotria* species, making field identification of *kōpiko* a challenge. Nevertheless, extensive searching of suitable forest habitat by keen-eyed field botanists has revealed that *Psychotria grandiflora* is critically endangered. Fortunately, these shrubs or small trees seem to self-pollinate and set seed, two per fruit. As birds eat the ripe orange fruits, plants must be regularly monitored to collect seed for propagation at the NTBG and Lyon Arboretum. • Special techniques such as embryo culture may facilitate propagation, enabling meager wild populations of *Psychotria grandiflora* to be augmented with young plants. Protection of wild populations from feral animals and weeds is also crucial, most likely using fenced exclosures like the two constructed by the Kaua'i DOFAW in Kōke'e State Park. Sadly, the last refuge for *Psychotria grandiflora* and other endangered Hawaiian species may be in managed and tended areas such as these.—*D.L.*

Psychotria hobdyi

Photograph: Mahanaloa Valley, Kaua'i
Range: Kaua'i
Habitat: diverse mesic forest
Population: five populations comprising about 70 plants
Threats: browsing from feral deer; rooting by feral pigs; competition from alien plants
Legal status: candidate for endangered status
Scale: corolla tube ¹/₂–³/₄ inch long

Containing more than 11,000 species, the Rubiaceae or coffee family is fourth-largest of the world's flowering plant families. The genus *Psychotria* alone comprises between 1,000 and 1,500 species worldwide, making their identification challenging, to say the least. Kaua'i is home to 8 of the 11 endemic Hawaiian *Psychotria* species. Of these, *Psychotria hobdyi* is clearly one of the most attractive, along with its close relative, *Psychotria grandiflora*. When in bloom, the branches of this small tree are adorned with large clusters of inch-long, tubular white flowers with five starlike petals. Flowers are later followed by plump, two-seeded fruits that ripen yellow to orange in color. • The species name honors former Kaua'i District forester Robert W. Hobdy, who first discovered plants growing in the diverse mesic forests of western Kaua'i. Browsing by introduced black-tailed deer prevents regeneration of young plants, as does rooting by pigs and competition from weedy alien plants. Several individuals of *Psychotria hobdyi* are protected by a fenced exclosure in Mahanaloa Valley. In addition, a number of young plants are thriving in cultivation at the NTBG's sites on Kaua'i.—*D.L.*

p. 149

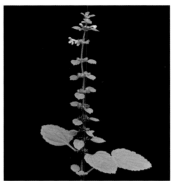

Phyllostegia bracteata

Photograph: Waikamoi, Maui
Range: Maui
Habitat: wet forest
Population: three populations with about 100 individuals total
Threats: destruction of the habitat by feral pigs; competition from alien plants
Legal status: candidate for endangered status
Scale: portion shown 6 inches tall

The mint genus *Phyllostegia* comprises both small- and large-flowered species. Most species have white- or pink-tinged flowers, but *P. floribunda* of Hawai'i Island has red flowers. *Phyllostegia bracteata* is from the small-white-flowered group. Mints have fruit that divide into four nutlets at maturity. All species of the related *Phyllostegia* and *Stenogyne* have unique enlarged, fleshy, greenish black nutlets that are thought to be an adaptation in their common ancestor as a way to attract birds for seed dispersal. • Historically *Phyllostegia bracteata* occurred at a number of widely separated localities on East and West Maui, but it is now apparently quite rare. It has only been collected several times in the 20th century, most recently in 1992. Today, when botanists go out specifically looking for it, at least a few of the delicate plants can be found. Part of the reason it is so difficult to assess the populations of this species is that it occurs in extremely wet environments of the Hawaiian wet forest. According to Joel Lau of The Nature Conservancy, there are several extant populations, including two in the Waikamoi Flume area and others in Kipahulu and the adjacent Manawainui Valleys. His estimates are most likely low because relatively large tracts of wet forest habitat still in comparatively good shape remain unexamined on East and West Maui.—*W.L.W.*

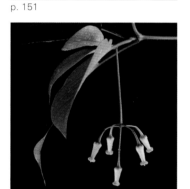

Phyllostegia warshaueri

Photograph: Volcano Rare Plant Facility, Center for Conservation Research and Training, University of Hawai'i, Volcano, Hawai'i
Range: Kohala Mountains and Hāmākua (O'ōkala Trail), Hawai'i; rediscovered in Laupāhoehoe
Habitat: wet forest
Population: three to four populations with about 10–20 individuals total
Threats: habitat destruction by pigs; competition from alien plants; ditch improvements and road clearing; small population size
Legal status: endangered
Scale: stem up to 10 feet; flower 1/2 inch across

Phyllostegia warshaueri was only described in 1987, partly because it is a very rare plant. But it had been known before then. In fact, it was first collected by Reverend John Lydgate prior to 1886 and named *Phyllostegia ambigua* var. *longipes* by Hillebrand in 1888. Based on newly collected material, Harold St. John considered this variety sufficiently different to warrant designation as the species *Phyllostegia warshaueri*. *Phyllostegia warshaueri* is a member of the mint family and shares a common ancestor with the bird-pollinated group *Stenogyne* (see p. 4). This vine produces 6 to 14 large flowers per stem, which are presumed to be insect pollinated. As with *Stenogyne*, species of *Phyllostegia* have unique fleshy fruits that apparently evolved for bird dispersal in these Hawaiian genera. *Phyllostegia* is among the Hawaiian genera most at risk of extinction despite the fact that there are 32 Hawaiian species, plus one in Tonga and one in Tahiti. Presently, only four species are apparently secure. • Historically, *Phyllostegia warshaueri* was known from the northeast slopes of Mauna Kea (Laupāhoehoe) and from the Kohala Mountains. It is currently known from two populations in the Kohala Mountains (5 to 10 individuals), and from Hāmākua (O'ōkala Trail). Since listing as an endangered species it has been rediscovered in Laupāhoehoe near Kīlau Stream (3 to 10 plants).—*W.L.W.*

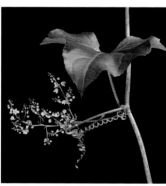

Labordia tinifolia var. wahiawaensis

Photograph: Wahiawa Mountains, Kaua'i
Range: Kaua'i
Habitat: wet forest
Population: one population of 20–30 plants within a 1/2- by 3/4-mile area
Threats: alien plants; feral pigs, landslides
Legal status: endangered
Scale: flower 3/5–3/4 inch long

Delicate, pale green flowers hang in chandelierlike clusters, the short, recurved petals revealing a darker greenness within. Fruits like small green jalapeño peppers dangle in clusters of five. These larger flowers and fruits characterize *Labordia tinifolia* var. *wahiawaensis*, setting it apart from the other two varieties of this species. Rarest of the three varieties, *wahiawaensis* is known from a single population in a small area of private land in the Wahiawa Mountains, Kaua'i. First collected in 1980 by Steve Perlman, this rather nondescript small tree is difficult to recognize in the field except for its leaves, which are markedly pale, almost silvery beneath. • Invasive alien plants, especially strawberry guava, are the greatest threat to this small population, although in 1992 Hurricane 'Iniki destroyed large areas of its pristine forest habitat and decimated the original population of about 100 plants. A critically endangered relative, *Labordia lydgatei*, also occurs in the Wahiawa Mountains. • Most *Labordia* species are difficult to cultivate by seeds or cuttings, but hopefully new propagation techniques will be discovered. Preservation of critical habitat is clearly the best means of saving not only these *Labordia* but also the myriad of plants and animals comprising the intricate ecosystems they inhabit. Product of millions of years of evolution, the Hawaiian endemic genus *Labordia* includes 15 named species and a newly discovered species from Kaua'i.—*D.L.*

'Ānunu
Sicyos alba

Photograph: Pu'u Maka'ala Natural Area Reserve, Hawai'i
Range: Hawai'i Island
Habitat: 3,200 to 3,720 feet; 'ōhi'a- and hāpu'u-dominated montane rain forests
Population: two populations with about 22 plants
Threats: habitat damage by feral pigs; trail clearing; competition from alien plants; volcanic activity; small population size
Legal status: endangered
Scale: vine up to 30 or more feet long; leaf 5 inches across

First collected by the U.S. Exploring Expedition of 1840 and 1841, *Sicyos alba* was considered a new variety of *Sicyos cucumerinus* by Asa Gray of Harvard in 1854. In 1978 Harold St. John, the foremost Hawaiian botanist of his day, named the plant to a new genus as *Sarx alba*. Ian Telford, a specialist on the gourd family of which *Sicyos* is a member, returned this species to *Sicyos*. The feature distinguishing *S. alba* from the other 13 Hawaiian species of the genus is the larger fruit up to 1 1/2 inches long, which becomes white and fleshy at maturity. It appears, as A. Gray's placement suggested, to be most closely related to *Sicyos cucumerinus*, which differs primarily in its firmly fleshy green fruit. The larger white fruit of *S. alba* perhaps represents an adaptation for dispersal of the seeds by birds. • Historically, the species was known only on Hawai'i, from Mauna Kea (now extirpated), Kīlauea, and the Pu'u Maka'ala area. Today, the two known populations are restricted to Pu'u Maka'ala and 'Ōla'a Forest Reserve, both on state-owned land. The number of individuals fluctuates from year to year because this species is an annual—a very odd life cycle for a rain forest plant. At last report, only one individual was growing at Pu'u Maka'ala, but 20 individuals are known from the 'Ōla'a population.—*W.L.W.*

Hawaiian Bonamia
Bonamia menziesii

Photograph: Waimea Arboretum and Botanical Garden, O'ahu
Range: all the main islands except Ni'ihau and Kaho'olawe, but considered extinct on Moloka'i
Habitat: dry to mesic forest, less often in wet forest
Population: 28 scattered populations totaling several hundred plants; populations sometimes consist of a single plant
Threats: alteration of habitat; human disturbance; alien plants; feral animals; fire
Legal status: endangered
Scale: flower 2/3–1 inch long

Golden hairs clothe the young leaves and twining stem tips of this robust forest vine. Seeking support to climb and scramble above the surrounding vegetation, the stems soon find their place in the sun. Once there, they thicken and produce masses of leathery foliage. Hanging funnel-shaped flowers an inch long appear among the leaves, downy and inconspicuous on the outside but pure white to greenish within, beckoning insect pollinators to visit. Round tan-colored capsules develop later, each containing a seed or two. • *Bonamia menziesii* is one of the few native lianas or truly woody vines to occur in Hawai'i. Rare throughout its range, *Bonamia menziesii* is endemic and currently known from five of the main islands. Only a few individual plants or small populations have been fenced to protect them from feral animals. This attractive vine is relatively easy to grow from seed; at least 25 individuals exist at three botanical gardens within the state. Although botanists actively map and collect seed from existing populations, reintroduction of cultivated plants into the wild has not yet been attempted. • The genus is named in honor of the French physician and botanist François Bonami, and the species name commemorates British surgeon and naturalist Archibald Menzies, who collected this and other plant species during his four visits to the Hawaiian Islands in the late 18th century.—*D.L.*

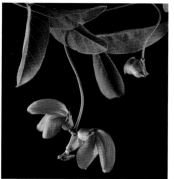

p. 155

Moloka'i Jack Bean
'Āwikiwiki; Puakauhi
Canavalia molokaiensis

Photograph: The Nature Conservancy, Kamakou Preserve, Moloka'i
Range: sites between Kalaupapa and Wai'ale'ia, and Kaunakakai and Kamakou, Moloka'i
Habitat: open, dry areas, mesic shrubland, and steep slopes of gulches
Population: four populations with up to 500 plants
Threats: destruction of the habitat by feral goats and pigs; competition from molasses grass
Legal status: endangered
Scale: perennial climber up to 10–15 feet or more

The species of the genus *Canavalia* are woody climbers, slender vines, or perennial herbs, often with twining branches. As a member of the legume or pea family they have fairly typical trifoliate leaves: a single leaf looks like three. The genus is pantropical in distribution with about 50 species, primarily in the Neotropics. In the Hawaiian Islands there are eight species: six native and two introduced species that have gone wild. The seeds of most species are reported to be poisonous, but those of some species, such as *Canavalia ensiformis* of the Old World tropics, are edible after cooking. The flowers of some species are used for *lei* making; the *lei maunaloa,* made from an introduced species of *Canavalia,* is one of the most attractive of Hawaiian *lei.* • *Canavalia molokaiensis,* like the other Hawaiian species, grows in upland habitats. It is a perennial climber and can be found clambering over other vegetation. It is distinguished from the other Hawaiian species in its narrow leaflets and the flowers, which are an attractive rose color. Flowers of other Hawaiian species range from dark carmine to dark purple. The conspicuous, compressed seedpods are up to six inches long. The seeds are also dark reddish brown, compressed, and up to nearly an inch long. *Canavalia molokaiensis* has never been known to be very common in the open, mesic shrubland, and steep slopes of gulches of eastern Moloka'i. —*W.L.W.*

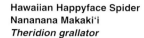

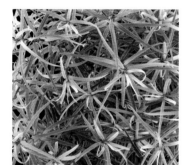

pp. 156, 157

Hawaiian Happyface Spider
Nananana Makaki'i
Theridion grallator

Photograph: Center for Conservation Research and Training Lab, University of Hawai'i at Mānoa, Honolulu, O'ahu
Range: O'ahu, Moloka'i, Lāna'i, Maui, Hawai'i
Habitat: 2,000–4,000 feet; moist and wet native forest
Population: locally rare
Threats: predation by alien ants; habitat loss
Legal status: none
Scale: body 1/4–1/5 inch long; 1-inch leg spread

Curiosity. In pursuit of knowledge, there's no substitute. In the 1890s R. C. L. Perkins discovered *Theridion grallator* and in 1900 French spider expert Eugene Simon named it from a preserved specimen. In 1972 Steven Lee Montgomery was looking for something else, but the facelike markings on this spider's back made him curious. Steve took it to photographer friend William Mull, who looked through his close-up lens and named the critter "Happyface." Today, this superior science teacher's assistant is the most recognized arthropod in Hawai'i. This spider has inspired song composers, playwrights, puppeteers, hula choreographers, painters, poets, and artists. A curious Hawai'i high school hiker and science student, Sam Gon III, became a successful Ph.D. candidate by studying this spider. • Luck. It was lucky that Montgomery spotted a *T. grallator* with facelike markings. Perkins and Simon probably looked at one of the two-thirds of spiders that mature in plain yellow dress. Of the one-third sporting red, white, and black abdomen spots and blotches, some are just spots and blotches, but many resemble faces—sad, startled, clownlike, or happy. For the spider the markings may be a way to avoid being eaten by foraging birds. For Hawaiian forests, the markings' popularity may be a way to avoid ecosystem destruction. "Save the forest, save the Happyface Spider!"—*A.M.*

p. 158

Kōlea
Myrsine linearifolia

Photograph: Koke'e State Park, Kaua'i
Range: Kaua'i
Habitat: mesic to wet *'ōhi'a* forests that are sometimes codominant with *'ōlapa* or *uluhe*
Population: seven populations with about 1,000 to 1,500 individuals total
Threats: competition from alien plants; habitat degradation by ungulates such as pigs and goats
Legal status: threatened
Scale: up to 26 feet high; leaf 2–3 inches long

Myrsine is a complex pantropical and subtropical genus occurring throughout most of the Pacific Basin, with perhaps as many as 150 to 200 species. There are 20 Hawaiian species presumably related to South Pacific species. The Hawaiians, who refer to all species as *kōlea,* formerly used the red sap and charcoal from the wood to dye *kapa* (a coarse cloth), used the wood itself for timber for houses, and used the logs for beating *kapa.* The nature of species in many genera of the Myrsine family is apparently different from that of many other flowering plant families in that the species vary only in rather minute floral features and in vegetative characteristics such as size, shape, or venation of leaves. Among the Hawaiian species, *Myrsine linearifolia* is therefore surprisingly distinctive with its long narrow leaves that are curved toward the tip. • *Myrsine linearifolia* was first collected on Kaua'i in 1912 but was described three decades later by botanist Edward Hosaka, who chose the specific epithet to describe its distinctive leaves. Many of the Hawaiian *Myrsine* species are trees or shrubs. *Myrsine linearifolia* is a branched shrub with greenish petals just 1/10 inch long and black fruits that are bird dispersed. • *Myrsine linearifolia* occurs in 10 scattered populations on Kaua'i, including Hā'upu, Kalualea, Kahuamaa Flat, Limahuli-Hanakāpi'ai Ridge, Koai'e Stream, and Nāmolokama Plateau. The largest remaining population, located in Kalalau Valley, contains several hundred individuals.—*W.L.W.*

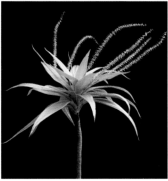

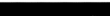

p. 159

Laukahi Kuahiwi; Ale
Plantago princeps var. *anomala*

Photograph: Koke'e State Park, Kalalau Valley rim, Kaua'i
Range: Kaua'i
Habitat: mesic to wet forest
Population: three populations comprising about 75 plants
Threats: feral pigs and goats; competition from alien weeds; rockslides
Legal status: endangered
Scale: plant 3–6 feet high

Readers familiar with the various naturalized or weedy plantain species might find it difficult to believe that *Plantago princeps* var. *anomala* belongs to the same genus. Its straplike leathery leaves 6 to 12 inches long are clustered atop a tall, unbranched stem, while slender spikes of small, diverging flowers and capsules project from the leaves. Yet they are members of the same genus, *Plantago,* which comprises about 250 species worldwide. On tropical islands, herbaceous plants occasionally evolve into woody life forms. Of the three endemic *Plantago* species of Hawai'i, *Plantago princeps* is the rarest and certainly the most distinctive, with its tall branched or unbranched canelike stems. • Botanists divide this variable species into four taxonomic varieties that variously occur on Kaua'i, O'ahu, Maui, Moloka'i, and Hawai'i. Var. *anomala,* named for its unusual features, is endemic to Kaua'i. Two populations occur in Kalalau and Pōhakuao Valleys along the Nā Pali coast and a third grows on Mount Kāhili on southern Kaua'i. This elegant plant is threatened by damage from feral pigs and goats and competition from invasive weeds. Efforts to propagate this *laukahi kuahiwi* from seed have little success, and therefore protection of the natural populations by fencing should be a conservation priority.—*D.L.*

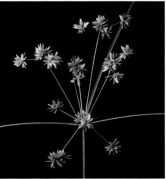

p. 160

Pu'uka'a
Cyperus trachysanthos

Photograph: National Tropical Botanical Garden Nursery, Lāwa'i, Kaua'i
Range: Kaua'i and O'ahu; originally widely distributed from five of the main islands
Habitat: wet sites such as mud flats, wet clay soil, or cliff seeps in coastal or low-elevation slopes
Population: five populations with fewer than 350 individuals total; currently declining
Threats: past threats include lowland habitat degradation and destruction; fire; alien plants
Legal status: endangered
Scale: plant 1/2–1 1/2 feet tall

Cyperus trachysanthos is a grasslike plant of the sedge family (Cyperaceae). Members of this family usually have three-angled stems and, as with grasses, their pollen is moved from plant to plant by the wind. Because wind pollination does not involve attracting insects or birds, these plants are less conspicuous than animal-pollinated plants and have relatively inconspicuous flowers. • Usually all of the Hawaiian species of a particular genus are closely related and evolved from a single ancestor that colonized over a considerable expanse of ocean. Hawaiian sedges are quite atypical in that many species of the same genus often are not closely related and result from multiple colonizations. For example, the 35 species of Hawaiian *Cyperus* probably result from no fewer than 18 separate colonizations. It is likely that Hawaiian sedges are so different in colonizing ability because they are food plants for migrating waterfowl, which bring seed from outside sources at a much higher and more regular rate than other means of long-distance dispersal. Plants like *Cyperus trachysanthos* have declined greatly this century primarily because of alteration or complete elimination of the specialized seasonally wet habitats.—*W.L.W.*

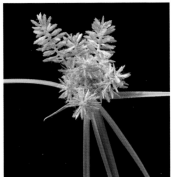

Puʻukaʻa
Cyperus pennatiformis* var. *bryanii

Photograph: Laysan Island
Range: Laysan
Habitat: dry sites such as sand dunes or low-elevation grasslands, ridges, or open sites in mesic forest
Population: one population with fewer than 100 individuals
Threats: past threats include lowland habitat degradation and destruction; small population size
Legal status: endangered
Scale: plant 1–4¹/₂ feet tall

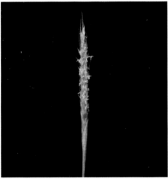

Hilo Ischaemum
Ischaemum byrone

Photograph: National Tropical Botanical Garden, Kahanu Garden, Maui
Range: Kauaʻi, Molokaʻi, Maui, Hawaiʻi
Habitat: windward coastal areas among rocks and on seeping cliffs near the ocean
Population: 18 populations comprising approximately 3,000 plants
Threats: coastal development; browsing from feral goats and deer; competition from alien weeds; landslides
Legal status: endangered
Scale: flower spike 2–3 inches long

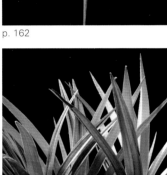

Paʻiniu
Astelia waialealae

Photograph: Sincock Bog, Kauaʻi
Range: central Alakaʻi Swamp area, Kauaʻi
Habitat: bogs and bog hummocks
Population: three populations of 10–15 plants total
Threats: rooting by feral pigs; invasion by alien weeds
Legal status: candidate for endangered status
Scale: leaf ¹/₂–1 inch wide

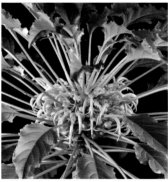

Delissea rhytidosperma

Photograph: National Tropical Botanical Garden, Limahuli Garden, Kauaʻi
Range: Kauaʻi
Habitat: 1,000–3,000 feet; lowland mesic forests or *koa* lowland dry forests
Population: one population with about 20 individuals total
Threats: habitat degradation by deer, goats, and pigs; predation by rats; fire; overcollecting; landslides; competition from alien plants
Legal status: endangered
Scale: up to to 8 feet tall; flower cluster 4 inches across

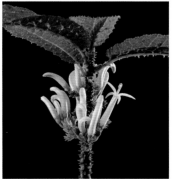

ʻAkūʻakū
Cyanea platyphylla

Photograph: Volcano Rare Plant Facility, Center for Conservation Research and Training, University of Hawaiʻi, Volcano, Hawaiʻi
Range: Hawaiʻi Island
Habitat: wet forest
Population: two populations comprising 27 plants
Threats: rooting by pigs; competition from alien weeds; predation by rats and slugs; loss of pollinators
Legal status: endangered
Scale: plant 3–10 feet high; corolla 1³/₅–2 inches long

Cyperus pennatiformis is a very rare sedge now restricted to several populations on three islands. *Cyperus pennatiformis* var. *bryanii* is endemic to the tiny northwestern Hawaiian island of Laysan. The initial decline of *Cyperus pennatiformis* var. *bryanii* was most likely caused by the release of the European hare on the island in 1903 by Max Schlemmer, superintendent of the bird guano operation for the Pacific Guano and Fertilizer Company, who came to Laysan in 1894. In 1904, when the guano resource was depleted, he bought the mining rights to this remote island and created a homestead. Unfortunately, one of his schemes was to initiate a rabbit-meat cannery. By 1911 visiting naturalists to Laysan noted a significant decrease in the island vegetation resulting from the exponential growth of the rabbit population Schlemmer had introduced. A biological expedition from 1912 to 1913 attempted to eradicate the rabbits, and although more than 5,000 were killed, many escaped by hiding in burrows. In 1923 another group of biologists, the Tanager Expedition, found the island essentially devoid of vegetation, and soon after that the remaining rabbits starved. Extensive efforts, particularly by the U.S. Fish and Wildlife Service, have restored much vegetation and bird populations have risen tremendously, but several species, like the flightless Laysan Rail, went extinct. The population of *Cyperus pennatiformis* var. *bryanii* has fluctuated widely and may still succumb.—*W.L.W.*

With about 10,000 species worldwide, the grasses represent the earth's fifth-largest flowering-plant family. Grasses are undisputedly the most useful plant group to humans, providing sugarcane and essential grains such as rice, corn, oats, wheat, barley, and rye. Furthermore, bamboos provide important construction materials in most tropical regions. Nevertheless, grasses are not particularly well represented in Hawaiʻi, which has only 47 native species including 39 endemics. Of these endemic Hawaiian grasses, nearly half (18 species) are considered either endangered, candidates for listing, or species of concern. • Flowers of most grasses are not particularly showy, and *Ischaemum byrone* is the only grass represented in this book. A clumping plant with sprawling, sparsely branching stems, it is well adapted to growing among lava rocks and on wet seeping cliffs in the ocean spray. With its wiry projecting awns, its paired flowering and fruiting spikes somewhat resemble those of wheat or barley in miniature. *Ischaemum byrone* thrives in cultivation and is represented by approximately 40 plants in the living collections at NTBG's McBryde Garden. The greatest threat to this species is alteration and destruction of its coastal habitat. *Ischaemum* is a genus of about 60 species, mainly in tropical Asia. Its genus name, the origin of which is uncertain, is derived from the Greek *ischiamos,* meaning "to quench the flow of blood."—*D.L.*

Rosettes of golden or silvery leaves, spikes of dark purple flowers, and berrylike orange fruits belong to the rare and elusive *Astelia waialealae*. Distinguished from the two commoner and more widespread *Astelia* species in Hawaiʻi by its shorter leaves folded into a V-shaped channel, this *paʻiniu* grows only in bogs and bog hummocks of the central Alakaʻi Swamp on the summit of Kauaʻi. The genus name *Astelia* is derived from the Greek root meaning *"stemless,"* although most species actually do have a short stem enclosed by leaves. About 25 species of *Astelia* occur from the Mascarene Islands near Madagascar eastward across the Pacific to Hawaiʻi and as far as Chile. All species have unisexual flowers produced on separate male and female plants. • *Astelia waialealae* is critically endangered, mostly due to feral pigs rooting in the fragile bogs it inhabits. Bogs are extremely slow to recover from damage, giving alien weeds an opportunity to colonize the disturbed areas. Conservation efforts by the U.S. Fish and Wildlife Service have focused on building fences around nine bogs in the Alakaʻi Swamp on Kauaʻi to exclude pigs from the three known populations of *Astelia waialealae*. It is possible that each population, seemingly of several plants, may actually represent a single clone. Because of its exacting habitat requirements, the rarest *paʻiniu* of Hawaiʻi has not yet been successfully grown in cultivation.—*D.L.*

This unique species with greenish white flowers about ³/₄ inch long was first collected on Kauaʻi in the 1850s. In 1867 Horace Mann Jr. chose the specific epithet to describe its wrinkled seeds inside globose purple fruits. *Delissea rhytidosperma* is a branched shrub with usually numerous large lance-shaped leaves. Historically, *Delissea rhytidosperma* was known from several sites on Kauaʻi, but, primarily due to habitat degradation and activities of feral animals that directly harmed plants, there remains only one population, located in state-owned land in Kuʻia Valley. The only other plant seen in recent years was a single individual in Limahuli Valley that subsequently died, and 20 plants in the Hāʻupu Range, which were destroyed by Hurricane ʻIniki in 1992. • *Delissea* is endemic to the Hawaiian Islands and is part of the largest radiation of plants from a single colonizing ancestor with over 125 species in six genera. Of those six, *Delissea* is probably in the greatest danger of going extinct in the near future. There are 10 species, 6 of which are already extinct; the remaining 4 probably consist of fewer than 100 individuals. • The genus commemorates M. Delisse, a physician from Mauritius, who served as naturalist on the D'Entrecasteaux expedition to the South Pacific from 1800 to 1804. • *Delissea rhytidosperma* occurs from as far north as Wainiha and Limahuli Valleys, as far east as Kapaʻa and Kealia, and as far south as Hāʻupu Range.—*W.L.W.*

Cyanea and its Hawaiian relatives, collectively known as lobelioids, are cousins to the common garden lobelia and cardinal flower. The Hawaiian lobelioids, with six genera and 115 species, are considered one of the most spectacular examples of island evolution in flowering plants. They include alpine rosette shrubs, bizarre cliff succulents, forest and bog shrubs, treelets, and even trees. Although the plants are diverse in growth form, leaf shape, and flower and fruit structure, molecular studies carried out by Tom Givnish and collaborators at the University of Wisconsin, Madison, suggest that all Hawaiian lobelioids have evolved from a single ancestor. • *Cyanea* is the largest plant genus native to the Hawaiian Islands with 74 species, most single-island endemics. The genus name refers to the supposedly blue flower color of the type species. Incredibly diverse, *Cyanea* species range in size from single-stemmed herbs or small shrubs to tall, palmlike trees 45 feet high like *Cyanea leptostegia* of Kauaʻi. Some species have deeply lobed, fernlike leaves, but most have smooth, straplike leaves. Still others, like *Cyanea platyphylla* and *C. tritomantha*, have stems and leaves armed with stout, spinelike prickles that presumably protected the plants from predation by now-extinct browsing birds such as the *Moa Nalo*. Conservation measures for *ʻakūʻakū* include fencing of one population and *ex situ* cultivation attempts.—*D.L.*

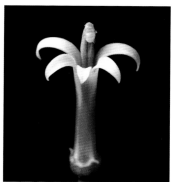

p. 166

Hāhā
Cyanea asarifolia

Photograph: Blue Hole, Kaua'i
Range: Kaua'i
Habitat: lowland wet forest, on moist cliff faces
Population: one population of 25–30 plants
Threats: landslides; herbivory by introduced slugs and rodents; competition from alien weeds; small population size
Legal status: endangered
Scale: corolla 3/4–4/5 inch long

Dark green, heart-shaped leaves resembling those of *Asarum* (wild ginger) give *Cyanea asarifolia* its name. Clusters of 30 to 40 gently curved, tubular purple and white flowers hang on stalks, followed by round purple berries. • *Cyanea asarifolia* was first collected in 1970 by former Kaua'i District forester Robert W. Hobdy, who discovered a small population growing in soil pockets on a cliff along Anahola Stream. Although this population has since disappeared, a second population was discovered in 1991 on the Wailua River, growing low on wet cliffs towering over 3,000 feet high. In 1992 this population was devastated by Hurricane 'Iniki. A post-hurricane visit to the site revealed many fallen plants lying at the cliff bases, decaying or being eaten by introduced slugs. Fortunately, seeds collected before the hurricane were successfully grown at the Lyon Arboretum of the University of Hawai'i to produce progeny thriving in propagation facilities at Lyon and NTBG. When planted outside, however, these tender plants fail to thrive, or succumb to snail and slug damage. • Attempts to reintroduce young *Cyanea asarifolia* into their natural habitat on Kaua'i have met with setbacks due to a large landslide at the outplanting site, which destroyed many plants. However, about 25 to 30 wild plants can be sighted on rock faces at the Wailua site, and additional plants likely occur higher up on the precipitous cliffs.—*D.L.*

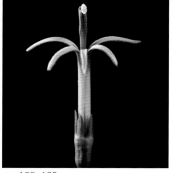

p. 167

Hāhā
Cyanea crispa

Photograph: National Tropical Botanical Garden Nursery, Lāwa'i, Kaua'i
Range: Ko'olau Mountains, O'ahu
Habitat: 600–2,400 feet; open lowland mesic forests and closed wet forests, usually in moist gullies
Population: five populations comprising 30–50 plants
Threats: invasive alien weeds; damage from feral pigs; predation by rats; possibly landslides
Legal status: endangered
Scale: corolla 1 1/2–2 1/3 inches long

As discussed under *Cyanea platyphylla* (see p. 250), *Cyanea* comprises 74 endemic species, making it the largest native plant genus of Hawai'i. Eleven species are considered extinct and most of the remaining species and subspecies are either threatened or endangered due to various factors including habitat destruction and loss of their native bird pollinators. Endemic to the Ko'olau Mountains of western O'ahu, *Cyanea crispa* is an endangered herb with stems one to four feet tall topped by a crown of fleshy leaves with crisped margins. Below the leaves, clusters of strongly curved purple and purplish white–striped flowers await pollination by Hawaiian honeycreepers. These birds had curved bills uniquely fitted to this floral shape, enabling them to drink nectar while transferring pollen deposited on their heads from flower to flower. • This species was originally described in the genus *Rollandia*, which was recently merged with *Cyanea* when comparative studies by botanists Thomas Lammers, Thomas Givnish, and Kenneth Systma revealed that the distinctions separating these two genera were not substantiated. Plants of *Cyanea crispa* are currently in cultivation at Lyon Arboretum on O'ahu, although unfortunately the plant photographed at NTBG succumbed to a fungal infection. *In situ* conservation efforts need to focus on fencing to exclude feral pigs and controlling rat predation and competing alien plant species.—*D.L.*

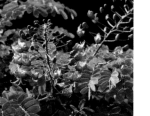

pp. 168, 169

'Akū
Cyanea tritomantha

Photograph: Pu'u Maka'ala Natural Area Reserve, Hawai'i; Tom's Trail, Pu'u Maka'ala, Upper Waiākea Forest Reserve, Hawai'i
Range: Hawai'i Island
Habitat: wet forest
Population: four or five widely scattered populations totaling 200–550 individuals
Threats: alien weeds; rooting by pigs; rats and slugs; human disturbance; loss of pollinators
Legal status: candidate for endangered status
Scale: plant 6–10 feet tall; corolla 2 1/2–3 inches long

Why do peculiar stout prickles cover the stems and leaves of *Cyanea tritomantha* and *Cyanea platyphylla?* Tom Givnish, botany professor at the University of Wisconsin, Madison, postulates that these species developed thornlike prickles to protect them from now-extinct browsing birds such as the *Moa Nalo*, a large gooselike bird with a tortoiselike bill. Known only from fossils, the *Moa Nalo* likely was hunted and driven to extinction by the ancient Hawaiians after they colonized Hawai'i around the fourth or fifth century A.D. • *Cyanea tritomantha* is known from widely scattered populations of several hundred or more plants on the Big Island of Hawai'i. Field botanist Steve Perlman of the NTBG stands proudly by plants growing under tree ferns in dense wet forest habitat. Some 'akū populations occur in the Natural Area Reserve System (NARS), but most are unprotected. NARS reserves include the most pristine natural habitats of Hawai'i and provide refuge for many rare and endangered species. Even so, fencing and constant monitoring are often required to protect the 'akū and other species against encroaching alien weeds and feral pigs. An astonishing 70 species and subspecies of *Cyanea* are threatened, endangered, or extinct, due in part to loss of their native bird pollinators. Fortunately many can be successfully grown in rare plant propagation facilities, including the one at Hawai'i Volcanoes National Park where *Cyanea tritomantha* is in cultivation.—*D.L.*

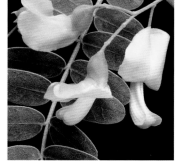

p. 176

Uhiuhi; Kāwa'u Kea
Caesalpinia kavaiensis

Photograph: Department of Land and Natural Resources, Division of Forestry and Wildlife, Uhi Uhi Enclosure, Hawai'i
Range: Kaua'i, O'ahu (Wai'anae Mountains), Lāna'i, West Maui, Hawai'i (North Kona District)
Habitat: dry or mesic forest
Population: eight populations with 60 individuals
Threats: goats, deer, rats, invertebrates, weeds, and fire damage either the habitat or the individual plant
Legal status: endangered
Scale: tree 15–35 feet tall

Caesalpinia kavaiensis is a medium-sized tree with rough, dark bark and a spreading crown. The flowers are a beautiful red and the fruit pod is broad, winged on one side, with a very pretty pinkish tinge when young and with a bluish waxy tinge when mature. As recently as 100 years ago there were still trees up to 35 feet tall, but now only small trees less than half that size remain. The wood is extremely hard, closed-grained, heavy, and very durable. Early Hawaiians took advantage of the wood's high density to make spears as well as *laau melomelo,* a club-shaped fishing implement that sinks. It was rubbed with a sticky substance to lure fish and dragged in the water; another person followed with a net to catch the fish attracted to it. It is unknown how much impact these uses had on the *uhiuhi,* but more likely the progressive clearing of the lowlands by Hawaiians and later many others, coupled with degradation of the remaining lowland forest, led to the great reduction of most populations. Only about 60 individuals of *C. kavaiensis* remain on islands of O'ahu, Lāna'i, and Hawai'i; it was once found also on Maui and Kaua'i but is now believed to be extinct on those islands. Most of the few remaining wild trees are growing in severely degraded habitat in dry forest on the slopes of Hualālai Volcano on Hawai'i.—*W.L.W.*

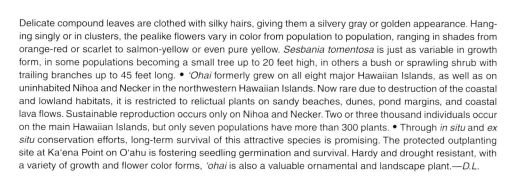

p. 177

'Ohai
Sesbania tomentosa

Photograph: South Point, Green Sand Beach, Hawai'i
Range: all eight major Hawaiian Islands, but extirpated on Ni'ihau and Lāna'i; Necker and Nihoa
Habitat: coastal dry shrublands and grasslands; mixed coastal dry cliffs; open forest
Population: 27 populations with 2,000–3,000 individuals total
Threats: cattle; feral deer; goats; off-road vehicles; alien plants; lack of pollination; rodents
Legal status: endangered
Scale: flower 1 inch long

Delicate compound leaves are clothed with silky hairs, giving them a silvery gray or golden appearance. Hanging singly or in clusters, the pealike flowers vary in color from population to population, ranging in shades from orange-red or scarlet to salmon-yellow or even pure yellow. *Sesbania tomentosa* is just as variable in growth form, in some populations becoming a small tree up to 20 feet high, in others a bush or sprawling shrub with trailing branches up to 45 feet long. • 'Ohai formerly grew on all eight major Hawaiian Islands, as well as on uninhabited Nihoa and Necker in the northwestern Hawaiian Islands. Now rare due to destruction of the coastal and lowland habitats, it is restricted to relictual plants on sandy beaches, dunes, pond margins, and coastal lava flows. Sustainable reproduction occurs only on Nihoa and Necker. Two or three thousand individuals occur on the main Hawaiian Islands, but only seven populations have more than 300 plants. • Through *in situ* and *ex situ* conservation efforts, long-term survival of this attractive species is promising. The protected outplanting site at Ka'ena Point on O'ahu is fostering seedling germination and survival. Hardy and drought resistant, with a variety of growth and flower color forms, 'ohai is also a valuable ornamental and landscape plant.—*D.L.*

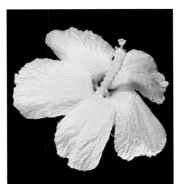

Ma'o Hau Hele
Hibiscus brackenridgei subsp. *brackenridgei*

Photograph: Waimea Arboretum and Botanical Garden, O'ahu
Range: Moloka'i, Lāna'i, Maui, Hawai'i
Habitat: dry forest and shrubland
Population: seven populations totaling fewer than 100 plants
Threats: competition from alien plants; alteration of habitat; fire; grazing by cattle; feral pigs, goats, and deer; introduced insects
Legal status: endangered
Scale: petal 1 1/2–2 inches long

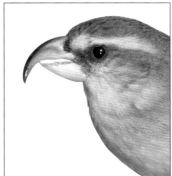
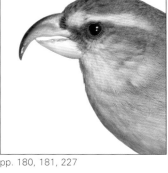

Ma'o Hau Hele
Hibiscus brackenridgei subsp. *mokuleianus*

Photograph: Waimea Arboretum and Botanical Garden, O'ahu
Range: O'ahu; formerly on Kaua'i
Habitat: dry forest and shrubland
Population: two populations of fewer than 100 individuals
Threats: destruction of habitat; competition from alien plants, pigs, goats; introduced insects; fire
Legal status: endangered
Scale: petal 2 1/3–3 1/5 inches long

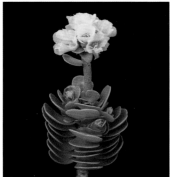

Maui Parrotbill
Pseudonestor xanthophrys

Photograph: Keauhou Bird Conservation Center, Volcano, Hawai'i
Range: East Maui; historic: southwest slopes of Maui's Haleakalā, Moloka'i
Habitat: 4,300–7,000 feet; *'ōhi'a* and *koa* rain forests
Population: about 500 in one population
Threats: predation by rats; disease (avian pox virus and malaria spread by *Culex* mosquitoes); habitat alteration by pigs, goats, alien plants
Legal status: endangered
Scale: 5 1/2 inches head to tail

Purslane
'Ihi
Portulaca molokiniensis

Photograph: National Tropical Botanical Garden, Native Hawaiian Plant Section, Lāwa'i, Kaua'i
Range: Molokini Islet, Pu'ukoa'e Islet, and Kaho'olawe
Habitat: dry coastal sites in leeward rainshadow
Population: several populations with about 500 individuals total
Threats: competition from alien plants; degradation of the narrow habitat
Legal status: none
Scale: flower cluster 1 1/2 inches across

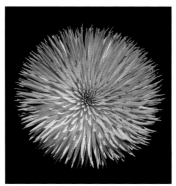

Haleakalā Silversword
'Āhinahina
Argyroxiphium sandwicense subsp. *macrocephalum*

Photograph: Haleakalā National Park, Maui
Range: Haleakalā National Park, Maui
Habitat: 7,000 to 8,000 feet; barren cinder cones and young *'a'ā* lava flows in alpine areas
Population: seven populations with about 65,000 individuals total
Threats: vandalism; overcollecting
Legal status: threatened
Scale: flower stalk 3–10 feet tall; plant 21 inches across

Hibiscus brackenridgei has been adopted as the official state flower of Hawai'i. Showy blooms of brilliant chrome yellow first catch the eye. Five delicately creped petals and a column of short stamens tipped by five stigmas signify that this plant belongs to the mallow family, more specifically to the large and diverse genus *Hibiscus,* which includes more than 200 species in the tropics and subtropics. Six native species occur in the Hawaiian Islands, five of which are endemic. Once found on all the main islands except Ni'ihau and Kaho'olawe, the *ma'o hau hele* shows considerable variation in number of features. • Based on this variation, Cornell University botanist Dr. David M. Bates recognizes two distinct types or subspecies: subspecies *brackenridgei* and subspecies *mokuleianus.* The first tends to be a shrub or small tree with less dense, non-spiny hairs on its leaves, flowers, and fruits, and somewhat shorter petals than those of the second subspecies. Both subspecies occur in dry forest and shrubland, a habitat that is as endangered as many of the species growing there. Conservation efforts include fencing populations and individual plants to exclude feral animals, although weed and fire control are still essential. Both subspecies are easily cultivated, and conservation collections are held at several botanical gardens in Hawai'i.—*D.L.*

Mature leaves of both *Hibiscus brackenridgei* subspecies are palmlike and deeply lobed, reminiscent of a maple or grape leaf. In contrast to subspecies *brackenridgei,* plants of subspecies *mokuleianus* are typically larger and treelike with a denser covering of fine, needlelike hairs on the leaves, stems, and especially the flowers and fruits. The flowers are also larger with more robust petals displaying a maroon spot at their base. • This subspecies of *ma'o hau hele* was recorded from dry forest and shrubland on Kaua'i, where it has presumably disappeared. Now fewer than 100 plants occur in two populations restricted to the Wai'anae Mountains of northern O'ahu. Threats are the same as for subspecies *brackenridgei,* and habitat preservation is key to conserving this subspecies of the Hawaiian state flower. Fortunately, both subspecies are hardy, drought-tolerant, and easily cultivated. At certain times of the year the introduced Chinese rose beetle riddles the leaves with lacey holes, but the plants seem to thrive in spite of the damage. Conservation collections are held at several botanical gardens in Hawai'i, and additional plants are likely cultivated in private collections. • This species was named in honor of William Dunlop Brackenridge, horticulturist and assistant botanist under the command of Commodore Charles Wilkes on the U. S. Exploring Expedition, which visited the Hawaiian Islands in 1840–41.—*D.L.*

The Maui Parrotbill illustrates two themes common to Hawaiian biology. • Adaptive radiation: The Maui Parrotbill is honeycreeper by heritage. An ancient founder finch survived the rigors of an ocean crossing to establish in Hawai'i. Breeding birds spread over varied ecosystems on many islands, successfully adapting beaks and behavior. This Hawaiian honeycreeper feeds and acts like a parrot, not a finch—it even hangs upside down. Searching for dinner, the Maui Parrotbill cracks open small branches and pries off bark. The narrower upper beak and tongue extract beetles and grubs. Moth larvae and pupae are also on the menu. • Habitat loss: The Maui Parrotbill once occupied a larger, drier habitat. After Polynesian settlers cleared lowlands for agriculture, 19th-century Europeans converted much of the forests of Maui and Moloka'i to grasslands by timber cutting, agriculture, and cattle ranching. Surviving birds contracted to higher, cooler, wetter forests than those for which they had adapted. Feral goats eating the forest, pigs rooting up understory, rats eating eggs, and disease weakening adults combine to make existence in even this last-stand location dangerous. Not surprisingly, the population is declining. • Today, Maui Parrotbill habitat is protected by a partnership of The Nature Conservancy and State and National Park Service land managers. Establishing a second habitat and reintroduced population is a long-term management goal.—*A.M./S.L.M.*

This distinctive species of *Portulaca,* described in 1987, actually was collected as early as 1913 by C. N. Forbes, a botanist at Bishop Museum who made some of the best and most extensive early collections of Hawaiian plants. It was collected a second time in 1925. These early collections were identified not as a new species but rather as the widespread Pacific strand plant *P. lutea,* which is also widespread in the Hawaiian Islands. In fact, a 1965 review of the Pacific species of the genus resulted only in pointing out that the seeds of one of these collections, featuring numerous tiny spines, were quite different than those of the smooth-surfaced *Portulaca lutea.* • Between 1978 and 1985 local botanists conducted surveys of Molokini and Kaho'olawe, and it was at this time that state forester Robert Hobdy recognized *Portulaca* as a quite distinct species from *P. lutea.* In 1987 he described it as a new species, *Portulaca molokiniensis.* It differs in its conspicuous stout vegetative growth and larger leaves, and especially in its dense headlike clusters of flowers and its spinose seeds. It is closely related to *P. lutea* and probably derived from it. It has a robust habit of thick succulent stems with clusters of closely spaced leaves. These features along with the conspicuous yellow flowers make *P. molokiniensis* an attractive plant for cultivation.—*W.L.W.*

The silverswords are the best known plants of the Hawaiian alpine, and have long been an icon for the unique and rare plants of Hawai'i. The most common of the five species is *A. sandwicense* from East Maui and Hawai'i. It was known as *'āhinahina* to the Hawaiians, meaning "gray" or "shining," referring to the dense layer of silvery hairs on the leaves. The leaves are arranged in a parabolic rosette that focuses the rays from the sun and elevates the temperature of leaves in the alpine environment as much as 68°F above the surrounding leaves. • The flowering of a silversword is a spectacular event. A plant may grow for 50 years or more as a compact rosette before it initiates a rapidly growing flowering stalk. The upper part of the flowering stalk is covered with hundreds of beautiful pink- to wine red–colored flower heads. Each head has several hundred tiny individual flowers. After the small fruits mature, the whole plant dies. This life style is referred to as *monocarpic.* Continuation of the species is contingent on the fate of the many seeds produced in this all-out effort. In any year the number of plants of this species ranges from zero to thousands.—*W.L.W.*

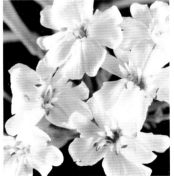

Catchfly; Campion
Silene perlmannii

Photograph: National Tropical Botanical Garden Nursery, Lāwa'i, Kaua'i
Range: presumed extinct in wild; a few individuals are in cultivation at NTBG and a research greenhouse in Irvine, California
Habitat: cliffs in mesic forest
Population: none in the wild (extirpated)
Threats: past threats include forest degradation and destruction; competition from alien plants; small population size
Legal status: endangered
Scale: flower 7/8 inch across

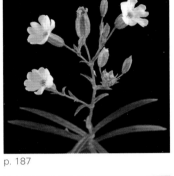

Catchfly; Campion
Silene lanceolata

Photograph: rim of Makolelau Gulch, Moloka'i
Range: Ohikilolo, O'ahu; Moloka'i; Pohakuloa Training Area, Mauna Kea, Hawai'i
Habitat: dry to mesic shrublands on cliff faces and ledges
Population: five populations on three islands and more than 2,600 individuals total
Threats: browsing and trampling by goats, pigs, and sheep; wildfires from military maneuvers; competition from alien plants
Legal status: endangered
Scale: flower 3/8 inch across

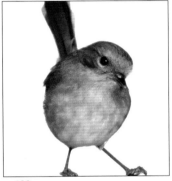

'Elepaio
Chasiempis sandwichensis

Photograph: Keauhou Bird Conservation Center, Volcano, Hawai'i
Range: Kaua'i, O'ahu, Hawai'i
Habitat: forests (wet to dry, native or alien)
Population: O'ahu: 1,900 birds and declining; Kaua'i: common; Hawai'i: fairly common
Threats: introduced diseases, especially avian pox virus; rat predation; habitat alteration by humans and pigs
Legal status: endangered on O'ahu
Scale: 5 1/2 inches head to tail

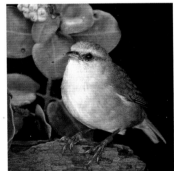

Hawai'i Creeper
Oreomystis mana

Photograph: Keauhou Bird Conservation Center, Volcano, Hawai'i
Range: Mauna Kea, Mauna Loa, and Hualālai Mountains, Hawai'i; formerly occupied larger habitats at lower elevations
Habitat: above 2,200 feet; 'ōhi'a and 'ōhi'a-koa forests
Population: 12,500
Threats: avian disease; rat predation; habitat alteration by pigs, goats; alien plant invasions
Legal status: endangered
Scale: 5 inches head to tail

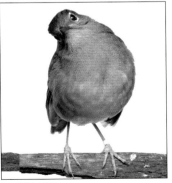

Small Kaua'i Thrush; Palmer's Thrush
Puaiohi
Myadestes palmeri

Photograph: Keauhou Bird Conservation Center, Volcano, Hawai'i
Range: only Alaka'i swamp, Kaua'i
Habitat: understory and fern-sedge covered stream banks in the wettest 'ōhi'a forest
Population: extremely rare; 50–200
Threats: cat and rat predation; avian disease; alien plants; habitat alteration by pigs
Legal status: endangered
Scale: 7 inches head to tail

On the island of O'ahu there are currently 116 species of plants listed by the U.S. federal government as endangered or threatened. The formal listing as endangered of one of these species, *Silene perlmanii*, may not have helped it survive in the face of continued and increasing pressures on its habitat; known from a single population near Palikea, southern Wai'anae Mountains, O'ahu, it appears to have gone extinct some time since 1996, when it was last observed in the wild. This attractive species is a member of the large and diverse genus *Silene*, the species of which are often known as campion or catchfly. The genus includes many cultivated ornamental annual and perennial species. • This unique Hawaiian species of considerable ornamental promise is a weakly woody perennial. It is capable of forming extensive festooning clumps of bright green lance-shaped leaves, each with a short upright stem terminated by a cluster of about 20 large white flowers. Steve Perlman and John Obata discovered it in 1987 in the Wai'anae Mountains in a steep, inaccessible area below a ridge-crest trail near Palikea. At the time of its discovery it was extremely rare, known from a single population of 20 individuals on a cliff face in a mesic forest at 2,600 feet. *Silene perlmanii* appears to be most closely related to *S. alexandri*, an extremely rare plant from Moloka'i.—*W.L.W.*

Silene, named by Linnaeus, is a genus of about 500 species. It is widely distributed in northern temperate regions, especially the Mediterranean climatic areas of Europe. The generic name was derived from Silenus, the mythological foster father of Bacchus. Silenus, who was always intoxicated, was described as covered with foam—suggested by the viscid excretions of many species of *Silene*. Most species are annual or perennial herbs; only rarely are they subshrubs or small shrubs like all seven of those in the Hawaiian Islands. All of the Hawaiian species may have evolved into diverse Hawaiian habitats from a single colonizing ancestor from Asia. Three of these white-flowered species are now considered to be extinct. • *Silene lanceolata* is a poorly known but very attractive clump-forming species. It has white flowers like most of the Hawaiian species, though smaller. What they lack in size is made up for by the presentation of usually numerous flowers in a cluster on a long, nearly leafless stem. It formerly had the widest distribution of any of the Hawaiian *Silene* and occurred on five of the main islands. By 1987 it had declined to a single known population in mesic shrubland below Pu'ukolekole, Moloka'i. Intensive plant surveys during the past decade have revealed three more populations. It is also in cultivation at NTBG and a research greenhouse in Irvine, California.—*W.L.W.*

'Elepaio is a small flycatcher with endemic subspecies on each island. It searches foliage and bark for insects, native or alien, and catches flying insects on the wing. Bold and curious, 'Elepaio may approach and even follow hikers. The birds are tolerant of disturbed forests and moderate human interaction. • In ancient times, when cutting logs for canoes, men looked to the 'Elepaio for help. If the bird landed on a tree selected for canoe making and pecked at it, the tree was considered unsound and was abandoned: *Ua 'Elepaio 'ia ka wa'a* ("The 'Elepaio has marked the log").[1] If the 'Elepaio landed and sang "'ono ka i'a" ("fish is delicious"), then the log was sound. Now it is time for people to repay the 'Elepaio for services rendered. • Although 'Elepaio on Kaua'i and Hawai'i are still fairly common, the O'ahu 'Elepaio (*Chasiempis sandwichensis ibidis*) continues to decline precipitously, occupying less than 4 percent of its original range. Decades of habitat loss have left the remaining birds in seven small isolated populations. A steady decline has occurred since the 1960s, caused by rat predation and high adult mortality from introduced diseases, especially avian pox. In May 2000 the once numerous O'ahu subspecies was placed on the federal endangered species list. Development of a recovery plan will be an important step in helping the 'Elepaio.—*A.M./S.L.M.*

1. M. K. Pukui, *'Ōlelo No'eau: Hawaiian Proverbs and Poetical Sayings*, Special Publication 71 (Honolulu: Bishop Museum Press, 1983), p. 306.

This shy spirit of the forest creeps among branches as it searches for insects (beetles, caterpillars, and moths) and spiders gleaned from branches and tree trunks and from under bark. They will eat an occasional snail found in their search and sometimes drink flower nectar, but eat mostly insects. The Hawai'i Creeper is sometimes mistaken for the common 'Amakihi (*Hemignathus virens*) or the Japanese White-eye (*Zosterops japonicus*) because of similar appearance and behavior in searching for food. • The bird's population is considered stable, but groups are isolated from one another and dispersal is poor. Birds tend to stay close to where they were raised and travel in family groups. State and federal agencies, working with community partners, are promoting healthy, continuous, multidistrict ecosystems as the best strategy to help the Hawai'i Creeper. Repeatedly, studies show that a strong native ecosystem is the foundation for nesting success and healthy, well-fed adults. Focus must be on eradication of introduced plants that compete with or smother key forest trees like 'ōhi'a and koa. Programs need to eliminate nest predators such as rats, and control mosquitoes that spread avian malaria and pox. Much more difficult is controlling introduced birds such as the Japanese White-eye that directly compete with creepers for food and may be reservoirs for disease.—*A.M./S.L.M.*

The secretive *Puaiohi's* coloring helps it blend into shadows and mossy branches in the wettest place on earth, the Alaka'i Wilderness Preserve. *Puaiohi* nutrition comes from fruits and seeds, especially the purple berries of native 'ōlapa. Late-19th-century biologist R. C. L. Perkins noted that while *Puaiohi* ate spiders and caterpillars, the bird especially liked beetles infesting koa trees (see also Lahaina Foliar Snout Beetle, p. 129). • Their singular call, described as a squeaking metal wheel in need of oil, is the easiest way to census the bird. These birds were described as rare by 19th-century bird collectors; their numbers fell dramatically in the 1970s and are declining today. With 75 percent of the wild *Puaiohi* in one location—Alaka'i swamp above 4,000 feet—establishing a second population is an especially important goal. • Help is on the way. Research and conservation efforts by state, federal, and private organizations aim to better understand the needs of the *Puaiohi* and Alaka'i ecosystem as a whole. Monitoring of threats, food sources, and breeding, together with predator control programs, will assist recovery of endangered plants and animals finding the Alaka'i a last refuge. The birds seem to respond to captive breeding programs. In 1999, newly released young birds found mates in two months, and some began nest building. *Puaiohi* is the first captive-bred Hawaiian forest bird species to successfully hatch chicks after release in the wild.—*A.M./S.L.M.*

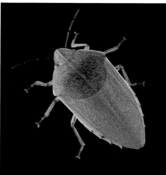

pp. 192, 193, 194, 195

Koa Bug
Pu'u Koa
Coleotichus blackburniae

Photograph: temporary studio, East–West Center, O'ahu; Betty Alberts residence, Pā'ia, Maui
Range: O'ahu, Moloka'i, Lāna'i, Maui, Hawai'i
Habitat: sea level to 6,000 feet; wet forests with *koa*, dry areas with '*a'ali'i*
Population: rare; perhaps only 1–5 percent of historic levels
Threats: introduced alien fly and wasp species
Legal status: species of concern
Scale: ³/₄ inch long

The koa bug is the largest of the "true bug" family in Hawai'i. Brilliantly colored koa bugs come in four iridescent, frosted colors: green with red markings and red with green, both on *koa;* yellow found on '*a'ali'i;* and a very rare blue phase. • A century ago, hundreds of adult koa bugs massed on tree branches feeding on juices of green pod. Available pods could still feed the robust populations that amazed biologists in 1899, but koa bug populations have steeply declined after 1962. • Their decrease is directly linked to 1960s state entomologists' importation and release of four biocontrol agents against the pestiferous southern green stink bug. In that era, scant concern was given to the well-being of native species as unintended victims. Agricultural officials actually used koa bugs to test and breed more parasites for releases. A tiny wasp *(Telonemus)* was introduced to parasitize stink bug eggs. Tests showed 27 of 28 koa bug eggs parasitized. The Florida stink bug tachinid fly, imported in 1962, parasitizes the adult green stink bug, but adult koa bugs are regular casualties. If only parasites were imported to attack the adult stages, at least koa bugs could reproduce before dying. A tinier wasp *(Ooencyrtus)* parasitized 25 of 28 koa bug eggs, producing 184 progeny. A project is underway to study the predator/prey interaction and determine survival options for the koa bug. The need for thorough study before irreversible release of biocontrol agents is obvious.—*A.M./S.L.M.*

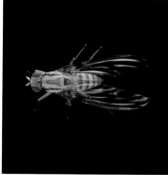

p. 196

Golden Picture-Wing Bird Lime Tree Fly
Ponalo Pāpala Kēpau
Drosophila ambochila

Photograph: Center for Conservation Research and Training Lab, University of Hawai'i at Mānoa, O'ahu
Range: southern Wai'anae Mountains, West O'ahu
Habitat: streamside forest in moist, shaded ravines
Population: rare, probably fewer than 3,000
Threats: alien swine uprooting host plants; competition for food from alien flies
Legal status: none
Scale: ¹/₈ inch long; ¹/₄-inch wing spread

The *Drosophila* (meaning "lovers of dew") or vinegar flies have long been favorite choices for probing the origin of species, and 1,000 kinds are unique to the Hawaiian archipelago. Of the 110 giant picture-wing pomace flies, 15 are quite provincial and undispersed, being found nowhere in the world save single, small home ranges. Even after 30 years of sampling—the species was discovered in 1970—*D. ambochila* has been found only on Wai'anae mountain range at 2,200 feet upland from Kunia, secreted in the shady glens below the tall peaks of Kaua, Hāpapa, and Kānehoa on O'ahu. • The cryptic colored, spotted wings assist in evading birds and larger predatory flies. Adults and young of this golden-yellow pomace fly feed on the fermenting succulent stems of the *pāpala kēpau,* which is a dominant tree in moist native lowland forests near streambeds. • Despite the availability of the host in many other locations, the insect's range is quite limited. Today *D. ambochila* faces a competitive threat from alien soldier flies now quite densely infesting the same feeding sites, calling for stronger quarantine inspection programs to prevent new invasions. Foraging feral swine have been uprooting many host seedlings, necessitating new fencing and control programs at The Nature Conservancy's Honouliuli Preserve. With vigilant management to stabilize regeneration of its sole host, this shy insect can continue occupying its home range.—*A.M./S.L.M.*

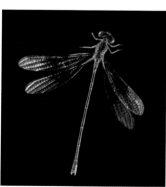

p. 197

Pointed Wing Pāpala Picture-Wing Fly
Ponalo Pāpala
Drosophila lanaiensis or relative

Photograph: Center for Conservation Research and Training Lab, Univ. of Hawai'i at Mānoa, O'ahu
Range: Hālawa and Nu'uanu Valleys in narrow ravines at base of Ko'olau Mountains, O'ahu
Habitat: head of moist ravines with host tree, *pāpala;* volcano summit ridgeline
Population: extremely rare
Threats: uprooting of young host plants by pigs; ant predation; competition from weeds
Legal status: none
Scale: ¹/₅ inch long; 1-inch wing spread

Rarest of the rare! A scientist had not seen this *Drosophila* species alive in over 100 years. It was discovered in 1894 on Lāna'i, then nothing. Scientists were ever watchful for this exceedingly longwinged fly, but without result. In 1940, a look-alike was collected on O'ahu, then nothing. In 1996 a survey in Hālawa Valley, O'ahu, found two more dead in a net. Still unknown were their larval and adult host plants. Then, success! In 1999, two were finally seen alive laying eggs on *pāpala* stems and young were lab-raised. This will allow solid identifications and eventual description of the dendrogram (family tree). It is likely that the tiny population on O'ahu will be a new species. • But has this *Drosophila* been found only to be declared endangered? Pigs are rooting up host plants. Brazilian guava trees have invaded the fly's forest habitat and are replacing the *pāpala.* Longlegged ants, indicted in other O'ahu forests with extirpating native flies, are marching upslope in this direction. Jackson's Chameleon, a cold-blooded predator on invertebrates, was imported from Africa and then illegally released by pet-trade partisans in forest margins. Perched by a branch where courtship or egg-laying occurs, a single reptile can decimate or even annihilate a population of flies. Control of alien agents of forest destruction must be improved.—*A.M./S.L.M.*

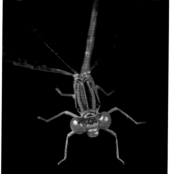

p. 198

Orangeblack Hawaiian Damselfly
Pinao Ma'alaea (adult); Lohelohe (naiad)
Megalagrion xanthomelas

Photograph: temporary studio, East–West Center, O'ahu
Range: Ni'ihau, O'ahu, Moloka'i, Lāna'i, Hawai'i; historic: Kaua'i, Maui
Habitat: coastal wetlands, tolerating a moderate salinity; lowland streamsides; artificial ponds
Population: near extinction on O'ahu; locally abundant on Moloka'i, Lāna'i, Hawai'i
Threats: predation on naiads by released alien fish
Legal status: candidate for endangered status
Scale: 2 inches long

In 1892 a consortium of British scientists sent a young biologist explorer, R. C. L. Perkins, to explore the "Sandwich Islands" fauna. Perkins investigated the fauna for most of a decade. In 1900 he reported that the orangeblack damselfly *(M. xanthomelas)* was common in Honolulu gardens and low wetlands on O'ahu. This predator was likely feasting on the swarms of alien mosquitoes and gnats. Out of a four-month damselfly life cycle, the immature stage spends more than three in water. By 1935 this colorful damselfly had disappeared from many localities where five alien, predatory fishes had been introduced into streams and ponds to control mosquito wrigglers. In 1990 Bishop Museum's Hawaii Biological Survey reported 15 new fish imported by pet shops were choking streams. Uninformed aquarium owners had released fish such as armored catfish, causing a drastic decline of damselflies. The best hope for recovery on O'ahu appears to be translocations of damselflies to streams freed of alien predators. • The cellophanelike wings are striking. In 1874 the world's damselfly expert determined the Hawaiian group was allied to South Pacific–Asian species. Calling it "the most magnificent species of the Legion," he erected a new group to account for the genus' unique wing veins. Rapid snapshots of wings in flight reveal that the front and back wings stroke independently, creating a smooth ride as air currents balance.—*A.M./S.L.M.*

Crimson Hawaiian Damselfly
Pinao 'Ula (adult); Lohelohe (naiad)
Megalagrion leptodemas

Photograph: temporary studio, East–West Center, O'ahu
Range: 1,500–2,000 feet, Ko'olau Mountains, O'ahu; historic: Wai'anae Mountains
Habitat: adults: stream banks and pools; naiads: midland freshwater streamsides in standing pools; slow sections of upper stream reaches
Population: very rare
Threats: predation on naiads by alien fish
Legal status: species of concern
Scale: 2 inches long

Slender and delicately beautiful, damselflies inspire artwork, stained glass, jewelry, and even films. In 1991 TV New Zealand filmed a Hawai'i damselfly for its natural history film *Splendid Isolation.* When senior cameraman Maurice Fisher looked in the viewfinder he exclaimed, "This is the most beautiful thing I've ever filmed—including our opera diva, Kiri Te Kanawa." • Flying damsels are graceful acrobats, flying backwards, racing prey, hovering, or flying in tandem while copulating in air. Damsels are deadly aerial predators whose beautiful legs, red with black spines, form a basket to capture prey. They pounce, or take prey on the wing, then begin to feed on their still-living lunch. Damselflies will catch and eat any insect smaller than they are: moths, leafhoppers, and crane flies. The larger damsels devour the smaller species and are, in turn, prey for the even larger dragonflies. • Bright colors make damselflies easy to spot. The vibrant hues of males may function to attract females and threaten rival males. Males aggressively patrol aerial corridors near breeding pools where females will lay eggs after mating. The males are fearless in this protection of their genetic posterity, undeterred by approaching humans, making them an easy insect to observe when hiking. *Megalagrion leptodemas* is the rarest of the O'ahu damselflies.—*A.M./S.L.M.*

p. 199

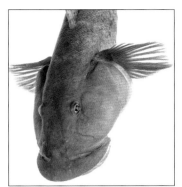

pp. 200, 203

'O'opu Nākea
Awaous guamensis

Photograph: National Tropical Botanical Garden, Limahuli Stream, Kaua'i
Range: major streams on all large Hawaiian Islands
Habitat: wide variety of stream types, rocky and soft-bottomed
Population: locally rare, especially on O'ahu
Threats: alien game fish and pet-trade fish; low stream flow, bank erosion, pollution, and sedimentation
Legal status: protected from commercial harvest and sale by state law
Scale: up to 14 inches long

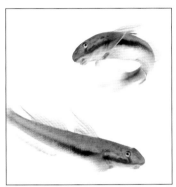

pp. 202, 204

'O'opu Nōpili
Sicyopterus stimpsoni

Photograph: National Tropical Botanical Garden, Limahuli Stream, Kaua'i
Range: all Hawaiian Islands
Habitat: lower/middle reaches of swift water in midstream with silt-free cobblestone bottoms
Population: rare; more abundant in wilder streams off O'ahu
Threats: low stream flow, stream bank erosion, pollution; alien freshwater fish
Legal status: protected from commercial harvest and sale by state law
Scale: about 7 inches long

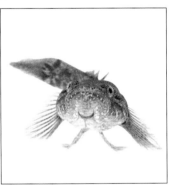

pp. 203, 205

'O'opu 'Akupa
Eleotris sandwicensis

Photograph: National Tropical Botanical Garden, Limahuli Stream, Kaua'i
Range: all Hawaiian Islands
Habitat: estuaries and lower streams below first waterfall
Population: rare
Threats: predatory alien gamefish and pet-trade fish; low stream flow, bank erosion, pollution, and sedimentation
Legal status: protected from commercial harvest and sale by state law
Scale: up to 10 inches long

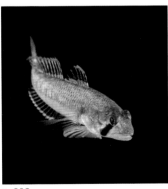

p. 206

'O'opu Naniha
Stenogobius hawaiiensis

Photograph: National Tropical Botanical Garden, Limahuli Stream, Kaua'i
Range: all Hawaiian Islands
Habitat: lower streams, often in brackish water or estuaries; soft- or hard-bottom streams
Population: rare
Threats: low stream flow; alien freshwater fish (as competition for food sources and as predators on 'o'opu)
Legal status: protected from commercial harvest and sale by state law
Scale: about 4 inches long

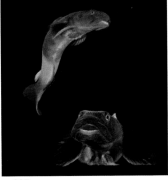

p. 207

'O'opu 'Alamo'o
Lentipes concolor

Photograph: National Tropical Botanical Garden, Limahuli Stream, Kaua'i
Range: all Hawaiian Islands
Habitat: up to 1,800 feet; perennial streams on wet, windward sides of islands
Population: rare on O'ahu; more abundant in wilder streams off O'ahu
Threats: low stream flow, stream pollution; silt in ocean; alien freshwater fish
Legal status: species of concern; protected from commercial harvest and sale by state law
Scale: about 2–4 inches long

Don't be fooled by a scientific name commemorating the Pacific island of Guam. *'O'opu nākea* is native to Hawaiian streams, although also found naturally elsewhere in the Pacific. • As their upper lip shows, these goby fish are bottom-feeders. In mucky stream bottoms they dine from a menu of primarily green algae, balanced with earthworms, snails, and insects. Most at home in the lower reaches of streams, they can swim to elevations up to 1,400 feet. Wherever they live, *'o'opu nākea* travel downstream with the first big winter rains. Eggs laid near the stream mouth are guarded by both sexes. The newly hatched larvae will wash out to sea, maturing over several months. When they return, between December and July, they will continue the cycle by swimming up a suitable stream to eventually lay eggs themselves. • *'O'opu nākea* were a favorite food in the traditional Hawaiian diet. Into the 19th century, basketry traps with a funnel mouth making escape difficult were laid in streams to catch them. Weighing in at up to a half-pound, these fish—largest of the gobies—are popular with modern pole fishers. *'O'opu nākea* were the first fish in Hawaiian fresh- or saltwater to receive protection. State conservation rules prohibit selling it commercially. Without this safeguard, *'o'opu nākea* would be overharvested for market.—*A.M./S.L.M.*

Fused pelvic fins under their bodies make these *'o'opu* especially talented (see p. 202). Using this suction cup they perform hard-to-believe feats. They grip stream-bottom rocks and hold stationary in swift water. They travel against the current, darting from rock to rock. They climb up waterfalls, even hanging upside down to go around undercut rocks in the falls. And they move quickly: They've been clocked at rates of 18 inches in 20 seconds! • The breakfast of champions? The *'o'opu nōpili* scrape algae from rocks in the stream bottom. Clean, fast-moving streams are required to provide the right temperature and nutrition to keep this aquatic athlete in shape. *'O'opu* are good indicator species of overall stream health. • A Hawaiian tale: An *'o'opu* is prepared for roasting. The cook turns away to find salt and returns to see the *'o'opu* "walking" back to his stream on his fins. The *'o'opu nōpili*'s strong grip was valued by Hawaiians as an ingredient in a charm used for *"hana aloha,"* a ceremony causing a lover to cling. • Like all native freshwater fishes, *'o'opu nōpili* juveniles return to streams after their time in the ocean. Stories relate that at times they were so numerous anyone stepping into a stream unavoidably brushed against the slithering fish, which could be scooped up by hand or in dip nets.—*A.M./S.M.*

'O'opu 'akupa is an eager and complete carnivore. Breakfast, lunch, and dinner find it consuming fish, freshwater invertebrates like shrimp, and aquatic insect larvae. Often smaller fish are on the menu. This strong appetite led to a Hawaiian proverb comparing a chubby person to an *'o'opu*. The photograph makes the aptness of the proverb quite obvious. • Unlike the true gobies, *'o'opu 'akupa* is part of a family of fish with unfused pelvic fins. Consequently the fish can't move beyond even the smallest waterfall. In some streams with a gradual rise, these fish are found as much as five miles inland. Fish like smallmouth bass, introduced for sport fishing, find *'o'opu* a ready food source. Since this *'o'opu* lives in the lower reaches of streams, it suffers more than those in mountain streams do from chemical runoff, stream bank collapse, and sedimentation of the stream.—*A.M./S.L.M.*

Since all Hawai'i life arrived by wind, wing, or wave, it is not surprising that *'o'opu naniha* occurs elsewhere in the Indian and Pacific Oceans. Native freshwater fishes start life as eggs in a streambed. Flushed by a heavy rain or strong current, newly hatched larvae enter the sea. They spend time in the saltwater before returning to freshwater streams as juveniles. They need not return to their birthstream; any stream will do. This ocean phase in the goby's life reminds us of its saltwater origins. Hawaiians recognized this life cycle in the *Kumulipo*, a Hawaiian creation story, with these poetic lines: *Hānau ka 'o'opukai noho i kai* (Born is the *'o'opu* living in the sea) / *Kia'i ia e ka 'o'opuwai noho i uka* (Guarded by the *'o'opu* living in the fresh water). • *'O'opu naniha* feeds on a plant and animal diet. More tolerant of sedimentation in streams, it is more abundant where other *'o'opu* could not survive. Living at lower elevations, *'o'opu naniha* is more vulnerable to alien, competing fish. One source of aliens is released aquarium fish. Those no longer able or interested in caring for an aquarium assume they are doing the right thing by releasing their unwanted pets in a stream. Returning the fish to a pet store, keeping them out of Hawaiian streams, is a far better action.—*A.M./S.L.M.*

This interesting fish is endemic to the Hawaiian Islands. Females are colored olive to brown overall. The males can display color to attract the females. Dark in front, they sport a rear that is a bright reddish orange or chalky white with red tinges. When aggression is needed, males can display brilliant white dorsal and anal fins, later reverting to dark with traces of color. • Healthy *'o'opu 'alamo'o* are omnivorous. Although they primarily eat "meat" such as insects, they also feed on algae and other plant matter. Clean, full, and free-flowing streams are necessary for healthy *'o'opu*. Low stream flow means warmer water with less oxygen. Fish may die of overheating or suffocation. The food of *'o'opu* may be poor or missing when streams are polluted. In the 1800s water from many major streams on all Hawaiian Islands was diverted and redirected to sugar fields. Recent debates and court cases on returning water once diverted for now-closed sugar plantations may result in stream restoration and a healthier *'o'opu* population. Recent recognition of the serious nature of "non-point sources" of stream pollution is now resulting in attention to up-stream sources of pollution.—*A.M./S.L.M.*

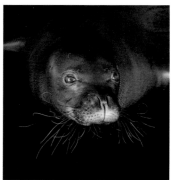

pp. 208, 209

Hawaiian Monk Seal
ʻĪlioholoikauaua
Monachus schauinslandi **(male)**

Photograph: Sea Life Park, Waimānalo, Oʻahu; Waikiki Aquarium, Honolulu, Oʻahu
Range: Northwestern Hawaiian Islands; rarer at scattered locations on other Hawaiian Islands
Habitat: sandy beaches and lava or coral benches with warm water and air temperature
Population: 1,300–1,400 seals
Threats: displacement and competition for food by humans; marine debris entanglements
Legal status: endangered
Scale: female 575 pounds; male 380 pounds

Large, oblong dark spots on white sand. That's the impression monk seal observers obtain in the wild. An hour's observation yields a concert of snuffles, snorts, and sneezes as the seal dozes. Rude, too-close visitors receive barked warnings, challenging jaws agape. • Life at sea for the ʻīlioholoikauaua ("dog running in rough surf") is poorly known. Humans observe and disturb seals beached on bits of sand to rest and give birth. They never form rookeries. Males do not make harems, but male groups occasionally mob scarce female partners. Single seals near the main islands are often antisocial males transported by wildlife agencies. • Habitat and diet requirements may have always restricted their numbers and range. In the main islands, Polynesian settlers' intensive shoreline use after A.D. 500 reduced the seal's range. Although Hawaiians did not hunt the seals, seals are extremely sensitive to human proximity. Hunting by European and American sealers depleted numbers. World War II and postwar occupation of atolls and islets kept seals off beaches. Eventual reduction in use of Pacific bases allowed monk seals to retake white sand beaches. With management of commercial fishing, marine debris cleanup, protection, and public education, it may not be too late. The newly created Northwest Hawaiian Coral Reef Ecosystem Reserve, which stretches for 1,200 miles north of Kauaʻi, protects the habitat of the monk seal and many other species.—*A.M./S.L.M.*

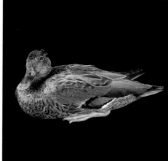

p. 210

Laysan Duck
Anas laysanensis

Photograph: Honolulu Zoo, Oʻahu
Range: Laysan in Northwestern Hawaiian Islands; pre-human: all major Hawaiian Islands
Habitat: 1,000 acres of low coral-sand atoll with a central depression and briny lagoon
Population: recent counts vary from 50 to 300
Threats: habitat alteration by human impact (alien plants, animals); natural disasters; disease
Legal status: endangered
Scale: 15–17 inches long head to tail

The Laysan Duck shares a Mallard ancestry with the Hawaiian Duck (see p. 211) but is a distinct species. The entire wild population lives on Laysan Island. From the 1890s to 1910s Laysan Ducks were hunted for food, feathers, and sport. Rabbits were introduced in 1903 and, before exterminated in 1923, stripped the island of plants, including a fan palm and sandalwood. Only seven ducks survived as of 1912, when more than 5,000 rabbits were shot. Duck populations fluctuate, but have been estimated at 600 in good years. Under 1993 El Niño drought conditions the population declined to 50 birds. Despite the genetic problems expected in a small population subjected to irregular depletions, many captive breeding programs have been successful. As early as 1957, Honolulu Zoo started a program with eight birds. Nevertheless, the species' concentration on one island makes risk of extinction high from disease or natural or accidental events. • Laysan Ducks are famous for their brine fly–catching technique. Seasonally, the flies are so abundant that to obtain a meal the ducks need only run across the mudflats of the central lagoon, snapping their bills. The basic diet is crustaceans and tide pool tidbits, insects, and other invertebrates. • The U.S. Fish and Wildlife Service manages the refuge to control alien species and encourage growth of native plants such as the bunch grasses used in nest building.—*A.M./S.L.M.*

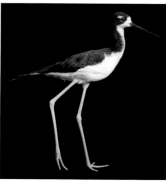

p. 211

Hawaiian Duck
Koloa Maoli
Anas wyvilliana

Photograph: Honolulu Zoo, Oʻahu
Range: Kauaʻi, Oʻahu, Maui, Hawaiʻi; possibly Niʻihau; historic: Molokaʻi
Habitat: lowland wetlands, river valleys, and mountain streams
Population: three populations, 2,500 individuals
Threats: rats, cats, dogs, mongoose; introduced avian pox virus and malaria; alien plants
Legal status: endangered
Scale: male 19–20 inches long; female 16–17 inches long

Koloa travel in pairs, eating mollusks, insects, and freshwater vegetation. This endemic species is believed to have evolved from the migratory, dimorphic Mallard *(A. platyrhynchos)*. Recent molecular study shows that the *Koloa* and Laysan Duck (see p. 210), once thought Mallard subspecies, are truly separate species. Observable *Koloa*-Mallard differences: Plumage is not dimorphic, the birds do not migrate, and they vocalize less frequently and more softly. • Waterbirds are quite vulnerable to altered environments and alien invasions. The list of threats to *Koloa* is long, but defenders are fighting back. State and federal agencies are working with private organizations and landowners to protect wetland habitats and enforce conservation rules. In predator-control programs, volunteers remove fast-growing alien plants that allow predators to cross water barriers and prey on nesting birds and ducklings. • Although the overall population is believed stable, a natural disaster or illness could severely reduce the species. The species is at special risk as long as 90 percent of the population lives on Kauaʻi. Protection of these birds, believed free of crossbreeding with alien Mallards, is especially important. *Koloa* were reestablished on Oʻahu and Hawaiʻi Islands through captive propagation programs, but are now breeding with Mallards. *Koloa* may be seen on Kauaʻi at Hanalei National Wildlife Refuge and on Oʻahu at wetlands in Kailua, Kahuku, Pearl Harbor, and Waialua.—*A.M./S.L.M.*

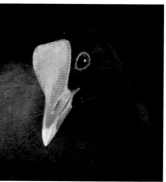

p. 212

Black-Necked Stilt; Hawaiian Stilt
Aeʻo; Kukuluaeʻo
Himantopus mexicanus knudseni

Photograph: Honolulu Zoo, Oʻahu
Range: Hawaiian Island chain
Habitat: shoreline and inland ponds with mudflats; temporary submerged or flooded areas
Population: rare; 1,200–1,600 in six populations; extremely rare on Lānaʻi
Threats: the loss of wetland habitats; rat, mongoose, cat, and dog predation
Legal status: endangered
Scale: 16 inches tall

Although many native birds were harmed by Polynesian alterations of coastal areas, the stilt's habitat increased with fishponds and the growing of *kalo* for *poi*. In the 1800s rice growing provided habitat. Draining of wetlands for public health (e.g., mosquito control) in the 1900s coincided with a decline of *kalo* and the ending of rice production, reducing habitat. Sport hunting, legal until 1939, contributed to a decline of the birds. Current populations appear stable, with 60 to 70 percent of the species on Maui and Oʻahu. At Kanahā Pond on Maui and the wetlands on the Mōkapu Peninsula, Oʻahu, predator control and habitat management have been implemented. • Moving daily to several locations, stilts feed on aquatic invertebrates, worms, brine shrimp, crabs, and small fish. They often feed at temporary shallow wetlands or flooded grassy areas associated with construction and poorly graded flats. They easily nab insects flushed to the surface. Open flats and flooded lands also provide clear visibility against predators. The birds are magnificent in flight with their long red legs trailing behind *(Kukuluaeʻo,* "standing tall on stilts"). Loud, sharp calls in preparation for landing give notice to other waterbirds: "Get out of my way, here I come." • In 1887 Dr. Leonhard Stejneger named this elegant bird for Kauaʻi resident Valdemar Knudsen, who sent many bird specimens to the Smithsonian collections and lent his mountain house and knowledge of Kauaʻi birdlife to visiting biologists.—*A.M./S.L.M.*

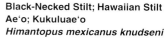

p. 213

Hawaiian Gallinule
ʻAlae ʻUla; Koki
Gallinula chloropus sandvicensis

Photograph: Honolulu Zoo, Oʻahu
Range: Kauaʻi, Oʻahu; historic: Molokaʻi, Maui, Hawaiʻi
Habitat: ponds, marshes, lowland wetlands, irrigation ditches, aquaculture ponds
Population: 200–400
Threats: rats, cats, dogs, and mongoose; introduced avian pox virus and malaria; alien plants
Legal status: endangered
Scale: 13–14 inches long head to tail

ʻAlae ʻula are often found with the Hawaiian Duck (see p. 211) and the Hawaiian coot. *ʻAlae ʻula* will feed in any fresh or brackish water on algae, tender shoots of plants, aquatic insects, and mollusks. The *ʻalae ʻula* can sometimes be seen using its large, unwebbed feet to walk on floating vegetation. Nesting on the edges of ponds makes them easy targets for predators such as rats and mongoose. Wildlife agencies attempt to manage wetlands to provide nesting sites on predator-free islets. Aggressive alien waterweeds must be cleared from wetlands or they provide bridges to nesting sites. Hanalei National Wildlife Refuge successfully combines wetland bird habitat and the growing of *kalo (taro)*, the traditional staple food in the Hawaiian diet. • Despite their unmistakable bright red foreheads, their secretive behavior makes an estimate of the birds' numbers unreliable. The dark gray body and almost black head contrast with a yellow beak and bright red *(ʻula)* frontal shield. The shield and secretive behavior gave the bird a central role in ancient Hawaiian legends telling how humans obtained the knowledge of fire: Maui, a legendary trickster and superhero, deceives the secretive bird, traps it, and forces it to reveal how to make fire. Once he is successful in extracting the secret, Maui punishes *ʻalae ʻula* by rubbing its face with a red coal, leaving the shield's color.—*A.M./S.L.M.*

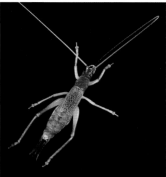

Kaua'i Tree Cricket
Ho'onēnē Palikū
***Prognathogryllus* new species**

Photograph: Mount Kekoiki, Kaua'i
Range: Makaleha Mountains and Mount Namahana, Kaua'i
Population: rare
Habitat: elfin cloud forest; wet cliffs
Threats: natural disasters; loss of habitat
Legal status: none
Scale: body 2 inches long

Placed in its own tribe of insects, this is the most peculiar contingent in the cricket and grasshopper order in Hawai'i. All are arboreal and graceful, with long antennae exceeding twice their body length (here one antenna is being licked clean in a female's mouth). Long antennae give more warning of what's ahead—helpful information when leaping about the canopy. Using sharp ovipositors, females inject slender eggs into leaf midribs. Hindwings are rudimentary, and tiny forewings have little function, but are a little larger in males. Males scrape together their forewings to sing for a mate. Incapable of flight, some species' total range is just a few acres, as learned from acoustic studies mapping the distinctive musical trills. With over 200 endemic crickets, island landscapes are alive with their songs day and night. • According to 1890s field biologist R. C. L. Perkins, birds hunted these large tree crickets, whose long, muscular hind jumping legs made them a tasty meal. To avoid being eaten, crickets hide by day in hollow stems of lobelias and *māmaki* or in tight leaf clusters. At night they emerge to feed on soft, decomposing vegetable matter. • This specimen was collected close to the collecting site of *Cyrtandra paliku* (see p. 50). Such remote and rarely visited places are reservoirs of wonderful unknown plants and animals awaiting discovery by curious naturalists.—*A.M./S.L.M.*

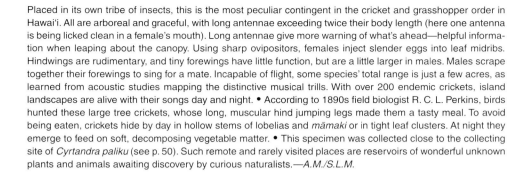

p. 215

Mauna Loa Vampire Bug
Mū Wēkiu 'A'ā
Nysius aa

Photograph: temporary studio, Helen Chellin Residence, Hawai'i
Range: Mauna Loa Mountain, Hawai'i
Habitat: 12,000–13,700 feet; alpine desert
Population: rare
Threats: possible predation by alien spiders
Legal status: none
Scale: 1/4 inch long

The alpine summit of Mauna Loa was once assumed to lack any resident living beings. Almost 14,000 feet high in the subtropics, each day's cool summer (49° to 57°F max.) is followed every night by winter (29° to 38°F min.). In 1935 University of California, Berkeley, biologist Robert Usinger found no resident life, but noted, "An abundance of weakened insects is continually blown up to these bleak heights to die. Such a situation should offer a veritable paradise to predacious bugs which are able to withstand the adverse climatic conditions." Dr. Dr. Wayne Gagné saw the potential for undiscovered life once colleagues reported an insect wonder on its sister peak, Mauna Kea. He found a single, long-legged nymph that inspired methodical searches yielding mature specimens soon named *Nysius aa* after the rugged 'a'ā lava in which it often lives. • On sunny days they scurry over the lava looking for lowland insects carried on thermal updrafts. Be they freshly arrived or smelly, stale ones, *N. aa* will suck their blood with their needlelike beaks. *N. aa* evolved from flighted bugs that suck seed juices, but its wings are now only tiny pads. Longer legs facilitate scrambling over cinders and lava in search of food and thermally buffered microniches. This bug's blood contains antifreeze that makes it cold-hardy with a low supercooling point, not freezing in experiments until cooled to −1.3°F.—*A.M./S.L.M.*

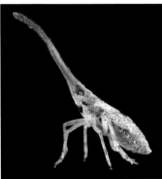

p. 215

'Akoko Planthopper
'Ūmi'i 'Akoko
Dictyophorodelphax mirabilis

Photograph: temporary studio, East–West Center, O'ahu
Range: west and southeast ridges, O'ahu
Habitat: 1,400–1,800 feet; dry and moist shrublands and forests with 'akoko plants
Population: rare
Threats: host plant destruction by deer; goats; brushfires
Legal status: none
Scale: 3/16 inch long

Headlong for gluttony and glory—that's the route taken by this most extraordinary of island mini-wildlife. This planthopper sucks white, sticky latex sap from 'akoko shrubs. When insects have thornlike horns, usually they are fooling birds by mimicking their host plants' harmful and inedible thorns. • What advantage does a creature that always feeds on thorn-free 'akoko stems find in a head taller than its body? The projection is mostly throat. Here milky sap is stored and predigestion breaks down the natural rubber, otherwise indigestible or even toxic. • Otto Swezey, a sugar scientist who added tremendous knowledge on Hawaiian insects, discovered and named this planthopper in 1907. In 1918 John Bridwell, intrigued by this peculiar form and limited localities, climbed an O'ahu ridge seeking its mysterious niche. He swept a few from 'akoko plants, and then he eyed 12 with two nymphs with smaller horns resting on one leaf. Having linked the bizarre insect and its food plant, he soon discovered a species on an eastern ridge, which he named *D. swezeyi* for his mentor. Bridwell predicted species on each island. He found and named *D. praedicta* on Maui below 'Īao needle. Others were discovered on Lāna'i and Kaua'i, 20 and 50 years later, respectively. All these miraculous 'akoko feeders are offshoots from a Hawai'i group of 80 other normal-headed insects.—*A.M./S.L.M.*

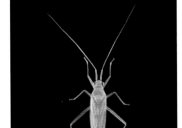

p. 215

Hawaiian Holly Leaf Bug
Mū Lau Kāwa'u O Ka'ala
Nesiomiris oahuensis

Photograph: temporary studio, East–West Center, O'ahu
Range: Mount Ka'ala summit, O'ahu
Habitat: 4,000 feet; stunted cloud forest
Population: rare
Threats: host plant destruction by pigs
Legal status: none
Scale: 3/8 inch long

Rising from the oldest part of O'ahu like a massive green pedestal is the island summit, Mount Ka'ala. Filled with natural treasures, the state's Ka'ala Natural Area Reserve protects a wet elfin cloud forest of stunted trees. Under the foliage of the native holly dwells this dainty leaf bug, its green coloring closely matching the spineless leaves. Camouflage helps it avoid being eaten by hungry native birds. Six sister species of *Nesiomiris* each live in a different geographic sector of O'ahu without overlap, a phenomenon evolution scholars call "competitive exclusion." • All but one of the 50 *Nesiomiris* names were given by Dr. Wayne Gagné, whose 20-year love affair with nature in Hawai'i created a monumental record of information. Longtime hiking partner John Obata found that following Wayne in the field meant getting "soaked or parboiled, depending on the mountain." Dr. Gagné blended the skills of a research biologist and a public educator, spreading the joy of bugs as he built environmental awareness and passion in those who met him. • The Hawai'i State Department of Land and Natural Resources built a protective fence to exclude pigs, and oversees volunteer weeding to assure the safety of all the creatures living in their gorgeous home in the mist.—*A.M./S.L.M.*

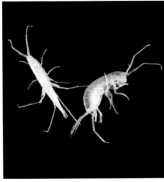

p. 215

Kaua'i Cave Sandhopper;
Kaua'i Cave Amphipod
'Uku Noho Ana
Spelaeorchestia koloana

Photograph: Kōloa Cave #2, Kaua'i
Range: Kōloa District, Kaua'i
Habitat: dark, moist subterranean caverns or lava tubes
Population: extremely rare
Threats: habitat loss; alien spiders, ants, and other predators; food competition from aliens
Legal status: endangered
Scale: 1/4–2/5 inch long

Life is tough at the bottom of the food chain. The Kaua'i cave amphipod is the prey of the Kaua'i cave wolf spider (see p. 59) and alien spiders and ants. The American cockroach invades many caves, preying on young amphipods. Both cockroaches and alien amphipods compete with this native for food. At five known amphipod locations, threats include overhead construction, road building, leaching pesticides, introduced diseases, and other human disturbance. • But all is not lost. Along with the Kaua'i cave wolf spider, this amphipod received federal endangered status protection in February 2000. Preservation actions include gates on cave openings to restrict human access, and planting native flora overhead to improve the root system on which the cave amphipod dines. Landowners entered into a cooperative agreement for habitat preservation and are considering the land overhead for a park or reserve. • Whereas noncave amphipods produce 10 or more eggs held in a pouch, the cave amphipods produce one egg so large it is held only by the mother's curving shell. The hatchling rides under the mother then leaves for an independent life. • Cave adaptation resulted in an eyeless, colorless slender-bodied crustacean with antennae, claws, and legs long and thin. Most sandhoppers jump defensively when disturbed, but cave amphipods walk away. Jumping in dark, low caves, where a predatory spider is listening for movement, may be dangerous, not protective.—*A.M./S.L.M.*

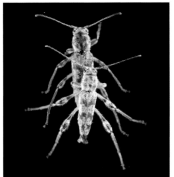

Hawai'i Euphorbia Longhorned Woodborer
(adult pair copulating)
Ponu 'Akoko
Plagithmysus montgomeryi

Photograph: temporary studio, East–West Center, O'ahu
Range: 6,500–7,500 feet between Mauna Kea and Mauna Loa Mountains, Hawai'i
Habitat: dry forest with 'akoko groves
Population: very rare
Threats: habitat alteration by sheep, goats, or fire
Legal status: none
Scale: male 1/2 inch long; female 3/4 inch long

For longhorned woodborer beetles, life is short and mating is active, rapid, and repetitive. Even risking being eaten by ravenous birds, the smaller-sized males "attempt to mate on seeing another individual, whether female or not, and continue to follow and mount one or another until successful," wrote Bishop Museum scientist Dr. Linsley Gressitt in his 1976 magnum opus. • Dark zigzag stripes and bands of pale downy hairs disrupt the woodborers' outline, camouflaging them on the gray bark of 'akoko trees. Blending into the background will not protect them if their host plant is eaten. Their range has been reduced by about 90 percent. Browsing sheep and goats are alien to Hawai'i; consequently, native plants did not evolve to survive being cropped. Dryland habitat is especially vulnerable to destruction in this way. • Millions of years ago a prolific founding North American beetle flew or blew to the Hawaiian Islands. Today, 140 vastly diverse species using 38 kinds of native plants have filled vacant niches through adaptive radiation. They live on 10-million-year-old Nihoa islet all down the island chain to the growing Big Island of Hawai'i. Imagine a chain of ecological theaters showing continuous evolutionary plays. Humans entered the theater late and, lacking a rewind button, scientists use comparative anatomy, host plant analysis, and biogeography to understand today's bounty of Hawaiian beetles.—*A.M./S.L.M.*

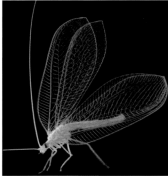

Sylvan Green Lacewing
Nalo Omao Lele Lihi
Anomalochrysa sylvicola

Photograph: Center for Conservation Research and Training Lab, University of Hawai'i at Mānoa, O'ahu
Range: forest reserves on Kaua'i and O'ahu
Habitat: lower fringes of dryland forest
Population: very rare—only three seen since a scientist found the pair in 1899 that led to species description
Threats: habitat loss; long-legged ants and other introduced predators
Legal status: none
Scale: 1 inch long; 2-inch wing spread

Wings of lacy intricacy inspire awe like artful cathedral windows. Astonishingly varied veins give rigidity to the four panes of cellophanelike chitin. Lacewings young and old are active and voracious predators on plant-feeding leafhoppers, mealybugs, and caterpillars. Continental farmers and gardeners release lacewings as natural pest control, but this method is rarely used in Hawai'i. • Native lacewings are seldom seen beyond forest borders. This handsome O'ahu example was discovered resting on a *lonomea* (soapberry) tree trunk on the southeast slope of the extinct Wai'anae volcano; the balance of native predator and prey continues within The Nature Conservancy's Honouliuli Preserve. Although lacewings are safe for now, ants and other alien aggressors are climbing this mountain, extirpating populations of native invertebrates in their path. • Lacewings are among the islands' finest endemic products of natural selection, but little is known about their life histories, and they are a challenge for biogeographers. Their name, *Anomalochrysa* ("golden anomaly"), marks a puzzling proliferation of species. Entomologist Elwood Zimmerman, attempting to clarify in his masterwork *Insects of Hawaii* what he called "a complex of complexes," spent the most lab time per species on lacewings. An ongoing study of all 19 species, half found only on the island of Hawai'i, will assist conservationists and land managers in securing the place of native lacewings in the future of Hawai'i.—*A.M./S.L.M.*

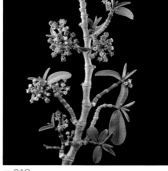

Spurge; Sandmat
'Akoko; Koko; 'Ekoko; Kokomalei
Chamaesyce celastroides var. *kaenana*

Photograph: Ka'ena Point, O'ahu
Range: Ka'ena Point, O'ahu; historically known on Wa'ianae Mountains and Ko'olau Mountains, O'ahu
Habitat: rocky slopes in coastal dry shrubland on windward slopes
Population: five populations with about 400 individuals total
Threats: competition from the alien plant species *koa haole;* fire; tourism
Legal status: endangered
Scale: plant 5 feet tall; leaf 1/2 inch long

Chamaesyce, a genus of mostly creeping herbs, is commonly known from species that are lawn weeds. All 250 species share what appear to be minute flowers and a three-lobed fruit on a small stalk. In fact, this structure, referred to as a cyathia, is a specialized cluster of one female flower and up to 30 or more male flowers. On Pacific oceanic islands the indigenous species are woody shrubs and even trees. As is often the case, the Hawaiian Islands have had the greatest insular radiation of the group; 16 endemic species inhabit virtually all habitats from the dry coast to rain forest and montane bogs. *Chamaesyce celastroides* var. *kaenana* is one of eight varieties of the most complex, widespread, and variable species. It has a restricted distribution, although its past distribution at opposite ends of O'ahu suggests that it may have been a component of the now-lost low dry forests. Most of the remaining individuals are in the Ka'ena Point Reserve. Situated at the base of sea cliffs of the Wai'anae Mountains, the reserve protects coastal sand dunes and boulder-slope ecosystems that harbor many native Hawaiian plant species. Over the past decades, jeeps, trucks, motorbikes, and other vehicles severely damaged the dunes and surrounding areas. Nearly six feet of sand were lost due to vehicular erosion in less than five years.—*W.L.W.*

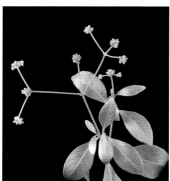

Kulu'ī
Nototrichium divaricatum

Photograph: Kalalau Valley rim, Nā Pali Coast State Park, Kaua'i
Range: Kaua'i
Habitat: cliff vegetation in diverse mesic forest
Population: three populations totaling 1,000–1,200 individuals
Threats: alien plant species; browsing by goats; landslides; falling rocks
Legal status: species of concern
Scale: plant 2–6 feet tall; leaf blade 1–13/4 inches long

Silvery green leaves covered with soft white down make this an attractive shrub. Clusters of tiny budlike flowers are borne in peculiar inflorescences with branches diverging at angles, resembling TV antennae. *Nototrichium divaricatum* was first named and published in 1996, demonstrating that exciting new species are still being discovered in Hawai'i, especially on Kaua'i, oldest of the main islands and richest in endemic plants and animals. • This unusual species was first collected on the Nā Pali Coast of Kaua'i by Steve Montgomery in 1985 and was relocated in 1991 by Ken Wood of the NTBG. Wood's exploration of this steep, rugged region has revealed individuals growing only on north-facing cliffs and ridges in remnants of diverse mesic forest that have escaped the ravages of feral goats. Large goat populations along the Nā Pali Coast are a major threat to this new species and many other rare and localized endemics restricted to Kalalau, Pohakuao, and Honopū Valleys. There is virtually no regeneration of young native plants in this floristically rich region of Kaua'i. • A Hawaiian endemic genus of silvery-leaved shrubs or small trees, *Nototrichium* includes a relatively widespread species found on all the main islands; an endangered species restricted to O'ahu and East Maui; and *Nototrichium divaricatum* of Kaua'i, a species of concern currently with no legal status although it is in cultivation at Lyon Arboretum and the NTBG.—*D.L.*

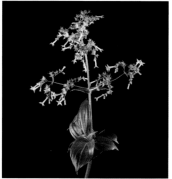

Pilo
Hedyotis mannii

Photograph: back of Hauola Gulch, Lāna'i
Range: Moloka'i, Lāna'i, West Maui
Habitat: mesic forest, possibly wet forest
Population: three populations totaling 50–65 individuals
Threats: feral pig damage; competition from alien weeds
Legal status: endangered
Scale: leaf 3/4–2 inches wide; corolla tube 3/16–9/16 inch long

Worldwide there are more than 150 *Hedyotis* species, with 21 species endemic to Hawai'i, making it the largest genus of Rubiaceae (coffee family) in the islands. Amazingly diverse, the Hawaiian species range in size from small herbs to shrubs and even large forest trees 30 feet tall. This provides an impressive example of island evolution or adaptive radiation, comparable to certain other plant genera in Hawai'i. A number of our *Hedyotis* species are known as *pilo* in Hawaiian, referring to the rather unpleasant or fetid smell produced by the crushed plant. • *Hedyotis mannii* is a subshrub with sharply four-angled or winged stems, shiny dark green leaves, and branching flower clusters or inflorescences up to one foot long. These produce numerous flowers with four pale yellow or greenish white petals fused into a trumpet-shaped white tube. Each flower is set on a colorful pinkish green calyx and ovary that later develops into a capsule. This species is named for botanist Horace Mann Jr., who first collected it on West Maui in the 1860s. This *pilo* inhabits moist, shady rock walls of narrow gulches in lowland to mid-elevation mesic and possibly wet forests. Previously widely scattered on Moloka'i, Lāna'i, and Maui, it has been reduced to a single small population on each island. No *in situ* conservation efforts have taken place to date.—*D.L.*

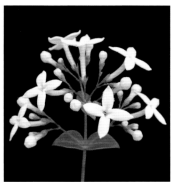

p. 221

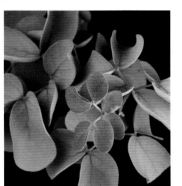

p. 222

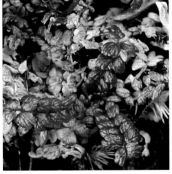

p. 226

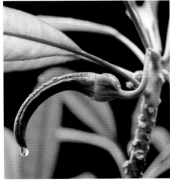

pp. 228, 229

Pilo
Hedyotis parvula

Photograph: National Tropical Botanical Garden Nursery, Lāwaʻi, Kauaʻi
Range: central and southern Waiʻanae Mountains, Oʻahu
Habitat: 2,350–2,730 feet; dry areas on and at base of cliff faces, rock outcrops, and ledges
Population: seven populations with 151 plants
Threats: browsing from feral goats; feral pigs; competition from alien weeds; fire from military training activities
Legal status: endangered
Scale: plant 1–2 feet tall; flower 1/2 inch across

Kanaloa
Palupalu O Kanaloa
Kanaloa kahoolawensis

Photograph: National Tropical Botanical Garden Nursery, Lāwaʻi, Kauaʻi
Range: Kahoʻolawe
Habitat: dry coastal vegetation
Population: two plants growing 50 feet apart
Threats: lack of reproductive vigor; seed predation by rats; drought stress; alien weeds; rockslides
Legal status: endangered
Scale: leaflets 1/2–1 1/4 inches long

Liliwai; Nani Waiʻaleʻale
Acaena exigua

Photograph: Liliwai Bog, Puʻu Kukui Preserve, Maui
Range: Mount Waiʻaleʻale, Kauaʻi; the bogs of Puʻu Kukui, West Maui
Habitat: 5,300–6,000 feet; montane bogs
Population: none known; one individual was rediscovered in 1997 but died in early 2000
Threats: habitat destruction by feral animals, especially pigs; competition for light and space with alien plants
Legal status: endangered
Scale: stem 3/10–1 1/2 inches long

ʻŌhā Wai
Clermontia peleana subsp. peleana

Photograph: Hilo Forest Reserve, Wailuku River, Hawaiʻi; Wailuku Drainage region, Hawaiʻi
Range: Hawaiʻi Island
Habitat: wet forest
Population: extinct in the wild
Threats: rooting by feral pigs; predation by rats (flowers, fruits); loss of pollinators
Legal status: endangered
Scale: leaf blade 38 inches long; corolla 23 inches long

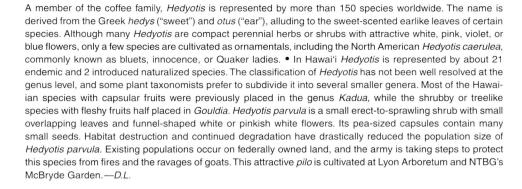

A member of the coffee family, *Hedyotis* is represented by more than 150 species worldwide. The name is derived from the Greek *hedys* ("sweet") and *otus* ("ear"), alluding to the sweet-scented earlike leaves of certain species. Although many *Hedyotis* are compact perennial herbs or shrubs with attractive white, pink, violet, or blue flowers, only a few species are cultivated as ornamentals, including the North American *Hedyotis caerulea*, commonly known as bluets, innocence, or Quaker ladies. • In Hawaiʻi *Hedyotis* is represented by about 21 endemic and 2 introduced naturalized species. The classification of *Hedyotis* has not been well resolved at the genus level, and some plant taxonomists prefer to subdivide it into several smaller genera. Most of the Hawaiian species with capsular fruits were previously placed in the genus *Kadua*, while the shrubby or treelike species with fleshy fruits half placed in *Gouldia*. *Hedyotis parvula* is a small erect-to-sprawling shrub with small overlapping leaves and funnel-shaped white or pinkish white flowers. Its pea-sized capsules contain many small seeds. Habitat destruction and continued degradation have drastically reduced the population size of *Hedyotis parvula*. Existing populations occur on federally owned land, and the army is taking steps to protect this species from fires and the ravages of goats. This attractive *pilo* is cultivated at Lyon Arboretum and NTBG's McBryde Garden.—*D.L.*

Smallest of the main Hawaiian Islands, Kahoʻolawe is dry, barren, and sparsely vegetated. Clearing for ranching, drastic overgrazing, and military target practice have decimated the native flora and caused massive soil erosion. During a botanical survey in 1992 NTBG field botanist Ken Wood discovered two unusual, low-growing shrubs on a steep, rocky talus slope harboring native coastal vegetation. Red-veined, grayish green leaves and small white flower heads suggested the legume family, but the heart-shaped seeds differed from those of other legumes. After determining the plant represented a new genus and species, we named it for Kanaloa, a Hawaiian deity closely associated with Kahoʻolawe. • Finding a new species is rare, but this exceptional plant is the first new Hawaiian genus discovered in nearly 90 years! Fossil pollen evidence indicates it was once abundant in lowland Oʻahu, Kauaʻi, and Maui. After humans populated Hawaiʻi, *kanaloa* became increasingly scarce, disappearing almost completely about eight centuries ago. • Of the two wild plants, one occasionally flowers and produces rare seeds, which have been successfully grown into three plants at NTBG's McBryde Garden. One cultivated plant flowers regularly, but its flowers are male and yield no fruits. Attempts to propagate *kanaloa* by cuttings, air layers, grafts, and tissue culture have failed. Nevertheless, there is still time for new techniques or technology to save this remarkable genus from extinction.—*D.L.*

Acaena is a southern circumpolar genus of more than 100 species. It is best represented in South America but has about 15 species in New Zealand, a few in Australia and New Guinea, and 1 each in California and the Hawaiian Islands. The four-parted flowers are minute and are presented in small tight clusters at the tip of the flowering stalk. The fruit has four or more, usually barbed, spines. Asa Gray described the Hawaiian species, *Acaena exigua*, in 1854 from a single specimen collected on Kauaʻi in 1840 by the U.S. Exploring Expedition. He chose the specific epithet in reference to the small size of the plant as compared to other members of the genus. This minute bog species, which can be easily overlooked among the tussocks of grasses and sedges with which it grows, was only collected twice in the 1800s on Kauaʻi and was not seen after 1957 on West Maui until 1997, when a single individual was discovered by Scott Meidell and Hank Oppenheimer of Maui Land & Pineapple Company, Inc. Similarities in the small spines on the fruits suggest that the Hawaiian species is related to the species in California and Andean South America. Birds could easily disperse the fruits: the small barbed spines act to attach the fruit to bird feathers for the long journey to the Hawaiian Islands.—*W.L.W.*

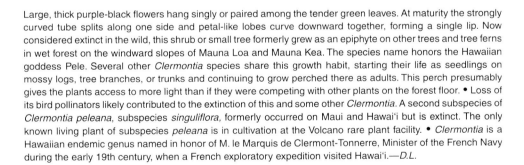

Large, thick purple-black flowers hang singly or paired among the tender green leaves. At maturity the strongly curved tube splits along one side and petal-like lobes curve downward together, forming a single lip. Now considered extinct in the wild, this shrub or small tree formerly grew as an epiphyte on other trees and tree ferns in wet forest on the windward slopes of Mauna Loa and Mauna Kea. The species name honors the Hawaiian goddess Pele. Several other *Clermontia* species share this growth habit, starting their life as seedlings on mossy logs, tree branches, or trunks and continuing to grow perched there as adults. This perch presumably gives the plants access to more light than if they were competing with other plants on the forest floor. • Loss of its bird pollinators likely contributed to the extinction of this and some other *Clermontia*. A second subspecies of *Clermontia peleana*, subspecies *singuliflora*, formerly occurred on Maui and Hawaiʻi but is extinct. The only known living plant of subspecies *peleana* is in cultivation at the Volcano rare plant facility. • *Clermontia* is a Hawaiian endemic genus named in honor of M. le Marquis de Clermont-Tonnerre, Minister of the French Navy during the early 19th century, when a French exploratory expedition visited Hawaiʻi.—*D.L.*

ACKNOWLEDGMENTS

What is held to be economical quite often has nothing to do with what's ethically or morally right. We are in pursuit of environmental quality, an ethical stance where our native biota is concerned, and for accepting each natural ecosystem on the planet for what it is—be it at the South Pole, in the Amazon jungle, or the native dry forest in Upper Mokuleia Valley—each a unique result of multifaceted ecological processes, past, present, and continuing.

—Wayne Gagné

To Wayne Gagné, whom we have come to know through the many people in Hawai'i he inspired.

Donors:
MacArthur Foundation
National Tropical Botanical Garden
The Nature Conservancy of Hawai'i

David Liittschwager and Susan Middleton would like to thank:

Fred Krupp for believing in this project, and for initiating the partnership with Environmental Defense that made it possible.

Steve Perlman for showing us the way.

E. O. Wilson for saying, in 1992, "Go next to Hawai'i."

Robert Hobdy for showing us our first native Hawaiian forest.

Bay & Paul Foundations for their support.

Arsenio Lopez, Sam Hoffman, Dan Oshima, and all the staff of The New Lab for their support, and for taking special care in processing our color film—especially Alson Tom and the digital department for making the highest quality scans from the original film; these scans were used to make the color separations for this book.

Son Do and Erica Aitken of Rods and Cones for their expert advice on color management.

The staff of Environmental Defense, especially Ed Bailey, who kept us solvent and who has always been there for us; David Wilcove, Michael Bean, and Robert Bonnie from the Wildlife Program; and Marcia Aronoff, Joel Plagens, Karen Kenyon, Rory Beelek, and Sherry Smith.

Paul Cox for his invaluable and indispensable support; the Seacology Foundation; the entire staff at National Tropical Botanical Garden, especially Ken Wood, Dave Lorence, Tim Flynn, Diane Ragone, Bob Nishek, Kerin Lilleeng-Rosenberger, Anne E. O'Malley, Melany Chapin, Rick Hanna, Dave Bender, Jeff Koppel, Charlie McDonald, Marilyn Asay, Sylvia Smith, and Chipper and Haole Wichman.

The Nature Conservancy of Hawai'i, especially Rex Johnson, Grady Timmons, Sam Gon, Pauline Sato, Brian Valley, Robin Baker, and Carol Gentry.

Roy and Betsy Eisenhardt for providing solid ground.

William and Paula Merwin for opening their doors to us.

Lisa Lytton, our editor, for seeing the vision and guiding it through National Geographic while giving birth to Arlie.

Jenny Barry for her expertise and grace in this long-awaited collaboration, and Kristen Wurz for her attention to every detail of production.

Veronica Andrew for her keen sensibility and faithful assistance, even while bringing Michael Andrew into the world.

Geneva Bumb for her diligent and cheerful assistance with the film handling, database management, and picture file preparation.

Beth Sudekum, Julia Babiarz, Brook Dillon, Patrice, and Yutaka Iwashita, in our office and darkroom in San Francisco.

Betty Alberts for her house on Maui.

Helen Chellin for her house, Red Cinder, on the Big Island.

Ken Wood for the cabin in Kōke'e.

Karen Ciabattoni for her hospitality and generous heart.

Gabriel Gandell for his Hawaiian heart and for those long talks on the front porch with his hunter friends while eating *lau laus*.

Maile Sakamoto, our first friend in Hawai'i.

Anita Manning, Steve Montgomery, David Lorence, and Warren L. Wagner for their patience, persistence, and expertise in writing the species descriptions.

Sam Gon and Jaan Lepson for their invaluable review of the text.

Gus Bodner for assistance with the Mount Ka'ala photograph.

Debby Ogden, Mary Koerner, and Ted Johnson for being wonderful neighbors.

Melissa Stein for her expert editorial assistance.

Lisa Kroeber for the boiler room where the computers are.

We would also like to express our deep appreciation to the following individuals:

Diane Ackerman
Tom Anderson
Richard Avedon
Robert Bettencourt
Adam Block
Dave and Sue Boynton
Pat Burke
John Burris
Kimo Campbell
Katie Cassel
Richard Chisolm
Gregory Clark
Tom Coffman
Linda Connor
John Culliney
Maria Eisner
Sumner Erdman
Mary Evanson
Ann Fielding
Suzanne Fritch
Susan Gabaree
Nancy Glover
Jody and Terry Grundy
Lisa Hadway
Gordon Hempton
Laurie Henneman
Cindi Hilke
Bob Hill
The Jack Hiner family, especially Janet, Nancy, Mindy, and Steve
Victoria Holt-Takamine
Liz Huppman
Gordon Joyce
Dierdre Kernan
Mike Kido
Moira and Steve Knox
Jill Laughlin
Tom Lovejoy
Tamia Marg
Tom Marioni and MOCA
Kim Martz
Rodney Marzullo
James Mejeur
Theresa Cabrera Menard
Tre Menard
Lydia Modi-Vitale
Bill Mull
Satoshi Nagase
Audrey Newman
Maria Perlman
John Plews and Truxton
Fred Powledge
Richard Press
Leslie Rainer
Brenda Ray
John A. Richards
The Frank Richardson family
Nan Richardson
George Saito
Lena Schnell

Demetrios Scourtis
Ralph Segal
Walter Sorrell
Forest Starr
Norma Stevens
Tilthon Sugi
Ann and Chuck Swanson
Patricia Tummons
Peter Van Dyke
Peter Warshall
Frederick and Lorita Wichman
Ann Wieseltier
Megan Wood
Alvin Yoshinaga

And we would like to express our gratitude to the following institutions and individuals:

Aloha Airlines
Julie King

ATA Airlines
Chip Tindall

Bishop Museum
Robert H. Cowie
Donald Duckworth
Richard Duggan
Ronald Englund
Neal Evenhuis
Francis Howarth
Gordon M. Nishida
Dan Polhemus
David Preston
Al Samuelson

Directorate of Public Works, Environmental Division, U.S. Army Garrison, Hawai'i
Alvin Char
Vince Costello
Jordan W. Jokiel
Kapua Kawelo
Matt Keir
Jobi Rohrer

East-West Center
Jeff Fox
June Kuramoto
Jim Maragos

Hawai'i Department of Land and Natural Resources
Nick Agorastos
Mike Buck
Vickie Caraway
Patrick Costales
Fern Duval II
Bill Evanson
Betsy Gagné
Bill Garnett
John Giffin

Donald Heacock
Galen Kawakami
Randy Kennedy
Fred Kraus
Brent Liesemeyer
Patty Moriyasu
Lyman Perry
Ed Petteys
Peter Shannon
Bill Stormont

Hawai'i Department of Transportation
Blain Kawamura

Helicopter pilots:
Duke Baldwin
Uli Bergman
Ken D'Attilio
Rodrigo Dill
Tom Hauptman
Greg Mattson
Eric Pacheco
Don Shearer
Ed Wagner

Honolulu Zoo
Peter Luscomb
Linda Santos

Just Film
Volker and Bernt Von Glasenapp

Kapiolani Community College
Daniel Chung

Keahou Bird Conservation Center
Peter Harrity
Cyndi Kuehler
Joe Kuhn
Marla Kuhn
Alan Lieberman
Paul Oesterle
Kristin Whittaker

Lyon Arboretum
Ray Baker
Greg Koob

Maui Land & Pineapple Company, Inc. Pu'u Kukui Watershed
Randy Bartlett
Scott Meidell
Hank Oppenheimer

Kapalua Nature Society
Linn Nishikawa

National Marine Fisheries Service
Bud Antonelis
Brenda Becker
Petra Bertilson-Friedman
Sheila Gummeson
Captain John Lamkin and the crew of the *Townsend Cromwell*

Panaewa Zoo
Eric Craig

Patagonia
Ron Hunter

U.S. Fish and Wildlife Service
Adam Asquith
Matt Berry
Marie Bruegman
Brendan Courtot
Beth Flint
Jack Jeffries
David Johnson
Barbara Maxfield
Bart McDermott
Arlene A. Pangelinan
Cindy Rehkemper
Eric Vanderwerf
Alex Wegman
Rebecca Woodward

U.S. Geological Survey Biological Resources Division
Paul Banko
Chuck Chimera
Lloyd Loope
Art Medeiros
Philip Thomas
Rick Warshauer

U.S. National Park Service
Steve Anderson
Darcy Hu
Ron Nagata

University of California at Berkeley
Rosie Gillespie

University of Hawai'i
Miquel Arnedo
Michael Hadfield
Tracy Johnson
Ken Kaneshiro

Waimea Arboretum and Botanical Garden
Winston Morton
David Orr
Jennifer Telford
Cissy Ufano
Keith Woolliams

West Virginia University
John Strazanac

INDEX

Steve Perlman, End of Waikamoi Flume, East Maui (page 264)

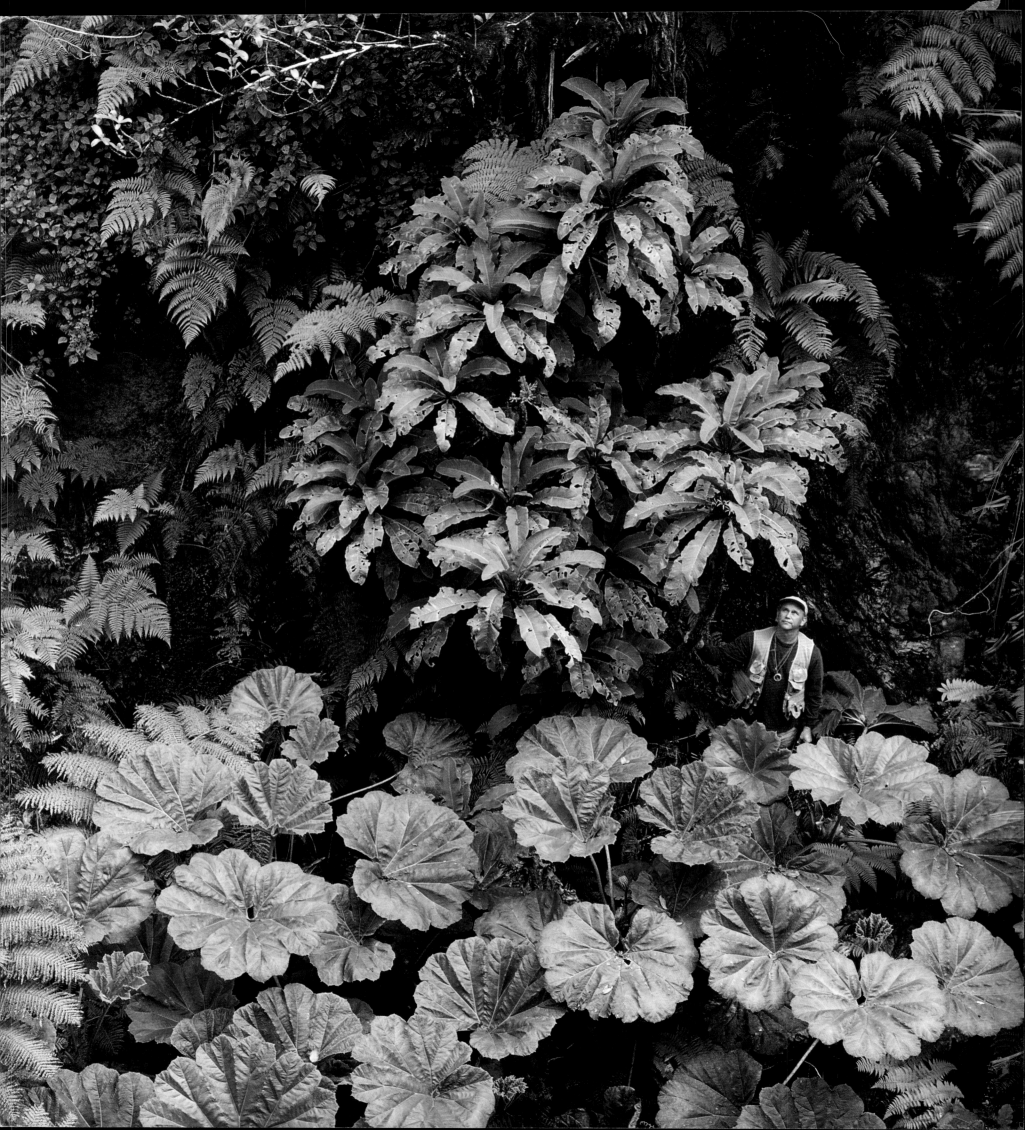